O9-ABI-059

Engage. Prepare. Succeed.

Aplia™ is an online interactive learning solution that improves comprehension and outcomes by increasing student effort and engagement. Founded by a professor to enhance his own courses, **Aplia** provides automatically graded assignments with detailed, immediate explanations on every question, and innovative teaching materials. **Aplia** saves instructors valuable time they'd otherwise spend on routine grading while giving students an easy way to stay on top of coursework with regularly scheduled assignments.

Aplia benefits include:

- Assessment analytics that track student participation, progress, and performance.
- Flexible gradebook tools compatible with other learning management systems.
- Automatically graded interactive problems that keep students engaged and on track throughout the term.

Learn more at:
www.cengage.com/aplia

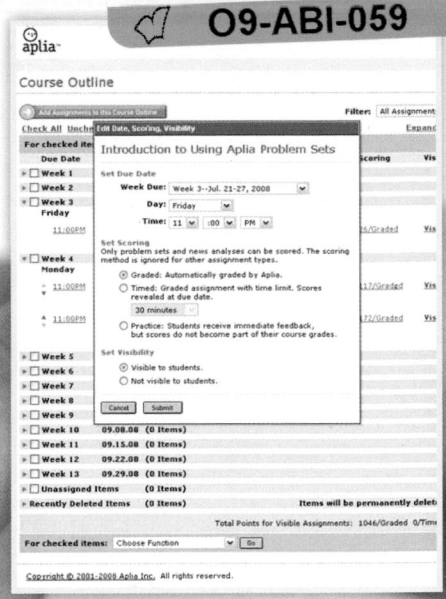

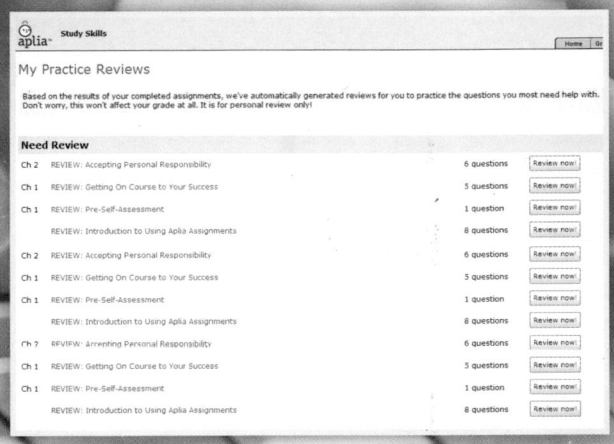

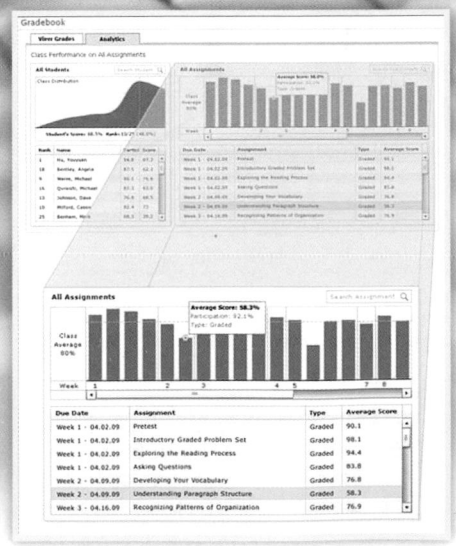

CENGAGE Learning®

CourseMate

Engaging. Trackable. Affordable.

Complement your text and course content with study and practice materials.

Cengage Learning's **CourseMate** brings course concepts to life with interactive learning, study, and exam preparation tools that support the printed textbook. Watch student comprehension soar as your class works with the printed textbook and the textbook-specific website. **CourseMate** goes beyond the book to deliver what you need!

CourseMate includes:

- An interactive eBook with highlighting, note taking, and an interactive glossary
- **Engagement Tracker**, a first-of-its-kind tool that monitors student engagement in the course
- Quizzes, videos, flashcards, and more

Learn more & view a demo at:

www.cengage.com/coursemate

CourseReader

Create an affordable and customized online reader in minutes!

CourseReader lets you choose from thousands of primary and secondary sources—including permissions-cleared readings, audio, and video selections.

With **CourseReader**, you can:

- Easily search and preview source material for your course
- Publish your notes to students, assign due dates, assemble and re-order selections, archive readers from previous terms and adapt them for future classes
- Provide students with pedagogical support, including descriptive introductions that add context to many of the primary source documents, and critical-thinking and multiple-choice questions that reinforce key points
- Utilize *Editor's Choice* selections as time-saving starting points

Learn more & view a demo at:

www.cengage.com/coursereader

TRANSFORMING LEARNING TRANSFORMING LIVES

CENGAGE Learning

WESTERN CIVILIZATION

A Brief History

Volume I: To 1715

EIGHTH EDITION

WESTERN CIVILIZATION

A Brief History

Volume I: To 1715

JACKSON J. SPIELVOGEL
The Pennsylvania State University

WADSWORTH
CENGAGE Learning

Australia • Brazil • Canada • Mexico • Singapore • Spain • United Kingdom • United States

WADSWORTH
CENGAGE Learning®

***Western Civilization: A Brief History, Volume I: To 1715*, Eighth Edition**
Jackson J. Spielvogel

Editor-in-Chief: Lyn Uhl

Senior Publisher: Suzanne Jeans

Acquiring Sponsoring Editor: Brooke Barbier

Senior Development Editor: Margaret McAndrew Beasley

Assistant Editor: Jamie Bushell

Editorial Assistant: Katie Coaster

Senior Media Editor: Lisa Ciccolo

Executive Brand Manager: Melissa Larmon

Marketing Coordinator: Lorreen Towle

Senior Marketing Communications Manager: Linda Yip Beckstrom

Senior Content Project Manager: Jane Lee

Senior Art Director: Cate Rickard Barr

Production Technology Analyst: Jeff Joubert

Manufacturing Planner: Sandra Milewski

Rights Acquisition Specialist, Image: Jennifer Meyer Dare

Rights Acquisition Specialist, Text: Jennifer Meyer Dare

Production Service: Orr Book Services

Text Designer: Shawn Girsberger

Cover Designer: Cyndy Patrick

Cover Image: Lorenzetti, Ambrogio, fl. 1317–48, Italian. Dancer, detail from the fresco *Effects of Good Government in the City*, 1338–40. Credit: Palazzo Pubblico Siena/Collection Dagli Orti/The Art Archive

Compositor: Cenveo Publisher Services

© 2014, 2011 Wadsworth, Cengage Learning

ALL RIGHTS RESERVED. No part of this work covered by the copyright herein may be reproduced, transmitted, stored, or used in any form or by any means graphic, electronic, or mechanical, including but not limited to photocopying, recording, scanning, digitizing, taping, Web distribution, information networks, or information storage and retrieval systems, except as permitted under Section 107 or 108 of the 1976 United States Copyright Act, without the prior written permission of the publisher.

For product information and technology assistance, contact us at
Cengage Learning Customer & Sales Support, 1-800-354-9706

For permission to use material from this text or product, submit all requests online at **www.cengage.com/permissions**. Further permissions questions can be emailed to **permissionrequest@cengage.com**.

Library of Congress Control Number: 2012946768

ISBN 13: 978-1-133-60792-2
ISBN 10: 1-133-60792-6

Wadsworth
20 Channel Center Street
Boston, MA 02210
USA

Cengage Learning is a leading provider of customized learning solutions with office locations around the globe, including Singapore, the United Kingdom, Australia, Mexico, Brazil and Japan. Locate your local office at **international.cengage.com/region**

Cengage Learning products are represented in Canada by Nelson Education, Ltd.

For your course and learning solutions, visit **www.cengage.com**.
Purchase any of our products at your local college store or at our preferred online store **www.cengagebrain.com**.
Instructors: Please visit **login.cengage.com** and log in to access instructor-specific resources.

Printed in Canada
1 2 3 4 5 6 7 16 15 14 13 12

ABOUT THE AUTHOR

JACKSON J. SPIELVOGEL is associate professor emeritus of history at The Pennsylvania State University. He received his Ph.D. from The Ohio State University, where he specialized in Reformation history under Harold J. Grimm. His articles and reviews have appeared in such journals as *Moreana*, *Journal of General Education*, *Catholic Historical Review*, *Archiv für Reformationsgeschichte*, and *American Historical Review*. He has also contributed chapters or articles to *The Social History of the Reformation*, *The Holy Roman Empire: A Dictionary Handbook*, the *Simon Wiesenthal Center Annual of Holocaust Studies*, and *Utopian Studies*. His work has been supported by fellowships from the Fulbright Foundation and the Foundation for Reformation Research. At Penn State, he helped inaugurate the Western civilization courses as well as a popular course on Nazi Germany. His book *Hitler and Nazi Germany* was published in 1987 (sixth edition, 2005). He is the author of *Western Civilization*, first published in 1991 (eighth edition, 2012), and the coauthor (with William Duiker) of *World History*, first published in 1994 (seventh edition, 2013). Professor Spielvogel has won five major university-wide teaching awards. During the year 1988–1989, he held the Penn State Teaching Fellowship, the university's most prestigious teaching award. In 1996, he won the Dean Arthur Ray Warnock Award for Outstanding Faculty Member, and in 2000, he received the Schreyer Honors College Excellence in Teaching Award.

TO DIANE,
WHOSE LOVE AND SUPPORT MADE IT ALL POSSIBLE
J.J.S.

BRIEF CONTENTS

DOCUMENTS XV

MAPS XVII

FEATURES XIX

PREFACE XXI

ACKNOWLEDGMENTS XXVI

INTRODUCTION TO STUDENTS OF WESTERN CIVILIZATION XXIX

STUDYING FROM PRIMARY SOURCE MATERIALS XXXI

1 THE ANCIENT NEAR EAST: THE FIRST CIVILIZATIONS 1

2 THE ANCIENT NEAR EAST: PEOPLES AND EMPIRES 26

3 THE CIVILIZATION OF THE GREEKS 45

4 THE HELLENISTIC WORLD 69

5 THE ROMAN REPUBLIC 89

6 THE ROMAN EMPIRE 113

7 LATE ANTIQUITY AND THE EMERGENCE OF THE MEDIEVAL WORLD 137

8 EUROPEAN CIVILIZATION IN THE EARLY MIDDLE AGES, 750–1000 162

9 THE RECOVERY AND GROWTH OF EUROPEAN SOCIETY IN THE HIGH MIDDLE AGES 184

10 THE RISE OF KINGDOMS AND THE GROWTH OF CHURCH POWER 205

11 THE LATER MIDDLE AGES: CRISIS AND DISINTEGRATION IN THE FOURTEENTH CENTURY 230

12 RECOVERY AND REBIRTH: THE AGE OF THE RENAISSANCE 253

13 REFORMATION AND RELIGIOUS WARFARE IN THE SIXTEENTH CENTURY 279

14 EUROPE AND THE WORLD: NEW ENCOUNTERS, 1500–1800 304

15 STATE BUILDING AND THE SEARCH FOR ORDER IN THE SEVENTEENTH CENTURY 331

16 TOWARD A NEW HEAVEN AND A NEW EARTH: THE SCIENTIFIC REVOLUTION AND THE EMERGENCE OF MODERN SCIENCE 357

GLOSSARY 376

NOTES 380

INDEX 384

DETAILED CONTENTS

DOCUMENTS XV

MAPS XVII

FEATURES XIX

PREFACE XXI

ACKNOWLEDGMENTS XXVI

INTRODUCTION TO STUDENTS OF WESTERN CIVILIZATION XXIX

STUDYING FROM PRIMARY SOURCE MATERIALS XXXI

1 THE ANCIENT NEAR EAST: THE FIRST CIVILIZATIONS 1

The First Humans 2
- The Hunter-Gatherers of the Old Stone Age 3
- The Neolithic Revolution (c. 10,000–4000 B.C.E.) 3

The Emergence of Civilization 5

Civilization in Mesopotamia 6
- The City-States of Ancient Mesopotamia 7
- Empires in Ancient Mesopotamia 9
- The Culture of Mesopotamia 11

Egyptian Civilization: "The Gift of the Nile" 13
- The Impact of Geography 13
- The Old and Middle Kingdoms 15
- Society and Economy in Ancient Egypt 16
- The Culture of Egypt 17
- Disorder and a New Order: The New Kingdom 19
- **IMAGES OF EVERYDAY LIFE**
- **THE EGYPTIAN DIET 20**
- **OPPOSING VIEWPOINTS**
- **AKHENATEN'S *HYMN TO ATEN* AND PSALM 104 OF THE HEBREW BIBLE 21**
- Daily Life in Ancient Egypt: Family and Marriage 22
- *Chapter Summary, Timeline, and Review* 23

2 THE ANCIENT NEAR EAST: PEOPLES AND EMPIRES 26

On the Fringes of Civilization 27
- The Impact of the Indo-Europeans 27

The Hebrews: "The Children of Israel" 28
- Was There a United Kingdom of Israel? 29
- The Kingdoms of Israel and Judah 29
- The Spiritual Dimensions of Israel 30
- The Neighbors of the Israelites 33

The Assyrian Empire 34
- Organization of the Empire 34
- The Assyrian Military Machine 35
- **OPPOSING VIEWPOINTS**
- **THE GOVERNING OF EMPIRES: TWO APPROACHES 36**
- Assyrian Society and Culture 37

The Persian Empire 38
- Cyrus the Great (559–530 B.C.E.) 38
- Expanding the Empire 39
- Governing the Empire 40
- The Great King 40
- Persian Religion 42
- *Chapter Summary, Timeline, and Review* 43

3 THE CIVILIZATION OF THE GREEKS 45

Early Greece 46
- Minoan Crete 46
- The First Greek State: Mycenae 47

The Greeks in a Dark Age (c. 1100–c. 750 B.C.E.) 48
- Homer and Homeric Greece 48
- Homer's Enduring Importance 49

The World of the Greek City-States (c. 750–c. 500 B.C.E.) 49
- The *Polis* 50
- A New Military System: The Greek Way of War 51
- Colonization and the Growth of Trade 51
- Tyranny in the Greek *Polis* 52
- Sparta 53
- Athens 53

The High Point of Greek Civilization: Classical Greece 55
- The Challenge of Persia 55
- The Growth of an Athenian Empire in the Age of Pericles 56

The Great Peloponnesian War 58
The Decline of the Greek States (404–338 B.C.E.) 58

The Culture and Society of Classical Greece 58
The Writing of History 58
Greek Drama 59
The Arts: The Classical Ideal 60
The Greek Love of Wisdom 61
Greek Religion 63
Daily Life in Classical Athens 63
OPPOSING VIEWPOINTS
WOMEN IN ATHENS AND SPARTA 65
Chapter Summary, Timeline, and Review 66

4 THE HELLENISTIC WORLD 69

Macedonia and the Conquests of Alexander 70
Philip and the Conquest of Greece 70
Alexander the Great 70
OPPOSING VIEWPOINTS
DEMOSTHENES AND ISOCRATES ADDRESS PHILIP OF MACEDONIA 71
FILM & HISTORY
***ALEXANDER* (2004) 75**

The World of the Hellenistic Kingdoms 76
Hellenistic Monarchies 76
The Threat from the Celts 76
Political Institutions 77
Hellenistic Cities 78
Economic Trends in the Hellenistic World 79
New Opportunities for Women 79

Culture in the Hellenistic World 81
New Directions in Literature 81
Hellenistic Art 82
A Golden Age of Science 82
Philosophy: New Schools of Thought 83

Religion in the Hellenistic World 85
Mystery Religions 85
Jews in the Hellenistic World 85
Chapter Summary, Timeline, and Review 86

5 THE ROMAN REPUBLIC 89

The Emergence of Rome 90
The Greeks in Italy 90
The Etruscans 91
Early Rome 91

The Roman Republic (c. 509–264 B.C.E.) 92
The Roman State 92
The Roman Conquest of Italy 93

The Roman Conquest of the Mediterranean (264–133 B.C.E.) 96
The Struggle with Carthage 97
The Eastern Mediterranean 97
The Nature of Roman Imperialism 98
Evolution of the Roman Army 98

Society and Culture in the Roman World 99
Roman Religion 99
The Growth of Slavery 100
The Roman Family 101
The Evolution of Roman Law 103
The Development of Literature 103
Roman Art 105
Values and Attitudes 105

The Decline and Fall of the Roman Republic (133–31 B.C.E.) 105
Background: Social, Economic, and Political Problems 105
The Reforms of the Gracchi 106
A New Role for the Roman Army: Marius and Sulla 106
The Death of the Republic 107
OPPOSING VIEWPOINTS
THE END OF THE REPUBLIC: THREE VIEWS 108
Chapter Summary, Timeline, and Review 110

6 THE ROMAN EMPIRE 113

The Age of Augustus (31 B.C.E.–14 C.E.) 114
The New Order 114
Augustan Society 116
The Augustan Age 117

The Early Empire (14–180) 117
The Julio-Claudians 117
The Five "Good Emperors" (96–180) 117
The Roman Empire at Its Height: Frontiers and Provinces 117
Prosperity in the Early Empire 120
IMAGES OF EVERYDAY LIFE
TRADE AND THE PRODUCTS OF TRADE 122

Roman Culture and Society in the Early Empire 123
The Golden Age of Latin Literature 123
The Silver Age of Latin Literature 124
The Upper-Class Roman Family 125
Imperial Rome 126
The Gladiatorial Shows 127
FILM & HISTORY
***GLADIATOR* (2000) 128**

Transformation of the Roman World: Crises in the Third Century 129
Political and Military Woes 129
Economic and Social Crises 130

Transformation of the Roman World: The Rise of Christianity 130
The Religious World of the Roman Empire 130
The Jewish Background 130
The Origins of Christianity 131
The Growth of Christianity 132
OPPOSING VIEWPOINTS
ROMAN AUTHORITIES AND A CHRISTIAN ON CHRISTIANITY 133
Chapter Summary, Timeline, and Review 135

7 LATE ANTIQUITY AND THE EMERGENCE OF THE MEDIEVAL WORLD 137

The Late Roman Empire 138
The Reforms of Diocletian and Constantine 138
The Empire's New Religion 140
The End of the Western Empire 140

The Germanic Kingdoms 141
OPPOSING VIEWPOINTS
TWO VIEWS OF THE HUNS 142
The Ostrogothic Kingdom of Italy 143
The Visigothic Kingdom of Spain 143
The Frankish Kingdom 143
Anglo-Saxon England 145
The Society of the Germanic Kingdoms 145

Development of the Christian Church 147
The Power of the Pope 147
The Monks and Their Missions 147
Christianity and Intellectual Life 151

The Byzantine Empire 152
The Reign of Justinian (527–565) 152
From Eastern Roman to Byzantine Empire 154

The Rise of Islam 155
Muhammad 156
The Teachings of Islam 156
The Spread of Islam 157
Chapter Summary, Timeline, and Review 159

8 EUROPEAN CIVILIZATION IN THE EARLY MIDDLE AGES, 750–1000 162

The World of the Carolingians 163
Charlemagne and the Carolingian Empire (700–814) 162
The Carolingian Intellectual Renewal 166
Life in the Carolingian World 167

Disintegration of the Carolingian Empire 169
Invasions of the Ninth and Tenth Centuries 169

The Emerging World of Lords and Vassals 171
Vassalage 171
Fief-Holding 172
OPPOSING VIEWPOINTS
LORDS AND VASSALS IN EUROPE AND JAPAN 173
The Manorial System 174

The Zenith of Byzantine Civilization 175
The Macedonian Dynasty 175

The Slavic Peoples of Central and Eastern Europe 177
Western Slavs 178
Southern Slavs 178
Eastern Slavs 179

The World of Islam 179
Islamic Civilization 180
Chapter Summary, Timeline, and Review 182

9 THE RECOVERY AND GROWTH OF EUROPEAN SOCIETY IN THE HIGH MIDDLE AGES 184

Land and People in the High Middle Ages 185
The New Agriculture 185
The Life of the Peasantry 187
The Aristocracy of the High Middle Ages 188

The New World of Trade and Cities 190
The Revival of Trade 191
The Growth of Cities 191
OPPOSING VIEWPOINTS
TWO VIEWS OF TRADE AND MERCHANTS 193
Life in the Medieval City 194
IMAGES OF EVERYDAY LIFE
LIFE IN A MEDIEVAL TOWN 195
Industry in Medieval Cities 196

The Intellectual and Artistic World of the High Middle Ages 196
The Rise of Universities 196
A Revival of Classical Antiquity 198
The Revival of Roman Law 199
The Development of Scholasticism 200
Literature in the High Middle Ages 200
Romanesque Architecture: "A White Mantle of Churches" 201
The Gothic Cathedral 201
Chapter Summary, Timeline, and Review 203

10 THE RISE OF KINGDOMS AND THE GROWTH OF CHURCH POWER 205

The Emergence and Growth of European Kingdoms, 1000–1300 206
- England in the High Middle Ages 206
- The Growth of the French Kingdom 207
- FILM & HISTORY
- ***The Lion in Winter* (1968) 208**
- Christian Reconquest: The Spanish Kingdoms 211
- The Lands of the Holy Roman Empire: Germany and Italy 212
- New Kingdoms in Northern and Eastern Europe 213
- Impact of the Mongol Empire 214
- The Development of Russia 215

The Recovery and Reform of the Catholic Church 216
- The Problems of Decline 216
- The Cluniac Reform Movement 216
- Reform of the Papacy 216

Christianity and Medieval Civilization 217
- Growth of the Papal Monarchy 217
- New Religious Orders and Spiritual Ideals 217
- Popular Religion in the High Middle Ages 220
- Voices of Protest and Intolerance 220

The Crusades 223
- Background to the Crusades 223
- The Early Crusades 223
- OPPOSING VIEWPOINTS
- **The Siege of Jerusalem: Christian and Muslim Perspectives 226**
- The Crusades of the Thirteenth Century 227
- Effects of the Crusades 227
- *Chapter Summary, Timeline, and Review 227*

11 THE LATER MIDDLE AGES: CRISIS AND DISINTEGRATION IN THE FOURTEENTH CENTURY 230

A Time of Troubles: Black Death and Social Crisis 231
- The Black Death: From Asia to Europe 231
- The Black Death in Europe 231
- OPPOSING VIEWPOINTS
- **Causes of the Black Death: Contemporary Views 232**
- Economic Dislocation and Social Upheaval 234

War and Political Instability 236
- The Hundred Years' War 236
- Political Instability 239
- FILM & HISTORY
- ***Joan of Arc* (1948) *The Messenger: The Story of Joan of Arc* (1999) 240**
- Western Europe: England and France 241
- The German Monarchy 242
- The States of Italy 242

The Decline of the Church 243
- Boniface VIII and the Conflict with the State 243
- The Papacy at Avignon (1305–1378) 245
- The Great Schism 245
- The Conciliar Movement 245

Culture and Society in an Age of Adversity 246
- The Development of Vernacular Literature 246
- Art and the Black Death 248
- Changes in Urban Life 248
- IMAGES OF EVERYDAY LIFE
- **Entertainment in the Middle Ages 249**
- Inventions and New Patterns 250
- *Chapter Summary, Timeline, and Review 250*

12 RECOVERY AND REBIRTH: THE AGE OF THE RENAISSANCE 253

Characteristics of the Italian Renaissance 254

The Making of Renaissance Society 255
- Economic Recovery 255
- Social Changes in the Renaissance 256
- The Family in Renaissance Italy 257

The Italian States in the Renaissance 259
- Machiavelli and the New Statecraft 261

The Intellectual Renaissance in Italy 261
- OPPOSING VIEWPOINTS
- **The Renaissance Prince: The Views of Machiavelli and Erasmus 262**
- Italian Renaissance Humanism 263
- Education in the Renaissance 264
- The Impact of Printing 264

The Artistic Renaissance 266
- Art in the Early Renaissance 266
- The Artistic High Renaissance 268
- The Northern Artistic Renaissance 269

The European State in the Renaissance 271
- The Renaissance State in Western Europe 271
- Central Europe: The Holy Roman Empire 273
- The Struggle for Strong Monarchy in Eastern Europe 273
- The Ottoman Turks and the End of the Byzantine Empire 273

The Church in the Renaissance 274
Dealing with Heresy and Reform 274
The Renaissance Papacy 275
Chapter Summary, Timeline, and Review 276

13 REFORMATION AND RELIGIOUS WARFARE IN THE SIXTEENTH CENTURY 279

Prelude to Reformation 280
Christian or Northern Renaissance Humanism 280
Church and Religion on the Eve of the Reformation 281

Martin Luther and the Reformation in Germany 282
The Early Luther 282
The Rise of Lutheranism 284
Organizing the Church 285
Germany and the Reformation: Religion and Politics 285

The Spread of the Protestant Reformation 287
The Zwinglian Reformation 287
The Radical Reformation: The Anabaptists 288
OPPOSING VIEWPOINTS
A REFORMATION DEBATE: CONFLICT AT MARBURG 289
The Reformation in England 290
John Calvin and the Development of Calvinism 291

The Social Impact of the Protestant Reformation 292
The Family 292
Religious Practices and Popular Culture 293

The Catholic Reformation 293
The Society of Jesus 293
A Revived Papacy 294
The Council of Trent 296

Politics and the Wars of Religion in the Sixteenth Century 296
The French Wars of Religion (1562–1598) 297
Philip II and Militant Catholicism 297
Revolt of the Netherlands 297
The England of Elizabeth 298
FILM & HISTORY
***ELIZABETH* (1998) 300**
Chapter Summary, Timeline, and Review 301

14 EUROPE AND THE WORLD: NEW ENCOUNTERS, 1500–1800 304

On the Brink of a New World 305
The Motives for Expansion 305
The Means for Expansion 306

New Horizons: The Portuguese and Spanish Empires 306
The Development of a Portuguese Maritime Empire 307
Voyages to the New World 308
IMAGES OF EVERYDAY LIFE
SPICES AND WORLD TRADE 309
The Spanish Empire in the New World 310

New Rivals on the World Stage 313
Africa: The Slave Trade 313
The West in Southeast Asia 315
OPPOSING VIEWPOINTS
WEST MEETS EAST: AN EXCHANGE OF ROYAL LETTERS 318
The French and British in India 319
China 320
Japan 320
The Americas 321

The Impact of European Expansion 322
The Conquered 323
FILM & HISTORY
***THE MISSION* (1986) 325**
The Conquerors 326

Toward a World Economy 327
Economic Conditions in the Sixteenth Century 327
The Growth of Commercial Capitalism 327
Mercantilism 328
Overseas Trade and Colonies: Movement Toward Globalization 328
Chapter Summary, Timeline, and Review 329

15 STATE BUILDING AND THE SEARCH FOR ORDER IN THE SEVENTEENTH CENTURY 331

Social Crises, War, and Rebellions 332
The Witchcraft Craze 332
The Thirty Years' War 334
Rebellions 335

The Practice of Absolutism: Western Europe 336
France: Foundations of Absolutism 336
The Reign of Louis XIV (1643–1715) 336
The Decline of Spain 338

Absolutism in Central and Eastern Europe 339
The German States 339
The Emergence of Austria 340
Russia: From Fledgling Principality to Major Power 340
The Ottoman Empire 343
The Limits of Absolutism 343

Limited Monarchy: The Dutch Republic and England 343
The Golden Age of the Dutch Republic 344
England and the Emergence of Constitutional Monarchy 344
IMAGES OF EVERYDAY LIFE
DUTCH DOMESTICITY 345
OPPOSING VIEWPOINTS
OLIVER CROMWELL: THREE PERSPECTIVES 347

The Flourishing of European Culture 350
The Changing Faces of Art 350
A Wondrous Age of Theater 352
Chapter Summary, Timeline, and Review 354

16 TOWARD A NEW HEAVEN AND A NEW EARTH: THE SCIENTIFIC REVOLUTION AND THE EMERGENCE OF MODERN SCIENCE 357

Background to the Scientific Revolution 358
Ancient Authors and Renaissance Artists 358
Technological Innovations and Mathematics 358
Renaissance Magic 359

Toward a New Heaven: A Revolution in Astronomy 359
Copernicus 359
Kepler 360
Galileo 360
Newton 361
OPPOSING VIEWPOINTS
A NEW HEAVEN? FAITH VERSUS REASON 363

Advances in Medicine and Chemistry 365
Vesalius 365
Harvey 365
Chemistry 365

Women in the Origins of Modern Science 366
Margaret Cavendish 366
Maria Winkelmann 367
Debates on the Nature of Women 367

Toward a New Earth: Descartes, Rationalism, and a New View of Humankind 368

The Spread of Scientific Knowledge 369
The Scientific Method 369
The Scientific Societies 370
Science and Society 371
Science and Religion 371
Chapter Summary, Timeline, and Review 373

GLOSSARY 376
NOTES 380
INDEX 384

DOCUMENTS

CHAPTER 1

THE CODE OF HAMMURABI 10

THE GREAT FLOOD 14

OPPOSING VIEWPOINTS: AKHENATEN'S *HYMN TO ATEN* AND PSALM 104 OF THE HEBREW BIBLE 21

A FATHER'S ADVICE 22

CHAPTER 2

THE COVENANT AND THE LAW: THE BOOK OF EXODUS 31

THE HEBREW PROPHETS: MICAH, ISAIAH, AND AMOS 32

OPPOSING VIEWPOINTS: THE GOVERNING OF EMPIRES: TWO APPROACHES 36

A DINNER WITH THE PERSIAN KING 41

CHAPTER 3

HOMER'S IDEAL OF EXCELLENCE 50

THE LYCURGAN REFORMS 54

ATHENIAN DEMOCRACY: THE FUNERAL ORATION OF PERICLES 57

OPPOSING VIEWPOINTS: WOMEN IN ATHENS AND SPARTA 65

CHAPTER 4

OPPOSING VIEWPOINTS: DEMOSTHENES AND ISOCRATES ADDRESS PHILIP OF MACEDONIA 71

ALEXANDER MEETS AN INDIAN KING 74

A NEW AUTONOMY FOR WOMEN? 80

THE STOIC IDEAL OF HARMONY WITH GOD 84

CHAPTER 5

CINCINNATUS SAVES ROME: A ROMAN MORALITY TALE 94

CATO THE ELDER ON WOMEN 102

THE TWELVE TABLES 104

OPPOSING VIEWPOINTS: THE END OF THE REPUBLIC: THREE VIEWS 108

CHAPTER 6

THE ACHIEVEMENTS OF AUGUSTUS 115

THE DAILY LIFE OF AN UPPER-CLASS ROMAN 123

OVID AND THE ART OF LOVE 125

OPPOSING VIEWPOINTS: ROMAN AUTHORITIES AND A CHRISTIAN ON CHRISTIANITY 133

CHAPTER 7

OPPOSING VIEWPOINTS: TWO VIEWS OF THE HUNS 142

GERMANIC CUSTOMARY LAW: THE ORDEAL 146

IRISH MONASTICISM AND THE PENITENTIAL 149

THE QUR'AN: THE PILGRIMAGE 157

CHAPTER 8

THE ACHIEVEMENTS OF CHARLEMAGNE 164

OPPOSING VIEWPOINTS: LORDS AND VASSALS IN EUROPE AND JAPAN 173

A WESTERN VIEW OF THE BYZANTINE EMPIRE 176

A MUSLIM'S DESCRIPTION OF THE RUS 178

CHAPTER 9

THE ELIMINATION OF MEDIEVAL FORESTS 186

WOMEN IN MEDIEVAL THOUGHT 190

OPPOSING VIEWPOINTS: TWO VIEWS OF TRADE AND MERCHANTS 193

UNIVERSITY STUDENTS AND VIOLENCE AT OXFORD 199

CHAPTER 10

MAGNA CARTA 209

A MIRACLE OF SAINT BERNARD 218

TREATMENT OF THE JEWS 222

OPPOSING VIEWPOINTS: THE SIEGE OF JERUSALEM: CHRISTIAN AND MUSLIM PERSPECTIVES 226

CHAPTER 11

OPPOSING VIEWPOINTS: CAUSES OF THE BLACK DEATH: CONTEMPORARY VIEWS 232

THE TRIAL OF JOAN OF ARC 239

BONIFACE VIII'S DEFENSE OF PAPAL SUPREMACY 244

DANTE'S VISION OF HELL 247

CHAPTER 12

A RENAISSANCE BANQUET 255

MARRIAGE NEGOTIATIONS 258

OPPOSING VIEWPOINTS: THE RENAISSANCE PRINCE: THE VIEWS OF MACHIAVELLI AND ERASMUS 262

A WOMAN'S DEFENSE OF LEARNING 265

CHAPTER 13

LUTHER AND THE NINETY-FIVE THESES 283

OPPOSING VIEWPOINTS: A REFORMATION DEBATE: CONFLICT AT MARBURG 289

LOYOLA AND OBEDIENCE TO "OUR HOLY MOTHER, THE HIERARCHICAL CHURCH" 295

QUEEN ELIZABETH ADDRESSES PARLIAMENT (1601) 299

CHAPTER 14

THE SPANISH CONQUISTADOR: CORTÉS AND THE CONQUEST OF MEXICO 312

THE ATLANTIC SLAVE TRADE 316

OPPOSING VIEWPOINTS: WEST MEETS EAST: AN EXCHANGE OF ROYAL LETTERS 318

THE MISSION 324

CHAPTER 15

A WITCHCRAFT TRIAL IN FRANCE 333

OPPOSING VIEWPOINTS: OLIVER CROMWELL: THREE PERSPECTIVES 347

THE BILL OF RIGHTS 349

WILLIAM SHAKESPEARE: IN PRAISE OF ENGLAND 354

CHAPTER 16

ON THE REVOLUTIONS OF THE HEAVENLY SPHERES 362

OPPOSING VIEWPOINTS: A NEW HEAVEN? FAITH VERSUS REASON 363

THE "NATURAL" INFERIORITY OF WOMEN 368

PASCAL: "WHAT IS A MAN IN THE INFINITE?" 372

MAPS

MAP 1.1 The Spread of *Homo sapiens sapiens* 2
SPOT MAP Harappa and Mohenjo-Daro 6
SPOT MAP The Yellow River, China 6
SPOT MAP Central Asian Civilization 6
SPOT MAP Caral, Peru 6
MAP 1.2 The Ancient Near East 7
SPOT MAP Hammurabi's Empire 9
MAP 1.3 Ancient Egypt 15
MAP 2.1 The Israelites and Their Neighbors in the First Millennium B.C.E. 29
SPOT MAP Phoenician Colonies and Trade Routes, c. 800 B.C.E. 33
MAP 2.2 The Assyrian and Neo-Babylonian Empires 35
MAP 2.3 The Persian Empire at the Time of Darius 39
MAP 3.1 Ancient Greece (c. 750–338 B.C.E.) 47
SPOT MAP Minoan Crete and Mycenaean Greece 48
MAP 4.1 The Conquests of Alexander the Great 73
MAP 4.2 The Hellenistic Kingdoms 77
MAP 5.1 Ancient Italy 91
SPOT MAP The City of Rome 91
SPOT MAP Roman Roads in Italy 95
MAP 5.2 Roman Conquests in the Mediterranean, 264–133 B.C.E. 96
MAP 5.3 Roman Dominions in the Late Republic, 31 B.C.E. 110
MAP 6.1 The Roman Empire from Augustus Through Trajan (14–117) 118
MAP 6.2 Trade Routes and Products in the Roman Empire, c. 200 120
SPOT MAP Silk Road 121
MAP 6.3 Imperial Rome 126
MAP 7.1 Divisions of the Late Roman Empire, c. 300 139
MAP 7.2 The Germanic Kingdoms of the Old Western Empire 144
MAP 7.3 The Spread of Christianity, 400–800 151
MAP 7.4 The Byzantine Empire in the Time of Justinian 153
SPOT MAP The Byzantine Empire, c. 750 155
MAP 7.5 The Spread of Islam 159
MAP 8.1 The Carolingian Empire 165
SPOT MAP Division of the Carolingian Empire by the Treaty of Verdun, 843 169
MAP 8.2 Invasions of the Ninth and Tenth Centuries 170
MAP 8.3 A Typical Manor 174
SPOT MAP The Byzantine Empire in 1025 177
MAP 8.4 The Migrations of the Slavs 177
SPOT MAP The Abbasid Caliphate at the Height of Its Power 180
SPOT MAP Flanders as a Trade Center 191
MAP 9.1 Medieval Trade Routes 192
MAP 9.2 Main Intellectual Centers of Medieval Europe 197
MAP 10.1 England and France, 1154–1337: (*left*) England and Its French Holdings; (*right*) Growth of the French State 210
MAP 10.2 Christian Reconquests in the Western Mediterranean 211
MAP 10.3 The Holy Roman Empire in the Twelfth Century 213
MAP 10.4 Northern and Eastern Europe, c. 1150 214
SPOT MAP The Mongol Empire in the Thirteenth Century 214
MAP 10.5 The Early Crusades 225
MAP 11.1 Spread of the Black Death 233
MAP 11.2 The Hundred Years' War 237
SPOT MAP The Holy Roman Empire in the Fourteenth Century 242
SPOT MAP The States of Italy in the Fourteenth Century 242
SPOT MAP Avignon 245
MAP 12.1 Renaissance Italy 260
MAP 12.2 Europe in the Second Half of the Fifteenth Century 272
MAP 13.1 The Empire of Charles V 286
SPOT MAP Zwingli's Zürich 288
SPOT MAP Calvin's Geneva 291
MAP 13.2 Catholics and Protestants in Europe by 1560 294
SPOT MAP The Netherlands 298
MAP 14.1 European Discoveries and Possessions in the Fifteenth and Sixteenth Centuries 307

SPOT MAP Lands of the Maya 310
SPOT MAP The Aztec Empire 311
SPOT MAP Lands of the Inca 311
MAP 14.2 Triangular Trade in the Atlantic Economy 315
SPOT MAP Southeast Asia, c. 1700 315
SPOT MAP The Mughal Empire 319
SPOT MAP The Qing Empire 320
SPOT MAP The West Indies 322
MAP 15.1 The Thirty Years' War 335
MAP 15.2 The Growth of Brandenburg-Prussia 340
MAP 15.3 The Growth of the Austrian Empire 341
MAP 15.4 Russia: From Principality to Nation-State 342
SPOT MAP Civil War in England 346

FEATURES

FILM & HISTORY

Alexander (2004) 75

Gladiator (2000) 128

The Lion in Winter (1968) 208

Joan of Arc (1948) *The Messenger: The Story of Joan of Arc* (1999) 240

Elizabeth (1998) 300

The Mission (1986) 325

OPPOSING VIEWPOINTS

Akhenaten's *Hymn to Aten* and Psalm 104 of the Hebrew Bible 21

The Governing of Empires: Two Approaches 36

Women in Athens and Sparta 65

Demosthenes and Isocrates Address Philip of Macedonia 71

The End of the Republic: Three Views 108

Roman Authorities and a Christian on Christianity 133

Two Views of the Huns 142

Lords and Vassals in Europe and Japan 173

Two Views of Trade and Merchants 193

The Siege of Jerusalem: Christian and Muslim Perspectives 226

Causes of the Black Death: Contemporary Views 232

The Renaissance Prince: The Views of Machiavelli and Erasmus 262

A Reformation Debate: Conflict at Marburg 289

West Meets East: An Exchange of Royal Letters 318

Oliver Cromwell: Three Perspectives 347

A New Heaven? Faith Versus Reason 363

IMAGES OF EVERYDAY LIFE

The Egyptian Diet 20

Trade and the Products of Trade 122

Life in a Medieval Town 195

Entertainment in the Middle Ages 249

Spices and World Trade 309

Dutch Domesticity 345

PREFACE

DURING A VISIT to Great Britain, where he studied as a young man, Mohandas Gandhi, the leader of the effort to liberate India from British colonial rule, was asked what he thought of Western civilization. "I think it would be a good idea," he replied. Gandhi's response was as correct as it was clever. Western civilization has led to great problems as well as great accomplishments, but it remains a good idea. And any complete understanding of today's world must take into account the meaning of Western civilization and the role Western civilization has played in history. Despite modern progress, we still greatly reflect our religious traditions, our political systems and theories, our economic and social structures, and our cultural heritage. I have written this brief history of Western civilization to assist a new generation of students in learning more about the past that has shaped them and the world in which they live.

At the same time, for the eighth edition, as in the seventh, I have added considerable new material on world history to show the impact other parts of the world have had on the West. Certainly, the ongoing struggle with terrorists since 2001 has dramatized the intricate relationship between the West and the rest of the world. It is important then to show not only how Western civilization has affected the rest of the world but also how it has been influenced and even defined since its beginnings by contacts with other peoples around the world.

Another of my goals was to write a well-balanced work in which the political, economic, social, religious, intellectual, cultural, and military aspects of Western civilization would be integrated into a chronologically ordered synthesis. Moreover, I wanted to avoid the approach that is quite common in other brief histories of Western civilization—an approach that makes them collections of facts with little continuity from section to section. Instead, I sought to keep the *story* in *history*. Narrative history effectively transmits the knowledge of the past and is the form that best enables students to remember and understand the past. At the same time, I have not overlooked the need for the kind of historical analysis that makes students aware that historians often disagree in their interpretations of the past.

Features of the Text

To enliven the past and let readers see for themselves the materials that historians use to create their pictures of the past, I have included in each chapter **primary sources** (boxed documents) that are keyed to the discussion in the text. The documents include examples of the religious, artistic, intellectual, social, economic, and political aspects of Western life. Such varied sources as a description of the life of an upper-class Roman, marriage negotiations in Renaissance Italy, a debate in the Reformation era, and the diary of a German soldier at Stalingrad all reveal in vivid fashion what Western civilization meant to the individual men and women who shaped it by their activities. Questions at the end of each source aid students in analyzing the documents.

A second primary source feature, **Opposing Viewpoints**, introduced in the seventh edition, presents comparisons of two or three primary sources along with focus questions to facilitate student analysis of historical documents. A visual feature, **Images of Everyday Life**, combines two or more illustrations with a lengthy caption to provide insight into various aspects of social life. Another boxed feature, **Film & History**, presents a brief analysis of a film's plot as well as its historical significance, value, and accuracy. (For more specifics about all of these features see "New to This Edition.")

A section entitled "Studying from Primary Source Materials" appears in the front of the book to introduce students to the language and tools of analyzing historical evidence—documents, photos, artwork, and maps.

Each chapter has an **introduction and an illustrated chapter summary** to help maintain the continuity of the narrative and to provide a synthesis of important themes. Anecdotes in the chapter introductions dramatically convey the major theme or themes of each chapter. **Detailed chronologies** reinforce the events discussed in the text, and a **timeline** at the end of each chapter enables students to review at a glance the chief developments of an era. Many of the timelines also show parallel developments in different cultures or nations. **Suggestions for Further Reading** at the end of each chapter review the most recent literature on each period and also point readers to some of the older "classic" works in each field. New **"Upon Reflection" Chapter Review questions and Key Terms lists** provide valuable study aids.

Updated maps and extensive illustrations serve to deepen readers' understanding of the text. **Detailed map captions** are designed to enrich students' awareness of the importance of geography to history, and numerous **spot maps** enable students to see at a glance the region or subject being discussed in the text. Map captions also include a map question to guide students' reading of the map. To facilitate understanding of cultural movements, illustrations of artistic works discussed in the text are placed near the discussions. Throughout the text, illustration captions have been revised and expanded to further students' understanding of the past. **Chapter outlines and focus questions, including critical thinking questions**, at the beginning of each chapter give students a useful overview and guide them to the main subjects of each chapter. The focus questions are then repeated at the beginning of each major section in the chapter. A **glossary of important terms** (boldfaced in the text when they are introduced and defined) is provided at the back of the book to maximize reader comprehension. A **guide to pronunciation** is now provided in the text in parentheses following the first mention of a complex name or term.

New to This Edition

As preparation for the revision of *Western Civilization: A Brief History*, I reexamined the entire book and analyzed the comments and reviews of colleagues who have found the book to be a useful instrument for introducing their students to the history of Western civilization. In making revisions for the eighth edition, I sought to build on the strengths of the previous editions and above all to maintain the balance, synthesis, and narrative qualities that characterized those editions. To keep up with the ever-growing body of historical scholarship, new or revised material has been added throughout the book on all of the following topics:

Chapter 1 Early human development; Sargon of Akkad; new Opposing Viewpoints feature on "Akhenaten's *Hymn to Aten* and Psalm 104 of the Hebrew Bible"; revision of Images of Everyday Life feature on "The Egyptian Diet."

Chapter 2 The Hittites; early history of the Israelites; Zoroastrianism; new Opposing Viewpoints feature on "The Governing of Empires: Two Approaches."

Chapter 3 The Persian Wars.

Chapter 4 Philip's military reforms; new Opposing Viewpoints feature on "Demosthenes and Isocrates Address Philip of Macedonia."

Chapter 5 Roman military success; new Opposing Viewpoints feature on "The End of the Republic: Three Views."

Chapter 6 The Roman army; new Film & History feature on *Gladiator*.

Chapter 7 Constantinople and the role of trade; the rise of Islam; new Opposing Viewpoints feature on "Two Views of the Huns."

Chapter 8 Charlemagne and the Carolingian Empire; new Opposing Viewpoints feature on "Lords and Vassals in Europe and Japan."

Chapter 9 New Opposing Viewpoints feature on "Two Views of Trade and Merchants."

Chapter 10 England in the High Middle Ages; revision of Film & History feature on *The Lion in Winter*; the Crusades.

Chapter 11 New section on "The Black Death: From Asia to Europe" with subsection on "Role of the Mongols"; revised section on "The Black Death in Europe"; new Opposing Viewpoints feature on "Causes of the Black Death: Contemporary Views."

Chapter 12 Women in the home in the Italian Renaissance; the impact of the Italian wars on Machiavelli; the *studia humanitatis*; the Spanish expulsion of the Jews and Muslims; the threat of the Ottoman Turks to the West.

Chapter 13 Luther and indulgences; Luther and the peasants; the empire of Charles V; the meaning of the Catholic Reformation.

Chapter 14 Revision of introduction to include a more concise road map of the chapter; the Portuguese maritime empire; new Images of Everyday Life feature on "Spices and World Trade"; the impact of the slave trade on Africa; the products of the Columbian Exchange; mercantilism.

Chapter 15 The Thirty Years' War; how "Western" Russia was before Peter the Great; new Opposing Viewpoints feature on "Oliver Cromwell: Three Perspectives."

Chapter 16 Antoine Lavoisier and his wife; the state and science.

Chapter 17 Travel literature and the concept of race.

Chapter 18 New Opposing Viewpoints feature on "Enlightened Absolutism: Enlightened or Absolute?"

Chapter 19 The Jacobins; women in the French Revolution.

Chapter 20 Iron production, especially pig iron and wrought iron; the Crystal Palace and colonization; new Opposing Viewpoints feature on "Attitudes of the

Industrial Middle Class in Britain and Japan"; new Images of Everyday Life on "Living Conditions of London's Poor."

Chapter 21 The corn laws in Great Britain.

Chapter 22 New Opposing Viewpoints feature on "The Practice of *Realpolitik*: Two Approaches"; new Film & History feature on *The Young Victoria*.

Chapter 23 The national state (in the introduction); the city; new section on "Mass Consumption."

Chapter 24 New introduction to the chapter; Modernism in literature and the arts.

Chapter 25 Enthusiasm for the outbreak of war; fighting in the African colonies; the motives of colonial subjects in fighting for their European rulers; revised material on the Turkish genocide of the Armenians; revision of the discussion of the peace settlement after World War I.

Chapter 26 The League of Nations; the Great Depression; women in the Middle East; self-rule for India; the Weimar Republic; the Spanish Civil War; new Opposing Viewpoints feature on "Spain Divided: The Poems of Two Brothers."

Chapter 27 The prelude to World War II and the course of the war; new illustration feature (two illustrations) on the pivotal Battle of Stalingrad.

Chapter 28 The origins of the Cold War; new section on "The Attempt to Revive Religion."

Chapter 29 New Opposing Viewpoints feature on "Czechoslovakia, 1968: Two Faces of Communism."

Chapter 30 New Opposing Viewpoints feature on "Islam and the West: Secularism in France"; Britain, Germany, France, the United States; the wars in Afghanistan and Iraq; gender issues and Muslim immigrants; technology in "The Digital Age"; new section on the global financial collapse titled "The End of Excess."

The enthusiastic response to the primary sources (boxed documents) led me to evaluate the content of each document carefully and add new documents throughout the text, including new comparative documents in the feature called **Opposing Viewpoints**. This feature has been expanded and now appears in every chapter, including such new topics as "Lords and Vassals in Europe and Japan," "Causes of the Black Death: Contemporary Views," "Attitudes of the Industrial Middle Class in Britain and Japan," and "Czechoslovakia, 1968: Two Faces of Communism." Two additional features have also been expanded. **Images of Everyday Life** can now be found in twelve chapters, including such new topics as "Spices and World Trade" and "Living Conditions of London's Poor." **Film & History features** now appear in eleven chapters, including such additions as *Gladiator* and *The Young Victoria*.

The **Suggestions for Further Reading** at the end of each chapter have been thoroughly updated and are organized under subheadings to make them more useful. Additional reading suggestions have been included online. New illustrations were added to every chapter. Chapter Notes have now been placed at the end of the book rather than at the end of each chapter.

A new format has been added at the end of each chapter. The **Chapter Summary** is illustrated with thumbnail images of chapter illustrations and combined with the **Chapter Timeline**. A **Chapter Review** has been added to assist students in studying the chapter. This review includes **Upon Reflection** essay question and a list of **Key Terms** from the chapter.

Because courses in Western civilization at American and Canadian colleges and universities follow different chronological divisions, the text is available in both one-volume and two-volume versions to fit the needs of instructors. Teaching and learning ancillaries include the following.

Instructor Resources

PowerLecture DVD with ExamView® and JoinIn® [ISBN: 9781133944058] This dual platform, all-in-one multimedia resource includes the Instructor's Resource Manual; Test Bank, prepared by Sarah K. Nytroe of DeSales University (includes key term identification, multiple-choice, true-false, and essay questions); Microsoft® PowerPoint® slides of both lecture outlines and images and maps from the text that can be used as offered or customized by importing personal lecture slides or other material; and *JoinIn®* PowerPoint® slides with clicker content. Also included is ExamView, an easy-to-use assessment and tutorial system that allows instructors to create, deliver, and customize tests in minutes. Instructors can build tests with as many as 250 questions using up to twelve question types, and using ExamView's complete word-processing capabilities, they can enter an unlimited number of new questions or edit existing ones.

eInstructor's Resource Manual Prepared by Sarah K. Nytroe of DeSales University, this manual has many features, including chapter outlines and summaries, lecture suggestions, suggested research topics, map exercises, discussion questions for primary source documents, and suggested readings and resources. Available on the instructor's companion website.

CourseMate Cengage Learning's History CourseMate brings course concepts to life with interactive learning, study, and exam preparation tools that support the printed textbook. History CourseMate includes an integrated ebook; interactive teaching and learning tools including quizzes, flashcards, videos, and more; and EngagementTracker, a first-of-its-kind tool that monitors student engagement in the course. Learn more at www.cengagebrain.com.

Aplia Aplia™ is an online interactive learning solution that improves comprehension and outcomes by increasing student effort and engagement. Founded by a professor to enhance his own courses, Aplia provides automatically graded assignments with detailed, immediate explanations on every question. The interactive assignments have been developed to address the major concepts covered in *Western Civilization: A Brief History* and are designed to promote critical thinking and engage students more fully in learning. Question types include questions built around animated maps, primary sources such as newspaper extracts, or imagined scenarios, such as engaging in a conversation with Benjamin Franklin or finding a diary and having to fill in some blank words; more in-depth primary source question sets that address a major topic with a number of related primary sources; and questions that promote deeper analysis of historical evidence. Images, video clips, and audio clips are incorporated into many of the questions. Students get immediate feedback on their work (not only what they got right or wrong, but why), and they can choose to see another set of related questions if they want to practice further. A searchable ebook is available inside the course as well so that students can easily reference it as they are working. Map-reading and writing tutorials are also available to get students off to a good start.

Aplia's simple-to-use course management interface allows instructors to post announcements, upload course materials, host student discussions, e-mail students, and manage the gradebook; a knowledgeable and friendly support team offers personalized assistance in customizing assignments to the instructor's course schedule. To learn more and view a demo for this book, visit www.aplia.com.

CourseReader CourseReader is an online collection of primary and secondary sources that lets you create a customized electronic reader in minutes. With an easy-to-use interface and assessment tool, you can choose exactly what your students will be assigned—simply search or browse Cengage Learning's extensive document database to preview and select your customized collection of readings. In addition to print sources of all types (letters, diary entries, speeches, newspaper accounts, and more), the collection includes a growing number of images and video and audio clips.

Each primary source document includes a descriptive headnote that puts the reading into context and is further supported by both critical thinking and multiple-choice questions designed to reinforce key points. For more information visit www.cengage.com/coursereader.

Cengagebrain.com Save your students time and money. Direct them to www.cengagebrain.com for a choice of formats and savings and a better chance to succeed in your class. *Cengagebrain.com*, Cengage Learning's online store, is a single destination for more than 10,000 new textbooks, eTextbooks, eChapters, study tools, and audio supplements. Students have the freedom to purchase à la carte exactly what they need when they need it. Students can save 50 percent on the electronic textbook and can pay as little as $1.99 for an individual eChapter.

Student Resources

Book Companion Site This website for students features a wide assortment of resources to help students master the subject matter. Prepared by Michael A. Sparks of Ivy Tech Community College—Central Indiana, the website includes learning objectives, a glossary, flashcards, tutorial quizzes, matching exercises, critical thinking exercises, weblinks, and suggested readings.

CL eBook This interactive multimedia ebook links out to rich media assets such as video and MP3 chapter summaries. Through this ebook, students can also access self-test quizzes, chapter outlines, matching exercises, critical thinking questions (for which the answers can be e-mailed to their instructors), primary source documents with critical thinking questions, and interactive (zoomable) maps. Available at www.cengagebrain.com.

Doing History: Research and Writing in the Digital Age, 2e [ISBN: 9781133587880] Prepared by Michael J. Galgano, J. Chris Arndt, and Raymond M. Hyser of James Madison University. Whether you're starting down the path as a history major or simply looking for a straightforward and systematic guide to writing a successful paper, you'll find this text to be an indispensable handbook to historical research. This text's "soup to nuts" approach to researching and writing about history addresses every step of the process, from locating your sources and gathering information, to writing clearly and making proper use of various citation styles to avoid plagiarism. You'll also learn how to make the most of every tool available to you—especially the technology that helps you conduct the process efficiently and effectively. The second edition includes a special appendix linked to CourseReader (see above), where you can examine and interpret primary sources online.

The History Handbook, 2e [ISBN: 9780495906766] Prepared by Carol Berkin of Baruch College, City University of New York, and Betty Anderson of Boston University. This book teaches students both basic and history-specific study skills such as how to take notes, get the most out of lectures and readings, read primary sources, research historical topics, and correctly cite sources. Substantially less expensive than comparable skill-building texts, *The History Handbook* also offers tips for Internet research and evaluating online sources. Additionally, students can purchase and download the *eAudio* version of *The History Handbook* or any of its eighteen individual units at www.cengagebrain.com to listen to on the go.

Writing for College History, 1e [ISBN: 9780618306039] Prepared by Robert M. Frakes of Clarion University. This brief handbook for survey courses in American history, Western Civilization/European history, and world civilization guides students through the various types of writing assignments they encounter in a history class. Providing examples of student writing and candid assessments of student work, this text focuses on the rules and conventions of writing for the college history course.

The Modern Researcher, 6e [ISBN: 9780495318705] Prepared by Jacques Barzun and Henry F. Graff of Columbia University. This classic introduction to the techniques of research and the art of expression is used widely in history courses, but is also appropriate for writing and research methods courses in other departments. Barzun and Graff thoroughly cover every aspect of research, from the selection of a topic through the gathering, analysis, writing, revision, and publication of findings. They present the process not as a set of rules but through actual cases that put the subtleties of research in a useful context. Part One covers the principles and methods of research; Part Two covers writing, speaking, and getting one's work published.

Reader Program Cengage Learning publishes a number of readers. Some contain exclusively primary sources, others are devoted to essays and secondary sources, and still others provide a combination of primary and secondary sources. All of these readers are designed to guide students through the process of historical inquiry. Visit Cengage.com/history for a complete list of readers.

Rand McNally Historical Atlas of Western Civilization, 2e [ISBN: 9780618841943] This valuable resource features more than forty-five maps, including maps highlighting Classical Greece and Rome; maps documenting European civilization during the Renaissance; maps following events in Germany, Russia, and Italy as they lead up to World Wars I and II; maps showing the dissolution of communism in 1989; maps depicting language and religion in the Western world; and maps describing the unification and industrialization of Europe.

Document Exercise Workbook [ISBN: V1: 9780534560836; V2: 9780534560843] Prepared by Donna Van Raaphorst, Cuyahoga Community College. This collection of exercises is based around primary sources. Available in two volumes.

Custom Options Nobody knows your students like you, so why not give them a text that is tailor-fit to their needs? Cengage Learning offers custom solutions for your course—whether it's making a small modification to *Western Civilization: A Brief History* to match your syllabus or combining multiple sources to create something truly unique. You can pick and choose chapters, include your own material, and add additional map exercises along with the *Rand McNally Atlas* to create a text that fits the way you teach. Ensure that your students get the most out of their textbook dollar by giving them exactly what they need. Contact your Cengage Learning representative to explore custom solutions for your course.

ACKNOWLEDGMENTS

I WOULD LIKE TO THANK the many teachers and students who have used previous editions of *Western Civilization: A Brief History*. I am gratified by their enthusiastic response to a textbook that was intended to put the *story* back in *history* and capture the imagination of the reader. I especially thank the many teachers and students who made the effort to contact me personally to share their enthusiasm. I am deeply grateful to John Soares for his assistance in preparing the map captions and to Charmarie Blaisdell of Northeastern University for her detailed suggestions on women's history. Daniel Haxall of Kutztown University provided valuable assistance with materials on postwar art, popular culture, Postmodern art and thought, and the Digital Age. I am especially grateful to Kathryn Spielvogel for her work as a research associate. Thanks to Wadsworth's comprehensive review process, many historians were asked to evaluate my manuscript and review each edition. I am grateful to the following for the innumerable suggestions that have greatly improved my work:

Patricia Adelle
William Paterson University

Paul Allen
University of Utah

Gerald Anderson
North Dakota State University

Susan L. H. Anderson
Campbell University

Letizia Argenteri
University of San Diego

Roy A. Austensen
Illinois State University

James A. Baer
Northern Virginia Community College—Alexandria

James T. Baker
Western Kentucky University

Patrick Bass
Morningside College

John F. Battick
University of Maine

Frederic J. Baumgartner
Virginia Polytechnic Institute

Phillip N. Bebb
Ohio University

Anthony Bedford
Modesto Junior College

F. E. Beemon
Middle Tennessee State University

Joel Benson
Northwest Missouri State University

Robert L. Bergman
Glendale Community College

Leonard R. Berlanstein
University of Virginia

Douglas T. Bisson
Belmont University

Charmarie Blaisdell
Northeastern University

Stephen H. Blumm
Montgomery County Community College

Hugh S. Bonar
California State University

Werner Braatz
University of Wisconsin—Oshkosh

Alfred S. Bradford
University of Missouri

Maryann E. Brink
College of William & Mary

Blaine T. Browne
Broward Community College

J. Holden Camp, Jr.
Hillyer College, University of Hartford

Jack Cargill
Rutgers University

Martha Carlin
University of Wisconsin—Milwaukee

Elizabeth Carney
Clemson University

Kevin K. Carroll
Arizona State University

Yuan-Ling Chao
Middle Tennessee State University

Eric H. Cline
Xavier University

Michael Clinton
Gwynedd Mercy College

Robert Cole
Utah State University

William J. Connell
Rutgers University

Nancy Conradt
College of DuPage

Marc Cooper
Southwest Missouri State

Caitlin Corning
George Fox University

Richard A. Cosgrove
University of Arizona

David A. Crain
South Dakota State University

Michael A. Crane, Jr. (student)
Everett Community College

Steve Culbertson
Owens Community College

Luanne Dagley
Pellissippi State Technical Community College

Marion F. Deshmukh
George Mason University

Michael F. Doyle
Ocean County College

Michael Duckett
Dawson College

Laura Dull
Delta College

Roxanne Easley
Central Washington University

James W. Ermatinger
University of Nebraska—Kearney

Charles T. Evans
Northern Virginia Community College

Porter Ewing
Los Angeles City College

Carla Falkner
Northeast Mississippi Community College

Steven Fanning
University of Illinois—Chicago

Ellsworth Faris
California State University—Chico

Gary B. Ferngren
Oregon State University

Mary Helen Finnerty
Westchester Community College

Eve Fisher
South Dakota State University

Lucien Frary
Rider University

A. Z. Freeman
Robinson College

Marsha Frey
Kansas State University

Frank J. Frost
University of California—Santa Barbara

Frank Garosi
California State University—Sacramento

Lorettann Gascard
Franklin Pierce College

Richard M. Golden
University of North Texas

Manuel G. Gonzales
Diablo Valley College

Amy G. Gordon
Denison University

Richard J. Grace
Providence College

Hanns Gross
Loyola University

John F. Guilmartin
Ohio State University

Jeffrey S. Hamilton
Gustavus Adolphus College

J. Drew Harrington
Western Kentucky University

James Harrison
Siena College

Derek Hastings
Oakland University

A. J. Heisserer
University of Oklahoma

Rowena Hernández-Múzquiz
Old Dominion University

Betsey Hertzler
Mesa Community College

Robert Herzstein
University of South Carolina

Shirley Hickson
North Greenville College

Martha L. Hildreth
University of Nevada

Boyd H. Hill, Jr.
University of Colorado—Boulder

Michael Hofstetter
Bethany College

Donald C. Holsinger
Seattle Pacific University

Frank L. Holt
University of Houston

W. Robert Houston
University of South Alabama

David R. C. Hudson
Texas A&M University

Paul Hughes
Sussex County Community College

Richard A. Jackson
University of Houston

Fred Jewell
Harding University

Jenny M. Jochens
Towson State University

Carolyn Johnston
Marian College

William M. Johnston
University of Massachusetts

Allen E. Jones
Troy State University

George Kaloudis
Rivier College

Jeffrey A. Kaufmann
Muscatine Community College

David O. Kieft
University of Minnesota

Patricia Killen
Pacific Lutheran University

William E. Kinsella, Jr.
Northern Virginia Community College—Annandale

James M. Kittelson
Ohio State University

Doug Klepper
Santa Fe Community College

Mark Klobas
Scottsdale Community College

Cynthia Kosso
Northern Arizona University

Clayton Miles Lehmann
University of South Dakota

Diana Chen Lin
Indiana University, Northwest

Ursula W. MacAffer
Hudson Valley Community College

Anthony Makowski
Delaware County Community College

Harold Marcuse
University of California—Santa Barbara

Mavis Mate
University of Oregon

Tom Maulucci
State University of New York—Fredonia

T. Ronald Melton
Brewton Parker College

Jack Allen Meyer
University of South Carolina

Eugene W. Miller, Jr.
The Pennsylvania State University—Hazleton

David Mock
Tallahassee Community College

John Patrick Montano
University of Delaware

Rex Morrow
Trident Technical College

Thomas M. Mulhern
University of North Dakota

Pierce Mullen
Montana State University

Frederick I. Murphy
Western Kentucky University

William M. Murray
University of South Florida

Otto M. Nelson
Texas Tech University

Sam Nelson
Willmar Community College

John A. Nichols
Slippery Rock University

Lisa Nofzinger
Albuquerque Technical Vocational Institute

Heather O'Grady-Evans
Elmira College

Chris Oldstone-Moore
Augustana College

Donald Ostrowski
Harvard University

James O. Overfield
University of Vermont

Matthew L. Panczyk
Bergen Community College

Kathleen Parrow
Black Hills State University

Michael Pascale
SUNY, Suffolk County Community College

Jonathan Perry
University of Central Florida

Carla Rahn Phillips
University of Minnesota

Keith Pickus
Wichita State University

Linda J. Piper
University of Georgia

Janet Polasky
University of New Hampshire

Thomas W. Porter
Randolph-Macon College

Charles A. Povlovich
California State University—Fullerton

Nancy Rachels
Hillsborough Community College

Charles Rearick
University of Massachusetts—Amherst

Jerome V. Reel, Jr.
Clemson University

Paul Reuter
Jefferson State Community College

Joseph Robertson
Gadsden State Community College

Jonathan Roth
San Jose State University

Constance M. Rousseau
Providence College

Julius R. Ruff
Marquette University

Richard Saller
University of Chicago

Magdalena Sanchez
Texas Christian University

Bonnie F. Saunders
Glendale Community College

Jack Schanfield
Suffolk County Community College

Richard Schellhammer
University of West Alabama

Linda Scherr
Mercer County Community College

Roger Schlesinger
Washington State University

Joanne Schneider
Rhode Island College

Thomas C. Schunk
University of Wisconsin—Oshkosh

Denise Scifres
Hinds Community College

Kyle C. Sessions
Illinois State University

Colleen M. Shaughnessy Zeena
Endicott College

Linda Simmons
Northern Virginia Community College—Manassas

Donald V. Sippel
Rhode Island College

Douglas R. Skopp
State University of New York—Plattsburgh

Glen Spann
Asbury College

John W. Steinberg
Georgia Southern University

Paul W. Strait
Florida State University

James E. Straukamp
California State University—Sacramento

Brian E. Strayer
Andrews University

Fred Suppe
Ball State University

Ruth Suyama
Los Angeles Mission College

Roger Tate
Somerset Community College

Tom Taylor
Seattle University

Jack W. Thacker
Western Kentucky University

Janet A. Thompson
Tallahassee Community College

David S. Trask
Guilford Technical Community College

Thomas Turley
Santa Clara University

John G. Tuthill
University of Guam

Maarten Ultee
University of Alabama

Donna L. Van Raaphorst
Cuyahoga Community College

Nancy G. Vavra
University of Colorado—Boulder

Janet Walmsley
George Mason University

Allen M. Ward
University of Connecticut

Richard D. Weigel
Western Kentucky University

Michael Weiss
Linn-Benton Community College

Richard S. Williams
Washington State University

Arthur H. Williamson
California State University—Sacramento

Katherine Workman
Wright State University

Judith T. Wozniak
Cleveland State University

Walter J. Wussow
University of Wisconsin—Eau Claire

Edwin M. Yamauchi
Miami University

The editors at Cengage Wadsworth have been both helpful and congenial at all times. I especially wish to thank Clark Baxter, whose clever wit, wisdom, gentle prodding, and good friendship have added much depth to our working relationship. Margaret McAndrew Beasley thoughtfully, wisely, efficiently, and pleasantly guided the overall development of the eighth edition. I also thank Brooke Barbier for her valuable insights. I want to express my gratitude to John Orr, whose good humor, well-advised suggestions, and generous verbal support made the production process easier. Pat Lewis was, as usual, a truly outstanding copyeditor. Abigail Baxter provided valuable assistance in obtaining permissions for the illustrations.

Above all, I thank my family for their support. The gifts of love, laughter, and patience from my daughters, Jennifer and Kathryn; my sons, Eric and Christian; my daughters-in-law, Liz and Laurie; and my sons-in-law, Daniel and Eddie, were enormously appreciated. I also wish to acknowledge my grandchildren, Devyn, Bryn, Drew, Elena, Sean, Emma, and Jackson, who bring great joy to my life. My wife and best friend, Diane, contributed editorial assistance, wise counsel, good humor, and the loving support that made it possible for me to accomplish a project of this magnitude. I could not have written the book without her.

INTRODUCTION TO STUDENTS OF WESTERN CIVILIZATION

CIVILIZATION, AS HISTORIANS define it, first emerged between five and six thousand years ago when people in different parts of the world began to live in organized communities with distinct political, military, economic, and social structures. Religious, intellectual, and artistic activities assumed important roles in these early societies. The focus of this book is on Western civilization, a civilization that many people identify with the continent of Europe.

Defining Western Civilization

Western civilization itself has evolved considerably over the centuries. Although the concept of the West did not yet exist at the time of the Mesopotamians and Egyptians, their development of writing, their drafting of law codes, and their practice of different roles based on gender all eventually influenced what became Western civilization. Although the Greeks did not conceive of Western civilization as a cultural entity, their artistic, intellectual, and political contributions were crucial to the foundations of Western civilization. The Romans produced a remarkable series of accomplishments that were fundamental to the development of Western civilization, which came to consist largely of lands in Europe conquered by the Romans, in which Roman cultural and political ideals were gradually spread. Nevertheless, people in these early civilizations viewed themselves as subjects of states or empires, not as members of Western civilization.

With the rise of Christianity during the Late Roman Empire, however, peoples in Europe began to identify themselves as part of a civilization different from other civilizations, such as that of Islam, leading to a concept of a Western civilization different from other civilizations. In the fifteenth century, Renaissance intellectuals began to identify this civilization not only with Christianity but also with the intellectual and political achievements of the ancient Greeks and Romans.

Important to the development of the idea of a distinct Western civilization were encounters with other peoples. Between 700 and 1500, encounters with the world of Islam helped define the West. But after 1500, as European ships began to move into other parts of the world, encounters with peoples in Asia, Africa, and the Americas not only had an impact on the civilizations found there but also affected how people in the West defined themselves. At the same time, as they set up colonies, Europeans began to transplant a sense of Western identity to other areas of the world, especially North America and parts of Latin America, that have come to be considered part of Western civilization.

As the concept of Western civilization has evolved over the centuries, so have the values and unique features associated with that civilization. Science played a crucial role in the development of modern Western civilization. The societies of the Greeks, the Romans, and the medieval Europeans were based largely on a belief in the existence of a spiritual order; a dramatic departure to a natural or material view of the universe occurred in the seventeenth-century Scientific Revolution. Science and technology have been important in the growth of today's modern and largely secular Western civilization, although antecedents to scientific development also existed in Greek and medieval thought and practice, and religion remains a component of the Western world today.

Many historians have viewed the concept of political liberty, belief in the fundamental value of every individual, and a rational outlook based on a system of logical, analytical thought as unique aspects of Western civilization. Of course, the West has also witnessed horrendous negations of liberty, individualism, and reason. Racism, slavery, violence, world wars, totalitarian regimes—these, too, form part of the complex story of what constitutes Western civilization.

The Dating of Time

In our examination of Western civilization, we also need to be aware of the dating of time. In recording the past, historians try to determine the exact time when events occurred. World War II in Europe, for example, began on September 1, 1939, when Hitler sent German troops into Poland, and ended on May 7, 1945, when Germany surrendered. By using dates, historians can place events in order and try to determine the development of patterns over periods of time.

If someone asked you when you were born, you would reply with a number, such as 1993. In the United States, we would all accept that number without question because it is part of the dating system followed in the Western world (Europe and the Western Hemisphere). In this system, events are dated by counting backward or forward from the the year 1. When the system was first devised, the year 1 was assumed to be the year of the birth of Jesus, and the abbreviations B.C. (before Christ) and A.D. (for the Latin words *anno Domini*, meaning "in the year of the Lord") were used to refer to the periods before and after the birth of Jesus, respectively. Historians now generally prefer to refer to the year 1 in nonreligious terms as the beginning of the "common era." The abbreviations B.C.E. (before the common era) and C.E. (common era) are used instead of B.C. and A.D., although the years are the same. Thus, an event that took place four hundred years before the year 1 would be dated 400 B.C.E. (before the common era)—or the date could be expressed as 400 B.C. Dates after the year 1 are labeled C.E. Thus, an event that took place two hundred years after the year 1 would be dated 200 C.E. (common era), or the date could be written A.D. 200. It can also be written simply as 200, just as you would not give your birth year as 1993 C.E. but simply as 1993.

Historians also make use of other terms to refer to time. A *decade* is ten years, a *century* is one hundred years, and a *millennium* is one thousand years. Thus "the fourth century B.C.E." refers to the fourth period of one hundred years counting backward from the year 1, the beginning of the common era. Since the first century B.C.E. would be the years 100 B.C.E. to 1 B.C.E., the fourth century B.C.E. would be the years 400 B.C.E. to 301 B.C.E. We could say, then, that an event in 350 B.C.E. took place in the fourth century B.C.E.

Similarly, the "fourth century C.E." refers to the fourth period of one hundred years after the beginning of the common era. Since the first period of one hundred years would be the years 1 to 100, the fourth period or fourth century would be the years 301 to 400. We could say, then, that an event in 350 took place in the fourth century. Likewise, the first millennium B.C.E. refers to the years 1000 B.C.E. to 1 B.C.E.; the second millennium C.E. refers to the years 1001 to 2000.

The dating of events can also vary from people to people. Most people in the Western world use the Western calendar, also known as the Gregorian calendar after Pope Gregory XIII, who refined it in 1582. The Hebrew calendar uses a different system in which the year 1 is the equivalent of the Western year 3760 B.C.E., considered to be the date of the creation of the world according to the Bible. Thus, the Western year 2012 is the year 5772 on the Hebrew calendar. The Islamic calendar begins year 1 on the day Muhammad fled Mecca, which is the year 622 on the Western calendar.

STUDYING FROM PRIMARY SOURCE MATERIALS

ASTRONOMERS INVESTIGATE THE universe through telescopes. Biologists study the natural world by collecting plants and animals in the field and then examining them with microscopes. Sociologists and psychologists study human behavior through observation and controlled laboratory experiments.

Historians study the past by examining historical "evidence" or "source" materials—church or town records, letters, treaties, advertisements, paintings, menus, literature, buildings, clothing—anything and everything written or created by our ancestors that give clues about their lives and the times in which they lived.

Historians refer to written material as "documents." Excerpts of more than 150 documents—some in shaded boxes and others in the text narrative itself—appear in every chapter of this textbook. Each chapter also includes several photographs of buildings, paintings, and/or other kinds of historical evidence.

As you read each chapter, the more you examine all this "evidence," the more you will understand the main ideas of the course. This introduction to studying historical evidence, along with the visual summaries at the end of each chapter, will help you learn how to look at evidence the way historians do. The better you become at reading evidence, the better the grade you will earn in your course.

Source Material Comes in Two Main Types: Primary and Secondary

Primary evidence is material that comes to us exactly as it left the pen of the person who wrote it. Letters between King Louis XIV of France and the king of Tonkin (now Vietnam) are primary evidence (p. 318). So is the court transcript of a witchcraft trial in France (p. 333), a play by Shakespeare (p. 354), or a diagram of the solar system drawn by Copernicus (p. 361).

Secondary evidence is an account by someone about the life or activity of someone else. A story about Abraham Lincoln written by his secretary of war would give us primary source information about Lincoln by someone who knew him. Reflections about Lincoln's presidency written by a historian might give us insights into how, for example, Lincoln governed during wartime. But because the historian did not know Lincoln in person, we would consider this a secondary source of information about Lincoln. Secondary sources such as historical essays (and textbooks such as this one) can therefore by very helpful in understanding the past. But it is important to remember that a secondary source can reveal as much about its author as it does about its subject.

Reading Documents

We will turn to a specific document in a moment and analyze it in some detail. For now, however, the following are a few basic things to be aware of—and to ask yourself—as you read any written document.

1. Who wrote it? The author of the textbook answers this question for you at the beginning of each document in the book. But your instructors may give you other documents to read, and the authorship of each document is the first question you need to answer.
2. What do we know about the author of the document? The more you know about the author, the more meaningful and reliable the information you can extract from the document.
3. Is it a primary or secondary document?
4. When was the document written?
5. What is the purpose of the document? Closely tied to the question of document type is the document's purpose. A work of fiction might have been written to entertain, whereas an official document was written to convey a particular law or decree to subjects, citizens, or believers.
6. Who was the intended audience? A play is meant to be performed by actors on a stage before a group of onlookers whereas Martin Luther's Ninety-Five Theses were posted publicly and intended to be seen by ordinary citizens.
7. Can you detect a bias in this document? As the two documents on the siege of Jerusalem (p. 226) suggest, firsthand accounts of the Crusades written by Christians and Muslims tend to differ. Each may be "accurate" as far as the writer is concerned, but your

job as a historian is to decide whether this written evidence gives a reliable account of what happened. You cannot always believe everything you read, but the more you read, the more you can decide what is, in fact, accurate.

"Reading" and Studying Photographs and Artwork

This book pays close attention to primary source and written documents, but contemporary illustrations can also be analyzed to provide an understanding of a historical period.

A historian might ask questions about a painting like the one at the right to learn more about life in a medieval town. The more you study and learn about medieval social history, the more information this painting will reveal. To help you look at and interpret art like a historian, ask yourself the following questions:

1. By looking closely at just the buildings, what do you learn about the nature of the medieval town dwellings and the allotment of space within the town? Why were medieval towns arranged in this fashion? Why would this differ from modern urban planning?
2. Based on the various activities shown, what kinds of groups would you expect to find in a medieval town? What do you learn about medieval methods of production? How do they differ from modern methods of production? What difference would this make in the nature of community organization and life?
3. Based on what the people in the street are wearing, what do you think their economic status was? Would that be typical of a medieval town? Why or why not?
4. What do you think the artist who created this piece was trying to communicate about life in a medieval town? Based on your knowledge of medieval towns, would you agree with the artist's assessment? Why or why not?
5. What do you think was the social class of the artist? Why?

Reading and Studying Maps

Historical events do not just "happen"; they happen in a specific place. It is important to learn all you can about that place, and a good map can help you do this.

Your textbook includes several kinds of maps. The map of Europe printed on the inside front cover of the textbook is a good place to start. Map basics include taking

Bibliothèque de l'Arsenal, Paris/© Snark/Art Resource, NY

Medieval Town

care to read and understand every label on whatever map you study. The map of Europe has labels for six kinds of information. Each of the following is important:

1. Names of countries.
2. Names of major cities.
3. Names of oceans and large bodies of water.
4. Names of rivers.
5. Longitude and latitude. Lines of longitude extend from the North Pole to the South Pole; one such line intersects Iceland in the top left (or northwest) corner of the map. Lines of latitude circle the globe east to west and intersect lines of longitude. These imaginary lines place countries and oceans in their approximate setting on the face of the earth. Not every map includes latitude and longitude.
6. Mileage scale. A mileage scale shows how far apart, in miles and kilometers, each location is from other locations.

Most Maps Include Three Basic Types of Information

1. The boundaries of countries, cities, empires, and other kinds of "political" information. A good map shows each political division in a different color to make them all easy to find. The color of each region or country is the decision of the mapmaker (also known as a cartographer).
2. Mountains, oceans, rivers, and other "physical" or "topographic" information. The mountains on this kind of map have been rendered by the cartographer:

Switzerland and Norway are mountainous; Germany and Belarus are relatively flat.

3. Latitude, longitude, a mileage scale, and other information. These elements help the reader place the information in some kind of context. Some maps include an "N" with an arrow that points north. Most maps show northern areas (Alaska, Norway, etc.) at the top. A map that does not do this is not misleading or wrong. But if an "N" arrow does not appear on the map, be sure you know where north is.

"Political" information tends to change a great deal: maps may change after a major war if the winners take more territory, for example. "Physical" information changes slowly: latitude, rivers, distances, and the like do not change or generally change only very slowly.

In addition, many maps include information about the spread of disease, the location of cathedrals and universities, trade routes, and any number of other things. There is no real limit to the kinds of information a map can show, and the more information a map can display clearly, the more useful it is. Any good map will include a "legend" stating the information that makes the map useful. The more detailed the map, the more information the mapmaker should provide in the legend.

Again, note that only the oceans, large bodies of water, and rivers—the "physical" features in a map—really exist in nature. They are relatively changeless. All other features on a map are made up and change fairly often. The maps you see here and on the next page all show the same familiar "boot" we call Italy. But all or part of this landmass has also been called Latium, Campania, the duchy of Benevento, the Papal States, the kingdom of the Two Sicilies, Tuscany, Lombardy, Piedmont, and Savoy. Populations and place names change; mountains and oceans do not, at least not much. Whenever you have trouble finding a region or a place on a map, look for a permanent feature to help you get your bearings.

In addition to kingdoms, cities, and mountains, maps can show the physical proximity of any two or more ideas, movements, or developments. Map 10.5 (p. 225) shows the routes of several Crusades of the eleventh and twelfth centuries. Note that the legend associates the color of a Crusade's route (shown as a line) with its duration in years. This map makes it possible to see a number of useful things at a glance that could take several maps to describe, including the following:

1. Where each Crusade began. (Note the places that send the most Crusades and those that send none.)
2. How far each Crusade traveled. (Note the mileage key.)
3. Which route each Crusade took. (Why did no crusaders make the trip only on land?)
4. How much time passed between the end of one Crusade and the beginning of another. (Did the rate of Crusades accelerate or slow down over time? What does this suggest?)

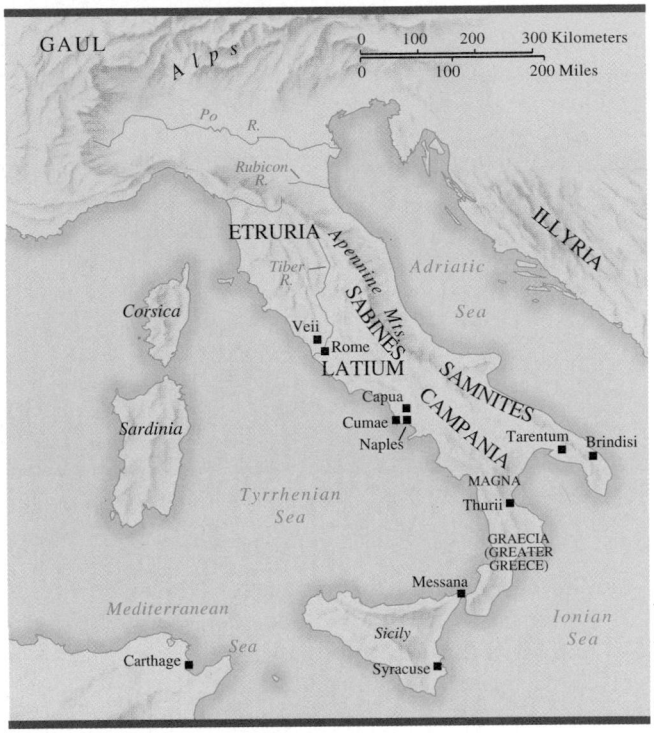

© Cengage Learning

Ancient Italy

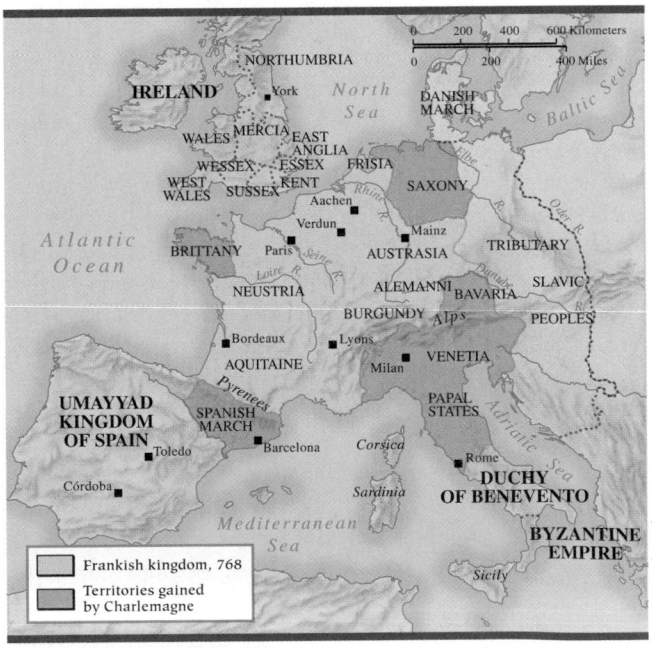

© Cengage Learning

The Carolingian Empire

© Cengage Learning

The Unification of Italy

5. Which crusaders actually made it to the eastern Mediterranean and which did not. (Consider any correlation between route and timing.)
6. The names of the Crusader States themselves.

Another kind of invasion appears in Map 11.1 (p. 233). This map shows the steady progress of the Black Death from the Black Sea and the Mediterranean north and west through Europe. Using the legend, find the shade of color that corresponds to the first outbreak of plague, in December 1347, and follow the spread of disease, shown here in six-month intervals, as you follow the colors northward.

The documents on p. 232 give a sense of how contemporaries tried to explain the plague, and the image on p. 234 vividly illustrates how some people responded to the horrors of the plague. Map 11.1 brings to mind another aspect of this horror by tracking the plague's ruthless and irresistible advance, month by month, year by year. The more information you can gather from the map, the more the document and illustrations can tell you about the horrors of the plague.

A happier kind of movement, the advance of learning, appears in Map 9.2 (p. 197). For this map, it is important to identify the symbols for universities and schools and to see where they appear on the map. Because education does not tend to move as a wave, as the plague did, each symbol represents a place where learning flourished more than it did in places without a symbol of some kind.

Map 11.1 makes it clear that the plague began in one part of Europe and touched nearly every region as it passed through it. Map 9.2 shows that education works differently; some people have better access to it than others. Your job as a historian is to recognize this and then to figure out why.

Putting It Together: Reading and Studying Documents, Supported by Images

Learning to read a document is no different from learning to read a restaurant menu. The more you practice, the quicker your eyes will find the lobster and pastries.

Let Us Explore a Pair of Primary Sources

As the introduction to the reading on the next page makes clear, King Louis XIV of France is writing the king of Tonkin to ask permission to send Christian missionaries to Southeast Asia. But this exchange of letters tells a great deal more than that.

Before you read this document, take a careful look at this portrait of Louis XIV. As this image makes clear, Louis lived during an age of flourishes and excess. Among many other questions, including some that appear later, you may ask yourself how Louis's manner of speaking reflects the public presentation you see in his portrait.

Chateaux de Versailles et de Trianon (Inv. MV3500), Versailles,//© Réunion des Musées Nationaux (Gérard Blot)/Art Resource, NY

King Louis XIV

A Letter to the King of Tonkin from Louis XIV

1 Most high, most excellent, most mighty and most magnanimous
2 Prince, our very dear and good friend, may it please God to increase
3 your greatness with a happy end!
4 We hear from our subjects who were in your Realm what pro-
5 tection you accorded them. We appreciate this all the more since we
6 have for you all the esteem that one can have for a prince as illustri-
7 ous through his military valor as he is commendable for the justice
8 which he exercises in his Realm. We have even been informed that
9 you have not been satisfied to extend this general protection to our
10 subjects but, in particular, that you gave effective proofs of it to
11 Messrs. Deydier and de Bourges. We would have wished that they
12 might have been able to recognize all the favors they received from
13 you by having presents worthy of you offered you; but since the war
14 which we have had for several years, in which all of Europe had
15 banded together against us, prevented our vessels from going to the
16 Indies, at the present time, when we are at peace after having gained
17 many victories and expanded our Realm through the conquest of
18 several important places, we have immediately given orders to the
19 Royal Company to establish itself in your kingdom as soon as possi-
20 ble, and have commanded Messrs. Deydier and de Bourges to re-
21 main with you in order to maintain a good relationship between
22 our subjects and yours, also to warn us on occasions that might
23 present themselves when we might be able to give you proofs of our
24 esteem and of our wish to concur with your satisfaction as well as
25 with your best interests.
26 By way of initial proof, we have given orders to have brought
27 to you some presents which we believe might be agreeable to you.
28 But the one thing in the world which we desire most, both for you
29 and for your Realm, would be to obtain for your subjects who have
30 already embraced the law of the only true God of heaven and earth,
31 the freedom to profess it, since this law is the highest, the noblest,
32 the most sacred and especially the most suitable to have kings reign
33 absolutely over the people.
34 We are even quite convinced that, if you knew the truths and
35 the maxims which it teaches, you would give first of all to your
36 subjects the glorious example of embracing it. We wish you this in-
37 comparable blessing together with a long and happy reign, and we
38 pray God that it may please Him to augment your greatness with
39 the happiest of endings.
40 Written at Saint-Germain-en-Laye, the 10th day of January, 1681,
41 Your very dear and good friend,
42 Louis

Answer from the King of Tonkin to Louis XIV

43 The King of Tonkin sends to the King of France a letter to express
44 to him his best sentiments, saying that he was happy to learn that
45 fidelity is a durable good of man and that justice is the most impor-
46 tant of things. Consequently practicing of fidelity and justice cannot
47 but yield good results. Indeed, though France and our Kingdom dif-
48 fer as to mountains, rivers, and boundaries, if fidelity and justice
49 reign among our villages, our conduct will express all of our good
50 feelings and contain precious gifts. Your communication, which
51 comes from a country which is a thousand leagues away, and which
52 proceeds from the heart as a testimony of your sincerity, merits re-
53 peated consideration and infinite praise. Politeness toward strangers
54 is nothing unusual in our country. There is not a stranger who is
55 not well received by us. How then could we refuse a man from
56 France, which is the most celebrated among the kingdoms of the
57 world and which for love of us wishes to frequent us and bring us
58 merchandise? These feelings of fidelity and justice are truly worthy
59 to be applauded. As regards your wish that we should cooperate in
60 propagating your religion, we do not dare to permit it, for there is
61 an ancient custom, introduced by edicts, which formally forbids it.
62 Now, edicts are promulgated only to be carried out faithfully;
63 without fidelity nothing is stable. How could we disdain a well-
64 established custom to satisfy a private friendship? . . .
65 We beg you to understand well that this is our communication
66 concerning our mutual acquaintance. This then is my letter. We send
67 you herewith a modest gift, which we offer you with a glad heart.
68 This letter was written at the beginning of winter and on a
69 beautiful day.

Your textbook does not show a corresponding portrait of the king of Tonkin, but you might try to create a picture of him in your mind as you read this response to the letter he receives from his fellow ruler.

The following questions about this document are the kinds of questions your instructor would ask about the document.

1. Why does Louis refer to the king of Tonkin, whom he never met, as his "very dear and good friend" (line 2)? Do you think that this French king would begin a conversation with, say, a French shopkeeper in quite the same way? If not, why does he identify more with a fellow king than with a fellow Frenchman?
2. How often do you imagine that the king of France had to persuade people to do what he wanted rather than order them to do so? Who might the people that he had to persuade have been?
3. Note that Louis uses what is referred to as the "royal *we*," referring to himself in the plural. When does the king of Tonkin refer to himself in the first person ("I"), and when does he refer to himself in the plural ("we")?
4. Why does Louis say that he is writing at that particular time rather than earlier (lines 13–18)?
5. Why does Louis say that Christian missionaries will be good for Tonkin and its people (lines 28–33)? What reason in Louis's own letter makes you wonder if converting the people of Tonkin to Christianity is "the one thing in the world which we desire most"?
6. Does the king of Tonkin seem pleased to hear from Louis and to receive his request (lines 43–53)? How does he refer to the gift Louis offers him?
7. Louis mentions his gratitude for the good treatment of some French subjects when they were "in your realm." What do you think these Frenchmen were

doing there? Do you think they were invited, or did they arrive on their own? How does the king of Tonkin respond when Louis mentions his appreciation for the "protection" they were accorded (lines 53–58)? Protection from what, do you suppose?

8. What reason does the king of Tonkin give for refusing Louis's offer of Christian missionaries (lines 59–64)? He takes care to explain to Louis that "edicts are promulgated . . . nothing is stable." What does this suggest about the king of Tonkin's attitude toward Louis and the "incomparable blessing" of faith in the Christian god? How many French people (or Europeans, for that matter) is the king of Tonkin likely to have met? What French person or persons might have already expressed to the king the ideas that Louis offers?
9. Compare the final lines of each letter. What significance do you draw from the fact that Louis names the day, month, year, and location in which he writes? Apart from later historians, to whom in particular would this information be of greatest interest? What is the significance of the king of Tonkin's closing line?

If you can propose thoughtful answers to these questions, you will have come to know the material very well and should be ready for whatever examinations and papers await you in your course.

CHAPTER 1

© Essam Al-Sudani/AFP/Getty Images

Excavation of Warka showing the ruins of Uruk

The Ancient Near East: The First Civilizations

CHAPTER OUTLINE AND FOCUS QUESTIONS

The First Humans

Q How did the Paleolithic and Neolithic Ages differ, and how did the Neolithic Revolution affect the lives of men and women?

The Emergence of Civilization

Q What are the characteristics of civilization, and what are some explanations for why early civilizations emerged?

Civilization in Mesopotamia

Q How are the chief characteristics of civilization evident in ancient Mesopotamia?

Egyptian Civilization: "The Gift of the Nile"

Q What are the basic features of the three major periods of Egyptian history? What elements of continuity are there in the three periods? What are their major differences?

CRITICAL THINKING

Q In what ways were the civilizations of Mesopotamia and Egypt alike? In what ways were they different?

IN 1849, A DARING YOUNG Englishman made a hazardous journey into the deserts and swamps of southern Iraq. Moving south down the banks of the Euphrates River while braving high winds and temperatures that reached 120 degrees Fahrenheit, William Loftus led a small expedition in search of the roots of civilization. As he said, "From our childhood we have been led to regard this place as the cradle of the human race."

Guided by native Arabs into the southernmost reaches of Iraq, Loftus and his small group of explorers were soon overwhelmed by what they saw. He wrote, "I know of nothing more exciting or impressive than the first sight of one of these great piles, looming in solitary grandeur from the surrounding plains and marshes." One of these piles, known to the natives as the mound of Warka, contained the ruins of Uruk, one of the first cities in the world and part of the world's first civilization.

Southwest Asia was one area in the world where civilization began. Although Western civilization did not yet exist, its origins can be traced back to the ancient Near East, where people in Southwest Asia and in Egypt, in northeastern Africa, developed organized societies, invented writing, and created the ideas and institutions that we associate with civilization. The later Greeks and Romans, who played such a crucial role in the development of Western civilization, were nourished and influenced by these older Near Eastern societies. It is appropriate, therefore, to begin our story of Western civilization with the early civilizations of Southwest Asia and Egypt. Before considering them, however, we must briefly examine prehistory and observe how human beings made the shift from hunting and gathering to agricultural communities and ultimately to cities and civilization.

The First Humans

Focus Question: How did the Paleolithic and Neolithic Ages differ, and how did the Neolithic Revolution affect the lives of men and women?

Historians rely primarily on documents to create their pictures of the past, but no written records exist for the prehistory of humankind. In their absence, the story of early humanity depends on archaeological and, more recently, biological information, which anthropologists and archaeologists use to formulate theories about our early past.

The earliest humanlike creatures—known as hominids—existed in Africa as long as 3 to 4 million years ago. Known as Australopithecines (aw-stray-loh-PITH-uh-synz), they flourished in East and South Africa and were the first hominids to make simple stone tools.

Another stage in early human development occurred around 1.5 million years ago when *Homo erectus* ("upright human being") emerged. *Homo erectus* made use of larger and more varied tools and was the first hominid to leave Africa and move into both Europe and Asia.

Around 250,000 years ago, a crucial stage in human development began with the emergence of *Homo sapiens* ((HOH-moh SAY-pee-unz) ("wise human being"). The first anatomically modern humans, known as *Homo sapiens sapiens* ("wise, wise human being"), appeared in Africa between 200,000 and 150,000 years ago. Recent evidence indicates that they began to spread outside Africa around 70,000 years ago. Map 1.1 shows probable dates for different movements, although many of these are still controversial.

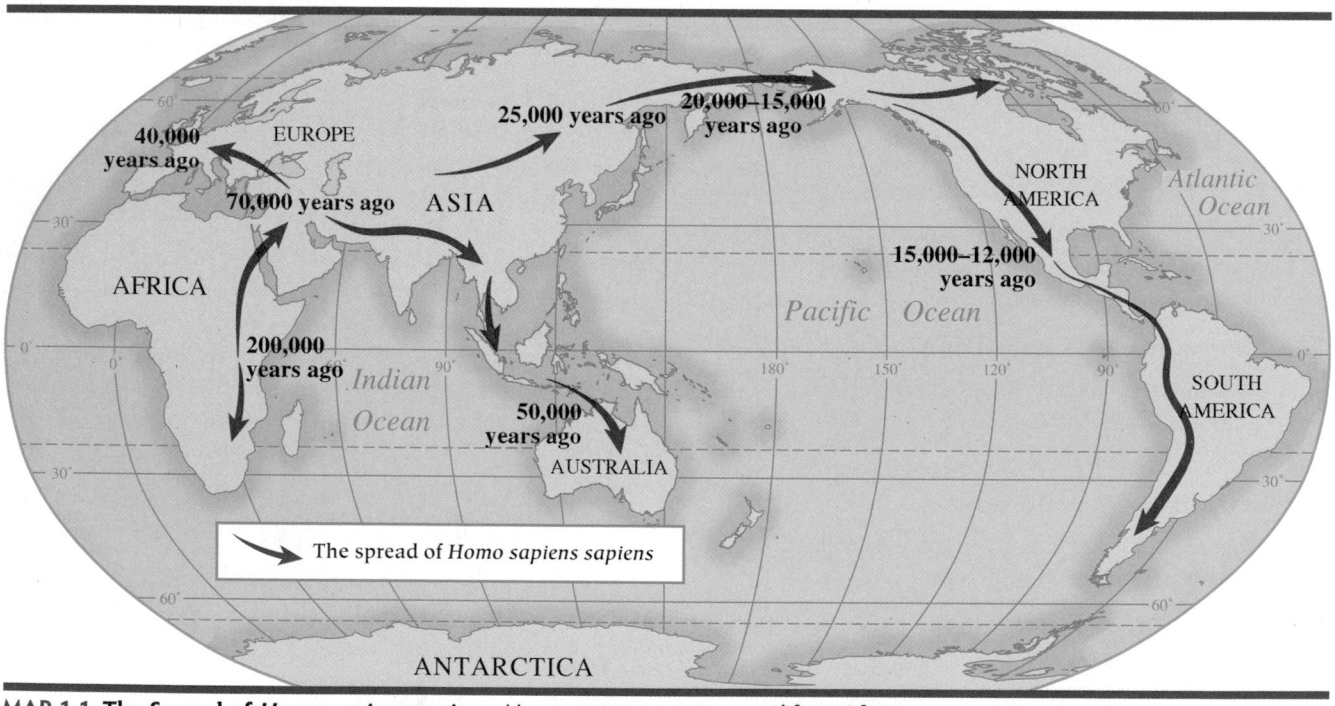

© Cengage Learning

MAP 1.1 The Spread of *Homo sapiens sapiens*. *Homo sapiens sapiens* spread from Africa beginning about 70,000 years ago. Living and traveling in small groups, these anatomically modern humans were hunter-gatherers. Although groups of people advanced beyond their old hunting grounds at a rate of only 2 or 3 miles per generation, this was enough to populate the world in tens of thousands of years.

Given that some diffusion of humans occurred during ice ages, how would such climate change affect humans and their movements, especially from Asia to Australia and Asia to North America?

These modern humans, who were our direct ancestors, soon encountered other hominids, such as the Neanderthals, whose remains were first found in the Neander valley in Germany. Neanderthal remains have since been found in both Europe and the western part of Asia and have been dated to between 200,000 and 30,000 B.C.E. Neanderthals relied on a variety of stone tools and were the first early people to bury their dead. By 30,000 B.C.E., *Homo sapiens sapiens* had replaced the Neanderthals, who had largely become extinct, and by 10,000 B.C.E., members of the *Homo sapiens sapiens* species could be found throughout the world. By that time, it was the only human species left. All humans today, whether they are Europeans, Australian Aborigines, or Africans, belong to the same subspecies of human being.

The Hunter-Gatherers of the Old Stone Age

One of the basic distinguishing features of the human species is the ability to make tools. The earliest tools were made of stone, and the term **Paleolithic** (Greek for "old stone") **Age** is used to designate this early period of human history (c. 2,500,000–10,000 B.C.E.).

For hundreds of thousands of years, humans relied on hunting and gathering for their daily food. Paleolithic peoples had a close relationship with the world around them, and over a period of time, they came to know which animals to hunt and which plants to eat. They did not know how to grow crops or raise animals, however. They gathered wild nuts, berries, fruits, and a variety of wild grains and green plants. Around the world, they hunted and consumed different animals, including buffalo, horses, bison, wild goats, and reindeer. In coastal areas, fish were a rich source of nourishment.

The hunting of animals and the gathering of wild plants no doubt led to certain patterns of living. Archaeologists and anthropologists have speculated that Paleolithic people lived in small bands of twenty to thirty. They were nomadic, moving from place to place to follow animal migrations and vegetation cycles. Hunting depended on careful observation of animal behavior patterns and required a group effort for success. Over the years, tools became more refined and more useful. The invention of the spear, and later the bow and arrow, made hunting considerably easier. Harpoons and fishhooks made of bone increased the catch of fish.

Both men and women were responsible for finding food—the chief work of Paleolithic people. Since women bore and raised the children, they generally stayed close to the camps, but they played an important role in acquiring food by gathering berries, nuts, and grains. Men hunted wild animals, an activity that often took them far from camp. Because both men and women played important roles in providing for the band's survival, scientists believe that a rough equality existed between men and women. Indeed, some speculate that both men and women made the decisions that affected the activities of the Paleolithic band.

CHRONOLOGY The First Humans

Australopithecines	flourished c. 3–4 million years ago
Homo erectus	flourished c. 100,000–1.5 million years ago
Neanderthals	flourished c. 200,000–30,000 B.C.E.
Homo sapiens sapiens	emerged c. 200,000 B.C.E.

Some groups of Paleolithic peoples, especially those who lived in cold climates, found shelter in caves. Over time, they created new types of shelter as well. Perhaps the most common was a simple structure of wood poles or sticks covered with animal hides. The systematic use of fire, which archaeologists believe began around 500,000 years ago, made it possible for the caves and human-made structures to have a source of light and heat. Fire also enabled early humans to cook their food, making it taste better, last longer, and in the case of some plants, such as wild grain, easier to chew and digest.

The making of tools and the use of fire—two important technological innovations of Paleolithic peoples—remind us how crucial the ability to adapt was to human survival. But Paleolithic peoples did more than just survive. The cave paintings of large animals found in southwestern France and northern Spain bear witness to the cultural activity of Paleolithic peoples. A cave discovered in southern France in 1994—known as the Chauvet (SHOH-vay) Cave, after the leader of the expedition that found it—contains more than three hundred paintings of lions, oxen, owls, bears, and other animals. Most of these are animals that Paleolithic people did not hunt, which suggests to some scholars that the paintings were made for religious or even decorative purposes. The discoverers were overwhelmed by what they saw: "There was a moment of ecstasy. . . . They overflowed with joy and emotion. . . . These were moments of indescribable madness."[1]

The Neolithic Revolution (c. 10,000–4000 B.C.E.)

The end of the last ice age around 10,000 B.C.E. was followed by what is called the **Neolithic Revolution**, a significant change in living patterns that occurred in the New Stone Age (the word *neolithic* is Greek for "new stone"). The name New Stone Age is misleading, however.

Although Neolithic peoples made a new type of polished stone ax, this was not the major change that occurred after 10,000 B.C.E.

AN AGRICULTURAL REVOLUTION The biggest change was the shift from hunting animals and gathering plants for sustenance (food gathering) to producing food by systematic agriculture (food production). The planting of grains and vegetables provided a regular supply of food, while the domestication of animals, such as sheep, goats, cattle, and pigs, added a steady source of meat, milk, and fibers such as wool for clothing. Larger animals could also be used as beasts of burden. The growing of crops and the taming of food-producing animals created a new relationship between humans and nature. Historians speak of this as an agricultural revolution. Revolutionary change is dramatic and requires great effort, but the ability to acquire food on a regular basis gave humans greater control over their environment. It also allowed them to give up their nomadic ways of life and begin to live in settled communities.

Systematic agriculture probably developed independently between 8000 and 7000 B.C.E. in various parts of the world. Different plants were cultivated: wheat, barley, and lentils in the Near East; rice and millet in southern Asia; millet and yams in western Africa; and beans, potatoes, and corn in the Americas. The Neolithic agricultural revolution needed a favorable environment. In the Near East, the upland areas above the Fertile Crescent (present-day northern Iraq and southern Turkey) were more conducive to systematic farming than the river valleys. This region received the necessary rainfall and was the home of two wild plant species (barley and wheat) and four wild animal species (pigs, cows, goats, and sheep) that humans eventually domesticated for their use.

CONSEQUENCES OF THE NEOLITHIC REVOLUTION The growing of crops on a regular basis gave rise to more permanent settlements, which historians refer to as Neolithic farming villages or towns. One of the oldest and largest agricultural villages was Çatal Hüyük (CHAHT-ahl hoo-YOOK), located in modern-day Turkey. Its walls enclosed 32 acres, and its population probably reached six thousand inhabitants during its high point from 6700 to 5700 B.C.E. People lived in simple mudbrick houses that were built so close to one another that there were few streets. To get to their homes, people had to walk along the rooftops and then enter the house through a hole in the roof.

Archaeologists have discovered twelve cultivated products in Çatal Hüyük, including fruits, nuts, and three kinds of wheat. Artisans made weapons and jewelry that were traded with neighboring people. Religious shrines housing figures of gods and goddesses have been found at Çatal Hüyük, as have a number of female statuettes. Molded with noticeably large breasts and buttocks, these "earth mothers" perhaps symbolically represented the fertility of both "mother earth" and human mothers. The shrines and the statues point to the role of religion in the lives of these Neolithic peoples.

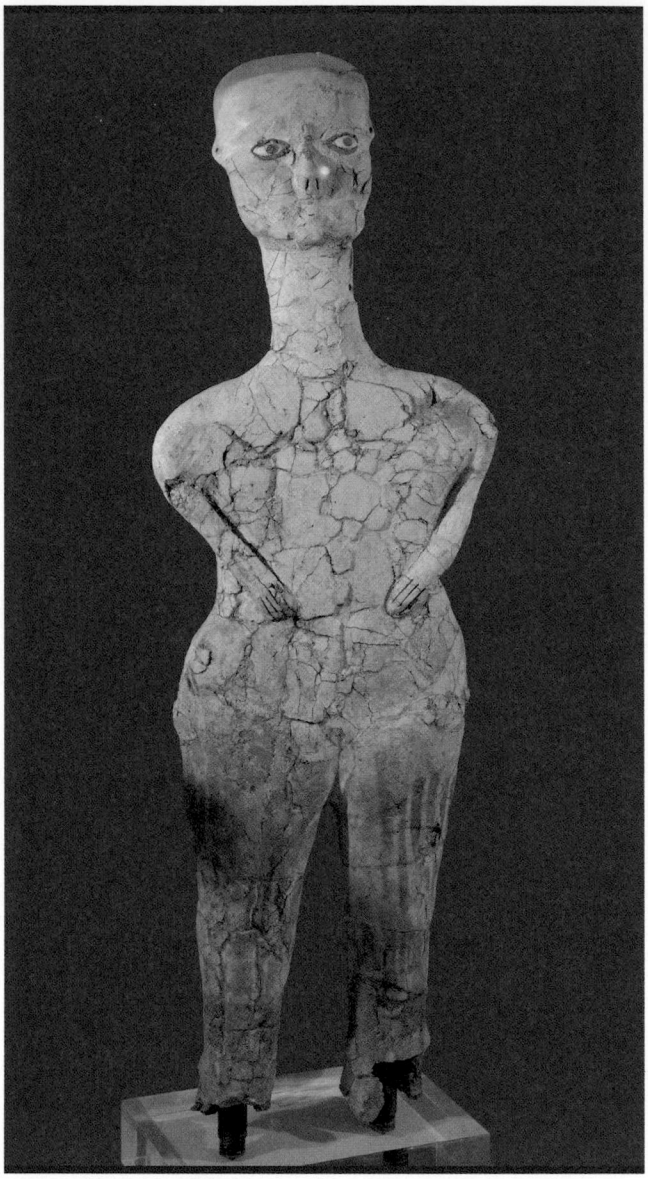

Archaeological Museum, Amman, Jordan//© Erich Lessing/Art Resource, NY

Statue from Ain Ghazal. This life-size statue made of plaster, sand, and crushed chalk was discovered in 1984 in Ain Ghazal (AYN gah-ZAL), an archaeological site near Amman, Jordan. Dating from 6500 B.C.E., it is among the oldest known statues of the human figure. Although it appears lifelike, its features are considered generic rather than a portrait of an individual face. The purpose and meaning of this sculpture may never be known.

The Neolithic Revolution had far-reaching consequences. Once people settled in villages or towns, they built permanent houses for protection and other structures for the storage of goods. As organized communities stockpiled food and accumulated material goods, they began to engage in trade. People also began to specialize in certain crafts, and a division of labor developed. Pottery was made from clay and baked in a fire to make it hard. The pots were used for cooking and to store grains. Woven baskets were also used for storage. Stone tools became refined as flint blades were employed to make sickles and hoes for use in the fields. Obsidian—a volcanic glass that was easily flaked—was also used to create very sharp tools. In the course of the Neolithic Age, many of the food plants still in use today began to be cultivated. Moreover, fibers from plants such as flax were used to make thread that was woven into cloth.

The change to systematic agriculture in the Neolithic Age also had consequences for the relationship between men and women. Men assumed the primary responsibility for working in the fields and herding animals, jobs that kept them away from the home. Although women also worked in the fields, many remained behind to care for the children, weave clothes, and perform other tasks that required labor close to home. In time, as work outside the home was increasingly perceived as more important than work done at home, men came to play the more dominant role in society, a basic pattern that would persist until our own times.

Other patterns set in the Neolithic Age also proved to be enduring elements of human history. Fixed dwellings, domesticated animals, regular farming, a division of labor, men holding power—all of these are part of the human story. For all our modern scientific and technological progress, human survival still depends on the growing and storing of food, an accomplishment of people in the Neolithic Age. The Neolithic Revolution was truly a turning point in human history.

NEW DEVELOPMENTS Between 4000 and 3000 B.C.E., significant technical developments began to transform the Neolithic towns. The invention of writing enabled records to be kept, and the use of metals marked a new level of human control over the environment and its resources. Already before 4000 B.C.E., craftspeople had discovered that certain rocks could be heated to liquefy metals embedded in them. The metals could then be cast in molds to produce tools and weapons that were more useful than stone instruments. Although copper was the first metal to be made into tools, after 4000 B.C.E., craftspeople in western Asia discovered that combining copper and tin created bronze, a much harder and more durable metal than copper. Its widespread use has led historians to call the period from around 3000 to 1200 B.C.E. the **Bronze Age**; thereafter, bronze was increasingly replaced by iron.

At first, Neolithic settlements were hardly more than villages. But as their inhabitants mastered the art of farming, more complex human societies began to emerge. As wealth increased, these societies began to develop armies and to build walled towns and cities. By the beginning of the Bronze Age, the concentration of larger numbers of people in the river valleys of Southwest Asia and Egypt was leading to a whole new pattern for human life.

The Emergence of Civilization

Q FOCUS QUESTION: What are the characteristics of civilization, and what are some explanations for why early civilizations emerged?

As we have seen, early human beings formed small groups that developed a simple culture that enabled them to survive. As human societies grew and developed greater complexity, a new form of human existence—called *civilization*—came into being. A **civilization** is a complex culture in which large numbers of human beings share a number of common elements. Historians have identified a number of basic characteristics of civilization. These include (1) an urban focus: cities became the centers of political, economic, social, cultural, and religious development; (2) a distinct religious structure: the gods were deemed crucial to the community's success, and professional priestly classes regulated relations with the gods; (3) new political and military structures: an organized government bureaucracy arose to meet the administrative demands of the growing population, and armies were organized to gain land and power and for defense; (4) a new social structure based on economic power: while kings and an upper class of priests, political leaders, and warriors dominated, there also existed a large group of free people (farmers, artisans, craftspeople) and at the very bottom, socially, a class of slaves; (5) the development of writing: kings, priests, merchants, and artisans used writing to keep records; and (6) new forms of significant artistic and intellectual activity: for example, monumental architectural structures, usually religious, occupied a prominent place in urban environments.

The civilizations that developed in Southwest Asia and Egypt, the forerunners of Western civilization, will be examined in detail in this chapter. But civilization also developed independently in other parts of the world. Between 3000 and 1500 B.C.E., the valley of the Indus River in India supported a flourishing civilization that extended hundreds of miles from the Himalayas to the coast of the Arabian Sea. Two major cities, Harappa (huh-RAP-uh) and Mohenjo-Daro (moh-HEN-joh-DAHR-oh), were at the heart of this South Asian civilization. Many written records of

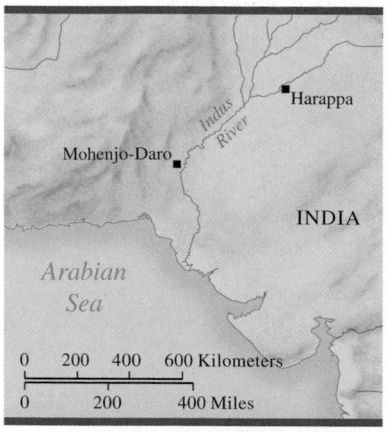

© Cengage Learning

Harappa and Mohenjo-Daro

the Indus valley civilization exist, but their language has not yet been deciphered. This Indus valley civilization carried on extensive trade with cities in Southwest Asia.

Another river valley civilization emerged along the Yellow River in northern China about 4,000 years ago. Under the Shang dynasty of kings, which ruled from 1750 to 1122 B.C.E., this civilization contained impressive cities with huge city walls, royal palaces, and large royal tombs. A system of irrigation enabled this early Chinese civilization to maintain a prosperous farming society ruled by an aristocratic class whose major concern was war.

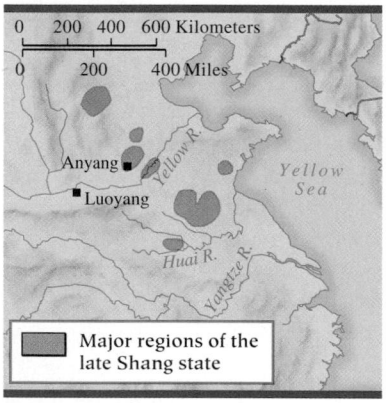

© Cengage Learning

The Yellow River, China

For a long time, scholars believed that civilization emerged in only four areas, the fertile river valleys of the Tigris and Euphrates, the Nile, the Indus, and the Yellow River—that is, in Southwest Asia, Egypt, India, and China. Recently, however, archaeologists have discovered two other early civilizations. One of these flourished in Central Asia (in what are now the republics of Turkmenistan and Uzbekistan) around 4,000 years ago. People in this civilization built mudbrick buildings, raised sheep and goats, had bronze tools, used a system of irrigation to grow wheat and barley, and had a writing system.

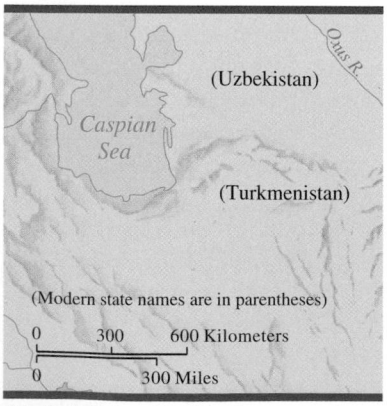

© Cengage Learning

Central Asian Civilization

Another early civilization was discovered in the Supe River valley of Peru. At the center of this civilization was the city of Caral, which flourished around 2600 B.C.E. It contained buildings for officials, apartment buildings, and grand residences, all built of stone. The inhabitants of Caral also developed a system of irrigation by diverting a river more than a mile upstream into their fields.

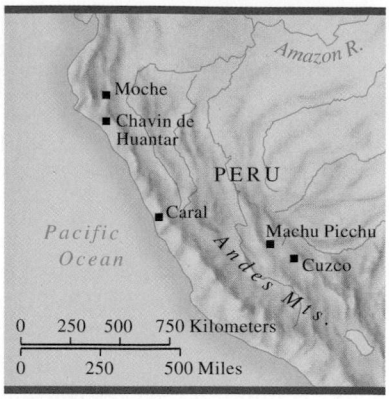

© Cengage Learning

Caral, Peru

Why early civilizations developed remains difficult to explain. One theory maintains that challenges forced human beings to make efforts that resulted in the rise of civilization. Some scholars have argued that material forces, such as the growth of food surpluses, made possible the specialization of labor and the development of large communities with bureaucratic organization. But the area of the Fertile Crescent (see Map 1.2), in which Mesopotamian civilization emerged, was not naturally conducive to agriculture. Abundant food could be produced only with a massive human effort to manage the water, an undertaking that required organization and led to civilized societies. Other historians have argued that nonmaterial forces, primarily religious, provided the sense of unity and purpose that made such organized living possible. And some scholars doubt that we will ever discover the actual causes of early civilization.

Civilization in Mesopotamia

Q FOCUS QUESTION: How are the chief characteristics of civilization evident in ancient Mesopotamia?

The Greeks spoke of the valley between the Tigris and Euphrates Rivers as Mesopotamia (mess-uh-puh-TAY-mee-uh), the "land between the rivers." The region receives little rain, but the soil of the plain of southern Mesopotamia was enlarged and enriched over the years by layers of silt deposited by the rivers. In late spring, the Tigris and Euphrates overflow their banks and deposit their fertile silt, but since this flooding depends on the melting of snows in the upland mountains where the rivers begin, it is irregular and sometimes catastrophic. In such circumstances, farming could be accomplished only with human intervention in the form of irrigation and drainage ditches.

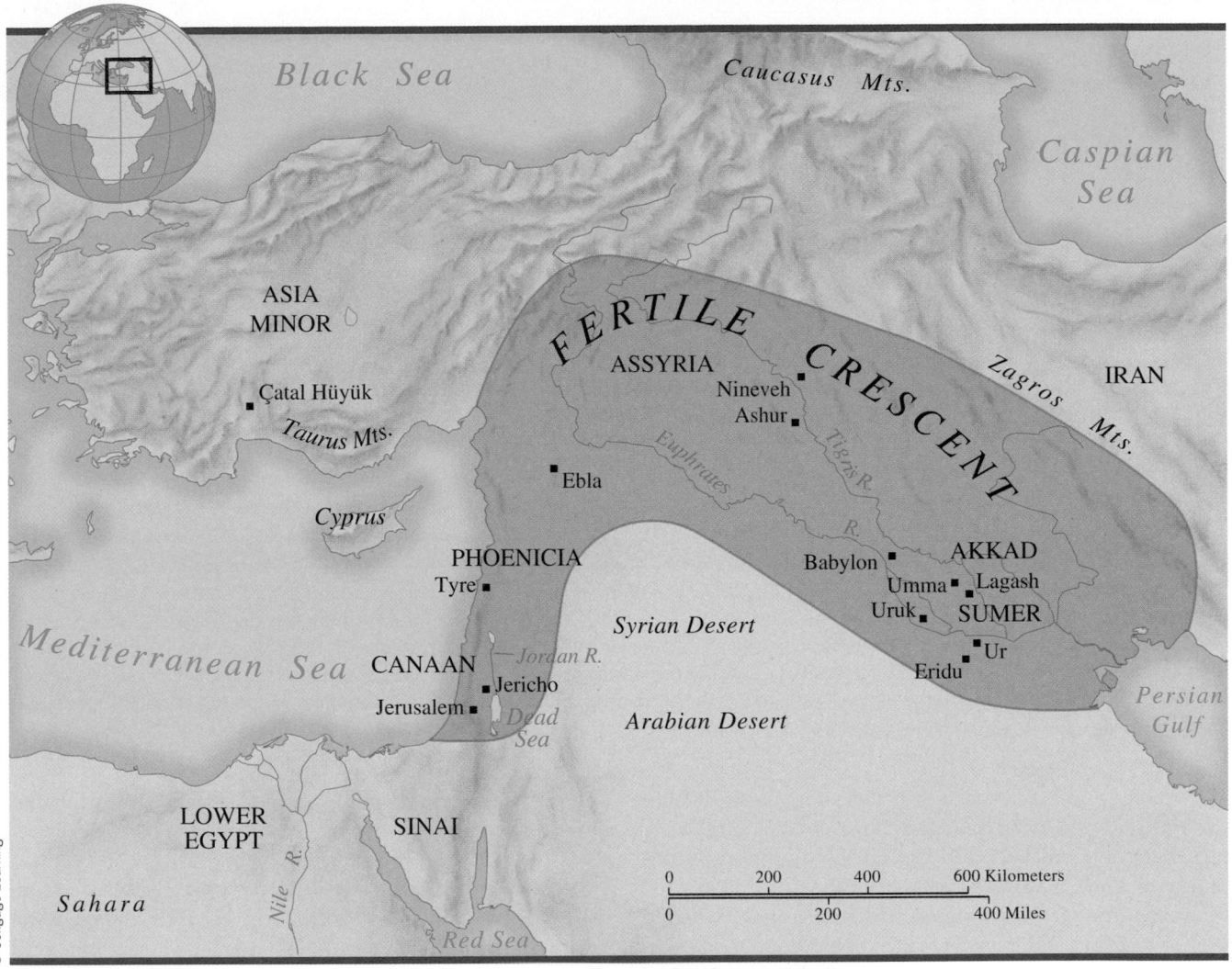

© Cengage Learning

MAP 1.2 The Ancient Near East. The Fertile Crescent encompassed land with access to water. Employing flood management and irrigation systems, the peoples of the region established civilizations based on agriculture. These civilizations developed writing, law codes, and economic specialization.

Q ***What geographic aspects of the Mesopotamian city-states made conflict between them likely?***

A complex system was required to control the flow of the rivers and produce the crops. Large-scale irrigation made possible the expansion of agriculture in this region, and the abundant food provided the material base for the emergence of civilization in Mesopotamia.

The City-States of Ancient Mesopotamia

The creators of Mesopotamian civilization were the Sumerians (soo-MER-ee-unz), a people whose origins remain unclear. By 3000 B.C.E., they had established a number of independent cities in southern Mesopotamia, including Eridu, Ur, Uruk, Umma, and Lagash. There is evidence that the Sumerians were not the first people in the region. A number of Sumerian agricultural and craft terms are not Sumerian in origin, indicating that the Sumerians adopted some aspects of preexisting settlements. As the Sumerian cities grew larger, they came to exercise political and economic control over the surrounding countryside, forming city-states. These city-states were the basic units of Sumerian civilization.

SUMERIAN CITIES Sumerian cities were surrounded by walls. Uruk, for example, occupied an area of approximately

© British Museum, London, UK/The Bridgeman Art Library

The "Royal Standard" of Ur. This detail is from the "Royal Standard" of Ur, a box dating from around 2700 B.C.E. that was discovered in a stone tomb from the royal cemetery of the Sumerian city-state of Ur. The scenes on one side of the box depict the activities of the king and his military forces. Shown in the bottom panel are four Sumerian battle chariots. Each chariot held two men, one who held the reins and the other armed with a spear for combat. A special compartment in the chariot held a number of spears. The charging chariots are seen defeating the enemy. In the middle band, the Sumerian soldiers round up the captured enemies. In the top band, the captives are presented to the king, who has alighted from his chariot and is shown standing above all the others in the center of the panel.

1,000 acres encircled by a wall 6 miles long with defense towers located every 30 to 35 feet along the wall. City dwellings, built of sun-dried bricks, included both the small flats of peasants and the larger dwellings of the civic and priestly officials. Although Mesopotamia had little stone or wood to use for building, it did have plenty of mud. Mudbricks, easily shaped by hand, were left to bake in the hot sun until they were hard enough to use for building. People in Mesopotamia were remarkably inventive with mudbricks, constructing some of the largest brick buildings in the world.

The most prominent building in a Sumerian city was the temple, which was dedicated to the chief god or goddess of the city and often built atop a massive stepped tower called a **ziggurat** (ZIG-uh-rat). The Sumerians believed that gods and goddesses owned the cities, and much wealth was used to build temples as well as elaborate houses for the priests and priestesses who served the gods. Priests and priestesses, who supervised the temples and their property, had great power. The temples owned much of the city land and livestock and served not only as the physical center of the city but also its economic and political center. In fact, historians believe that in the early stages of a few city-states, priests and priestesses may have played an important role in ruling. The Sumerians believed that the gods ruled the cities, making the state a **theocracy** (government by a divine authority). Ruling power, however, was primarily in the hands of worldly figures known as kings.

KINGSHIP Sumerians viewed kingship as divine in origin; they believed kings derived their power from the gods and were the agents of the gods. As one person said in a petition to his king, "You in your judgment, you are the son of Anu [god of the sky]; your commands, like the word of a god, cannot be reversed; your words, like rain pouring down from heaven, are without number."[2] Regardless of their origins, kings had power—they led armies, initiated legislation, supervised the building of public works, provided law courts, and organized workers for the irrigation projects on which Mesopotamian agriculture depended. The army, the government bureaucracy, and the priests and priestesses all aided the kings in their rule.

ECONOMY AND SOCIETY The economy of the Sumerian city-states was primarily agricultural, but commerce and industry became important as well. The people of Mesopotamia produced woolen textiles, pottery, and metalwork. Foreign trade, which was primarily a royal monopoly, could be extensive. Royal officials imported luxury items, such as copper and tin, aromatic woods, and fruit trees, in exchange for dried fish, wool, barley, wheat, and goods produced by Mesopotamian metalworkers. Traders traveled by land to the Mediterranean in the west and by sea to India in the east. The invention of the wheel around 3000 B.C.E. led to carts with wheels that made the transport of goods easier.

Sumerian city-states probably contained four major social groups: elites, dependent commoners, free commoners, and slaves. Elites included royal and priestly officials and their families. Dependent commoners included the elites' clients, who worked for the palace and temple estates. Free commoners worked as farmers, merchants, fishers, scribes, and craftspeople. Farmers probably made up 90 percent or more of the population. They could exchange their crops for the goods of the artisans in town markets. Slaves belonged to palace officials, who used them mostly in building projects; temple officials, who used mostly female slaves to weave cloth and grind grain; and rich landowners, who used them for farming and domestic work.

Empires in Ancient Mesopotamia

As the number of Sumerian city-states grew and the states expanded, conflicts arose as city-state fought city-state for control of land and water. The fortunes of various city-states rose and fell over the centuries. The constant wars, with their burning and sacking of cities, left many Sumerians in deep despair, as is evident in the words of this Sumerian poem from the city of Ur: "Ur is destroyed, bitter is its lament. The country's blood now fills its holes like hot bronze in a mold. Bodies dissolve like fat in the sun. Our temple is destroyed; the gods have abandoned us, like migrating birds. Smoke lies on our city like a shroud."

Located on the flat land of Mesopotamia, the Sumerian city-states were also open to invasion. To the north of the Sumerian city-states lived the Akkadians (uh-KAY-dee-unz). We call them a Semitic people because of the language they spoke (see Table 1.1). Around 2340 B.C.E., Sargon, leader of the Akkadians, overran the Sumerian city-states and established a dynastic empire. Sargon used the former rulers of the conquered city-states as his governors. His power was based on the military, namely, his army of 5,400 men. Sargon's empire included most of Mesopotamia as well as lands westward to the Mediterranean. But the Akkadian empire eventually disintegrated, and its end by 2100 B.C.E. brought a return to the system of warring city-states until Ur-Nammu of Ur succeeded in reunifying most of Mesopotamia. But this final flowering of Sumerian culture collapsed with the coming of the Amorites. Under Hammurabi (ham-uh-RAH-bee), the Amorites, or Old Babylonians, a large group of Semitic-speaking seminomads, created a new empire.

Hammurabi (1792–1750 B.C.E.) employed a well-disciplined army of foot soldiers who carried axes, spears, and copper or bronze daggers. He learned to divide his opponents and subdue them one by one. Using such methods, he gained control of Sumer and Akkad and reunified Mesopotamia almost to the old borders created by Sargon of Akkad. After his conquests, he called himself "the sun of Babylon, the king who has made the four quarters of the world subservient," and established a new capital at Babylon, north of Akkad. He also built temples, defensive walls, and irrigation canals; encouraged trade; and brought about an economic revival. Indeed, Hammurabi saw himself as a shepherd to his people: "I am indeed the shepherd who brings peace, whose scepter is just. My benevolent shade was spread over my city. I held the people of the lands of Sumer and Akkad safely on my lap."[3] Hammurabi left his dynasty strong enough that it survived until the 1550s B.C.E., when the Kassites from the northeast took over.

TABLE 1.1 Some Semitic Languages

Akkadian	*Canaanitic*
Arabic	Hebrew
Aramaic	*Phoenician*
Assyrian	*Syriac*
Babylonian	

NOTE: Languages in italic type are no longer spoken.

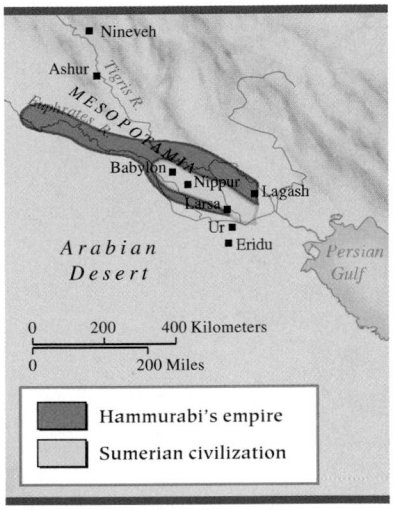

Hammurabi's Empire

© Cengage Learning

THE CODE OF HAMMURABI Hammurabi is best remembered for his law code, a collection of 282 laws. For centuries, laws had regulated people's relationships with one another in the lands of Mesopotamia, but only fragments of these earlier codes survive. Although many scholars today view Hammurabi's collection less as a code of laws and more as the attempt of Hammurabi to portray himself as the source of justice to the people, the code still gives us a glimpse of the Babylonian society of his time (see the box on p. 10).

The Code of Hammurabi reveals a society with a system of strict justice. Penalties for criminal offenses were severe and varied according to the social class of the victim. A crime against a member of the upper class (a noble) was punished more severely than the same offense against a member of the lower class. Moreover, the principle of

The Code of Hammurabi

Hammurabi's is the most complete Mesopotamian law code, although not the earliest. It was inscribed on a stone stele (STEE-lee *or* STEEL) topped by a bas-relief picturing Hammurabi receiving the inspiration for the law code from the sun god Shamash, who was also the god of justice. The law code emphasizes the principle of "an eye for an eye" and punishments that vary according to social status. Punishments could be severe. The following examples illustrate these concerns.

The Code of Hammurabi

25. If fire broke out in a free man's house and a free man, who went to extinguish it, cast his eye on the goods of the owner of the house and has appropriated the goods of the owner of the house, that free man shall be thrown into that fire.
129. If the wife of a free man has been caught while lying with another man, they shall bind them and throw them into the water. If the husband of the woman wishes to spare his wife, then the king in turn may spare his subject.
131. If a free man's wife was accused by her husband, but she was not caught while lying with another man, she shall make affirmation by god and return to her house.
196. If a free man has destroyed the eye of a member of the aristocracy, they shall destroy his eye.
198. If he has destroyed the eye of a commoner or broken the bone of a commoner, he shall pay one mina of silver.
199. If he has destroyed the eye of a free man's slave or broken the bone of a free man's slave, he shall pay one-half his value.
209. If a free man struck another free man's daughter and has caused her to have a miscarriage, he shall pay ten shekels of silver for her fetus.
210. If that woman has died, they shall put his daughter to death.
211. If by a blow he has caused a commoner's daughter to have a miscarriage, he shall pay five shekels of silver.
212. If that woman has died, he shall pay one-half mina of silver.
213. If he struck a free man's female slave and has caused her to have a miscarriage, he shall pay two shekels of silver.
214. If that female slave has died, he shall pay one-third mina of silver.

What do these laws from the Code of Hammurabi reveal about Mesopotamian society?

Source: PRITCHARD, JAMES; *ANCIENT NEAR EASTERN TEXTS RELATED TO THE OLD TESTAMENT–THIRD EDITION WITH SUPPLEMENT.* © 1950, 1955, 1969, renewed 1978 by Princeton University Press. Reprinted by permission of Princeton University Press.

"an eye for an eye, a tooth for a tooth" was fundamental to this system of justice. This meant that punishments should fit the crime: "If a freeman has destroyed the eye of a member of the aristocracy, they shall destroy his eye." Hammurabi's code also had an impact on legal ideas in Southwest Asia for hundreds of years, as the following verse from the Hebrew Bible demonstrates: "If anyone injures his neighbor, whatever he has done must be done to him: fracture for fracture, eye for eye, tooth for tooth. As he has injured the other, so he is to be injured" (Leviticus 24:19–20).

Hammurabi's code took the responsibilities of public officials very seriously. The governor of an area and city officials were expected to catch burglars. If they failed to do so, the officials in the district where the crime was committed had to replace the lost property. If murderers were not found, the officials had to pay a fine to the relatives of the murdered person.

The law code also furthered the proper performance of work with what amounted to consumer protection laws. Builders were held responsible for the buildings they constructed. If a house collapsed and caused the death of the owner, the builder was put to death. If the collapse caused the death of the son of the owner, the son of the builder was put to death. If goods were destroyed by the collapse, they had to be replaced and the house itself reconstructed at the builder's expense.

The largest number of laws in the Code of Hammurabi focused on marriage and the family. Parents arranged marriages for their children. After marriage, the parties involved signed a marriage contract; without it, no one was considered legally married. The husband made a bridal payment, and the woman's parents were responsible for providing a dowry to the new husband.

As in many patriarchal societies, women had far fewer privileges and rights in marriage than men. A woman's place was in the home, and failure to fulfill her expected duties was grounds for divorce. If she was not able to bear children, her husband could divorce her, but he did have to return the dowry to her family. If his wife tried to leave home to engage in business, thus neglecting her house, her husband could divorce her and did not have to repay the dowry. Furthermore, a wife who was a "gadabout, . . . neglecting her house [and] humiliating her husband," could be drowned. We do know that in practice not all women remained at home. Some worked in the fields and others in business, where they were especially prominent in running taverns.

Women were guaranteed some rights, however. If a woman was divorced without good reason, she received the dowry back. A woman could seek divorce and get her dowry back if her husband was unable to show that she had done anything wrong. In theory, a wife was guaranteed use of her husband's property in the event of his death. The mother could also decide which of her sons would receive an inheritance.

Sexual relations were strictly regulated as well. Husbands, but not wives, were permitted sexual activity outside marriage. A wife and her lover caught committing adultery were pitched into the river, although if the husband pardoned his wife, the king could pardon the guilty man. Incest was strictly forbidden. If a father had incestuous relations with his daughter, he would be banished. Incest between a son and mother resulted in both being burned.

Fathers ruled their children as well as their wives. Obedience was duly expected: "If a son has struck his father, they shall cut off his hand." If a son committed a serious enough offense, his father could disinherit him, although fathers were not permitted to disinherit their sons arbitrarily.

The Culture of Mesopotamia

A spiritual worldview was of fundamental importance to Mesopotamian culture. To the peoples of Mesopotamia, the gods were living realities who affected all aspects of life. It was crucial, therefore, that the correct hierarchies be observed. Leaders could prepare armies for war, but success depended on a favorable relationship with the gods. This helps explain the importance of the priestly class and is the reason why even the kings took great care to dedicate offerings and monuments to the gods.

THE IMPORTANCE OF RELIGION One of the most famous accounts of the creation of the universe from the ancient Near East was the Babylonian creation epic known as the *Enuma Elish*. The name comes from the first three words of the first two lines of the poem:

> *When on high the heavens were not yet named,*
> *And below, the earth was not called by a name.*

The *Enuma Elish* tells how the god Marduk was endowed with absolute power by the other gods to do battle with Tiamat, a primordial goddess who personified the forces of watery chaos. Marduk defeats Tiamat in battle and proceeds to create the universe by dividing Tiamat in two, one part becoming the heavens and the other the earth, with her breasts as mountains. From her eyes came the Tigris and Euphrates Rivers. The *Enuma Elish* was recited during the New Year festival celebrated in honor of Marduk in the city of Babylon, which the all-powerful god founded as an earthly residence for the gods after his creation of the universe.

The Mesopotamians viewed their city-states as earthly copies of a divine model and order. Each city-state was sacred because it was linked to a god or goddess. Hence, Nippur, the earliest center of Sumerian religion, was dedicated to Enlil (EN-lil), the god of wind. Moreover, located at the heart of each city-state was a temple complex. Occupying several acres, this sacred area consisted of a ziggurat with a temple at the top dedicated to the god or goddess who owned the city. The temple complex was the true center of the community. The main god or goddess dwelt there symbolically in the form of a statue, and the ceremony of dedication included a ritual that linked the statue to the god or goddess and thus supposedly harnessed the power of the deity for the city's benefit. Considerable wealth was poured into the construction of temples and other buildings used for the residences of priests and priestesses who helped the gods. Although the gods literally owned the city, the temple complex used only part of the land and rented out the remainder. The temples dominated individual and commercial life, an indication of the close relationship between Mesopotamian religion and culture.

The physical environment had an obvious impact on the Mesopotamian view of the universe. Ferocious floods, heavy downpours, scorching winds, and oppressive humidity were all part of the local climate. These conditions and the resulting famines easily convinced Mesopotamians that this world was controlled by supernatural forces and that the days of human beings "are numbered; whatever he may do, he is but wind," as *The Epic of Gilgamesh* laments. In the presence of nature, Mesopotamians could easily feel helpless, as this poem relates:

> *The rampant flood which no man can oppose,*
> *Which shakes the heavens and causes earth to tremble,*
> *In an appalling blanket folds mother and child,*
> *Beats down the canebrake's full luxuriant greenery,*
> *And drowns the harvest in its time of ripeness.*[4]

The Mesopotamians discerned cosmic rhythms in the universe and accepted its order but perceived that it was not completely safe because of the presence of willful, powerful cosmic powers that they identified with gods and goddesses.

With its numerous gods and goddesses animating all aspects of the universe, Mesopotamian religion was **polytheistic**. The four most important deities were An, Enlil, Enki (EN-kee), and Ninhursaga (nin-HUR-sah-guh). An was the god of the sky and hence the most important force in the universe. Since his basic essence was authority, he was also viewed as the source or active principle of all authority, including the earthly power of rulers and fathers alike. Enlil, god of wind, was considered the second greatest power of the visible universe. In charge of the wind and thus an expression of the legitimate use of force, Enlil became the symbol of the proper use of force on earth as well. Enki was god of the earth. Since the earth was the source of life-giving waters, Enki was also god of rivers, wells, and canals. More generally, he represented the waters of creativity and was responsible for inventions and crafts. Ninhursaga began as a goddess associated with soil, mountains, and vegetation. Eventually, however, she was worshiped as a mother goddess, a "mother of all children," who manifested her power by giving birth to kings and conferring the royal insignia on them.

Human beings' relationship with their gods was based on subservience since, according to Sumerian myth, human beings were created to do the manual labor the gods were unwilling to do for themselves. Moreover, humans were insecure because they could never be sure what the gods would do. But humans did make attempts to circumvent or relieve their anxiety by discovering the intentions of the gods; these efforts gave rise to the development of the arts of **divination**.

Divination took a variety of forms. A common form, at least for kings and priests who could afford it, involved killing animals, such as sheep or goats, and examining their livers or other organs. Supposedly, features seen in the organs of the sacrificed animals foretold events to come. One handbook predicted that if the animal organ had shape *x*, the outcome of the military campaign would be *y*. Private individuals relied on cheaper divinatory

Louvre (Hervé Lewandowski), Paris//© Réunion des Musées Nationaux/Art Resource, NY

The Development of Cuneiform Writing. Pictured here is the cone of Urukagina (oo-ROOK-uh-gee-nuh), an example of cuneiform writing from an early Sumerian dynasty. The inscription announces reductions in taxes. The table shows the development of writing from pictographic signs to cuneiform characters.

Pictographic sign, c. 3100 B.C.E.									
Interpretation	star	?sun over horizon	?stream	ear of barley	bull's head	bowl	head + bowl	lower leg	?shrouded body
Cuneiform sign, c. 2400 B.C.E.									
Cuneiform sign c. 700 B.C.E. (turned through 90°)									
Phonetic value*	dingir, an	u_4, ud	a	še	gu_4	nig_2, ninda	ku_2	du, gin, gub	lu_2
Meaning	god, sky	day, sun	water, seed, son	barley	ox	food, bread	to eat	to walk, to stand	man

*Some signs have more than one phonetic value and some sounds are represented by more than one sign; for example, u_4 means the fourth sign with the phonetic value *u*.

From the *Cultural Atlas of Mesopotamia & the Ancient Near East* by Michael Roaf/Courtesy of Andromeda Oxford Limited, Oxford, England techniques. These included interpreting patterns of smoke from burning incense or the pattern formed when oil was poured into water. The Mesopotamian arts of divination arose out of the desire to discover the purposes of the gods: if people could decipher the signs that foretold events, the events would be predictable, and humans could act wisely.

THE CULTIVATION OF NEW ARTS AND SCIENCES The realization of writing's great potential was another aspect of Mesopotamian culture. The oldest Mesopotamian texts date to around 3000 B.C.E. and were written by the Sumerians, who used a **cuneiform** (kyoo-NEE-uh-form) ("wedge-shaped") system of writing. Using a reed stylus, they made wedge-shaped impressions on clay tablets, which were then baked or dried in the sun. Once dried, these tablets were virtually indestructible, and the several hundred thousand that have been discovered have served as a valuable source of information for modern scholars. Sumerian writing evolved from drawings of physical objects to simplified and stylized signs, leading eventually to a phonetic system that made possible the written expression of abstract ideas.

Mesopotamian peoples used writing primarily for record keeping. They also produced monumental texts, documents that were intended to last forever, such as inscriptions etched in stone on statues and royal buildings. Numerous texts were prepared for teaching purposes. Schools for scribes were in operation by 2500 B.C.E. They were necessary because much time was needed to master the cuneiform system of writing. The primary goal of scribal education was to produce professionally trained scribes for careers in the temples and palaces, the military, and government. Pupils were male and primarily from wealthy families.

Writing was important because it enabled a society to keep records and maintain knowledge of previous practices and events. Writing also made it possible for people to communicate ideas in new ways, which is especially evident in Mesopotamian literary works. The most famous piece of Mesopotamian literature was *The Epic of Gilgamesh,* an elaborate poem that records the exploits of a legendary king of Uruk. Gilgamesh—wise, strong, and perfect in body, part man, part god—befriends a hairy beast named Enkidu. Together they set off in pursuit of heroic deeds. When Enkidu dies, Gilgamesh experiences the pain of mortality and embarks on a search for the secret of immortality. But his efforts fail (see the box on p. 14), and Gilgamesh remains mortal. The desire for immortality, one of humankind's great searches, ends in complete frustration. Everlasting life, this Mesopotamian epic makes clear, is only for the gods.

People in Mesopotamia also made outstanding achievements in mathematics and astronomy. In math, the Sumerians devised a number system based on 60, using combinations of 6 and 10 for practical solutions. Geometry was used to measure fields and erect buildings. In astronomy, the Sumerians made use of units of 60 and charted the heavenly constellations. Their calendar was based on twelve lunar months and was brought into harmony with the solar year by adding an extra month from time to time.

Egyptian Civilization: "The Gift of the Nile"

FOCUS QUESTIONS: What are the basic features of the three major periods of Egyptian history? What elements of continuity are there in the three periods? What are their major differences?

Although contemporaneous with Mesopotamia, civilization in Egypt evolved along somewhat different lines. Of central importance to the development of Egyptian civilization was the Nile River. That the Egyptian people recognized its significance is apparent in this *Hymn to the Nile*: "The bringer of food, rich in provisions, creator of all good, lord of majesty, sweet of fragrance. . . . He who . . . fills the magazines, makes the granaries wide, and gives things to the poor. He who makes every beloved tree to grow. . . ."[5] Egypt, like Mesopotamia, was a river valley civilization.

The Impact of Geography

The Nile is a unique river, beginning in the heart of Africa and coursing northward for thousands of miles. It is the longest river in the world. Thanks to the Nile, an area several miles wide on both banks of the river was capable of producing abundant harvests. The "miracle" of the Nile was its annual flooding. The river rose in the summer from rains in Central Africa and the Ethiopian highlands, crested in Egypt in September and October, and left a deposit of silt that enriched the soil. The Egyptians called this fertile land the "Black Land" because it was dark from the silt and the lush crops that grew on it. Beyond these narrow strips of fertile fields lay the deserts (the "Red Land").

Unlike the floods of Mesopotamia's rivers, the flooding of the Nile was gradual and usually predictable, and the river itself was seen as life-enhancing, not life-threatening. Although a system of organized irrigation was still necessary, the small villages along the Nile could make the effort without the massive state intervention that was required in Mesopotamia. Egyptian civilization consequently tended to remain more rural, with many small population centers congregated along a narrow band on both sides of the Nile. About 100 miles before it empties into the Mediterranean, the river splits into two major branches, forming the delta,

The Great Flood

The great poem of Mesopotamian literature, *The Epic of Gilgamesh,* includes an account by Utnapishtim (a Mesopotamian forerunner of the biblical Noah), who had built a ship and survived the flood unleashed by the gods to destroy humankind. This selection recounts how the god Ea (Sumerian Enki, god of the waters) advised Utnapishtim to build a boat and how he came to land his boat at the end of the flood. In this section, Utnapishtim is telling his story to Gilgamesh.

The Epic of Gilgamesh

"In those days the world teemed, the people multiplied, the world bellowed like a wild bull, and the great god was aroused by the clamor. Enlil heard the clamor and he said to the gods in council, 'The uproar of mankind is intolerable and sleep is no longer possible by reason of the babel.' So the gods agreed to exterminate mankind. Enlil did this, but Ea because of his oath warned me in a dream . . . , 'Tear down your house and build a boat, abandon possessions and look for life, despise worldly goods and save your soul alive. Tear down your house, I say, and build a boat. . . . Then take up into the boat the seed of all living creatures. . . .' [Utnapishtim did as he was told, and then the destruction came.]

"For six days and six nights the winds blew, torrent and tempest and flood overwhelmed the world, tempest and flood raged together like warring hosts. When the seventh day dawned the storm from the south subsided, the sea grew calm, the flood was stifled; I looked at the face of the world and there was silence, all mankind was turned to clay. The surface of the sea stretched as flat as a rooftop; I opened a hatch and the light fell on my face. Then I bowed low, I sat down and I wept, the tears streamed down my face, for on every side was the waste of water. I looked for land in vain, but fourteen leagues distant there appeared a mountain, and there the boat grounded; on the mountain of Nisir the boat held fast, she held fast and did not budge. . . . When the seventh day dawned I loosed a dove and let her go. She flew away, but finding no resting-place she returned. Then I loosed a swallow, and she flew away but finding no resting-place she returned. I loosed a raven, she saw that the waters had retreated, she ate, she flew around, she cawed, and she did not come back. Then I threw everything open to the four winds, I made a sacrifice and poured out a libation on the mountain top."

Q What does this selection from *The Epic of Gilgamesh* tell you about the relationship between the Mesopotamians and their gods? How might you explain the differences between this account and the biblical flood story in Genesis?

Source: From *THE EPIC OF GILGAMESH* translated with an introduction by N. K. Sandars (Penguin Classics 1960, Third edition 1972). Copyright © N. K. Sandars, 1960, 1964, 1972. Reproduced by permission of Penguin Books Ltd.

a triangular-shaped territory called Lower Egypt to distinguish it from Upper Egypt, the land upstream to the south (see Map 1.3). Egypt's important cities developed at the tip of the delta. Even today, most of Egypt's people are crowded along the banks of the Nile River.

The surpluses of food that Egyptian farmers grew in the fertile Nile valley made Egypt prosperous. But the Nile also served as a unifying factor in Egyptian history. In ancient times, the Nile was the fastest way to travel through the land, making both transportation and communication easier. Winds from the north pushed sailboats south, and the current of the Nile carried them north. Often when they headed downstream (north), people used long poles or paddles to propel their boats forward.

Unlike Mesopotamia, which was subject to constant invasion, Egypt was blessed by natural barriers that fostered isolation, protected it from invasion, and gave it a sense of security. These barriers included the deserts to the west and east; the cataracts (rapids) on the southern part of the Nile, which made defense relatively easy; and the Mediterranean Sea to the north. These barriers, however, were effective only when combined with Egyptian fortifications at strategic locations. Nor did they prevent the development of trade. Indeed, there is evidence of very early trade between Egypt and Mesopotamia.

In essence, Egyptian geography and topography played important roles in the early history of the country. The regularity of the Nile floods and the relative isolation of the Egyptians created a sense of security that was accompanied by a feeling of changelessness. To the ancient Egyptians, when the Nile flooded each year, "the fields laugh and people's faces light up." Unlike people in Mesopotamia, Egyptians faced life with a spirit of confidence in the stability of things. Egyptian civilization was characterized by a remarkable degree of continuity over thousands of years.

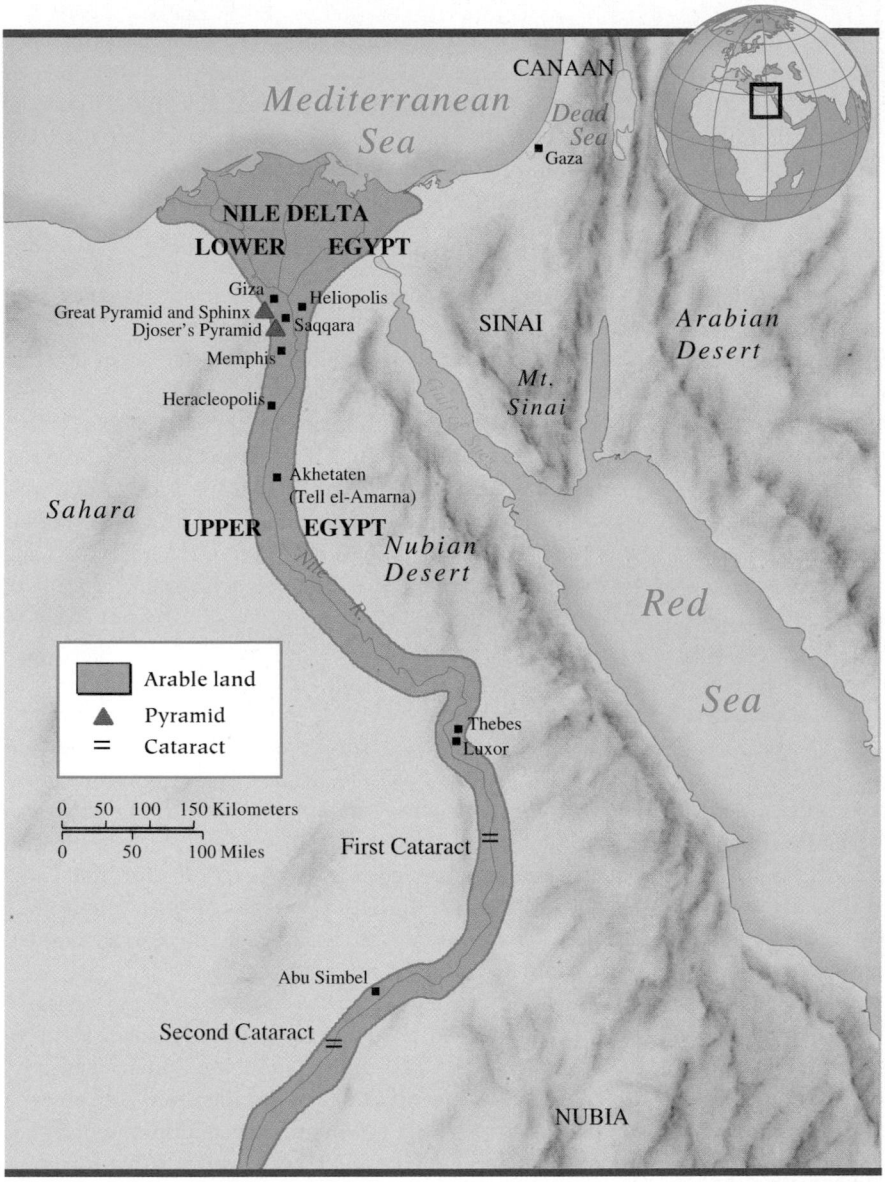

© Cengage Learning

MAP 1.3 Ancient Egypt. Egyptian civilization centered on the life-giving water and flood silts of the Nile River, with most of the population living in Lower Egypt, where the river splits to form the Nile delta. Most of the pyramids, built during the Old Kingdom, are clustered at the entrance to the delta.

How did the lands to the east and west of the river help to protect Egypt from invasion?

The Old and Middle Kingdoms

The basic framework for the study of Egyptian history was provided by Manetho (MAN-uh-thoh), an Egyptian priest and historian who lived in the early third century B.C.E. He divided Egyptian history into thirty-one dynasties of kings. Using Manetho's and other lists of kings, modern historians have divided Egyptian history into three major periods known as the Old Kingdom, the Middle Kingdom, and the New Kingdom. These were periods of long-term stability characterized by strong monarchical authority, competent bureaucracy, freedom from invasion, much construction of temples and pyramids, and considerable intellectual and cultural activity. But between the periods of stability were ages known as the Intermediate Periods, which were characterized by weak political structures and rivalry for leadership, invasions, a decline in building activity, and a restructuring of society.

According to the Egyptians' own tradition, their land consisted initially of numerous populated areas ruled by tribal chieftains. Around 3100 B.C.E., the first Egyptian royal dynasty, under a king called Menes, united Upper and Lower Egypt into a single kingdom. Henceforth the king would be called "king of Upper and Lower Egypt," and one of the royal crowns would be the Double Crown, combining the White Crown of Upper Egypt and the Red Crown of Lower Egypt. Just as the Nile served to unite Upper and Lower Egypt physically, kingship served to unite the two areas politically.

THE OLD KINGDOM The Old Kingdom encompassed the third through sixth dynasties of Egyptian kings, lasting from around 2686 to 2181 B.C.E. It was an age of prosperity and splendor, made visible in the construction of the greatest and largest pyramids in Egypt's history. The capital of the Old Kingdom was located at Memphis, south of the delta.

Kingship was a divine institution in ancient Egypt and formed part of a universal cosmic scheme: "What is the king of Upper and Lower Egypt? He is a god by whose dealings one lives, the father and mother of all men, alone by himself, without an equal."[6] In obeying their king, subjects helped maintain the cosmic order. A breakdown in royal power could only mean that citizens were offending divinity and weakening the universal structure. Among the various titles of Egyptian kings, *pharaoh* (originally meaning "great house" or "palace") eventually came to be the most common.

Although they possessed absolute power, Egyptian kings were supposed to rule according to set principles and not arbitrarily. The chief principle was called *Ma'at,* a spiritual precept that conveyed the idea of truth and justice, especially right order and harmony. To ancient Egyptians, this fundamental order and harmony had existed throughout the universe since the beginning of time. Pharaohs were the divine instruments who maintained it and were themselves subject to it.

Although theoretically absolute in their power, in practice Egyptian kings did not rule alone. Initially, members of the king's family performed administrative tasks, but by the fourth dynasty, a bureaucracy with regular procedures had developed. Especially important was the office of vizier, "steward of the whole land." Directly responsible to the king, the vizier was in charge of the bureaucracy, with its numerous departments, including police, justice, river transport, and public works. Agriculture and the treasury were the most important departments. Agriculture was, of course, the backbone of Egyptian prosperity, and the treasury collected taxes, which were paid in kind. A careful assessment of land and tenants was undertaken to establish the tax base.

For administrative purposes, Egypt was divided into provinces or nomes, as they were later called by the Greeks—twenty-two in Upper Egypt and twenty in Lower Egypt. A governor, called by the Greeks a nomarch, was head of each nome and was responsible to the king and vizier. Nomarchs, however, tended to build up large holdings of land and power within their nomes, creating a potential rivalry with the pharaohs.

THE MIDDLE KINGDOM Despite the theory of divine order, the Old Kingdom eventually collapsed, ushering in a period of disorder. Eventually, a new royal dynasty managed to pacify all Egypt and inaugurated the Middle Kingdom, a new period of stability lasting from around 2055 to 1650 B.C.E. Several factors contributed to its vitality. The nome structure was reorganized. The boundaries of each nome were now settled precisely, and the obligations of the nomes to the state were clearly delineated. Nomarchs were confirmed as hereditary officeholders but with the understanding that their duties must be performed faithfully. These included the collection of taxes for the state and the recruitment of labor forces for royal projects, such as stone quarrying.

The Middle Kingdom was characterized by a new concern on the part of the pharaohs for the people. In the Old Kingdom, the pharaoh had been viewed as an inaccessible god-king. Now he was portrayed as the shepherd of his people with the responsibility to build public works and provide for the public welfare. As one pharaoh expressed it, "He [a particular god] created me as one who should do that which he had done, and to carry out that which he commanded should be done. He appointed me herdsman of this land, for he knew who would keep it in order for him."[7]

CHRONOLOGY The Egyptians

Early Dynastic Period (dynasties 1–2)	c. 3100–2686 B.C.E.
Old Kingdom (dynasties 3–6)	c. 2686–2181 B.C.E.
First Intermediate Period (dynasties 7–10)	c. 2180–2055 B.C.E.
Middle Kingdom (dynasties 11–12)	c. 2055–1650 B.C.E.
Second Intermediate Period (dynasties 13–17)	c. 1650–1550 B.C.E.
New Kingdom (dynasties 18–20)	c. 1550–1070 B.C.E.
Postempire Egypt (dynasties 21–31)	1070–30 B.C.E.

Society and Economy in Ancient Egypt

Egyptian society had a simple structure in the Old and Middle Kingdoms; basically, it was organized along hierarchical lines with the god-king at the top. The king was surrounded by an upper class of nobles and priests who participated in the elaborate rituals of life that surrounded the pharaoh. The members of this ruling class ran the government and managed their own landed estates, which provided much of their wealth.

Below the upper classes were merchants and artisans. Merchants engaged in active trade up and down the Nile as well as in town and village markets. Some merchants also engaged in international trade; they were sent by the king to Crete and Syria, where they obtained wood and other products. Expeditions traveled into Nubia for ivory and down the Red Sea to Punt for incense and spices. Egyptian artisans displayed unusually high standards of craftsmanship and beauty and produced an incredible variety of goods: stone dishes; beautifully painted boxes made of clay; wooden furniture; gold, silver, and copper tools and containers; paper and rope made of papyrus; and linen clothing.

The great majority of people in Egypt simply worked the land. In theory, the king owned all the land but granted portions of it to his subjects. Large sections were in the possession of nobles and the temple complexes. Most of the lower classes were serfs or common people who were bound to the land and cultivated the estates. They paid taxes in the form of crops to the king, nobles, and priests; lived in small villages or towns; and provided military service and forced labor for building projects.

The Culture of Egypt

Egypt produced a culture that dazzled and awed its later conquerors. The Egyptians' technical achievements alone, especially visible in the construction of the pyramids, demonstrated a measure of skill unique in the world at that time. To the Egyptians, all of these achievements were part of a cosmic order suffused with the presence of the divine.

SPIRITUAL LIFE IN EGYPTIAN SOCIETY The Egyptians had no word for religion because it was an inseparable aspect of existence in the world in which they lived. The Egyptians possessed a remarkable number of gods associated with heavenly bodies and natural forces—hardly unusual in view of the importance to Egypt's well-being of the sun, the river, and the fertile land along its banks. The sun was the source of life and hence worthy of worship. A sun cult developed, and the sun god took on different forms and names, depending on his specific function. He was worshiped as Atum in human form and as Re, who had a human body but the head of a falcon. The pharaoh took the title "Son of Re" because he was regarded as the earthly embodiment of Re.

River and land deities included Osiris (oh-SY-russ) and Isis (Y-sis) with their child Horus, who was related to the Nile and to the sun as well. Osiris became especially important as a symbol of resurrection. A famous Egyptian myth told of the struggle between Osiris, who brought civilization to Egypt, and his evil brother Seth, who killed him, cut his body into fourteen parts, and tossed them into the Nile. Isis, the faithful wife of Osiris, found the pieces and, with help from other gods, restored Osiris to life. As a symbol of resurrection and as judge of the dead, Osiris took on an important role for the Egyptians. By identifying with Osiris, one could hope to gain new life, just as Osiris had done. The dead, embalmed and mummified, were placed in tombs (in the case of kings, in pyramidal tombs), given the name of Osiris, and by a process of magical identification became Osiris. Like Osiris, they would then be reborn. The flood of the Nile and the new life it brought to Egypt were symbolized by Isis gathering all of the parts of Osiris together and were celebrated each spring in the festival of the new land.

Later Egyptian spiritual practice began to emphasize morality by stressing the role of Osiris as judge of the dead. The dead were asked to give an account of their

© The Trustees of the British Museum, London/Art Resource, NY

Osiris as Judge of the Dead. According to the *Book of the Dead,* after making a denial of offenses (the "negative confession"), the deceased experienced the "weighing of the heart." Shown here is a scene from the *Book of the Dead* depicting the judgment of Hunefer, a royal scribe who died around 1285 B.C.E. Hunefer's heart is placed on one side of a balance scale; on the other side is the feather of Ma'at, the goddess of truth. For Hunefer, heart and feather are of equal weight, so the god Anubis ushers him into the presence of Osiris, seated on his throne at the right. A "swallowing monster," a hybrid creature combining crocodile, lion, and hippopotamus, stood ready at the scale to devour the deceased if he failed the test.

earthly deeds to show whether they deserved a reward. Other means were also employed to gain immortality. Magical incantations, preserved in the *Book of the Dead* from the period of the New Kingdom, were used to ensure a favorable journey to a happy afterlife. Specific instructions explained what to do when confronted by the judge of the dead. These instructions had two aspects. The negative confession gave a detailed list of what one had not done:

> *I have not committed evil against men.*
> *I have not mistreated cattle.*
> *I have not blasphemed a god*
> *I have not done violence to a poor man. . . .*
> *I have not made anyone sick. . . .*
> *I have not killed*
> *I have not caused anyone suffering. . . .*
> *I have not had sexual relations with a boy.*
> *I have not defiled myself*[8]

Later the supplicant made a speech listing his good actions: "I have done that which men said and that with which gods are content. . . . I have given bread to the hungry, water to the thirsty, clothing to the naked, and a ferry-boat to him who was marooned. I have provided divine offerings for the gods and mortuary offerings for the dead."[9]

THE PYRAMIDS One of the great achievements of Egyptian civilization, the building of pyramids, occurred during the Old Kingdom. Pyramids were not built in isolation but as part of a larger complex dedicated to the dead—in effect, a city of the dead. The area included a large pyramid for the king's burial, smaller pyramids for his family, and mastabas, rectangular structures with flat roofs, as tombs for the pharaoh's noble officials. The tombs were well prepared for their residents. The rooms were furnished and stocked with numerous supplies, including chairs, boats, chests, weapons, games, dishes, and a variety of foods. The Egyptians believed that human beings had two bodies, a physical one and a spiritual one, which they called the *ka*. If the physical body was properly preserved (that is, mummified) and the tomb furnished with all the various objects of regular life, the *ka* could return and continue its life despite the death of the physical body.

To preserve the physical body after death, the Egyptians practiced mummification, a process of slowly drying a dead body to prevent it from decomposing. Special workshops, run by priests, performed this procedure, primarily for the wealthy families who could afford it. According to Herodotus, an ancient Greek historian (see Chapter 3) who visited Egypt around 450 B.C.E., "The most refined method is as follows: first of all they draw out the brain through the nostrils with an iron hook. . . . Then they make an incision in the flank with a sharp Ethiopian stone through which they extract all the internal organs."[10] The liver, lungs, stomach, and intestines were placed in four special jars that were put in the tomb with the mummy. The priests then covered the corpse with a natural salt that absorbed the body's water. Later, they filled the body with spices and wrapped it with layers of linen soaked in resin. At the end of the process, which took about seventy days, a lifelike mask was placed over the head and shoulders of the mummy, which was then sealed in a case and placed in its tomb in a pyramid.

The largest and most magnificent of all the pyramids was built under King Khufu (KOO-foo). Constructed at Giza around 2540 B.C.E., the famous Great Pyramid covers almost 13 acres, measures 756 feet at each side of its base, and stands 481 feet high. Its four sides are almost precisely oriented to the four points of the compass. The interior included a grand gallery to the burial chamber, which was built of granite with a lidless sarcophagus for the pharaoh's body. The Great Pyramid still stands as a visible symbol of the power of Egyptian kings and the spiritual conviction that underlay Egyptian society. No later pyramid ever matched its size or splendor. But an Egyptian pyramid was not just the king's tomb; it was also an important symbol of royal power. It could be seen for miles as a visible reminder of the glory and might of the ruler, who was a living god on earth.

ART AND WRITING Commissioned by kings or nobles for use in temples and tombs, Egyptian art was largely functional. Wall paintings and statues of gods and kings in temples served a strictly spiritual purpose. They were an integral part of the performance of ritual, which was thought necessary to preserve the cosmic order and hence the well-being of Egypt. Likewise, the mural scenes and sculptured figures found in the tombs had a specific function. They were supposed to aid the journey of the deceased into the afterworld. Because they often depicted scenes from the life of the deceased, they provide us with much information about the Egyptian lifestyle (see Images of Everyday Life on p. 20).

Egyptian art was also formulaic. Artists and sculptors were expected to observe a strict canon of proportions that determined both form and presentation. This canon gave Egyptian art a distinctive appearance for thousands of years. Especially characteristic was the convention of combining the profile, semiprofile, and frontal views of the human body in relief work and painting in order to represent each part of the body accurately. The result was an art that was highly stylized yet still allowed distinctive features to be displayed.

© Will and Deni McIntyre/Photo Researchers, Inc.

The Pyramids at Giza. The three pyramids at Giza, across the Nile River from Cairo, are the most famous in Egypt. At the rear is the largest of the three pyramids, the Great Pyramid of Khufu. Next to it is the pyramid of Khafre (KAF-ray). In the foreground is the smaller pyramid of Menkaure (men-KOW-ray) standing behind the even smaller pyramids for the pharaohs' wives. Covering almost 13 acres, the Great Pyramid of Khufu is immense. It is estimated that the Great Pyramid contains 2.3 million stone blocks, each weighing about 2.5 tons.

Writing in Egypt emerged during the first two dynasties. The Greeks later labeled Egyptian writing **hieroglyphics**, meaning "priest carvings" or "sacred writings." Hieroglyphs (HY-uh-roh-glifs) were symbols that depicted objects and had a sacred value at the same time. Although hieroglyphs were later simplified into two scripts for writing purposes, they never developed into an alphabet. Egyptian hieroglyphs were initially carved in stone, but later the two simplified scripts were written on papyrus, a paper made from the papyrus reed that grew along the Nile. Most of the ancient Egyptian literature that has come down to us was written on papyrus rolls and wooden tablets.

Disorder and a New Order: The New Kingdom

The Middle Kingdom was brought to an end by a new period of instability. An incursion into the delta region by a people known as the Hyksos (HIK-sohs) initiated this second age of disorder. The Hyksos, a Semitic-speaking people, infiltrated Egypt in the seventeenth century B.C.E. and came to dominate much of Egypt. The presence of the Hyksos was not entirely negative for Egypt, however. They taught the Egyptians to make bronze for use in new agricultural tools and weapons. The Hyksos also brought new forms of military equipment to Egypt, including the horse-drawn war chariot, a heavier sword, and the compound bow. Eventually, a new line of pharaohs—the eighteenth dynasty—made use of the new weapons to throw off Hyksos domination, reunite Egypt, establish the New Kingdom (c. 1550–1070 B.C.E.), and launch the Egyptians along a new militaristic and imperialistic path. During the period of the New Kingdom, Egypt became the most powerful state in the Middle East. The Egyptians occupied Canaan and Syria but permitted local princes to rule under Egyptian control. Egyptian armies also moved westward into Libya and extended Egypt's border to the south by conquering the African kingdom of Nubia.

The eighteenth dynasty was not without its own troubles, however. Amenhotep (ah-mun-HOH-tep) IV (c. 1364–1347 B.C.E.) introduced the worship of Aten, god of the sun disk, as the chief god and pursued his worship with great enthusiasm (see the box on p. 21). Changing his own name to Akhenaten (ah-kuh-NAH-tun) ("Servant of Aten"), the pharaoh closed the temples of other gods and especially endeavored to lessen the power of Amon-Re and his priesthood at Thebes. Akhenaten strove to reduce the priests' influence by replacing Thebes as the capital of Egypt with Akhetaten ("Horizon of Aten"), a new city located at modern Tell el-Amarna, 200 miles north of Thebes.

Akhenaten's attempt at religious change failed. It went too far in asking Egyptians to ignore their traditional ways and beliefs, especially since they saw the destruction of the old gods as subversive of the very cosmic order on which Egypt's survival and continuing prosperity depended. Moreover, the priests at Thebes were unalterably opposed to the changes, which diminished their influence and power. At the same time, Akhenaten's preoccupation with religion caused him to ignore foreign affairs and led to the loss of both Syria and Canaan. Akhenaten's changes were soon undone after his death by those who influenced his successor, the boy-pharaoh Tutankhamun (toot-ahng-KAH-muhn) (1347–1338 B.C.E.). Tutankhamun returned the government to Thebes and restored the old gods. The Aten experiment had failed to take hold, and the eighteenth dynasty itself came to an end in 1333 B.C.E.

IMAGES OF EVERYDAY LIFE

The Egyptian Diet

The diets of the upper and lower classes in ancient Egypt differed considerably. Various types of meat and fowl, including beef, goat, pork, goose, and pigeon, were on the tables of the rich. Fish was also an important part of the upper-class Egyptian diet. Although done for sport as well as food, hunting waterfowl in the stands of papyrus reeds that grew along the river's banks was a favorite pastime of the Egyptian upper classes. Shown below is a hunting scene from the eighteenth-dynasty tomb of Nebamun in Thebes. Nebamun, a nobleman, is seen standing in his boat using his throwstick to hunt birds. He holds three birds in his right hand while a cat retrieves two in its claws and holds the wings of another in its teeth.

The basic diet of the poor consisted chiefly of bread, beer made from barley, and onions. The baking of bread was an important task in all households. The tomb painting at the lower right from the eighteenth-dynasty tomb of Mennah shows two men carrying grain while slave girls fight over leftovers in the background.

Vegetables and fruits were also part of the Egyptian diet. Among the vegetables were lettuce, radishes, squash, and cucumbers. Fruits included figs, dates, and grapes, which were mainly used by the upper classes for making wine. The third illustration shows peasants harvesting grapes from grapevines that have been attached to a trellis. Both sweet and dry wines were produced from a variety of dark and pale grapes.

Tombs of the Nobles, Thebes, Egypt//© Erich Lessing/Art Resource, NY

British Museum, London//© Werner Forman/Art Resource, NY

Tombs of the Nobles, Thebes, Egypt//© Erich Lessing/Art Resource, NY

Akhenaten's *Hymn to Aten* and Psalm 104 of the Hebrew Bible

Amenhotep IV, more commonly known as Akhenaten, created a religious upheaval in Egypt by introducing the worship of Aten, god of the sun disk, as the chief god. Akhenaten's reverence for Aten is evident in this hymn. Some authorities have noted a similarity in spirit and wording to the 104th Psalm of the Old Testament. In fact, some scholars have argued that there might be a connection between the two.

Hymn to Aten

Your rays suckle every meadow.
When you rise, they live, they grow for you.
You make the seasons in order to rear all that you have made.
The winter to cool them,
And the heat that they may taste you.
You have made the distant sky in order to rise therein,
In order to see all that you do make.
While you were alone,
Rising in your form as the living Aten,
Appearing, shining, withdrawing or approaching,
You made millions of forms of yourself alone.

Cities, towns, fields, road, and river—
Every eye beholds you over against them,
For you are the Aten of the day over the earth. . . .
The world came into being by your hand,
According as you have made them.
When you have risen they live,
When you set they die.
You are lifetime your own self,
For one lives only through you.
Eyes are fixed on beauty until you set.
All work is laid aside when you set in the west.
But when you rise again,
Everything is made to flourish for the king . . .
Since you did found the earth
And raise them up for your son,
Who came forth from your body: the King of Upper
and Lower Egypt, . . . Akh-en-Aten, . . . and the
Chief Wife of the King . . . Neferti-iti, living and
youthful forever and ever.

Psalm 104:19–25, 27–30

The moon marks off the seasons,
and the sun knows when to go down.

You bring darkness, it becomes night,
and all the beasts of the forest prowl.

The lions roar for their prey
and seek their food from God.

The sun rises, and they steal away;
they return and lie down in their dens.

Then man goes out to his work,
to his labor until evening.

How many are your works, O Lord!
In wisdom you made them all;
the earth is full of your creatures.

There is the sea, vast and spacious,
teeming with creatures beyond number—
living things both large and small. . . .

These all look to you
to give them their food at the proper time.

When you give it to them,
they gather it up;
when you open your hand,
they are satisfied with good things.

When you hide your face,
they are terrified;
when you take away their breath,
they die and return to the dust.

When you send your Spirit,
they are created,
and you renew the face of the earth.

Q What similarities do you see between Akhenaten's *Hymn to Aten* and Psalm 104 of the Hebrew Bible? How do you explain the similarities? What significant differences do you find between the two, and what do they tell you about the differences between the religion of the Egyptians and the religion of ancient Israel?

Source: PRITCHARD, JAMES; *ANCIENT NEAR EASTERN TEXTS RELATED TO THE OLD TESTAMENT– THIRD EDITION WITH SUPPLEMENT.* © 1950, 1955, 1969, renewed 1978 by Princeton University Press. Reprinted by permission of Princeton University Press.
Scripture taken from the HOLY BIBLE, NEW INTERNATIONAL VERSION®. Copyright © 1973, 1978, 1984 Biblica. Used by permission of Zondervan. All rights reserved. The "NIV" and "New International Version" trademarks are registered in the United States Patent and Trademark Office by Biblica. Use of either trademark requires the permission of Biblica.

A Father's Advice

Upper-class Egyptians enjoyed compiling collections of wise sayings to provide guidance for leading an upright and successful life. This excerpt is taken from *The Instruction of the Vizier Ptah-hotep* and dates from around 2450 B.C.E. The vizier was the pharaoh's chief official. In this selection, Ptah-hotep advises his son on how to be a successful official.

The Instruction of the Vizier Ptah-hotep

Then he said to his son:

Let not your heart be puffed-up because of your knowledge; be not confident because you are a wise man. Take counsel with the ignorant as well as the wise. The full limits of skill cannot be attained, and there is no skilled man equipped to his full advantage. Good speech is more hidden than the emerald, but it may be found with maidservants at the grindstones. . . .

If you are a leader commanding the affairs of the multitude, seek out for yourself every beneficial deed, until it may be that your own affairs are without wrong. Justice is great, and its appropriateness is lasting; it has been disturbed since the time of him who made it, whereas there is punishment for him who passes over its laws. It is the right path before him who knows nothing. Wrongdoing has never brought its undertaking into port. It may be that it is fraud that gains riches, but the strength of justice is that it lasts. . . .

If you are a man of intimacy, whom one great man sends to another, be thoroughly reliable when he sends you. Carry out the errand for him as he has spoken. Do not be reserved about what is said to you, and beware of any act of forgetfulness. Grasp hold of truth, and do not exceed it. Mere gratification is by no means to be repeated. Struggle against making words worse, thus making one great man hostile to another through vulgar speech. . . .

If you are a man of standing and found a household and produce a son who is pleasing to god, if he is correct and inclines toward your ways and listens to your instruction, while his manners in your house are fitting, and if he takes care of your property as it should be, seek out for him every useful action. He is your son, . . . you should not cut your heart off from him.

But a man's seed often creates enmity. If he goes astray and transgresses your plans and does not carry out your instruction, so that his manners in your household are wretched, and he rebels against all that you say, while his mouth runs on in the most wretched talk, quite apart from his experience, while he possesses nothing, you should cast him off: he is not your son at all. He was not really born to you. Thus, you enslave him entirely according to his own speech. He is one whom god has condemned in the very womb.

Q According to this document, what social and political skills were prized by members of the Egyptian governing elite? What does the passage reveal about Egyptian bureaucrats?

Source: PRITCHARD, JAMES; *ANCIENT NEAR EASTERN TEXTS RELATED TO THE OLD TESTAMENT– THIRD EDITION WITH SUPPLEMENT.* © 1950, 1955, 1969, renewed 1978 by Princeton University Press. Reprinted by permission of Princeton University Press.

The nineteenth dynasty managed to restore Egyptian power one more time. Under Ramesses (RAM-uh-seez) II (c. 1279–1213 B.C.E.), the Egyptians regained control of Canaan but were unable to reestablish the borders of their earlier empire. New invasions in the thirteenth century by the "Sea Peoples," as the Egyptians called them, destroyed Egyptian power in Canaan and drove the Egyptians back within their old frontiers. The days of Egyptian empire were ended, and the New Kingdom itself expired with the end of the twentieth dynasty in 1070 B.C.E. For the next thousand years, despite periodic revivals of strength, Egypt was dominated by Libyans, Nubians, Persians, and finally Macedonians after the conquest of Alexander the Great (see Chapter 4). In the first century B.C.E., Egypt became a province in Rome's mighty empire.

Daily Life in Ancient Egypt: Family and Marriage

Ancient Egyptians had a very positive attitude toward daily life on earth and followed the advice of the wisdom literature, which suggested that people marry young and establish a home and family (see the box above). Monogamy was the general rule, although a husband was allowed to keep additional wives if his first wife was childless. Pharaohs were entitled to harems; the queen, however, was acknowledged as the Great Wife, with a status higher than that of the other wives. The husband was master in the house, but wives were very much respected and in charge of the household and education of the children. From a book of wise sayings came this advice:

> If you are a man of standing, you should found your household and love your wife at home as is fitting. Fill her belly; clothe her back. Ointment is the prescription for her body. Make her heart glad as long as you live. She is a profitable field for her lord. You should not contend with her at law, and keep her far from gaining control. . . . Let her heart be soothed through what may accrue to you; it means keeping her long in your house.[11]

Women's property and inheritance remained in their hands, even in marriage. Although most careers and public offices were closed to women, some did operate businesses. Peasant women worked long hours in the fields and at numerous domestic tasks, especially weaving cloth. Upper-class women could function as priestesses, and a few queens even became pharaohs in their own right. Most famous was Hatshepsut (hat-SHEP-soot) in the New Kingdom. She first served as regent for her stepson Thutmosis (thoot-MOH-suss) III but assumed the throne for herself and remained in power until her death.

Hatshepsut's reign was a prosperous one, as is especially evident in her building activity. She is most famous for the temple dedicated to herself at Deir el Bahri on the west bank of the Nile at Thebes. As pharaoh, Hatshepsut sent out military expeditions, encouraged mining, fostered agriculture, and sent a trading expedition up the Nile. Hatshepsut's official statues sometimes show her clothed and bearded like a king. She was referred to as "His Majesty." That Hatshepsut was aware of her unusual position is evident from an inscription she had placed on one of her temples. It read, "Now my heart turns to and fro, in thinking what will the people say, they who shall see my monument in after years, and shall speak of what I have done."

Marriages were arranged by parents. The primary concerns were family and property, and clearly the chief purpose of marriage was to produce children, especially sons. From the New Kingdom came this piece of wisdom: "Take to yourself a wife while you are a youth, that she may produce a son for you."[12] Daughters were not slighted, however. Numerous tomb paintings show the close and affectionate relationship parents had with both sons and daughters. Although marriages were arranged, some of the surviving love poems from ancient Egypt indicate an element of romance in some marriages. Marriages could and did end in divorce, which was allowed, apparently with compensation for the wife. Adultery, however, was strictly prohibited, and punishments were severe, especially for women, who could have their noses cut off or be burned at the stake.

CHAPTER SUMMARY

Humanlike creatures first emerged in Africa more than 3 to 4 million years ago. Over a long period of time, Paleolithic people learned how to create more sophisticated tools, to use fire, and to adapt to and even change their physical environment. Paleolithic people were primarily nomads, who hunted animals and gathered wild plants for survival. Nevertheless, they created a culture that included sophisticated cave paintings.

The agricultural revolution of the Neolithic Age, which began around 10,000 B.C.E., dramatically changed human patterns of living. The growing of food on a regular basis and the taming of animals made it possible for humans to stop their nomadic ways and settle in more permanent settlements. These organized communities gradually gave rise to more complex human societies.

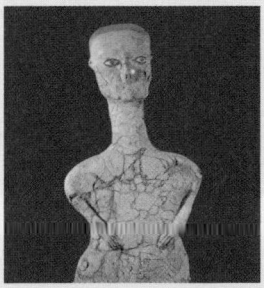

These more complex human societies, which we call the first civilizations, emerged around 3000 B.C.E. in the river valleys of Mesopotamia, Egypt, India, and China. An increase in food production in these regions led to a significant growth in human population and the rise of cities. Efforts to control the flow of water for farming also led to organized governments in these new urban civilizations.

The peoples of Southwest Asia and Egypt laid the foundations of Western civilization. They developed cities and struggled with the problems of organized states as they moved from individual communities to larger territorial units and eventually to empires. They invented writing to keep records and created literature. They constructed monumental buildings to please their gods, give witness to their power, and preserve their culture. They developed new political, military, social, and religious structures to deal with the basic problems of human existence and organization. These first civilizations left detailed records that allow us to view how they grappled with three of the fundamental problems that humans have pondered: the nature of human relationships, the nature of the universe, and the role of divine forces in that cosmos. Although later people would provide different answers from those of the Mesopotamians and Egyptians, it was they who first posed the questions, gave answers, and wrote them down.

By the middle of the second millennium B.C.E., much of the creative impulse of the Mesopotamian and Egyptian civilizations was beginning to wane. As we shall see in Chapter 2, by 1200 B.C.E. a whole new pattern of petty states and new kingdoms would lead to the largest empires the ancient Near East had seen.

CHAPTER TIMELINE

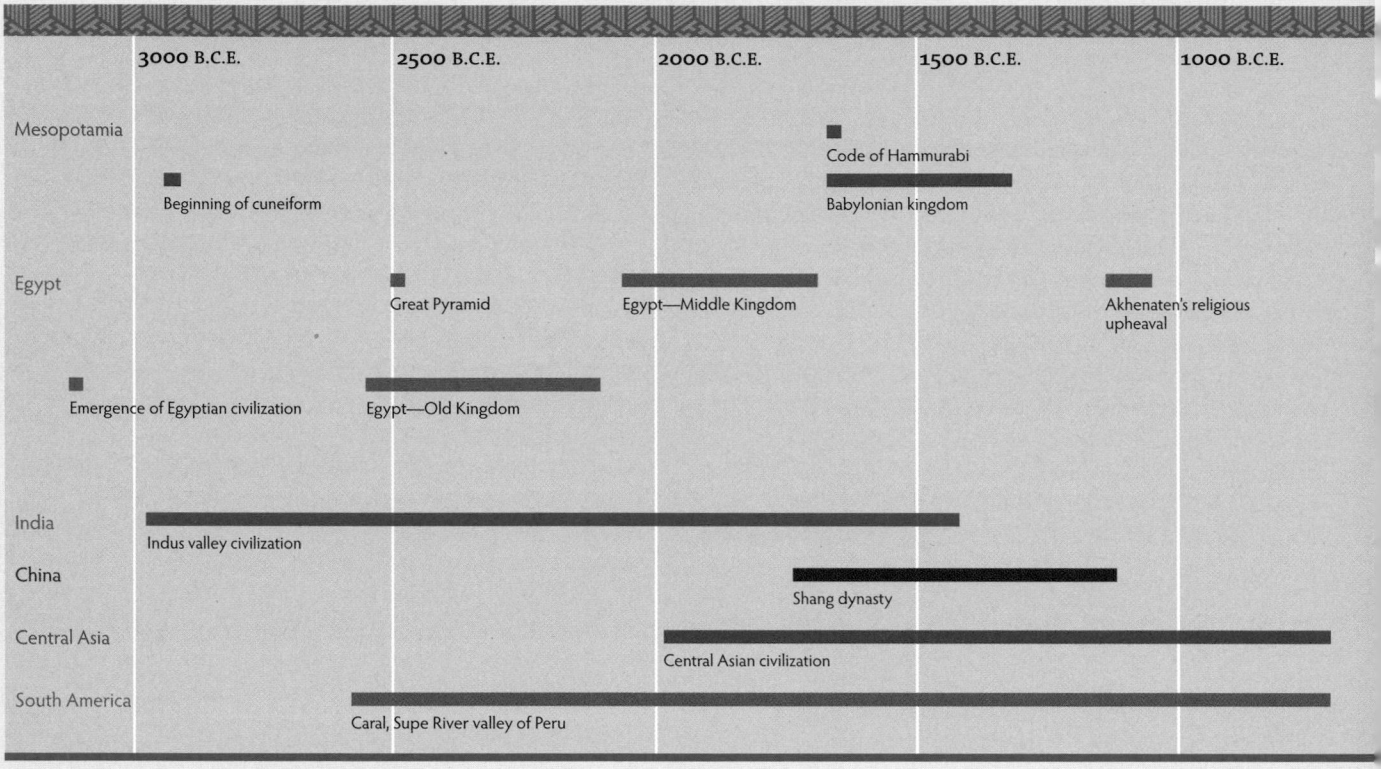

CHAPTER REVIEW

Upon Reflection

Q What achievements did early humans make during the Paleolithic and Neolithic Ages, and how did those achievements eventually make possible the emergence of civilization?

Q What roles did geography, environmental conditions, religion, politics, economics, and women and families play in the civilizations of Southwest Asia and Egypt?

Q What do you think Western civilization has derived from the civilizations of the ancient Near East?

Key Terms

Paleolithic Age (p. 3)
Neolithic Revolution (p. 3)
Bronze Age (p. 5)
civilization (p. 5)
ziggurat (p. 8)
theocracy (p. 8)
polytheistic (p. 12)
divination (p. 12)
cuneiform (p. 13)
hieroglyphics (p. 19)

Suggestions for Further Reading

THE PREHISTORIC WORLD For a brief but sound survey, see **I. Tattersall, *The World from Beginnings to 4000 B.C.E.*** The following works are also of considerable value in examining the prehistory of humankind: **S. Mithen, *After the Ice: A Global Human History, 20,000–5000 B.C.*** (Cambridge, Mass., 2006), and **N. Wade, *Before the Dawn: Recovering the Lost History of Our Ancestors*** (New York, 2006). On the role of women in prehistory, see **J. M. Adovasio, O. Soffer,** and **J. Page, *The Invisible Sex: Uncovering the True Roles of Women in Prehistory*** (New York, 2007).

THE ANCIENT NEAR EAST An excellent reference tool on the ancient Near East can be found in **P. Bienkowski** and **A. Milward, eds., *Dictionary of the Ancient Near East*** (Philadelphia, 2000). For a detailed survey, see **A. Kuhrt, *The Ancient Near East, c. 3000–330 B.C.,*** 2 vols. (London, 1995). A brief recent survey can be found in **M. van de Mieroop, *A History of the Ancient Near East, ca. 3000–323 B.C.,*** 2nd ed. (Oxford, 2006). **G. Leick, *The Babylonians*** (London, 2003), provides an overview of the peoples of ancient Mesopotamia. On the economic and social history of the ancient Near East, see **D. C. Snell, *Life in the Ancient Near East*** (New Haven, Conn., 1997).

ANCIENT MESOPOTAMIA A beautifully illustrated survey of ancient Mesopotamia can be found in **M. Roaf, *Cultural Atlas of Mesopotamia and the Ancient Near East*** (New York, 1996). The world of the Sumerians is examined in **H. Crawford, *Sumer and the Sumerians***, 2nd ed. (Cambridge, 2004). On the spiritual perspective of ancient Mesopotamia, see **J. Bottero, *Religion in Ancient Mesopotamia*** (Chicago, 2001). On daily life, see **S. Bertman, *Handbook to Life in Ancient Mesopotamia*** (New York, 2003).

ANCIENT EGYPT For a good introduction to ancient Egypt, see the beautifully illustrated work by **M. Millman, *Imagining Egypt*** (New York, 2007). Other general surveys include **I. Shaw, ed., *The Oxford History of Ancient Egypt*** (New York, 2000), and **D. J. Brewer, *Ancient Egypt: Foundations of a Civilization*** (New York, 2005), on Egypt before the period of the Old Kingdom. Egyptian religion is covered in **J. Assmann, *The Search for God in Ancient Egypt,*** trans. **D. Lorton** (Ithaca, N.Y., 2001). An important study on women is **G. Robins, *Women in Ancient Egypt*** (Cambridge, Mass., 1993). Daily life can be examined in **E. Strouhal, *Life of the Ancient Egyptians*** (Norman, Okla., 1992).

Visit the CourseMate website at **www.cengagebrain.com** for additional study tools and review materials for this chapter.

CHAPTER 2

Stanza della Segnatura, Stanze di Raffaello, Vatican Palace, Vatican State/© Scala/Art Resource, NY

The judgment of Solomon as painted by Raphael in the sixteenth century

The Ancient Near East: Peoples and Empires

CHAPTER OUTLINE AND FOCUS QUESTIONS

On the Fringes of Civilization

Q What is the significance of the Indo-European-speaking peoples?

The Hebrews: "The Children of Israel"

Q To what extent did the Israelites establish a united state, and what became of it? In what ways was the Jewish faith unique in the ancient Near East, and how did it evolve over time? Who were the neighbors of the Israelites, and what was their significance?

The Assyrian Empire

Q What methods and institutions did the Assyrians use to amass and maintain their empire?

The Persian Empire

Q What methods and institutions did the Persians use to amass and maintain their empire, and how did these methods and institutions differ from those of the Assyrians?

CRITICAL THINKING

Q What is the relationship between the political history of the Israelites and the evolution of their religious beliefs?

AROUND 970 B.C.E., Solomon came to the throne of Israel, a small state in western Asia. He was lacking in military prowess but excelled in many other ways. Through trade and a series of foreign alliances, he created a strong, flourishing state. But he was especially famed for his skill as a judge. When two women came before him, each claiming that the same infant was her natural child, Solomon ordered his servant to cut the child in half and give half to each woman. The first woman objected: "Please, my lord, give her the living baby! Don't kill him!" The second woman replied, "Neither I nor you shall have him. Cut him in two!" Then Solomon rendered his judgment: "Give the living baby to the first woman. Do not kill him; she is his mother." According to the biblical account, "When all Israel heard the verdict the king had given, they held the king in awe, because they saw that he had wisdom from God to administer justice." After Solomon's death, Israel began to disintegrate. But how had such a small nation been able to survive as long as it did in a Near East dominated by mighty empires?

The weakening of Egypt around 1200 B.C.E. left no dominant powers in the Near East, allowing a patchwork of petty kingdoms and city-states to emerge, especially in Syria and Canaan. One of these small states, the Hebrew nation known as Israel, has played a role in Western civilization completely disproportionate to its size. The Hebrews played a minor part in the politics of the ancient Near East, but their spiritual heritage, in the form of Judeo-Christian values, is one of the basic pillars of Western civilization.

The small states did not last. Ever since the first city-states had arisen in the Near East around 3000 B.C.E., there had been a movement toward the creation of larger territorial states with more sophisticated systems of control. This process reached a high point in the first millennium B.C.E. with the assembling of vast empires. Between 1000 and 500 B.C.E., the Assyrians, the Chaldeans, and the Persians all established empires that encompassed large areas of the ancient Near East. Each had impressive and grandiose capital cities that emphasized the power and wealth of its rulers. Each brought peace and order for a time by employing new administrative techniques. Each eventually fell to other conquerors. In the long run, these large empires had less impact on Western civilization than the Hebrew people. In human history, the power of ideas is often more significant than the power of empires.

© Adam Woolfitt/CORBIS

Stonehenge. The Bronze Age in northwestern Europe is known for its megaliths, or large standing stones. Between 3200 and 1500 B.C.E., standing stones arranged in circles or lined up in rows were erected throughout the British Isles and northwestern France. The most famous of these megalithic constructions is Stonehenge in England.

On the Fringes of Civilization

Focus Question: What is the significance of the Indo-European-speaking peoples?

Western civilization took root in Mesopotamia and Egypt, but significant developments were also taking place on the fringes of these cultures. Farming had spread into the Balkan peninsula of Europe by 6500 B.C.E., and by 4000 B.C.E. it was well established in southern France, central Europe, and the coastal regions of the Mediterranean. Although migrating farmers from the Near East may have brought some farming techniques into Europe, historians now believe that the Neolithic peoples of Europe domesticated animals and began to farm largely on their own.

One outstanding feature of late Neolithic Europe was the building of megalithic structures. *Megalith* is Greek for "large stone." Radiocarbon dating, a technique that allows scientists to determine the age of objects, shows that the first megalithic structures were built around 4000 B.C.E., more than a thousand years before the great pyramids were built in Egypt. Between 3200 and 1500 B.C.E., standing stones that were placed in circles or lined up in rows were erected throughout the British Isles and northwestern France. Other megalithic constructions have been found as far north as Scandinavia and as far south as the islands of Corsica, Sardinia, and Malta. Some archaeologists have demonstrated that the stone circles were used as observatories to detect not only such simple astronomical phenomena as the midwinter and midsummer sunrises but also such sophisticated observations as the major and minor standstills of the moon.

By far the most famous of these megalithic constructions is Stonehenge in England. Stonehenge consists of a series of concentric rings of standing stones. Its construction sometime between 2100 and 1900 B.C.E. was no small accomplishment. The eighty bluestones used at Stonehenge weigh 4 tons each and were transported to the site from their original source 135 miles away. Like other megalithic structures, Stonehenge indicates a remarkable awareness of astronomy on the part of its builders, as well as an impressive coordination of workers.

The Impact of the Indo-Europeans

For many historians, both the details of construction and the purpose of the megalithic structures of Europe remain a mystery. Also puzzling is the role of the Indo-European

TABLE 2.1 Some Indo-European Languages

SUBFAMILY	LANGUAGES
Indo-Iranian	*Sanskrit*, Persian
Balto-Slavic	Russian, Serbo-Croatian, Czech, Polish, Lithuanian
Hellenic	Greek
Italic	*Latin*, Romance languages (French, Italian, Spanish, Portuguese, Romanian)
Celtic	Irish, Gaelic
Germanic	Swedish, Danish, Norwegian, German, Dutch, English

NOTE: Languages in italic type are no longer spoken.

people. The name *Indo-European* refers to people who used a language derived from a single parent tongue. Indo-European languages include Greek, Latin, Persian, Sanskrit, and the Germanic languages (see Table 2.1). It has been suggested that the original Indo-European-speaking peoples were based somewhere in the steppe region north of the Black Sea or in southwestern Asia, in modern Iran or Afghanistan. Although there had been earlier migrations, around 2000 B.C.E. they began major nomadic movements into Europe (including present-day Italy and Greece), India, and western Asia. One group of Indo-Europeans who moved into Asia Minor and Anatolia (modern Turkey) around 1750 B.C.E. coalesced with the native peoples to form the Hittite kingdom with its capital at Hattusha (Boğazkale in modern Turkey).

THE HITTITE EMPIRE The Hittites began to spread outward around 1600 B.C.E., but it was not until around two hundred years later that a new line of kings created the Hittite New Kingdom or Hittite empire. Especially notable was Suppiluliumas (suh-PIL-oo-LEE-uh-muss) I (c. 1370–1330 B.C.E.), one of the strongest rulers of the era, who established Hittite control from western Turkey to northern Syria. Suppiluliumas formed an alliance with the Egyptians and then conquered Syria. The Hittites were the first of the Indo-European peoples to make use of iron, enabling them to construct weapons that were stronger and cheaper to make because of the widespread availability of iron ore. The end of Hittite power came in part from internal problems but also as a result of attacks by the Sea Peoples from the west around 1200 B.C.E. and by a group of aggressive tribespeople known as the Gasga, who raided Hittite cities. By 1190 B.C.E., Hittite power had come to an end.

During its heyday, however, the Hittite empire was one of the great powers in western Asia. The Hittite ruler, known as the Great King, controlled the core areas of the kingdom, but in western and southern Anatolia and Syria, he allowed local rulers to swear allegiance to him as vassals. Constant squabbling over succession to the throne, however, tended to weaken royal authority at times.

At its height, the Hittite empire also demonstrated an interesting ability to assimilate other cultures into its own. In language, literature, art, law, and religion, the Hittites borrowed much from Mesopotamia as well as from the native peoples that they had subdued. Hittite religion, for example, combined Indo-European deities and Mesopotamian gods. Recent scholarship has stressed the important role of the Hittites in transmitting Mesopotamian culture, as they transformed it, to later Western civilizations in the Mediterranean area, especially to the Mycenaean Greeks (see Chapter 3).

The crumbling of the Hittite kingdom and the weakening of Egypt after 1200 B.C.E. left a power vacuum in western Asia, allowing a patchwork of petty kingdoms and city-states to emerge, especially in the area at the eastern end of the Mediterranean Sea. The Hebrews were one of these peoples.

The Hebrews: "The Children of Israel"

FOCUS QUESTIONS: To what extent did the Israelites establish a united state, and what became of it? In what ways was the Jewish faith unique in the ancient Near East, and how did it evolve over time? Who were the neighbors of the Israelites, and what was their significance?

The Hebrews were a Semitic-speaking people who had a tradition concerning their origins and history that was eventually written down as part of the Hebrew Bible, known to Christians as the Old Testament. Describing themselves originally as nomads organized in clans, the Hebrews' tradition states that they were descendants of the patriarch Abraham, who had migrated from Mesopotamia to Canaan, where they became identified as the "Children of Israel." Again according to tradition, a drought in Canaan caused many Hebrews to migrate to Egypt, where they lived peacefully until they were enslaved by pharaohs who used them as laborers on building projects. These Hebrews remained in bondage until Moses led them eastward out of Egypt in the Exodus, which some historians have argued would have occurred in the first half of the thirteenth century B.C.E. According to the biblical account, the Hebrews then wandered for many years in the desert until they entered Canaan. Organized into twelve tribes, they became embroiled in conflict with the Philistines, a people who had settled in the coastal area of Canaan but were beginning to move into the inland areas.

Many scholars today doubt that the early books of the Hebrew Bible reflect the true history of the early Israelites. They argue that the early books of the Bible, written centuries after the events described, preserve only what the Israelites came to believe about themselves and that recent archaeological evidence often contradicts the details of the biblical account. Some of these scholars have even argued that the Israelites were not nomadic invaders but indigenous peoples in the Canaanite hill country. What is generally agreed, however, is that between 1200 and 1000 B.C.E., the Israelites emerged as a distinct group of people, possibly organized in tribes or a league of tribes.

Was There a United Kingdom of Israel?

According to the Hebrew Bible, the Israelites established a united kingdom of Israel beginning with Saul (c. 1020–1000 B.C.E.), who supposedly achieved some success in the ongoing struggle with the Philistines. But after his death, a brief period of anarchy ensued until one of Saul's lieutenants, David (c. 1000–970 B.C.E.), reunited the Israelites, defeated the Philistines, and established control over all of Canaan. According to the biblical account, some of his conquests led to harsh treatment for the conquered people: "David also defeated the Moabites. He made them lie down on the ground and measured them off with a length of cord. Every two lengths of them were put to death, and the third length was allowed to live. So the Moabites became subject to David and brought tribute."[1] Among David's conquests was the city of Jerusalem, which he supposedly made into the capital of a united kingdom.

According to the biblical account, David's son Solomon (c. 970–930 B.C.E.) did even more to strengthen royal power. He expanded the political and military establishments and extended the trading activities of the Israelites. Solomon is portrayed as a great builder, who was responsible for the Temple in the city of Jerusalem. The Israelites viewed the Temple as the symbolic center of their religion and hence of the kingdom of Israel itself. Under Solomon, ancient Israel was supposedly at the height of its power (see Map 2.1).

The accuracy of this biblical account of the united kingdom of Israel under Saul, David, and Solomon has recently been challenged by a new generation of archaeologists and historians. Although they mostly accept Saul, David, and Solomon as historical figures, they portray them more as chief warlords than as kings. If a kingdom of Israel did exist during these years, it was not as powerful or as well organized as the Hebrew Bible says. Furthermore, they argue, there is no definitive archaeological evidence that Solomon built the Temple in Jerusalem.

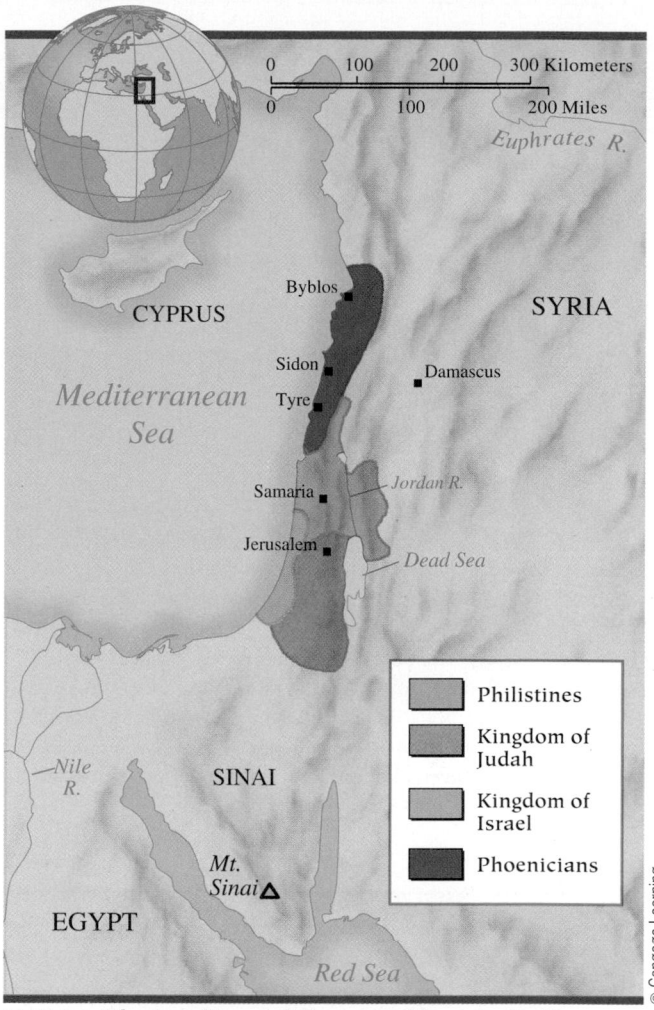

© Cengage Learning

MAP 2.1 The Israelites and Their Neighbors in the First Millennium B.C.E. After the death of Solomon, tensions between the tribes in Israel led to the creation of two kingdoms—a northern kingdom of Israel and a southern kingdom of Judah. With power divided, the Israelites could not resist invasions that dispersed many Jews from Canaan. Some, such as the "ten lost tribes," never returned. Others were sent to Babylon but were later allowed to return under the rule of the Persians.

Q ***Why was Israel more vulnerable to the Assyrian Empire than Judah was?***

The Kingdoms of Israel and Judah

There may or may not have been a united kingdom of Israel, but after Solomon's death, tensions between the northern and southern tribes led to the establishment of two separate kingdoms—the kingdom of Israel, composed of the ten northern tribes, with its capital eventually at Samaria, and the southern kingdom of Judah, consisting of two tribes, with its capital at Jerusalem. In 722 or

British Museum, London/© Erich Lessing/Art Resource, NY

Exiles from Judah. The Assyrians overran the kingdom of Israel in 722 or 721 B.C.E., destroyed the capital city of Samaria, and then began an assault on the kingdom of Judah. In this eighth-century B.C.E. relief from the palace of Sennacherib at Nineveh, captives with baggage are shown on their way into exile, escorted by an Asssyrian soldier (third figure from the left), after the Assyrian conquest of the fortified town of Lachish in Judah in 701 B.C.E. The Assyrians failed to take Jerusalem, however, and Judah remained independent, although it was forced to pay tribute to the Assyrians.

721 B.C.E., the Assyrians destroyed Samaria, overran the kingdom of Israel, and deported many Israelites to other parts of the Assyrian Empire. These dispersed Israelites (the "ten lost tribes") merged with neighboring peoples and gradually lost their identity.

The southern kingdom of Judah was also forced to pay tribute to Assyria but managed to retain its independence as Assyrian power declined. A new enemy, however, appeared on the horizon. The Chaldeans (kal-DEE-unz) brought the final destruction of Assyria, conquered the kingdom of Judah, and completely destroyed Jerusalem in 586 B.C.E. Many people from Judah were deported to Babylonia; the memory of their exile is still evoked in the stirring words of Psalm 137:

> *By the rivers of Babylon, we sat and wept when we remembered Zion. . . .*
> *How can we sing the songs of the Lord while in a foreign land?*
> *If I forget you, O Jerusalem, may my right hand forget its skill.*
> *May my tongue cling to the roof of my mouth if I do not remember you, if I do not consider Jerusalem my highest joy.*[2]

But the Babylonian captivity of the people of Judah did not last. A new set of conquerors, the Persians, destroyed the Chaldean kingdom but allowed the people of Judah to return to Jerusalem and rebuild their city and temple. The revived kingdom of Judah remained under Persian control until the conquests of Alexander the Great in the fourth century B.C.E. The people of Judah survived, eventually becoming known as the Jews and giving their name to Judaism, the religion of Yahweh (YAH-way), the Israelite God.

CHRONOLOGY The Israelites

Saul	c. 1020–1000 B.C.E.
David	c. 1000–970 B.C.E.
Solomon	c. 970–930 B.C.E.
Northern kingdom of Israel destroyed by Assyria	722 or 721 B.C.E.
Southern kingdom of Judah falls to Chaldeans; destruction of Jerusalem	586 B.C.E.
Return of exiles to Jerusalem	538 B.C.E.

The Spiritual Dimensions of Israel

The spiritual perspective of the Israelites evolved over time. Early Israelites probably worshiped many gods, including nature spirits dwelling in trees and rocks. For some Israelites, Yahweh was the chief god of Israel, but many, including kings of Israel and Judah, worshiped other gods as well. It was among the Babylonian exiles that Yahweh, the God of Israel, came to be regarded as the only God. After the return of these exiles to Judah, their point of view eventually became dominant, and pure **monotheism**, the belief that there is only one God, came to be the major tenet of Judaism.

"I AM THE LORD YOUR GOD": RULER OF THE WORLD

According to the Jewish conception, there is but one God, whom the Jews called Yahweh. God is the creator of the world and everything in it. To the Jews, the gods of all other peoples were merely idols. The Jewish God ruled the world; he was subject to nothing. All peoples were his servants, whether they knew it or not. This God was also transcendent. He had created nature but was not in nature. The stars, moon, rivers, wind, and other natural phenomena were not divinities or suffused with divinity, as other peoples of the ancient Near East believed, but they were God's handiwork. All of God's creations could be admired for their awesome beauty but not worshiped as gods.

This omnipotent creator of the universe was not removed from the life he had created, however, but was a just and good God who expected goodness from his people. If they did not obey his will, they would be punished.

The Covenant and the Law: The Book of Exodus

According to the biblical account, it was during the Exodus from Egypt that the Israelites supposedly made their covenant with Yahweh. They agreed to obey their God and follow his law. In return, Yahweh promised to take special care of his chosen people. These selections from the Book of Exodus describe the making of the covenant and God's commandments to the Israelites.

Exodus 19:1–8

In the third month after the Israelites left Egypt—on the very day—they came to the desert of Sinai. After they set out from Rephidim, they entered the desert of Sinai, and Israel camped there in the desert in front of the mountain. Then Moses went up to God, and the Lord called to him from the mountain, and said, "This is what you are to say to the house of Jacob and what you are to tell the people of Israel: 'You yourselves have seen what I did to Egypt, and how I carried you on eagles' wings and brought you to myself. Now if you obey me fully and keep my covenant, then out of all nations you will be my treasured possession. Although the whole earth is mine, you will be for me a kingdom of priests and a holy nation.' These are the words you are to speak to the Israelites." So Moses went back and summoned the elders of the people and set before them all the words the Lord had commanded him to speak. The people all responded together, "We will do everything the Lord has said." So Moses brought their answer back to the Lord.

Exodus 20:1–17

And God spoke all these words: "I am the Lord your God, who brought you out of Egypt, out of the land of slavery. You shall have no other gods before me. You shall not make for yourself an idol in the form of anything in heaven above or on the earth beneath or in the waters below. You shall not bow down to them or worship them; for I, the Lord your God, am a jealous God, punishing the children for the sin of the fathers to the third and fourth generation of those who hate, but showing love to a thousand generations of those who love me and keep my commandments. You shall not misuse the name of the Lord your God, for the Lord will not hold anyone guiltless who misuse his name. Remember the Sabbath day by keeping it holy. Six days you shall labor and do all your work, but the seventh day is a Sabbath to the Lord your God. On it you shall not do any work, neither you, nor your son or daughter, nor your manservant or maidservant, nor your animals, nor the alien within your gates. For in six days the Lord made the heavens and the earth, the sea, and all that is in them, but he rested on the seventh day. Therefore the Lord blessed the Sabbath day and made it holy. Honor your father and your mother, so that you may live long in the land the Lord your God is giving you. You shall not murder. You shall not commit adultery. You shall not steal. You shall not give false testimony against your neighbor. You shall not covet your neighbor's house. You shall not covet your neighbor's wife, or his manservant or maidservant, his ox or donkey, or anything that belongs to your neighbor."

Q What was the nature of the covenant between Yahweh and the Israelites? What was its moral significance for the Israelites? How does it differ from Hammurabi's code, and how might you explain those differences?

Source: Scripture taken from the HOLY BIBLE, NEW INTERNATIONAL VERSION®. Copyright © 1973, 1978, 1984 Biblica. Used by permission of Zondervan. All rights reserved. The "NIV" and "New International Version" trademarks are registered in the United States Patent and Trademark Office by Biblica. Use of either trademark requires the permission of Biblica.

But he was also a God of mercy and love: "The Lord is gracious and compassionate, slow to anger and rich in love. The Lord is good to all; he has compassion on all he has made."[3] Despite the powerful dimensions of God as creator and sustainer of the universe, the Jewish message also emphasized that each person could have a personal relationship with this powerful being. As the psalmist sang, "My help comes from the Lord, the Maker of heaven and earth. He will not let your foot slip—he who watches over you will not slumber."[4]

"YOU ONLY HAVE I CHOSEN": COVENANT AND LAW

Three aspects of the Hebrew religious tradition had special significance: the covenant, the law, and the prophets. The Israelites believed that during the Exodus from Egypt, when Moses supposedly led his people out of bondage into the "promised land," a special event occurred that determined the Jewish experience for all time. According to tradition, God entered into a covenant or contract with the tribes of Israel, who believed that Yahweh had spoken to them through Moses (see the box above). The Israelites

The Hebrew Prophets: Micah, Isaiah, and Amos

The Hebrew prophets warned the Israelites that they must obey God's commandments or face being punished for breaking their covenant with God. These selections from the biblical prophets Micah, Isaiah, and Amos make clear that God would punish the Israelites for their sins. Even the Assyrians, as Isaiah indicated, would be used as God's instrument to punish them.

Micah 6:9–16

Listen! The Lord is calling to the city—and to fear your name is wisdom—"Heed the rod and the One who appointed it. Am I still to forget, O wicked house, your ill-gotten treasures . . . ? Shall I acquit a man with dishonest scales, with a bag of false weights? Her rich men are violent; her people are liars and their tongues speak deceitfully. Therefore, I have begun to destroy you, to ruin you because of your sins. You will eat but not be satisfied; your stomach will still be empty. You will store up but save nothing, because what you save I will give to the sword. You will plant but not harvest; you will press olives but not use the oil on yourselves, you will crush grapes but not drink the wine. . . . Therefore I will give you over to ruin and your people to derision; you will bear the scorn of the nations."

Isaiah 10:1–6

Woe to those who make unjust laws, to those who issue oppressive decrees, to deprive the poor of their rights and withhold justice from the oppressed of my people, making widows their prey and robbing the fatherless. What will you do on the day of reckoning, when disaster comes from afar? To whom will you run for help? Where will you leave your riches? Nothing will remain but to cringe among the captives or fall among the slain. Yet for all this, his anger is not turned away, his hand is still upraised. "Woe to the Assyrian, the rod of my anger, in whose hand is the club of my wrath! I send him against a godless nation, I dispatch him against a people who anger me, to seize loot and snatch plunder, and to trample them down like mud in the streets."

Amos 3:1–2

Hear this word the Lord has spoken against you, O people of Israel—against the whole family I brought up out of Egypt: "You only have I chosen of all the families of the earth; therefore, I will punish you for all your sins."

Q What did the Hebrew prophets see as the chief transgressions of the Israelites? What do these selections tell you about the nature of the Israelites as a "chosen" people?

Source: Scripture taken from the HOLY BIBLE, NEW INTERNATIONAL VERSION®. Copyright © 1973, 1978, 1984 Biblica. Used by permission of Zondervan. All rights reserved. The "NIV" and "New International Version" trademarks are registered in the United States Patent and Trademark Office by Biblica. Use of either trademark requires the permission of Biblica.

promised to obey Yahweh and follow his law. In return, Yahweh promised to take special care of his chosen people, "a peculiar treasure unto me above all people."

This covenant between Yahweh and his chosen people could be fulfilled, however, only by obedience to the law of God. Law became a crucial element of the Jewish world and had a number of different dimensions. In some instances, it set forth specific requirements, such as payments for offenses. Most important, since the major characteristic of God was his goodness, ethical concerns stood at the center of the law. Sometimes these took the form of specific standards of moral behavior: "You shall not murder. You shall not commit adultery. You shall not steal."[5] But these concerns were also expressed in decrees that regulated the economic, social, religious, and political life of the community, since God's laws of morality applied to all areas of life. These laws made no class distinctions and emphasized the protection of the poor, widows, orphans, and slaves.

THE PROPHETS The Israelites believed that certain religious leaders or "holy men," called prophets, were sent by God to serve as his voice to his people. The golden age of the prophets began in the mid-eighth century B.C.E. and continued during the time when the people of Israel and Judah were threatened by Assyrian and Chaldean conquerors. These "men of God" went through the land warning the Israelites that they had failed to keep God's commandments and would be punished for breaking the covenant: "I will punish you for all your iniquities." Amos prophesied the fall of the northern kingdom of Israel to Assyria; twenty years later, Isaiah said the kingdom of Judah too would fall (see the box above).

National & University Library, Jerusalem/© Bridgeman-Giraudon/Art Resource, NY

Hebrew Law. Because of the supposed covenant between Yahweh and the Israelites, law became an important part of Jewish life. Seen here is a twelfth-century manuscript page of the *Mishneh Torah*, a fourteen-volume study of all of Jewish law by Moses Maimonides, the foremost Jewish philosopher of the Middle Ages.

Out of the words of the prophets came new concepts that enriched the Jewish tradition and ultimately Western civilization, including a notion of universalism and a yearning for social justice. Although the Jews' religious practices gave them a sense of separateness from other peoples, the prophets transcended this by embracing a concern for all humanity. All nations would someday come to the God of Israel: "All the earth shall worship you." A universal community of all people under God would someday be established by Israel's effort. This vision encompassed the elimination of war and the establishment of peace for all the nations of the world. In the words of the prophet Isaiah, "He will judge between the nations and will settle disputes for many people. They will beat their swords into plowshares and their spears into pruning hooks. Nation will not take up sword against nation, nor will they train for war anymore."[6]

The prophets also cried out against social injustice. They condemned the rich for causing the poor to suffer, denounced luxuries as worthless, and warned of dire punishments for these sins. God's command was to live justly, share with one's neighbors, care for the poor and the unfortunate, and act with compassion. When God's command was not followed, the social fabric of the community was threatened. These proclamations by Israel's prophets became a source for Western ideals of social justice, even if they have never been perfectly realized.

Although the prophets eventually developed a sense of universalism, the demands of the Jewish religion—the obligation to obey their God—encouraged a separation between the Jews and their non-Jewish neighbors. Unlike most other peoples of the Near East, Jews could not simply be amalgamated into a community by accepting the gods of their conquerors and their neighbors. To remain faithful to the demands of their God, they might even have to refuse loyalty to political leaders.

The Neighbors of the Israelites

The Israelites were not the only people living in Canaan. The Philistines, who invaded from the sea, established five towns on the coastal plain of the region. They settled down as farmers and eventually entered into conflict with the Israelites. Although the Philistines were newcomers to the area, the Phoenicians (fuh-NEE-shuns) had resided there for some time but now found themselves with a new independence. A Semitic-speaking people, the Phoenicians resided along the Mediterranean coast on a narrow band of land 120 miles long. They had rebuilt their major cities after destruction by the Sea Peoples. Their newfound political independence helped the Phoenicians expand the trade that was already the foundation of their prosperity. In fact, the Phoenician city of Byblos had been the principal distribution center for Egyptian papyrus outside Egypt (the Greek word for book, *biblos*, is derived from the name Byblos).

All three chief cities of Phoenicia—Byblos, Tyre, and Sidon—were seaports on the eastern Mediterranean, but they also served as distribution centers for the lands to the east in Mesopotamia. The Phoenicians themselves produced a number of goods for foreign markets, including

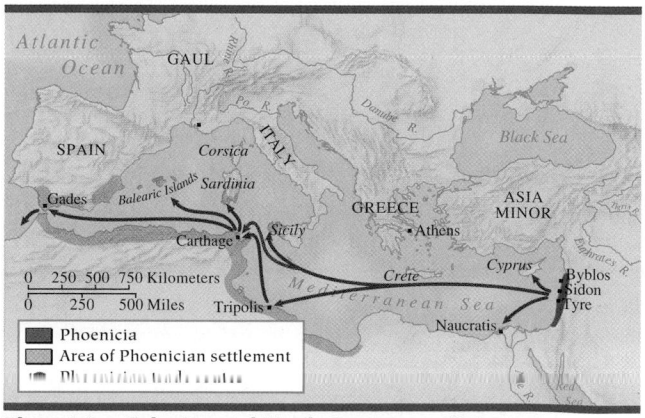

© Cengage Learning

Phoenician Colonies and Trade Routes, c. 800 B.C.E.

TABLE 2.2 A Comparison of the Phoenician, Greek, and Latin Alphabets (Letters A–F)

PHOENICIAN			GREEK			LATIN	
Phoenician	*Phoenician Name*	*Modern Symbol*	*Early Greek*	*Classical Greek*	*Greek Name*	*Early Latin*	*Classical Latin*
	'aleph	'		A	alpha	A	A
	beth	b		B	beta		B
	gimel	g		Γ	gamma		C
	daleth	d		Δ	delta		D
	he	h		E	epsilon		E
	waw	w			digamma		F

SOURCE: Andrew Robinson, *The Story of Writing* (London: Thames & Hudson, 1995), p. 170.

purple dye, glass, wine, and lumber from the famous cedars of Lebanon. In addition, the Phoenicians improved their ships and became great international sea traders. They charted new routes, not only in the Mediterranean but also in the Atlantic Ocean, where they sailed south along the west coast of Africa. The Phoenicians established a number of colonies in the western Mediterranean, including settlements in southern Spain, Sicily, and Sardinia. Carthage, the Phoenicians' most famous colony, was located on the North African coast.

Culturally, the Phoenicians are best known as transmitters. Instead of using pictographs or signs to represent whole words and syllables as the Mesopotamians and Egyptians did, the Phoenicians simplified their writing by using twenty-two different signs to represent the sounds of their speech. These twenty-two characters or letters could be used to spell out all the words in the Phoenician language. Although the Phoenicians were not the only people to invent an alphabet, theirs would have special significance because it was eventually passed on to the Greeks. From the Greek alphabet was derived the Roman alphabet that we still use today (see Table 2.2). The Phoenicians achieved much while independent, but they ultimately fell subject to the Assyrians, Chaldeans, and Persians.

The Assyrian Empire

FOCUS QUESTION: What methods and institutions did the Assyrians use to amass and maintain their empire?

The existence of independent states in Canaan was possible only because of the power vacuum existing in the ancient Near East after the demise of the Hittite kingdom and the weakening of Egypt. But this condition did not last; new empires soon came to dominate vast stretches of the ancient Near East. The first of these empires emerged in Assyria, an area whose location on the upper Tigris River brought it into both cultural and political contact with southern Mesopotamia.

Although part of Mesopotamia, Assyria, with its hills and adequate, if not ample, rainfall, had a different terrain and climate. The Assyrians were a Semitic-speaking people who exploited the use of iron weapons to establish an empire that by 700 B.C.E. included Mesopotamia, parts of the Iranian plateau, sections of Asia Minor, Syria, Canaan, and Egypt down to Thebes (see Map 2.2). Yet the empire's size contributed to its undoing. Ashurbanipal (ah-shur-BAH-nuh-pahl) (669–627 B.C.E.) was one of the strongest Assyrian rulers, but it was already becoming apparent during his reign that the Assyrian Empire was greatly overextended. Internal strife intensified as powerful Assyrian nobles gained control of vast territories and waged their own private military campaigns. Moreover, subject peoples, such as the Babylonians, greatly resented Assyrian rule and rebelled against it. Soon after Ashurbanipal's reign, the Assyrian Empire began to disintegrate rapidly. The capital city of Nineveh fell to a coalition of Chaldeans and Medes in 612 B.C.E., and in 605 B.C.E. the rest of the empire was finally divided between the coalition powers.

Organization of the Empire

At its height, the Assyrian Empire was ruled by kings whose power was considered absolute. Under their leadership, the empire became well organized. By eliminating governorships held by nobles on a hereditary basis and instituting a new hierarchy of local officials directly responsible to the king, the Assyrian kings gained greater control over the resources of the empire. The Assyrians also developed an efficient system of communication to administer their empire more effectively. A network of

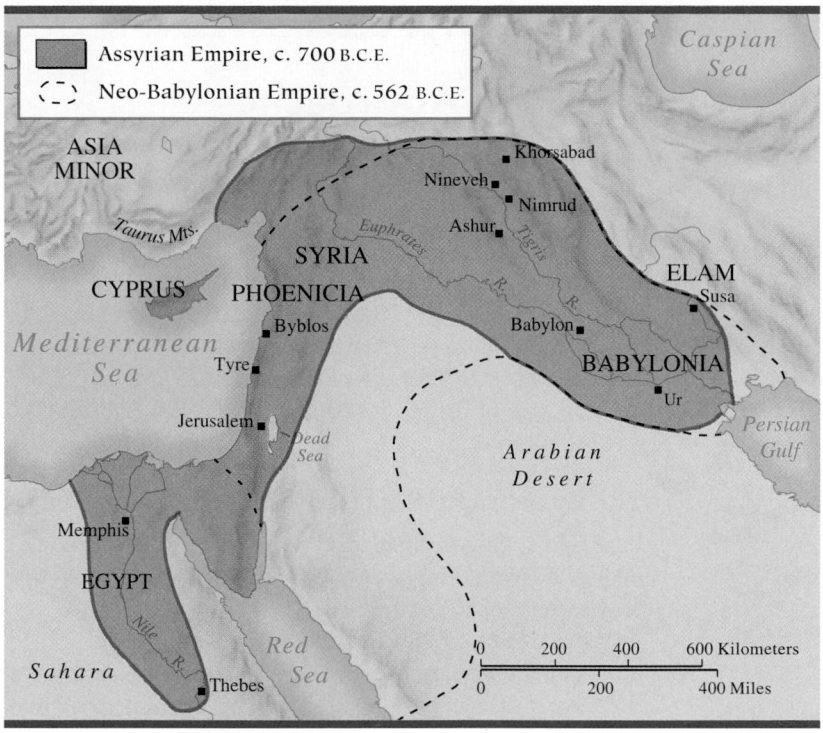

MAP 2.2 The Assyrian and Neo-Babylonian Empires. The Assyrian Empire expanded in large part due to its brutal military methods. It maintained its rule through use of a common language and religion, along with extremely violent suppression of internal revolts. It was overthrown by Chaldeans in Babylonia, leading to the Neo-Babylonian Empire epitomized by Nebuchadnezzar.

Why was control of Babylonia crucial to both empires?

© Cengage Learning

posting stages was established throughout the empire that used relays of horses (mules or donkeys in mountainous terrain) to carry messages. The system was so effective that a provincial governor anywhere in the empire (except Egypt) could send a query and receive an answer from the king within a week.

The Assyrian Military Machine

The ability of the Assyrians to conquer and maintain an empire was due to a combination of factors. Over many years of practice, the Assyrians developed effective military leaders and fighters. They were able to enlist and deploy troops numbering in the hundreds of thousands, although most campaigns were not conducted on such a large scale. In 845 B.C.E., an Assyrian army of 120,000 men crossed the Euphrates on a campaign. Size alone was not decisive, however.

The Assyrian army was extremely well organized and disciplined. It had a standing army of infantry as its core, accompanied by cavalry and horse-drawn war chariots that were used as mobile platforms for shooting arrows. Moreover, the Assyrians had the advantage of having the first large armies equipped with iron weapons. The Hittites had been the first to develop iron metallurgy, but iron was used extensively only after new methods for hardening it came into common use after 1000 B.C.E.

Another factor in the Assyrians' success was their ability to use various military tactics. The Assyrians were skilled at waging guerrilla war in the mountains and set battles on open ground and were especially renowned for siege warfare. They would hammer a city's walls with heavy, wheeled siege towers and armored battering rams while sappers dug tunnels to undermine the walls' foundations and cause them to collapse. The besieging Assyrian armies learned to cut off supplies so effectively that if a city did not fall to them, the inhabitants could be starved into submission.

A final factor that made the Assyrian military machine so effective was its ability to create a climate of terror as an instrument of war. The Assyrians became famous for their terror tactics, although some historians believe that their policies were no worse than those of other conquerors. As a matter of regular policy, the Assyrians laid waste the land in which they were fighting, smashing dams, looting and destroying towns, setting crops on fire, and cutting down trees, particularly fruit trees. The Assyrians were especially known for the atrocities inflicted on their captives. King Ashurnasirpal (ah-shur-NAH-zur-pahl) II recorded this account of his treatment of prisoners:

> 3000 of their combat troops I felled with weapons. . . . Many of the captives taken from them I burned in a fire. Many I took alive; from some of these I cut off their hands to the wrist, from others I cut off their noses, ears and fingers; I put out the eyes of many of the soldiers. . . . I burned their young men and women to death.[7]

After conquering another city, the same king wrote, "I fixed up a pile of corpses in front of the city's gate. I flayed the nobles, as many as had rebelled, and spread their skins out on the piles. . . . I flayed many within my land and spread their skins out on the walls."[8] (Obviously not a king to play games with!) Note that this policy of extreme cruelty to prisoners was not used against all enemies but was reserved primarily for those who were already part of the empire and then rebelled against Assyrian rule (see the box on p. 36).

OPPOSING VIEWPOINTS

The Governing of Empires: Two Approaches

Both the Assyrians and the Persians created large empires that encompassed large areas of the ancient Near East. Although both Assyrian and Persian rulers used military force and violence to attain their empires, their approaches to conquest and ruling sometimes differed. Assyrian rulers were known for their terror tactics and atrocities, as described in the first two selections. The kings of Persia had a reputation for less cruelty and more tolerance. Especially noteworthy was Cyrus, as is evident in this selection from a decree (known as the Cyrus Cylinder) that he issued in 538 B.C.E. The propaganda value of his words is also apparent, however.

King Sennacherib (704–681 B.C.E.) Describes His Siege of Jerusalem (701 B.C.E.)

As to Hezekiah, the Jew, he did not submit to my yoke, I laid siege to 46 of his strong cities, walled forts and to the countless small villages in their vicinity, and conquered them by means of well-stamped earth-ramps, and battering-rams brought thus near to the walls combined with the attack by foot soldiers, using mines, breaches as well as sapper work. I drove out of them 200,150 people, young and old, male and female, horses, mules, donkeys, camels, big and small cattle beyond counting, and considered them booty. Himself I made a prisoner in Jerusalem, his royal residence, like a bird in a cage. I surrounded him with earthwork in order to molest those who were leaving his city's gate.

King Ashurbanipal (669–627 B.C.E.) Describes His Treatment of Conquered Babylon

I tore out the tongues of those whose slanderous mouths had uttered blasphemies against my god Ashur and had plotted against me, his god-fearing prince; I defeated them completely. The others, I smashed alive with the very same statues of protective deities with which they had smashed my own grandfather Sennacherib—now finally as a belated burial sacrifice for his soul. I fed their corpses, cut into small pieces, to dogs, pigs, . . . vultures, the birds of the sky and also to the fish of the ocean. After I . . . thus made quiet again the hearts of the great gods, my lords, I removed the corpses of those whom the pestilence had felled, whose leftovers after the dogs and pigs had fed on them were obstructing the streets, filling the places of Babylon, and of those who had lost their lives through the terrible famine.

The Cyrus Cylinder

I am Cyrus, king of the world, great king, legitimate king, king of Babylon, king of Sumer and Akkad, king of the four corners of the earth. . . .

When I entered Babylon as a friend and when I established the seat of the government in the palace of the ruler under jubilation and rejoicing, Marduk, the great lord [the chief Babylonian god], caused the magnanimous inhabitants of Babylon to love me, and I was daily endeavoring to worship him. My numerous troops walked around in Babylon in peace. I did not allow anybody to terrorize any place of the country of Sumer and Akkad. I strove for peace in Babylon and in all his other sacred cities. As to the inhabitants of Babylon . . . I brought relief to their dilapidated housing, putting thus an end to their main complaints. . . .

As to the region from as far as Ashur and Susa . . . I returned to these sacred cities on the other side of the Tigris, the sanctuaries of which have been ruins for a long time, the images which used to live therein and established for them permanent sanctuaries. I also gathered all their former inhabitants and returned to them their dwellings.

Q Both Ashurbanipal and Cyrus entered Babylon as conquerors. How did their treatment of the conquered city differ? How do you explain the differences? Which method do you think was more effective? Why?

Sources: King Sennacherib (704–681 B.C.E.) Describes His Siege of Jerusalem (701 B.C.E.) and King Ashurbanipal (669–627 B.C.E.) Describes His Treatment of Conquered Babylon. PRITCHARD, JAMES; *ANCIENT NEAR EASTERN TEXTS RELATED TO THE OLD TESTAMENT–THIRD EDITION WITH SUPPLEMENT.* © 1950, 1955, 1969, renewed 1978 by Princeton University Press. Reprinted by permission of Princeton University Press. The Cyrus Cylinder. PRITCHARD, JAMES; *ANCIENT NEAR EASTERN TEXTS RELATED TO THE OLD TESTAMENT–THIRD EDITION WITH SUPPLEMENT.* © 1950, 1955, 1969, renewed 1978 by Princeton University Press. Reprinted by permission of Princeton University Press, pp. 315–316.

British Museum, London//© Werner Forman/Art Resource, NY

King Ashurbanipal's Lion Hunt. This relief, sculptured on alabaster as a decoration for the northern palace in Nineveh, depicts King Ashurbanipal engaged in a lion hunt. Lion hunts were not conducted in the wild but were held under controlled circumstances. The king and his retainers faced lions released from cages in an arena. The purpose was to glorify the king as a conqueror of the king of beasts. Relief sculpture, one of the best-known forms of Assyrian art, reached its high point under Ashurbanipal at about the time that the Assyrian Empire began to disintegrate.

Assyrian Society and Culture

Unlike the Hebrews, the Assyrians were not fearful of mixing with other peoples. In fact, the Assyrian policy of deporting many prisoners of newly conquered territories to Assyria created a polyglot society in which ethnic differences were not very important. It has been estimated that over a period of three centuries, between 4 and 5 million people were deported to Assyria, resulting in a population that was very racially and linguistically mixed. What gave identity to the Assyrians themselves was their language, although even that was akin to that of their southern neighbors in Babylonia, who also spoke a Semitic tongue. Religion was also a cohesive force. Assyria was literally "the land of Ashur," a reference to its chief god. The king, as the human representative of the god Ashur, provided a unifying focus.

Agriculture formed the principal basis of Assyrian life. Assyria was a land of farming villages with relatively few significant cities, especially in comparison with southern Mesopotamia. Unlike the river valleys, where farming required the minute organization of large numbers of people to maintain the irrigation systems, Assyrian farms received sufficient moisture from regular rainfall.

Trade was second to agriculture in economic importance. For internal trade, metals, such as gold, silver, copper, and bronze, were used as a medium of exchange. Various agricultural products also served as a form of payment or exchange. Because of their geographic location, the Assyrians served as middlemen and participated in an international trade in which they imported timber, wine, and precious metals and stones while exporting textiles produced in palaces, temples, and private villas.

Assyrian culture was a hybrid. The Assyrians assimilated much of Mesopotamian civilization and saw themselves as guardians of Sumerian and Babylonian culture. Ashurbanipal, for example, established a large library at Nineveh that included the available works of Mesopotamian history. Assyrian religion reflected this assimilation of other cultures as well. Although the Assyrians' national god Ashur was their chief deity, virtually all the other gods and goddesses were Mesopotamian.

Among the best-known objects of Assyrian art are the relief sculptures found in the royal palaces in three of the Assyrian capital cities, Nimrud, Nineveh, and Khorsabad. These reliefs, which were begun in the ninth century B.C.E. and reached their high point in the reign of Ashurbanipal in the seventh, depicted two different kinds of subject matter: ritual or ceremonial scenes, revolving around the person of the king, and scenes of hunting and war. The latter show realistic action scenes of the king and his warriors engaged in battle or hunting animals, especially lions. These pictures depict a strongly masculine world where discipline, brute force, and toughness are the enduring values, indeed, the very values of the Assyrian military monarchy.

The Persian Empire

Focus Question: What methods and institutions did the Persians use to amass and maintain their empire, and how did these methods and institutions differ from those of the Assyrians?

The Chaldeans, a Semitic-speaking people, had gained ascendancy in Babylonia by the seventh century and came to form the chief resistance to Assyrian control of Mesopotamia. After the collapse of the Assyrian Empire, the Chaldeans, under their king Nebuchadnezzar (neb-uh-kud-NEZZ-ur) II (605–562 B.C.E.), regained for Babylonia a position as the leading power in the ancient Near East.

Nebuchadnezzar rebuilt Babylon as the center of his empire, making it one of the most magnificient cities of the ancient world. Babylon was surrounded by great walls, 8 miles in length, encircled by a moat filled by the Euphrates River. The city was adorned with temples and palaces; most famous of all were the Hanging Gardens, one of the Seven Wonders of the ancient world. These were supposedly built to satisfy Nebuchadnezzar's wife, a princess from the land of Media, who missed the mountains of her homeland. A series of terraces led to a plateau, an artificial mountain, at the top of which grew the lush gardens irrigated by water piped to the top. According to the account of a first-century C.E. author, the gardens made a remarkable impression when seen from a distance:

> On the top of the citadel are the hanging gardens, a wonder celebrated in the tales of the Greeks. . . . Columns of stone were set up to sustain the whole work, and on these was laid a floor of squared blocks, strong enough to hold the earth which is thrown upon it to a great depth, as well as the water with which they irrigate the soil; and the structure supports trees of such great size that the thickness of their trunks equals a measure of eight cubits [about 12 feet]. They tower to a height of fifty feet, and they yield as much fruit as if they were growing in their native soil. . . . To those who look upon the trees from a distance, real woods seem to be overhanging their native mountains.[9]

But the splendor of the Neo-Babylonian Empire proved to be short-lived as Babylon fell to the Persians in 539 B.C.E.

The Persians were an Indo-European-speaking people related to the Medes. Both peoples probably formed part of the great waves of Indo-European migrations into the Mediterranean, the Near East, and India. The Persians lived to the southeast of the Medes, who occupied the western Iranian plateau south of the Caspian Sea. Primarily nomadic, both Medes and Persians were organized in clans. Both peoples were led by petty kings assisted by a group of warriors who formed a class of nobles.

By 735 B.C.E., the Medes had begun to form a confederation of the various tribes, and around the beginning of the seventh century, they became unified under a monarchy. The Persians did likewise under the Achaemenid (ah-KEE-muh-nud) dynasty established in Persis in southern Iran. About fifty years later, the Persians were made subject to the Medes. The Medes now constituted a powerful state and joined the Babylonians in attacking the Assyrians. After the capture of Nineveh in 612 B.C.E., King Cyaxares (si-AK-suh-reez) established a Median empire, the first Iranian empire known to the ancient Near East.

Cyrus the Great (559–530 B.C.E.)

In 559 B.C.E., Cyrus became the leader of the Persians, united them under his rule, and went on the offensive against the Medes. In 550 B.C.E., he established Persian control over Media, making it the first Persian **satrapy**, or province. Three years later, Cyrus defeated the prosperous Lydian kingdom in western Asia Minor, and Lydia became another Persian satrapy (see Map 2.3). Cyrus's forces then went on to conquer the Greek city-states that had been established on the Ionian coast of western Asia Minor. Cyrus then turned eastward, subduing the eastern part of the Iranian plateau, Sogdia, and even western India. His eastern frontiers secured, Cyrus entered Mesopotamia in 539 and captured Babylon. His treatment of Babylonia showed remarkable restraint and wisdom. Babylonia was made into a Persian province under a Persian satrap, but many government officials were kept in their positions. Cyrus took the title "King of All, Great King, Mighty King, King of Babylon, King of the Land of Sumer and Akkad, King of the Four Rims [of the earth], the Son of Cambyses the Great King, King of Anshan"[10] and insisted that he stood in the ancient, unbroken line of Babylonian kings. By appealing to the vanity of the Babylonians, he won their loyalty. Cyrus also issued an edict permitting the Jews, who had been brought to Babylon earlier in the sixth century B.C.E., to return to Jerusalem with their sacred temple objects and to rebuild their temple as well.

To his contemporaries, Cyrus the Great was deserving of his epithet. The Greek historian Herodotus recounted that the Persians viewed him as a "father," a ruler who was "gentle, and procured them all manner of goods."[11] Certainly, Cyrus must have been an unusual ruler for his time, a man who demonstrated considerable wisdom and compassion in the conquest and organization of his empire. Cyrus gained the favor of the priesthoods in his conquered lands by restoring temples and permitting religious toleration. He won approval by using not only Persians but also native peoples as government officials in their own states. Unlike the Assyrian rulers of an earlier empire, he had a reputation for mercy. Medes, Babylonians, and Hebrews all

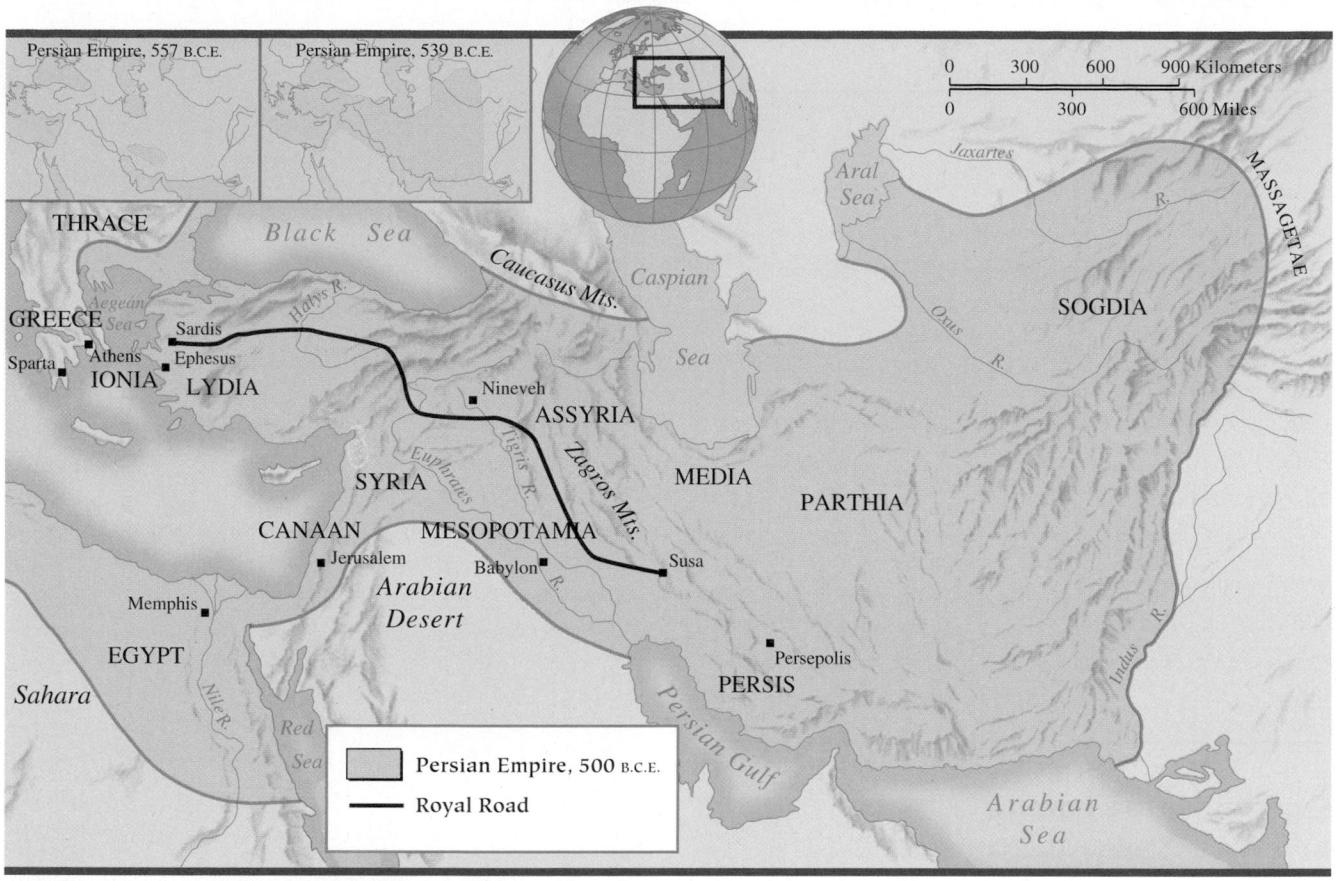

© Cengage Learning

MAP 2.3 The Persian Empire at the Time of Darius. Cyrus the Great united the Persians and led them in the successful conquest of much of the Near East. By the time of Darius, the Persian Empire was the largest the world had yet seen. The Persians allowed religious tolerance and gave some government positions to natives of conquered territories.

How did Persian policies attempt to overcome the difficulties of governing far-flung provinces?

accepted him as their legitimate ruler. Indeed, the Hebrews regarded him as the anointed one of God:

> I am the Lord who says of Cyrus, "He is my shepherd and will accomplish all that I please"; he will say of Jerusalem, "Let it be rebuilt"; and of the temple, "Let its foundations be laid." This is what the Lord says to his anointed, to Cyrus, whose right hand I take hold of to subdue nations before him.[12]

Cyrus had a genuine respect for ancient civilizations—in building his palaces, he made use of Assyrian, Babylonian, Egyptian, and Lydian practices.

Expanding the Empire

Cyrus's successors extended the territory of the Persian Empire. His son Cambyses (kam-BY-seez) (530–522 B.C.E.) undertook a successful invasion of Egypt and made it into a satrapy with Memphis as its capital. Darius (duh-RY-uss) (521–486 B.C.E.) added a new Persian province in western India that extended to the Indus River and moved into Europe proper, conquering Thrace and making the Macedonian king a vassal. A revolt of the Ionian Greek cities in 499 B.C.E. resulted in temporary freedom for these communities in western Asia Minor. Aid from the Greek mainland, most notably from Athens, encouraged the Ionians to invade Lydia and burn Sardis, center of the Lydian satrapy. This event led to Darius's involvement with the mainland Greeks. After reestablishing control of the Ionian Greek cities, Darius undertook an invasion of the Greek mainland, which culminated in the famous Athenian victory in the Battle of Marathon in 490 B.C.E. (see Chapter 3).

CHRONOLOGY The Ancient Empires

The Assyrians	
Height of power	700 B.C.E.
Ashurbanipal	669–627 B.C.E.
Capture of Nineveh by Medes and Chaldeans	612 B.C.E.
Destruction of the Assyrian Empire	605 B.C.E.
The Chaldeans	
Ascendancy in Babylonia	600s B.C.E.
Height of Neo-Babylonian Empire under King Nebuchadnezzar II	605–562 B.C.E.
Fall of Babylon	539 B.C.E.
The Persians	
Unification under Achaemenid dynasty	600s B.C.E.
Persian control over Medes	550 B.C.E.
Conquests of Cyrus the Great	559–530 B.C.E.
Cambyses and conquest of Egypt	530–522 B.C.E.
Reign of Darius	521–486 B.C.E.

Governing the Empire

By the reign of Darius, the Persians had created the largest empire the world had yet seen. As noted earlier, it not only included all the old centers of power in the Near East, Egypt, Mesopotamia, and Assyria but also extended into Thrace and Asia Minor in the west and into India in the east. For administrative purposes, the empire had been divided into around twenty satrapies. Each of these provinces was ruled by a governor or **satrap**, literally, a "protector of the kingdom." Although Darius had not introduced the system of satrapies, he organized it more rationally. He created a sensible system for calculating the tribute that each satrapy owed to the central government and gave the satraps specific civil and military duties. They collected tributes, were responsible for justice and security, raised military levies for the royal army, and normally commanded the military forces within their satrapies. In terms of real power, the satraps were miniature kings with courts imitative of the Great King's.

From the time of Darius on, satraps were all of Persian descent. The major satrapies were given to princes of the royal family, and their position became essentially hereditary. The minor satrapies were placed in the hands of Persian nobles. Their offices, too, tended to pass from father to son. The hereditary nature of the governors' offices made it necessary to provide some checks on their power. Consequently, royal officials at the satrapal courts acted as spies for the Great King.

© The Art Archive/Giami Dagli Orti

Darius, the Great King. Darius ruled the Persian Empire from 521 to 486 B.C.E. He is shown here on his throne in Persepolis, a new capital city that he built. In his right hand, Darius holds the royal staff; in his left, he holds a lotus blossom with two buds, a symbol of royalty.

An efficient system of communication was crucial to sustaining the Persian Empire. Well-maintained roads facilitated the rapid transit of military and government personnel. One in particular, the so-called Royal Road, stretched from Sardis, the center of Lydia in Asia Minor, to Susa, the chief capital of the Persian Empire. Like the Assyrians, the Persians established staging posts equipped with fresh horses for the king's messengers.

The Great King

In this vast administrative system, the Persian king occupied an exalted position. All subjects were the king's servants, and he was the source of all justice, possessing the

A Dinner with the Persian King

The Persian kings lived in luxury as a result of their conquests and ability to extract taxes from their conquered subjects. In this selection, we read a description of how a Persian king dined with his numerous guests.

Athenaeus, *The Deipnosophists*

Heracleides of Cumae, author of the *Persian History*, writes in the second book of the work entitled *Equipment*: "All who attend upon the Persian kings when they dine first bathe themselves and then serve in white clothes, and spend nearly half the day on preparations for the dinner. Of those who are invited to eat with the king, some dine outdoors, in full sight of anyone who wishes to look on; others dine indoors in the king's company. Yet even these do not eat in his presence, for there are two rooms opposite each other, in one of which the king has his meal, in the other the invited guests. The king can see them through the curtain at the door, but they cannot see him. Sometimes, however, on the occasion of a public holiday, all dine in a single room with the king, in the great hall. And whenever the king commands a symposium [drinking bout following the dinner], which he does often, he has about a dozen companions at the drinking. When they have finished dinner, that is, the king by himself, the guests in the other room, these fellow-drinkers are summoned by one of the eunuchs; and entering they drink with him, though even they do not have the same wine; moreover, they sit on the floor, while he reclines on a couch supported by feet of gold, and they depart after having drunk to excess. In most cases the king breakfasts and dines alone, but sometimes his wife and some of his sons dine with him. And throughout the dinner his concubines sing and play the lyre; one of them is the soloist, the others sing in chorus. And so . . . the 'king's dinner,' as it is called, will appear prodigal to one who merely hears about it, but when one examines it carefully it will be found to have been got up with economy and even with parsimony; and the same is true of the dinners among other Persians of high station. For one thousand animals are slaughtered daily for the king; these comprise horses, camels, oxen, asses, deer, and most of the small animals; many birds are also consumed, including Arabian ostriches—and the creature is large—geese, and cocks. And of all these only moderate portions are served to each of the king's guests, and each of them may carry home whatever he leaves untouched at the meal. But the greater part of these meats and other foods are taken into the courtyard for the body-guard and light-armed troopers maintained by the king; there they divide all the half-eaten remnants of meat and bread and share them in equal portions."

Q What does this description of a royal dinner tell you about the nature of Persian kingship?

Source: Reprinted by permission of the publishers and the Trustees of the Loeb Classical Library from *Athenaeus: The Deipnosophists*, Loeb Classical Library Vol. II, trans. by C. B. Gulick, Cambridge, Mass.: Harvard University Press, Copyright © 1928, by the President and Fellows of Harvard College. The Loeb Classical Library is a registered trademark of the President and Fellows of Harvard College.

power of life and death over everyone. Persian kings were largely secluded and not easily accessible. They resided in a series of splendid palaces. Darius in particular was a palace builder on a grand scale. His description of the construction of a palace in the chief Persian capital of Susa demonstrated what a truly international empire Persia was:

> This is the . . . palace which at Susa I built. From afar its ornamentation was brought. . . . The cedar timber was brought from a mountain named Lebanon. . . . Teakwood was brought from Gandara and from Carmania. The gold which was used here was brought from Sardis and from Bactria. The stone—lapis lazuli and carnelian—was brought from Sogdiana. . . . The silver and copper were brought from Egypt. The ornamentation with which the wall was adorned was brought from Ionia. The ivory was brought from Ethiopia, from India, and from Arachosia. The stone pillars were brought from . . . Elam. The artisans who dressed the stone were Ionians and Sardians. The goldsmiths who wrought the gold were Medes and Egyptians. . . . Those who worked the baked brick [with figures] were Babylonians. The men who adorned the wall were Medes and Egyptians. At Susa here a splendid work was ordered; very splendid did it turn out.[13]

But Darius was unhappy with Susa. He did not really consider it his homeland, and it was oppressively hot in the summer months. He built another residence at Persepolis, a new capital located to the southeast of the old one at a higher elevation.

The policies of Darius also tended to widen the gap between the king and his subjects (see the box above). As the Great King himself said of all his subjects, "What was said to

Louvre (Chuzeville), Paris/© Réunion des Musées Nationaux/Art Resource, NY

Archers of the Persian Guard. One of the main pillars supporting the Persian Empire was the military. This frieze, composed of enameled brick, depicts members of the famous infantry force known as the Immortals, so called because their number was never allowed to drop below 10,000. Anyone killed would be replaced immediately. The men in the frieze carry the standard lance and bow and arrow of the infantry.

them by me, night and day it was done."[14] Over a period of time, the Great Kings in their greed came to hoard immense quantities of gold and silver in the various treasuries located in the capital cities. Both their hoarding of wealth and their later overtaxation of their subjects are seen as crucial factors in the ultimate weakening of the Persian Empire.

In its heyday, however, the empire stood supreme, and much of its power depended on the military. By the time of Darius, the Persian monarchs had created a standing army of professional soldiers. This army was truly international, composed of contingents from the various peoples who made up the empire. At its core was a cavalry force of 10,000 and an elite infantry force of 10,000 Medes and Persians known as the Immortals because they were never allowed to fall below 10,000 in number. When one was killed, he was immediately replaced. The Persians made effective use of their cavalry, especially for operating behind enemy lines and breaking up lines of communication.

Persian Religion

Of all the Persians' cultural contributions, the most original was their religion, **Zoroastrianism**. According to Persian tradition, its founder, Zoroaster (ZOR-oh-ass-tur) (also known as Zarathustra), was born in 660 B.C.E. After a period of wandering and solitude, he experienced revelations that caused him to be revered as a prophet of the "true religion." His teachings were eventually written down in the third century C.E. in the Zend Avesta.

Like the Hebrews, Zoroaster taught a spiritual message of monotheism. To Zoroaster, the religion he preached was the only perfect one, and Ahuramazda (uh-HOOR-uh-MAHZ-duh) was the only god. Ahuramazda (the "Wise Lord") was the supreme deity who brought all things into being:

> *This I ask of You, O Ahuramazda; answer me well:*
> *Who at the Creation was the first father of Justice?—*
> *Who assigned their path to the sun and the stars?—*
> *Who decreed the waxing and waning of the moon,*
> *if it was not You?— . . .*
> *Who has fixed the earth below, and the heaven above*
> *with its clouds that it might not be moved?—*
> *Who has appointed the waters and the green things*
> *upon the earth?—*
> *Who has harnessed to the wind and the clouds their*
> *steeds?— . . .*
> *Thus do I strive to recognize in You, O Wise One,*
> *Together with the Holy Spirit, the Creator of all*
> *things.*[15]

According to Zoroaster, Ahuramazda also possessed abstract qualities or states that all humans should aspire to, such as good thought, right, and piety. Although Ahuramazda was supreme, he was not unopposed. At the beginning of the world, the good spirit of Ahuramazda was opposed by the evil spirit, known as Ahriman.

Humans also played a role in this cosmic struggle between good and evil. Ahuramazda, the creator, gave all humans free will and the power to choose between right and wrong. The good person chooses the right way of Ahuramazda. Zoroaster taught that there would be an end to the struggle between good and evil. Ahuramazda would eventually triumph, and at the last judgment at the end of the world, the final separation of good and evil would occur. Individuals, too, would be judged. Each soul faced a final evaluation of its actions. The soul of a person who had performed good deeds would achieve paradise, but if the person's deeds had been evil, the soul would be thrown into an abyss of torment. Some historians believe that Zoroastrianism, with its emphasis on good and evil, heaven and hell, and a last judgment, had an impact on Christianity, a religion that eventually surpassed it in signficance.

CHAPTER SUMMARY

By 1500 B.C.E., much of the creative impulse of the Mesopotamian and Egyptian civilizations was beginning to decline. And by 1200 B.C.E., the decline of the Hittites and Egyptians had created a power vacuum that allowed a patchwork of petty kingdoms and city-states to emerge, especially in the area of Syria and Canaan. One was that of the Phoenicians, who created a trading empire in the Mediterranean as well as an alphabet that was later adapted by the Greeks and the Romans.

Of these small states, however, perhaps the most important was that of the Israelites, who created a kingdom under Saul, David, and Solomon. By the tenth century B.C.E., the inhabitants of Israel had divided into a northern kingdom of Israel and a southern kingdom of Judah, but the rise of larger states in the region led eventually to their demise. Israel fell to the Assyrians at the end of the eighth century B.C.E. and Judah to the Chaldeans in the sixth century. Nevertheless, although the Israelites created no empire and were dominated by the Assyrians, Chaldeans, and eventually the Persians, they left a spiritual legacy that influenced much of the later development of Western civilization. The evolution of Hebrew monotheism created in Judaism one of the world's great religions; it influenced the development of both Christianity and Islam. When we speak of the Judeo-Christian heritage of Western civilization, we refer not only to the concept of monotheism but also to ideas of law, morality, and social justice that have become important parts of Western culture.

All of these small states were eventually overshadowed by the rise of the great empires of the Assyrians, Chaldeans, and Persians. The Assyrian Empire, built upon the effective use of military force, was the first to unite almost all of the ancient Near East. Nevertheless, after reaching the height of its power by 700 B.C.E., it gradually succumbed to internal dissension and was overrun by the armies of the Medes and the Chaldeans near the end of the seventh century B.C.E. The latter created a Neo-Babylonian Empire, which in turn was short-lived and soon conquered by the Persians. Although the Persian Empire owed much to the administrative organization developed by the Assyrians, the Persian Empire had its own peculiar strengths. Persian rule was tolerant as well as efficient. Conquered peoples were allowed to keep their own religions, customs, and methods of doing business. The two centuries of relative peace that the Persian Empire brought to the Near East facilitated trade and the general well-being of its peoples. Many Near Eastern peoples, including the Israelites, expressed gratitude for being subjects of the Great Kings of Persia.

CHAPTER TIMELINE

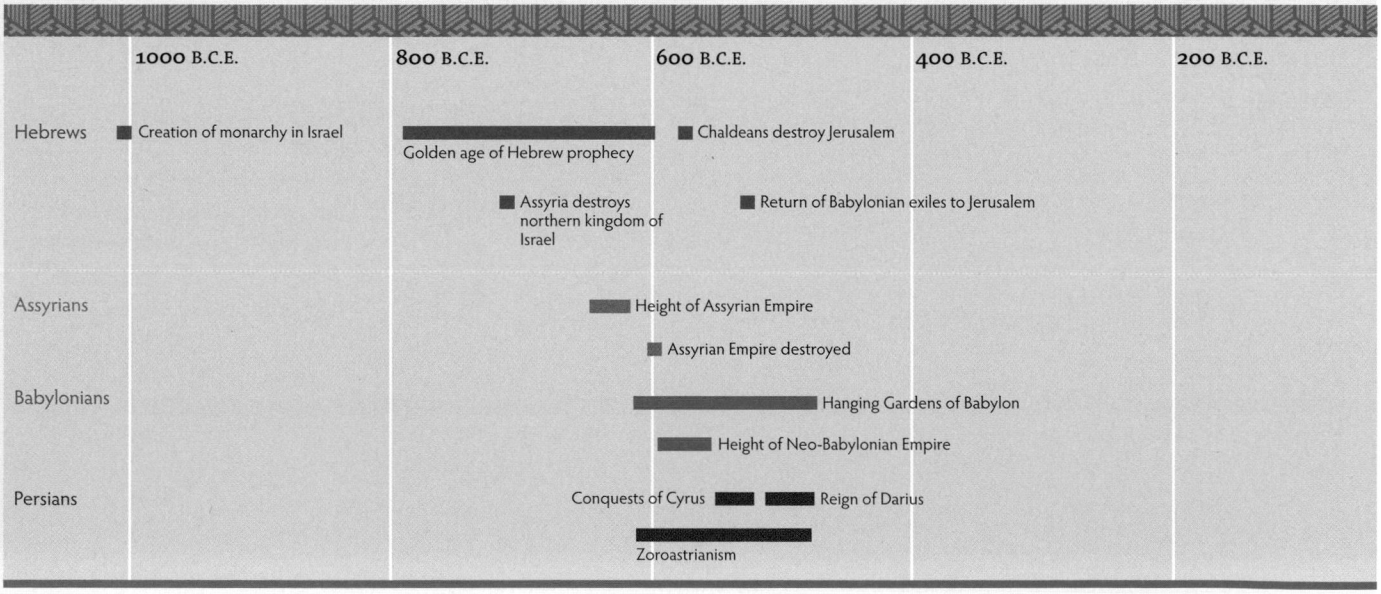

CHAPTER REVIEW

Upon Reflection

Q What were the major characteristics of the civilization established by the Israelites?

Q Compare and contrast the administrative and military structure and attitudes toward subject peoples of the Assyrian and Persian Empires.

Q If the large empires of the Assyrians and Persians dominated the entire Near East for centuries, why did the small state of the Israelites have a greater impact on Western civilization?

Key Terms

monotheism (p. 30)
satrapy (p. 38)
satrap (p. 40)
Zoroastrianism (p. 42)

Suggestions for Further Reading

THE HITTITES On the Hittites, see **T. Bryce, *The Kingdom of the Hittites,*** 2nd ed. (Oxford, 2006), and ***Life and Society in the Hittite World*** (Oxford, 2002).

ANCIENT ISRAEL There is an enormous literature on ancient Israel. For an important revisionist view on the archaeological aspects, see **I. Finkelstein** and **N. Silberman, *The Bible Unearthed: Archaeology's New Vision of Ancient Israel*** (New York, 2002). For a historical narrative, see **H. Shanks, *Ancient Israel: A Short History from Abraham to the Roman Destruction of the Temple,*** rev. ed. (Englewood Cliffs, N.J., 1999). On the origins of the Israelites, see **W. G. Dever, *Who Were the Early Israelites and Where Did They Come From?*** (Grand Rapids, Mich., 2003). On controversies surrounding the history of the Israelites, see **J. M. Golden, *Ancient Canaan and Israel*** (Oxford, 2004).

RELIGION OF ISRAEL For a general study on the religion of Israel, see **W. J. Doorly, *The Religion of Israel*** (New York, 1997).

THE PHOENICIANS For a good account of Phoenician domestic and overseas expansion, see **D. Harden, *The Phoenicians,*** rev. ed. (Harmondsworth, England, 1980). See also **M. E. Aubet, *The Phoenicians and the West: Politics, Colonies and Trade,*** 2nd ed. (Cambridge, 2001), and **G. Markoe, *Phoenicians*** (London, 2000), on Phoenician society.

THE ASSYRIAN EMPIRE A detailed account of Assyrian political, economic, social, military, and cultural history is **H. W. F. Saggs, *The Might That Was Assyria*** (London, 1984). The Neo-Babylonian Empire can be examined in **H. W. F. Saggs, *Babylonians*** (Norman, Okla., 1995).

THE PERSIAN EMPIRE The classic work on the Persian Empire is **A. T. Olmstead, *History of the Persian Empire*** (Chicago, 1948), but see also **L. Allen, *The Persian Empire*** (Chicago, 2005), and **J. M. Cook, *The Persian Empire*** (New York, 1983), for new material and fresh interpretations. On the history of Zoroastrianism, see **S. A. Nigosian, *The Zoroastrian Faith: Tradition and Modern Research*** (New York, 1993).

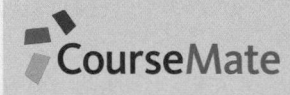

Visit the CourseMate website at www.cengagebrain.com for additional study tools and review materials for this chapter.

Museo Pio Clementino, Vatican Museums, Vatican State/© Scala/Art Resource, NY

A bust of Pericles

CHAPTER 3

The Civilization of the Greeks

CHAPTER OUTLINE AND FOCUS QUESTIONS

Early Greece

Q How did the geography of Greece affect Greek history?

The Greeks in a Dark Age (c. 1100–c. 750 B.C.E.)

Q Who was Homer, and why was his work used as the basis for Greek education?

The World of the Greek City-States (c. 750–c. 500 B.C.E.)

Q What were the chief features of the *polis*, or city-state, and how did the major city-states of Athens and Sparta differ?

The High Point of Greek Civilization: Classical Greece

Q What did the Greeks mean by *democracy*, and in what ways was the Athenian political system a democracy? What effect did the two great conflicts of the fifth century B.C.E.—the Persian Wars and the Peloponnesian War—have on Greek civilization?

The Culture and Society of Classical Greece

Q Upon what ideals was Classical Greek art based, and how were these ideals expressed? What questions did the Greek philosophers pose, and what answers did they suggest?

CRITICAL THINKING

Q Why are the Greeks considered the cornerstone of the Western intellectual tradition?

IN 431 B.C.E., WAR ERUPTED as two dramatically different Greek city-states—Athens and Sparta—fought for domination of the Greek world. The people of Athens felt secure behind their walls and in the first winter of the war held a public funeral to honor those who had died in battle. On the day of the ceremony, the citizens of Athens joined in a procession, with the relatives of the dead wailing for their loved ones. As was the custom in Athens, one leading citizen was asked to address the crowd, and on this day it was Pericles who spoke to the people. He talked about the greatness of Athens and reminded the Athenians of the strength of their political system: "Our constitution," he said, "is called a democracy because power is in the hands not of a minority but of the whole people. When it is a question of settling private disputes, everyone is equal before the law. Just as our political life is free and open, so is our day-to-day life in our relations with each other. . . . Here each individual is interested not only in his own affairs but in the affairs of the state as well."

In this famous Funeral Oration, Pericles gave voice to the ideal of democracy and the importance of the individual. It was the Greeks who created the intellectual foundations of our Western heritage. They asked some basic questions about human life that still dominate our own intellectual pursuits: What is the nature of the universe? What is the purpose of human existence? What is our relationship to divine forces? What constitutes a community? What constitutes a state? What is true education? What are the true sources of law? What is truth itself, and how do we realize it? Not only did the Greeks provide answers to these questions, but they created a system of logical, analytical thought to examine them. This rational outlook has remained an important feature of Western civilization.

The story of ancient Greek civilization is a remarkable one that begins with the first arrival of the Greeks around 2000 B.C.E. By the eighth century B.C.E., the characteristic institution of ancient Greek life, the *polis* or city-state, had emerged. Greek civilization flourished and reached its height in the Classical era of the fifth century B.C.E., which has come to be closely identified with the achievements of Athenian democracy.

Early Greece

Focus Question: How did the geography of Greece affect Greek history?

Geography played an important role in Greek history. Compared to the landmasses of Mesopotamia and Egypt, Greece was compact: its mountainous peninsula encompassed only 45,000 square miles of territory, about the same as the state of Louisiana. The mountains and the sea were especially significant. Much of Greece consists of small plains and river valleys surrounded by mountain ranges 8,000 to 10,000 feet high. The mountainous terrain had the effect of isolating Greeks from one another. Consequently, Greek communities tended to follow their own separate paths and develop their own way of life. As time went on, these communities became attached to their independence and were only too willing to fight one another to gain advantage. No doubt the small size of these independent Greek communities fostered participation in political affairs and unique cultural expressions, but the rivalry among these communities also led to the bitter warfare that ultimately devastated Greek society.

The sea also influenced the evolution of Greek society. Greece had a long seacoast, dotted by bays and inlets that provided numerous harbors. The Greeks also inhabited a number of islands to the west, south, and particularly the east of the Greek mainland. It is no accident that the Greeks became seafarers who sailed out into the Aegean and the Mediterranean first to make contact with the outside world and later to establish colonies that would spread Greek civilization throughout the Mediterranean region.

Topography helped determine the major territories into which Greece was ultimately divided. South of the Gulf of Corinth was the Peloponnesus (pel-uh-puh-NEE-suss), which was virtually an island (see Map 3.1). Consisting mostly of hills, mountains, and small valleys, the Peloponnesus was the location of Sparta, as well as the site of Olympia, where famous athletic games were held. Northeast of the Peloponnesus was the Attic peninsula (or Attica), the home of Athens, hemmed in by mountains to the north and west and surrounded by the sea to the south and east. Northwest of Attica was Boeotia (bee-OH-shuh) in central Greece with its chief city of Thebes (THEEBZ). To the north of Boeotia was Thessaly, which contained the largest plains and became a great producer of grain and horses. To the north of Thessaly lay Macedonia, which was not of much importance in Greek history until 338 B.C.E., when a Macedonian king, Philip II, conquered the Greeks.

Minoan Crete

The earliest civilization in the Aegean region emerged on the large island of Crete, southeast of the Greek mainland. A Bronze Age civilization that used metals, especially bronze, in making weapons had been established there by 2800 B.C.E. This forgotten civilization was rediscovered at the turn of the twentieth century by the English archaeologist Arthur Evans, who named it "Minoan" (mi-NOH-un) after Minos, a legendary king of Crete. In language and religion, the Minoans were not Greek, although they did have some influence on the peoples of the Greek mainland.

Evans's excavations on Crete at the beginning of the twentieth century led to the discovery of an enormous palace complex at Knossus (NOSS-suss), near modern Heracleion, that was most likely the center of a far-ranging "sea empire," probably largely commercial. We know from archaeological remains that the people of Minoan Crete were accustomed to sea travel and had made contact with the more advanced civilization of Egypt.

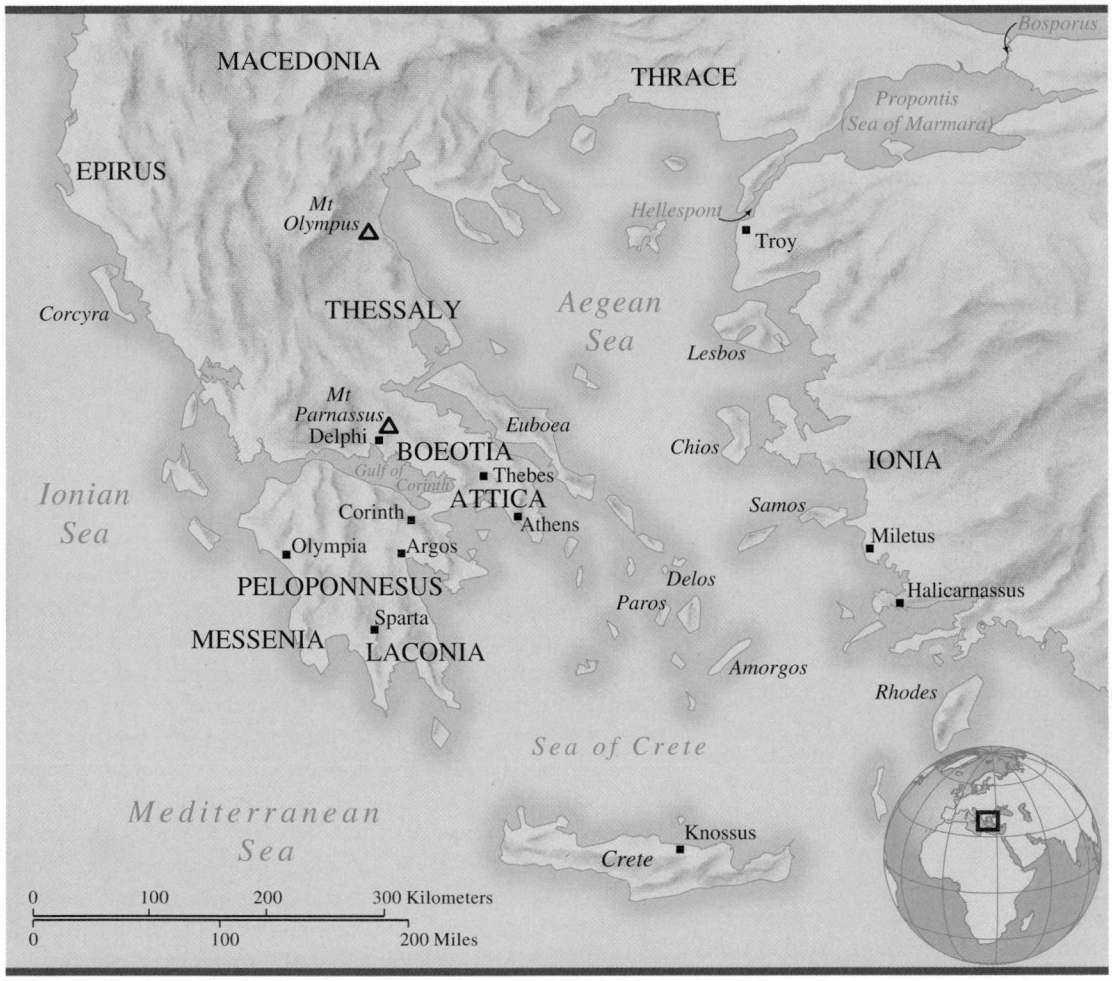

© Cengage Learning

MAP 3.1 Ancient Greece (c. 750–338 B.C.E.). Between 750 and 500 B.C.E., the city-state emerged as the central institution in Greek life. Classical Greece lasted from about 500 to 338 B.C.E. and encompassed the high points of Greek civilization in the arts, science, philosophy, and politics, but also the Persian Wars and the Peloponnesian War.

How does the geography of Greece help explain the rise and development of the Greek city-state?

The Minoan civilization reached its height between 2000 and 1450 B.C.E. The palace at Knossus, the royal seat of the kings, demonstrates the prosperity and power of this civilization. It was an elaborate structure built around a central courtyard and included numerous private living rooms for the royal family and workshops for making decorated vases, small sculptures, and jewelry. Even bathrooms, with elaborate drains, were part of the complex. The rooms were decorated with frescoes in bright colors showing sporting events and naturalistic scenes that have led some observers to conclude that the Cretans had a great love of nature.

The centers of Minoan civilization on Crete suffered a sudden and catastrophic collapse around 1450 B.C.E. The cause of this destruction has been vigorously debated. Some historians believe that a tsunami triggered by a powerful volcanic eruption on the island of Thera was responsible for the devastation. Most historians, however, maintain that the destruction was the result of invasion and pillage by mainland Greeks known as the Mycenaeans.

The First Greek State: Mycenae

The term *Mycenaean* (my-suh-NEE-un) is derived from Mycenae (my-SEE-nee), a remarkable fortified site first excavated by the amateur German archaeologist Heinrich Schliemann (HYN-rikh SHLEE-mahn). Mycenae was one center in a Greek civilization that flourished between 1600 and 1100 B.C.E. The Mycenaean Greeks were part of the Indo-European family of peoples (see Chapter 2) who spread from their original location into southern and western Europe, India, and Iran. One group entered the territory of Greece from the north around 1900 B.C.E. and managed to gain control of the Greek mainland and develop a civilization.

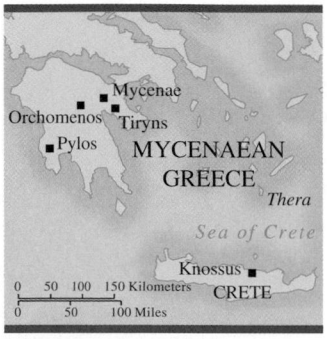

© Cengage Learning

Minoan Crete and Mycenaean Greece

Mycenaean civilization, which reached its high point between 1400 and 1200 B.C.E., consisted of a number of powerful monarchies based in fortified palace complexes. Like Mycenae itself, the palaces were built on hills and surrounded by gigantic stone walls. These various centers of power probably formed a loose confederacy of independent states, with Mycenae being the strongest. Next in importance to the kings in these states were the army commanders, priests, and the bureaucrats who kept careful records. The free citizenry included peasants, soldiers, and artisans, and the lowest rung of the social ladder consisted of serfs and slaves.

The Mycenaeans were, above all, a warrior people who prided themselves on their heroic deeds in battle. Some scholars believe that the Mycenaeans, led by Mycenae itself, spread outward militarily, conquering Crete and making it part of the Mycenaean world. The most famous of all their supposed military adventures has come down to us in the epic poetry of Homer (discussed in the next section). Did the Mycenaean Greeks, led by Agamemnon (ag-uh-MEM-non), king of Mycenae, indeed sack the city of Troy on the northwestern coast of Asia Minor around 1250 B.C.E., as Homer described? Since the excavations of Heinrich Schliemann, begun in 1870, scholars have debated this question. Many believe that Homer's account does have a basis in fact.

By the late thirteenth century B.C.E., Mycenaean Greece was showing signs of serious trouble. Mycenae itself was torched around 1190 B.C.E., and other Mycenaean centers show similar patterns of destruction as new waves of Greek-speaking invaders moved in from the north. By 1100 B.C.E., the Mycenaean culture was coming to an end, and the Greek world was entering a new period of considerable insecurity.

The Greeks in a Dark Age (c. 1100–c. 750 B.C.E.)

Q FOCUS QUESTION: Who was Homer, and why was his work used as the basis for Greek education?

After the collapse of Mycenaean civilization, Greece entered a difficult period in which the population declined and food production dropped. Because of the dire conditions and our meager knowledge about the period, historians call it the Dark Age. Not until 850 B.C.E. did farming revive. At the same time, some new developments were forming the basis for a revived Greece.

During the Dark Age, large numbers of Greeks left the mainland and migrated across the Aegean Sea to various islands and especially to the western shores of Asia Minor, a strip of territory that came to be called Ionia (eye-OH-nee-uh). The Greeks who resided there were called Ionians. Two other major groups of Greeks settled in established parts of Greece. The Aeolian (ee-OH-lee-un) Greeks, located in northern and central Greece, colonized the large island of Lesbos and the adjacent territory of the mainland. The Dorians (DOR-ee-unz) established themselves in southwestern Greece, especially in the Peloponnesus, as well as on some of the islands in the south Aegean Sea, including Crete.

Other important activities occurred in the Dark Age as well. Greece saw a revival of some trade and some economic activity besides agriculture. Iron came into use for the construction of weapons. And at some point in the eighth century B.C.E., the Greeks adopted the Phoenician alphabet to give themselves a new system of writing. Near the very end of this Dark Age appeared the work of Homer, who has come to be viewed as one of the great poets of all time.

Homer and Homeric Greece

The *Iliad* and the *Odyssey*, the great epic poems of early Greece, were based on stories that had been passed down from generation to generation. It is generally assumed that early in the eighth century B.C.E., Homer made use of these oral traditions to compose the *Iliad*, his epic of the Trojan War. The war was precipitated by Paris, a prince of Troy, whose kidnapping of Helen, wife of the king of the Greek state of Sparta, outraged all the Greeks. Under the leadership of the Spartan king's brother, Agamemnon of Mycenae, the Greeks attacked Troy. Ten years later, the Greeks finally won and sacked the city.

But the *Iliad* is not so much the story of the war itself as it is the tale of the Greek hero Achilles (uh-KIL-eez) and how the "wrath of Achilles" led to disaster. As is true of

© The Trustees of the British Museum/Art Resource, NY

The Slaying of Hector. This scene from a late-fifth-century B.C.E. Athenian vase depicts the final battle between Achilles and the Trojan hero Hector. Achilles is shown lunging forward with his spear to deliver the fatal blow to the Trojan prince, a scene taken from Homer's *Iliad*. The *Iliad* is Homer's masterpiece and was important to later Greeks as a means of teaching the aristocratic values of courage and honor.

all great literature, the *Iliad* abounds in universal lessons. Underlying them all is the clear message, as one commentator has observed, that "men will still come and go like the generations of leaves in the forest; that [man] will still be weak, and the gods strong and incalculable; that the quality of a man matters more than his achievement; that violence and recklessness will still lead to disaster, and that this will fall on the innocent as well as on the guilty."[1]

The *Odyssey*, Homer's other masterpiece, is an epic romance that recounts the journeys of a Greek hero named Odysseus (oh-DIS-see-us) after the fall of Troy and his ultimate return to his wife. But there is a larger vision here as well: the testing of the heroic stature of Odysseus until, by both cunning and patience, he prevails. In the course of this testing, the underlying moral message is "that virtue is a better policy than vice."[2]

Although the *Iliad* and the *Odyssey* supposedly deal with the heroes of the Mycenaean age of the thirteenth century B.C.E., many scholars believe that they really describe the social conditions of the Dark Age. According to the Homeric view, Greece was a society based on agriculture in which a landed warrior-aristocracy controlled much wealth and exercised considerable power. Homer's world reflects the values of aristocratic heroes.

Homer's Enduring Importance

This, of course, explains the importance of Homer to later generations of Greeks. Homer did not so much record history as make it. The Greeks regarded the *Iliad* and the *Odyssey* as authentic history recorded by one poet, Homer. These masterpieces gave the Greeks an idealized past with a cast of heroes and came to be used as standard texts for the education of generations of Greek males. As one Athenian stated, "My father was anxious to see me develop into a good man . . . and as a means to this end he compelled me to memorize all of Homer."[3] The values Homer taught were essentially the aristocratic values of courage and honor (see the box on p. 50). A hero strives for excellence, which the Greeks called *arete* (ahr-uh-TAY). In the warrior-aristocratic world of Homer, *arete* is won in struggle or contest. Through his willingness to fight, the hero protects his family and friends, preserves his own honor and that of his family, and earns his reputation.

In the Homeric world, aristocratic women, too, were expected to pursue excellence. Penelope, for example, the wife of Odysseus, the hero of the *Odyssey*, remains faithful to her husband and displays great courage and intelligence in preserving their household during her husband's long absence. Upon his return, Odysseus praises her: "Madame, there is not a man in the wide world who could find fault with you. For your fame has reached heaven itself, like that of some perfect king, ruling a populous and mighty state with the fear of god in his heart, and upholding the right."[4] Homer gave the Greeks a model of heroism, honor, and nobility. But in time, as a new world of city-states emerged in Greece, new values of cooperation and community also transformed what the Greeks learned from Homer.

The World of the Greek City-States (c. 750–c. 500 B.C.E.)

Q Focus Question: What were the chief features of the *polis*, or city-state, and how did the major city-states of Athens and Sparta differ?

In the eighth century B.C.E., Greek civilization burst forth with new energies, beginning the period that historians have called the Archaic Age of Greece. Two major

Homer's Ideal of Excellence

The *Iliad* and the *Odyssey*, epics that the Greeks believed were written by Homer, were used as basic texts for the education of Greeks for hundreds of years in antiquity. This passage from the *Iliad*, describing a conversation between Hector, prince of Troy, and his wife, Andromache (an-DRAH-muh-kee), illustrates the Greek ideal of gaining honor through combat. At the end of the passage, Homer also reveals what became the Greek attitude toward women: women are supposed to spin and weave and take care of their households and their children.

Homer, *Iliad*

Hector looked at his son and smiled, but said nothing. Andromache, bursting into tears, went up to him and put her hand in his. "Hector," she said, "you are possessed. This bravery of yours will be your end. You do not think of your little boy or your unhappy wife, whom you will make a widow soon. Some day the Achaeans [Greeks] are bound to kill you in a massed attack. And when I lose you I might as well be dead. . . . I have no father, no mother, now. . . . I had seven brothers too at home. In one day all of them went down to Hades' House. The great Achilles of the swift feet killed them all. . . .

"So you, Hector, are father and mother and brother to me, as well as my beloved husband. Have pity on me now; stay here on the tower; and do not make your boy an orphan and your wife a widow. . . ."

"All that, my dear," said the great Hector of the glittering helmet, "is surely my concern. But if I hid myself like a coward and refused to fight, I could never face the Trojans and the Trojan ladies in their trailing gowns. Besides, it would go against the grain, for I have trained myself always, like a good soldier, to take my place in the front line and win glory for my father and myself. . . ."

As he finished, glorious Hector held out his arms to take his boy. But the child shrank back with a cry to the bosom of his girdled nurse, alarmed by his father's appearance. He was frightened by the bronze of the helmet and the horsehair plume that he saw nodding grimly down at him. His father and his lady mother had to laugh. But noble Hector quickly took his helmet off and put the dazzling thing on the ground. Then he kissed his son, dandled him in his arms, and prayed to Zeus and the other gods: "Zeus; and you other gods, grant that this boy of mine may be, like me, preeminent in Troy, as strong and brave as I; a mighty king of Ilium. May people say, when he comes back from battle, 'Here is a better man than his father.' Let him bring home the bloodstained armor of the enemy he has killed, and make his mother happy."

Hector handed the boy to his wife, who took him to her fragrant breast. She was smiling through her tears, and when her husband saw this he was moved. He stroked her with his hand and said: "My dear, I beg you not to be too much distressed. No one is going to send me down to Hades before my proper time. But Fate is a thing that no man born of woman, coward or hero, can escape. Go home now, and attend to your own work, the loom and the spindle, and see that the maidservants get on with theirs. War is men's business; and this war is the business of every man in Ilium, myself above all."

Q What important ideals for Greek men and women are revealed in this passage from the *Iliad*?

Source: From *THE ILIAD* by Homer, translated by E. V. Rieu, Revised and updated by Peter Jones with D. C. H. Rieu, Edited with an introduction and notes by Peter Jones (Penguin Classics, 1950, Revised translation 2003). Copyright © the Estate of E. V. Rieu, 1946. Revised translation and Introduction and Notes copyright © Peter V. Jones, 2003. Reproduced by permission of Penguin Books Ltd.

developments stand out in this era: the evolution of the *polis* (POH-liss) as the central institution in Greek life and the Greeks' colonization of the Mediterranean and Black Seas.

The *Polis*

The Greek ***polis*** (plural, *poleis*) developed slowly during the Dark Age but by the eighth century B.C.E. had emerged as a truly unique and fundamental institution in Greek society. In a physical sense, the *polis* encompassed a town or city or even a village and its surrounding countryside. But the town or city or village served as the focus or central point where the citizens of the *polis* could assemble for political, social, and religious activities. In some *poleis*, this central meeting point was a hill, which could serve as a place of refuge during an attack and later in some sites came to be the religious center on which temples and public monuments were erected. Below this *acropolis* would be an *agora*, an open space that served both as a place where citizens could assemble and as a market.

Poleis varied greatly in size, from a few square miles to a few hundred square miles. The larger ones were the product of consolidation. The territory of Attica, for example, had once had twelve *poleis* but eventually became a single *polis* (Athens) through a process of amalgamation. The population of Athens grew to about 250,000 by the fifth century B.C.E. Most *poleis* were much smaller, consisting of only a few hundred to several thousand people.

Although our word *politics* is derived from the Greek term *polis*, the *polis* itself was much more than just a political institution. It was, above all, a community of citizens in which all political, economic, social, cultural, and religious activities were focused. As a community, the *polis* consisted of citizens with political rights (adult males), citizens with no political rights (women and children), and noncitizens (slaves and resident aliens). All citizens of a *polis* possessed basic rights, but these were coupled with responsibilities. The Greek philosopher Aristotle argued that the citizen did not just belong to himself; "we must rather regard every citizen as belonging to the state." The unity of citizens was important and often meant that states would take an active role in directing the patterns of life. The loyalty that citizens had to their *poleis* also had a negative side, however. *Poleis* distrusted one another, and the division of Greece into fiercely patriotic sovereign units helped bring about its ruin. Greece was not a united country but a geographic concept. The cultural unity of the Greeks did not mean much politically.

A New Military System: The Greek Way of War

As the *polis* developed, so did a new military system. In earlier times, wars in Greece had been fought by aristocratic cavalry—nobles on horseback. These aristocrats, who were large landowners, also dominated the political life of their *poleis*. But by the end of the eighth century and the start of the seventh, a new military order came into being that was based on **hoplites** (HAHP-lyts), heavily armed infantrymen who wore bronze or leather helmets, breastplates, and greaves (shin guards). Each carried a round shield, a short sword, and a thrusting spear about 9 feet long. Hoplites advanced into battle as a unit, forming a phalanx (a rectangular formation) in tight order, usually eight ranks deep. As long as the hoplites kept their order, were not outflanked, and did not break, they either secured victory or, at the very least, suffered no harm. The phalanx was easily routed, however, if it broke its order. The safety of the phalanx depended on the solidarity and discipline of its members. As one seventh-century B.C.E. poet noted, a good hoplite was "a short man firmly placed upon his legs, with a courageous heart, not to be uprooted from the spot where he plants his legs."[5]

The hoplite force had political as well as military repercussions. The aristocratic cavalry was now outdated. Since each hoplite provided his own armor, men of property, both aristocrats and small farmers, made up the new phalanx. Those who could become hoplites and fight for the state could also challenge aristocratic control.

In the new world of the Greek city-states, war became an integral part of the Greek way of life. The Greek philosopher Plato described war as "always existing by nature between every Greek city-state."[6] The Greeks created a tradition of warfare that became a prominent element of Western civilization. For example, the Greeks devised excellent weapons and body armor, making effective use of technological improvements. Greek armies included a large number of citizen-soldiers, who gladly accepted the need for training and discipline, giving them an edge over their opponents' often far-larger armies of mercenaries. Moreover, the Greeks displayed a willingness to engage the enemy head-on, deciding a battle quickly and with as few casualties as possible. Finally, the Greeks demonstrated the effectiveness of heavy infantry in determining the outcome of battle. All of these features of Greek warfare remained characteristic of Western military tactics for centuries.

Colonization and the Growth of Trade

Between 750 and 550 B.C.E., large numbers of Greeks left to settle in distant lands. Poverty and land hunger created by the growing gulf between rich and poor, overpopulation, and the development of trade were all factors that led to the establishment of colonies. Some Greek colonies were simply trading posts or centers for the transshipment of goods to Greece. Most were larger settlements that included fertile agricultural land taken from the native populations in those areas. Each colony was founded as a *polis* and was usually independent of the mother *polis* (*metropolis*) that had established it.

In the western Mediterranean, new Greek settlements were established along the coastline of southern Italy, southern France, eastern Spain, and northern Africa west of Egypt. To the north, the Greeks set up colonies in Thrace, where they sought good farmland to grow grains. Greeks also settled along the shores of the Black Sea and secured the approaches to it with cities on the Hellespont and Bosporus, most noticeably Byzantium, site of the later Constantinople (Istanbul). By establishing these settlements, the Greeks spread their culture throughout the Mediterranean basin. Colonization also led to increased trade and industry. The Greeks on the mainland sent their pottery, wine, and olive oil to these areas; in return, they

Museo Nazionale di Villa Giulia, Rome,//© Scala/Art Resource, NY

The Hoplite Forces. The Greek hoplites were infantrymen equipped with large round shields and long thrusting spears. In battle, they advanced in tight phalanx formation and were dangerous opponents as long as this formation remained unbroken. This vase painting of the seventh century B.C.E. shows two groups of hoplite warriors engaged in battle. The piper on the left is leading another line of soldiers preparing to enter the fray.

received grains and metals from the west and fish, timber, wheat, metals, and slaves from the Black Sea region. In many *poleis*, the expansion of trade and industry created a new group of rich men who desired political privileges commensurate with their wealth but found them impossible to gain because of the power of the ruling aristocrats.

Tyranny in the Greek *Polis*

The desires of these new groups opened the door to the rise of **tyrants** in the seventh and sixth centuries B.C.E. They were not necessarily oppressive or wicked, as our word *tyrant* connotes. Greek tyrants were rulers who seized power by force and who were not subject to the law. Support for the tyrants came from the new rich, who made their money in trade and industry, as well as from poor peasants, who were in debt to landholding aristocrats. Both groups were opposed to the domination of political power by aristocratic **oligarchies**.

Tyrants usually achieved power by a local coup d'état and maintained it by using mercenary soldiers. Once in power, they built marketplaces, temples, and walls that created jobs, glorified the city, and enhanced their own popularity. Tyrants also favored the interests of merchants and traders. Despite these achievements, however, tyranny fell out of favor by the end of the sixth century B.C.E. Its very nature as a system outside the law seemed contradictory to the ideals of the Greek community. Although tyranny did not last, it played a significant role in the course of Greek history by ending the rule of narrow aristocratic oligarchies. The end of tyranny opened the door to greater numbers of people in government. Although this trend culminated in the development of democracy in some communities, in other states expanded oligarchies of one kind or another managed to remain in power. Greek states exhibited considerable variety in their governmental structures; this can perhaps best be seen by examining the two most famous and most powerful Greek city-states, Sparta and Athens.

Sparta

Located in the southeastern Peloponnesus, in an area known as Laconia (luh-KOH-nee-uh), the Spartans had originally occupied four small villages that eventually became unified into a single *polis* (a fifth soon joined the others). This unification made Sparta a strong community in Laconia and enabled the Spartans to conquer the neighboring Laconians. Many Laconians became ***perioikoi*** (per-ee-EE-koh-ee), free inhabitants who were required to pay taxes and perform military service for Sparta but were not citizens. Other Laconians became known as **helots** (HEL-uts) (derived from a Greek word for "capture"). They were bound to the land and forced to work on farms and as household servants for the Spartans.

When the land in Laconia proved unable to support the growing number of Spartan citizens, the Spartans looked for land nearby and, beginning around 730 B.C.E., undertook the conquest of neighboring Messenia despite its larger size and population. Messenia possessed a spacious, fertile plain ideal for growing grain. After its conquest, which was not completed until the seventh century B.C.E., the Messenians were made helots and forced to work for the Spartans.

THE NEW SPARTA To ensure control over their conquered Laconian and Messenian helots, the Spartans decided to create a military state. By the early sixth century B.C.E., they had transformed Sparta into a military camp (see the box on p. 54). The lives of all Spartans were now rigidly organized. At birth, each child was examined by state officials who decided whether it was fit to live. Infants judged unfit were left to die. Boys were taken from their mothers at the age of seven and put under control of the state. They lived in military-style barracks, where they were subjected to harsh discipline to make them tough and given an education that stressed military training and obedience to authority. At twenty, Spartan males were enrolled in the army for regular military service. Although allowed to marry, they continued to live in the barracks and ate all their meals in public dining halls with their fellow soldiers. Meals were simple; the famous Spartan black broth consisted of a piece of pork boiled in blood, salt, and vinegar, causing a visitor who ate in a public mess to remark that he now understood why Spartans were not afraid to die. At thirty, Spartan males were allowed to vote in the assembly and live at home, but they stayed in the army until the age of sixty.

While their husbands remained in military barracks until age thirty, Spartan women lived at home. Because of this separation, Spartan women had greater freedom of movement and greater power in the household than was common for women elsewhere in Greece. They were encouraged to exercise and remain fit to bear and raise healthy children. Like the men, Spartan women engaged in athletic exercises in the nude. Many Spartan women upheld the strict Spartan values, expecting their husbands and sons to be brave in war. The story is told that as a Spartan mother was burying her son, an old woman came up to her and said, "You poor woman, what a misfortune." "No," replied the other, "because I bore him so that he might die for Sparta and that is what has happened, as I wished."[7] Another Spartan woman, as she was handing her son his shield, told him to come back carrying his shield or carried on it.

THE SPARTAN STATE The Spartan government was headed by two kings, who led the Spartan army on its campaigns. A group of five men, known as the *ephors* (EFF-urz), were elected each year and were responsible for the education of youth and the conduct of all citizens. A council of elders, composed of the two kings and twenty-eight citizens over the age of sixty, decided on the issues that would be presented to an assembly. This assembly of all male citizens did not debate but only voted on the issues put before it by the council of elders.

To make their new military state secure, the Spartans deliberately turned their backs on the outside world. Foreigners, who might bring in new ideas, were discouraged from visiting Sparta. Nor were Spartans, except for military reasons, encouraged to travel abroad where they might pick up new ideas that might prove dangerous to the stability of the state. Likewise, Spartan citizens were discouraged from studying philosophy, literature, or the arts—subjects that might encourage new thoughts. The art of war and of ruling was the Spartan ideal; all other arts were frowned on.

In the sixth century, Sparta used its military might and the fear it inspired to gain greater control of the Peloponnesus by organizing an alliance of almost all the Peloponnesian states. Sparta's strength enabled it to dominate this Peloponnesian League and determine its policies. By 500 B.C.E., the Spartans had organized a powerful military state that maintained order and stability in the Peloponnesus. Raised from early childhood to believe that total loyalty to the Spartan state was the basic reason for existence, the Spartans viewed their strength as justification for their militaristic ideals and regimented society.

Athens

By 700 B.C.E., Athens had established a unified *polis* on the peninsula of Attica. Although early Athens had been ruled by a monarchy, by the seventh century it had fallen under

The Lycurgan Reforms

To maintain control over the conquered Messenians, the Spartans instituted the reforms that created their military state. These reforms are associated with the name of the lawgiver Lycurgus (ly-KUR-guss), although historians are not sure that he ever actually existed. In this account of Lycurgus, the ancient Greek historian Plutarch discusses the effect of these reforms on the treatment and education of boys.

Plutarch, *Lycurgus*

Lycurgus was of another mind; he would not have masters bought out of the market for his young Spartans, . . . nor was it lawful, indeed, for the father himself to breed up the children after his own fancy; but as soon as they were seven years old they were to be enrolled in certain companies and classes, where they all lived under the same order and discipline, doing their exercises and taking their play together. Of these, he who showed the most conduct and courage was made captain; they had their eyes always upon him, obeyed his orders, and underwent patiently whatsoever punishment he inflicted; so that the whole course of their education was one continued exercise of a ready and perfect obedience. The old men, too, were spectators of their performances, and often raised quarrels and disputes among them, to have a good opportunity of finding out their different characters, and of seeing which would be valiant, which a coward, when they should come to more dangerous encounters. Reading and writing they gave them just enough to serve their turn; their chief care was to make them good subjects, and to teach them to endure pain and conquer in battle. To this end, as they grew in years, their discipline was proportionately increased; their heads were close-clipped, they were accustomed to go barefoot, and for the most part to play naked.

After they were twelve years old, they were no longer allowed to wear any undergarments, they had one coat to serve them a year; their bodies were hard and dry, with but little acquaintance of baths and unguents; these human indulgences they were allowed only on some few particular days in the year. They lodged together in little bands upon beds made of the rushes which grew by the banks of the river Eurotas, which they were to break off with their hands with a knife; if it were winter, they mingled some thistledown with their rushes, which it was thought had the property of giving warmth. By the time they were come to this age there was not any of the more hopeful boys who had not a lover to bear him company. The old men, too, had an eye upon them, coming often to the grounds to hear and see them contend either in wit or strength with one another, and this as seriously . . . as if they were their fathers, their tutors, or their magistrates; so that there scarcely was any time or place without someone present to put them in mind of their duty, and punish them if they had neglected it.

[Spartan boys were also encouraged to steal their food.] They stole, too, all other meat they could lay their hands on, looking out and watching all opportunities, when people were asleep or more careless than usual. If they were caught, they were not only punished with whipping, but hunger, too, being reduced to their ordinary allowance, which was but very slender, and so contrived on purpose, that they might set about to help themselves, and be forced to exercise their energy and address. This was the principal design of their hard fare.

Q What does this passage from Plutarch's account of Lycurgus tell you about the nature of the Spartan state? Why would the entire program have been distasteful to the Athenians?

Source: From *The Lives of the Noble Grecians and Romans* by Plutarch, translated by John Dryden and edited by Arthur H. Clough.

the control of its aristocrats. They possessed the best land and controlled political and religious life by means of a council of nobles, assisted by a board of nine archons. Although there was an assembly of full citizens, it possessed few powers.

Near the end of the seventh century B.C.E., Athens faced political turmoil because of serious economic problems. Many Athenian farmers found themselves sold into slavery when they were unable to repay the loans they had borrowed from their aristocratic neighbors, pledging themselves as collateral. Over and over, cries arose to cancel the debts and give land to the poor. Athens seemed on the verge of civil war.

THE REFORMS OF SOLON Hoping to avoid tyranny, the ruling Athenian aristocrats responded to this crisis by choosing Solon (SOH-lun), a reform-minded aristocrat, as sole archon in 594 B.C.E. and giving him full power to make changes. Solon canceled all current land debts, outlawed new loans based on humans as collateral, and freed people who had fallen into slavery for debts. He refused, however, to carry out any redistribution of the land and hence failed to deal with the basic cause of the economic crisis.

Like his economic reforms, Solon's political measures were also a compromise. Though by no means eliminating the power of the aristocracy, they opened the door to the participation of new people, especially the nonaristocratic wealthy, in the government. But Solon's reforms, though popular, did not solve Athens's problems. Aristocratic factions continued to vie for power, and the poorer peasants resented Solon's failure to institute land redistribution. Internal strife finally led to the very institution Solon had hoped to avoid—tyranny. Pisistratus (puh-SIS-truh-tuss), an aristocrat, seized power in 560 B.C.E. Pursuing a foreign policy that aided Athenian trade, Pisistratus remained popular with the merchants. But the Athenians rebelled against his son Hippias and ended the tyranny in 510 B.C.E. Although the aristocrats attempted to reestablish an oligarchy, Cleisthenes (KLYSS-thuh-neez), another aristocratic reformer, opposed this plan and, with the backing of the Athenian people, gained the upper hand in 508 B.C.E. The reforms of Cleisthenes now established the basis for Athenian democracy.

THE REFORMS OF CLEISTHENES A major aim of Cleisthenes's reforms was to weaken the power of traditional localities and regions, which had provided the foundation for aristocratic strength. He made the *demes*, the villages and townships of Attica, the basic units of political life. Cleisthenes enrolled all the citizens of the demes in ten new tribes, each of which contained inhabitants located in the rural districts of Attica, the coastal areas, and Athens. Each tribe thus contained a cross section of the population and reflected all of Attica, a move that gave local areas a basic role in the political structure. Each of the ten tribes chose fifty members by lot each year for a new Council of Five Hundred, which was responsible for the administration of both foreign and financial affairs and prepared the business that would be handled by the assembly. This assembly of all male citizens had final authority in the passing of laws after free and open debate; thus, Cleisthenes's reforms strengthened the central role of the assembly of citizens in the Athenian political system.

The reforms of Cleisthenes laid the foundations for Athenian democracy. More changes would come in the fifth century B.C.E. when the Athenians themselves would begin to use the word *democracy* to describe their system (from the Greek words *demos*, "people," and *kratia*, "power"—thus, "power to the people"). By 500 B.C.E., Athens was more united than it had ever been and was about to assume a more important role in Greek affairs.

CHRONOLOGY Archaic Greece: Sparta and Athens	
Sparta	
Conquest of Messenia	c. 730–710 B.C.E.
Beginning of Peloponnesian League	c. 560–550 B.C.E.
Athens	
Solon's reforms	594–593 B.C.E.
Tyranny of Pisistratus	c. 560–556 and 546–527 B.C.E.
Deposition of Hippias—end of tyranny	510 B.C.E.
Cleisthenes's reforms	c. 508–501 B.C.E.

The High Point of Greek Civilization: Classical Greece

FOCUS QUESTIONS: What did the Greeks mean by *democracy*, and in what ways was the Athenian political system a democracy? What effect did the two great conflicts of the fifth century B.C.E.—the Persian Wars and the Peloponnesian War—have on Greek civilization?

Classical Greece is the name given to the period from around 500 B.C.E. to the conquest of Greece by the Macedonian king Philip II in 338 B.C.E. It was a time of brilliant achievement, much of it associated with the flowering of democracy in Athens under the leadership of Pericles. Many of the lasting contributions of the Greeks occurred during this period. The age began with a mighty confrontation between the Greek states and the mammoth Persian Empire.

The Challenge of Persia

As Greek civilization expanded throughout the Mediterranean, it was inevitable that it would come into contact with the Persian Empire to the east. The Ionian Greek cities in southwestern Asia Minor had already fallen subject to the Persian Empire by the mid-sixth century B.C.E. An unsuccessful revolt by the Ionian cities in 499, assisted by the Athenian navy, led the Persian ruler Darius to seek revenge by attacking the mainland Greeks in 490. Darius may also have wished to expand his empire westward. The Persians landed an army on the plain of Marathon, only 26 miles from Athens. There a mostly Athenian army, though clearly outnumbered, went on the attack. Led by

Miltiades (mil-TY-uh-deez), one of the Greek leaders who insisted on attacking, the Greek hoplites charged across the plain of Marathon and crushed the Persian forces.

Xerxes (ZURK-seez), the new Persian monarch after the death of Darius in 486 B.C.E., vowed revenge and renewed the invasion of Greece. In preparation for the attack, some of the Greek states formed a defensive league under Spartan leadership, while the Athenians pursued a new military policy by developing a navy. By the time of the Persian invasion in 480 B.C.E., the Athenians had produced a fleet of about two hundred vessels.

Xerxes led a massive invasion force into Greece: close to 150,000 troops, almost seven hundred naval ships, and hundreds of supply ships to keep the large army fed. The Greeks hoped to stop the Persians at the pass of Thermopylae (thur-MAHP-ul-lee) along the main road into central Greece. A Greek force numbering close to nine thousand, under the leadership of the Spartan king Leonidas (lee-ON-uh-duss) and his contingent of three hundred Spartans, held off the Persian army for several days. The Spartan troops were especially brave. When told that Persian arrows would darken the sky in battle, one Spartan warrior supposedly responded, "That is good news. We will fight in the shade!" Unfortunately for the Greeks, a traitor told the Persians how to use a mountain path to outflank the Greek force. King Leonidas and the three hundred Spartans fought to the last man.

The Athenians, now threatened by the onslaught of the Persian forces, abandoned their city. While the Persians sacked and burned Athens, the Greek fleet remained offshore near the island of Salamis (SAL-uh-mis) and challenged the Persian navy to fight. Although the Greeks were outnumbered, they managed to outmaneuver the Persian fleet and utterly defeated it. A few months later, early in 479 B.C.E., the Greeks formed the largest Greek army seen up to that time and decisively defeated the Persian army at Plataea (pluh-TEE-uh), northwest of Attica. The Greeks had won the war and were now free to pursue their own destiny.

The Growth of an Athenian Empire in the Age of Pericles

After the defeat of the Persians, Athens stepped in to provide new leadership against the Persians by forming a confederation called the Delian League. Organized in the winter of 478-477 B.C.E., the Delian League was dominated by the Athenians from the beginning. Its main headquarters was the island of Delos, but its chief officials, including the treasurers and commanders of the fleet, were Athenian. Under the leadership of the Athenians, the Delian League pursued the attack against the Persian Empire. Virtually all of the Greek states in the Aegean were liberated from Persian control. Arguing that the Persian threat was now over, some members of the Delian League wished to withdraw. But the Athenians forced them to remain in the league and to pay tribute. "No secession" became Athenian policy. The Delian League was rapidly becoming an instrument of Athenian imperialism and the nucleus of an Athenian empire.

At home, Athenians favored the new imperial policy, especially in the 450s B.C.E., when an aristocrat named Pericles (PER-i-kleez) began to play an important political role. Under Pericles, Athens embarked on a policy of expanding democracy at home while severing its ties with Sparta and expanding its new empire abroad. This period of Athenian and Greek history, which historians have subsequently labeled the Age of Pericles, witnessed the height of Athenian power and the culmination of its brilliance as a civilization.

During the Age of Pericles, the Athenians became deeply attached to their democratic system. The sovereignty of the people was embodied in the assembly, which consisted of all male citizens over eighteen years of age. In the 440s, that was probably a group of about 43,000. Not all attended, however, and the number present at the meetings, which were held every ten days on a hillside east of the Acropolis, seldom reached 6,000. The assembly passed all laws and made final decisions on war and foreign policy.

Routine administration of public affairs was handled by a large body of city magistrates, usually chosen by lot without regard to class and usually serving one-year terms. This meant that many male citizens held public office at some time in their lives. A board of ten officials known as generals—*strategoi* (strah-tay-GOH-ee)—were elected by public vote to guide affairs of state, although their power depended on the respect they had attained. Generals were usually wealthy aristocrats, even though the people were free to select others. The generals could be reelected, enabling individual leaders to play an important political role. Pericles's frequent reelection (fifteen times) as one of the generals made him one of the leading politicians between 461 and 429 B.C.E.

All public officials were subject to scrutiny and could be deposed from office if they lost the people's confidence. After 488 B.C.E., the Athenians occasionally made use of a tactic called ostracism. Members of the assembly could write on a broken pottery fragment (*ostrakon*) the name of the person they most disliked or considered most harmful to the *polis*. A person who received a majority (if at least six thousand votes were cast) was exiled for ten years.

Pericles expanded the Athenians' involvement in *democracy*, which was what Athenians had come to call their

Athenian Democracy: The Funeral Oration of Pericles

In his *History of the Peloponnesian War*, the Greek historian Thucydides presented his reconstruction of the eulogy given by Pericles in the winter of 431–430 B.C.E. to honor the Athenians killed in the first campaigns of the Great Peloponnesian War. It is a magnificent, idealized description of the Athenian democracy at its height.

Thucydides, *History of the Peloponnesian War*

Our constitution is called a democracy because power is in the hands not of a minority but of the whole people. When it is a question of settling private disputes, everyone is equal before the law; when it is a question of putting one person before another in positions of public responsibility, what counts is not membership of a particular class, but the actual ability which the man possesses. No one, so long as he has it in him to be of service to the state, is kept in political obscurity because of poverty. And just as our political life is free and open, so is our day-to-day life in our relations with each other. We do not get into a state with our next-door neighbor if he enjoys himself in his own way, nor do we give him the kind of black looks which, though they do no real harm, still do hurt people's feeling. We are free and tolerant in our private lives; but in public affairs we keep to the law. This is because it commands our deep respect.

We give our obedience to those whom we put in positions of authority, and we obey the laws themselves, especially those which are for the protection of the oppressed, and those unwritten laws which it is an acknowledged shame to break. . . . Here each individual is interested not only in his own affairs but in the affairs of the state as well: even those who are mostly occupied with their own business are extremely well-informed on general politics—this is a peculiarity of ours: we do not say that a man who takes no interest in politics is a man who minds his own business; we say that he has no business here at all. We Athenians, in our own persons, take our decisions on policy or submit them to proper discussions: for we do not think that there is an incompatibility between words and deeds; the worst thing is to rush into action before the consequences have been properly debated. . . . Taking everything together, then, I declare that our city is an education to Greece, and I declare that in my opinion each single one of our citizens, in all the manifold aspects of life, is able to show himself the rightful lord and owner of his own person and do this, moreover, with exceptional grace and exceptional versatility. And to show that this is no empty boasting for the present occasion, but real tangible fact, you have only to consider the power which our city possesses and which has been won by those very qualities which I have mentioned.

Q In the eyes of Pericles, what were the ideals of Athenian democracy? In what ways did Pericles exaggerate his claims? Why would the Athenian passion for debate described by Pericles have been distasteful to the Spartans?

Source: From *THE HISTORY OF THE PELOPONNESIAN WAR* by Thucydides, translated by Rex Warner, with an introduction and notes by M. I. Finley (Penguin Classics, 1954, Revised edition 1972). Translation copyright © Rex Warner, 1954. Introduction and Appendices copyright © 1972. Reproduced by permission of Penguin Books, Ltd.

form of government (see the box above). Power was in the hands of the people: male citizens voted in the assemblies and served as jurors in the courts. Lower-class citizens were now eligible for public offices formerly closed to them. Pericles also introduced state pay for officeholders, including the widely held jury duty. This meant that even poor citizens could hold public office and afford to participate in public affairs. Nevertheless, although the Athenians developed a system of government that was unique in its time in which citizens had equal rights and the people were the government, aristocrats continued to hold the most important offices, and many people, including women, slaves, and foreigners residing in Athens, were not given the same political rights.

The Athenian pursuit of democracy at home was coupled with increasing imperialism abroad. Citing the threat of the Persian fleet in the Aegean, the Athenians moved the Delian League treasury from the island of Delos to Athens itself in 454 B.C.E. Members were charged a fee (tribute) for the Athenian claim of protection. Pericles also used the money in the league treasury, without the approval of its members, to build new temples in Athens, an arrogant reminder that the Delian League had become the Athenian empire. But Athenian imperialism alarmed the other Greek states, and soon all Greece was confronted with a new war.

The Great Peloponnesian War

During the forty years after the defeat of the Persians, the Greek world divided into two major camps: Sparta and its supporters and the Athenian empire. In his classic *History of the Peloponnesian War*, the great Greek historian Thucydides (thoo-SID-uh-deez) pointed out that the fundamental, long-range cause of the war that began in 431 B.C.E. was the fear that Athens and its empire inspired in Sparta. Then, too, Athens and Sparta had built two very different kinds of societies, and neither state was able to tolerate the other's system. A series of disputes finally led to the outbreak of war.

At the beginning of the war in 431 B.C.E., both sides believed they had winning strategies. The Athenians planned to remain behind the protective walls of Athens while the overseas empire and the navy kept them supplied. Pericles knew perfectly well that the Spartans and their allies could beat the Athenians in pitched battles, which was the chief aim of the Spartan strategy. The Spartans and their allies attacked Athens, hoping that the Athenians would send out their army to fight beyond the walls. But Pericles was convinced that Athens was secure behind its walls and retaliated by sending out naval excursions to ravage the seacoast of the Peloponnesus.

In the second year of the war, however, plague devastated the crowded city of Athens and wiped out possibly one-third of the population. Pericles himself died the following year (429 B.C.E.), a severe loss to Athens. Despite the ravages of the plague, the Athenians fought on in a struggle that dragged on for twenty-seven years. A crushing blow came in 405 B.C.E. when the Athenian fleet was destroyed at Aegospotami (ee-guh-SPAH-tuh-my) on the Hellespont. Athens was besieged and surrendered in 404. Its walls were torn down, the navy was disbanded, and the Athenian empire was destroyed. The great war was finally over.

The Decline of the Greek States (404–338 B.C.E.)

The Great Peloponnesian War weakened the major Greek states and led to new alliances among the *poleis*. After the defeat of Athens in 404 B.C.E., the Spartans established control over Greece. Oligarchies of local leaders in cooperation with Spartan garrisons were imposed on states "liberated" from Athenian imperialism. But the harsh policies of the oligarchs soon led to a reaction. In Athens, a rebellion enabled the Athenians to reestablish their democracy in 403 B.C.E. and even to rebuild their navy and again become an important force in the Greek world.

To maintain its newly organized leadership in Greek affairs, Sparta encouraged a Greek crusade against the Persians as a common enemy. But the Persians had learned the lessons of Greek politics and offered financial support to Athens and other Greek states to oppose Spartan power within Greece itself, thus beginning a new war that finally ended in 386 B.C.E.

The city-state of Thebes, in Boeotia, north of Athens, now began to exert its influence. Under their leader Epaminondas (eh-PAM-uh-NAHN-duss), the Thebans dramatically defeated the Spartan army at the Battle of Leuctra in 371 B.C.E. Spartan power declined, but Theban ascendancy was short-lived. After the death of Epaminondas in the Battle of Mantinea in 362 B.C.E., the Thebans could no longer dominate Greek politics. Yet the Greek states continued their petty wars, seemingly oblivious to the growing danger to the north, where King Philip II of Macedonia was developing a unified state that would finally end the destructive fratricide of the Greek states by imposing Macedonian authority.

The Culture and Society of Classical Greece

Focus Questions: Upon what ideals was Classical Greek art based, and how were these ideals expressed? What questions did the Greek philosophers pose, and what answers did they suggest?

Classical Greece saw a period of remarkable intellectual and cultural growth throughout the Greek world. Historians agree, however, that Periclean Athens was the most important center of Classical Greek culture.

The Writing of History

History as we know it, the systematic analysis of past events, was a Greek creation. Herodotus (huh-ROD-uh-tuss) (c. 484–c. 425 B.C.E.) was the author of *The Persian Wars*, a work commonly regarded as the first real history in Western civilization. The Greek word *historia* (from which we derive our word *history*) means "research" or "investigation," and it is in the opening line of Herodotus's work that we find the first recorded use of the word:

> These are the researches [*historia*] of Herodotus of Halicarnassus, which he publishes, in the hope of thereby preserving from decay the remembrance of what men have done, and of preventing the great and wonderful actions of the Greeks and the Barbarians from losing their due meed [reward] of glory; and withal to put on record what were their grounds of feud.[8]

The central theme of Herodotus's work is the conflict between the Greeks and the Persians, which he viewed as a struggle between freedom and despotism. Herodotus traveled extensively and questioned many people to obtain his information. Although he was a master storyteller and sometimes included considerable fanciful material, Herodotus was also capable of exhibiting a critical attitude toward the materials he used.

Thucydides (c. 460–c. 400 B.C.E.) was a far better historian, indeed, the greatest of the ancient world. Thucydides was an Athenian and a participant in the Peloponnesian War. He had been elected a general, but a defeat in battle led the Athenian assembly to send him into exile, which gave him the opportunity to concentrate on writing his *History of the Peloponnesian War*.

Unlike Herodotus, Thucydides was not concerned with divine forces or gods as causal factors in history. He saw war and politics in purely rational terms, as the activities of human beings. He examined the causes of the Peloponnesian War in a clear and objective fashion, placing much emphasis on the accuracy of his facts. As he stated:

> And with regard to my factual reporting of the events of the war I have made it a principle not to write down the first story that came my way, and not even to be guided by my own general impressions; either I was present myself at the events which I have described or else I heard of them from eye-witnesses whose reports I have checked with as much thoroughness as possible.[9]

Thucydides also provided remarkable insight into the human condition. He believed that political situations recur in similar fashion and that the study of history is therefore of great value in understanding the present.

Greek Drama

Drama, as we know it, was created by the Greeks and was clearly intended to do more than entertain. It was used to educate citizens and was supported by the state for that reason. Plays were presented in outdoor theaters as part of a religious festival. The form of Greek plays remained rather stable. Three male actors who wore masks acted all the parts. A chorus, also male, played the role of groups of people or served as narrators. Action was very limited because the emphasis was on the story and its meaning.

The first Greek dramas were tragedies, plays based on the suffering of a hero and usually ending in disaster. Aeschylus (ESS-kuh-luss) (525–456 B.C.E.) is the first tragedian whose plays are known to us. Although he wrote ninety tragedies, only seven have survived. As was customary in Greek tragedy, his plots were simple. The entire drama focused on a single tragic event and its meaning. Greek tragedies were sometimes presented in a trilogy (a set of three plays) built around a common theme. The only complete trilogy we possess, called the *Oresteia* (uh-res-TY-uh), was written by Aeschylus. The theme of this trilogy is derived from Homer. Agamemnon, the king of Mycenae, returns a hero from the defeat of Troy. His wife, Clytemnestra (kly-tuhm-NES-truh), avenges the sacrificial death of her daughter Iphigenia (if-uh-juh-NY-uh) by murdering Agamemnon, who had been responsible for Iphigenia's death. In the second play of the trilogy, Agamemnon's son Orestes (aw-RES-teez) avenges his father by killing his mother. Orestes is now pursued by the Furies, who torment him for killing his mother. Evil acts breed evil acts and suffering is one's lot, suggests Aeschylus. But Orestes is put on trial and acquitted by Athena, the patron goddess of Athens. Personal vendetta has been eliminated, and law has prevailed.

Another great Athenian playwright was Sophocles (SAHF-uh-kleez) (c. 496–406 B.C.E.), whose most famous play is *Oedipus the King*. The oracle of Apollo foretells how a man (Oedipus) will kill his own father and marry his mother. Despite all attempts at prevention, the tragic events occur. Although it appears that Oedipus suffered the fate determined by the gods, Oedipus also accepts that he himself as a free man must bear responsibility for his actions: "It was Apollo, friends, Apollo, that brought this bitter bitterness, my sorrows, to completion. But the hand that struck me was none but my own."[10]

The third outstanding Athenian tragedian, Euripides (yoo-RIP-i-deez) (c. 485–406 B.C.E.), moved beyond his predecessors in creating more realistic characters. His plots also became more complex and reflected a greater interest in real-life situations. Perhaps the greatest of all his plays was *The Bacchae*, which dealt with the introduction of the hysterical rites associated with Dionysus (dy-uh-NY-suss), god of wine. Euripides is often seen as a skeptic who questioned traditional moral and religious values. Euripides was also critical of the traditional view that war was glorious. He portrayed war as brutal and barbaric.

Greek tragedies dealt with universal themes still relevant in our day. They probed such problems as the nature of good and evil, the conflict between spiritual values and the demands of the state or family, the rights of the individual, the nature of divine forces, and human nature. Over and over, the tragic lesson was repeated: humans were free and yet could operate only within limitations imposed by the gods. The real task was to cultivate the balance and moderation that led to awareness of one's true position. But the pride in human accomplishment and independence is real. As the chorus chants in Sophocles's *Antigone*, "Is there anything more wonderful on earth, our marvelous planet, than the miracle of man?"[11]

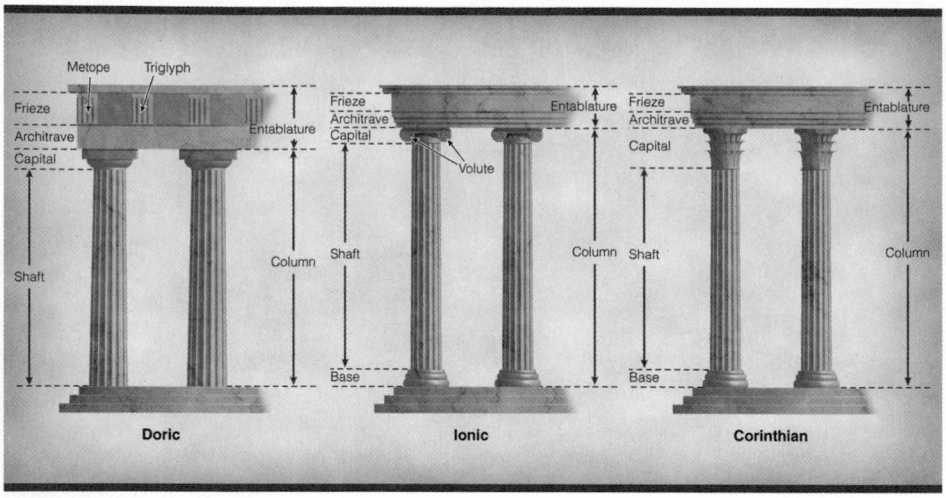

© Art Resource, NY

Doric, Ionic, and Corinthian Orders. The size and shape of a column constituted one of the most important aspects of Greek temple architecture. The Doric order, with plain capitals and no base, developed first in the Dorian Peloponnesus and was rather simple in comparison to the slender Ionic column, which had an elaborate base and spiral-shaped capitals, and the Corinthian column, which featured leaf-shaped capitals.

Greek comedy developed later than tragedy. The plays of Aristophanes (ar-is-STAH-fuh-neez) (c. 450–c. 385 B.C.E.), who used both grotesque masks and obscene jokes to entertain the Athenian audience, are examples of Old Comedy, which was used to attack or savagely satirize both politicians and intellectuals. In *The Clouds*, for example, Aristophanes characterized the philosopher Socrates as the operator of a thought factory where people could learn deceitful ways to handle other people. Of special importance to Aristophanes was his opposition to the Peloponnesian War. *Lysistrata*, performed in 411 B.C.E., at a time when Athens was in serious danger of losing the war, has a comic but effective message against the war.

© Adam Crowley/Photodisc/GettyImages

The Parthenon. The arts in Classical Greece were designed to express the eternal ideals of reason, moderation, symmetry, balance, and harmony. In architecture, the most important form was the temple, and the classic example of this kind of architecture is the Parthenon, built between 447 and 432 B.C.E. Located on the Acropolis in Athens, the Parthenon was dedicated to Athena, the patron goddess of the city, but it also served as a shining example of the power and wealth of the Athenian empire.

The Arts: The Classical Ideal

The arts of the Western world have been largely dominated by the artistic standards established by the Greeks of the Classical period. Classical Greek art did not aim at experimentation for experiment's sake but was concerned with expressing eternally true ideals. The subject matter was the human being, presented as an object of great beauty. The Classical style, based on the ideals of reason, moderation, balance, and harmony in all things, was meant to civilize the emotions.

In architecture, the most important structure was the temple dedicated to a god or goddess. Because Greek religious ceremonies were held at altars in the open air, temples were not used to enclose the faithful, as modern churches are. At the center of Greek temples were walled rooms that housed the statues of deities and treasuries in which gifts to the gods and goddesses were safeguarded. These central rooms were surrounded by a screen of columns that give Greek temples their open structure. The columns were originally made of wood but were

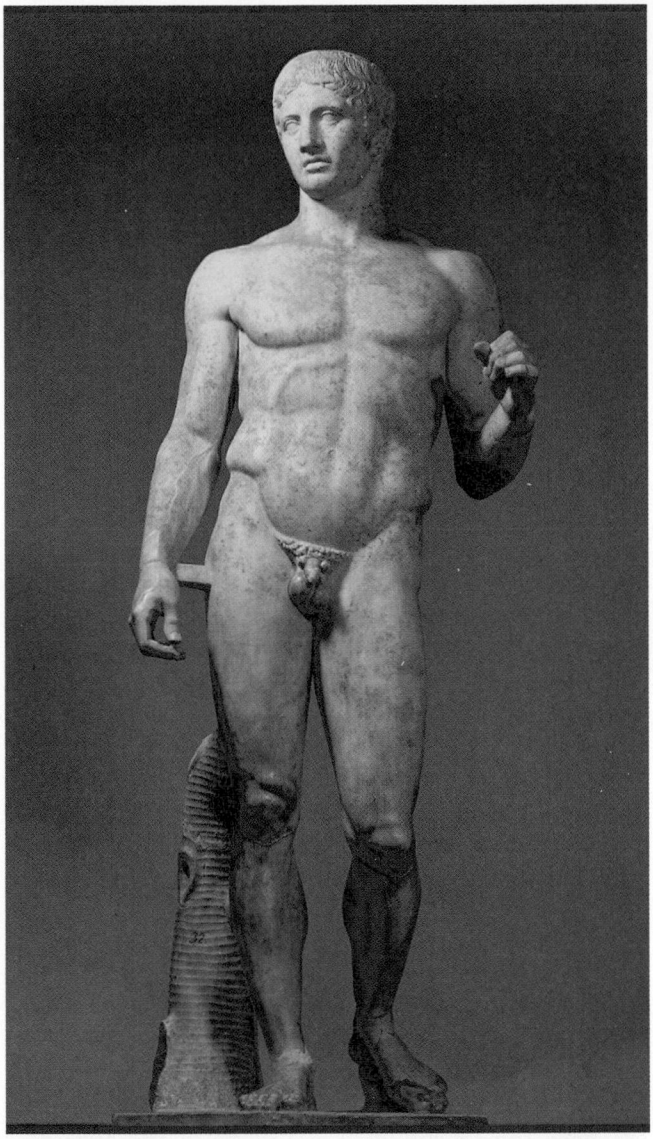

Museo Archeologico Nazionale, Naples//© Scala/Art Resource, NY

Doryphoros. This statue, known as the *Doryphoros*, or spear carrier, is a Roman copy of the original work by the fifth-century B.C.E. sculptor Polyclitus, who believed it illustrated the ideal proportions of the human figure. Classical Greek sculpture moved away from the stiffness of earlier figures but retained the young male nude as the favorite subject. The statues became more lifelike, with relaxed poses and flexible, smooth-muscled bodies. The aim of sculpture, however, was not realism but rather the expression of ideal beauty.

changed to limestone in the seventh century and to marble in the fifth century B.C.E.

Some of the finest examples of Greek Classical architecture were built in fifth-century Athens. The most famous building, regarded as the greatest example of the Classical Greek temple, is the Parthenon, built between 447 and 432 B.C.E. and consecrated to Athena, the patron goddess of Athens. The Parthenon typifies the principles of Classical architecture: the search for calm, clarity, and freedom from superfluous detail. The individual parts of the temple were constructed in accordance with certain mathematical ratios also found in nature. The architects' concern with these laws of proportion is paralleled by the attempt of Greek philosophers to understand the general laws underlying the natural world.

Greek sculpture also developed a Classical style that differed significantly from the artificial stiffness of earlier periods. Statues of the male nude, the favorite subject of Greek sculptors, now exhibited more relaxed attitudes; their faces were self-assured, their bodies flexible and smooth-muscled. Although the figures possessed natural features that made them lifelike, Greek sculptors sought to achieve not realism but a standard of ideal beauty. Polyclitus (pahl-ee-KLY-tuss), a fifth-century B.C.E. sculptor, wrote a treatise (now lost) on a canon of proportions that he illustrated in a work known as the *Doryphoros* (doh-RIF-uh-rohss). His theory maintained that the use of ideal proportions, based on mathematical ratios found in nature, could produce an ideal human form, beautiful in its perfected and refined features. This search for ideal beauty was the dominant feature of the Classical standard in sculpture.

The Greek Love of Wisdom

Philosophy is a Greek word that literally means "love of wisdom." Early Greek philosophers were concerned with the development of critical or rational thought about the nature of the universe and the place of divine forces in it. The **Sophists**, however, were a group of philosophical teachers in fifth-century Athens who rejected such speculation as foolish; they argued that understanding the universe was beyond the reach of the human mind. It was more important for individuals to improve themselves, so the only worthwhile object of study was human behavior. The Sophists were wandering scholars who sold their services as professional teachers to the young men of Greece, especially those of Athens. The Sophists stressed the importance of **rhetoric** (the art of persuasive speaking) in winning debates and swaying an audience, a skill that was especially valuable in democratic Athens. To the Sophists, there was no absolute right or wrong—what was right for one individual might be wrong for another. True wisdom consisted of being able to perceive and pursue one's own good. Because of these ideas, many people viewed the Sophists as harmful to society and especially dangerous to the values of young people.

One of the critics of the Sophists was Socrates (SAHK-ruh-teez) (469–399 B.C.E.). Because he left no writings of his own, we know about him only from his pupils, especially his most famous one, Plato. By occupation, Socrates was a stonemason, but his true love was philosophy. He taught a number of pupils, but not for pay, because he believed that the only goal of education was to improve the individual. He made use of a teaching method that is still known by his name. The **Socratic method** employs a question-and-answer technique to lead pupils to see things for themselves using their own reason. Socrates believed that all real knowledge is within each person; only critical examination was needed to call it forth. This was the real task of philosophy, since "the unexamined life is not worth living."

Socrates's questioning of authority led him into trouble. Athens had had a tradition of free thought and inquiry, but the defeat in the Peloponnesian War had created an environment much less tolerant of open debate and soul-searching. Socrates was accused of corrupting the youth of Athens by his teaching. An Athenian jury convicted him and sentenced him to death.

One of Socrates's disciples was Plato (PLAY-toh) (c. 429–347 B.C.E.), considered by many the greatest philosopher of Western civilization. Unlike his master Socrates, who wrote nothing, Plato wrote a great deal. He was fascinated with the question of reality: How do we know what is real? According to Plato, a higher world of eternal, unchanging Ideas or Forms has always existed. To know these Forms is to know truth. These ideal Forms constitute reality and can be apprehended only by a trained mind, which, of course, is the goal of philosophy. The objects that we perceive with our senses are simply reflections of the ideal Forms. Hence, they are shadows, while reality is found in the Forms themselves.

Plato's ideas of government were set out in a dialogue he titled *The Republic*. Based on his experience in Athens, Plato had come to distrust the workings of democracy. It was obvious to him that individuals could not attain an ethical life unless they lived in a just and rational state. Plato's search for the just state led him to construct an ideal state in which the population was divided into three basic groups. At the top was an upper class, a ruling elite composed of the philosopher-kings: "Unless either philosophers become kings in their countries or those who are now called kings and rulers come to be sufficiently inspired with a genuine desire for wisdom; unless, that is to say, political power and philosophy meet together . . . there can be no rest from troubles . . . for states, nor yet, as I believe, for all mankind."[12] The second group consisted of citizens who showed courage, the warriors who protected the society. All the rest made up the masses, essentially people driven not by wisdom or courage but by desire. They would be the producers of society—the artisans, tradesmen, and farmers.

In Plato's ideal state, each group fulfilled its assigned role, creating a society that functioned harmoniously The needs of the community, rather than the happiness of the individual, were Plato's concern, and he focused on the need for the guardians or rulers, above all, to be removed from any concerns for wealth or prestige so that they could strive for what was best for the community. To rid the guardians of these desires, Plato urged that they live together, forgoing both private property and family life. Plato believed that women, too, could be rulers; in this he departed radically from the actual practices of the Greek states.

Plato established a school at Athens known as the Academy. One of his pupils, who studied there for twenty years, was Aristotle (AR-iss-tot-ul) (384–322 B.C.E.), who later became a tutor to Alexander the Great. Aristotle did not accept Plato's theory of ideal Forms. Instead, he believed that by examining individual objects, we can perceive their form and arrive at universal principles; however, these principles do not exist as a separate higher world of reality beyond material things but are a part of things themselves. Aristotle's interests, then, lay in analyzing and classifying things based on thorough research and investigation. His interests were wide-ranging, and he wrote treatises on an enormous number of subjects: ethics, logic, politics, poetry, astronomy, geology, biology, and physics.

Like Plato, Aristotle wished for an effective form of government that would rationally direct human affairs. Unlike Plato, he did not seek an ideal state based on the embodiment of an ideal Form of justice; he tried to find the best form of government through a rational examination of existing governments. For his *Politics*, Aristotle examined the constitutions of 158 states and arrived at general categories for organizing governments. He identified three good forms of government: monarchy, aristocracy, and constitutional government. But based on his examination, he warned that monarchy can easily turn into tyranny, aristocracy into oligarchy, and constitutional government into radical democracy or anarchy. He favored constitutional government as the best form for most people.

Aristotle's philosophical and political ideas played an enormous role in the development of Western thought during the Middle Ages (see Chapter 9). So did his ideas on women. Aristotle believed that marriage was meant to provide mutual comfort between man and woman and contributed to the overall happiness of a community: "The community needs both male and female excellences or it can only be half-blessed."[13] Nevertheless, Aristotle maintained that women were biologically inferior to men: "A woman is, as it were, an infertile male. She is female in fact on account of a kind of inadequacy." Therefore, according to Aristotle, women must be subordinated to men, not only in the community but also in marriage: "The association between husband and wife is clearly an aristocracy. The man rules by virtue of merit, and in the sphere that is his by right; but he hands over to this wife such matters as are suitable for her."[14]

Greek Religion

Greek religion was intricately connected to every aspect of daily life; it was both social and practical. Public festivals, which originated in religious practices, served specific functions: boys were prepared to be warriors, girls to be mothers. Since religion was related to every aspect of life, citizens had to have a proper attitude toward the gods. Religion was a civic cult necessary for the well-being of the state. Temples dedicated to a god or goddess were the major buildings in Greek society.

Homer gave an account of the gods that provided Greek religion with a definite structure. Over a period of time, most Greeks came to accept a common religion based on twelve chief gods and goddesses who were thought to live on Mount Olympus, the highest mountain in Greece. Among the twelve were Zeus, the chief deity and father of the gods; Athena, goddess of wisdom and crafts; Apollo, god of the sun and poetry; Aphrodite, goddess of love; and Poseidon, brother of Zeus and god of the seas and earthquakes.

The twelve Olympian gods were common to all Greeks, who thus shared a basic polytheistic religion. Each *polis* usually singled out one of the twelve Olympians as a guardian deity of its community. Athena was the patron goddess of Athens, for example. Because it was desirable to have the gods look favorably on one's activities, ritual assumed enormous proportions in Greek religion. Prayers were often combined with gifts to the gods based on the principle "I give to you, the gods, so that you will give in return." Ritual also meant sacrifices of animals or food. Animals were burned on an altar in front of a temple or a small altar in front of a home.

Festivals also developed as a way to honor the gods and goddesses. Some of these (the Panhellenic celebrations) were important to all Greeks and were held at special locations, such as those dedicated to the worship of Zeus at Olympia or to Apollo at Delphi. Numerous events were held in honor of the gods at the great festivals, including athletic competitions to which all Greeks were invited. The first such games were held at the Olympic festival in 776 B.C.E. and then held every four years thereafter to honor Zeus. Initially, the Olympic contests consisted of foot races and wrestling, but later, boxing, javelin throwing, and various other contests were added.

The Greeks also had a great desire to know the will of the gods. To do so, they made use of the oracle, a sacred shrine dedicated to a god or goddess who revealed the future. The most famous was the oracle of Apollo at Delphi, located on the side of Mount Parnassus, overlooking the Gulf of Corinth. At Delphi, a priestess listened to questions while in a state of ecstasy that was believed to be induced by Apollo. Her responses were interpreted by the priests and given in verse form to the person asking questions. Representatives of states and individuals traveled to Delphi to consult the oracle of Apollo. States might inquire whether they should undertake a military expedition; individuals might raise such questions as "Heracleidas asks the god whether he will have offspring from the wife he has now." Responses were often enigmatic and at times even politically motivated. Croesus (KREE-suss), the king of Lydia in Asia Minor who was known for his vast wealth, sent messengers to the oracle at Delphi, asking whether he should go to war with the Persians. The oracle replied that if Croesus attacked the Persians, a mighty empire would be destroyed. Overjoyed to hear these words, Croesus made war on the Persians but was crushed by the enemy forces. A mighty empire was indeed destroyed—his own.

Daily Life in Classical Athens

The Greek city-state was, above all, a male community: only adult male citizens took part in public life. In Athens, this meant the exclusion of women, slaves, and foreign residents, or roughly 85 percent of the population in Attica. Of the 150,000 citizens in Athens, about 43,000 were adult males who exercised political power. Resident foreigners, who numbered about 35,000, received the protection of the laws but were also subject to some of the responsibilities of citizens, namely, military service and the funding of festivals. The remaining social group, the slaves, numbered around 100,000. Most slaves in Athens worked in the home as cooks and maids or toiled in the fields. Some were owned by the state and worked on public construction projects.

ECONOMY AND LIFESTYLE The Athenian economy was largely agricultural but highly diversified. Athenian farmers grew grains, vegetables, and fruit for local consumption; cultivated vines and olive trees for wine and olive oil, which were exportable products; and grazed sheep and goats for wool and milk products. Given the size of its population and the lack of abundant fertile land, Athens had to import between 50 and 80 percent of its grain, a staple in the Athenian diet. Trade was thus highly important to the Athenian economy. The building of the port at Piraeus and the Long Walls (a series of defensive walls nearly 5 miles long connecting Athens and Piraeus) created the physical conditions that made Athens the leading trade center in the Greek world of the fifth century B.C.E.

Artisans were more important to the Athenian economy than their relatively small numbers might suggest. Athens was the chief producer of high-quality painted pottery at the time. Other crafts had moved beyond the small workshop into the factory through the use of slave labor. The shield factory of Lysias, for example, employed 120 slaves. Public works projects also provided jobs for Athenians. The building program of Pericles, financed from the Delian League treasury, made possible the hiring of both skilled and unskilled labor.

The Athenian lifestyle was simple. Houses were furnished with necessities bought from artisans, such as beds, couches, tables, chests, pottery, stools, baskets, and cooking utensils. Wives and slaves made clothes and blankets at home. The Athenian diet was rather plain and relied on such basic foods as barley, wheat, millet, lentils, grapes, figs, olives, almonds, bread made at home, vegetables, eggs, fish, cheese, and chicken. Olive oil was widely used, not only for eating but also for lighting lamps and rubbing on the body after washing and exercise. Although country houses kept animals, they were used for reasons other than their flesh: oxen for plowing, sheep for wool, goats for milk and cheese.

FAMILY AND RELATIONSHIPS The family was an important institution in ancient Athens. Husband, wife, and children constituted the nuclear family, although other dependent relatives and slaves often shared the household. The family's primary social function was to produce new citizens. Strict laws stipulated that a citizen must be the offspring of a legally acknowledged marriage between two Athenian citizens whose parents were also citizens.

Women were citizens who could participate in most religious cults and festivals but were otherwise excluded from public life. They could not own property beyond personal items and always had a male guardian. The function of the Athenian woman as wife was very clear. Her foremost obligation was to bear children, especially male children who would preserve the family line. The marriage formula that Athenians used put it succinctly: "I give this woman for the procreation of legitimate children." A wife was also expected to take care of her family and her house, either doing the household work herself or supervising the slaves who did the actual work (see the box on p. 65).

Louvre, Paris//© Erich Lessing/Art Resource, NY

Women in the Loom Room. In Athens, women were considered citizens and could participate in religious cults and festivals, but they were barred from any political activity. Women were thought to belong in the home, caring for the children and the needs of the household. A principal activity of Greek women was the making of clothes. This scene from the side of a fifth-century B.C.E. Greek vessel shows one woman spinning while another holds a small hand loom.

Women were kept under strict control. Since they were married at fourteen or fifteen, they were taught about their responsibilities at an early age. Although many managed to learn to read and play musical instruments, they were often cut off from any formal education. And women were supposed to remain at home, out of sight, except when attending funerals or festivals. If they left the house, they were to be accompanied.

Male homosexuality was also a prominent feature of Athenian life. The Greek homosexual ideal was a relationship between a mature man and a young male. It is most likely that this was an aristocratic ideal and not one practiced by the common people. Although the relationship was frequently physical, the Greeks also viewed it as educational. The older male (the "lover") won the love of his "beloved" by his value as a teacher and by the devotion he demonstrated in training his charge. In a sense, this love relationship was seen as a way of initiating young men into the male world of political and military dominance. The Greeks did not feel that the coexistence of homosexual and heterosexual predilections created any special problems for individuals or their society.

OPPOSING VIEWPOINTS

Women in Athens and Sparta

In Classical Athens, a woman's place was in the home. She had two major responsibilities as a wife—bearing and raising children and managing the household. In the first selection, from a dialogue on estate management, Xenophon (ZEN-uh-fun) relates the instructions of an Athenian to his new wife. Although women in Sparta had the same responsibilities as women in Athens, they assumed somewhat different roles as a result of the Spartan lifestyle. The second, third, and fourth selections demonstrate these differences as seen in the accounts of three ancient Greek writers.

Xenophon, *Oeconomicus*

[Ischomachus addresses his new wife:] For it seems to me, dear, that the gods with great discernment have coupled together male and female, as they are called, chiefly in order that they may form a perfect partnership in mutual service. For, in the first place that the various species of living creatures may not fail, they are joined in wedlock for the production of children. Secondly, offspring to support them in old age is provided by this union, to human beings, at any rate. Thirdly, human beings live not in the open air, like beasts, but obviously need shelter. Nevertheless, those who mean to win stores to fill the covered place, have need of someone to work at the open-air occupations; since plowing, sowing, planting and grazing are all such open-air employments; and these supply the needful food. . . . For he made the man's body and mind more capable of enduring cold and heat, and journeys and campaigns; and therefore imposed on him the outdoor tasks. To the woman, since he had made her body less capable of such endurance, I take it that God has assigned the indoor tasks. And knowing that he had created in the woman and had imposed on her the nourishment of the infants, he meted out to her a larger portion of affection for newborn babes than to the man. . . .

Your duty will be to remain indoors and send out those servants whose work is outside, and superintend those who are to work indoors, and to receive the incomings, and distribute so much of them as must be spent, and watch over so much as is to be kept in store, and take care that the sum laid by for a year be not spent in a month. And when wool is brought to you, you must see that cloaks are made for those that want them. You must see too that the dry corn [grain] is in good condition for making food. One of the duties that fall to you, however, will perhaps seem rather thankless: you will have to see that any servant who is ill is cared for.

Xenophon, *Constitution of the Spartans*

First, to begin at the beginning, I will start with the begetting of children. Elsewhere those girls who are going to have children and are considered to have been well brought up are nourished with the plainest diet which is practicable and the smallest amount of luxury good possible; wine is certainly not allowed them at all, or only if well diluted. Just as the majority of craftsmen are sedentary, the other Greeks expect their girls to sit quietly and work wool. But how can one expect girls brought up like this to give birth to healthy babies? Lycurgus (see p. 54) considered slave girls quite adequate to produce clothing, and thought that for free women the most important job was to bear children. In the first place, therefore, he prescribed physical training for the female sex no less than for the male; and next, just as for men, he arranged competitions of racing and strength for women also, thinking that if both parents were strong their children would be more robust.

Aristotle, *Politics*

Now, this license of the [Spartan] women, from the earliest times, was to be expected. For the men were absent from home for long periods of time on military expeditions, fighting the war against the Argives and again against the Arkadians and Messenians; . . . . And nearly two-fifths of the whole country is in the hands of women, both because there have been numerous heiresses, and because large dowries are customary. And yet it would have been better to have regulated them, and given none at all or small or even moderate ones. But at present it is possible for a man to give an inheritance to whomever he chooses.

Plutarch, *Lycurgus*

Since Lycurgus regarded education as the most important and finest duty of the legislator, he began at the earliest stage by looking at matters relating to marriages and

(Continued)

(Opposing Viewpoints continued)

births. . . . For he exercised the girls' bodies with races and wrestling and discus and javelin throwing, so that the embryos formed in them would have a strong start in strong bodies and develop better, and they would undergo their pregnancies with vigor and would cope well and easily with childbirth. He got rid of daintiness and sheltered upbringing and effeminacy of all kinds, by accustoming the girls no less than the young men to walking naked in processions and dancing and singing at certain festivals, when young men were present and watching. . . . The nudity of the girls had nothing disgraceful in it for modesty was present and immorality absent, but rather it made them accustomed to simplicity and enthusiastic as to physical fitness, and gave the female sex a taste of noble spirit, inasmuch as they too had a share in valor and ambition.

Q In what ways were the lifestyles of Athenian and Spartan women the same? In what ways were they different? How did the Athenian and Spartan views of the world shape their conceptions of gender and gender roles, and why were those conceptions different?

Sources: Xenophon, *Oeconomicus*. Reprinted by permission of the publishers and the Trustees of the Loeb Classical Library from *Xenophon, Memorabilia and Oeconomicus*, Loeb Classical Library Vol. IV, translated by E.C. Marchant and O.J. Todd, Cambridge, Mass.: Harvard University Press, Copyright © 1930, by the President and Fellows of Harvard College. The Loeb Classical Library is a registered trademark of the President and Fellows of Harvard College. Xenophon, *Constitution of the Spartans*, Aristotle, *Politics*, and Plutarch, *Lycurgus*. From *Ancient Greece: Social and Historical Documents from Archaic Times to the Death of Socrates*. Edited by Matthew Dillon and Lynda Garland. London: Routledge, 1994, pp. 393–95. Copyright 1994 Matthew Dillon and Lynda Garland.

CHAPTER SUMMARY

The earliest Greek-speaking people migrated into Greece about 2000 B.C.E., and by 1600 B.C.E. they had established a Greek civilization, known as Mycenaean civilization from Mycenae, one of its major cities. After its collapse in the twelfth century B.C.E., Greece entered a Dark Age. With the end of the Dark Age around 800 B.C.E., the era of the *polis*, or city-state, began. The *polis* was a community of citizens ruled by its male citizens. The two most famous city-states were Sparta, a militaristic *polis* ruled by an oligarchy, and Athens, which became known for its democratic institutions in spite of the fact that many slaves and women had no political rights.

The Greek city-states flourished and reach their height in the Classical era of the fifth century B.C.E. The century began with the Persian Wars, which temporarily unified the Greeks, who were victorious against the powerful Persian Empire. But the growth of an Athenian empire led to a mighty conflict with Sparta—the Great Peloponnesian War—that weakened the Greek city-states and ultimately opened the door to an invasion by Philip II of Macedonia that put an end to their freedom in 338 B.C.E.

The civilization of the ancient Greeks was the fountainhead of Western culture. Socrates, Plato, and Aristotle established the foundations of Western philosophy. Herodotus and Thucydides created the discipline of history. Our literary forms are largely derived from Greek poetry and drama. Greek notions of harmony, proportion, and beauty have remained the touchstones for all subsequent Western art and architecture. A rational method of inquiry, so important to modern science, was conceived in ancient Greece. Many of our political terms are Greek in origin, and so are our concepts of the rights and duties of citizenship, especially as they were conceived in Athens, which gave the idea of democracy to the Western world. Especially during the Classical period, the Greeks raised and debated fundamental questions about the purpose of human existence, the structure of human society, and the nature of the universe that have concerned Western thinkers every since. Although the Greeks did not conceive of Western civilization as a cultural entity, their artistic, intellectual, and political contributions were crucial to the foundations of Western civilization.

All of these achievements came from a group of small city-states in ancient Greece. And yet there remains an element of tragedy about Greek civilization. For all of their brilliant accomplishments, the Greeks were unable to rise above the divisions and rivalries that caused them to fight each other and undermine their own civilization. Luckily, their contributions to Western civilization survived their political struggles.

CHAPTER TIMELINE

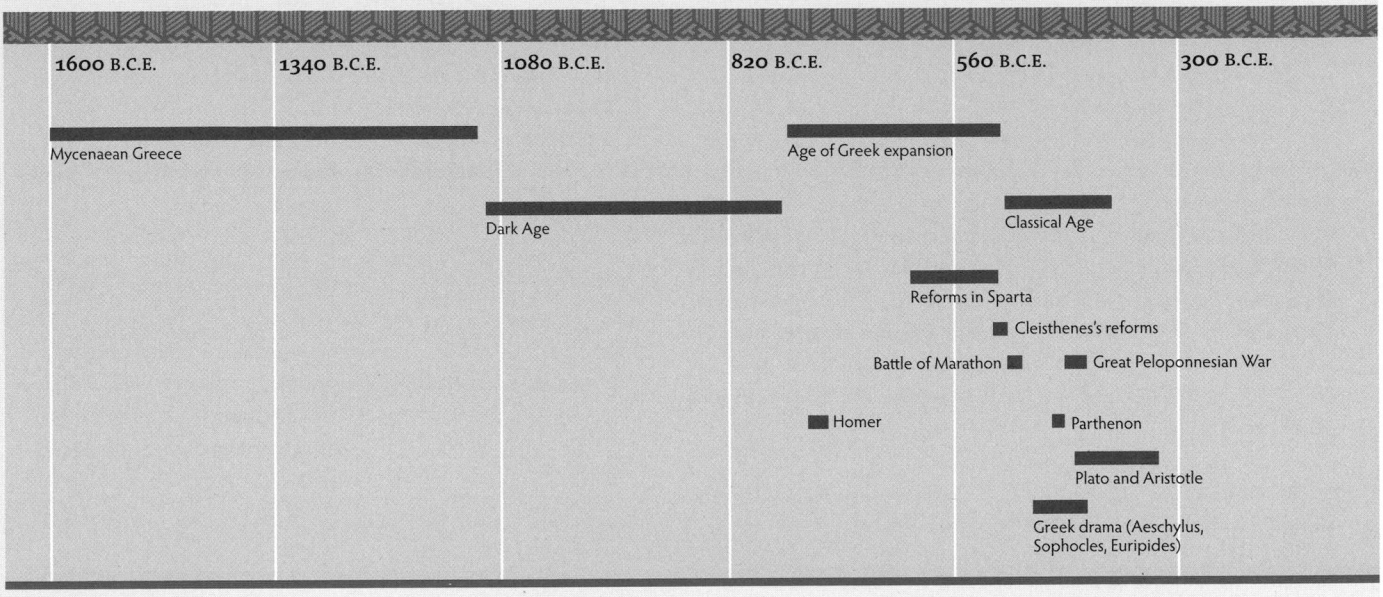

CHAPTER REVIEW

Upon Reflection

Q What was the *polis*, and why is it considered by many historians to be an important development in the political history of Western civilization?

Q Discuss the organization of the Athenian democratic system. Was it truly a democracy? In what ways was Athenian democracy similar to U.S. democracy? In what ways was it different?

Q The period of the Classical Age in Greece is known for its literary, artistic, and intellectual achievements. What basic characteristics of Greek culture are reflected in the major achievements of the Greeks in the writing of history, drama, the arts, and philosophy? What universal human concerns did these same achievements reflect?

Key Terms

polis (p. 50)
hoplites (p. 51)
tyrants (p. 52)
oligarchies (p. 52)
perioikoi (p. 53)
helots (p. 53)
Sophists (p. 61)
rhetoric (p. 61)
Socratic method (p. 62)

Suggestions for Further Reading

GENERAL WORKS Good general introductions to Greek history include **P. Cartledge, *The Cambridge Illustrated History of Ancient Greece*** (Cambridge, 1998), and **W. Donlan et al., *Ancient Greece: A Political, Social, and Cultural History*** (New York, 1998). On the Greek way of war, see **V. D. Hanson, *The Wars of the Ancient Greeks,*** rev. ed. (London, 2006).

EARLY GREEK HISTORY Early Greek history is examined in **O. Murray, *Early Greece,*** 2nd ed. (Cambridge, Mass., 1993). On the Trojan War, see **B. Strauss, *The Trojan War: A New History*** (New York, 2006).

ARCHAIC GREECE A good general work on Archaic Greece is **J. Hall, *History of the Archaic Greek World, c. 1200–479 B.C.E.*** (London, 2006). On Sparta, see **P. A. Cartledge, *Sparta and Laconia: A Regional History, 1300–362 B.C.E.***, 2nd ed. (London, 2002) and ***The Spartans*** (New York, 2003). On early Athens, see **R. Osborne, *Demos*** (New York, 1985). The Persian Wars are examined in **P. Green, *The Greco-Persian Wars*** (Berkeley, Calif., 1996).

CLASSICAL GREECE A general history of Classical Greece can be found in **P. J. Rhodes, *A History of the Greek Classical World, 478–323 B.C.*** (London, 2006). Valuable works on Athens include **D. Kagan, *Pericles of Athens and the Birth of Democracy*** (New York, 1991), and **K. A. Raaflaub et al., *Origins of Democracy in Ancient Greece*** (Berkeley, Calif., 2007). For a recent account of the Great Peloponnesian War, see **J. F. F. Lazenby, *The Peloponnesian War*** (New York, 2004).

GREEK CULTURE For a history of Greek art, see **M. Fullerton, *Greek Art*** (Cambridge, 2000). On Greek drama, see the general work by **J. De Romilly, *A Short History of Greek Literature*** (Chicago, 1985). On Greek history writing, see **D. Shanske, *Thucydides and the Philosophical Origins of History*** (Cambridge, 2006).

FAMILY AND GENDER ISSUES On the family and women, see **C. B. Patterson, *The Family in Greek History*** (New York, 1998); **E. Fantham et al., *Women in the Classical World*** (New York, 1994); and **S. Blundell, *Women in Ancient Greece*** (London, 1995).

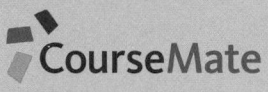

Visit the CourseMate website at **www.cengagebrain.com** for additional study tools and review materials for this chapter.

CHAPTER 4

Louvre (MA 2301), Paris/© Réunion des Musées Nationaux (Bulloz)/Art Resource, NY

Roman statuette of Alexander the Great wearing a helmet

The Hellenistic World

CHAPTER OUTLINE AND FOCUS QUESTIONS

Macedonia and the Conquests of Alexander

Q How was Alexander able to amass his empire, and what might his rule have been like if he had lived longer?

The World of the Hellenistic Kingdoms

Q What were the main features of the political and military organization of the Hellenistic kingdoms, and how did the new political systems differ from those of the Greek city-states? What were the main social developments in the Hellenistic world?

Culture in the Hellenistic World

Q What achievements in literature, art, science, and philosophy occurred during the Hellenistic period?

Religion in the Hellenistic World

Q Which religions were prominent during the Hellenistic period, and what does their popularity suggest about Hellenistic society?

CRITICAL THINKING

Q How was the Hellenistic period different from the Greek Classical Age?

IN 334 B.C.E., ALEXANDER THE GREAT led an army of Greeks and Macedonians into western Asia to launch his attack on the Persian Empire. Years of campaigning resulted in the complete defeat of the Persians, and in 327, Alexander and his troops pushed east into India. But two more years of fighting in an exotic and difficult terrain exhausted his troops, who rebelled and refused to go on. Reluctantly, Alexander turned back, leading his men across the arid lands of southern Persia. Conditions in the desert were appalling; the blazing sun and lack of water led to thousands of deaths. At one point, when a group of his soldiers found a little water, they scooped it up in a helmet and gave it to Alexander. Then, according to Arrian, an ancient Greek historian, Alexander, "with a word of thanks for the gift, took the helmet and, in full view of his troops, poured the water on the ground. So extraordinary was the effect of this action that the water wasted by Alexander was as good as a drink for every man in the army." Ever the great military leader, Alexander had found yet another way to inspire his troops.

Alexander the Great was the son of King Philip II of Macedonia, who in 338 B.C.E. had defeated the Greeks and established his control over the Greek peninsula. When Alexander became king after Philip's death, he led the Macedonians and Greeks on a spectacular conquest of the Persian Empire, opening the door to the spread of

Greek culture throughout the ancient Near East. Greek settlers poured into the Near Eastern lands to work as bureaucrats, traders, soldiers, and scholars. Alexander's triumph gave rise to a new series of kingdoms that blended the achievements of the eastern world with the cultural outlook and attitudes of the Greeks. We use the term **Hellenistic** to designate this new order. The Hellenistic world was the world of Greeks and non-Greek easterners, and it resulted, in its own way, in a remarkable series of accomplishments that are sometimes underestimated. They form the story of this chapter.

Macedonia and the Conquests of Alexander

Focus Question: How was Alexander able to amass his empire, and what might his rule have been like if he had lived longer?

While the Greek city-states were continuing their fratricidal warfare, to their north a new and ultimately powerful kingdom was emerging. The Macedonians were probably not Greek; scholars are still unsure whether the Macedonian language was an archaic dialect of Greek or an altogether separate language. The Greeks certainly viewed the Macedonians as barbarians, although the Greeks allowed them to participate as "Greeks" in the Olympic Games beginning in the fifth century B.C.E.

Unlike the Greeks, the Macedonians were mostly rural folk and were organized in tribes, not city-states. Not until the end of the fifth century B.C.E., during the reign of King Archelaus (c. 413–399 B.C.E.), did Macedonia emerge as an important kingdom. But his reign was followed by decades of foreign invasions and internal strife until King Philip II (359–336 B.C.E.) took control and turned Macedonia into the chief power of the Greek world.

Philip instituted military reforms that transformed Macedonia into a major military power. He created a new phalanx of infantrymen who were more lightly armed than Greek hoplites; each carried a smaller shield and a shorter sword. But the Macedonian infantryman's chief weapon was a long thrusting spear—18 feet in length, or twice as long as the Greek hoplite's spear. In this way, Macedonian infantrymen could impale an opposing hoplite force before the hoplites could even reach them. The Macedonian phalanx was supported by strong cavalry contingents that served to break the opposing line of battle and create disorder in the enemy's ranks. Philip also strengthened the bonds between the army and its leaders. Even the king shared in the dangers of battle, as is evident from his many wounds. Philip's new army defeated the Illyrians to the west and the Thracians to the north and east and was then drawn into the Greeks' interstate conflicts.

Philip and the Conquest of Greece

The Greeks had mixed reactions to Philip's growing strength. Many Athenians, especially the orator Demosthenes (duh-MAHSS-thuh-neez), came to have a strong distrust of the Macedonian leader's intentions. Demosthenes delivered a series of orations, known as the *Philippics*, in which he portrayed Philip as ruthless, deceitful, treacherous, and barbaric and called on the Athenians to undertake a struggle against him. Other Athenians, such as Isocrates (eye-SAHK-ruh-teez), a teacher of rhetoric, viewed Philip as a savior who would rescue the Greeks from themselves by uniting them (see the box on p. 71).

Demosthenes's repeated calls for action, combined with Philip's rapid expansion, finally spurred Athens to action. Allied with a number of other Greek states, Athens fought the Macedonians at the Battle of Chaeronea (ker-uh-NEE-uh), near Thebes, in 338 B.C.E. The Macedonian army crushed the Greeks, and Philip was now free to consolidate his control over the Greek peninsula. The independent Greek *polis*, long the basic political unit of the Greek world, came to an end as Philip formed an alliance of the Greek states that we call the Corinthian League because it met at Corinth. All members took an oath of loyalty: "I swear by Zeus, Earth, Sun, Poseidon, Athena, Ares, and all the gods and goddesses, I will abide by the peace, and I will not break the agreements with Philip the Macedonian, nor will I take up arms with hostile intent against any one of those who abide by the oaths either by land or by sea."[1]

Although Philip allowed the Greek city-states autonomy in domestic affairs, he retained the general direction of their foreign affairs. Philip insisted that the Greek states end their bitter rivalries and cooperate with him in a war against Persia. Before Philip could undertake his invasion of Asia, however, he was assassinated, leaving the task to his son Alexander.

Alexander the Great

Alexander was only twenty when he became king of Macedonia. The illustrious conqueror had in many ways been prepared for kingship by his father, who had taken Alexander along on military campaigns and had put him in command of the cavalry at the important Battle of Chaeronea. After his father's assassination, Alexander moved quickly to assert his authority, securing the Macedonian frontiers and

OPPOSING VIEWPOINTS

Demosthenes and Isocrates Address Philip of Macedonia

Among the Greeks, Demosthenes reacted most strongly to the growing strength and expansionary policies of the Macedonian king Philip II. Demosthenes delivered a series of orations to the Athenian assembly in which he portrayed Philip as a ruthless and barbaric man. The first selection is from Demosthenes's *Third Philippic*, delivered around 341 B.C.E. Isocrates saw Philip in a different light and appealed to him to lead both Greeks and Macedonians in a war against the Persians. The second selection is from Isocrates's *Address to Philip*, written in 346 B.C.E.

Demosthenes, *The Third Philippic*

I observe, however, that all men, and you first of all, have conceded to him something which has been the occasion of every war that the Greeks have ever waged. And what is that? The power of doing what he likes, of calmly plundering and stripping the Greeks one by one, and of attacking their cities and reducing them to slavery. Yet your hegemony in Greece lasted seventy-three years, that of Sparta twenty-nine, and in these later times Thebes too gained some sort of authority after the battle of Leuctra. But neither to you nor to the Thebans nor to the Spartans did the Greeks ever yet, men of Athens, concede the right of unrestricted action, or anything like it. On the contrary, when you, or rather the Athenians of that day, were thought to be showing a want of consideration in dealing with others, all felt it their duty, even those who had no grievance against them, to go to war in support of those who had been injured. . . . Yet all the faults committed by the Spartans in those thirty years, and by our ancestors in their seventy years of supremacy, are fewer, men of Athens, than the wrongs which Philip has done to the Greeks in the thirteen incomplete years in which he has been coming to the top—or rather, they are not a fraction of them. . . . Ay, and you know this also, that the wrongs which the Greeks suffered from the Spartans or from us, they suffered at all events at the hands of true-born sons of Greece, and they might have been regarded as the acts of a legitimate son, born to great possessions, who should be guilty of some fault or error in the management of his estate: so far he would deserve blame and reproach, yet it could not be said that it was not one of the blood, not the lawful heir who was acting thus. But if some slave or illegitimate bastard had wasted and squandered what he had no right to, heavens! How much more monstrous and exasperating all would have called it! Yet they have no such qualms about Philip and his present conduct, though he is not only no Greek, nor related to the Greeks, but not even a barbarian from any place that can be named with honor, but a pestilent knave from Macedonia, from where it was never yet possible to buy a decent slave.

Isocrates, *Address to Philip*

I chose to address to you what I have to say . . . I am going to advise you to champion the cause of concord among the Hellenes and of a campaign against the barbarians; and as persuasion will be helpful in dealing with the Hellenes, so compulsion will be useful in dealing with the barbarians. . . .

I affirm that, without neglecting any of your own interests, you ought to make an effort to reconcile Argos and Sparta and Thebes and Athens; for if you can bring these cities together, you will not find it hard to unite the others as well. . . .

You see how utterly wretched these states have become because of their warfare, and how like they are to men engaged in a personal encounter; for no one can reconcile the parties to a quarrel while their wrath is rising; but after they have punished each other badly, they need no mediator, but separate of their own accord. And that is just what I think these states also will do unless you first take them in hand. . . .

Now regarding myself, and regarding the course which you should take toward the Hellenes, perhaps no more need be said. But as to the expedition against Asia, we shall urge upon the cities which I have called upon you to reconcile that it is their duty to go to war with the barbarians.

Q What are Demosthenes's criticisms of Philip II? What appeal does Isocrates make to Philip? What do these documents tell you about the persistent factionalism and communal tensions within the Greek world? In light of subsequent events, who—Demosthenes or Isocrates—made the stronger argument? Why?

Sources: Demosthenes, *The Third Philippic*. Reprinted by permission of the publishers and the Trustees of the Loeb Classical Library from *Demosthenes*, Loeb Classical Library Vol. I, trans. by J.H. Vince, Cambridge, Mass.: Harvard University Press, copyright © 1930, by the President and Fellows of Harvard College. The Loeb Classical Library is a registered trademark of the President and Fellows of Harvard College. Isocrates, *Address to Philip*. Reprinted by permission of the publishers and the Trustees of the Loeb Classical Library from *Isocrates*, vol. 1, Loeb Classical Library Vol. 209, translated by George Norlin, Cambridge, Mass.: Harvard University Press, Copyright © 1928, by the President and Fellows of Harvard College. The Loeb Classical Library is a registered trademark of the President and Fellows of Harvard College.

© The Trustees of the British Museum (GR 1872.5-15.1), London/AHP/Art Resource, NY

Alexander the Great. This marble head of Alexander the Great was made in the second or first century B.C.E. The long hair and tilt of his head reflect the descriptions of Alexander in the literary sources of the time. This portrait shows a youthful and even godlike appearance. Alexander claimed to be descended from Heracles, a Greek hero worshiped as a god, and as pharaoh of Egypt, he gained recognition as a living deity. It is reported that one statue, now lost, showed Alexander gazing at Zeus. At the base of the statue were the words "I place the earth under my sway; you, O Zeus, keep Olympus."

smothering a rebellion in Greece. He then turned to his father's dream, the invasion of the Persian Empire.

THE CONQUESTS OF ALEXANDER There is no doubt that Alexander was taking a chance in attacking the Persian Empire. Although weakened in some respects, it was still a strong state. Alexander's fleet was inferior to the Persian navy, and his finances were shaky at best. In the spring of 334 B.C.E., Alexander entered Asia Minor with an army of some 37,000 men. About half were Macedonians, the rest Greeks and other allies. The cavalry, which would play an important role as a strike force, numbered about 5,000.

Alexander's first confrontation with the Persians, in a battle at the Granicus River in 334 B.C.E. (see Map 4.1), nearly cost him his life but resulted in a major victory. By spring 333, the entire western half of Asia Minor was in Alexander's hands, and the Ionian Greek cities of western Asia Minor had been "liberated" from the Persian oppressor. Meanwhile, the Persian king, Darius III, mobilized his forces to stop Alexander's army. Although the Persian troops outnumbered Alexander's, the Battle of Issus was fought on a narrow field that canceled the advantage of superior numbers and resulted in another Macedonian success. The Persian cause was certainly not helped when Darius made a spectacular exit from the battlefield before it was even clear who would win. After his victory at Issus in 333 B.C.E., Alexander turned south, and by the winter of 332, Syria, Palestine, and Egypt were under his domination. He took the traditional title of pharaoh of Egypt and founded the first of a series of cities named after him (Alexandria) as the Greek administrative capital of Egypt. It became (and remains today) one of Egypt's and the Mediterranean world's most important cities.

The next year, Alexander renewed his offensive, moving into the territory of the ancient Mesopotamian kingdoms and fighting a decisive battle with the Persians not far from Babylon. At Gaugamela (gaw-guh-MEE-luh), Alexander's men were clearly outnumbered by the Persian forces, which had established the battle site on a broad, open plain where their war chariots could maneuver to best advantage. Alexander was able to break through the center of the Persian line with his heavy cavalry, followed by the infantry. The battle turned into a rout, although Darius managed to escape. After his victory, Alexander entered Babylon and then proceeded to the Persian capitals at Susa and Persepolis, where he acquired the Persian treasuries and took possession of vast quantities of gold and silver.

By 330, Alexander was again on the march. After Darius was killed by one of his own men, Alexander took the title and office of the Great King of the Persians. But he was not content to rest with the spoils of the Persian Empire. During the next three years, he moved east and northeast, as far as modern Pakistan. By the summer of 327 B.C.E., he had entered India, which at that time was divided into a number of warring states. In 326 B.C.E., Alexander and his armies arrived in the plains of northwestern India. At the Battle of the Hydaspes River, Alexander won a brutally fought battle (see the box on p. 74). When Alexander made clear his determination to march east to conquer more of India, his soldiers, weary of campaigning year after year, mutinied and refused to go further. Alexander acceded to their demands and agreed to return, leading his troops through southern Persia across the Gedrosian Desert, where they suffered heavy losses from appalling desert conditions. Alexander and the remnants of his army went to Susa and then Babylon, where he planned still more campaigns. But in June 323 B.C.E., weakened from wounds, fever, and probably excessive alcohol, he died at the age of thirty-two.

Museo Archeologico Nazionale, Naples,//© Erich Lessing/Art Resource, NY

Alexander and Darius at the Battle of Issus. This late-second- or early-first-century B.C.E. mosaic from the floor of a Roman villa at Pompeii is thought to be a copy of a panel painting made by Philoxenos of Eretria about 310 B.C.E. The mosaic depicts the battle between Alexander and Darius III, king of Persia, at Issus in 333 B.C.E. Alexander is seen at the left on horseback, recklessly leading his troops into battle. Darius is shown in his chariot, already turning around to flee from the enemy.

© Cengage Learning

Alexander's empire
Battle sites
Alexander's route
0 300 600 900 Kilometers
0 300 600 Miles
MACEDONIA
Pella
Black Sea
Caspian Sea
Aral Sea
Jaxartes R.
Oxus R.
Caucasus Mts.
Aegean Sea
Granicus River 334 B.C.E.
Halys R.
Pergamum
Ancyra
Ephesus
LYDIA
Rhodes
Issus 333 B.C.E.
Gaugamela 331 B.C.E.
Tigris R.
Euphrates R.
Cyprus
SYRIA
MEDIA
Epiphaneia
PARTHIA
330 B.C.E.
329 B.C.E.
BACTRIA
327 B.C.E.
Hydaspes R.
Hydaspes River 326 B.C.E.
Mediterranean Sea
Tyre 332 B.C.E.
Damascus
Babylon 323 B.C.E. (Alexander's death)
Seleucia
Paraetonium
Alexandria
PALESTINE
Gaza
Susa
PERSIA
Arabian Desert
Siwah
EGYPT
Alexandria
Pasargadae 324 B.C.E.
Persepolis
Gedrosian Desert
Indus R.
INDUS VALLEY
Patala 325 B.C.E.
Nile R.
Persian Gulf
ARABIA
Red Sea
Arabian Sea

MAP 4.1 The Conquests of Alexander the Great. In just twelve years, Alexander the Great conquered vast territories. Dominating lands from west of the Nile to east of the Indus, he brought the Persian Empire, Egypt, and much of the Middle East under his control and laid the foundations for the Hellenistic world.

Q ***Approximately how far did Alexander and his troops travel during those twelve years?***

Alexander Meets an Indian King

In his campaigns in India, Alexander fought a number of difficult battles. At the Battle of the Hydaspes River, he faced a strong opponent in the Indian king Porus. After defeating Porus, Alexander treated him with respect, according to Arrian, Alexander's ancient biographer.

Arrian, *The Campaigns of Alexander*

Throughout the action Porus had proved himself a man indeed, not only as a commander but as a soldier of the truest courage. When he saw his cavalry cut to pieces, most of his infantry dead, and his elephants killed or roaming riderless and bewildered about the field, his behavior was very different from that of the Persian King Darius: unlike Darius, he did not lead the scramble to save his own skin, but so long as a single unit of his men held together, he fought bravely on. It was only when he was himself wounded that he turned the elephant on which he rode and began to withdraw. . . . Alexander, anxious to save the life of this great and gallant soldier, sent . . . [to him] an Indian named Meroes, a man he had been told had long been Porus's friend. Porus listened to Meroes's message, stopped his elephant, and dismounted; he was much distressed by thirst, so when he had revived himself by drinking, he told Meroes to conduct him with all speed to Alexander.

Alexander, informed of his approach, rode out to meet him. . . . When they met, he reined in his horse and looked at his adversary with admiration: he was a magnificent figure of a man, over seven feet high and of great personal beauty; his bearing had lost none of its pride; his air was of one brave man meeting another, of a king in the presence of a king, with whom he had fought honorably for his kingdom.

Alexander was the first to speak. "What," he said, "do you wish that I should do with you?" "Treat me as a king ought," Porus is said to have replied. "For my part," said Alexander, pleased by his answer, "your request shall be granted. But is there not something you would wish for yourself? Ask it." "Everything," said Porus, "is contained in this one request."

The dignity of these words gave Alexander even more pleasure, and he restored to Porus his sovereignty over his subjects, adding to his realm other territory of even greater extent. Thus, he did indeed use a brave man as a king ought, and from that time forward found him in every way a loyal friend.

Q What do we learn from Arrian's account about Alexander's military skills and Indian methods of fighting?

Source: From *THE CAMPAIGNS OF ALEXANDER THE GREAT* by Arrian, translated by Aubrey de Selincourt and revised with an introduction and notes by J.R. Hamilton (Penguin Classics 1958, Revised edition 1971). Copyright © the Estate of Aubrey de Selincourt, 1958. Introduction and Notes copyright © J. R. Hamilton, 1971. Reproduced by permission of Penguin Books Ltd.

CHRONOLOGY Macedonia and the Conquests of Alexander

Reign of Philip II	359–336 B.C.E.
Battle of Chaeronea; Philip II conquers Greece	338 B.C.E.
Reign of Alexander the Great	336–323 B.C.E.
Alexander invades Asia; Battle of Granicus River	334 B.C.E.
Battle of Issus	333 B.C.E.
Battle of Gaugamela	331 B.C.E.
Fall of Persepolis, the Persian capital	330 B.C.E.
Alexander enters India	327 B.C.E.
Battle of Hydaspes River	326 B.C.E.
Death of Alexander	323 B.C.E.

THE LEGACY OF ALEXANDER Alexander is one of the most puzzling great figures in history. Historians relying on the same sources give vastly different pictures of him. Some portray him as an idealistic visionary and others as a ruthless Machiavellian. No doubt he was a great military leader—a master of strategy and tactics, fighting in every kind of terrain and facing every kind of opponent. Alexander was a brave and even reckless fighter who was quite willing to lead his men into battle and risk his own life. His example inspired his troops to follow him into unknown lands and difficult situations. We know that he sought to imitate Achilles, the warrior-hero of Homer's *Iliad*, an important ideal in Greek culture. Alexander kept a copy of the *Iliad*—and a dagger—under his pillow. He also claimed to be descended from Heracles, the Greek hero who came to be worshiped as a god. Alexander also aspired to divine honors; as pharaoh of Egypt, he became a living

FILM & HISTORY

Alexander (2004)

Alexander is a product of director Oliver Stone's lifelong fascination with Alexander, the king of Macedonia who conquered the Persian Empire in the fourth century B.C.E. and initiated the Hellenistic era. Stone's epic film cost $150 million, which resulted in an elaborate and often visually beautiful film. Narrated by the aging Ptolemy (Anthony Hopkins), Alexander's Macedonian general who took control of Egypt after his death, the film tells the life of Alexander (Colin Farrell) through an intermix of battle scenes, scenes showing the progress of Alexander and his army through the Middle East and India, and flashbacks to his early years. Stone portrays Alexander's relationship with his mother, Olympias (Angelina Jolie), as instrumental in his early development while also focusing on his rocky relationship with his father, King Philip II (Val Kilmer). The movie elaborates on the major battle at Gaugamela in 331 B.C.E., where the Persian leader Darius is forced to flee, and then follows Alexander as he conquers the rest of the Persian Empire and continues east into India. After his troops begin to mutiny, Alexander finally returns to the Persian capital of Babylon, where he dies on June 10, 323 B.C.E.

The enormous amount of money spent on the film enabled Stone to achieve a stunning visual spectacle, but as history, the film leaves much to be desired. The character of Alexander is never developed in depth. He is shown at times as a weak character who is plagued by doubts over his own decisions and often seems obsessed with his desire for glory. Alexander is also portrayed as an idealistic leader who believed that the people he conquered wanted change, that he was "freeing the people of the world," and that Asia and Europe would grow together into a single community. But was Alexander an idealistic dreamer, as Stone apparently believes, or was he a military leader who, following the dictum that "fortune favors the bold," ran roughshod over the wishes of his soldiers in order to follow his dream and was responsible for mass slaughter in the process? The latter is a perspective that Stone glosses over, but Ptolemy probably expresses the more realistic notion that "none of us believed in his dream." The movie also does not elaborate on Alexander's wish to be a god. Certainly, Alexander aspired to divine honors; at one point he sent instructions to the Greek cities to "vote him a god." Stone's portrayal of Alexander is perhaps most realistic in presenting Alexander's drinking binges and his bisexuality, which was common in the Greco-Roman world. His marriage to Roxane (Rosario Dawson), daughter of a Bactrian noble, is shown, as well as his love for his lifelong companion Hephaestion (Jared Leto) and his sexual relationship with the Persian male slave Bagoas (Francisco Bosch).

Warner Bros/The Kobal Collection/Jaap Buitendijk

Alexander (Colin Farrell) on his horse Bucephalus, reviewing the troops before the Battle of Gaugamela.

The film contains a number of inaccurate historical details. Alexander's first encounters with the Persian royal princesses and Bagoas did not occur when he entered Babylon for the first time. Alexander did not kill Cleitas in India, and he was not wounded in India at the Battle of the Hydaspes River but at the siege of Malli. Specialists in Persian history have also argued that Persian military forces were much more disciplined than they are depicted in the movie.

god according to Egyptian tradition and at one point even sent instructions to the Greek cities to "vote him a god."

Regardless of his ideals, motives, or views about himself, one fact stands out: Alexander ushered in a new age, the Hellenistic era (see the Film & History feature above). The word *Hellenistic* is derived from a Greek word meaning "to imitate Greeks." It is an appropriate way, then, to describe an age that saw the extension of the Greek language and ideas to the non-Greek world of the Near East. Alexander's destruction of the Persian monarchy had extended Greco-Macedonian rule over an enormous area. It created opportunities for Greek engineers, intellectuals, merchants, soldiers, and administrators. While the Greeks on the mainland might remain committed to the ideals of their city-states, those who followed Alexander and his successors participated in a new political unity based on the principle of monarchy. Alexander had transformed his army from a Macedonian force into an international one, owing loyalty only to himself. His successors used force to establish military monarchies that dominated the Hellenistic world after his death. Autocratic power, based on military strength and pretensions of divine rule, became a regular feature of those Hellenistic monarchies and was among Alexander's political contributions to the Hellenistic world. His vision of empire no doubt inspired the Romans, who were the ultimate heirs of Alexander's legacy.

But Alexander also left a cultural legacy. As a result of his conquests, Greek language, art, architecture, and literature spread throughout the Near East. The urban centers of the Hellenistic Age, many founded by Alexander and his successors, became springboards for the diffusion of Greek culture. Alexander had established a number of cities and military colonies named Alexandria to guard strategic points and supervise wide areas. Most of the settlers were Greek mercenaries. It has been estimated that in the course of his campaigns, Alexander summoned 60,000 to 65,000 additional mercenaries from Greece, at least 36,000 of whom took up residence in the garrisons and new cities. While the Greeks spread their culture in the east, they were also inevitably influenced by eastern ways. Thus, Alexander's legacy became one of the hallmarks of the Hellenistic world: the clash and fusion of different cultures.

The World of the Hellenistic Kingdoms

Q Focus Questions: What were the main features of the political and military organization of the Hellenistic kingdoms, and how did the new political systems differ from those of the Greek city-states? What were the main social developments in the Hellenistic world?

The united empire that Alexander created by his conquests disintegrated after his death. All too soon, Macedonian military leaders were engaged in a struggle for power. By 300 B.C.E., any hope of unity was dead.

Hellenistic Monarchies

Eventually, four Hellenistic kingdoms emerged as the successors to Alexander (see Map 4.2). In Macedonia, the struggles for power led to the extermination of Alexander's dynasty. Not until 276 B.C.E. did Antigonus Gonatus (an-TIG-oh-nuss guh-NAH-tuss), the grandson of one of Alexander's generals, succeed in establishing the Antigonid (an-TIG-uh-nid) dynasty as rulers of Macedonia. The Antigonids viewed control of Greece as essential to their power but did not see outright conquest as necessary.

Another Hellenistic monarchy was founded by the general Seleucus (suh-LOO-kuss), who established the Seleucid (suh-LOO-sid) dynasty of Syria. This was the largest of the Hellenistic kingdoms and controlled much of the old Persian Empire from Turkey in the west to India in the east, although the Seleucids found it increasingly difficult to maintain control of the eastern territories. In fact, an Indian ruler named Chandragupta Maurya (chun-druh-GOOP-tuh MOWR-yuh) (324–301 B.C.E.) created a new Indian state, the Mauryan Empire, and drove out the Seleucid forces. The Seleucid rulers maintained relations with the Mauryan Empire, however. Trade was fostered, especially in such luxuries as spices and jewels.

A third Hellenistic kingdom came into being by freeing itself from the Seleucids. This was the kingdom of Pergamum (PURR-guh-mum) in western Asia Minor under the Attalid (AT-uh-lid) dynasty. In 133 B.C.E., the last member of the Attalid dynasty bequeathed his kingdom to Rome in his will.

The fourth Hellenistic monarchy was Egypt, which had come under the control of Ptolemy (TAHL-uh-mee), another Macedonian general. Named governor of Egypt after Alexander's death, Ptolemy had established himself as king by 305 B.C.E., founding the Ptolemaic (tahl-uh-MAY-ik) dynasty of pharaohs. Hellenistic Egypt lasted longer than all the other Hellenistic monarchies; it was not until the reign of Cleopatra VII, who allied herself with the wrong side in the Roman civil wars (see Chapter 5), that Egypt fell to the Romans in 30 B.C.E.

The Threat from the Celts

The Celts, also known as the Gauls, were a people who had occupied large areas of Europe north of the Alps during the early Iron Age (c. 800–500 B.C.E.), especially the region to the south and west of the Rhine River, west of the Alps, and north of the Pyrenees (a region known as Gaul).

At the end of the fifth century B.C.E., possibly as the result of overpopulation, Celtic peoples began to migrate south and east. One group sacked the city of Rome in 390 B.C.E. (see Chapter 5). After the death of Alexander the Great, other groups of Celts began to threaten the Hellenistic world.

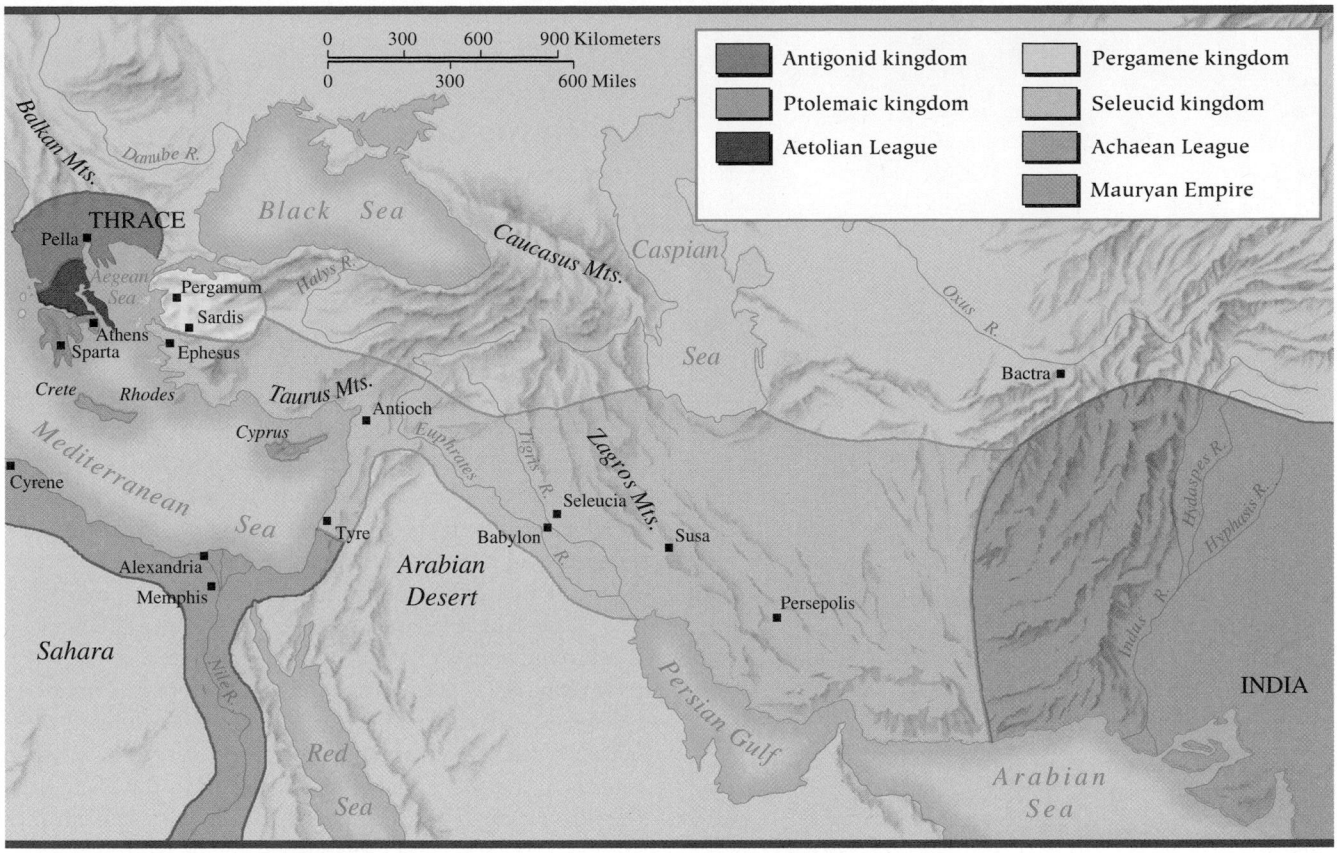

© Cengage Learning

MAP 4.2 The Hellenistic Kingdoms. Alexander died unexpectedly at the age of thirty-two and did not designate a successor. Upon his death, his generals struggled for power, eventually establishing four monarchies that spread Hellenistic culture and fostered trade and economic development.

Q *Which kingdom encompassed most of the old Persian Empire?*

Celts attacked Macedonia early in the third century B.C.E., as one ancient writer reported: "When the defeated Macedonians had fixed themselves within the walls of their cities, the victorious Brennus ravaged the fields of the whole of Macedonia with no one to oppose him."[2] Brennus also led a group of 30,000 Celts into Greece itself and caused considerable damage until being defeated in 278 B.C.E.

Other groups of Celts later attacked Asia Minor, where Attalus I defeated them in 230 B.C.E. After his victory, Attalus gained control of much of Asia Minor and declared himself king of Pergamum. Such attacks led the Celts to be feared everywhere in the Hellenistic world.

Political Institutions

The Hellenistic monarchies created a semblance of stability for several centuries, even though Hellenistic kings refused to accept the new status quo and periodically engaged in wars to alter it. At the same time, an underlying strain always existed between the new Greco-Macedonian ruling class and the native populations. Together, these factors generated a certain degree of tension that was never truly ended until the vibrant Roman state to the west stepped in and imposed a new order.

The Hellenistic kingdoms shared a common political system that represented a break with their Greek past. To the Greeks, monarchy was an institution for barbarians, associated in their minds with people like the Persians. Although they retained democratic forms of government in their cities, the Greeks of the Hellenistic world were forced to accept monarchy as a new fact of political life.

Although Alexander the Great had apparently hoped to fuse Greeks and easterners—he used Persians as administrators and encouraged his soldiers to marry easterners, as he himself did—Hellenistic monarchs relied primarily on Greeks and Macedonians to form the

Museo Nazionale Romano (Palazzo Altemps), Rome/© Araldo de Luca/CORBIS

A Celt and His Wife: Monument to the Victory of a Hellenistic King. This statue of a Celtic chieftain and his wife is a Roman copy of a bronze original that was part of a larger monument erected in the 220s B.C.E. to commemorate the victory of Attalus I of Pergamum over the Celts, a victory that gave Pergamum control over much of Asia Minor. In this scene, the defeated Celtic leader plunges a sword into his chest just after he has killed his wife to prevent her from being sold into slavery.

new ruling class. It has been estimated that in the Seleucid kingdom, for example, only 2.5 percent of the people in authority were non-Greek, and most of them were commanders of local military units. Those who did advance to important administrative posts had learned Greek (all government business was transacted in Greek) and had become Hellenized in a cultural sense. The policy of excluding non-Greeks from leadership positions, it should be added, was not due to the incompetence of the natives but to the determination of the Greek ruling class to maintain its privileged position. It was the Greco-Macedonian ruling class that provided the only unity in the Hellenistic world.

Hellenistic Cities

Cities played an especially important role in the Hellenistic kingdoms. Throughout his conquests, Alexander had founded a series of new cities and military settlements, and Hellenistic kings did likewise. The new population centers varied considerably in size and importance. Military settlements were meant to maintain order and might consist of only a few hundred men who were strongly dependent on the king. But there were also new independent cities with thousands of inhabitants. Alexandria in Egypt was the largest city in the Mediterranean region by the first century B.C.E.

Hellenistic rulers encouraged this massive spread of Greek colonists to the Near East because of their intrinsic value to the new monarchies. Greeks (and Macedonians) provided not only a recruiting ground for the army but also a pool of civilian administrators and workers who would contribute to economic development. Even architects, engineers, dramatists, and actors were in demand in the new Greek cities. Many Greeks and Macedonians were quick to see the advantages of moving to the new urban centers and gladly sought their fortunes in the Near East. Greeks of all backgrounds joined the exodus, at least until around 250 B.C.E., when the outpouring began to slow.

In the Hellenistic cities, the culture was primarily Greek. The political institutions of the cities were modeled after those of the Greek *polis*. Greeks of the Classical period would easily have recognized the councils, assemblies, and codes of law. The physical layouts of the new cities were also modeled after those of the Greek homeland. Using the traditional rectilinear grid, cities were laid out with temples, altars, and stone theaters.

Many of the new urban centers were completely dominated by Greeks while the native populations remained cut off from all civic institutions. The Greeks commissioned purely Greek sculpture, read literature of the Classical period, and had separate law courts for themselves. Complaints from resentful natives have survived. An Egyptian camel driver, for example, complained bitterly that he was not paid regularly because he did "not know how to behave like a Greek." Not only was it difficult for easterners to enter the ranks of the ruling class, but those who did so had to become thoroughly Hellenized. This often required alienation from their own culture.

The Greeks' belief in their own cultural superiority provided an easy rationalization for their political dominance of the eastern cities. But Greek control of the new cities of the Near East was also necessary because the kings frequently used the cities as instruments of government, enabling them to rule considerable territory without an extensive bureaucracy. At the same time, for security reasons, the Greeks needed the support of the kings. After all, the Hellenistic cities were islands of Greek culture in a sea of non-Greeks. The relationship between rulers and cities, therefore, was a symbiotic one that had serious consequences for the cities.

In the political system, religious practices, and architecture of their new cities, the Greeks tried to re-create the *poleis* of their homeland. But it was no longer possible to do so. The new cities were not autonomous entities and soon found themselves dependent on the power of the Hellenistic monarchies. Although the kings did not rule the cities directly, they restricted freedom in other ways. Cities knew they could not conduct an independent foreign policy and did not try to do so. The kings also demanded tribute, which could be a heavy burden.

The Greek cities of the Hellenistic era were the chief agents for the spread of Greek culture in the Near East, as far, in fact, as modern Afghanistan and India. These cities were also remarkably vibrant despite their subordination to the Hellenistic monarchies and continued to be a focal point for the loyalty of their citizens.

Economic Trends in the Hellenistic World

Agriculture was still of primary importance to both the native populations and the new Greek cities of the Hellenistic world. The Greek cities continued their old agrarian patterns. A well-defined citizen body owned land and worked it with the assistance of slaves. But these farms were isolated units in a vast area of land ultimately owned by the king or assigned to large estate owners and worked by native peasants dwelling in villages. Overall, then, neither agricultural patterns nor methods of production underwent significant changes.

Few new products or manufacturing methods were introduced during the Hellenistic era, but the centers of manufacturing shifted significantly. Industry spread from Greece to the east—especially to Asia Minor, Rhodes, and Egypt. New textile centers were set up at Pergamum, while glass and silver crafts were developed in Syria. Leading all cities in manufacturing was Alexandria in Egypt, which became the center for the production of parchment, textiles, linens, oil, metalwork, and glass.

Commerce expanded considerably in the Hellenistic era. Indeed, trading contacts linked much of the Hellenistic world. The decline in the number of political barriers encouraged more commercial traffic. Although Hellenistic monarchs still fought wars, the conquests of Alexander and the policies of his successors made possible greater trade between east and west. Two major trade routes connected the east with the Mediterranean. The central route was the major one: it proceeded by sea from India to the Persian Gulf and then up the Tigris River to Seleucia, which had replaced Babylon as the center for waterborne traffic from the Persian Gulf and overland caravan routes as well. Overland routes from Seleucia then led to Antioch and Ephesus. The southern route also wound its way from India by sea but went around Arabia and up the Red Sea to Petra or later Berenice. Caravan routes then led overland to Coptos on the Nile and from there to Alexandria and the Mediterranean.

An incredible variety of products were traded: gold and silver from Spain; iron from northern Armenia; salt from Asia Minor; timber from Macedonia; purple dye from Tyre; ebony, gems, ivory, and spices from India; frankincense (used on altars) from Arabia; slaves from Thrace, Syria, and Asia Minor; fine wines from Syria and western Asia Minor; olive oil from Athens; and numerous exquisite foodstuffs, such as the famous prunes of Damascus. The greatest trade, however, was in the basic staple of life—grain. The great exporting areas were Egypt, Sicily, and the Black Sea region.

New Opportunities for Women

One of the significant features of social life in the Hellenistic world was the emergence of new opportunities for women—at least, for upper-class women—especially in economic matters. Documents reveal increasing numbers of women involved in managing slaves, selling property, and making loans. Even then, legal contracts made by women had to include their official male guardians, although in numerous instances these men no longer played an important function but were listed only to satisfy legal requirements. In Sparta, women were allowed to own land and manage their own economic affairs. Because many of their husbands were absent or had died in war, many Spartan women became wealthy; females owned 40 percent of the land in Sparta.

Spartan women, however, were an exception, especially on the Greek mainland. Women in Athens, for example, still remained highly restricted and supervised. Although a few philosophers welcomed female participation in men's affairs, many philosophers rejected equality between men and women and asserted that the traditional roles of wives and mothers were most satisfying for women. In her treatise "On Chastity," Phintys (FIN-tiss) wrote that "serving as generals, public officials, and statesmen is appropriate for men," but "keeping house, remaining within, and taking care of husbands belongs to women."[3]

A New Autonomy for Women?

Upper-class women made noticeable gains in Hellenistic society. But even in the lives of ordinary women, a new assertiveness came to the fore despite the continuing domination of society by men. The first selection is taken from the letter of a wife to her husband, complaining about his failure to return home. In the second selection, a father complains that his daughter has abandoned him, contrary to Egyptian law providing that children who have been properly raised should support their parents.

Letter from Isias to Hephaistion, 168 B.C.E.

If you are well and other things are going right, it would accord with the prayer that I make continually to the gods. I myself and the child and all the household are in good health and think of you always. When I received your letter from Horos, in which you announce that you are in detention in the Serapeum at Memphis, for the news that you are well I straightway thanked the gods, but about your not coming home, when all the others who had been secluded there have come, I am ill-pleased, because after having piloted myself and your child through such bad times and been driven to every extremity owing to the price of wheat, I thought that now at least, with you at home, I should enjoy some respite, whereas you have not even thought of coming home nor given any regard to our circumstances, remembering how I was in want of everything while you were still here, not to mention this long lapse of time and these critical days, during which you have sent us nothing. As, moreover, Horos who delivered the letter has brought news of your having been released from detention, I am thoroughly ill-pleased. Notwithstanding, as your mother also is annoyed, for her sake as well as for mine please return to the city, if nothing more pressing holds you back. You will do me a favor by taking care of your bodily health. Farewell.

Letter from Ktesikles to King Ptolemy, 220 B.C.E.

I am wronged by Dionysios and by Nike my daughter. For though I raised her, my own daughter, and educated her and brought her to maturity, when I was stricken with bodily ill-health and was losing my eyesight, she was not minded to furnish me with any of the necessities of life. When I sought to obtain justice from her in Alexandria, she begged my pardon, and in the eighteenth year she swore me a written royal oath to give me each month twenty drachmas, which she was to earn by her own bodily labor. . . . But now corrupted by Dionysios, who is a comic actor, she does not do for me anything of what was in the written oath, despising my weakness and ill-health. I beg you, therefore, O King, not to allow me to be wronged by my daughter and by Dionysios the actor who corrupted her, but to order Diophanes the strategus [a provincial administrator] to summon them and hear us out; and if I am speaking the truth, let Diophanes deal with her corrupter as seems good to him and compel my daughter Nike to do justice to me. If this is done I shall no longer be wronged but by fleeing to you, O King, I shall obtain justice.

Q What specific complaints are contained in each letter? What do these complaints reveal about some women in the Hellenistic world? Judging by the content of these letters, what freedoms did Hellenistic women enjoy? How autonomous were they? Based on your knowledge of gender and gender roles in shaping earlier cultures, how did Hellenistic civilization differ in its conceptions of what was "proper" for men and women?

Source: From *The Hellenistic Period: Historical Sources in Translation* by Roger S. Bagnall and Peter Derow, pp. 281–82, 246. Copyright © 1981, 2004 by Roger S. Bagnall and Peter Derow. Published 2004 by Blackwell Publishing.

But the opinions of philosophers did not prevent upper-class women from making gains in areas other than the economic sphere (see the box above). New possibilities for females arose when women in some parts of the Hellenistic world were allowed to pursue education in the traditional fields of literature, music, and even athletics. Education, then, provided new opportunities for women: several female poets were active in the third century B.C.E., and there are instances of women involved in both scholarly and artistic activities.

The creation of the Hellenistic monarchies, which represented a considerable departure from the world of the

© The Art Archive/Jean Vinchon Numismatist Paris/Alfredo Dagli Orti

Queen Arsinoë II. Arsinoë II, sister and wife of King Ptolemy II, played an active role in Egyptian political affairs. Arsinoë was the first Egyptian queen whose portrait appeared on coins with her husband. This illustration of a gold coin from the kingdom of Egypt in 263 B.C.E. shows the queen's portrait on the reverse side of the coin.

polis, also gave new scope to the role played by the monarchs' wives, the Hellenistic queens. In Macedonia, a pattern of alliances between mothers and sons provided openings for women to take an active role in politics, especially in political intrigue. In Egypt, opportunities for royal women were even greater because the Ptolemaic rulers reverted to an Egyptian custom of kings marrying their own sisters. Of the first eight Ptolemaic rulers, four wed their sisters. Ptolemy II and his sister-wife Arsinoë (ahr-SIN-oh-ee) II were both worshiped as gods in their lifetimes. Arsinoë played an energetic role in government and was involved in the expansion of the Egyptian navy. She was also the first Egyptian queen whose portrait appeared on coins with her husband. Hellenistic queens also showed an intense interest in culture. They wrote poems, collected art, and corresponded with intellectuals.

Culture in the Hellenistic World

Focus Question: What achievements in literature, art, science, and philosophy occurred during the Hellenistic period?

Although the Hellenistic kingdoms encompassed vast areas and many diverse peoples, the Greeks provided a sense of unity as a result of the diffusion of Greek culture throughout the region. The Hellenistic era was a period of considerable cultural accomplishment in many areas—literature, art, science, and philosophy. Although these achievements occurred everywhere in the Hellenistic world, certain centers, especially the great cities of Alexandria and Pergamum, stood out. In both cities, cultural developments were encouraged by the rulers themselves. Rich Hellenistic kings had considerable resources with which to patronize culture.

The Ptolemies in Egypt made Alexandria an especially important cultural center. The library became the largest in ancient times, housing more than half a million scrolls. The museum (literally, "temple of the Muses") created a favorable environment for scholarly research. Alexandria became home to scholars of all kinds—poets, writers, philosophers, and scientists.

New Directions in Literature

The Hellenistic Age produced an enormous quantity of literature, most of which has not survived. Hellenistic monarchs, who held literary talent in high esteem, subsidized writers on a grand scale. The Ptolemaic rulers of Egypt were particularly lavish. The combination of their largess and the famous library drew a host of scholars and authors to Alexandria, including a circle of poets. Theocritus (thee-AHK-ruh-tuss) (c. 315–250 B.C.E.), originally a native of the island of Sicily, wrote "little poems" or idylls dealing with erotic subjects, lovers' complaints, and pastoral themes expressing his love of nature and its beauty.

In the Hellenistic era, Athens remained the theatrical center of the Greek world. As tragedy withered, writers invented New Comedy, which rejected political themes and sought only to entertain and amuse. The Athenian playwright Menander (muh-NAN-dur) (c. 342–291 B.C.E.) was perhaps the best representative of New Comedy. Plots were simple: typically, a hero falls in love with a not-really-so-bad prostitute who turns out eventually to be the long-lost daughter of a rich neighbor. The hero marries her, and they live happily ever after.

The Hellenistic period saw a great outpouring of historical and biographical literature. The chief historian of the Hellenistic Age was Polybius (puh-LIB-ee-uss) (c. 203–c. 120 B.C.E.), a Greek who lived for some years in Rome. He is regarded as second only to Thucydides among Greek historians. His major work consisted of forty books narrating the history of the "inhabited Mediterranean world" from 221 to 146 B.C.E. Only the first five books are extant, although long extracts from the other books survive. His history focuses on the growth of

Rome from a city-state to a vast empire. It is apparent that Polybius understood the significance of the Romans' achievement. He followed Thucydides in seeking rational motives for historical events. He also approached his sources critically and used firsthand accounts.

Hellenistic Art

In addition to being patrons of literary talent, the Hellenistic monarchs were eager to spend their money to beautify and adorn the cities in their states. The founding of new cities and the rebuilding of old ones provided numerous opportunities for Greek architects and sculptors. The structures of the Greek homeland—gymnasia, baths, theaters, and, of course, temples—lined the streets of these cities. Most noticeable in the temples was the use of the more ornate Corinthian order, which became especially popular during the Hellenistic Age (see the illustration in Chapter 3 on p. 60).

Sculptors were commissioned by Hellenistic kings and rich citizens. Thousands of statues, many paid for by the people honored, were erected in towns and cities all over the Hellenistic world. While maintaining the technical skill of the Classical period, Hellenistic sculptors moved away from the idealism of fifth-century classicism to a more emotional and realistic art, seen in numerous statues of old women, drunks, and little children at play.

Alexander the Great's incursion into the western part of India resulted in some Greek cultural influences there, especially during the Hellenistic era. In the first century B.C.E., Indian sculptors began to create statues of the Buddha. The impact of Greek sculpture was especially evident in the Buddhist statues made in Gandhara, which is today part of Pakistan.

Musei Capitolini, Rome/© Araldo de Luca/CORBIS

Drunken Old Woman. Hellenistic sculptors no longer tried to capture ideal beauty in their work, a quest that characterized Greek classicism, but moved toward a more emotional and realistic art. This statue of a drunken old woman is typical of this new trend in art. Old and haggard, mired in poverty, she struggles just to go on living.

A Golden Age of Science

The Hellenistic era witnessed a more conscious separation of science from philosophy. In Classical Greece, what we would call the physical and life sciences had been divisions of philosophical inquiry. Nevertheless, by the time of Aristotle, the Greeks had already established an important principle of scientific investigation—empirical research, or systematic observation, as the basis for generalization. In the Hellenistic Age, the sciences tended to be studied in their own right.

One of the traditional areas of Greek science was astronomy, and two Alexandrian scholars continued this exploration. Aristarchus (ar-iss-TAR-kus) of Samos (c. 310–230 B.C.E.) developed a *heliocentric* view of the universe, contending that the sun and the fixed stars remained stationary while the earth rotated around the sun in a circular orbit. This view was not widely accepted, and most scholars clung to the earlier *geocentric* view of the Greeks, which held that the earth was at the center of the universe. Another astronomer, Eratosthenes (er-uh-TAHSS-thuh-neez) (c. 275–194 B.C.E.), determined that the earth was round and calculated its circumference at 24,675 miles, within 200 miles of the actual figure.

A third Alexandrian scholar was Euclid (YOO-klid), who lived around 300 B.C.E. He established a school in Alexandria but is primarily known for his *Elements*. This was a systematic organization of the fundamental elements of geometry as they had already been worked out; it became the standard textbook of plane geometry and was used up to modern times.

The most famous of the scientists of the Hellenistic period, Archimedes (ahr-kuh-MEE-deez) (287–212 B.C.E.), came from the western Mediterranean region. Archimedes

© The Art Archive/Kanellopoulos Museum, Athens/Gianni Dagli Orti

National Museum of Pakistan, Karachi/© Borromeo/Art Resource, NY

Hellenistic Sculpture and a Greek-Style Buddha. Greek architects and sculptors were highly valued throughout the Hellenistic world. Shown on the left is a terra-cotta statuette of a draped young woman, made as a tomb offering near Thebes, probably around 300 B.C.E. The incursion of Alexander into the western part of India resulted in some Greek cultural influences there. During the first century B.C.E., Indian sculptors in Gandhara began to make statues of the Buddha in a style that combined Indian and Hellenistic artistic traditions, evident in the stone sculpture of the Buddha on the right. Note the wavy hair topped by a bun tied with a ribbon, also a feature of earlier statues of Greek deities. This Buddha is also seen wearing a Greek-style toga.

was especially important for his work on the geometry of spheres and cylinders, for establishing the value of the mathematical constant pi, and for creating the science of hydrostatics. Archimedes was also a practical inventor. He may have devised the so-called Archimedean screw, used to pump water out of mines and to lift irrigation water, as well as a compound pulley for transporting heavy weights. During the Roman siege of his native city of Syracuse, he constructed a number of devices to thwart the attackers. According to Plutarch's account, the Romans became so frightened "that if they did but see a little rope or a piece of wood from the wall, instantly crying out, that there it was again, Archimedes was about to let fly some device at them, they turned their backs and fled."[4]

Archimedes's accomplishments inspired a wealth of semilegendary stories. Supposedly, he discovered specific gravity by observing the water he displaced in his bath and became so excited by his realization that he jumped out of the water and ran home naked, shouting "Eureka!" ("I have found it!"). He is said to have emphasized the importance of levers by proclaiming to the king of Syracuse, "Give me a lever and a place to stand on, and I will move the earth." The king was so impressed that he encouraged Archimedes to lower his sights and build defensive weapons instead.

Philosophy: New Schools of Thought

While Alexandria and Pergamum became the renowned cultural centers of the Hellenistic world, Athens remained the prime center for philosophy and continued to attract the most illustrious philosophers, who chose to establish their schools there. Two entirely new schools of philosophical thought reinforced Athens's reputation as a philosophical center.

EPICUREANISM Epicurus (ep-i-KYOOR-uss) (341–270 B.C.E.), the founder of **Epicureanism** (ep-i-kyoo-REE-uh-ni-zum), established a school in Athens before 300 B.C.E. Epicurus's famous belief in a doctrine of pleasure began with his view of the world. Though he did not deny the existence of the gods, he did not believe they played any active role in the world. The universe ran on its own. This left human beings free to follow self-interest as a basic motivating force. Happiness was the goal of life, and the means to achieving it was the pursuit of pleasure, the only true good. But the pursuit of pleasure was not meant in a physical, hedonistic sense:

> When, therefore, we maintain that pleasure is the end, we do not mean the pleasures of profligates and those that consist in sensuality, as is supposed by some who are either ignorant or disagree with us or do not understand, but freedom from pain in the body and from trouble in the mind. For it is not continuous drinkings and revellings, nor the satisfaction of lusts, nor the enjoyment of fish and other luxuries of the wealthy table, which produce a pleasant life, but sober

The Stoic Ideal of Harmony with God

The Stoic Cleanthes (klee-AN-theez) (331–232 B.C.E.) succeeded Zeno as head of this school of philosophy. One historian of Hellenistic civilization has called this work by Cleanthes the greatest religious hymn in Greek literature. Certainly, it demonstrates that Stoicism, unlike Epicureanism, did have an underlying spiritual foundation. This poem has been compared to the great psalms of the Hebrews.

Cleanthes, *Hymn to Zeus*

Nothing occurs on the earth apart from you, O God,
nor in the heavenly regions nor on the sea,
except what bad men do in their folly;
but you know to make the odd even,
and to harmonize what is dissonant; to you the alien is akin.
And so you have wrought together into one all things that are good and bad,
So that there arises one eternal logos [rationale] of all things,
Which all bad mortals shun and ignore.
Unhappy wretches, ever seeking the possession of good things,
They neither see nor hear the universal law of God,
By obeying which they might enjoy a happy life.

Q Based on Cleanthes's poem, what are some of the beliefs of the Stoics? How do they differ from the beliefs of the Epicureans?

Source: From *Hellenistic Philosophy: Stoics, Epicureans, Sceptics*, Second Edition, A. A. Long. Copyright © 1986 by A. A. Long. Reprinted by permission of the University of California Press.

> reasoning, searching out the motives for all choice and avoidance, and banishing mere opinions, to which are due the greatest disturbance of the spirit.[5]

Pleasure was not satisfying one's desire in an active, gluttonous fashion but rather freedom from emotional turmoil and freedom from worry—the freedom that came from a mind at rest. To achieve this passive pleasure, one had to free oneself from public activity: "We must release ourselves from the prison of affairs and politics." They were too strenuous to give peace of mind. But this was not a renunciation of all social life, for to Epicurus, a life could be complete only when it was centered on the basic ideal of friendship: "Of all the things which wisdom acquires to produce the blessedness of the complete life, far the greatest is the possession of friendship."[6] Epicurus's own life in Athens was an embodiment of his teachings. He and his friends created their own private community where they could pursue their ideal of true happiness.

STOICISM Epicureanism was eventually overshadowed by another school of thought known as **Stoicism** (STOH-i-siz-um), which became the most popular philosophy of the Hellenistic world and later flourished in the Roman Empire as well. It was the product of a teacher named Zeno (335–263 B.C.E.), who came to Athens and began to teach in a public colonnade known as the Painted Portico (the *Stoa Poikile*—hence, *Stoicism*). Like Epicureanism, Stoicism was concerned with how individuals find happiness. But Stoics took a radically different approach to the problem. To them, happiness, the supreme good, could be found only in virtue, which meant essentially living in harmony with the divine will. To the Stoics, following the divine will meant abiding by the natural laws that the gods established to run the universe.

Virtuous living, then, was living in accordance with the laws of nature (see the box above). This led to the acceptance of whatever one received in life, since the divine will was by its very nature good. By accepting divine law, people mastered themselves and gained inner peace. Life's problems could not disturb such individuals, and they could bear whatever life offered (hence, our word *stoic*).

Unlike Epicureans, Stoics did not believe in the need to separate oneself from the world and politics. Public service was regarded as noble. The real Stoic was a good citizen and could even be a good government official. Because Stoics believed that a divine principle was present throughout the universe, each human being also contained a divine spark. This led to a belief in the oneness of humanity. The world constituted a single society of equal human beings. Although they were not equal in the outer world, all were free to follow the divine will (what was best for each individual). All persons, then, even slaves, though unfree in body, were equal at the level of the soul.

Epicureanism and especially Stoicism appealed to large numbers of people in the Hellenistic world. Both of these philosophies focused primarily on the problem of human happiness. Their popularity would suggest a fundamental change in the character of the Greek lifestyle. In the Classical Greek world, the happiness of individuals and the meaning of life were closely associated with the life of the *polis*. One found fulfillment within the community. In the Hellenistic kingdoms, although the *polis* continued to exist, the sense that one could find satisfaction and fulfillment through life in the *polis* had weakened. Not only did individuals seek new philosophies that offered personal happiness, but in the cosmopolitan world of the Hellenistic states, with their mixtures of peoples, a new openness to thoughts of universality could also emerge. For some people, Stoicism embodied this larger sense of community. The appeal of new philosophies in the Hellenistic era can also be explained by the apparent decline in certain aspects of traditional religion.

Religion in the Hellenistic World

Focus Question: Which religions were prominent during the Hellenistic period, and what does their popularity suggest about Hellenistic society?

When the Greeks spread throughout the Hellenistic kingdoms, they took their gods with them. Although the construction of temples may have been less important than in Classical times, there were still many demonstrations of a lively religious faith. But over time, there was a noticeable decline in the vitality of the traditional Greek Olympian religion. The civic cults based on the traditional gods no longer seemed sufficient to satisfy people's emotional needs.

This left Greeks receptive to the numerous religious cults of the eastern world. The Greeks were always tolerant of other existing religious institutions. Hence, in the Hellenistic cities of the Near East, the traditional civic cults of their own gods and foreign cults existed side by side. Alexandria had cults of the traditional Greek gods, Egyptian deities such as Isis and Horus, the Babylonian Astarte, and the Syrian Atargatis.

But for many people, the search for personal meaning remained unfulfilled. Among educated Greeks, the philosophies of Epicureanism and especially Stoicism offered help. Another source of solace came in the form of **mystery religions**.

Mystery Religions

Mystery cults, with their secret initiations and promises of individual salvation, were not new to the Greek world. But the Greeks of the Hellenistic era were strongly influenced by eastern mystery cults, such as those of Egypt, which offered a distinct advantage over the Greek mystery religions. The latter had usually been connected to specific locations (such as Eleusis), which meant that a would-be initiate had to undertake a pilgrimage in order to participate in the rites. In contrast, the eastern mystery religions were readily available since temples to their gods and goddesses were located throughout the Greek cities of the east.

All of the mystery religions were based on the same fundamental premises. Individuals could pursue a path to salvation and achieve eternal life by being initiated into a union with a savior god or goddess who had died and risen again. The ritual of initiation, by which the seeker identified with the god or goddess, was, no doubt, a highly emotional experience.

The Egyptian cult of Isis was one of the most popular of the mystery religions. The cult of Isis was very ancient but became truly universal in Hellenistic times. Isis was the goddess of women, marriage, and children, as one of her hymns states: "I am she whom women call goddess. I ordained that women should be loved by men: I brought wife and husband together, and invented the marriage contract. I ordained that women should bear children."[7] Isis was also portrayed as the giver of civilization who had brought laws and letters to all humankind. The cult of Isis offered a precious commodity to its initiates—the promise of eternal life. In many ways, the mystery religions of the Hellenistic era helped pave the way for Christianity.

Jews in the Hellenistic World

In observing the similarities among their gods and goddesses, Greeks and easterners tended to assume they were the same beings with different names, giving rise to a process of **syncretism**. But a special position was occupied in the Hellenistic world by the Jews, whose monotheistic religion was exclusive and did not accommodate this kind of fusion of spiritual beings.

The Jewish province of Judaea (which embraced the lands of the old Hebrew kingdom of Judah) was ruled by the Ptolemies until it fell under the control of the Seleucids by 200 B.C.E. In the reign of the Seleucid king

Antiochus (an-TY-uh-kuss) IV (175–163 B.C.E.), conflict erupted in Judaea. Hellenistic monarchs were generally tolerant of all religions, but problems with Rome prompted Antiochus to try to impose more cultural and religious unity throughout his kingdom. When he sent troops to Jerusalem and seized the Temple, he sparked a Jewish uprising led by Judas Maccabaeus (JOO-dus mak-uh-BEE-uss). The rebels succeeded in recapturing the Temple in 164 B.C.E., a joyous event that has been celebrated every year since in the Jewish holiday of Hanukkah (HAH-nuh-kuh) (Hebrew for "rededication"). Although the conflict in Judaea continued, the Seleucids ultimately made concessions and allowed the Jews considerable freedom.

But large numbers of Jews no longer lived in Judaea. There was a large Jewish population in Egypt, particularly in Alexandria, as well as Jewish settlements throughout the cities of Asia Minor and Syria. In each city, Jews generally set up a synagogue and formed a private association for worship as other foreigners did. But some city authorities also allowed the Jews to form a political corporation that gave them greater rights than other resident aliens. Most important, they gained the privilege to live by their own laws and their own judicial system. The Jews were not really interested in citizenship in the cities in which they resided because full citizenship required worship of the city's gods, anathema to Jews, who believed only in Yahweh.

CHAPTER SUMMARY

While the Greek city-states were pursuing their squabbles, to their north a new and powerful kingdom—Macedonia—emerged. Under King Philip II, the Macedonians undertook military reforms, defeated a Greek allied army in 338 B.C.E., and then consolidated their control over the Greek peninsula. Although the independent Greek city-states lost their freedom when they were conquered by the Macedonians, Greek culture did not die, and a new age, known as the Hellenistic era, eventually came into being.

That era began with the conquest of the Persian Empire by Alexander the Great, the young successor to his father, Philip II. Alexander, vowing to avenge the Persian attacks on Greece, crossed into Asia Minor with his army in 334 B.C.E. By 330 B.C.E., the Persian Empire had been defeated, but Alexander, never at rest, moved eastward into India, where a rebellion by his exhausted troops forced him to return to Babylon, where he died in 323 B.C.E. Though a great military leader, Alexander was not a good political administrator. He failed to establish any definite structure for the empire he had conquered, and four Hellenistic kingdoms eventually emerged as his successors.

Within those kingdoms, the resulting society is known as *Hellenistic*, meaning Greek-like or "to imitate Greeks." The Greek language became dominant throughout the area as Greek ideas became influential. Greek merchants, artists, philosophers, and soldiers found opportunities and rewards throughout the Near East, now a world of kingdoms rather than independent city-states.

The Hellenistic period was, in its own way, a vibrant one. New cities arose and flourished. New philosophical doctrines—such as Epicureanism and Stoicism—captured the minds of many. Sculptors and architects found many opportunities under the patronage of kings and other wealthy individuals. Significant achievements occurred in literature and science, as is evident in the work of Polybius, Euclid, and Archimedes. Greek culture spread throughout the Near East and made an impact wherever it was carried. In some areas of the Hellenistic world, queens played an active role in political life, and many upper-class women found new avenues for expressing themselves. Although the Hellenistic era achieved a degree of political stability, by the late third century B.C.E., signs of decline were beginning to multiply, and the growing power of Rome eventually endangered the Hellenistic world.

CHAPTER TIMELINE

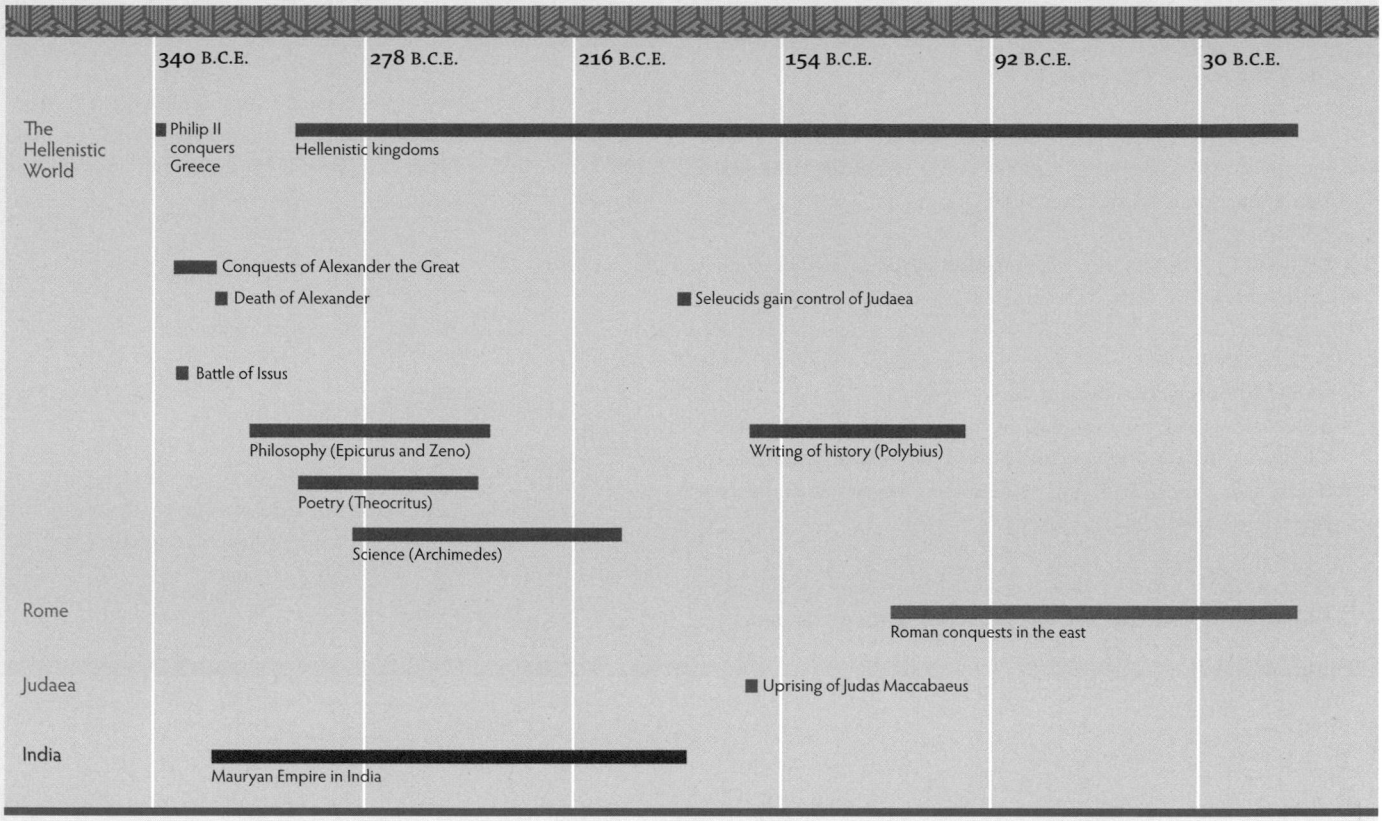

CHAPTER REVIEW

Upon Reflection

Q What role did Alexander the Great play in the creation of the Hellenistic kingdoms?

Q What were the main achievements of the Hellenistic kingdoms, and why did they fail to bring any lasting order to the lands of the Near East?

Q It can be said that the Hellenistic Age witnessed a shift from the *polis* to the *cosmopolis*. What does this mean, and what effects did it have on Greek life?

Key Terms

Hellenistic (p. 70)
Epicureanism (p. 83)
Stoicism (p. 84)
mystery religions. (p. 85)
syncretism (p. 85)

Suggestions for Further Reading

GENERAL WORKS For good introductions to the Hellenistic era, see **P. Green, *The Hellenistic Age: A Short History*** (New York, 2007), and **G. Shipley, *The Greek World After Alexander, 323–30 B.C.*** (London, 2000). See also **A. Erskine, ed., *A Companion to the Hellenistic World*** (Oxford 2005).

ALEXANDER There are considerable differences of opinion on Alexander the Great. Good biographies include **P. Cartledge, *Alexander the Great*** (New York, 2004); **P. Green, *Alexander of Macedon*** (Berkeley, Calif., 1991); and **G. M. Rogers, *Alexander: The Ambiguity of Greatness*** (New York, 2004).

HELLENISTIC MONARCHIES On the various Hellenistic monarchies, see the collection of essays in **C. Habicht, *Hellenistic Monarchies*** (Ann Arbor, Mich., 2006).

THE CELTS On the Celts, see the beautifully illustrated brief study by **J. Davies, *The Celts*** (London, 2000).

ECONOMIC AND SOCIAL TRENDS On economic and social trends, see **M. I. Finley, *The Ancient Economy,*** 2nd ed. (London, 1985). Hellenistic women are examined in two works by **S. B. Pomeroy, *Goddesses, Whores, Wives, and Slaves: Women in Classical Antiquity*** (New York, 1975), pp. 120–148, and ***Women in Hellenistic Egypt*** (New York, 1984).

HELLENISTIC CULTURE For a general introduction to Hellenistic culture, see **J. Onians, *Art and Thought in the Hellenistic Age*** (London, 1979). On art, see **J. J. Pollitt, *Art in the Hellenistic Age*** (New York, 1986). On Hellenistic philosophy, see **R. W. Sharples, *Stoics, Epicureans, and Skeptics: An Introduction to Hellenistic Philosophy*** (London, 1996).

HELLENISTIC RELIGION On various facets of Hellenistic religion, see **L. Martin, *Hellenistic Religions: An Introduction*** (New York, 1987), and **A. Tripolitis, *Religions of the Hellenistic-Roman Age*** (Ann Arbor, Mich., 2001).

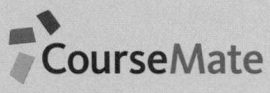

Visit the CourseMate website at **www.cengagebrain.com** for additional study tools and review materials for this chapter.

CHAPTER 5

Musei Capitolini, Rome//© Giraudon/The Bridgeman Art Library

Horatius defending the bridge as envisioned by Tommaso Laureti, a sixteenth-century Italian painter

The Roman Republic

CHAPTER OUTLINE AND FOCUS QUESTIONS

The Emergence of Rome

Q What impact did geography have on the history of Rome, and what influence did the Etruscans and Greeks have on early Roman history?

The Roman Republic (c. 509–264 B.C.E.)

Q What were the major political institutions of the Roman Republic, and what policies and institutions help explain the Romans' success in conquering Italy?

The Roman Conquest of the Mediterranean (264–133 B.C.E.)

Q How did Rome achieve its empire from 264 to 133 B.C.E., and what is meant by the phrase "Roman imperialism"?

Society and Culture in the Roman World

Q How did the acquisition of an empire affect Roman social and economic institutions, values and attitudes, and art and literature?

The Decline and Fall of the Roman Republic (133–31 B.C.E.)

Q What were the main problems Rome faced during the last century of the Republic, and how were they ultimately resolved?

CRITICAL THINKING

Q What did the Roman poet Horace mean when he wrote, "Captive Greece took captive her rude conqueror"?

EARLY ROMAN HISTORY is filled with legendary tales of the heroes who made Rome great. One of the best known is the story of Horatius at the bridge. Threatened by attack from the neighboring Etruscans, Roman farmers abandoned their fields and moved into the city, where they would be protected by the walls. One weak point in the Roman defenses, however, was a wooden bridge over the Tiber River. Horatius was on guard at the bridge when the Etruscans made a sudden assault, causing many Roman troops to throw down their weapons and flee. Horatius urged them to make a stand at the bridge to protect Rome; when they hesitated, as a last resort he told them to destroy the bridge behind him while he held the Etruscans back. Astonished at the sight of a single defender, the confused Etruscans threw their spears at Horatius, who caught them on his shield and barred the way. By the time the Etruscans had regrouped and were about to overwhelm the lone defender, the Roman soldiers brought down the bridge. When Horatius heard the bridge crash into the river behind him, he dived fully armed into the water and swam safely to the other side through a hail of arrows. Rome had been saved by the courageous act of a Roman who knew his duty and was determined to carry it out. Courage, duty, determination—these qualities would also serve the many Romans who believed that it was their mission to rule nations and peoples.

In the first millennium B.C.E., a group of Latin-speaking people established a small community on the plain of Latium on the Italian peninsula. This community, called Rome, was one of the numerous settlements founded by Latin-speaking peoples throughout Latium and the rest of Italy. Roman history is basically the story of the Romans' conquest of the plain of Latium, then Italy, and finally the entire Mediterranean region. Why were the Romans able to do this? The Romans made the right decisions at the right time; in other words, the Romans had political wisdom.

The Romans were also practical. Unlike the Greeks, who reserved their citizenship for small, select groups, the Romans often offered citizenship to the peoples they conquered, thus laying the groundwork for a strong, integrated empire. The Romans also did not hesitate to borrow ideas and culture from the Greeks. Roman strength lay in government, law, and engineering. The Romans knew how to govern people, establish legal structures, and construct the roads that took them to the ends of the known world. Throughout their empire, they carried their law, their political institutions, their engineering skills, and their Latin language. And even after the Romans were gone, those same gifts continued to play an important role in the continuing saga of Western civilization.

The Emergence of Rome

Q Focus Question: What impact did geography have on the history of Rome, and what influence did the Etruscans and Greeks have on early Roman history?

Italy is a peninsula extending about 750 miles from north to south (see Map 5.1). It is not very wide, however, averaging about 120 miles across. The Apennine Mountains traverse the peninsula from north to south, forming a ridge down the middle that divides west from east. Nevertheless, Italy has some fairly large fertile plains ideal for farming. Most important were the Po River valley in the north, probably the most fertile agricultural area; the plain of Latium (LAY-shee-um), on which Rome was located; and Campania (kam-PAY-nee-uh *or* kahm-PAHN-yuh), to the south of Latium. To the east of the Italian peninsula is the Adriatic Sea, and to the west, the Tyrrhenian Sea with the nearby large islands of Corsica and Sardinia. Sicily lies just west of the toe of the boot-shaped Italian peninsula. Geography had an impact on Roman history. Although the Apennines bisect Italy, they are less rugged than the mountain ranges of Greece and so did not divide the peninsula into many small isolated communities. Italy also possessed considerably more productive farmland than Greece and thus could support a large population. Rome's location was favorable from a geographic point of view. Located 18 miles inland on the Tiber River, Rome had access to the sea and yet was far enough inland to be safe from pirates. Built on seven hills, it was easily defended, and because it was situated where the Tiber could be readily forded, Rome became a natural crossing point for north-south traffic in western Italy. All in all, Rome had a good central location in Italy from which to expand.

Moreover, the Italian peninsula juts into the Mediterranean, making it an important crossroads between the western and eastern parts of that sea. Once Rome had unified Italy, involvement in affairs throughout the region was natural. And after the Romans had conquered their Mediterranean empire, Italy's central location made their task of governing that empire considerably easier.

The Greeks in Italy

We know little about the Indo-European peoples who moved into Italy during the second half of the second millennium B.C.E. By the first millennium B.C.E., other peoples had also settled in Italy, the two most notable being the Greeks and the Etruscans (i-TRUSS-kunz). The Greeks arrived on the Italian peninsula in large numbers during the age of Greek colonization (750–550 B.C.E.; see Chapter 3). Initially, the Greeks settled in southern Italy and gradually migrated around the coast and up the peninsula as far as Brindisi. They also occupied the eastern two-thirds of Sicily. Ultimately, the Greeks had considerable influence on Rome. They cultivated olives and grapes, passed on their alphabetic system of writing, and provided artistic and cultural models through their sculpture, architecture, and literature. Indeed, many historians view Roman culture as a continuation of Greek culture. Whereas Greek influence had initially touched Rome indirectly through the Etruscans, the Roman conquest of southern Italy and Sicily brought the Romans into direct contact with Greeks.

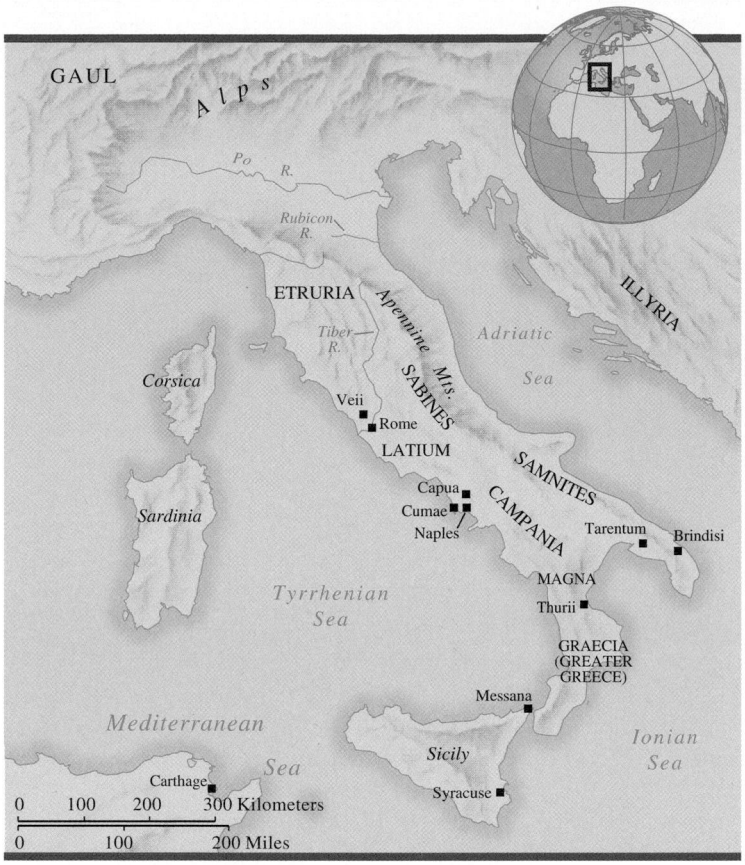

© Cengage Learning

MAP 5.1 Ancient Italy. Ancient Italy was home to several groups. Both the Etruscans in the north and the Greeks in the south had a major influence on the development of Rome.

Once Rome conquered the Etruscans, Sabines, Samnites, and other local groups, what aspects of the Italian peninsula helped make it defensible against outside enemies?

The Etruscans

The initial development of Rome was influenced most by the Etruscans, who had settled north of Rome in Etruria. The origins of the Etruscans are not clear, but after 650 B.C.E., they expanded in Italy and became the dominant cultural and economic force in a number of areas. To the north, they moved into north-central Italy, including the Po valley. To the south, according to Roman tradition and archaeological evidence, they controlled Rome and possibly all of Latium. From Latium they moved south and came into direct conflict with Greek colonists in southern Italy. In the sixth century B.C.E., the Etruscans were at the height of their power. But by 480 B.C.E., their power had begun to decline, and by 400 B.C.E., they were confined to Etruria itself. Later they were invaded by Celts from Gaul and then conquered by the Romans. But by then the Etruscans had made an impact. By transforming villages into towns and cities, they brought urbanization to northern and central Italy (as the Greeks had done in southern Italy). Rome was the Etruscans' most enduring product.

Early Rome

According to Roman legend, Rome was founded by twin brothers, Romulus and Remus, in 753 B.C.E., and archaeologists have found that around that time, there was a settlement consisting of huts on the tops of several of Rome's hills. The early Romans, basically a pastoral people, spoke Latin, which, like Greek, belongs to the Indo-European family of languages (see Table 2.1 in Chapter 2). The Roman historical tradition also maintained that early Rome (753–509 B.C.E.) had been under the control of seven kings and that two of the last three had been Etruscans. Some historians believe that the king list may have some historical accuracy. What is certain is that Rome did fall under the influence of the Etruscans for about one hundred years during the period of the kings.

By the beginning of the sixth century, under Etruscan influence, Rome began to change from a pastoral community to an actual city. The Etruscans were responsible for an outstanding building program. They constructed the first roadbed of the chief street through Rome—the Sacred Way—before 575 B.C.E. and oversaw the development of temples, markets, shops, streets, and

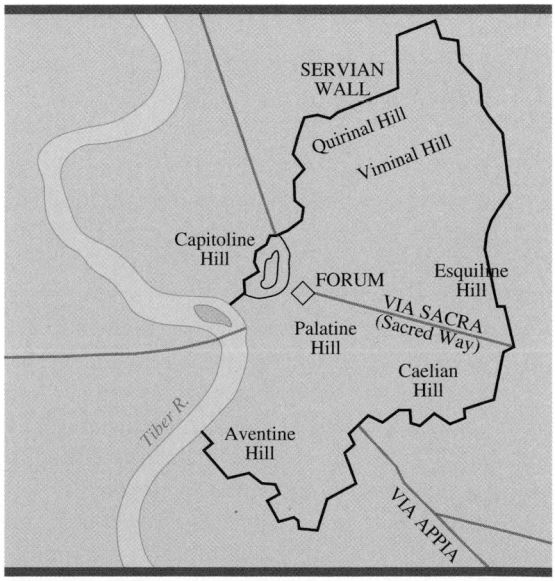

© Cengage Learning

The City of Rome

Tomb of the Leopards, Tarquinia, Italy//© Scala/Art Resource, NY

Etruscan Tomb Mural. Like the Egyptians, the Etruscans filled their tombs with furniture, bowls, and other objects of daily life, as well as murals showing diversions experienced in life and awaiting the dead in the afterlife. Shown in this mural found in an Etruscan tomb at Tarquinia are servants and musicians at a banquet. This mural was painted in the first half of the fifth century B.C.E.

houses. By 509 B.C.E., the date when the monarchy was supposedly overthrown and a republican form of government was established, a new Rome had emerged, essentially as a result of the fusion of Etruscan and native Roman elements. After Rome had expanded over its seven hills and the valleys in between, the Servian Wall was built to surround the city in the fourth century B.C.E.

The Roman Republic (c. 509–264 B.C.E.)

FOCUS QUESTION: What were the major political institutions of the Roman Republic, and what policies and institutions help explain the Romans' success in conquering Italy?

The transition from a monarchy to a republican government was not easy. Rome felt threatened by enemies from every direction and, in the process of meeting these threats, embarked on a course of military expansion that led to the conquest of the entire Italian peninsula. During this period of expansion in Italy, the Roman Republic developed political institutions that were in many ways determined by the social divisions that existed within the community.

The Roman State

In politics and law, as in conquest, the Romans took a practical approach and fashioned political institutions in response to problems as they arose. Hence, it is important to remember that the political institutions we will discuss evolved over a period of centuries.

POLITICAL INSTITUTIONS The chief executive officers of the Roman Republic were the **consuls** (KAHN-sulls) and **praetors** (PREE-turs). Two consuls, chosen annually, administered the government and led the Roman army into battle. They possessed ***imperium*** (im-PEE-ree-um), "the right to command." The office of the praetor was created in 366 B.C.E. The praetor also possessed *imperium* and could govern Rome when the consuls were away from the city and could also lead armies. The praetor's primary function, however, was the execution of justice. He was in charge of the civil law as it applied to Roman citizens. In 242 B.C.E., reflecting Rome's growth, another praetor was added to judge cases in which one or both parties were noncitizens.

As Rome expanded into the Mediterranean, additional praetors were established to govern the newly conquered provinces (two in 227, two more in 197). But as the number of provinces continued to grow, the Romans devised a new system in which ex-consuls and ex-praetors who had served their one-year terms were given the title of *proconsul* and *propraetor* and sent out as provincial governors. This demonstrates once again the Romans' practical solution to an immediate problem. It was reasonable to assume that officials with governmental experience would make good provincial administrators, although this was not always true in practice due to the opportunities for financial corruption in the provinces.

The Roman state also had administrative officials with specialized duties. **Quaestors** (QUES-turs) were assigned to assist the consuls and praetors in the administration of financial affairs. **Aediles** (EE-dylz) supervised the public games and watched over the the city's grain supply, a major problem for a rapidly growing urban community that relied on imported grain to feed its population.

The Roman **senate** held an especially important position in the Roman Republic. The senate, or council of elders, was a select group of about three hundred men who served for life. The senate was not a legislative body and could only advise the magistrates. The advice of the senate was not taken lightly, however, and by the third century B.C.E., it had virtually the force of law. No doubt the prestige of the senate's members furthered this development. But it also helped that the senate met continuously, whereas the chief magistrates changed annually and the popular assemblies operated slowly and met only periodically.

The Roman Republic possessed a number of popular assemblies. The most important was the **centuriate assembly**, essentially the Roman army functioning in its political role. Organized by classes based on wealth, it was structured in such a way that the wealthiest citizens always had a majority. The centuriate assembly elected the chief magistrates and passed laws. Another assembly, the council of the plebs, came into being in 471 B.C.E. as a result of the struggle of the orders (see the next section).

The government of the Roman Republic, then, consisted of three major elements. Two consuls and later other elected officials served as magistrates and ran the state. An assembly of adult males (the centuriate assembly), controlled by the wealthiest citizens, elected these officials, while the senate, a small group of large landowners, advised them. Thus, the Roman state was an aristocratic republic controlled by a relatively small group of privileged people.

THE STRUGGLE OF THE ORDERS: SOCIAL DIVISIONS IN THE ROMAN REPUBLIC The most noticeable element in the social organization of early Rome was the division between two groups—the **patricians** and the **plebeians** (pli-BEE-unz). The patrician class in Rome consisted of families who were descended from the original senators appointed during the period of the kings. Their initial prominence was probably due to their wealth as great landowners. Thus, the patricians constituted an aristocratic governing class. Only they could be consuls, magistrates, and senators. Through their patronage of large numbers of dependent clients, they could control the centuriate assembly and many other facets of Roman life.

The plebeians constituted the considerably larger group of "independent, unprivileged, poorer, and vulnerable men" as well as nonpatrician large landowners, less wealthy landholders, craftspeople, merchants, and small farmers. Although they were citizens, they did not possess the same rights as the patricians. Both patricians and plebeians could vote, but only the patricians could be elected to governmental offices. Both had the right to make legal contracts and marriages, but intermarriage between patricians and plebeians was forbidden. At the beginning of the fifth century B.C.E., the plebeians began a struggle to obtain both political and social equality with the patricians.

The plebeians' first success came in 494 B.C.E., when they withdrew physically from the state. The patricians, realizing that they could not defend Rome by themselves, were forced to compromise. Two new officials known as **tribunes of the plebs** were instituted (later the number was raised to five and then to ten). These tribunes were given the power to protect plebeians against arrest by patrician magistrates. Moreover, after a new popular assembly for plebeians only, called the **council of the plebs**, was created in 471 B.C.E., the tribunes became responsible for convoking it and placing proposals before it. If adopted, these measures became ***plebiscita*** (pleb-i-SEE-tuh) ("it is the opinion of the plebs"), but they were binding only on the plebeians, not the patricians. Nevertheless, the council of the plebs gave the plebeians considerable political leverage. After 445 B.C.E., when a law allowed patricians and plebeians to intermarry, the division between the two groups became less important. In the fourth century B.C.E., the consulship was opened to plebeians. The climax of the struggle between the orders came in 287 B.C.E. with the passage of a law that stipulated that all *plebiscita* passed by the council of the plebs had the force of law and were binding on the entire community, including patricians.

The struggle between the orders had a significant impact on the development of the Roman constitution. Plebeians achieved the right to hold the highest offices of state, to intermarry with the patricians, and to pass laws binding on the entire Roman community. Although the struggle had been long, the Romans had handled it by compromise, not violent revolution. Theoretically, by 287 B.C.E., all Roman citizens were equal under the law, and all could strive for political office. But in reality, as a result of the right of intermarriage, a select number of patrician and plebeian families formed a new senatorial aristocracy that came to dominate the political offices. The Roman Republic had not become a democracy.

The Roman Conquest of Italy

At the beginning of the Republic, Rome was surrounded by enemies, including the Etruscans to the north and the Sabines (SAY-bynz), Volscians (VOL-shunz), and Aequi

Cincinnatus Saves Rome: A Roman Morality Tale

There is perhaps no better account of how the virtues of duty and simplicity enabled good Roman citizens to prevail during the travails of the fifth century B.C.E. than Livy's account of Cincinnatus. He was chosen dictator, supposedly in 457 B.C.E., to defend Rome against the attacks of the Aequi. The position of dictator was a temporary expedient used only in emergencies; the consuls would resign, and a leader with unlimited power would be appointed for a fixed period (usually six months). In this account, Cincinnatus did his duty, defeated the Aequi, and returned to his simple farm in just fifteen days.

Livy, *The Early History of Rome*

The city was thrown into a state of turmoil, and the general alarm was as great as if Rome herself were surrounded. Nautius was sent for, but it was quickly decided that he was not the man to inspire full confidence; the situation evidently called for a dictator, and, with no dissenting voice, Lucius Quinctius Cincinnatus was named for the post.

Now I would solicit the particular attention of those numerous people who imagine that money is everything in this world, and that rank and ability are inseparable from wealth: let them observe that Cincinnatus, the one man in whom Rome reposed all her hope of survival, was at that moment working a little three-acre farm . . . west of the Tiber, just opposite the spot where the shipyards are today. A mission from the city found him at work on his land—digging a ditch, maybe, or plowing. Greetings were exchanged, and he was asked—with a prayer for divine blessing on himself and his country—to put on his toga and hear the Senate's instructions. This naturally surprised him, and, asking if all were well, he told his wife Racilia to run to their cottage and fetch his toga. The toga was brought, and wiping the grimy sweat from his hands and face he put it on; at once the envoys from the city saluted him, with congratulations, as Dictator, invited him to enter Rome, and informed him of the terrible danger of Municius's army. A state vessel was waiting for him on the river, and on the city bank he was welcomed by his three sons who had come to meet him, then by other kinsmen and friends, and finally by nearly the whole body of senators. Closely attended by all these people and preceded by his lictors he was then escorted to his residence through streets lined with great crowds of common folk who, be it said, were by no means so pleased to see the new Dictator, as they thought his power excessive and dreaded the way in which he was likely to use it.

[Cincinnatus proceeds to raise an army, march out, and defeat the Aequi.]

In Rome the Senate was convened by Quintus Fabius the City Prefect, and a decree was passed inviting Cincinnatus to enter in triumph with his troops. The chariot he rode in was preceded by the enemy commanders and the military standards, and followed by his army loaded with its spoils. . . . Cincinnatus finally resigned after holding office for fifteen days, having originally accepted it for a period of six months.

Q What values did Livy emphasize in his account of Cincinnatus? How important were those values to Rome's success? Why did Livy say he wrote his history?

Source: From THE EARLY HISTORY OF ROME: BOOKS I–V OF THE HISTORY OF ROME FROM ITS FOUNDATION by Livy, translated by Aubrey de Selincourt with an introduction by R. M. Ogilvie (Penguin Classics 1960, Reprinted with a new introduction 1971). Copyright © the Estate of Aubrey de Selincourt, 1960. Reproduced by permission of Penguin Books Ltd.

(EYE-kwee *or* EE-kwy) to the east and south. The Latin communities on the plain of Latium posed an even more immediate threat. If we are to believe Livy, one of the chief ancient sources for the history of the early Roman Republic, Rome was engaged in almost continuous warfare with its neighbors for the next hundred years.

In his account of these years, Livy provided a detailed narrative of Roman efforts. Many of Livy's stories were legendary in character and indeed were modeled on events in Greek history. But Livy, writing in the first century B.C.E., used such stories to teach Romans the moral values and virtues that had made Rome great. These included tenacity, duty, courage, and especially discipline (see the box above). Indeed, Livy recounted stories of military leaders who executed their own sons for leaving their place in battle, a serious offense, because the success of the hoplite infantry depended on maintaining a precise order. These stories had little basis in fact, but like the story of George Washington and the cherry tree in American history, they provided mythic images to reinforce Roman patriotism.

By 338 B.C.E., Rome had crushed the Latin states in Latium. During the next fifty years, the Romans waged a fierce struggle with the Samnites (SAM-nyts), a hill people from the central Apennines, some of whom had settled in Campania, south of Rome. Rome was again victorious. The conquest of the Samnites gave the Romans considerable control over a large part of Italy and also brought them into direct contact with the Greek communities of southern Italy. Soon after their conquest of the Samnites, the Romans were involved in hostilities with some of these Greek cities and by 267 B.C.E. had completed their conquest of southern Italy. After overrunning the remaining Etruscan states to the north in 264 B.C.E., Rome had conquered all of modern Italy except the extreme north.

To rule Italy, the Romans devised the Roman Confederation. Under this system, Rome allowed some peoples—especially the Latins—to have full Roman citizenship. Most of the remaining communities were made allies. They remained free to run their own local affairs but were required to provide soldiers for Rome. Moreover, the Romans made it clear that loyal allies could improve their status and even aspire to becoming Roman citizens. Thus, the Romans had found a way to give conquered peoples a stake in Rome's success.

The Romans' conquest of Italy can hardly be said to be the result of a direct policy of expansion. Much of it was opportunistic. The Romans did not hesitate to act when they felt that their security was threatened. And surrounded by potential enemies, Rome in a sense never felt secure. Yet once embarked on a course of expansion, the Romans pursued consistent policies that help explain their success. The Romans excelled at making wise diplomatic decisions. Though firm and even

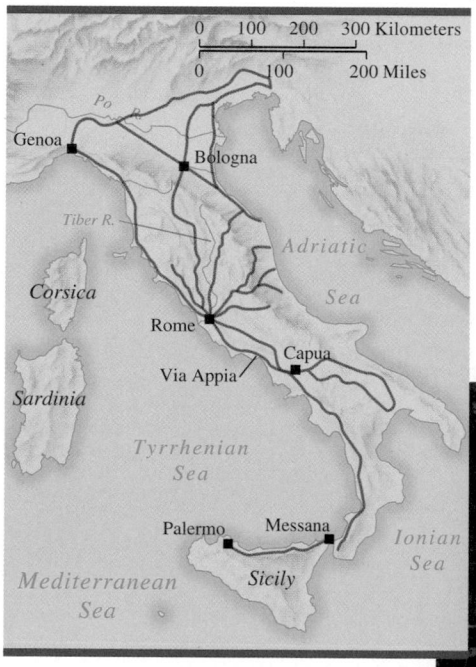

© Cengage Learning

Roman Roads in Italy. The Romans built a remarkable system of roads. After laying a foundation with gravel, which allowed for drainage, the Roman builders placed flagstones, closely fitted together. Unlike other peoples who built similar kinds of roads, the Romans did not follow the contours of the land but made their roads as straight as possible to facilitate communications and transportation, especially for military purposes. Seen here is a view of the Via Appia (Appian Way), built in 312 B.C.E. under the leadership of the censor and consul Appius Claudius (Roman roads were often named after the great Roman families who encouraged their construction). The Via Appia (shown on the map) was meant to make it easy for Roman armies to march from Rome to the newly conquered city of Capua, a distance of 152 miles.

© Jon Arnold Images Ltd (Walter Bibikow)/Alamy

cruel when necessary—rebellions were put down without mercy—they were also shrewd in extending citizenship and allowing autonomy in domestic affairs. In addition, the Romans were not only good soldiers but persistent ones as well. The loss of an army or a fleet did not cause them to quit but instead spurred them on to build new armies and new fleets. Finally, the Romans had a practical sense of strategy. As they conquered, they settled Romans and Latins in new communities outside Latium. By 264 B.C.E., the Romans had established fortified towns at all strategic locations. By building roads to these settlements and connecting them, the Romans assured themselves of an impressive military and communications network that enabled them to rule effectively and efficiently. Insisting on military service from the allies in the Roman Confederation, Rome essentially mobilized the entire military manpower of all Italy for its wars.

The Roman Conquest of the Mediterranean (264–133 B.C.E.)

Q FOCUS QUESTION: How did Rome achieve its empire from 264 to 133 B.C.E., and what is meant by the phrase "Roman imperialism"?

After their conquest of the Italian peninsula, the Romans found themselves face to face with a formidable Mediterranean power—Carthage (KAR-thij). Founded around 800 B.C.E. by Phoenicians from Tyre, Carthage in North Africa was located in a favorable position for commanding Mediterranean trade routes and had become an important commercial center (see Map 5.2). It had become politically and militarily strong as well. By the third century B.C.E., the Carthaginian empire included the coast of northern Africa, southern Spain, Sardinia, Corsica, and western Sicily. With its monopoly of western Mediterranean trade,

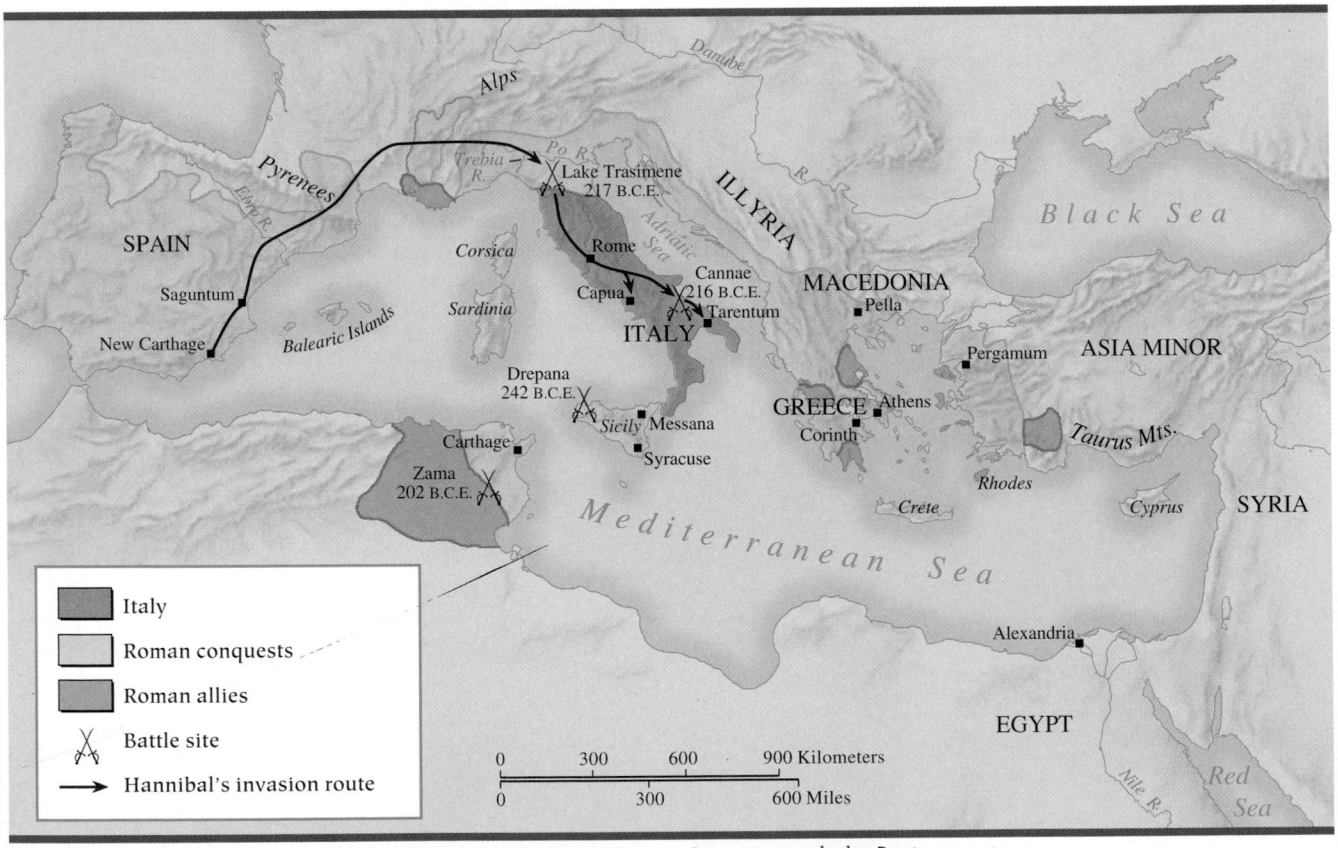

© Cengage Learning

MAP 5.2 Roman Conquests in the Mediterranean, 264–133 B.C.E. Beginning with the Punic Wars in 264 B.C.E., Rome expanded its holdings, first in the western Mediterranean at the expense of Carthage and later in Greece and western Asia Minor.

Q ***What aspects of Mediterranean geography, combined with the territorial holdings and aspirations of Rome and the Carthaginians, made the Punic Wars more likely?***

Carthage was the largest and richest state in the area. The presence of Carthaginians in Sicily made the Romans apprehensive about Carthaginian encroachment on the Italian coast. In 264 B.C.E., mutual suspicions drove the two powers into a lengthy struggle for control of the western Mediterranean.

The Struggle with Carthage

The First Punic (PYOO-nik) War (264–241 B.C.E.) (the Latin word for Phoenician was *Punicus)* began when the Romans decided to intervene in a struggle between two Sicilian cities by sending an army to Sicily. The Carthaginians, who considered Sicily within their own sphere of influence, deemed this just cause for war. In going to war, both sides determined on the conquest of Sicily. The Romans realized that the war would be long and drawn out if they could not supplement land operations with a navy and promptly developed a substantial fleet. The Carthaginians, for their part, had difficulty finding enough mercenaries to continue the fight. After a long struggle in which both sides lost battles in northern Africa and Sicily, a Roman fleet defeated the Carthaginian navy off Sicily, and the war quickly came to an end. In 241 B.C.E., Carthage gave up all rights to Sicily and had to pay an indemnity.

HANNIBAL AND THE SECOND PUNIC WAR After the war, Carthage made an unexpected recovery and extended its domains in Spain to compensate for the territory lost to Rome. The Carthaginians proceeded to organize a formidable land army in the event of a second war with Rome, because they realized that defeating Rome on land was essential to victory. When the Romans encouraged one of Carthage's Spanish allies to revolt against Carthage, Hannibal (HAN-uh-bul), the greatest of the Carthaginian generals, struck back, beginning the Second Punic War (218–201 B.C.E.).

This time the Carthaginians decided to bring the war home to the Romans by fighting in their own backyard. Hannibal went into Spain, marched east, and crossed the Alps with an army of 30,000 to 40,000 men and 6,000 horses and elephants. The Alps took a toll on the Carthaginian army, and most of the elephants did not survive the trip. The remaining army, however, posed a real threat. At Cannae (KAN-ny *or* KAN-nee) in 216 B.C.E., the Romans lost an army of almost 40,000 men. Rome seemed on the brink of disaster but refused to give up, raised yet another army, and gradually recovered. Although Hannibal remained free to roam in Italy, he had neither the men nor the equipment to lay siege to Rome or any other major cities. The Romans began to reconquer some of the Italian cities that had rebelled against Roman rule after Hannibal's successes. More important, the Romans pursued a strategy that aimed at undermining the Carthaginian empire in Spain. By 206 B.C.E., the Romans had pushed the Carthaginians out of Spain.

The Romans then took the war directly to Carthage. Late in 204 B.C.E., a Roman army under Publius Cornelius Scipio, later known as Scipio Africanus (SEE-pee-oh af-ree-KAY-nuss), moved from Sicily into northern Africa and forced the Carthaginians to recall Hannibal from Italy. At the Battle of Zama in 202 B.C.E., the Romans decisively defeated Hannibal's forces, and the war was essentially over. Eventually, Hannibal left Carthage and went to help Antiochus, the ruler of the Seleucid kingdom, in his struggle with Rome. After Antiochus made peace with the Romans, Hannibal fled to Bithynia, near the Black Sea. Pursued by the Romans, Hannibal declared, "Let us free Rome of her dread of one old man," and committed suicide.

By the peace treaty signed with the Romans in 201 B.C.E., Carthage lost Spain, agreed to pay an indemnity, and promised not to go to war without Rome's permission. Spain, like Sicily, Corsica, and Sardinia earlier, was made into a Roman province. Rome had become the dominant power in the western Mediterranean.

THE DESTRUCTION OF CARTHAGE But some Romans wanted even more. A number of prominent Romans, especially the conservative politician Cato, advocated the complete destruction of Carthage. Cato ended every speech he made to the senate with the words, "And I think Carthage must be destroyed." When the Carthaginians technically broke their peace treaty with Rome by going to war against one of Rome's North African allies who had been encroaching on Carthage's home territory, the Romans declared war. Roman forces undertook their third and last war with Carthage (149–146 B.C.E.). This time Carthage was no match for the Romans, who seized the opportunity to carry out the final destruction of Carthage in 146 B.C.E. The territory was made a Roman province called Africa.

The Eastern Mediterranean

During the Punic Wars, Rome had become acutely aware of the Hellenistic states of the eastern Mediterranean when the king of Macedonia made an alliance with Hannibal after the Roman defeat at Cannae. But Rome was preoccupied with the Carthaginians, and it was not until after the defeat of Carthage that Rome became involved in the world of Hellenistic politics as an advocate of the freedom of the Greek states. This support of the Greeks brought the Romans into conflict with both Macedonia and the kingdom of the Seleucids. Roman military victories and diplomatic negotiations rearranged the territorial boundaries of the Hellenistic kingdoms and brought the Greek states their freedom in 196 B.C.E. For fifty years, the

CHRONOLOGY The Roman Conquest of Italy and the Mediterranean	
Defeat of the Latin states	340–338 B.C.E.
Samnite Wars	343–290 B.C.E.
Defeat of Greek states in southern Italy	281–267 B.C.E.
First Punic War	264–241 B.C.E.
Second Punic War	218–201 B.C.E.
Battle of Cannae	216 B.C.E.
Completion of Roman seizure of Spain	206 B.C.E.
Battle of Zama	202 B.C.E.
Third Punic War	149–146 B.C.E.
Incorporation of Macedonia as a Roman province	148 B.C.E.
Destruction of Carthage	146 B.C.E.
Roman acquisition of Pergamum	133 B.C.E.

Romans tried to be a power broker in the affairs of the Greeks without direct control of their lands. When the effort failed, the Romans changed their policy. Macedonia was made a Roman province in 148 B.C.E., and when some of the Greek states rose in revolt against Rome's restrictive policies, Rome acted decisively. The city of Corinth, leader of the revolt, was destroyed in 146 B.C.E. to teach the Greeks a lesson, and Greece was placed under the control of the Roman governor of Macedonia. Thirteen years later, in 133 B.C.E., the king of Pergamum deeded his kingdom to Rome, giving Rome its first province in Asia. Rome was now master of the Mediterranean Sea.

The Nature of Roman Imperialism

Rome's empire was built in three stages: the conquest of Italy, the conflict with Carthage and expansion into the western Mediterranean, and the involvement with and domination of the Hellenistic kingdoms in the eastern Mediterranean. The Romans did not have a master plan for the creation of an empire; as in Italy, much of their continued expansion was opportunistic, carried out in response to perceived threats to their security. The more they expanded, the more threats to their security appeared on the horizon, involving them in yet more conflicts. Indeed, the Romans liked to portray themselves as declaring war only for defensive reasons or to protect allies. That is only part of the story, however. It is likely, as some historians have suggested, that at some point a group of Roman aristocratic leaders emerged who favored expansion both for the glory it offered and for the economic benefits it provided. Certainly, by the second century B.C.E., aristocratic senators perceived new opportunities for lucrative foreign commands, enormous spoils of war, and an abundant supply of slave labor for their growing landed estates. By that same time, the destruction of Corinth and Carthage indicated that Roman imperialism had become more arrogant and brutal as well. Rome's foreign success also had enormous repercussions for the internal development of the Roman Republic.

Evolution of the Roman Army

By the fourth century B.C.E., the Roman army consisted of four legions, each made up of 4,000 to 5,000 men; each legion had about 300 cavalry and the rest infantry. The infantry consisted of three lines of battle. The *hastati* (hahs-TAH-tee) (spearmen), made up of the youngest recruits, formed the front line; they were armed with heavy spears and short swords and were protected by a large oval shield, helmet, breastplate, and greaves (shin guards). The *principes* (prin-KI-pays *or* prin-SI-pays) (chief men), armed and protected like the *hastati*, formed the second line. The third line of battle was formed by the *triarii* (tri-AR-ee-ee) (third-rank men), who knelt behind the first two lines, ready to move up and fill any gaps. A fourth group of troops, poor citizens who wore cloaks but no armor and were lightly armed, functioned as skirmishers who usually returned to the rear lines after their initial contact with the enemy to form backup reserves.

In the early Republic, the army was recruited from citizens between the ages of eighteen and forty-six who had the resources to equip themselves for battle. Since most of them were farmers, they enrolled for only a year, campaigned during the summer months, and returned home in time for the fall harvest. Later, during the Punic Wars of the third century B.C.E., the period of service had to be extended, although this was resisted by farmers whose livelihoods could be severely threatened by a long absence. Nevertheless, after the disastrous defeat at Cannae in 216 B.C.E., the Romans were forced to recruit larger armies, and the number of legions rose to twenty-five.

In the early centuries of the Republic, then, the Roman army was basically a citizen army led by the Republic's elected magistrates. The ancient historian Polybius believed that the Roman army was more successful than others because it was an army of citizens who wanted to defend their homeland. Roman military success may also have been due to the aggressive behavior of the Roman military leaders, although this could be detrimental at sea. Major changes in recruitment would not come until the first century B.C.E. with the military reforms of Marius (see "A New Role for the Roman Army: Marius and Sulla" later in this chapter).

© The Art Archive/Museo della Civiltà Romana, Rome/Gianni Dagli Orti

Bibliothèque Nationale (FA-5853113), Paris/© Roger-Viollet/The Image Works

Roman Legionaries. Roman legionaries, famed for their courage and tenacity, made possible Roman domination of the Mediterranean Sea. At the time of the Punic Wars, a Roman legionary wore chain-mail armor and a plumed helmet and carried an oval shield, as in the bronze statue from the second or first century B.C.E. Heavy javelins and swords were their major weapons. This equipment remained standard until the time of Julius Caesar. The illustration on the right shows a Roman legion on the march from Trajan's column, erected in the second century C.E.

Society and Culture in the Roman World

Q Focus Question: How did the acquisition of an empire affect Roman social and economic institutions, values and attitudes, and art and literature?

One of the most noticeable features of Roman culture and society is the impact of the Greeks. The Romans had experienced Greek influence early on through the Greek cities in southern Italy. By the end of the third century B.C.E., however, Greek civilization was playing an ever-increasing role in Roman culture. Greek ambassadors, merchants, and artists traveled to Rome and spread Greek thought and practices. After their conquest of the Hellenistic kingdoms, Roman military commanders shipped Greek manuscripts and artworks back to Rome. Multitudes of educated Greek slaves were used in Roman households. Virtually every aspect of Roman life, from literature and philosophy to religion and education, was affected by Greek models. Rich Romans hired Greek tutors and sent their sons to Athens to study. As the Roman poet Horace said, "Captive Greece took captive her rude conqueror." Greek thought captivated the less sophisticated Roman minds, and the Romans became willing transmitters of Greek culture—not, however, without some resistance from Romans who had nothing but contempt for Greek politics and who feared the end of old Roman values. Even those who favored Greek culture blamed the Greeks for Rome's new vices, including a taste for luxury and homosexual practices.

Roman Religion

Every aspect of Roman society was permeated with religion. The official state religion focused on the worship of a pantheon of gods and goddesses, including Jupiter, Juno, Minerva, and Mars. As Rome developed and came into contact with other peoples and gods, the community simply adopted new deities. Hence, the Greek Hermes became the Roman Mercury. Eventually, a complete amalgamation of Greek and Roman religion occurred, giving the Romans and the Greeks essentially a single "Greco-Roman" religion.

Roman religion focused on the worship of the gods for a very practical reason—human beings were thought to be totally dependent on them. The exact performance of ritual was crucial to establishing a right relationship with the gods. What was true for individuals was also valid for the state: it also had to observe correct ritual to receive its reward. The rituals were performed by a college of priests or pontiffs, who thus bore the responsibility for maintaining the right relationship between the state and the gods. If the rituals were performed correctly, the Romans would obtain the "peace of the gods." No doubt the Roman success in creating an empire was a visible confirmation of divine favor. As Cicero, the first-century B.C.E. politician and writer, claimed, "We have overcome all the nations of the world, because we have realized that the world is directed and governed by the gods."[1]

Just as the state had an official cult, so did families. Because the family was regarded as a small state within the state, it had its own household cults, which included Janus, the spirit of the doorway, and Vesta, goddess of the hearth. Here, too, proper ritual was important, and it was the responsibility of the ***paterfamilias*** (pay-ter-fuh-MIL-ee-uss) as head of the family to ensure that religious obligations were properly fulfilled.

Religious festivals were an important part of Roman religious practice. There were two kinds: public festivals ordained and paid for by the state and private festivals celebrated by individuals and families. By the mid-second century B.C.E., six public festivals were celebrated annually, each lasting several days. The practice of holding games also grew out of religious festivals. The games were inaugurated in honor of Jupiter Optimus Maximus (JOO-puh-tur AHP-tuh-muss MAK-suh-muss) ("best and greatest"), the patron deity of Rome, but had become annual events by 366 B.C.E. In the late Republic, both the number of games and the number of days they lasted were increased. Originally, the games consisted of chariot racing in the Circus Maximus; later, animal hunts and theatrical performances were added. In the empire, gladiatorial contests would become the primary focus (see Chapter 6).

Forum Boarium, Rome/© Scala/Art Resource, NY

Temple of Portunus. The Romans considered the proper worship of the gods an important key to success. Typical of Roman religious architecture was the small urban temple located in the midst of a crowded commercial center. Pictured here is a rectangular temple built in Rome in the late second or early first century B.C.E. and dedicated to Portunus, the god of harbors. The temple was located in the cattle market close to the Tiber River.

The Growth of Slavery

Slavery was a common institution throughout the ancient world, but no people possessed more slaves or relied so much on slave labor as the Romans eventually did. Before the third century B.C.E., a small Roman farmer might possess one or two slaves who would help farm his few acres and perform domestic chores. These slaves would most likely be from Italy and be regarded as part of the family household. Only the very rich would have large numbers of slaves.

The Roman conquest of the Mediterranean brought a drastic change in the use of slaves. Large numbers of foreign slaves were brought back to Italy. During the Republic, then, the chief source of slaves was from capture in war, followed by piracy. Of course, the children of slaves also became slaves. Although some Roman generals brought back slaves to be sold to benefit the public treasury, ambitious generals of the first century B.C.E., such as Pompey and Caesar, made personal fortunes by treating slaves captured by their armies as private property.

Slaves were used in many ways in Roman society. The rich, of course, owned the most and the best. In the late

Republic, it became a badge of prestige to be attended by many slaves. Greeks were in much demand as tutors, musicians, doctors, and artists. Roman businessmen would employ them as shop assistants or artisans. Slaves were also used as farm laborers; huge gangs of slaves living in pitiful conditions worked the large landed estates known as ***latifundia*** (lat-i-FOON-dee-uh). Cato the Elder argued that it was cheaper to work slaves to death and then replace them than to treat them well. Many slaves of all nationalities were used as menial household workers, such as cooks, valets, waiters, cleaners, and gardeners. Roads, aqueducts, and other public facilities were constructed by contractors using slave labor. The total number of slaves is difficult to judge—estimates range from 20 to 30 percent of the population.

It is also difficult to generalize about the treatment of Roman slaves. There are numerous instances of humane treatment by masters and situations where slaves even protected their owners from danger out of gratitude and esteem. But slaves were also subject to severe punishments, torture, abuse, and hard labor that drove some to run away or even revolt against their owners. The Republic had stringent laws against aiding a runaway slave. The murder of a master by a slave might mean the execution of all the other household slaves. Near the end of the second century B.C.E., large-scale slave revolts occurred in Sicily, where enormous gangs of slaves were subjected to horrible working conditions on large landed estates. Slaves were branded, beaten, inadequately fed, worked in chains, and housed at night in underground prisons. One revolt of 70,000 slaves lasted three years (135–132 B.C.E.) before it was crushed, and the great revolt on Sicily (104–101 B.C.E.) involved most of the island and took a Roman army of 17,000 men to suppress. The most famous revolt on the Italian peninsula occurred in 73 B.C.E. Led by Spartacus, a slave who had been a Thracian gladiator, the revolt broke out in southern Italy and involved 70,000 slaves. Spartacus managed to defeat several Roman armies before he was finally trapped and killed in southern Italy in 71 B.C.E. Six thousand of his followers were crucified, the traditional form of execution for slaves.

The Roman Family

At the heart of the Roman social structure stood the family, headed by the *paterfamilias*—the dominant male. The household also included the wife, sons with their wives and children, unmarried daughters, and slaves. A family was virtually a small state within the state, and the power of the *paterfamilias* was parallel to that of the state magistrates over citizens. Like the Greeks, Roman males believed that the weakness of the female sex necessitated male guardians (see the box on p. 102). The *paterfamilias* exercised that authority; on his death, sons or close male relatives assumed the role of guardians. By the late Republic, however, although the rights of male guardians remained legally in effect, upper-class women found numerous ways to circumvent the power of their guardians.

Fathers arranged the marriages of daughters, although there are instances of mothers and daughters having influence on the choice. In the Republic, women married *cum manu*, "with legal control" passing from father to husband. By the mid-first century B.C.E., the dominant practice had changed to *sine manu*, "without legal control," which meant that married daughters officially remained within the father's legal power. Since the fathers of most married women were dead, not being in the "legal control" of a husband made possible independent property rights that forceful women could translate into considerable power within the household and outside it. Traditionally, Roman marriages were intended to be for life, but divorce

© The Art Archive/Alfredo Dagli Orti

A Roman Woman. Roman women, especially those of the upper class, had comparatively more freedom than women in Classical Athens despite the persistent male belief that women required guardianship. This portrait of a Roman woman is from a Roman mosaic dating from the first century B.C.E.

Cato the Elder on Women

During the Second Punic War, the Romans enacted the Oppian Law, which limited the amount of gold women could possess and restricted their dress and use of carriages. In 195 B.C.E., an attempt was made to repeal the law, and women demonstrated in the streets on behalf of the effort. According to the Roman historian Livy, the conservative Roman official Cato the Elder spoke against repeal and against the women favoring it. Although the words are probably not Cato's own, they do reflect a traditional male Roman attitude toward women.

Livy, *The History of Rome*

"If each of us, citizens, had determined to assert his rights and dignity as a husband with respect to his own spouse, we should have less trouble with the sex as a whole; as it is, our liberty, destroyed at home by female violence, even here in the Forum is crushed and trodden underfoot, and because we have not kept them individually under control, we dread them collectively. . . . But from no class is there not the greatest danger if you permit them meetings and gatherings and secret consultations. . . .

"Our ancestors permitted no woman to conduct even personal business without a guardian to intervene in her behalf; they wished them to be under the control of fathers, brothers, husbands; we (Heaven help us!) allow them now even to interfere in public affairs, yes, and to visit the Forum and our informal and formal sessions. What else are they doing now on the streets and at the corners except urging the bill of the tribunes and voting for the repeal of the law? Give loose rein to their uncontrollable nature and to this untamed creature and expect that they will themselves set bounds to their license; unless you act, this is the least of the things enjoined upon women by custom or law and to which they submit with a feeling of injustice. It is complete liberty or rather, if we wish to speak the truth, complete license that they desire.

"If they win in this, what will they not attempt? Review all the laws with which your forefathers restrained their license and made them subject to their husbands; even with all these bonds you can scarcely control them. What of this? If you suffer them to seize these bonds one by one and wrench themselves free and finally to be placed on a parity with their husbands, do you think you will be able to endure them? The moment they begin to be your equals, they will be your superiors. . . .

"Now they publicly address other women's husbands, and, what is more serious, they beg for law and votes, and from various men they get what they ask. In matters affecting yourself, your property, your children, you, Sir, can be importuned; once the law has ceased to set a limit to your wife's expenditures you will never set it yourself. Do not think, citizens, that the situation which existed before the law was passed will ever return."

Q What particular actions of the women protesting this law angered Cato? What more general concerns did he have about Roman women? What did he believe was women's ultimate goal in regard to men?

Source: Reprinted by permission of the publishers and the Trustees of the Loeb Classical Library from *Livy: History of Rome, Book 34, Loeb Classical Library Vol. II–V*, trans. by B.O. Foster, Cambridge, Mass.: Harvard University Press, Copyright © 1935 by the President and Fellows of Harvard College. The Loeb Classical Library is a registered trademark of the President and Fellows of Harvard College.

was introduced in the third century B.C.E. and became relatively easy to obtain: either party could initiate it, and no one needed to prove the breakdown of the marriage. Divorce became especially prevalent in the first century B.C.E.—a period of political turmoil, when marriages were used to cement political alliances.

Some upper-class parents provided education for their daughters. Some girls had private tutors, and others may have gone to primary schools. But at the age when boys were entering secondary schools, girls were pushed into marriage. The legal minimum age for marriage was twelve, although fourteen was a more common age in practice. Although some Roman doctors warned that early pregnancies could be dangerous for young girls, early marriages persisted due to the desire to benefit from dowries as soon as possible and the reality of early mortality. A good example is Tullia, Cicero's beloved daughter. She was married at sixteen, widowed at twenty-two, remarried one year later, divorced at twenty-eight, remarried at twenty-nine, and divorced at thirty-three. She died at thirty-four, not a particularly young age for females in Roman society.

The Evolution of Roman Law

One of Rome's chief gifts to the Mediterranean world of its day and to succeeding generations was its development of law. The Twelve Tables of 450 B.C.E. were the first codification of Roman law (see the box on p. 104), and although inappropriate for later times, they were never officially abrogated and were still memorized by schoolboys in the first century B.C.E. Civil law derived from the Twelve Tables proved inadequate for later Roman needs, however, and gave way to corrections and additions by the praetors. On taking office, a praetor issued an edict listing his guidelines for dealing with different kinds of legal cases. The praetors were knowledgeable in law, but they also relied on Roman jurists—amateur law experts—for advice in preparing their edicts. The interpretations of the jurists, often embodied in the edicts of the praetors, created a body of legal principles.

In 242 B.C.E., the Romans appointed a second praetor who was responsible for examining suits between a Roman and a non-Roman as well as between two non-Romans. The Romans found that although some of their rules of law could be used in these cases, special rules were often needed. These rules gave rise to a body of law known as the law of nations, defined by the Romans as "that part of the law which we apply both to ourselves and to foreigners." But the influence of Greek philosophy, primarily Stoicism, led Romans in the late Republic to develop the idea of the law of nature—or universal divine law derived from right reason. The Romans came to view their law of nations as derived from or identical to this law of nature, thus giving Roman jurists a philosophical justification for systematizing Roman law according to basic principles.

The Development of Literature

The Romans produced little literature before the third century B.C.E., and the Latin literature that emerged in that century was strongly influenced by Greek models. The demand for plays at public festivals eventually led to a growing number of native playwrights. One of the best known was Plautus (PLAW-tuss) (c. 254–184 B.C.E.), who used plots from Greek New Comedy (see Chapter 4) for his own plays. The actors wore Greek costumes and Greek masks and portrayed the same basic stock characters: lecherous old men, skillful slaves, prostitutes, and young men in love. Plautus wrote for the masses and became a very popular playwright in Rome.

In the last century of the Republic, the Romans began to produce a new poetry, less dependent on epic themes and more inclined to personal expression. Latin poets were now able to use various Greek forms to express their own feelings about people, social and political life, and love. The finest example of this can be seen in the work of Catullus (kuh-TULL-uss) (c. 87–54 B.C.E.), Rome's "best lyric poet" and one of the greatest in world literature.

Catullus became a master at adapting and refining Greek forms of poetry to express his emotions. He wrote a variety of poems on, among other things, political figures, social customs, the use of language, the death of his brother, and the travails of love. Catullus became infatuated with Clodia, the promiscuous sister of a tribune and wife of a provincial governor, and addressed a number of poems to her (he called her Lesbia), describing his passionate love and hatred for her (Clodia had many other lovers besides Catullus):

> *You used to say that you wished to know only Catullus,*
> *Lesbia, and wouldn't take even Jove before me!*
> *I didn't regard you just as my mistress then: I cherished you*
> *as a father does his sons or his daughters' husbands.*
> *Now that I know you, I burn for you even more fiercely,*
> *though I regard you as almost utterly worthless.*
> *How can that be, you ask? It's because such cruelty forces*
> *lust to assume the shrunken place of affection.*[2]

Catullus's ability to express in simple fashion his intense feelings and curiosity about himself and his world had a noticeable impact on later Latin poets.

The development of Roman prose was greatly aided by the practice of oratory. Romans had great respect for oratory because the ability to persuade people in public debate meant success in politics. Oratory was brought to perfection in a literary fashion by Cicero (SIS-uh-roh) (106–43 B.C.E.), the best exemplar of the literary and intellectual interests of the senatorial elite of the late Republic and, indeed, the greatest prose writer of that period. For Cicero, oratory was not simply skillful speaking. An orator was a statesman, a man who achieved his highest goal by pursuing an active life in public affairs.

Later, when the turmoil of the late Republic forced him into semiretirement from politics, Cicero became more interested in writing philosophical treatises. He performed a valuable service for Roman society by popularizing and making understandable the works of Greek philosophers. In his philosophical works, Cicero, more than anyone else, transmitted the Classical intellectual heritage to the Western world. Cicero's original contributions came in the field of politics. His works *On the Laws* and *On the Republic* provided fresh insights into political thought, including the need for a mixed constitution: "a moderate and well-balanced form of government which is a combination of the three simple good forms (monarchy, aristocracy, and democracy) is preferable even to monarchy."[3] His emphasis on the need to pursue an active life to benefit and improve society later would greatly influence the Italian Renaissance.

The Twelve Tables

In 451 B.C.E., plebeian pressure led to the creation of a special commission of ten men who were responsible for codifying Rome's laws and making them public. In so doing, the plebeians hoped that they could restrict the arbitrary power of the patrician magistrates, who alone had access to the laws. The Twelve Tables represent the first formal codification of Roman laws and customs. The laws dealt with litigation procedures, debt, family relations, property, and other matters of public and sacred law. The code was inscribed on bronze plaques, which were eventually destroyed. These selections are taken from reconstructions of the code preserved in later writings.

Selections from the Twelve Tables

Table III: Execution; Law of Debt

When a debt has been acknowledged, or judgment about the matter has been pronounced in court, thirty days must be the legitimate time of grace. After that, the debtor may be arrested by laying on of hands. Bring him into court. If he does not satisfy the judgment, or no one in court offers himself as surety in his behalf, the creditor may take the defaulter with him. He may bind him either in stocks or in fetters. . . .

Unless they make a settlement, debtors shall be held in bond for sixty days. During that time they shall be brought before the praetor's court in the meeting place on three successive market days, and the amount for which they are judged liable shall be announced; on the third market day they shall suffer capital punishment or be delivered up for sale abroad, across the Tiber.

Table IV: Rights of Head of Family

Quickly kill . . . a dreadfully deformed child.

If a father three times surrenders a son for sale, the son shall be free from the father.

A child born ten months after the father's death will not be admitted into legal inheritance.

Table V: Guardianship; Succession

Females shall remain in guardianship even when they have attained their majority.

A spendthrift is forbidden to exercise administration over his own goods. . . . A person who, being insane or a spendthrift, is prohibited from administering his own goods shall be under trusteeship of agnates [nearest male relatives].

Table VII: Rights Concerning Land

Branches of a tree may be lopped off all round to a height of no more than 15 feet. . . . Should a tree on a neighbor's farm be bent crooked by a wind and lean over your farm, action may be taken for removal of that tree.

It is permitted to gather up fruit falling down on another man's farm.

Table VIII: Torts or Delicts

If any person has sung or composed against another person a song such as was causing slander or insult to another, he shall be clubbed to death.

If a person has maimed another's limb, let there be retaliation in kind unless he makes agreement for settlement with him.

Any person who destroys by burning any building or heap of corn [grain] deposited alongside a house shall be bound, scourged, and put to death by burning at the stake, provided that he has committed the said misdeed with malice aforethought, but if he shall have committed it by accident, that is, by negligence, it is ordained that he repair the damage.

Table IX: Public Law

The penalty shall be capital punishment for a judge or arbiter legally appointed who has been found guilty of receiving a bribe for giving a decision.

Table XI: Supplementary Laws

Intermarriage shall not take place between plebeians and patricians.

Q What do the selections from the Twelve Tables reveal about Roman society? In what ways do these laws differ from those in the Code of Hammurabi? In what ways are they similar?

Source: From *Roman Civilization, Vol. I*, Naphtali Lewis and Meyer Reinhold. Copyright © 1955 Columbia University Press. Reprinted by permission of the publisher.

Roman Art

The Romans were also dependent on the Greeks for artistic inspiration. During the third and second centuries B.C.E., they adopted many features of the Hellenistic style of art. The Romans developed a taste for Greek statues, which they installed in their homes as well as in public buildings. Once demand outstripped the supply of original works, reproductions of Greek statues became fashionable. The Romans' own portrait sculpture was characterized by an intense realism that included even unpleasant physical details. Wall paintings and frescoes in the houses of the rich realistically depicted landscapes, portraits, and scenes from mythological stories.

The Romans excelled in architecture, a highly practical art. Although they continued to employ Greek styles and made use of colonnades, rectangular structures, and post-and-lintel construction, the Romans were also innovative. They made considerable use of curvilinear forms: the arch, vault, and dome. The Romans were also the first people in antiquity to use concrete on an enormous scale. By combining concrete and curvilinear forms, they were able to construct massive buildings—public baths and amphitheaters, the most famous of which was the Coliseum in Rome, which could seat 50,000 spectators. These large buildings were made possible by Roman engineering skills. These same skills were put to use in constructing roads (the Romans built a network of 50,000 miles of roads throughout their empire), aqueducts (in Rome, almost a dozen aqueducts kept a population of one million supplied with water), and bridges.

Values and Attitudes

The Romans were by nature a conservative people. They were very concerned about maintaining the *mos maiorum* (MOHSS my-YOR-um), the customs or traditions of their ancestors. They emphasized parental authority and, above all, their obligations to the state. The highest virtue was *pietas* (PY-i-tas)—the dutiful execution of one's obligations to one's fellow citizens, to the gods, and to the state.

By the second century B.C.E., however, the creation of an empire had begun to weaken the old values. The Romans began to focus more on affluence, status, and material possessions. Emphasis shifted toward individualism and away from collective well-being, the old public spirit that had served Rome so well. Romans who worried about the decline of the old values blamed it on different causes. Some felt that after the destruction of Carthage, the Romans no longer had any strong enemies to challenge them. Others believed that the Romans had simply been overwhelmed by the affluence afforded by the new empire. And some blamed everything on the Greeks for importing ideas and practices baneful to the Romans. Of course, there were also many Romans who, though desirous of maintaining traditional values, were also well aware that the acquisition of an empire had created a new world with new demands and values.

The Decline and Fall of the Roman Republic (133–31 B.C.E.)

Focus Question: What were the main problems Rome faced during the last century of the Republic, and how were they ultimately resolved?

By the mid-second century B.C.E., Roman domination of the Mediterranean Sea was well established. Yet the process of building an empire had weakened and threatened the internal stability of Rome. This internal instability characterizes the period of Roman history from 133 until 31 B.C.E., when Octavian defeated Mark Antony and stood supreme over the Roman world. By that time, the constitution of the Roman Republic was in shambles.

Background: Social, Economic, and Political Problems

By the second century B.C.E., the senate had become the effective governing body of the Roman state. It consisted of three hundred men, drawn primarily from the landed aristocracy; they remained senators for life and held the chief magistracies of the Republic. During the wars of the third and second centuries, the senate came to exercise enormous power. It directed the wars and took control of both foreign and domestic policy, including financial affairs.

Moreover, the magistracies and senate were increasingly controlled by a relatively select circle of wealthy and powerful families, both patrician and plebeian, called the ***nobiles*** (NAW-bee-lays) ("nobles"). In the hundred years from 233 to 133 B.C.E., 80 percent of the consuls came from twenty-six families; moreover, 50 percent came from only ten families. Hence, the *nobiles* constituted a governing oligarchy whose members managed, through landed wealth, patronage, and intimidation, to maintain their hold over the magistracies and senate and thus guide the destiny of Rome while running the state in their own interests.

By the end of the second century B.C.E., two types of aristocratic leaders, called the ***optimates*** (ahp-tuh-MAH-tayz) ("the best men") and the ***populares*** (PAWP-oo-lahr-ayss) ("favoring the people"), became prominent. *Optimates* and *populares* were terms of political rhetoric that were used by individuals within the aristocracy against fellow aristocratic rivals to distinguish one set of tactics from another. The *optimates* controlled the senate and wished to maintain their oligarchical privileges, while the *populares* were usually other ambitious aristocrats who used the people's assemblies as instruments to break the domination of the *optimates*. The conflicts between these aristocratic leaders and their supporters engulfed the first century B.C.E. in political turmoil.

Of course, the aristocrats formed only a tiny minority of the Roman people. The backbone of the Roman state and army had traditionally been the small farmers. But economic changes that began in the period of the Punic Wars increasingly undermined the position of that group. Their lands had been severely damaged during the Second Punic War when Hannibal invaded Italy. Moreover, in order to win the wars, Rome had to increase the term of military service from two to six years. When they returned home, many farmers found their farms so deteriorated that they chose to sell out instead of remaining on the land. By this time, capitalistic agriculture was also increasing rapidly. Landed aristocrats had been able to develop large estates (the *latifundia)* by taking over state-owned land and by buying out small peasant owners. These large estates relied on slave and tenant labor and frequently concentrated on cash crops, such as grapes for wine, olives, and sheep for wool, which small farmers could not afford to do. Thus, the rise of the *latifundia* contributed to the decline in the number of small citizen farmers. Because the latter group traditionally provided the foundation of the Roman army, the number of men available for military service declined. Moreover, many of these small farmers drifted to the cities, especially Rome, forming a large class of day laborers who possessed no property. This new class of urban proletariat formed a highly unstable mass with the potential to create much trouble in depressed times.

The Reforms of the Gracchi

In 133 B.C.E., Tiberius Gracchus (ty-BEER-ee-uss GRAK-us), himself a member of the aristocracy and a new tribune, came to believe that the underlying cause of Rome's problems was the decline of the small farmer. Consequently, Tiberius bypassed the senate, where he knew his rivals would oppose his proposal, and had the council of the plebs pass a land reform bill that authorized the government to reclaim public land held by large landowners and to distribute it to landless Romans. Many senators, themselves large landowners whose estates included large tracts of public land, were furious, and a group of them took the law into their own hands and assassinated Tiberius.

The efforts of Tiberius Gracchus were continued by his brother Gaius (GY-uss), elected tribune for 123 and 122 B.C.E. Gaius, too, pushed for the distribution of land to displaced farmers. But he broadened his reform program with measures that would benefit the **equestrian order**, a rising group of wealthy citizens who wanted a share in the political power held by the ruling aristocracy. Many senators, hostile to Gaius's reforms and fearful of his growing popularity, instigated mob action that resulted in the death of the reformer and many of his friends in 121 B.C.E. The attempts of the Gracchus brothers to bring reforms had opened the door to more instability and further violence.

A New Role for the Roman Army: Marius and Sulla

In the closing years of the second century B.C.E., a series of military disasters gave rise to a fresh outburst of popular anger against the old leaders of the senate. Military defeats in northern Africa under a senate-appointed general encouraged Marius (MAR-ee-uss)—a "new man" from the equestrian order—to run for the consulship on a "win the war" campaign slogan. Marius won and became a consul for 107 B.C.E. Marius took command of the army in Africa and brought the war to a successful conclusion. He was then called on to defeat the Celts, who threatened an invasion of Italy. Marius was made consul for five years, from 104 to 100 B.C.E.; raised a new army; and decisively defeated the Celts, leaving him in a position of personal ascendancy in Rome.

In raising a new army, Marius initiated military reforms that proved to have drastic consequences. The Roman army had traditionally been a conscript army of small landholders. Marius recruited volunteers from both the urban and rural proletariat who possessed no property. These volunteers swore an oath of loyalty to the general, not the senate, and thus inaugurated a professional-type army that might no longer be subject to the state. Moreover, to recruit these men, a general would promise them land, so the generals had to play politics to get legislation passed that would provide land for their veterans. Marius left a powerful legacy. He had created a new system of military recruitment that placed much power in the hands of the individual generals.

Lucius Cornelius Sulla (SULL-uh) was the next general to take advantage of the new military system. The senate had placed him in charge of a war in Asia Minor, but when the council of the plebs tried to transfer command of this war to Marius, a civil war ensued. Sulla won and seized Rome itself in 82 B.C.E. He forced the senate to grant him the title of dictator to "reconstitute the Republic." After conducting a reign of terror to wipe out all opposition, Sulla revised the constitution to restore power to the senate and eliminated most of the powers of the popular assemblies and the tribunes of the plebs. In 79 B.C.E., believing that he had restored the traditional Republic governed by a powerful senate, he retired. But his real legacy was quite different from what he had intended. His example of using an army to seize power would prove most attractive to ambitious men.

The Death of the Republic

For the next fifty years, Roman history would be characterized by two important features: the jostling for power by a number of strong individuals and the civil wars generated by their conflicts. Three men came to hold enormous military and political power—Crassus (KRASS-uss), Pompey (PAHM-pee), and Julius Caesar. Crassus, who was known as the richest man in Rome, had successfully put down the major slave rebellion led by Spartacus. Pompey had returned from a successful military command in Spain in 71 B.C.E. and had been hailed as a military hero. Julius Caesar had been a spokesman for the *populares* from the beginning of his political career and had a military command in Spain. In 60 B.C.E., Caesar joined with Crassus and Pompey to form a coalition that historians call the First Triumvirate.

Though others had made political deals before, the combined wealth and power of these three men was enormous, enabling them to dominate the political scene and achieve their basic aims: Pompey received lands for his veterans and a command in Spain, Crassus was given a command in Syria, and Caesar was granted a special military command in Gaul (modern France). When Crassus was killed in battle in 53 B.C.E., his death left two powerful men with armies in direct competition. Caesar had used his time in Gaul wisely. He had conquered all of Gaul and gained fame, wealth, and military experience as well as an army of seasoned veterans who were loyal to him. When leading senators fastened on Pompey as the less harmful to their cause and voted for Caesar to lay down his command and return as a private citizen to Rome, Caesar refused. Such a step was intolerable to Caesar, as it would leave him totally vulnerable to his enemies (see the box on p. 108). He chose to keep his army and moved into Italy by illegally crossing the Rubicon, the river that formed the southern boundary of his province. (The phrase "crossing the Rubicon" is still used today to mean taking a decisive action from which there is no turning back.) According to his ancient biographer Suetonius, Caesar said to his troops, "Even now we could turn back; but once we cross that tiny bridge, then everything will depend on armed force."[4] Caesar marched on Rome, starting a civil war between his forces and those of Pompey and his allies. The defeat of Pompey's forces left Caesar in complete control of the Roman government.

Caesar had officially been made dictator in 47 B.C.E., and three years later he was made dictator for life. He continued to hold elections for offices but saw to it that his supporters chose the people he recommended. Upon becoming Rome's ruler, he quickly instituted a number of ambitious reforms. He increased the senate to nine hundred members by filling it with many of his supporters and granted citizenship to a number of people in the provinces who had helped him. By establishing colonies of Roman citizens in North Africa, Gaul, and Spain, he initiated a process of Romanization in those areas. He also reorganized the administrative structures of cities in Italy in an attempt to create a sense of order in their government. Caesar was a generous victor and pardoned many of the republican leaders who had opposed him, allowing

Museo Archeologico Nazionale, Naples/© Scala/Art Resource, NY

Caesar. Conqueror of Gaul and member of the First Triumvirate, Julius Caesar is perhaps the best-known figure of the late Republic. Caesar became dictator of Rome in 47 B.C.E. and after his victories in the civil war was made dictator for life. Some members of the senate who resented his power assassinated him in 44 B.C.E. Pictured is a marble copy of a bust of Caesar.

OPPOSING VIEWPOINTS

The End of the Republic: Three Views

Although Rome stood supreme over the Mediterranean world by 133 B.C.E., the internal structure of the Republic had begun to disintegrate. During the next hundred years, the Republic was afflicted with mob violence, assassinations, civil wars, and unscrupulous politicians who seized every opportunity to advance their own interests. The Roman historian Sallust (86–35 B.C.E.), who lived through many of these crises, reflected on the causes of Rome's problems. In the first selection below, he discusses the moral decline that set in after the destruction of Carthage in 146 B.C.E. Sallust presented a broad, philosophical view of the problem, but some figures directly involved in the struggles of the last century—namely, Caesar and Cicero—had their own ideas about the immediate crisis that led to the end of the Republic. In the second selection, taken from *The Civil Wars*, Caesar presents a defense of his decision to move into Italy with his troops. In the third selection, a letter from Cicero to his friend Atticus, Cicero indicates what he thinks of Caesar's action.

Sallust, *The War with Catiline*

Good morals were cultivated at home and in the field; [in the early Republic] there was the greatest harmony and little or no avarice; justice and honesty prevailed among them, thanks not so much to laws as to nature. Quarrels, discord, and strife were reserved for their enemies; citizen vied with citizen only for the prize of merit. They were lavish in their offerings to the gods, frugal in the home, loyal to their friends. By practicing these two qualities, boldness in warfare and justice when peace came, they watched over themselves and their country. . . .

But when our country had grown great through toil and the practice of justice, when great kings had been vanquished in war, savage tribes and mighty people subdued by force of arms, when Carthage, the rival of Rome's sway, had perished root and branch, and all seas and lands were open, then Fortune began to grow cruel and to bring confusion into all our affairs. Those who had found it easy to bear hardships and dangers, anxiety and adversity, found leisure and wealth, desirable under other circumstances, a burden and a curse. Hence the lust for power first, then for money, grew upon them; these were, I may say, the root of all evils. For avarice destroyed honor, integrity, and all other noble qualities; taught in their place insolence, cruelty, to neglect the gods, to set a price on everything. Ambition drove many men to become false; to have one thought locked in the breast, another ready on the tongue; to value friendships and enmities not on their merits but by the standard of self-interest, and to show a good front rather than a good heart. At first these vices grew slowly; from time to time they were punished; finally, when the disease had spread like a deadly plague, the state was changed and a government second to none in justice and excellence became cruel and intolerable.

Caesar, *The Civil Wars*

Having called the senate together, he [Caesar, who refers to himself in the third person] recounts the wrongs done him by his personal enemies. He explains that he had sought no extraordinary office, but, waiting for the legitimate time of his consulship, had been content with privileges open to all the citizens. . . . He sets forth his own patience when under no pressure he had made the request about the disbandment of the armies, a point in which he was ready to make a personal sacrifice of dignity and position. He tells them of the bitterness of his foes who refused in his case what they demanded in the other, and preferred utter confusion to the surrender of military power and armed force. He tells of their injustice in robbing him of his legions, of their cruelty and insolence in infringing the rights of the tribunes; he enumerates the terms that he had offered, the conferences asked for and refused. On these considerations he exhorts and charges them to take up the burden of state and administer it with his help; but if they shrink through fear he will not burden them, and will administer the state himself. Envoys should be sent to Pompey to effect a settlement, nor was he afraid of the remark made by Pompey a little before in the senate, to the effect that undue influence is attributed to those to whom envoys are sent and fear argued on the part of those that send them. Such considerations seemed to belong to a poor and weak spirit. His own wish was to be superior to others in justice and equity as he had striven to surpass them in action.

Cicero, *Letter to Atticus*

Pray, what's all this? What is going on? I am in the dark. Is it a Roman general or Hannibal we are talking of? Deluded wretch, with never in his [Caesar's] life a glimpse of even the shadow of Good! And he says he is doing all this for his honor's sake! Where is honor without moral

(Continued)

good? And is it good to have an army without public authority, to seize Roman towns by way of opening the road to the mother city, to plan debt cancellations, recall of exiles, and a hundred other villainies "all for that first of deities, Sole Power"? He is welcome to his greatness. I would rather a single hour with you, warming myself in that "bonus" sunshine of yours, than all such autocracies, or rather I had sooner die a thousand deaths than entertain one such thought.

Q How did Caesar view the steps he had taken? How did Cicero view those steps? What do the differences between Caesar and Cicero tell you about the end of the Republic? How do the views of Caesar and Cicero give support to Sallust's argument? What do these three selections have in common in regard to the fall of the Republic? How do they differ?

Sources: Sallust, *The War with Catiline*. Reprinted from *Sallust*, Loeb Classical Library, trans. by J. C. Rolfe, Cambridge, Mass.: Harvard University Press, 1921. The Loeb Classical Library is a registered trademark of the President and Fellows of Harvard College. Caesar, *The Civil Wars*. Reprinted from Caesar, *The Civil Wars*, Cambridge, Mass.: Harvard University Press, 1966. The Loeb Classical Library is a registered trademark of the President and Fellows of Harvard College. Cicero's *Letter to Atticus*. Reprinted from Cicero's *Letters to Atticus*, Vol. IV, D.R. Shackleton Bailey, ed., Cambridge, Mass.: Harvard University Press, 1968. The Loeb Classical Library is a registered trademark of the President and Fellows of Harvard College.

them to return to Rome. He also reformed the calendar by introducing the Egyptian solar year of 365 days (with changes implemented in 1582 C.E., it became the basis of our current calendar). He planned much more in the way of building projects and military adventures in the east, but in 44 B.C.E., a group of leading senators who resented his domination assassinated him in the belief that they had struck a blow for republican liberty. In truth, they had set the stage for another civil war that delivered the death blow to the Republic.

Within a few years after Caesar's death, two men had divided the Roman world between them—Octavian (ahk-TAY-vee-un), Caesar's heir and grandnephew, took the west, and Antony, Caesar's ally and assistant, the east. But the empire of the Romans, large as it was, was still too small for two masters, and Octavian and Antony eventually came into conflict. Antony allied himself with the Egyptian queen Cleopatra VII, with whom, like Caesar before him, he fell in love. Octavian began a propaganda campaign, accusing Antony of catering to Cleopatra and giving away Roman territory to this "whore of the east." Finally, at the Battle of Actium in Greece in 31 B.C.E., Octavian's forces smashed the army and navy of Antony and Cleopatra. Both fled to Egypt, where, according to the account of the Roman historian Florus, they committed suicide a year later:

> Antony was the first to commit suicide, by the sword. Cleopatra threw herself at Octavian's feet, and tried her best to attract his gaze: in vain, for his self-control was impervious to her beauty. It was not her life she was after, for that had already been granted, but a portion of her kingdom. When she realized this was hopeless and that she had been earmarked to feature in Octavian's triumph in Rome, she took advantage of her guard's carelessness to get herself into the mausoleum, as the royal tomb is called. Once there, she put on the royal robes which she was accustomed to wear, and lay down in a richly perfumed coffin beside her Antony. Then she applied poisonous snakes to her veins and slipped into death as though into a sleep.[5]

Octavian, at the age of thirty-two, stood supreme over the Roman world (see Map 5.3). The civil wars had ended. And so had the Republic.

CHRONOLOGY The Decline and Fall of the Roman Republic

Reforms of Tiberius Gracchus	133 B.C.E.
Reforms of Gaius Gracchus	123–122 B.C.E.
Marius: First consulship	107 B.C.E.
Marius: Consecutive consulships	104–100 B.C.E.
Sulla as dictator	82–79 B.C.E.
Pompey's command in Spain	77–71 B.C.E.
Campaign of Crassus against Spartacus	73–71 B.C.E.
First Triumvirate (Caesar, Pompey, Crassus)	60 B.C.E.
Caesar in Gaul	59–49 B.C.E.
Murder of Crassus by Parthians	53 B.C.E.
Caesar's crossing of the Rubicon	49 B.C.E.
Caesar named dictator	47 B.C.E.
End of civil war	45 B.C.E.
Assassination of Caesar	44 B.C.E.
Octavian's defeat of Antony at Actium	31 B.C.E.

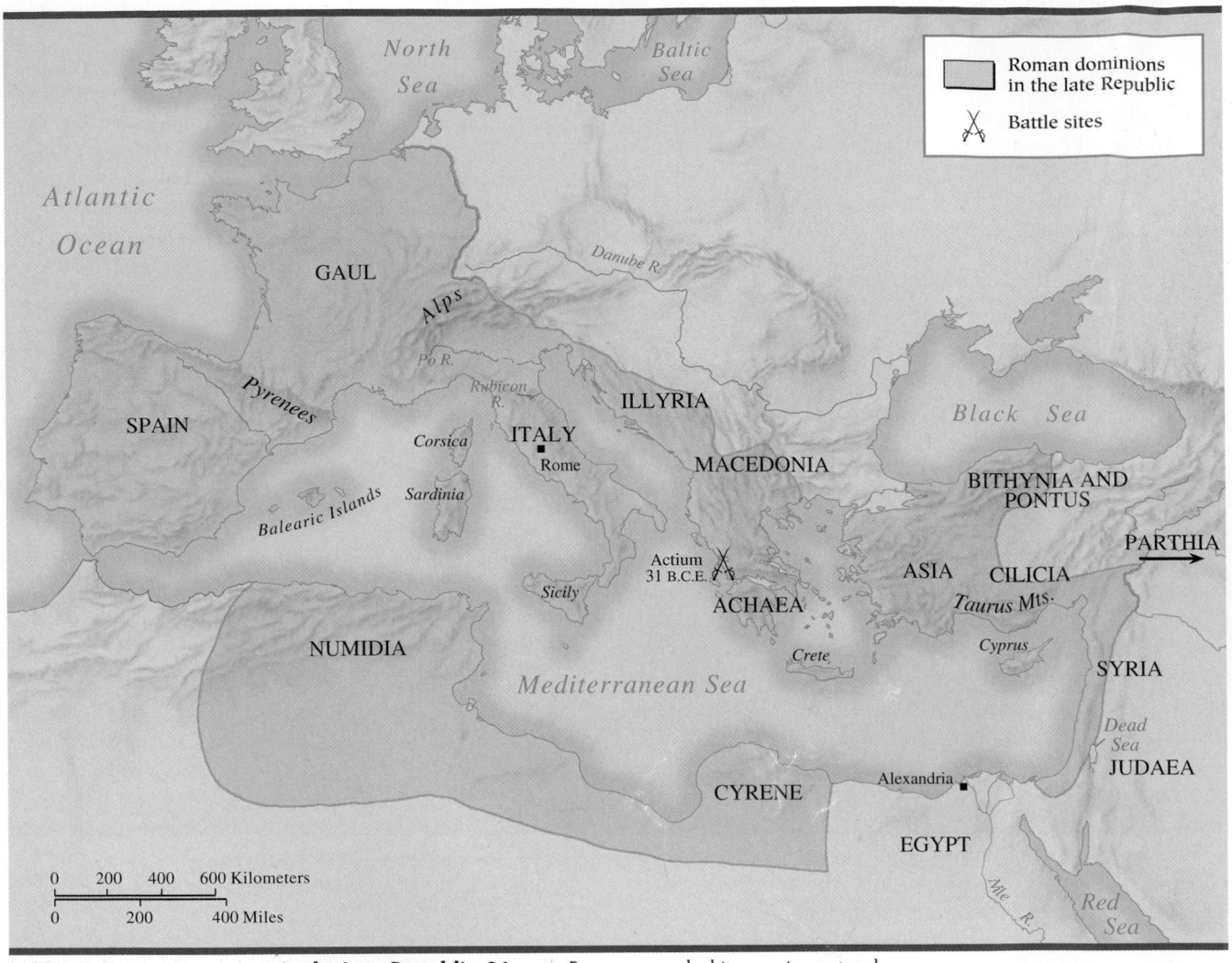

MAP 5.3 Roman Dominions in the Late Republic, 31 B.C.E. Rome expanded its empire not only in response to military threats on its borders but also for increased access to economic resources and markets, in addition to the vanity of conquest itself.

Q ***For comparison, look back at Map 5.2. In what areas did the Romans gain the greatest amount of territory, and how?***

CHAPTER SUMMARY

Sometime in the eighth century B.C.E., a group of Latin-speaking people built a small community called Rome on the Tiber River in Italy. Between 509 and 264 B.C.E., this city expanded and united almost all of Italy under its control. Diplomacy was as important as the Roman armies in this achievement, and the Romans made their rule acceptable by allowing local autonomy and gradually granting Roman citizenship to non-Romans. During this time of conquest, Rome also developed the political institutions of a republic ruled by an aristocratic oligarchy.

Although Rome had no master plan for expansion, its relationship with its neighbors outside Italy soon led to involvement in new wars. Its first challenge was Carthage and the Carthaginian empire in Spain and Africa. Rome was victorious after the three long and bloody Punic Wars. In the east, Rome conquered Macedonia and also took control of the Greek states. Thus, between 264 and 133 B.C.E., Rome expanded to the west and east and became master of the Mediterranean Sea.

Religion and law permeated Roman life. Ritual was at the focus of religion, for ritual established the correct relationship with the gods, both for individuals and for the state. Roman law was among Rome's most enduring accomplishments. The early laws, written in the Twelve Tables, constituted civil law for Romans. As Rome expanded, the Romans developed a new body of law, the law of nations, that applied to Romans and non-Romans alike. Republican Rome was also influenced by Hellenistic Greece, especially in literature, art, and philosophy.

In the second century B.C.E., the conservative, traditional values of Rome declined as affluence and individualism increased. After 133 B.C.E., Rome's republican institutions proved inadequate for the task of ruling an empire. In the breakdown that ensued, ambitious individuals such as Pompey, Crassus, and Caesar saw opportunities for power unparalleled in Roman history and succumbed to the temptations. The military reforms of Marius at the beginning of the first century had made possible the creation of professional armies that were loyal to the generals who recruited them, rather than to the state. Bloody civil war ensued as powerful individuals jockeyed for power. Peace was finally achieved when Octavian defeated Antony and Cleopatra. Octavian, who came to be known by the title of Augustus, would soon create a new system of government that seemed to preserve the Republic while establishing the basis for a new system that would rule the empire in an orderly fashion.

CHAPTER TIMELINE

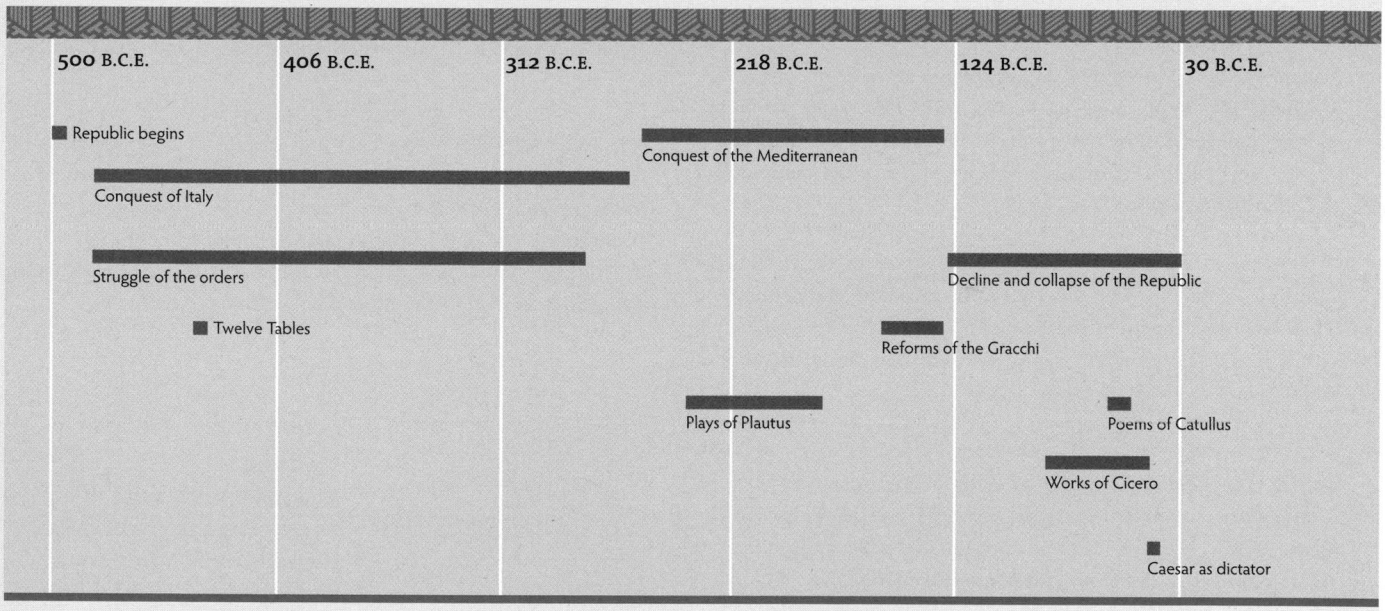

CHAPTER REVIEW

Upon Reflection

Q How did Rome's contact with the Hellenistic world affect Roman civilization in the second and first centuries B.C.E.?

Q How did Rome achieve its empire from 264 to 133 B.C.E., and in the course of its expansion, what happened to the political structure and the political values of the Roman Republic?

Q Was the fall of the Roman Republic due to systemic institutional weaknesses or the personal ambitions of generals and politicians? Why?

Key Terms

consuls (p. 92)
praetors (p. 92)
imperium (p. 92)
quaestors (p. 92)
aediles (p. 93)
senate (p. 93)
centuriate assembly (p. 93)
patricians (p. 93)
plebeians (p. 93)
tribunes of the plebs (p. 93)
council of the plebs (p. 93)
plebiscita (p. 93)
paterfamilias (p. 100)
latifundia (p. 101)
nobiles (p. 105)
optimates (p. 105)
populares (p. 105)
equestrian order (p. 106)

Suggestions for Further Reading

GENERAL SURVEYS Good surveys of Roman history include **C. S. Mackay, *Ancient Rome: A Military and Political History*** (Cambridge, 2004), and **M. T. Boatwright, D. J. Gargola,** and **R. J. A. Talbert, *The Romans: From Village to Empire*** (New York, 2004). See also **H. I. Flower, ed., *The Cambridge Companion to the Roman Republic*** (Cambridge, 2003).

EARLY ROME The history of early Rome is well covered in **T. J. Cornell, *The Beginnings of Rome: Italy and Rome from the Bronze Age to the Punic Wars (c. 1000–264 B.C.)*** (London, 1995). A good work on the Etruscans is **S. Haynes, *Etruscan Civilization: A Cultural History*** (Los Angeles, 2005).

POLITICAL AND SOCIAL STRUCTURE Aspects of the Roman political structure can be studied in **R. E. Mitchell, *Patricians and Plebeians: The Origin of the Roman State*** (Ithaca, N.Y., 1990). On the Roman social structure, see **G. Alfoldy, *The Social History of Rome*** (London, 1985).

THE EXPANSION OF ROME On the conquest of Italy, see **J.-M. David, *The Roman Conquest of Italy,*** trans. **A. Nevill** (Oxford, 1996). On Rome's struggle with Carthage, see **N. Bagnall, *The Punic Wars*** (Oxford, 2002). On Roman military forces, see **A. Goldsworthy, *The Complete Roman Army*** (London, 2003).

ROMAN SOCIETY AND CULTURE Roman religion can be examined in **E. M. Orlin, *Temples, Religion, and Politics in the Roman Republic*** (New York, 2002. On the Roman family, see **S. Dixon, *The Roman Family*** (Baltimore, 1992). On slavery and its consequences, see **K. R. Bradley, *Slavery and Rebellion in the Roman World, 140–70 B.C.*** (Bloomington, Ind., 1989). For a brief, readable survey of Latin literature, see **R. M. Ogilvie, *Roman Literature and Society*** (Harmondsworth, England, 1980). On Roman art and architecture, see **F. S. Kleiner, *A History of Roman Art*** (Belmont, Calif., 2006).

THE LATE REPUBLIC An excellent account of basic problems in the late Republic can be found in **M. Beard** and **M. H. Crawford, *Rome in the Late Republic*** (London, 1985). Also valuable are **D. Shorter, *The Fall of the Roman Republic*** (London, 1994), and **E. Hildinger, *Swords Against the Senate: The Rise of the Roman Army and the Fall of the Republic*** (Cambridge, Mass., 2002).

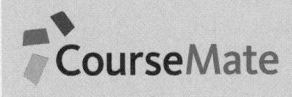

Visit the CourseMate website at **www.cengagebrain.com** for additional study tools and review materials for this chapter.

CHAPTER 6

Galleria degli Uffizi, Florence/© Alinari/The Bridgeman Art Library

A second-century Roman marble bust of Hadrian

The Roman Empire

CHAPTER OUTLINE AND FOCUS QUESTIONS

The Age of Augustus (31 B.C.E.–14 C.E.)

Q In his efforts to solve the problems Rome had faced during the late Republic, what changes did Augustus make in Rome's political, military, and social institutions?

The Early Empire (14–180)

Q What were the chief features of the Roman Empire at its height during the second century?

Roman Culture and Society in the Early Empire

Q What were the chief intellectual, artistic, and social developments in the Early Empire? How did these differ from the intellectual, artistic, and social developments of the Republic?

Transformation of the Roman World: Crises in the Third Century

Q What political, military, economic, and social problems did the Roman Empire face during the third century?

Transformation of the Roman World: The Rise of Christianity

Q What characteristics of Christianity enabled it to grow and ultimately to triumph?

CRITICAL THINKING

Q How did Christianity transform the Roman Empire?

WITH THE VICTORIES OF OCTAVIAN, peace finally settled on the Roman world. Although civil conflict still erupted occasionally, the new imperial state constructed by Octavian experienced a period of remarkable stability for the next two hundred years. To the Romans, their divine mission was clearly to rule nations and peoples. Hadrian, one of the emperors of the second century C.E., was but one of many Roman rulers who believed in Rome's mission. He was a strong and intelligent ruler who took his responsibilities seriously. Between 121 and 132, he visited all of the provinces in the empire. According to his Roman biographer, Aelius Spartianus, "Hardly any emperor ever traveled with such speed over so much territory." When he arrived in a province, Hadrian dealt firsthand with any problems and bestowed many favors on the local population. He also worked to establish the boundaries of the provinces and provide for their defense. New fortifications, such as the 80-mile-long Hadrian's Wall across northern Britain, were built to defend the borders. Hadrian insisted on rigid discipline for frontier armies and demanded that the soldiers be kept in training "just as if war were imminent." He also tried to lead by personal example; according to his biographer, he spent time with the troops and "cheerfully ate out of doors such camp food as bacon, cheese, and vinegar." Moreover, he "would walk as much as twenty miles fully armed."

The Romans imposed their peace on the largest empire established in antiquity. Indeed, Rome's writers proclaimed that "by heaven's will my Rome shall be capital of the world."[1] Those writers were not quite accurate, but few Romans were aware of the Han Empire, which flourished at the same time (202 B.E.C.–221 C.E.) and extended from Central Asia to the Pacific. Although there was little contact between them, the Han and Roman Empires had remarkable similarities: they both lasted for centuries; they both had great success in establishing centralized control; and they both maintained their law and political institutions, technical skills, and languages throughout their empires.

By the third century C.E., however, Rome's ability to rule nations and people began to weaken as the Roman Empire began to experience renewed civil war, economic chaos, and invasions. In the meantime, the growth of Christianity, one of the remarkable success stories of Western civilization, led to the emergence of a new and vibrant institution.

The Age of Augustus (31 B.C.E.–14 C.E.)

Focus Question: In his efforts to solve the problems Rome had faced during the late Republic, what changes did Augustus make in Rome's political, military, and social institutions?

In 27 B.C.E., Octavian proclaimed the "restoration of the Republic." He understood that only traditional republican forms would satisfy the senatorial aristocracy. At the same time, Octavian was aware that the Republic could not be fully restored and managed to arrive at a compromise that worked at least during his lifetime. In 27 B.C.E., the senate awarded him the title of Augustus, "revered one." He preferred the title *princeps* (PRIN-keps *or* PRIN-seps), meaning "chief citizen" or "first among equals." The system of rule that Augustus established is sometimes called the **principate**, conveying the idea of a constitutional monarch as coruler with the senate. But while Augustus worked to maintain this appearance, in reality power was heavily weighted in favor of the *princeps*.

The New Order

In the new constitutional order that Augustus created, the basic governmental structure consisted of the *princeps* (Augustus) and an aristocratic senate. Augustus retained the senate as the chief deliberative body of the Roman

Braccio Nuovo, Vatican Museums, Vatican State/© Scala/Art Resource, NY

Augustus. Octavian, Caesar's adopted son, emerged victorious from the civil conflict that rocked the Republic after Caesar's assassination. The senate awarded him the title Augustus. This marble statue from Prima Porta, an idealized portrait, is based on Greek rather than Roman models. The statue was meant to be a propaganda piece, depicting a youthful general addressing his troops. At the bottom stands Cupid, the son of Venus, goddess of love, meant to be a reminder that the Julians, Caesar's family, claimed descent from Venus, thus emphasizing the ruler's divine background.

The Achievements of Augustus

This excerpt is taken from a text written by Augustus and inscribed on a bronze tablet at Rome. Copies of the text were displayed in stone in many provincial capitals. Called "the most famous ancient inscription," the *Res Gestae* (RAYS GES-ty *or* REEZ JES-tee) of Augustus summarizes his accomplishments in three major areas: his offices, his private expenditures on behalf of the state, and his exploits in war and peace. Though factual in approach, it is a highly subjective account.

Augustus, *Res Gestae*

Below is a copy of the accomplishments of the deified Augustus by which he brought the whole world under the empire of the Roman people, and of the moneys expended by him on the state and the Roman people, as inscribed on two bronze pillars set up in Rome.

1. At the age of nineteen, on my own initiative and at my own expense, I raised an army by means of which I liberated the Republic, which was oppressed by the tyranny of a faction [Mark Antony and his supporters]. . . .
2. Those who assassinated my father [Julius Caesar, his adoptive father] I drove into exile, avenging their crime by due process of law; and afterwards when they waged war against the state, I conquered them twice on the battlefield.
3. I waged many wars throughout the whole world by land and by sea, both civil and foreign, and when victorious I spared all citizens who sought pardon. . . .
5. The dictatorship offered to me . . . by the people and the senate, both in my absence and in my presence, I refused to accept.
17. Four times I came to the assistance of the treasury with my own money, transferring to those in charge of the treasury 150,000,000 sesterces. And in the consulship of Marcus Lepidus and Lucius Arruntius I transferred out of my own patrimony 170,000,000 sesterces to the soldiers' bonus fund, which was established on my advice for the purpose of providing bonuses for soldiers who had completed twenty or more years of service. . . .
22. I gave a gladiatorial show three times in my own name, and five times in the names of my sons or grandsons; at these shows about 10,000 fought. . . .
25. I brought peace to the sea by suppressing the pirates. In that war I turned over to their masters for punishment nearly 30,000 slaves who had run away from their owners and taken up arms against the state. . . .
26. I extended the frontiers of all the provinces of the Roman people on whose boundaries were peoples not subject to our empire. . . .
27. I added Egypt to the empire of the Roman people. . . .
28. I established colonies of soldiers in Africa, Sicily, Macedonia, in both Spanish provinces, in Achaea, Asia, Syria, Narbonese Gaul, and Pisidia. Italy, moreover, has twenty-eight colonies established by me, which in my lifetime have grown to be famous and populous. . . .
35. When I held my thirteenth consulship, the senate, the equestrian order, and the entire Roman people gave me the title of "father of the country." . . . At the time I wrote this document I was in my seventy-sixth year.

Q What were the achievements of Augustus? To what extent did these accomplishments create the "job" of being emperor? In what sense could this document be called a piece of propaganda?

Source: From *Roman Civilization, Vol. I*, Naphtali Lewis and Meyer Renhold. Copyright © 1955 Columbia University Press. Reprinted by permission of the publisher.

state. Its decrees, screened in advance by the *princeps*, now had the effect of law. The title of *princeps* carried no power in itself, but Augustus held the office of consul each year until 23 B.C.E., when he assumed the power of a tribune, which enabled him to propose laws and veto any item of public business. By observing proper legal forms for his power, Augustus proved highly popular. As the Roman historian Tacitus commented, "Indeed, he attracted everybody's goodwill by the enjoyable gift of peace. . . . Opposition did not exist."[2] No doubt the ending of the civil wars had greatly bolstered Augustus's popularity (see the box above). At the same time, his continuing control of the army, while making possible the Roman peace, was a crucial source of his power.

THE MILITARY As a result of the civil wars of the first century B.C.E., the Roman army increased in size and became more professional with legionaries who served for a longer period. Under the empire, the shift to a professional army was completed when early emperors created a bureaucracy that could train and administer such an army. The peace of the Roman Empire depended on the army and so did the security of the *princeps*. Though primarily responsible for guarding the frontiers of the empire, the army was also used to maintain domestic order within the provinces. Augustus maintained a standing army of twenty-eight legions, or about 150,000 men. Roman legionaries were recruited only from the citizenry and, under Augustus, largely from Italy. Augustus also maintained a large contingent of auxiliary forces—around 130,000—enlisted from the subject peoples. Augustus was also responsible for establishing the **praetorian guard**. Although nominally a military reserve, these "nine cohorts of elite troops," roughly 9,000 men, had the important task of guarding the person of the *princeps*. Eventually, the praetorian guard would play an important role in making and deposing emperors.

The role of the *princeps* as military commander gave rise to a title by which this ruler eventually came to be known. When victorious, a military commander was acclaimed by his troops as *imperator* (im-puh-RAH-tur). Augustus was so acclaimed on a number of occasions. *Imperator* is our word *emperor*. Although this title was applied to Augustus and his successors, Augustus still preferred to use the title *princeps*.

ROMAN PROVINCES AND FRONTIERS Augustus inaugurated a new system for governing the provinces. Under the Republic, the senate had appointed the provincial governors. Now certain provinces were allotted to the *princeps*, who assigned deputies known as legates to govern them. These legates were from the senatorial class and held office as long as the emperor chose. The senate continued to designate the governors of the remaining provinces, but the authority of Augustus enabled him to overrule the senatorial governors and establish a uniform imperial policy.

Augustus also stabilized the frontiers of the Roman Empire. He conquered the central and maritime Alps and then expanded Roman control of the Balkan peninsula up to the Danube River. His attempt to conquer Germany failed, however, when three Roman legions under Varus were massacred in 9 C.E. in the Teutoburg Forest by a coalition of German tribes. The defeat severely dampened Augustus's enthusiasm for continued expansion in central Europe. Thereafter, the Romans were content to use the Rhine as the frontier between the Roman province of Gaul and the German tribes to the east. In fact, Augustus's difficulties had convinced him that "the empire should not be extended beyond its present frontiers."[3] His defeats in Germany taught Augustus that Rome's power was not unlimited. They also left him devastated; for months afterward he would beat his head against a door, shouting "Varus, give me back my legions!"

Augustan Society

Society in the Early Roman Empire was characterized by a system of social stratification, inherited from the Republic, in which Roman citizens were divided into three basic classes: the senatorial, equestrian, and lower classes. Augustus had accepted the senatorial order as a ruling class for the empire. Senators filled the chief magistracies of the Roman government, held the most important military posts, and governed the provinces. One needed to possess property worth 1 million sesterces (an unskilled laborer in Rome received 3 sesterces a day; a Roman legionary, 900 sesterces a year in pay) to belong to the senatorial order. The equestrian order was open to all Roman citizens of good standing who possessed property valued at 400,000 sesterces. They, too, could now hold military and governmental offices, but the positions open to them were less important than those of the senators.

Citizens not of the senatorial or equestrian order belonged to the lower classes, who made up the overwhelming majority of free citizens. The diminution of the power of the Roman assemblies ended whatever political power the lower classes may have possessed earlier in the Republic. Many of these people were provided with free grain and public spectacles to keep them from creating disturbances. Nevertheless, by gaining wealth and serving as lower officers in the Roman legions, it was sometimes possible for them to advance to the equestrian order.

Augustus's belief that Roman morals had been corrupted during the late Republic led him to initiate social legislation to arrest the decline. He thought that increased luxury had undermined traditional Roman frugality and simplicity and caused a loosening of morals, evidenced by easy divorce, a falling birthrate among the upper classes, and lax behavior manifested in hedonistic parties and the love affairs of prominent Romans with fashionable women and elegant boys.

Through his new social legislation, Augustus hoped to restore respectability to the upper classes and reverse the declining birthrate as well. Expenditures for feasts were limited, and other laws made adultery a criminal offense. In fact, Augustus's own daughter Julia was exiled for adultery. Augustus also revised the tax laws to penalize bachelors, widowers, and married persons who had fewer than three children.

The Augustan Age

The Augustan Age was a lengthy one. Augustus died in 14 C.E. after dominating the Roman world for forty-five years. He had created a new order while placating the old by restoring and maintaining traditional values, a fitting combination for a leader whose favorite maxim was "make haste slowly." By the time of his death, his new order was so well established that few agitated for an alternative. Indeed, as the Roman historian Tacitus pointed out, "Actium had been won before the younger men were born. Even most of the older generation had come into a world of civil wars. Practically no one had ever seen truly Republican government. . . . Political equality was a thing of the past; all eyes watched for imperial commands."[4] The Republic was now only a memory and, given its last century of warfare, an unpleasant one at that. The new order was here to stay.

The Early Empire (14–180)

Focus Question: What were the chief features of the Roman Empire at its height during the second century?

There was no serious opposition to Augustus's choice of his stepson Tiberius (ty-BEER-ee-uss) as his successor. By designating a family member as *princeps*, Augustus established the Julio-Claudian dynasty; the next four successors of Augustus were related either to his own family or to that of his wife, Livia.

The Julio-Claudians

Several major tendencies emerged during the reigns of the Julio-Claudians (14–68). In general, more and more of the responsibilities that Augustus had given to the senate were taken over by the emperors, who also instituted an imperial bureaucracy, staffed by talented freedmen, to run the government on a daily basis. As the Julio-Claudian successors of Augustus acted more openly as real rulers rather than "first citizens of the state," the opportunity for arbitrary and corrupt acts also increased. Nero (NEE-roh) (54–68) freely eliminated people he wanted out of the way, including his own mother, whose murder he arranged. Without troops, the senators proved unable to oppose these excesses. Eventually, however, Nero's extravagances provoked a revolt of the Roman legions. Abandoned by his guards, Nero chose to commit suicide by stabbing himself in the throat after uttering his final words: "What an artist the world is losing in me." A new civil war erupted in 69, known as the year of the four emperors. Finally, Vespasian (vess-PAY-shun), commander of the legions in the east, established himself as sole ruler and his family as a new dynasty known as the Flavians, which ruled from 69 to 96. The significance of the year 69 was summed up precisely by Tacitus when he stated that "a well-hidden secret of the principate had been revealed: it was possible, it seemed, for an emperor to be chosen outside Rome."[5]

The Five "Good Emperors" (96–180)

At the beginning of the second century, a series of five so-called **good emperors** presided over a period of peace and prosperity that lasted almost a hundred years. These men—Nerva (NUR-vuh), Trajan (TRAY-jun), Hadrian (HAY-dree-un), Antoninus Pius (an-tuh-NY-nuss PY-uss), and Marcus Aurelius (MAR-kuss aw-REE-lee-uss)—treated the ruling classes with respect, cooperated with the senate, ended arbitrary executions, maintained peace throughout the empire, and supported domestic policies generally beneficial to the empire. Though absolute monarchs, they were known for their tolerance and diplomacy. By adopting capable men as their successors, the first four good emperors reduced the chances of succession problems.

Under the five good emperors, the powers of the emperor continued to be extended at the expense of the senate. Increasingly, imperial officials appointed and directed by the emperor took over the running of the government. The good emperors also extended the scope of imperial administration to areas previously untouched by the imperial government. Trajan (98–117) established a program that provided state funds to assist poor parents in raising and educating their children.

The good emperors were widely praised by their subjects for their extensive building programs. Trajan and Hadrian (117–138) were especially active in constructing public works—aqueducts, bridges, roads, and harbor facilities—throughout the provinces and in Rome. Trajan built a new forum in Rome to provide a setting for his celebrated victory column. Hadrian's Pantheon, a temple of "all the gods," is one of the grandest ancient buildings surviving in Rome.

The Roman Empire at Its Height: Frontiers and Provinces

Although Trajan broke with Augustus's policy of defensive imperialism by extending Roman rule into Dacia (modern Romania), Mesopotamia, and the Sinai peninsula, his conquests represent the high-water mark of Roman expansion (see Map 6.1). His successors recognized that the empire was overextended and pursued a policy of retrenchment. Hadrian withdrew Roman forces from much of Mesopotamia. Although he retained Dacia and Arabia, he went on the

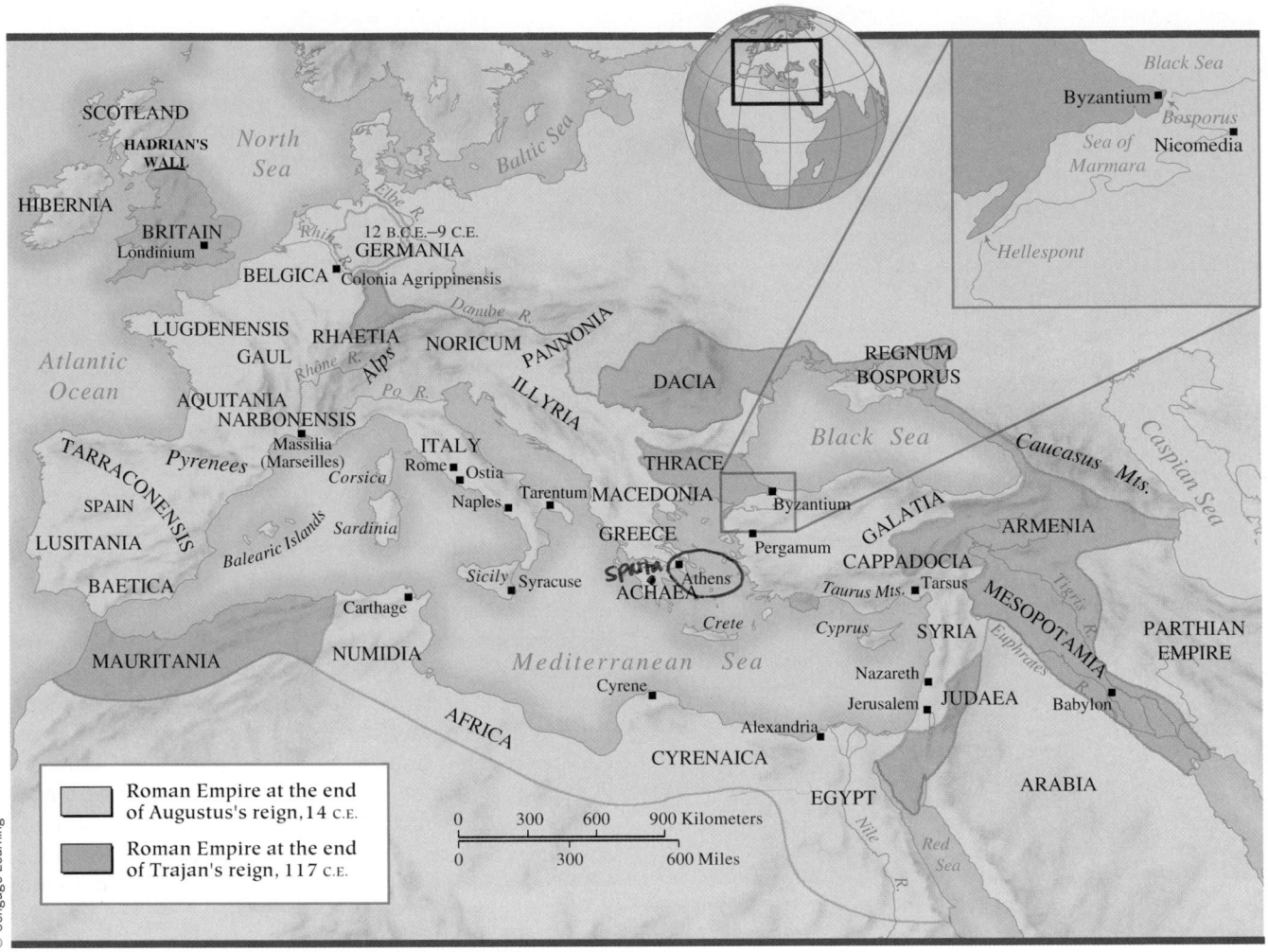

© Cengage Learning

MAP 6.1 The Roman Empire from Augustus Through Trajan (14–117). Augustus and later emperors continued the expansion of the Roman Empire, adding more resources but also increasing the burdens of administration and keeping the peace. Compare this map with Map 5.3.

Which territories were conquered by Augustus, and which were added by the end of Trajan's reign?

defensive in his frontier policy, reinforcing the fortifications along a line connecting the Rhine and Danube Rivers and building a defensive wall 80 miles long to keep the Scots out of Roman Britain. By the end of the second century, the vulnerability of the empire had become apparent. Frontiers were stabilized, and the Roman forces were established in permanent bases behind the frontiers. But when one frontier was attacked, troops had to be drawn from other frontiers, leaving those borders vulnerable to attack. The empire lacked a real strategic reserve, and in the next century its weakness would be ever more apparent.

At its height in the second century, the Roman Empire was one of the greatest states the world had seen. It covered about 3.5 million square miles, and like the empire of Han China, it had a population estimated at more than 50 million. While the emperors and the imperial administration provided a degree of unity, considerable leeway was given to local customs, and the privileges of Roman citizenship were extended to many people throughout the empire. In 212, the emperor Caracalla (kar-uh-KAL-uh) completed the process by giving Roman citizenship to every free inhabitant of the empire. Latin was the language of the western part of the empire, while Greek was used in the east. Although Roman culture spread to all parts of the empire, there were limits to Romanization because local languages persisted and many of the empire's residents spoke neither Latin nor Greek.

CITIES AND ROMANIZATION The administration and cultural life of the Roman Empire depended greatly on cities and towns. A provincial governor's staff was not large, so local city officials were expected to act as Roman agents in carrying out many government functions, especially those related to taxes. Most towns and cities were not large by modern standards. The biggest was Rome, but there were also some large cities in the east: Alexandria in Egypt numbered over 300,000 inhabitants, Ephesus in Asia Minor had 200,000, and Antioch in Syria housed around 150,000. In the west, cities were usually small, with only a few thousand inhabitants. Cities were important in the spread of Roman culture, law, and the Latin language. They were also uniform in physical appearance, with similar temples, markets, amphitheaters, and other public buildings.

Magistrates and town councillors chosen from the ranks of the wealthy upper classes directed municipal administration. These municipal offices were unsalaried but were nevertheless sought by wealthy citizens because they conferred prestige and power at the local level as well as Roman citizenship. Roman municipal policy effectively tied the upper classes to Roman rule and ensured that these classes would retain control over the rest of the population.

The process of Romanization in the provinces was reflected in significant changes in the governing classes of the empire. In the course of the first century, there was a noticeable decline in the number of senators from Italian families. Increasingly, the Roman senate was being recruited from wealthy provincial equestrian families. The provinces also provided many of the legionaries for the Roman army and, beginning with Trajan, supplied many of the emperors.

The speed and the extent of Romanization varied widely in different parts of the empire. In the west, including Spain, Africa, and parts of Gaul, where Greeks and Phoenicians had established cities centuries earlier, Romanization occurred quickly. Temples, aqueducts, amphitheaters, and the Latin language rapidly became fixtures in these areas. Moreover, men from these western territories, especially Spain and parts of Gaul, began serving as officials in Rome as early as the first century C.E.

The process of Romanization was less extensive in other parts of the empire, especially in Asia, where towns and cities had their own traditions long before the arrival of the Romans. Their common language was Greek, not Latin, and many people outside urban areas spoke neither Latin nor Greek. Even more important than geography in determining the degree of Romanization, however, was class status. By 200 C.E., the upper classes everywhere in the empire had become Romanized, sharing a common culture as well as similar economic and social interests.

ROMAN LAW AND ROMANIZATION As Roman citizenship spread in the cities, new citizens themselves became subject to Roman law, which in itself became an important instrument in the process of Romanization. The Early Empire had experienced great progress in the study and codification of law. The second and early third centuries C.E. witnessed the "classical age of Roman law," when a number of great jurists compiled and classified basic legal principles that have remained extremely valuable in the Western world. Most jurists emphasized the emperor as the source of law: "What has pleased the emperor has the force of law." The identification of the law of nations with

© DeA Picture Library (M. Borchi) /Art Resource, NY

Rome in Germany. The Roman army helped bring Roman culture and institutions to the provinces. Local production and trade grew up around the military camps to meet the soldiers' needs, and cities often developed from the bases themselves or from colonies located nearby. Pictured are the remains of the imperial thermal baths in the Roman city of Augusta Treverorum (modern Trier). Trier became the headquarters of the imperial procurator of Belgica and the two Germanies and flourished as one of the most significant cities in the western Roman Empire. Public baths were a prominent feature of any Roman city.

natural law led to a concept of natural rights. According to the jurist Ulpian (d. 228), natural rights implied that all men are born equal and should therefore be equal before the law. Although that principle was not applied in practice, the Romans did establish standards of justice applicable to all people, many of which we would immediately recognize today. A person was regarded as innocent until proved otherwise. People accused of wrongdoing were allowed to defend themselves before a judge. A judge was expected to weigh evidence carefully before arriving at a decision. These principles lived on in Western civilization long after the fall of the Roman Empire.

For Roman citizens, Roman law provided a uniform system of principles by which they conducted their affairs and led their lives. When the emperor Caracalla gave Roman citizenship to every free person in the empire, Roman law became an even more significant factor in binding the entire empire together.

Prosperity in the Early Empire

The Early Empire was a period of considerable prosperity. Internal peace resulted in unprecedented levels of trade (see Map 6.2). Merchants from all over the empire came

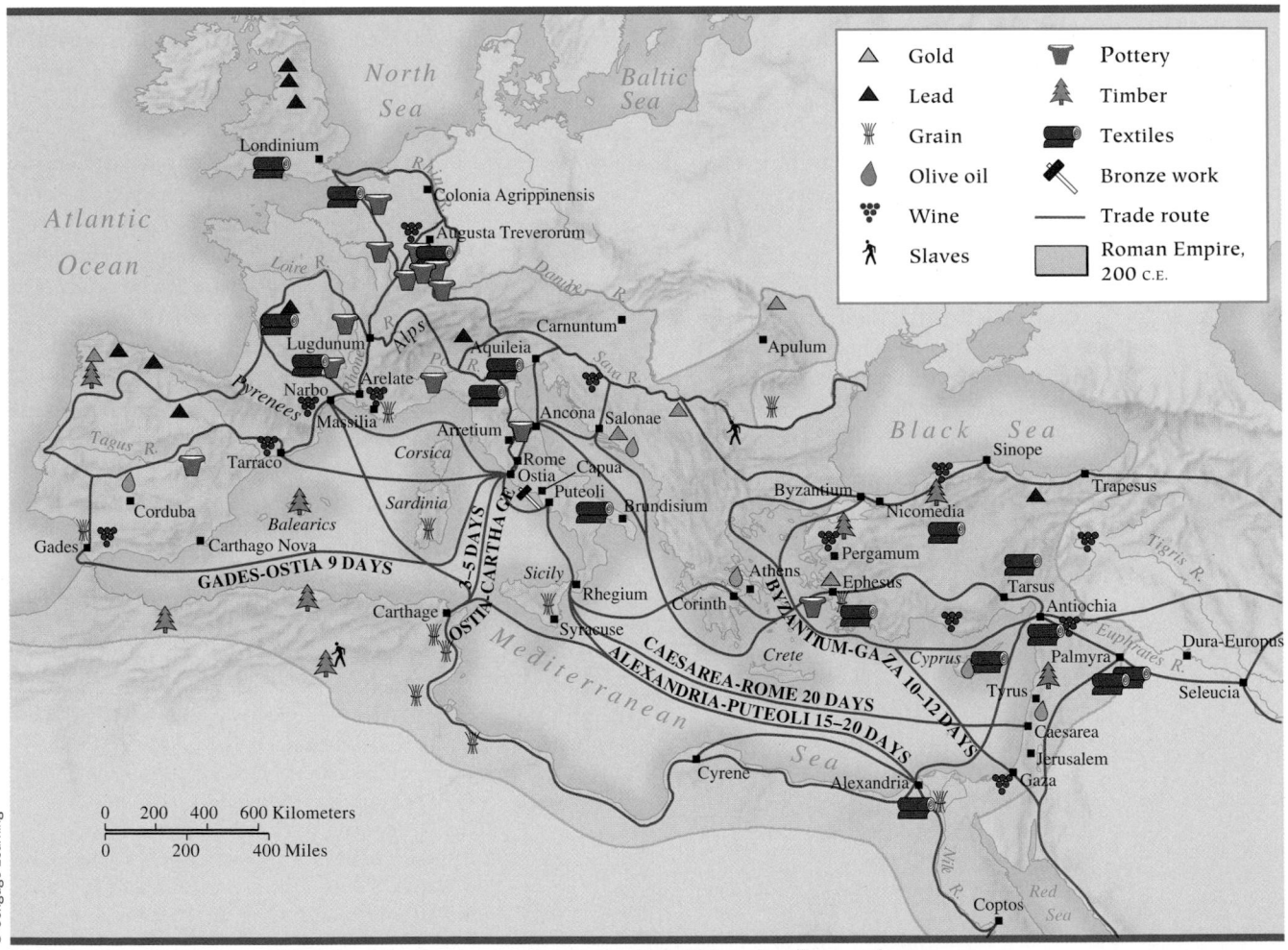

© Cengage Learning

MAP 6.2 Trade Routes and Products in the Roman Empire, c. 200. Although still primarily an agrarian economy, the Roman Empire provided the single currency and stable conditions necessary for an expansion of trade in various commodities and products. An extensive system of roads and shipping routes also facilitated trade.

Q *What truth is there to the statement that "All roads lead to Rome"?*

to the chief Italian ports of Puteoli on the Bay of Naples and Ostia at the mouth of the Tiber. The importation of large quantities of grain to feed the people of Rome and an incredible quantity of luxury items for the wealthy upper classes in the west led to a steady drain of gold and silver coins from Italy and the west to the eastern part of the empire.

Long-distance trade beyond the Roman frontiers also developed during the Early Empire. Developments in both the Roman and Chinese Empires helped foster the growth of this trade. Although both empires built roads chiefly for military purposes, these arteries also came to be used to facilitate trade. Moreover, by creating large empires, the Romans and Chinese not only established internal stability but also pacified bordering territories, thus reducing the threat that bandits posed to traders. As a result, merchants developed a network of trade routes that brought these two great empires into commercial contact. Most important was the overland Silk Road, a regular caravan route between West and East.

The Silk Road was the route used to transport Chinese exports of silk cloth to the West. Silk became a craze among Roman elites, leading to a vast outpouring of silver from Rome to China and provoking the Roman emperor Tiberius to grumble that "the ladies and their baubles are transferring our money to foreigners." The silk trade also stimulated a degree of mutual curiosity between the two great civilizations but not much mutual knowledge or understanding. So far as is known, no personal or diplomatic contacts between the two civilizations ever took place.

Increased trade helped stimulate manufacturing. The cities of the east still produced the items made in Hellenistic times. The first two centuries of the empire also witnessed the high point of industrial development in Italy. Some industries became concentrated in certain areas, such as bronze work in Capua and pottery in Arretium in Etruria (see Images of Everyday Life on p. 122). Other industries, such as brickmaking, were pursued in rural areas on large landed estates. Much production remained small-scale and was done by individual craftsmen, usually freedmen or slaves. In the course of the first century, Italian centers of industry began to experience increasing competition from the provinces.

Despite the extensive trade and commerce, agriculture remained the chief occupation of most people and the underlying basis of Roman prosperity. While the large landed estates called *latifundia* still dominated agriculture, especially in southern and central Italy, small peasant farms persisted, particularly in Etruria and the Po valley. Although large estates concentrating on sheep and cattle raising used slaves, the lands of some *latifundia* were worked by free tenant farmers who paid rent in labor, produce, or sometimes cash.

In considering the prosperity of the Roman world, it is important to remember the enormous gulf between rich and poor (see the box on p. 123). The development of towns and cities, so important to the creation of any civilization, is based in large degree on the agricultural surpluses of the countryside. In ancient times, the margin of surplus produced by each farmer was relatively small.

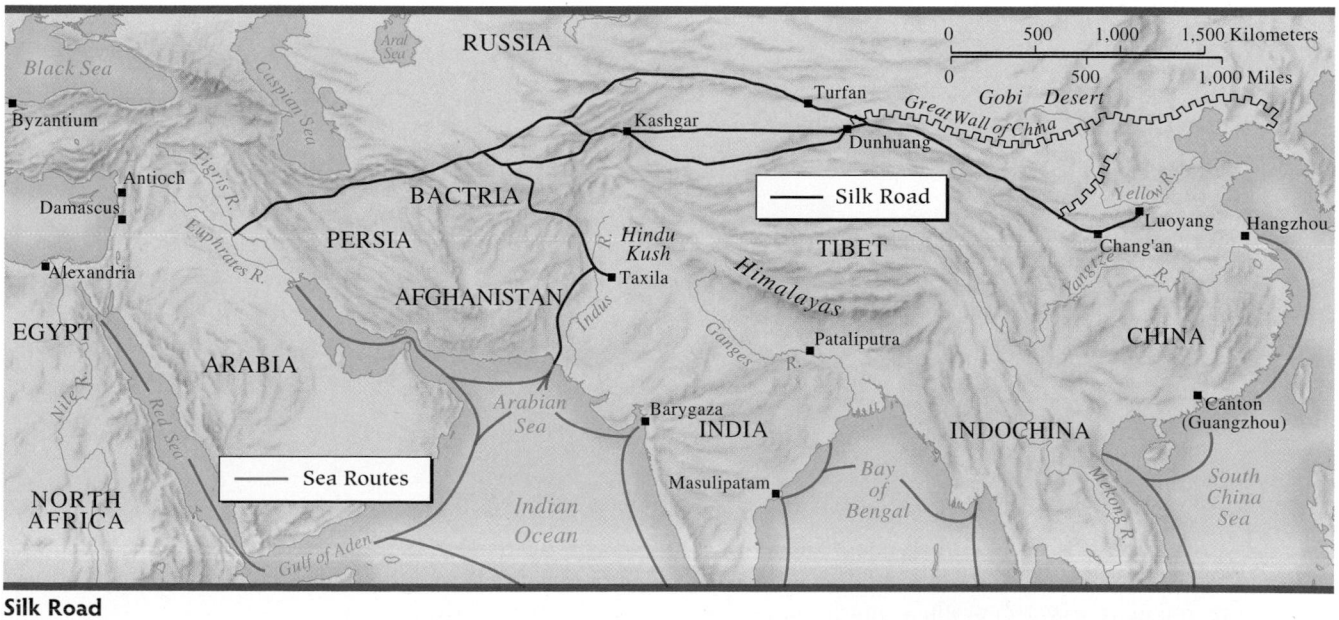

© Cengage Learning

Silk Road

IMAGES OF EVERYDAY LIFE

Trade and the Products of Trade

© The Art Archive/Bardo Museum, Tunis/Gianni Dagli Orti

Museo Civico, Albenga, Italy//© Scala/Art Resource, NY

Trade was an important component in the prosperity of the Early Roman Empire. Although Roman roads were excellent, most goods traveled by boat throughout the Mediterranean and beyond. This third-century C.E. Roman mosaic from Sousse, Tunisia, shows workers unloading a cargo of iron ore from a ship. Vast numbers of amphorae, large two-handled pottery jars, were used to transport olive oil and wine, as well as such luxury items as pepper, cloves, and incense. As can be seen in the illustration at the right from excavations done near Pisa, amphorae could be stacked to transport large quantities of goods. Roman merchant ships could stack between 5,000 and 10,000 of them in their holds. Rome itself became, as one Greek observed, "the warehouse of the world," where "whatever is raised or manufactured by every people is always here in superabundance." In addition to the imported grain that fed the populace, numerous luxury goods were available in the shops. Since many Romans held merchants in low regard, most shops were run by slaves or freedmen. The stone relief from Ostia in the second century C.E. shows a shopkeeper selling groceries and livestock. In addition to the local produce, two monkeys from overseas are available as pets.

Museo Ostiense, Ostia, Italy//
© Erich Lessing/Art Resource, NY

Therefore, the upper classes and urban populations had to be supported by the labor of a large number of farmers who never found it easy to produce much more than enough for themselves. In lean years, when there were no surpluses, the townspeople often took what they wanted, leaving little for the peasants.

The Daily Life of an Upper-Class Roman

There was an enormous gulf between rich and poor in Roman society. The upper classes lived lives of great leisure and luxury in their villas and on their vast estates. Pliny the Younger (c. 62–c. 113) was an upper-class Roman who rose to the position of governor of Bithynia in Asia Minor. In this excerpt from one of his letters, Pliny describes a typical day vacationing at one of his Italian villas. Although Pliny owned four villas in Italy, he did not belong to the ranks of the really rich in Roman society.

Pliny, Letter to Fuscus Salinator

You want to know how I plan the summer days I spend in Tuscany. I wake when I like, usually about sunrise, often earlier but rarely later. My shutters stay closed, for in the stillness and darkness I feel myself surprisingly detached from any distractions and left to myself in freedom. . . . If I have anything on hand I work it out in my head, choosing and correcting the wording, and the amount I achieve depends on the ease or difficulty with which my thoughts can be marshaled and kept in my head. Then I call my secretary, the shutters are opened, and I dictate what I have put into shape; he goes out, is recalled, and again dismissed. Three or four hours after I first wake (but I don't keep to fixed times) I betake myself according to the weather either to the terrace or the covered arcade, work out the rest of my subject, and dictate it. I go for a drive, and spend the time in the same way as when walking or lying down; my powers of concentration do not flag and are in fact refreshed by the change. After a short sleep and another walk I read a Greek or Latin speech aloud and with emphasis, not so much for the sake of my voice as my digestion, though of course both are strengthened by this. Then I have another walk, am oiled, take exercise, and have a bath. If I am dining alone with my wife or with a few friends, a book is read aloud during the meal and afterward we listen to a comedy or some music; then I walk again with the members of my household, some of whom are educated. Thus, the evening is prolonged with varied conversations, and even when the days are at their longest, comes to a satisfying end.

Sometimes I vary this routine, for, if I have spent a long time on my couch or taking a walk, after my siesta and reading I go out on horseback instead of a carriage so as to be quicker and take less time. Part of the day is given up to friends who visit me from neighboring towns and sometimes come to my aid with a welcome interruption when I am tired. Occasionally I go hunting, but not without my notebooks so that I shall have something to bring home even if I catch nothing. I also give some time to my tenants (they think it should be more) and the boorishness of their complaints gives fresh zest to our literary interests and the more civilized pursuits of town.

Q What does Pliny's letter tell you about the lifestyle of upper-class Romans? Could this lifestyle be related to the decline of the Roman Empire? Why or why not?

Source: From THE LETTERS OF THE YOUNGER PLINY, translated with an introduction by Betty Radice (Penguin Classics 1963, Reprinted 1969). Copyright © Betty Radice, 1963, 1969. Reproduced by permission of Penguin Books Ltd.

Roman Culture and Society in the Early Empire

Q **Focus Questions:** What were the chief intellectual, artistic, and social developments in the Early Empire? How did these differ from the intellectual, artistic, and social developments of the Republic?

The shift from republic to empire not only transformed the Roman political world but also affected its cultural and social life. Intellectuals found ways to accommodate the autocratic rule of emperors, while Roman architects created massive buildings befitting an empire. Gladiatorial games increased dramatically in size and number in the Early Empire, and upper-class women acquired greater independence.

The Golden Age of Latin Literature

The most distinguished poet of the Augustan Age was Virgil (VUR-jul) (70–19 B.C.E.). The son of a small landholder in northern Italy, he welcomed the rule of Augustus and wrote his greatest work in the emperor's honor. Virgil's masterpiece was the *Aeneid*, an epic poem clearly meant to rival the work of Homer. The connection between Troy and Rome is made explicitly. Aeneas (i-NEE-uss), the son of Anchises of Troy, survives the destruction of Troy and eventually settles in Latium; hence, Roman civilization is linked to Greek history. The character of Aeneas is portrayed as the ideal Roman—his virtues are duty, piety, and faithfulness. Virgil's overall purpose was to show that Aeneas had fulfilled his mission to establish the Romans in Italy and thereby start Rome on its divine mission to rule the world.

> *Let others fashion from bronze more lifelike, breathing images—*
> *For so they shall—and evoke living faces from marble;*
> *Others excel as orators, others track with their instruments*
> *The planets circling in heaven and predict when stars will appear.*
> *But, Romans, never forget that government is your medium!*
> *Be this your art:—to practice men in the habit of peace,*
> *Generosity to the conquered, and firmness against aggressors.*[6]

As Virgil expressed it, ruling was Rome's gift.

Another prominent Augustan poet was Horace (HOR-uss) (65–8 B.C.E.), a friend of Virgil's. Horace was a sophisticated writer whose overriding concern was to point out to his contemporaries the "follies and vices of his age." In the *Satires*, a medley of poems on a variety of subjects, Horace is revealed as a detached observer of human weaknesses. He directed his attacks against movements, not living people, and took on such subjects as sexual immorality, greed, and job dissatisfaction ("How does it happen, Maecenas, that no man alone is content with his lot?"). Horace mostly laughs at the weaknesses of humankind and calls for forbearance: "Supposing my friend has got liquored and wetted my couch, . . . is he for such a lapse to be deemed less dear as a friend, or because when hungry he snatched up before me a chicken from my side of the dish?"[7]

Ovid (OH-vid) (43 B.C.E.–18 C.E.) was the last of the great poets of the golden age. He belonged to a youthful, privileged social group in Rome that liked to ridicule old Roman values. In keeping with the spirit of this group, Ovid wrote a frivolous series of love poems known as the *Amores*. Intended to entertain and shock, they achieved their goal. Another of Ovid's works was *The Art of Love*. This was essentially a takeoff on didactic poems. Whereas authors of earlier didactic poems had written guides to farming, hunting, or some such subject, Ovid's work was a handbook on the seduction of women (see the box on p. 125).

The most famous Latin prose work of the golden age was written by the historian Livy (LIV-ee) (59 B.C.E.–17 C.E.). Livy's masterpiece was his *History of Rome*, covering the years from the foundation of the city (in the seventh century B.C.E.) to 9 B.C.E. Only 35 of the original 142 books have survived, although we do possess brief summaries of the whole work from other authors. Livy perceived history in terms of moral lessons. As he stated in the preface:

> The study of history is the best medicine for a sick mind; for in history you have a record of the infinite variety of human experience plainly set out for all to see; and in that record you can find for yourself and your country both examples and warnings: fine things to take as models, base things, rotten through and through, to avoid.[8]

For Livy, human character was the determining factor in history.

Livy's history celebrated Rome's greatness. He built scene upon scene that not only revealed the character of the chief figures but also demonstrated the virtues that had made Rome great. Of course, he had serious weaknesses as a historian. He was not always concerned about the factual accuracy of his stories. But he was an excellent storyteller, and his work remained the standard history of Rome for centuries.

The Silver Age of Latin Literature

In the history of Latin literature, the century and a half after Augustus is often labeled the "silver age" to indicate that the literary efforts of the period, though good, were not equal to the high standards of the Augustan "golden age." The popularity of rhetorical training encouraged the use of clever literary expressions at the expense of original content. A good example of this trend can be found in the works of Seneca.

Educated in Rome, Seneca (c. 4 B.C.E.–65 C.E.) became strongly attached to the philosophy of Stoicism. In letters written to a young friend, he expressed the basic tenets of Stoicism: living according to nature, accepting events dispassionately as part of the divine plan, and universal love for all humanity. Thus, "the first thing philosophy promises us is the feeling of fellowship, of belonging to mankind and being members of a community. . . . Philosophy calls for simple living, not for doing penance, and the simple way of life need not be a crude one."[9] Viewed in retrospect, Seneca displays some glaring inconsistencies. While preaching the virtues of simplicity, he amassed a fortune and was ruthless at times in protecting it. His letters show humanity, benevolence, and fortitude, but his sentiments are often undermined by an attempt to be clever with words.

The greatest historian of the silver age was Tacitus (c. 56–120). His main works included the *Annals* and *Histories*, which presented a narrative account of Roman history from the reign of Tiberius through the assassination of the emperor Domitian (doh-MISH-un) in 96. Tacitus believed that history had a moral purpose: "It seems to me a historian's foremost duty to ensure that merit is recorded, and to confront evil deeds and words with the fear of posterity's denunciations."[10] As a member of the senatorial class, Tacitus was disgusted with the abuses of power perpetrated

Ovid and the Art of Love

Ovid has been called the last great poet of the Augustan golden age of literature. One of his most famous works was *The Art of Love*, a guidebook for the seduction of women. Unfortunately for Ovid, the work appeared at a time when Augustus was eager to improve the morals of the Roman upper class. Augustus considered the work offensive, and Ovid soon found himself in exile.

Ovid, *The Art of Love*

Now I'll teach you how to captivate and hold the woman of your choice. This is the most important part of all my lessons. Lovers of every land, lend an attentive ear to my discourse; let goodwill warm your hearts, for I am going to fulfill the promises I made you.

First of all, be quite sure that there isn't a woman who cannot be won, and make up your mind that you will win her. Only you must prepare the ground. Sooner would the birds cease their song in the springtime, or the grasshopper be silent in the summer, . . . than a woman resist the tender wooing of a youthful lover. . . .

Now the first thing you have to do is to get on good terms with the fair one's maid. She can make things easy for you. Find out whether she is fully in her mistress's confidence, and if she knows all about her secret dissipations. Leave no stone unturned to win her over. Once you have her on your side, the rest is easy. . . .

In the first place, it's best to send her a letter, just to pave the way. In it you should tell her how you dote on her; pay her beauty compliments and say all the nice things lovers always say. . . . Even the gods are moved by the voice of entreaty. And promise, promise, promise. Promises will cost you nothing. Everyone's a millionaire where promises are concerned. . . .

If she refuses your letter and sends it back unread, don't give up; hope for the best and try again. . . .

Don't let your hair stick up in tufts on your head; see that your hair and your beard are decently trimmed. See also that your nails are clean and nicely filed; don't have any hair growing out of your nostrils; take care that your breath is sweet, and don't go about reeking like a billy-goat. All other toilet refinements leave to the women or to perverts. . . .

When you find yourself at a feast where the wine is flowing freely, and where a woman shares the same couch with you, pray to that god whose mysteries are celebrated during the night, that the wine may not overcloud your brain. 'Tis then you may easily hold converse with your mistress in hidden words whereof she will easily divine the meaning. . . .

By subtle flatteries you may be able to steal into her heart, even as the river insensibly overflows the banks which fringe it. Never cease to sing the praises of her face, her hair, her taper fingers and her dainty foot. . . .

Tears, too, are a mighty useful resource in the matter of love. They would melt a diamond. Make a point, therefore, of letting your mistress see your face all wet with tears.

Howbeit, if you can't manage to squeeze out any tears—and they won't always flow just when you want them to—put your finger in your eyes.

Q What were Ovid's principles of love? Why do you think Augustus found *The Art of Love* so offensive?

Source: From *The Love Books of Ovid*, translated by J. Lewis May. Published 1930 by Rarity Press.

by the emperors and was determined that the "evil deeds" of wicked men would not be forgotten. Many historians believe he went too far in projecting the evils of his own day into his account of the past. His work *Germania* is especially important as a source of information about the early Germans. But it too is colored by Tacitus's attempt to depict the Germans as noble savages in contrast to the decadent Romans.

The Upper-Class Roman Family

By the second century C.E., significant changes were occurring in the Roman family. The foundations of the authority of the *paterfamilias* over his family, which had already begun to weaken in the late Republic, were further undermined. The *paterfamilias* no longer had absolute authority over his children; he could no longer sell his children into slavery or have them put to death. Moreover, the husband's absolute authority over his wife also disappeared, a process that had begun in the late Republic. In the Early Empire, the idea of male guardianship continued to weaken significantly, and by the late second century, it had become a formality.

Upper-class Roman women in the Early Empire had considerable freedom and independence. They had acquired

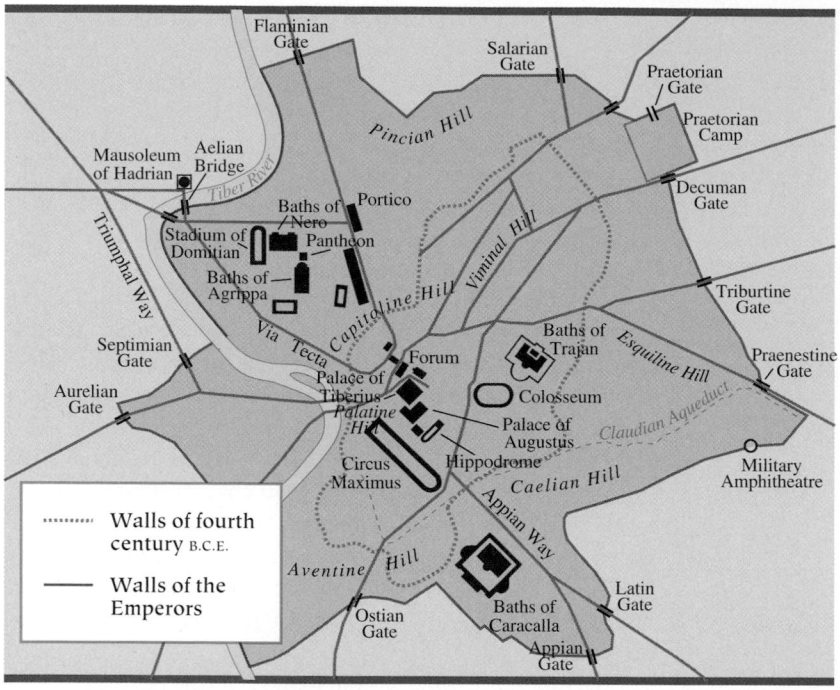

© Cengage Learning

MAP 6.3 Imperial Rome. A large, overcrowded, and dirty city, Rome was the political, economic, social, and cultural hub of the Roman Empire. Squalid and desperate living conditions for the poor contrasted dramatically with the city's aristocratic villas and magnificent architectural works.

How did roads from outside enter Rome, and what could possibly explain this?

the right to own, inherit, and dispose of property. Upper-class women could attend races, the theater, and events in the amphitheater, although in the latter two places they were forced to sit in sections apart from the men. Moreover, ladies of rank were still accompanied by maids and companions when they went out. Some women operated businesses, such as shipping firms. Women could still not participate in politics, but the Early Empire saw a number of important women who influenced politics through their husbands, including Livia, the wife of Augustus; Agrippina, the mother of Nero; and Plotina, the wife of Trajan.

Imperial Rome

At the center of the colossal Roman Empire was the ancient city of Rome (see Map 6.3). Truly a capital city, Rome had the largest population of any city in the empire. It is estimated that it was home to close to one million people by the time of Augustus. For anyone with political ambitions, Rome was the place to be. Extremely cosmopolitan, it was a magnet to people far and near. Nationalities from all over the empire resided there, with entire neighborhoods inhabited by specific groups, such as Greeks and Syrians.

But for all its sophistication, Rome was an overcrowded and noisy city. Because of the congestion, cart and wagon traffic was banned from the streets during the day. The noise from the resulting vehicular movement at night often made sleep difficult. Evening pedestrian travel was dangerous. Although Augustus had organized a police force, lone travelers could be assaulted, robbed, or soaked by filth thrown out of the upper-story windows of Rome's massive apartment buildings.

An enormous gulf existed between rich and poor in the city of Rome. While the rich had comfortable villas, the poor lived in apartment blocks called *insulae*, which might be six stories high. Constructed of concrete, they were often poorly built and prone to collapse. The use of wooden beams in the floors and movable stoves, torches, candles, and lamps in the rooms for heat and light created a constant danger of fire. Once started, fires were extremely difficult to put out. The famous conflagration of 64, which Nero was unjustly accused of starting, devastated a good part of the city. Besides the hazards of collapse and fire, living conditions were miserable. High rents forced entire families into one room. The absence of plumbing and central heating made life so uncomfortable that poorer Romans spent most of their time outdoors in the streets.

Fortunately for these people, Rome boasted public buildings unequaled elsewhere in the empire. Its temples, forums, markets, baths, theaters, triumphal arches, governmental buildings, and amphitheaters gave parts of the city an appearance of grandeur and magnificence.

Though the center of a great empire, Rome was also a great parasite. Beginning with Augustus, the emperors accepted responsibility for providing food for the urban populace, with about 200,000 people receiving free grain. Even with the free grain, conditions were grim for the poor. Early in the second century, a Roman doctor noted that rickets was common among children in the city.

In addition to food, entertainment was provided on a grand scale for the inhabitants of Rome. The poet Juvenal said of the Roman masses, "But nowadays, with no vote to sell, their motto is 'Couldn't care less.' Time was when their plebiscite elected generals, heads of state, commanders of legions: but now they've pulled in their horns, there's only two things that concern them: Bread and Circuses."[11] Public

© Thomas S. England/Photo Researchers, Inc.

Interior of the Colosseum of Rome. The Colosseum was a large amphitheater constructed under the emperor Vespasian and his son Titus. Such amphitheaters, in which gladiatorial contests were held, were built throughout the empire. They varied in size, but the one at Rome was the largest. The Colosseum was named after the Colossus of Nero, a large statue of the first-century C.E. emperor that stood nearby. The scene of many bloody gladiatorial combats, the Colosseum could be used for other spectacles as well. It was flooded for a spectacular naval battle when the emperor Titus held the first games there.

spectacles were provided by the emperor and other state officials as part of the great festivals—most of them religious in origin—celebrated by the state. More than one hundred days a year were given over to these public holidays. The festivals included three major types of entertainment. At the Circus Maximus, horse and chariot races attracted hundreds of thousands of spectators, while dramatic and other performances were held in theaters. But the most famous of all the public spectacles were the gladiatorial shows.

The Gladiatorial Shows

The gladiatorial shows were an integral part of Roman society. They took place in amphitheaters; the first permanent one was constructed at Rome in 29 B.C.E. Perhaps the most famous was the Flavian amphitheater, called the Colosseum, which could seat 50,000 spectators. Similar amphitheaters, with capacities ranging from a few thousand to tens of thousands, were built throughout the empire. In most cities and towns, the amphitheaters were the biggest buildings, rivaled only by the circuses for races and the public baths. Where a society invests its money gives an idea of its priorities. Since the amphitheater was the primary location for the gladiatorial games, it is fair to say that public slaughter was an important part of Roman culture.

Gladiatorial games were held from dawn to dusk. The main events were contests to the death between trained fighters. Most gladiators were slaves or condemned criminals and were trained for combat in special gladiatorial schools (see the Film & History feature on p. 128).

Gladiatorial games included other forms of entertainment as well. Criminals of all ages and both sexes were sent into the arena without weapons to face certain death from wild animals who would tear them to pieces. Numerous kinds of animal contests were also staged: wild beasts against each other, such as bears against buffaloes; staged hunts with men shooting safely from behind iron bars; and gladiators in the arena with bulls, tigers, and lions. Reportedly, five thousand beasts were killed in one day of games when the emperor Titus inaugurated the Colosseum in 80 C.E. Enormous resources were invested in the capture and shipment of wild animals for slaughter, and whole species were hunted to extinction in parts of the empire.

These bloodthirsty spectacles were wildly popular with the Roman people. The Roman historian Tacitus said, "Few indeed are to be found who talk of any other subjects in their homes, and whenever we enter a classroom, what else is the conversation of the youths."[12] But the gladiatorial games served a purpose beyond mere entertainment. Like the other forms of public entertainment, they fulfilled both a political and a social function by diverting the thoughts of the idle masses from political unrest. It was said of the emperor Trajan that he understood that although the distribution of grain and money satisfied the individual, spectacles were necessary for the "contentment of the masses."

FILM & HISTORY

Gladiator (2000)

The film *Gladiator*, directed by Ridley Scott, is a fictional story set in the Roman Empire near the end of the second century C.E. In the movie, Emperor Marcus Aurelius (Richard Harris) informs his son Commodus (Joaquin Phoenix) that he intends to turn over imperial power to his successful and respected general, Maximus (Russell Crowe), in the hope that this decent and honest man can restore the Roman Senate and revive the Republic. Commodus reacts by killing his father, assuming the position of emperor, and ordering the deaths of Maximus, his wife, and son. Maximus escapes but returns to Spain too late to save his wife and child. He is captured and then sold into slavery to Proximo (Oliver Reed), who trains him to be a gladiator. Maximus is eventually sent to Rome, where he becomes a superhero in the gladiatorial games in the Roman Colosseum, all the while awaiting an opportunity to avenge the deaths of his wife and son by killing Commodus. Maximus becomes involved in a plot with Lucilla (Connie Nielsen), the emperor's sister, and Gracchus (Derek Jacobi), a Roman senator, to rejoin his army, march on Rome, and overthrow the emperor. When Commodus discovers the plot, he challenges the captured Maximus to a duel in the Colosseum but stabs him first to ensure his own success. Despite his injury, Maximus kills the emperor in combat.

Gladiator is a relatively exciting story, but how much of it is based on historical facts? With the exception of Marcus Aurelius, Commodus, and Lucilla, all of the characters are fictional. Marcus Aurelius was a kind emperor with a love of philosophy and died in 180 C.E., probably of plague, and certainly not by his son's hands, as depicted in the film. Commodus ruled from 180 to 192, although he was only eighteen when he became emperor, not in his late twenties as in the movie; and he had blond hair, not dark hair. Commodus was an unstable and cruel young man who was strongly attracted to gladiatorial contests. He was obsessed with performing in the arena, especially with slaughtering animals. He was not killed in the Colosseum, however, but was strangled by his wrestling partner on the last day of 192.

Contrary to the movie, Marcus Aurelius had no intention of restoring the Republic; by 180, most Romans had become well accustomed to the empire. In fact, Marcus Aurelius had already made his son Commodus a joint ruler in 177. Nor had Marcus Aurelius banned gladiatorial games, as the movie claims. And although Commodus's sister Lucilla did enter into a plot with some senators to assassinate her brother in 182, the plot failed, and the conspirators, including Lucilla, were executed.

Maximus (Russell Crowe) triumphs in the Roman Colosseum.

© DreamWorks/Courtesy Everett Collection

Although *Gladiator* shows little concern for historical facts, the movie did demonstrate that many people are still interested in ancient history. It became one of the highest earning films of 2000 and won numerous awards including Academy Awards for Best Picture and Best Actor for Russell Crowe. Moreover, the film helped to renew interest in Roman history—sales of biographies of historical Roman figures and Marcus Aurelius's *Meditations* increased noticeably in the years after the movie was released.

Transformation of the Roman World: Crises in the Third Century

Focus Question: What political, military, economic, and social problems did the Roman Empire face during the third century?

At the end of the second century, a number of natural catastrophes struck Rome. Floods of the Tiber, famine, and plague brought back from the east by the army led to a considerable loss of population and a shortage of military manpower. To many Romans, these natural disasters seemed to portend an ominous future for Rome, and indeed, in the course of the third century, the Roman Empire came near to collapse.

Political and Military Woes

After a series of civil wars, Septimius Severus (sep-TIM-ee-uss se-VEER-uss) (193–211), who was born in North Africa and spoke Latin with an accent, used his legions to seize power. On his deathbed, Septimius Severus advised his sons, "Live in harmony, make the soldiers rich, and don't give a damn for anything else." His advice set the tone for the new dynasty he established. The Severan rulers (193–235) began to create a military monarchy. The army was expanded, soldiers' pay was increased, and military officers were appointed to important government positions. A new stability seemed at hand, but the increased power of the military led new military leaders to aspire to become emperor, and the military monarchy of the Severan rulers degenerated into military anarchy.

For the next fifty years (235–284), the empire was mired in the chaos of continual civil war. Contenders for the imperial throne found that bribing soldiers was an effective way to become emperor. In these five decades, there were twenty-two emperors, only two of whom did not meet a violent end. At the same time, the empire was beset by a series of invasions, no doubt encouraged by the internal turmoil. In the east, the Sassanid Persians made inroads into Roman territory. A fitting symbol of Rome's crisis was the capture of the Roman emperor, Valerian (253–260), by the Persians and his death in captivity, an event unprecedented in Roman history. Valerian's body was displayed in the chief towns of Persia. Germanic tribes also poured into the empire. The Goths overran the Balkans and moved into Greece and Asia Minor. The Franks advanced into Gaul and Spain. Not until the reign of Aurelian (aw-REEL-yun) (270–275) were most of the boundaries restored. Although he abandoned the Danubian province of Dacia, Aurelian reconquered Gaul and

Antikensammlung (Johannes Laurentius), Staatliche Museen zu Berlin/© Bildarchiv Preussischer Kulturbesitz /Art Resource, NY

Septimius Severus and His Family. This portrait, painted on wood about 200 C.E., is the only existing painted likeness of a Roman emperor. The painting, which was found in Egypt, portrays the emperor with gray hair and beard in memory of Marcus Aurelius. To legitimize his authority, Septimius Severus had himself adopted into the Antonine dynasty, calling himself the son of Marcus Aurelius. The emperor stands next to his wife with their two sons in front of them. The face of his son Geta has been blotted out, no doubt by order of the other son standing next to him, Caracalla, who had his brother killed when he succeeded to the throne.

reestablished order in the east and along the Danube. Grateful citizens hailed him as "restorer of the world."

As civil wars and invasions wore down the central government, provinces began to break away from the empire. A military commander named Postumus seized control of Gaul and then gained the support of Britain and Spain. He defended his "Gallic empire" until he was killed by his own soldiers in 269. In the east, Zenobia (zuh-NOH-bee-uh), the wife of the ruler of Syria, seized power after his death and then in 270 extended her control over Egypt and much of Asia Minor. In 272, Emperor Aurelian ended this threat to imperial power by defeating Zenobia and her forces in Syria.

Economic and Social Crises

Invasions, civil wars, and a recurrence of the plague came close to causing an economic collapse of the Roman Empire in the third century. The population declined drastically, possibly by as much as one-third. There was a noticeable decline in trade and small industry. The labor shortage created by the plague affected both military recruiting and the economy. Farm production deteriorated as fields were ravaged by Germanic tribes and even more often by the defending Roman armies. Many farmers complained that Roman commanders and their soldiers were confiscating produce and livestock. Provincial governors seemed powerless to stop these depredations, and some even joined in the extortion. The monetary system began to show signs of collapse as a result of debased coinage and the beginnings of serious inflation.

Armies were needed more than ever, but financial strains made it difficult to enlist and pay the necessary soldiers. Short of cash, the imperial government paid its soldiers with produce, causing bitter resentment. Whereas in the second century the Roman army had been recruited among the inhabitants of frontier provinces, by the mid-third century the state had to rely on hiring barbarians to fight under Roman commanders. These soldiers had no understanding of Roman traditions and no real attachment to either the empire or the emperors. By the end of the third century, a new political structure would emerge (see Chapter 7).

Transformation of the Roman World: The Rise of Christianity

Q Focus Question: What characteristics of Christianity enabled it to grow and ultimately to triumph?

The advent of Christianity marks a fundamental break with the dominant values of the Greco-Roman world. Christian views of God, human beings, and the world were quite different from those of the Greeks and Romans. Nevertheless, to understand the rise of Christianity, we must first examine both the religious environment of the Roman world and the Jewish background from which Christianity emerged.

The Religious World of the Roman Empire

Augustus had taken a number of steps to revive the Roman state religion, which had declined during the turmoil of the late Republic. The official state religion focused on the worship of a pantheon of gods and goddesses. Observance of proper ritual by state priests theoretically established the proper relationship between Romans and the gods and guaranteed security, peace, and prosperity. The polytheistic Romans were extremely tolerant of other religions. The Romans allowed the worship of native gods and goddesses throughout their provinces and even adopted some of the local gods. In addition, the imperial cult of Rome and Augustus was developed to bolster support for the emperors. After Augustus, deceased emperors deified by the Roman senate were included in the official imperial cult.

The desire for a more emotional spiritual experience led many people to the mystery religions of the Hellenistic east, which flooded into the western Roman world during the Early Empire. The mystery religions offered secret teachings that promised their followers advantages unavailable through Roman religion: entry into a higher world of reality and the promise of a future life superior to the present one. They also featured elaborate rituals with deep emotional appeal. By participating in their ceremonies and performing their rites, an adherent could achieve communion with spiritual beings and undergo purification that opened the door to life after death.

Although many mystery cults competed for the attention of the Roman world, perhaps the most important was Mithraism. Mithra was the chief agent of Ahuramazda, the supreme god of light in Persian Zoroastrianism (see Chapter 2). In the Roman world, Mithra came to be identified with the sun god and was known by his Roman title, the Unconquered Sun. Mithraism had spread rapidly in Rome and the western provinces by the second century C.E. and was especially favored by soldiers, who viewed Mithra as their patron deity. Mithraists paid homage to the sun on the first day of the week (Sunday), commemorated the sun's birthday around December 25, and celebrated ceremonial meals. All of these practices had parallels in Christianity.

The Jewish Background

In Hellenistic times, the Jewish people had been granted considerable independence by their Seleucid rulers (see Chapter 4). Roman involvement with the Jews began in

63 B.C.E., and by 6 C.E., Judaea had been made a province and placed under the direction of a Roman procurator. But unrest continued, augmented by divisions among the Jews themselves. The Sadducees believed in rigid adherence to Hebrew law, rejected the possibility of personal immortality, and favored cooperation with the Romans. The Pharisees adhered strictly to Jewish ritual, and although they wanted Judaea to be free from Roman control, they did not advocate violent means to achieve this goal. The Essenes were a Jewish sect that lived in a religious community near the Dead Sea. As revealed in the Dead Sea Scrolls, a collection of documents first discovered in 1947, the Essenes, like many other Jews, awaited a Messiah who would save Israel from oppression, usher in the kingdom of God, and establish a true paradise on earth. A fourth group, the Zealots, were militant extremists who advocated the violent overthrow of Roman rule. A Jewish revolt in 66 C.E. was crushed by the Romans four years later. The Jewish Temple in Jerusalem was destroyed, and Roman power once more stood supreme in Judaea.

The Origins of Christianity

In the midst of the confusion and conflict in Judaea, Jesus of Nazareth (c. 6 B.C.E.–30 C.E.) began his public preaching. Jesus grew up in Galilee, an important center of the militant Zealots. Jesus's message was straightforward. He reassured his fellow Jews that he did not plan to undermine their traditional religion: "Do not think that I have come to abolish the Law or the Prophets; I have not come to abolish them but to fulfill them."[13] According to Jesus, what was important was not strict adherence to the letter of the law and attention to rules and prohibitions but the transformation of the inner person: "So in everything, do to others what you would have them do to you, for this sums up the Law and the Prophets."[14] God's command was simple—to love God and one another: "Love the Lord your God with all your heart and with all your soul and with all your mind and with all your strength. The second is this: Love your neighbor as yourself."[15] In his Sermon on the Mount, Jesus presented the ethical concepts—humility, charity, and brotherly love—that would form the basis for the value system of medieval Western civilization. As we have seen, these were not the values of Classical Greco-Roman civilization.

Although some Jews welcomed Jesus as the Messiah who would save Israel from oppression and establish God's kingdom on earth, Jesus spoke of a heavenly kingdom, not an earthly one: "My kingdom is not of this world."[16] In this he disappointed the radicals. At the same time, conservative religious leaders believed that Jesus was another false Messiah who was undermining respect for traditional Jewish religion. To the Roman authorities of Palestine and their local allies, the Nazarene was a potential revolutionary who might transform Jewish expectations of a messianic kingdom into a revolt against Rome. Jesus thus found himself denounced on many sides and was given over to the Roman authorities. The procurator Pontius Pilate ordered his crucifixion. But that did not solve the problem. A few loyal disciples spread the story that Jesus had overcome death, had been resurrected, and had then ascended into heaven. The belief in Jesus's resurrection became an important tenet of Christian doctrine. Jesus was now hailed by his followers as the

Catacomb of S. Domitilla, Rome, Italy/© Scala/Art Resource, NY

Jesus and His Apostles. Pictured is a fourth-century fresco from a Roman catacomb depicting Jesus and his apostles. Catacombs were underground cemeteries where early Christians buried their dead. Christian tradition holds that in times of imperial repression, Christians withdrew to the catacombs to pray and hide.

"anointed one" (*Christ* in Greek), the Messiah who would return and usher in the kingdom of God on earth.

THE IMPORTANCE OF PAUL Christianity began, then, as a religious movement within Judaism and was viewed that way by Roman authorities for many decades. Although tradition holds that one of Jesus's disciples, Peter, founded the Christian church at Rome, the most important figure in early Christianity after Jesus was Paul of Tarsus (c. 5–c. 67). Paul reached out to non-Jews and transformed Christianity from a Jewish sect into a broader religious movement.

Called the "second founder of Christianity," Paul was a Jewish Roman citizen who had been strongly influenced by Hellenistic Greek culture. He believed that the message of Jesus should be preached not only to Jews but to Gentiles (non-Jews) as well. Paul was responsible for founding Christian communities throughout Asia Minor and along the shores of the Aegean.

It was Paul who provided a universal foundation for the spread of Jesus's ideas. He taught that Jesus was, in effect, a savior-God, the son of God, who had come to earth to save all humans, who were basically sinners as a result of Adam's original sin of disobedience against God as recorded in the Old Testament. By his death, Jesus had atoned for the sins of all humans and made it possible for all men and women to experience a new beginning with the potential for individual salvation. By accepting Jesus Christ as their savior, they too could be saved.

THE SPREAD OF CHRISTIANITY At first, Christianity spread slowly. Although the teachings of early Christianity were disseminated primarily by the preaching of convinced Christians, written materials also appeared. Paul had written a series of epistles (letters) outlining Christian beliefs for different Christian communities. Some of Jesus's disciples may also have preserved some of the sayings of the master in writing and would have passed on personal memories that became the basis of the written gospels—the "good news" concerning Jesus as recorded by Matthew, Mark, Luke, and John—which eventually became the authoritative record of Jesus's life and teachings and formed the core of the New Testament. Recently, some scholars have argued that other gospels, such as that of Thomas, were rejected because they deviated from the beliefs about Jesus held by the emerging church leaders.

Although Jerusalem was the first center of Christianity, its destruction by the Romans in 70 C.E. left individual Christian churches with considerable independence. By 100, Christian churches had been established in most of the major cities of the east and in some places in the western part of the empire. Many early Christians came from the ranks of Hellenized Jews and the Greek-speaking populations of the east. But in the second and third centuries, an increasing number of followers came from Latin-speaking cultures. A Latin translation of the Greek New Testament that appeared soon after 200 aided this process.

Although some of the fundamental values of Christianity differed markedly from those of the Greco-Roman world, the Romans initially did not pay much attention to the Christians and regarded them at first as simply another sect of Judaism. The structure of the Roman Empire itself aided the growth of Christianity. Christian missionaries, including some of Jesus's original twelve disciples, known as apostles, used Roman roads to travel throughout the empire spreading their "good news."

As the popular appeal of Christianity grew, the Roman attitude toward it began to change. The Romans were tolerant of other religions except when they threatened public order or public morals. Many Romans came to view Christians as harmful to the order of the Roman state. Because Christians held their meetings in secret and seemed to be connected to Christian groups in distant areas, the government could view them as potentially dangerous to the state.

Some Romans felt that Christians were overly exclusive and hence harmful to the community and public order. The Christians did not recognize other gods and therefore abstained from public festivals honoring these divinities. Finally, Christians refused to participate in the worship of the state gods and the imperial cult. Since the Romans regarded these as important to the state, the Christians' refusal undermined the security of the state and hence constituted an act of treason, punishable by death. But to the Christians, who believed there was only one real God, the worship of state gods and the emperors was idolatry and would endanger their own salvation.

Nevertheless, Roman persecution of Christians in the first and second centuries was never systematic but only sporadic and local. It began during the reign of Nero. After the fire that destroyed much of Rome, the emperor used the Christians as scapegoats, accusing them of arson and hatred of the human race and subjecting them to cruel deaths in Rome. In the second century, Christians were largely ignored as harmless (see the box on p. 133). By the end of the reigns of the five good emperors, Christians still represented a small minority, but one of considerable strength.

The Growth of Christianity

The sporadic persecution of Christians by the Romans in the first and second centuries did nothing to stop the growth of Christianity. In fact, it served to strengthen Christianity as an institution in the second and third centuries by causing it to shed the loose structure of the first century and move toward a more centralized organization of its various church communities. Crucial to this change

Roman Authorities and a Christian on Christianity

At first, Roman authorities were uncertain how to deal with the Christians. In the second century, as seen in the following exchange between Pliny the Younger and the emperor Trajan, Christians were often viewed as harmless and yet were subject to persecution if they persisted in being Christians. Pliny was governor of the province of Bithynia in northwestern Asia Minor (present-day Turkey). He wrote to the emperor for advice about how to handle people accused of being Christians. Trajan's response reflects the general approach toward Christians by the emperors of the second century. The final selection is taken from *Against Celsus*, written about 246 by Origen of Alexandria. In it, Origen defended the value of Christianity against Celsus, a philosopher who had written an attack on Christians and their teachings.

An Exchange Between Pliny and Trajan

Pliny to Trajan

It is my custom to refer all my difficulties to you, Sir, for no one is better able to resolve my doubts and to inform my ignorance.

I have never been present at an examination of Christians. Consequently, I do not know the nature or the extent of the punishments usually meted out to them, nor the grounds for starting an investigation and how far it should be pressed. . . .

For the moment this is the line I have taken with all persons brought before me on the charge of being Christians. I have asked them in person if they are Christians, and if they admit it, I repeat the question a second and third time, with a warning of the punishment awaiting them. If they persist, I order them to be led away for execution; for, whatever the nature of their admission, I am convinced that their stubbornness and unshakable obstinacy ought not to go unpunished. . . .

Now that I have begun to deal with this problem, as so often happens, the charges are becoming more widespread and increasing in variety. An anonymous pamphlet has been circulated which contains the names of a number of accused persons. . . .

I have therefore postponed any further examination and hastened to consult you. The question seems to me to be worthy of your consideration, especially in view of the number of persons endangered; for a great many individuals of every age and class, both men and women, are being brought to trial, and this is likely to continue. It is not only the towns, but villages and rural districts too which are infected through contact with this wretched cult. I think though that it is still possible for it to be checked and directed to better ends, for there is no doubt that people have begun to throng the temples which had been almost entirely deserted for a long time. . . . It is easy to infer from this that a great many people could be reformed if they were given an opportunity to repent.

Trajan to Pliny

You have followed the right course of procedure, my dear Pliny, in your examination of the cases of persons charged with being Christians, for it is impossible to lay down a general rule to a fixed formula. These people must not be hunted out; if they are brought before you and the charge against them is proved, they must be punished, but in the case of anyone who denies that he is a Christian, and makes it clear that he is not by offering prayers to our gods, he is to be pardoned as a result of his repentance however suspect his past conduct may be. But pamphlets circulated anonymously must play no part in any accusation. They create the worst sort of precedent and are quite out of keeping with the spirit of our age.

Origen, *Against Celsus*

He [Celsus] says that Christians perform their rites and teach their doctrines in secret, and they do this with good reason to escape the death penalty that hangs over them. He compares the danger to the risks encountered for the sake of philosophy as by Socrates. . . . I reply to this that in Socrates's case the Athenians at once regretted what they had done, and cherished no grievance against him. . . . But in the case of the Christians the Roman Senate, the contemporary emperors, the army, . . . and the relatives of believers fought against the gospel and would have hindered it; and it would have been defeated by the combined force of so many unless it had overcome and risen above the opposition by divine power, so that it has conquered the whole world that was conspiring against it. . . .

He [also] ridicules our teachers of the gospel who try to elevate the soul in every way to the Creator of the universe. . . . He compares them [Christians] to wool-workers in houses, cobblers, laundry-workers, and the most obtuse yokels, as if they called children quite in

(Continued)

(Opposing Viewpoints continued)

infancy and women to evil practices, telling them to leave their father and teachers and to follow them. But let Celsus . . . tell us how we make women and children leave noble and sound teaching, and call them to wicked practices. But he will not be able to prove anything of any kind against us. On the contrary, we deliver women from licentiousness and from perversion caused by their associates, and from all mania for theaters and dancing, and from superstition.

Q What were Pliny's personal opinions of Christians? Why was he willing to execute them? What was Trajan's response, and what were its consequences for the Christians? What major points did Origen make about the benefits of the Christian religion?Why did the Roman authorities consider these ideas dangerous to the Roman state?

Sources: An Exchange Between Pliny and Trajan. From THE LETTERS OF THE YOUNGER PLINY, translated with an introduction by Betty Radice (Penguin Classics 1963, Reprinted 1969). Copyright © Betty Radice, 1963, 1969. Reproduced by permission of Penguin Books Ltd. Origen, *Against Celsus*. From Origen, Contra Celsum. Trans Henry Chadwick. Copyright © 1953. Reprinted with the permission of Cambridge University Press.

was the emerging role of the bishops, who began to assume more control over church communities. The Christian church was creating a well-defined hierarchical structure in which the bishops and clergy were salaried officers separate from the laity or regular church members.

THE APPEAL OF CHRISTIANITY Christianity grew slowly in the first century, took root in the second, and had spread widely by the third. Why was Christianity able to attract so many followers? First of all, the Christian message had much to offer the Roman world. The promise of salvation, made possible by Jesus's death and resurrection, had immense appeal in a world full of suffering and injustice. Christianity seemed to imbue life with a meaning and purpose beyond the simple material things of everyday reality. Second, Christianity was not entirely unfamiliar. It could be viewed as simply another eastern mystery religion, offering immortality as the result of the sacrificial death of a savior-God. At the same time, it offered advantages that the other mystery religions lacked. Jesus had been a human figure, not a mythological one, such as Mithra. Moreover, Christianity had universal appeal. Unlike Mithraism, it was not restricted to men. Furthermore, it did not require a painful or expensive initiation rite as other mystery religions did. Initiation was accomplished simply by baptism—a purification by water—by which one entered into direct communion with Jesus. In addition, Christianity gave new meaning to life and offered what the Roman state religions could not—a personal relationship with God and a link to higher worlds.

Finally, Christianity fulfilled the human need to belong. Christians formed communities bound to one another in which people could express their love by helping each other and offering assistance to the poor, the sick, widows, and orphans. Christianity satisfied the need to belong in a way that the huge, impersonal, and remote Roman Empire could never do.

Christianity proved attractive to all classes. The promise of eternal life was for all—rich, poor, aristocrats, slaves, men, and women. As Paul stated in his Epistle to the Colossians: "And [you] have put on the new self, which is being renewed in knowledge in the image of its Creator. Here there is no Greek nor Jew, circumcised or uncircumcised, barbarian, Scythian, slave or free, but Christ is all, and is in all."[17] Although it did not call for revolution or social upheaval, Christianity emphasized a sense of spiritual equality for all people.

WOMEN AND EARLY CHRISTIANITY First-century Christian communities had allowed both men and women to play significant roles, often as preachers for the community. By the second century, however, men had gained control of church organization and relegated women to secondary roles. Women, as Paul had argued, should be subject to men.

Nevertheless, many women found that Christianity offered them new roles and new forms of companionship with other women. Christian women fostered the new religion in their own homes and preached their convictions to other people in their towns and villages. Many also died for their faith. Perpetua was an aristocratic woman who converted to Christianity. Her pagan family begged her to renounce her new faith, but she refused. Arrested by the Roman authorities, she chose instead to die for her faith and was one of a group of Christians who were slaughtered by wild beasts in the arena at Carthage on March 7, 203.

THE FAILURE OF PERSECUTION As the Christian church became more organized, some emperors in the third century responded with more systematic persecutions, but their schemes failed to work. The last great persecution was by Diocletian at the beginning of the fourth century. But even he had to admit what had become apparent in the course of the third century: Christianity had become too strong to be eradicated by force.

CHAPTER SUMMARY

The Roman Republic had created one of the largest empires in antiquity, but its republican institutions had proved inadequate for the task of ruling an empire. After a series of bloody civil wars, Augustus created a new order that began the Roman Empire. Although he never declared the Republic dead and continued to give the senate a role in governing, most political power remained in the hands of the *princeps*, or chief citizen, as Augustus called himself. Significantly, the army swore loyalty to him, and the restoration of peace soon made the new political order acceptable to most people in the empire.

Augustus established the Julio-Claudian dynasty, which lasted until 68. In 69, Vespasian, a successful general, founded the Flavian dynasty after a year of civil war. This dynasty began to openly use the title of *imperator*, or emperor. In the second century, five "good emperors" maintained a period of peace and prosperity when trade flourished and the provinces were governed efficiently. Within their empire, the Romans were responsible for a remarkable series of achievements that were bequeathed to the future.

These achievements were fundamental to the development of Western civilization, a civilization that would arise for the most part in the lands in Europe conquered by the Romans, where Roman culture and political ideals were gradually spread. The Romance languages of today (French, Italian, Spanish, Portuguese, and Romanian) are based on Latin. Western practices of impartial justice and trial by jury owe much to Roman law. As great builders, the Romans left monuments to their skills throughout Europe, some of which, including aqueducts and roads, are still in use today. Other monuments provided models for public buildings in the West for hundreds of years. Aspects of Roman administrative practices survived in the Western world for centuries. The Roman also preserved the intellectual heritage of the Greco-Roman world of antiquity.

By the third century, however, the Roman world was suffering an era of decline. Generals fought each other in civil wars. Between the years 235 and 284, there were twenty-two emperors, and only two of them did not suffer a violent end. German tribes and Persian armies invaded the empire. There were plagues, population decline, and economic problems. At the same time, a new religion—Christianity—was spreading throughout the empire. Beginning among the followers of Jesus of Nazareth, Christianity, with its promise of salvation, its similarity to many mystery religions, and its universality as a religion for all—rich and poor, men and women, Greek and Roman—slowly gained acceptance. As we shall see in the next chapter, the response to the crises of the third century and the rise of Christianity would gradually bring a transformation of the Roman Empire in the fourth and fifth centuries.

CHAPTER TIMELINE

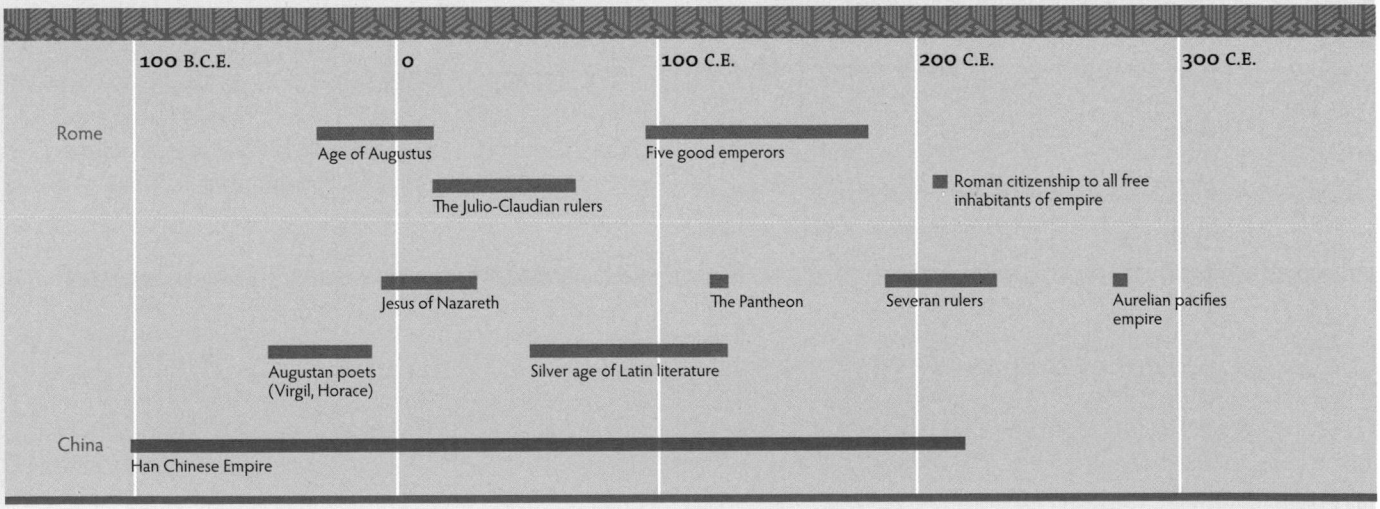

CHAPTER REVIEW

Upon Reflection

Q Was Augustus the last of the republicans or the first of the emperors? Why do you think so?

Q In what ways was the rule of the Roman emperors in the first and second centuries C.E. an improvement over the Republic of the first century B.C.E.? In what ways was their rule not an improvement over the last century of the Republic?

Q How do you explain the spread of Christianity in the Roman Empire?

Key Terms

principate (p. 114)
praetorian guard (p. 116)
good emperors (p. 117)

Suggestions for Further Reading

GENERAL HISTORIES OF THE ROMAN EMPIRE For a good survey of the Early Empire, see **M. Goodman, *The Roman World, 44 B.C.–A.D. 180*** (London, 1997). On the crises of the third century, see **D. S. Potter, *The Roman Empire at Bay, A.D. 180–395*** (New York, 2004).

ROMAN EMPERORS Studies of Roman emperors of the first and second centuries include **A. Everitt, *Augustus: Life of Rome's First Emperor*** (New York, 2006); **E. Champlin, *Nero*** (Cambridge, Mass., 2003); **E. Speller, *Following Hadrian*** (Oxford, 2003); and **P. Matyszak, *The Sons of Caesar: Imperial Rome's First Dynasty*** (London, 2006), on the Julio-Claudian rulers.

ROMAN ARMY AND PROVINCES The Roman army is examined in **J. B. Campbell, *The Emperor and the Roman Army*** (Oxford, 1984). On warfare, see **A. Goldsworthy, *Roman Warfare*** (New York, 2005). On the provinces and Roman foreign policy, see **B. Isaac, *The Limits of Empire: The Roman Empire in the East*** (Oxford, 1990), and **S. L. Dyson, *The Creation of the Roman Frontier*** (Princeton, N.J., 1985).

ROMAN SOCIETY Various aspects of Roman society are covered in **L. Adkins** and **R. A. Adkins, *Handbook to Life in Ancient Rome*** (New York, 1994). On the gladiators, see **F. Meijer, *The Gladiators: History's Most Deadly Sport*** (Boston, 2005). On Roman women, see **S. Dixon, *Reading Roman Women*** (London, 2001).

EARLY CHRISTIANITY For a general introduction to early Christianity, see **J. Court** and **K. Court, *The New Testament World*** (Cambridge, 1990). On Christian women, see **R. Kraemer, *Her Share of the Blessings: Women's Religion Among the Pagans, Jews and Christians in the Graeco-Roman World*** (Oxford, 1995). On the controversies surrounding the Christian gospels in the early history of Christianity, see **E. Pagels, *Beyond Belief: The Secret Gospel of Thomas*** (New York, 2003).

Visit the CourseMate website at **www.cengagebrain.com** for additional study tools and review materials for this chapter.

© The Art Archive/Bibliothèque Municipale Besançon/Kharbine-Tapabor/Collection Jean Vigne

A fifteenth-century manuscript illustration of Clovis, his wife Clotilde, and their four sons

CHAPTER 7

Late Antiquity and the Emergence of the Medieval World

CHAPTER OUTLINE AND FOCUS QUESTIONS

The Late Roman Empire

Q What reforms did Diocletian and Constantine institute, and to what extent were the reforms successful?

The Germanic Kingdoms

Q What changes did the Germanic peoples make to the political, economic, and social conditions of the Western Roman Empire? What were the main features of Germanic law and society, and how did they differ from those of the Romans?

Development of the Christian Church

Q How and why did the organization of the Christian church and its relations with the state change during the fourth and fifth centuries? What were the chief characteristics of Benedictine monasticism, and what role did monks play in both the conversion of Europe to Christianity and the intellectual life of the Germanic kingdoms?

The Byzantine Empire

Q How did the Byzantine Empire that had emerged by the eighth century differ from the empire of Justinian and from the Germanic kingdoms in the west?

The Rise of Islam

Q What was the basic message of Islam, and why was it able to expand so successfully?

CRITICAL THINKING

Q In what ways were the Byzantine and Islamic civilizations different from the civilization developing in western Europe? In what ways were they similar?

BY THE THIRD CENTURY, the Roman Empire was experiencing a number of problems as well as witnessing the growth of a new religion—Christianity. To restore the empire, the emperors Diocletian and Constantine initiated a number of reforms that created the so-called Late Empire. Constantine also converted to Christianity, starting a process that gave the Late Empire a new state religion.

After Constantine, the Late Roman Empire survived, but in the west it increasingly faced incursions of Germanic tribes. By the second half of the fifth century, new political arrangements were taking shape that brought the collapse of the old imperial structure in the west and the emergence of a series of Germanic kingdoms in western Europe that would form the basis of a new civilization. In these kingdoms, the Christian church also played a role as it drew these Germanic tribes to its faith.

The conversion to Christianity of the pagan leaders of German tribes was sometimes dramatic, at least as reported by the sixth-century historian Gregory of Tours. Clovis (KLOH-viss), leader of the Franks, married Clotilde, daughter of the king of the Burgundians. She was a Christian, but Clovis refused her pleas to become a Christian, telling her, "Your god can do nothing." But during a battle with the Alemanni (al-uh-MAH-nee), when Clovis's army was close to utter destruction, "he saw the danger; his heart was stirred; and he raised his eyes to heaven, saying, 'Jesus Christ, I beseech the glory of your aid. If you shall grant me victory over these enemies, I will believe in you and be baptized in your name.'" When he had uttered these words, the Alemanni began to flee. Clovis kept his vow and became a Christian.

While the Germanic kingdoms were putting down roots in the west, the eastern part of the old Roman Empire, increasingly Greek in culture, continued as the Byzantine Empire. Serving as a buffer between Europe and the peoples to the east, the Byzantine or Eastern Roman Empire also preserved the intellectual and legal accomplishments of Greek and Roman antiquity. At the same time, a new culture centered on Islam emerged in the east; it spread through large parts of the old Roman Empire, preserved much of Greek culture, and created its own flourishing civilization. This chapter, then, concerns the transformation of the Roman world in late antiquity, the heirs of the Roman Empire, and the new world—the medieval world—they began to create.

The Late Roman Empire

Focus Question: What reforms did Diocletian and Constantine institute, and to what extent were the reforms successful?

At the end of the third century and beginning of the fourth, the Roman Empire gained a new lease on life through the efforts of two strong emperors, Diocletian (dy-uh-KLEE-shun) and Constantine, who restored order and stability. The empire was virtually transformed into a new state, the Late Roman Empire, which included a new governmental structure, a rigid economic and social system, and a new state religion—Christianity.

The Reforms of Diocletian and Constantine

Diocletian had risen through the ranks to become a prominent military leader. After the murder of the emperor Numerian by his praetorian prefect, Diocletian executed the prefect and was then hailed as emperor by his soldiers. Diocletian's own rise to power led him to see the need for a new system for ruling the Roman Empire.

POLITICAL REFORMS Believing that the empire had grown too large for a single ruler, Diocletian (284–305) divided it into four administrative units (see Map 7.1); each had its own prefect with the title of either "Augustus" or "Caesar." Despite the appearance of four-man rule, however, Diocletian's military seniority enabled him to claim a higher status and hold the ultimate authority. Constantine (306–337) continued and even expanded the autocratic policies of Diocletian. Both rulers greatly strengthened and enlarged the administrative bureaucracies of the Roman Empire. Henceforth, civil and military bureaucracies were sharply separated. Each contained a hierarchy of officials who exercised control at the various levels. The emperor presided over both hierarchies of officials and served as the only link between them. New titles of nobility—such as *illustres* ("illustrious ones") and *illustrissimi* ("most illustrious ones")—were instituted to dignify the holders of positions in the civil and military bureaucracies.

MILITARY REFORMS Additional military reforms were also instituted. The army was enlarged to 400,000 men, including units composed of Germans. By the end of Constantine's reign, the army had also been reorganized. Military forces were divided into two kinds: garrison troops, which were located on the frontiers and intended as a first line of defense against invaders, and mobile units, which were located behind the frontier but could be quickly moved to support frontier troops when the borders were threatened. This gave the empire greater flexibility in responding to invasion.

ECONOMIC AND SOCIAL TRENDS The political and military reforms of Diocletian and Constantine greatly enlarged two institutions—the army and the civil service—that drained most of the public funds. Alhough more revenues were needed to pay for the army and bureaucracy, the population was not growing, so the tax base could not be expanded. Diocletian and Constantine devised new economic and social policies to deal with these financial burdens, but like their political policies, they were all based on coercion and loss of individual freedom. To fight **inflation**, Diocletian resorted to issuing a price edict in

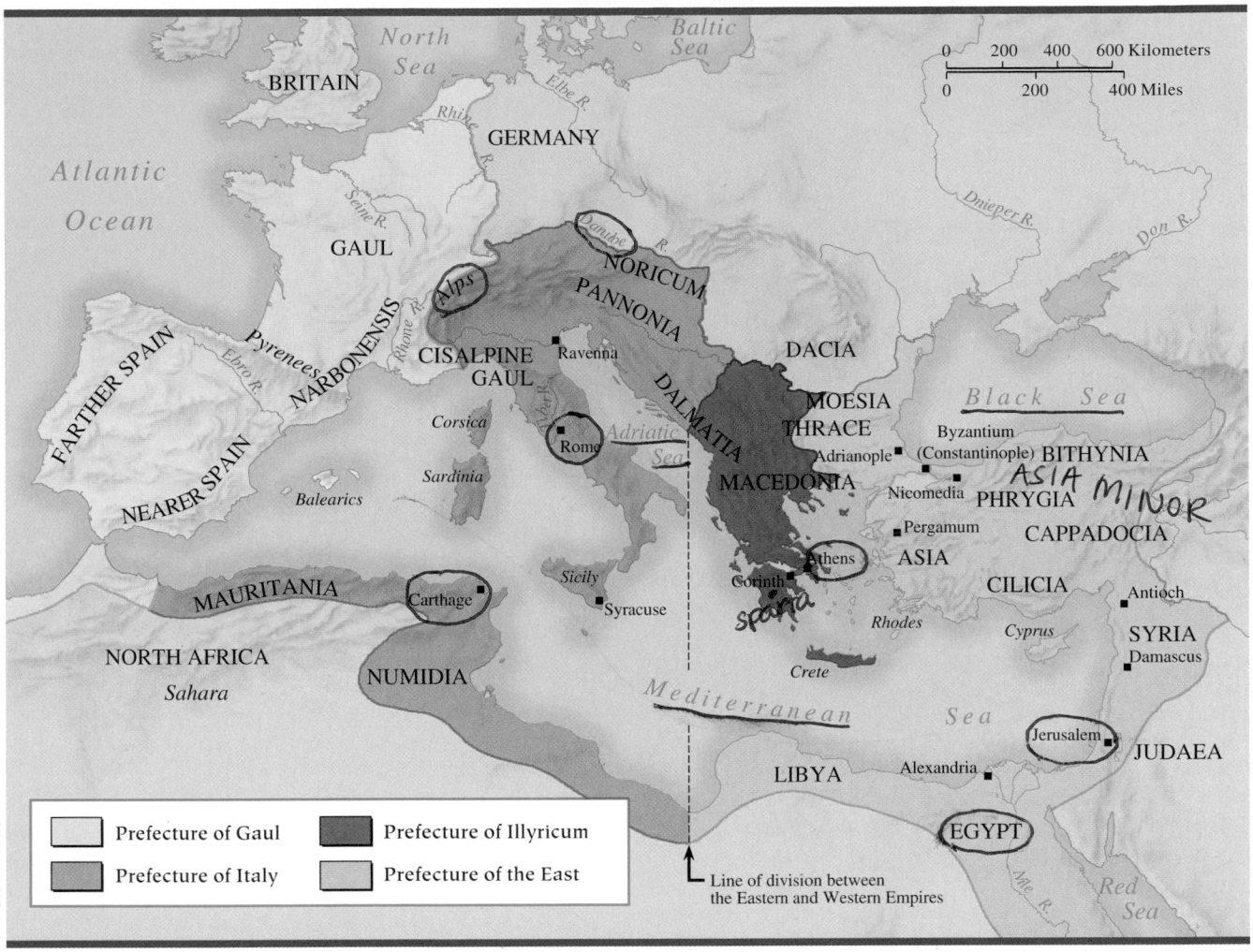

© Cengage Learning

MAP 7.1 Divisions of the Late Roman Empire, c. 300. Diocletian imposed order and a new economic and administrative structure on the Late Empire. He divided the Roman Empire into four regions, each ruled by either an "Augustus" or a "Caesar," although Diocletian retained supreme power.

Q *Compare this map with Map 6.1. How much territory had been lost by the time of Diocletian?*

301 that established maximum wages and prices for the entire empire, but despite severe penalties, it was unenforceable and failed to work.

Coercion also came to form the underlying basis for numerous occupations in the Late Roman Empire. To maintain the tax base and keep the empire going despite the shortage of labor, the emperors issued edicts that forced people to remain in their designated vocations. Hence, basic jobs, such as bakers and shippers, became hereditary. Free tenant farmers continued to decline and soon found themselves bound to the land by large landowners who took advantage of depressed agricultural conditions to enlarge their landed estates.

In general, the economic and social policies of Diocletian and Constantine were based on an unprecedented degree of control and coercion. Though temporarily successful, in the long run such authoritarian policies stifled the very vitality the Late Empire needed to revive its sagging fortunes.

CONSTANTINE'S BUILDING PROGRAM Constantine was especially interested in building programs despite the strain they placed on the budget. Between 324 and 330, he engaged in his biggest project, the construction of a new capital city in the east, on the site of the Greek city of Byzantium (buh-ZAN-tee-um), on the shores of the Bosporus. Named the "city of Constantine," or Constantinople

Palazzo dei Conservatori, Rome//© Scala/Art Resource, NY

The Emperor Constantine. Constantine played an important role in restoring order and stability to the Roman Empire at the beginning of the fourth century. This marble head of Constantine, which is 8 feet 6 inches high, was part of an enormous 30-foot-tall seated statue of the emperor in the New Basilica in Rome. Constantine used these awe-inspiring statues throughout the empire to build support for imperial policies by reminding his subjects of his position as an absolute ruler with immense power. The depiction of Constantine with his eyes turned toward heaven emphasized the emperor's special relationship with God.

(modern Istanbul), it was developed for defensive reasons; it had an excellent strategic location. Calling it his "New Rome," Constantine endowed the city with a forum, large palaces, and a vast amphitheater. It was officially dedicated on May 11, 330, "by the commandment of God," and in the following years, many Christian churches were built there.

The Empire's New Religion

Christianity flourished after Constantine became the first Christian emperor. According to the traditional story, before a crucial battle, he saw a vision of a Christian cross inscribed "In this sign you will conquer." Having won the battle, the story goes, Constantine was convinced of the power of the Christian God. Although he was not baptized until the end of his life, in 313 he issued the famous Edict of Milan, officially tolerating the existence of Christianity. Under Theodosius (thee-uh-DOH-shuss) "the Great" (378–395), it was made the official religion of the Roman Empire. Christianity had triumphed.

ORGANIZATION AND RELIGIOUS DISPUTES By the fourth century, the Christian church had developed a system of government. The Christian community in each city was headed by a bishop, whose area of jurisdiction was known as a bishopric or diocese. The bishoprics of each Roman province were clustered together under the direction of an archbishop. The bishops of four great cities, Rome, Jerusalem, Alexandria, and Antioch, held positions of special power in church affairs because the churches in these cities all asserted that they had been founded by the original apostles sent out by Jesus.

One reason the church needed a more formal organization was the problem of **heresy**. As Christianity developed and spread, contradictory interpretations of important doctrines emerged. Heresy came to be viewed as a teaching different from the official "catholic" (universal) beliefs of the church. In a world where people were concerned about salvation, questions such as whether Jesus's nature was divine or human took on great significance. These doctrinal differences also became political issues, creating political factions that actually warred with one another. It is highly unlikely, though, that ordinary people understood the issues in these debates.

One of the major heresies of the fourth century was **Arianism** (AR-ee-uh-niz-uhm), which arose among the followers of Arius, a priest from Alexandria in Egypt. Arius believed that Jesus had been human and thus not truly God. Arius was opposed by Athanasius (ath-uh-NAY-shuss), a bishop of Alexandria, who argued that Jesus was human but also truly God. Emperor Constantine, disturbed by the controversy, called the first ecumenical council of the church, a meeting composed of representatives from the entire Christian community. The Council of Nicaea (ny-SEE-uh), held in 325, condemned Arianism and stated that Jesus was of "the same substance" as God:

> We believe in one God the Father All-sovereign, maker of all things visible and invisible; And in one Lord Jesus Christ, the Son of God, begotten of the Father, only-begotten, that is, of the substance of the Father, God of God, Light of Light, true God of true God, begotten not made, of one substance with the Father.[1]

The Council of Nicaea did not end the controversy, however; not only did Arianism persist in some parts of the Roman Empire for many years, but many of the Germanic Goths who established states in the west converted to Arian Christianity (see "The Germanic Kingdoms" later in this chapter). As a result of these fourth-century theological controversies, the Roman emperor came to play an increasingly important role in church affairs.

The End of the Western Empire

Constantine had reunited the Roman Empire and restored a semblance of order. After his death, however, the empire continued to divide into western and eastern parts, and by 395, they had become two virtually independent states. In the fifth century, the empire in the east remained intact under the Roman emperor in Constantinople (see "The Byzantine Empire" later in this chapter), but the empire in the west collapsed and was replaced by a series of Germanic kingdoms.

During the first and second centuries C.E., the Romans had established the Rhine and Danube Rivers as the empire's northern boundary. The Romans called all the peoples to the north of the rivers "Germans" and regarded them as uncivilized barbarians. In fact, the Germans consisted of different groups with their own customs and identities, but these constantly changed as tribes broke up and came together in new configurations. At times, they formed larger confederations under strong warrior leaders. The Germans lived by herding and farming and also traded with people living along the northern frontiers of the empire. Their proximity to the Romans also led to some Romanization of the tribes. They were familiar with the Roman use of coins rather than barter and also gained some knowledge of both the Latin language and Roman military matters.

Although the Romans had established a series of political frontiers along the Rhine and Danube Rivers, Romans and Germans often came into contact across these boundaries. For some time, the Romans had hired Germanic tribes to fight other Germanic tribes that threatened Rome or enlisted groups of Germans to fight for Rome. In any case, until the fourth century, the empire had proved capable of absorbing these people without harm to its political structure. As that century wore on, however, the situation began to change as the Germanic tribes came under new pressures from invaders.

In the late fourth century, the Germanic tribes came under new pressure when the Huns, a fierce tribe of nomads from the steppes of Asia (see the box on p. 142), began moving into the Black Sea region. One of the groups displaced by the Huns was the Visigoths (VIZ-uh-gahths), who crossed the Danube into German territory and settled down as Roman allies. Ill-treated by Roman officials, the Visigoths soon revolted, and the attempt to stop them at Adrianople in 378 led to a crushing defeat for the Romans. Soon the Visigoths were again on the move. Under their king Alaric (AL-uh-rik), they moved into Italy and sacked Rome in 410. Then, at the urging of the emperor, they moved into Spain and southern Gaul as Roman allies.

The Romans' experience with the Visigoths established a precedent. The emperors in the first half of the fifth century made alliances with whole groups of Germanic peoples, who settled peacefully in the western part of the empire. The Burgundians settled in much of eastern Gaul, just south of another German tribe called the Alemanni. Only the Vandals consistently remained hostile to the Romans. They ravaged parts of Gaul and crossed the Pyrenees into Spain. Defeated by incoming Visigoths, the Vandals crossed the Strait of Gibraltar and conquered the province of Africa. In 455, the Vandals even attacked Rome, sacking it more ferociously than the Visigoths had in 410.

CHRONOLOGY The Late Roman Empire	
Diocletian	284–305
Constantine	306–337
Edict of Milan	313
Construction of Constantinople	324–330
Battle of Adrianople	378
Theodosius the Great	378–395
Division of the empire	395
Alaric and Visigoths sack Rome	410
Vandals sack Rome	455
Odoacer deposes Romulus Augustulus	476

Increasingly, German military leaders dominated the imperial courts of the western empire, treating the Roman emperors as puppet rulers under their control. One such German leader finally ended the charade of Roman imperial rule. Odoacer (oh-doh-AY-sur) deposed the Roman emperor, Romulus Augustulus (RAHM-yuh-luss ow-GOOS-chuh-luss), in 476 and began to rule on his own. Meanwhile, the Ostrogoths (AHSS-truh-gahths), another branch of the Goths, under their king Theodoric (thee-AHD-uh-rik) (493–526), marched into Italy, killed Odoacer, and established control of Italy in 493.

By the end of the fifth century, Roman imperial authority in the west had ceased. Nevertheless, the intellectual, governmental, and cultural traditions of the Late Roman Empire continued to live in the new Germanic kingdoms.

The Germanic Kingdoms

Q FOCUS QUESTIONS: What changes did the Germanic peoples make to the political, economic, and social conditions of the Western Roman Empire? What were the main features of Germanic law and society, and how did they differ from those of the Romans?

By 500, the Western Roman Empire was being replaced politically by a series of kingdoms ruled by German kings (see Map 7.2). Although the Germans now ruled, they were greatly outnumbered by the Romans, who still controlled most of the economic resources. Both were

OPPOSING VIEWPOINTS

Two Views of the Huns

The first selection is a description of the Huns by Ammianus Marcellinus (c. 330–c. 393), who has been called the "last great Roman historian." Ammianus wrote a history of Rome from 96 C.E. to his own day. Only the chapters that deal with the period from 354 to 378 have survived. Historians believe that his account of the Huns is largely based on stereotypes. The second selection is taken from an account by Priscus, an envoy from the Eastern Roman Empire to the court of Attila (AT-uh-luh *or* uh-TIL-uh), king of the Huns from 434 to 453. His description of the Huns in 448 is quite different from that of Ammianus Marcellinus.

Ammianus Marcellinus, *The Later Roman Empire*

The Huns . . . are quite abnormally savage. From the moment of their birth they make deep gashes in their children's cheeks, so that when in due course hair appears its growth is checked by the wrinkled scars. . . . They have squat bodies, strong limbs, and thick necks, and are so prodigiously ugly and bent that they might be two-legged animals, or the figures crudely carved from stumps which are seen on the parapets of bridges. Still, their shape, however disagreeable, is human; but their way of life is so rough that they have no use for fire or seasoned food, but live on the roots of wild plants and the half-raw flesh of any sort of animal, which they warm a little by placing it between their thighs and the backs of their horses. They have no buildings to shelter them, but avoid anything of the kind; . . . not so much as a hut thatched with reeds is to be found among them. . . . They wear garments of linen or of the skins of field-mice stitched together, and there is no difference between their clothing whether they are at home or abroad. Once they have put their necks in some dingy shirt they never take it off or change it till it rots and falls to pieces from incessant wear. They have round caps of fur on their heads, and protect their hairy legs with goatskins. Their shapeless shoes . . . make it hard to walk easily. In consequence they are ill-fitted to fight on foot, and remain glued to their horses, hardy but ugly beasts, on which they sometimes sit like women to perform their everyday business. Buying or selling, eating or drinking, are all done by day or night on horseback, and they even bow forward over their beasts' narrow necks to enjoy a deep and dreamy sleep. . . .

They sometimes fight by challenging their foes to single combat, but when they join battle they advance in packs, uttering their various warcries. Being lightly equipped and very sudden in their movements they can deliberately scatter and gallop about at random, inflicting tremendous slaughter; their extreme nimbleness enables them to force a rampart or pillage an enemy's camp before one catches sight of them. . . . None of them plows or ever touches a plow-handle. They have no fixed abode, no home or law or settled manner of life, but wander like refugees with the wagons in which they live. In these their wives weave their filthy clothing, mate with their husbands, and give birth to their children, and rear them to the age of puberty.

Priscus, *An Account of the Court of Attila the Hun*

[We were invited to a banquet with Attila.] When the hour arrived we went to Attila's palace, along with the embassy from the western Romans, and stood on the threshold of the hall in the presence of Attila. The cupbearers gave us a cup, according to the national custom, that we might pray before we sat down. Having tasted the cup, we proceeded to take our seats, all the chairs being ranged along the walls of the room on either side. Attila sat in the middle on a couch; a second couch was set behind him, and from it steps led up to his bed, which was covered with linen sheets and coverlets. . . .

[First the king and his guests pledged one another with the wine.] When this ceremony was over the cupbearers retired and tables, large enough for three or four, or even more, to sit at, were placed next the table of Attila, so that each could take of the food on the dishes without leaving his seat. The attendant of Attila first entered with a dish full of meat, and behind him came the other attendants with bread and other dishes, which they laid

(Continued)

(Opposing Viewpoints continued)

on the tables. A luxurious meal, served on silver plate, had been made ready for us and the other guests, but Attila ate nothing but meat on a wooden platter. In everything else, too, he showed himself temperate; his cup was of wood, while to the guests were given goblets of gold and silver. His dress, too, was quite simple, affecting only to be clean.

Q What motives may have prompted Ammianus Marcellinus to describe the Huns so harshly? How does the account of Priscus differ, and what strategies of the Huns do you detect here to impress and overawe foreigners? How reliable do you think these descriptions of the Huns are? Why?

Sources: Ammianus Marcellinus, *The Later Roman Empire.* From THE LATER ROMAN EMPIRE by Ammianus Marcellinus, selected and translated by Walter Hamilton (Penguin Classics, 1986). Translation copyright © Walter Hamilton, 1986. Reproduced by permission of Penguin Books Ltd. Priscus, *An Account of the Court of Attila the Hun,* from Fragmenta Historicorum Graecorum, trans. J. B. Bury.

Christian, but many of the Germans were Arian Christians, considered heretics by Roman Christians, who belonged to the Christian church in Rome, which had become known as the Roman Catholic Church. Gradually, the two groups merged into a common culture, although the pattern of settlement and the fusion of the Romans and Germans took different forms in the various Germanic kingdoms.

The Ostrogothic Kingdom of Italy

More than any other Germanic state, the Ostrogothic kingdom of Italy managed to maintain the Roman tradition of government. The Ostrogothic king, Theodoric, had received a Roman education while a hostage in Constantinople. After taking control of Italy, he was eager to create a synthesis of Ostrogothic and Roman practices. In addition to maintaining the entire structure of imperial Roman government, he established separate systems of rule for the Ostrogoths and the Romans. The Italian population lived under Roman law administered by Roman officials. The Ostrogoths were governed by their own customs and their own officials.

After Theodoric's death in 526, it quickly became apparent that much of his success had been due to the force of his personality. His successors soon found themselves facing opposition from the imperial forces of the Byzantine or Eastern Roman Empire. Under Emperor Justinian (juh-STIN-ee-un) (527–565) (see "The Byzantine Empire" later in this chapter), Byzantine armies reconquered Italy between 535 and 552, devastating much of the peninsula and in the process destroying Rome as one of the great urban centers of the Mediterranean world. The Byzantine reconquest proved ephemeral, however. Another German tribe, the Lombards, invaded in 568 and conquered much of northern and central Italy. Unlike the Ostrogoths, the Lombards were harsh rulers who cared little for Roman structures and traditions.

The Visigothic Kingdom of Spain

The Visigothic kingdom in Spain demonstrated a number of parallels with the Ostrogothic kingdom of Italy. Both favored coexistence between the Roman and German populations, both featured a warrior caste dominating a larger native population, and both continued to maintain much of the Roman structure of government while largely excluding Romans from power. There were also noticeable differences, however. Laws preventing intermarriage were dropped, and the Visigothic and Hispano-Roman peoples began to blend. A new body of law common to both peoples also developed.

The Visigothic kingdom possessed one fatal weakness. With no established procedure for choosing new rulers, powerful Visigoths fought constantly to lay claim to the kingship. Church officials tried to help develop a sense of order, as this decree illustrates: "No one of us shall dare to seize the kingdom; no one shall arouse sedition among the citizenry; no one shall think of killing the king." Church edicts failed to stop the feuds, however, and assassinations remained a way of life in Visigothic Spain. In 711, Muslim invaders destroyed the Visigothic kingdom itself (see "The Rise of Islam" later in this chapter).

The Frankish Kingdom

Only one of the German states on the European continent proved long-lasting—the kingdom of the Franks. The establishment of a Frankish kingdom was the work of Clovis (c. 482–511), a member of the Merovingian (meh-ruh-VIN-jee-un) dynasty who became a Catholic Christian around 500. He was not the first German king to convert to Christianity, but the others had joined the Arian sect of Christianity. The Roman Catholic Church regarded the Arians as heretics whose beliefs diverged from official

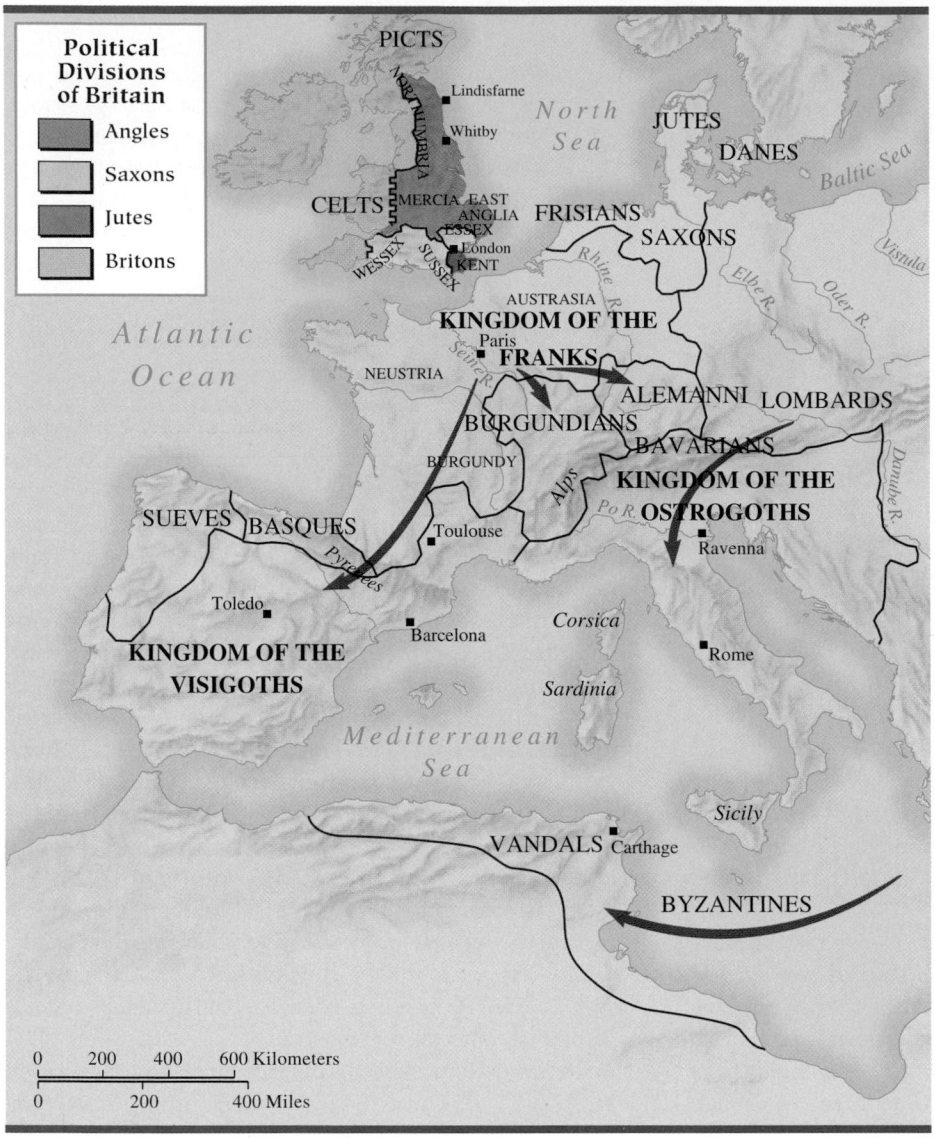

© Cengage Learning

MAP 7.2 The Germanic Kingdoms of the Old Western Empire. The Germanic tribes filled the power vacuum created by the demise of the Roman Empire, building states that blended elements of Germanic customs and laws with those of Roman culture, including large-scale conversions to Christianity. The Franks established the most durable of these Germanic states.

Q *How did the movements of the Franks during this period correspond to the borders of present-day France?*

church doctrine. Clovis's conversion to Catholic Christianity gained him the support of the Roman Catholic Church, which was eager to obtain the friendship of a major Germanic ruler who was a Catholic Christian. By 510, Clovis had established a powerful new Frankish kingdom stretching from the Pyrenees in the west to German lands in the east (modern-day France and western Germany). After the death of Clovis, however, his sons divided the newly created kingdom among themselves, as was the Frankish custom. Thus, during the sixth and seventh centuries, the once-united Frankish kingdom came to be partitioned into three major areas: Neustria (NOO-stree-uh) in northern Gaul; Austrasia (au-STRAY-zhuh), consisting of the ancient Frankish lands on both sides of the Rhine; and the former kingdom of Burgundy.

During the sixth and seventh centuries, the Frankish kingdom witnessed a process of fusion between Gallo-Roman and Frankish cultures and peoples, a process accompanied by a significant decline in Roman standards of civilization and commercial activity. The Franks were

CHRONOLOGY The Germanic Kingdoms

Theodoric establishes Ostrogothic kingdom in Italy	493
Frankish king Clovis converts to Christianity	c. 500
Reconquest of Italy by Byzantines	535–552
Lombards begin conquest of Italy	568
Muslims shatter Visigothic kingdom in Spain	711

warriors and did little to encourage either urban life or trade. By 750, Frankish Gaul was basically an agricultural society in which the old Roman estates of the Late Empire had continued unimpeded. Institutionally, however, Germanic concepts of kingship and customary law replaced the Roman governmental structure.

Anglo-Saxon England

The barbarian pressures on the Western Roman Empire had forced the emperors to withdraw the Roman armies and abandon Britain by the beginning of the fifth century. This opened the door to the Angles and Saxons, Germanic tribes from Denmark and northern Germany. Although these same peoples had been conducting plundering raids for a century, the withdrawal of the Roman armies enabled them to establish settlements instead. They met with resistance from the Celtic Britons, however, who still controlled the western regions of Cornwall, Wales, and Cumberland at the beginning of the seventh century. The German invaders eventually succeeded in carving out small kingdoms throughout the island, Kent in southeastern England being one of them.

The Society of the Germanic Kingdoms

As Germans and Romans intermarried and began to create a new society, some of the social customs of the Germanic people began to play an important role. The crucial social bond among the Germanic peoples was the family, especially the extended or patriarchal family of husbands, wives, children, brothers, sisters, cousins, and grandparents. In addition to working the land together and passing it down to succeeding generations along male lines, the extended family provided protection, which was sorely needed in the violent atmosphere of Merovingian times.

The German conception of family affected the way Germanic law treated crime and punishment. In the Roman system, as in our own, a crime such as murder was considered an offense against society or the state and was handled by a court that heard evidence and arrived at a decision. Germanic law tended to be personal. If one person injured another, the result could be a blood feud in which the family of the injured party took revenge on the kin of the wrongdoer. Feuds could involve savage acts of revenge, such as hacking off hands or feet, gouging out eyes, or slicing off ears and noses. Because this system could easily get out of control, an alternative system arose that made use of a fine called ***wergeld*** (WURR-geld), which was paid by a wrongdoer to the family of the person he had injured or killed. *Wergeld* (literally, "man money") was the value of a person in monetary terms. That value varied according to social status. An offense against a nobleman, for example, cost considerably more than one against a freeman or a slave.

Under German customary law, compurgation and the ordeal were the two most commonly used procedures for determining whether an accused person was guilty and should have to pay *wergeld*. Compurgation was the swearing of an oath by the accused person, backed up by a group of "oath helpers," numbering twelve or twenty-five, who would also swear that the accused person should be believed. The ordeal functioned in a variety of ways, all of which were based on the principle of divine intervention—the assumption was that divine forces (pagan or Christian) would not allow an innocent person to be harmed (see the box on p. 146).

THE FRANKISH FAMILY AND MARRIAGE For the Franks, like other Germanic peoples, the extended family was at the center of social organization. The Frankish family structure was simple. Males were dominant and made all the important decisions. A woman obeyed her father until she married and then fell under the legal domination of her husband. A widow, however, could hold property without a male guardian. In Frankish law, the *wergeld* of a wife of childbearing age—of value because she could produce children—was considerably higher than that of a man. The law stated, "If any one killed a free woman after she had begun bearing children, he shall be sentenced to 24,000 denars. . . . After she can have no more children, he who kills her shall be sentenced to 8,000 denars."[2]

Because marriage affected the extended family group, fathers or uncles could arrange marriages for the good of the family without considering their children's wishes. Most important was the engagement ceremony in which a prospective son-in-law made a payment symbolizing the purchase of paternal authority over the bride. The essential feature of the marriage itself was the placing of the married couple in bed to achieve their physical union. In first marriages, it was considered important that the wife be a virgin, which ensured that any children would be the husband's. A virgin symbolized the ability of the bloodline to continue. Accordingly, adultery was viewed as pollution of the woman and her offspring, poisoning their future. Adulterous wives were severely punished (an adulterous woman could be strangled or even burned alive); adulterous husbands were not. Divorce was relatively simple and was initiated primarily by the husband. Divorced wives simply returned to their original families.

Germanic Customary Law: The Ordeal

In Germanic customary law, the ordeal came to be a means by which accused persons might clear themselves. Although the ordeal took different forms, all involved a physical trial of some sort, such as holding a red-hot iron. It was believed that God would protect the innocent and allow them to come through the ordeal unharmed. This sixth-century account by Gregory of Tours describes an ordeal by hot water.

Gregory of Tours, "An Ordeal of Hot Water" (c. 580)

An Arian presbyter disputing with a deacon of our religion made venomous assertions against the Son of God and the Holy Ghost, as is the habit of that sect [the Arians]. But when the deacon had discoursed a long time concerning the reasonableness of our faith and the heretic, blinded by the fog of unbelief, continued to reject the truth, . . . the former said: "Why weary ourselves with long discussions? Let acts approve the truth; let a kettle be heated over the fire and someone's ring be thrown into the boiling water. Let him who shall take it from the heated liquid be approved as a follower of the truth, and afterward let the other party be converted to the knowledge of the truth. And do you also understand, O heretic, that this our party will fulfill the conditions with the aid of the Holy Ghost; you shall confess that there is no discordance, no dissimilarity in the Holy Trinity." The heretic consented to the proposition and they separated after appointing the next morning for the trial. But the fervor of faith in which the deacon had first made this suggestion began to cool through the instigation of the enemy. Rising with the dawn he bathed his arm in oil and smeared it with ointment. But nevertheless he made the round of the sacred places and called in prayer on the Lord. . . . About the third hour they met in the marketplace. The people came together to see the show. A fire was lighted, the kettle was placed upon it, and when it grew very hot the ring was thrown into the boiling water. The deacon invited the heretic to take it out of the water first. But he promptly refused, saying, "You who did propose this trial are the one to take it out." The deacon all of a tremble bared his arm. And when the heretic presbyter saw it besmeared with ointment he cried out: "With magic arts you have thought to protect yourself, that you have made use of these salves, but what you have done will not avail." While they were thus quarreling there came up a deacon from Ravenna named Iacinthus and inquired what the trouble was about. When he learned the truth he drew his arm out from under his robe at once and plunged his right hand into the kettle. Now the ring that had been thrown in was a little thing and very light so that it was thrown about by the water as chaff would be blown about by the wind; and searching for it a long time he found it after about an hour. Meanwhile the flame beneath the kettle blazed up mightily so that the greater heat might make it difficult for the ring to be followed by the hand; but the deacon extracted it at length and suffered no harm, protesting rather that at the bottom the kettle was cold while at the top it was just pleasantly warm. When the heretic beheld this he was greatly confused and audaciously thrust his hand into the kettle saying, "My faith will aid me." As soon as his hand had been thrust in all the flesh was boiled off the bones clear up to the elbow. And so the dispute ended.

Q What was the purpose of the ordeal of hot water? What does it reveal about the nature of the society that used it? What conception of justice do you think was held by this society?

Source: From *Translations and Reprints from the Original Sources of European History*, Series I, Vol. 4. Trans. A. C. Howland. (Philadelphia: University of Pennsylvania Press, 1898).

For most women in the new Germanic kingdoms, their legal status reflected the material conditions of their lives. Archaeological evidence suggests that most women had life expectancies of only thirty to forty years, and 10 to 15 percent of women died in their childbearing years, no doubt due to complications associated with childbirth. For most women, life consisted of domestic labor: providing food and clothing for the household, caring for the children, and assisting with numerous farming chores. Of all women's duties, the most important was childbearing, because it was crucial to the perpetuation of the family and its possessions.

Development of the Christian Church

Focus Questions: How and why did the organization of the Christian church and its relations with the state change during the fourth and fifth centuries? What were the chief characteristics of Benedictine monasticism, and what role did monks play in both the conversion of Europe to Christianity and the intellectual life of the Germanic kingdoms?

By the end of the fourth century, Christianity had become the predominant religion of the Roman Empire. As the official Roman state disintegrated, the Christian church played an increasingly important role in the new civilization built on the ruins of the old Roman Empire.

The Power of the Pope

One of the far-reaching developments in the history of the Christian church was the emergence of one bishop—that of Rome—as the recognized leader of the western Christian church. According to church tradition, Jesus had given the keys to the kingdom of heaven to Peter, who was considered the chief apostle and the first bishop of Rome. Subsequent bishops of Rome were considered Peter's successors and came to be known as popes (from the Latin word *papa*, meaning "father") of the Catholic Church.

Although western Christians came to accept the bishop of Rome as the head of the church in the fourth and fifth centuries, there was no unanimity on the extent of the powers the pope possessed as a result of this position. Nevertheless, the emergence of a strong pope, Gregory I (590–604), known as Gregory the Great, in the sixth century set the papacy and the Roman Catholic Church on an energetic path that enabled the church to play an increasingly prominent role in civilizing the Germans and aiding the emergence of a distinctly new European civilization in the seventh and eighth centuries.

As pope, Gregory I took charge of Rome and its surrounding area and made it into an administrative unit that eventually came to be known as the Papal States. Gregory also pursued a policy of extending papal authority over the Christian church in the west. He intervened in ecclesiastical conflicts throughout Italy and corresponded with the Frankish rulers, urging them to reform the church in Gaul. He successfully initiated the efforts of missionaries to convert England to Christianity and was especially active in converting the pagan peoples of Germanic Europe. His primary instrument was the monastic movement.

© Bettmann/CORBIS

Pope Gregory I. Pope Gregory the Great became one of the most important popes of the Early Middle Ages. As a result of his numerous writings, he is considered the last of the Latin Fathers of the church. This twelfth-century manuscript illustration shows Gregory dictating a work to a monk. On Gregory's shoulder is a dove, symbol of the Holy Spirit, which is providing divine inspiration for what he is dictating.

The Monks and Their Missions

A **monk** (Latin *monachus*, meaning "someone who lives alone") was a person who sought to live a life divorced from the world, cut off from ordinary human society, in order to pursue an ideal of godliness or total dedication to the will of God. Christian **monasticism** was initially based on the model of the solitary hermit who forsakes all civilized society to pursue spirituality. Saint Anthony (c. 250–350) was a prosperous Egyptian peasant who decided to follow Jesus's injunction in the Gospel of Mark: "Go your way, sell whatsoever you have, and give to the poor, and you shall have treasure in heaven: and come, take up the cross, and follow me." Anthony gave away his

300 acres of land to the poor and went into the desert to pursue his ideal of holiness. Others did likewise, often to extremes. Saint Simeon the Stylite lived for three decades in a basket atop a pillar more than 60 feet high. These spiritual gymnastics established a new ideal for Christianity. Whereas the early Christian model had been the martyr who died for the faith and achieved eternal life in the process, the new ideal was the monk who died to the world and achieved spiritual life through denial, asceticism, and mystical experience of God. These early monks, however, soon found themselves unable to live in solitude. Their feats of holiness attracted followers on a wide scale, and as the monastic ideal spread throughout the east, a new form of monasticism based on communal life soon became the dominant form. Monastic communities came to be seen as the ideal Christian society that could provide a moral example to the wider society around them.

BENEDICTINE MONASTICISM Saint Benedict of Nursia (c. 480–c. 543), who founded a monastic house for which he wrote a set of rules in the 520s, established the fundamental form of monastic life in the western Christian church. The Benedictine rule came to be used by other monastic groups and was crucial to the growth of monasticism in the western Christian world.

Benedict's rule favored an ideal of moderation. In Chapter 40 of the rule, on the amount a monk should drink, this sense of moderation becomes apparent:

> "Every man has his proper gift from God, one after this manner, another after that." And therefore it is with some misgiving that we determine the amount of food for someone else. Still, having regard for the weakness of some brothers, we believe that a hemina of wine [a quarter liter] per day will suffice for all. Let those, however, to whom God gives the gift of abstinence, know that they shall have their proper reward. But if either the circumstances of the place, the work, or the heat of summer necessitates more, let it lie in the discretion of the abbot to grant it. But let him take care in all things lest satiety or drunkenness supervene.[3]

At the same time, moderation did not preclude a disciplined existence based on the ideals of poverty, chastity, and obedience.

The Benedictine rule divided each day into a series of activities, with primary emphasis on prayer and manual labor. Physical work of some kind was required of all monks for several hours a day because idleness was "the enemy of the soul." At the very heart of community practice was prayer, the proper "work of God." While this included private meditation and reading, all monks gathered together seven times during the day for common prayer and chanting of psalms. A Benedictine life was a communal one; monks ate, worked, slept, and worshiped together.

Each Benedictine monastery was strictly ruled by an **abbot**, or "father" of the monastery, who held complete authority over the monks; each monk owed unquestioning obedience to the will of the abbot. Every Benedictine monastery owned lands that enabled it to be a self-sustaining community, isolated from and independent of the world surrounding it. Within the monastery, however, monks were to fulfill their vow of poverty: "Let all things be common to all, as it is written, lest anyone should say that anything is his own or arrogate it to himself."[4] By the eighth century, Benedictine monasticism had spread throughout the west.

Although the original monks were men, women soon followed suit in withdrawing from the world to dedicate themselves to God. The first monastic rule for western women was produced by Caesarius of Arles for his sister in the fifth century. It strongly emphasized a rigid cloistering of these women, known as **nuns**, to protect them from dangers.

Monasticism played an indispensable role in early medieval civilization. Monks became the new heroes of Christian civilization. Their dedication to God became the highest ideal of Christian life. Monks copied Latin works and passed on the legacy of the ancient world to Western civilization in its European stage. Moreover, the monks played an increasingly significant role in spreading Christianity to all of Europe.

MONKS AS MISSIONARIES The British Isles, in particular, became an important center of Christian culture and missionary fervor. After their conversion, the Celts of Ireland and Anglo-Saxons of England created new centers of Christian learning and in turn themselves became enthusiastic missionaries.

By the sixth century, Irish monasticism was a flourishing institution with its own unique characteristics. Unlike Benedictine monasticism, it was strongly ascetic. Monks performed strenuous fasts, prayed and meditated frequently under extreme privations, and confessed their sins on a regular basis to their superiors. In fact, Irish monasticism gave rise to the use of penitentials or manuals that provided a guide for examining one's life to see what sins, or offenses against the will of God, one had committed (see the box on p. 149). A great love of learning also characterized Irish monasticism. The Irish eagerly absorbed both Latin and Greek culture and fostered education as a major part of their monastic life.

Their emphasis on asceticism led many Irish monks to go into voluntary exile. This "exile for the love of God" was not into isolation, however, but into missionary activity. Irish monks became fervid missionaries. Saint Columba (521–597) left Ireland in 565 as a "pilgrim for

Irish Monasticism and the Penitential

Irish monasticism became well known for its ascetic practices. Much emphasis was placed on careful examination of conscience to determine if one had committed a sin against God. To facilitate this examination, penitentials were developed that listed possible sins with appropriate penances. Penance usually meant fasting—consuming nothing but bread and water—for a certain number of days each week. Although these penitentials were eventually used throughout Christendom, they were especially important in Irish Christianity. This excerpt from the Penitential of Cummean, an Irish abbot, was written about 650 and demonstrates a distinctive feature of the penitentials, an acute preoccupation with sexual sins.

The Penitential of Cummean

A bishop who commits fornication shall be degraded and shall do penance for twelve years.

A presbyter or a deacon who commits natural fornication, having previously taken the vow of a monk, shall do penance for seven years. He shall ask pardon every hour; he shall perform a special fast during every week except in the days between Easter and Pentecost.

He who defiles his mother shall do penance for three years, with perpetual pilgrimage.

So shall those who commit sodomy do penance every seven years.

He who merely desires in his mind to commit fornication, but is not able, shall do penance for one year, especially in the three forty-day periods.

He who is willingly polluted during sleep shall arise and sing nine psalms in order, kneeling. On the following day, he shall live on bread and water.

A cleric who commits fornication once shall do penance for one year on bread and water; if he begets a son he shall do penance for seven years as an exile; so also a virgin.

He who loves any woman, but is unaware of any evil beyond a few conversations, shall do penance for forty days.

He who is in a state of matrimony ought to be continent during the three forty-day periods and on Saturday and on Sunday, night and day, and in the two appointed week days [Wednesday and Friday], and after conception, and during the entire menstrual period.

After a birth he shall abstain, if it is a son, for thirty-three [days]; if a daughter, for sixty-six [days].

Boys talking alone and transgressing the regulations of the elders [in the monastery] shall be corrected by three special fasts.

Children who imitate acts of fornication, twenty days; if frequently, forty.

But boys of twenty years who practice masturbation together and confess [shall do penance] twenty or forty days before they take communion.

Q What does the Penitential of Cummean reveal about the nature of Irish monasticism? What do you think was the theory of human sexuality held by early Irish Christianity?

Source: From *Medieval Handbooks of Penance*, edited by John T. McNeill and Helena M. Garner. Copyright © 1990 by Columbia University Press. Reprinted by permission of the publisher.

Christ" and founded an influential monastic community off the coast of Scotland on the island of Iona. From there Irish missionaries went to northern England to begin the process of converting the Angles and Saxons. Other Irish monks traveled to the European continent. New monasteries founded by the Irish became centers of learning wherever they were located.

At the same time the Irish monks were busy bringing their version of Christianity to the Anglo-Saxons of Britain, Pope Gregory the Great had set into motion an effort to convert England to Roman Christianity. His most important agent was Augustine, a monk from Rome, who arrived in England in 597. England at that time had a number of Germanic kingdoms. Augustine went first to Kent, where he converted King Ethelbert; most of the king's subjects then followed suit. Pope Gregory's conversion techniques emphasized persuasion rather than force, and as seen in this excerpt from one of his letters, he was willing to assimilate old pagan practices in order to coax the pagans into the new faith:

> We wish you [Abbot Mellitus] to inform him [Augustine] that we have been giving careful thought to the affairs of the English, and have come to the conclusion that the temples of the idols among that people should on no account be destroyed. The idols are to be destroyed, but the temples themselves are to be aspersed with holy water, altars set up

© The Board of Trinity College, Dublin/The Bridgeman Art Library

The Book of Kells. Art historians use the term *Hiberno-Saxon* (Hibernia was the ancient name for Ireland) or *Insular* to refer to works produced primarily in the monasteries of the British Isles, especially Ireland. The best example of Hiberno-Saxon art is *The Book of Kells*, a richly decorated illuminated manuscript of the Christian gospels. Though owned by the monastery of Kells, the work was produced by the monks of Iona, who combined Celtic and Anglo-Saxon abstract designs with elaborate portrayals of human figures and animals. A twelfth-century priest who viewed it observed: "Look . . . keenly at it and you . . . will make out intricacies, so delicate and subtle, so exact and compact, so full of knots and links, with colors so fresh and vivid, that you might say that all this was the work of an angel, and not of a man." This page from the Gospel of Luke shows the devil tempting Jesus to cast himself down from the Temple.

> in them, and relics deposited there. For if these temples are well-built, they must be purified from the worship of demons and dedicated to the service of the true God.[5]

Freed of their pagan past, temples became churches, as one Christian commentator noted with joy: "The dwelling place of demons has become a house of God. The saving light has come to shine, where shadows covered all. Where sacrifices once took place and idols stood, angelic choirs now dance. Where God was angered once, now God is made content."[6] Likewise, old pagan feasts were given new names and incorporated into the Christian calendar. The Christian feast of Christmas, for example, was held on December 25, the day of the pagan celebration of the winter solstice.

As Roman Christianity spread northward in Britain, it encountered Irish Christianity moving southward. Roman Christianity prevailed, although the English church, despite its newfound unity and loyalty to Rome, retained some Irish features. Most important was the concentration on monastic culture with special emphasis on learning and missionary work. By 700, the English clergy had become the best trained and most learned in western Europe.

Following the Irish example, English monks journeyed to the European continent to carry on the work of conversion (see Map 7.3). Most important was Boniface (c. 680–755), who undertook the conversion of pagan Germans in Frisia, Bavaria, and Saxony. By 740, Saint Boniface, the "Apostle of the Germans," had become the most famous churchman in Europe. Fifteen years later, he was killed while trying to convert the pagan Frisians. Boniface was a brilliant example of the numerous Irish and English monks whose tireless efforts made Europe the bastion of the Roman Catholic faith.

WOMEN AND MONASTICISM Women played an important role in the monastic missionary movement and the conversion of the Germanic kingdoms. Double monasteries, where monks and nuns lived in separate houses but attended church services together, were found in both the English and Frankish kingdoms. The monks and nuns followed a common rule under a common head. Frequently, this leader was an **abbess** rather than an abbot. Many of these abbesses belonged to royal houses, especially in Anglo-Saxon England. In the kingdom of Northumbria, for example, Saint Hilda founded the monastery of Whitby in 657. As abbess, she was responsible for giving learning an important role in the life of the monastery; five future bishops were educated under her tutelage. For female intellectuals, monasteries offered opportunities for learning not found elsewhere in the society of their day.

Nuns of the seventh and eighth centuries also played an important role in the spread of Christianity. The great English missionary Boniface relied on nuns in England for books and money. He also asked the abbess of Wimborne to send groups of nuns to establish convents in newly converted German lands. A nun named Leoba established the first convent in Germany at Bischofsheim.

THE PATH OF CELIBACY The monastic movement enabled some women to pursue a new path to holiness. Cloisters

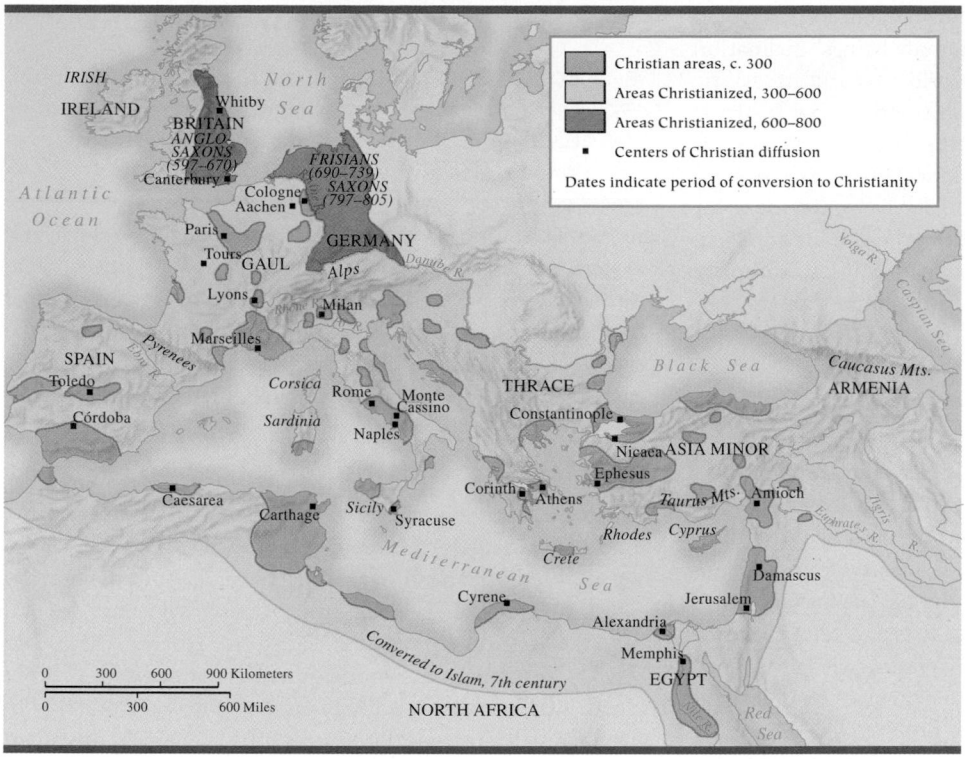

© Cengage Learning

MAP 7.3 The Spread of Christianity, 400–800. The Christian church had penetrated much of the Roman Empire by the end of the fifth century. It emerged as a major base of power after the fall of the empire, and it pushed its influence into new areas through the activities of missionaries.

Q ***What aspects of geography help explain the relatively late conversions of the Anglo-Saxons in Britain and the Frisians and Saxons east of the Rhine River?***

for both men and women offered the ideal place to practice the new Christian ideal of celibacy. This newfound emphasis on abstaining from sexual relations, especially evident in the emphasis on virginity, created a new image of the human body in late antiquity. To many Greeks and Roman, the human body had been a source of beauty, joy, and pleasure, an attitude evident in numerous works of art. Many Christians, however, regarded the body as a hindrance to establishing a spiritual connection with God. The refusal to have sex was a victory over the desires of the flesh and thus an avenue to holiness.

In the fourth and fifth centuries, a cult of virginity also moved beyond the walls of monasteries and convents. Throughout the Mediterranean world, groups of women met together to learn about the importance and benefits of celibacy. In Rome, a woman named Marcella supported a group of aristocratic women in their studies of celibacy.

Christianity and Intellectual Life

Many early Christians expressed considerable hostility toward the pagan culture of the Classical world. Tertullian (c. 160–c. 225), a Christian writer from Carthage, had proclaimed, "What has Jerusalem to do with Athens, the Church with the Academy, the Christian with the heretic? . . . After Jesus Christ we have no need of speculation, after the Gospel no need of research."[7] To many early Christians, the Bible (see Chapter 6) contained all the knowledge anyone needed. Others, however, thought it was not possible to separate Christian thought from Classical traditions and education and encouraged Christianity to absorb the Classical heritage. As it spread in the eastern Roman world, Christianity adopted Greek as its language; the New Testament was written in Greek. Christians also turned to Greek thought for help in expressing complicated theological concepts. In many ways, then, Christianity served to preserve Greco-Roman culture.

THE WORK OF AUGUSTINE The work of Augustine (354–430) provides one of the best examples of how Christian intellectuals used pagan culture in the service of Christianity. Augustine came to be revered as one of the Latin Fathers of the Catholic Church, intellectuals who wrote in Latin and profoundly influenced the development of Christian thought in the west.

Born in North Africa, Augustine was reared by his mother, an ardent Christian. He eventually became a professor of rhetoric at Milan in 384. After experiencing a profound and moving religious experience, he gave up his teaching position and went back to North Africa, where he became bishop of Hippo from 396 until his death in 430.

Augustine's most famous work, *The City of God*, was a profound expression of a Christian philosophy of government and history. In it, he theorized on the ideal relations between two kinds of societies existing throughout time—the City of God and the City of the World. Those who loved God would be loyal to the City of God, whose ultimate location was the kingdom of heaven. Earthly society would always be uncertain because of human beings' inclination to sin. And yet the City of the World was still necessary, for it was the duty of rulers to curb the depraved instincts of sinful humans and maintain the peace necessary for Christians to live in the world. Hence, Augustine posited that secular government and authority were necessary for the pursuit of the true Christian life on earth; in doing so, he provided a justification for secular political authority that would play an important role in medieval thought.

JEROME AND THE BIBLE Another important intellectual of the early church was Jerome (345–420), who pursued literary studies in Rome and became a master of Latin prose. Jerome had mixed feelings about his love for Classical studies, however, and like Augustine, he experienced a spiritual conversion after which he tried to dedicate himself more fully to Jesus. Ultimately, Jerome found a compromise by purifying the literature of the pagan world and then using it to further the Christian faith. Jerome was a great scholar, and his extensive knowledge of both Hebrew and Greek enabled him to translate the Old and New Testaments into Latin. In the process, he created the so-called Latin Vulgate, or common text, of the Scriptures that became the standard edition for the Catholic Church in the Middle Ages.

CASSIODORUS Although the Christian church came to accept Classical culture, it was not easy to do so in the world of the new Germanic kingdoms. Nevertheless, some Christian scholars managed to keep learning alive. Most prominent was Cassiodorus (c. 490–c. 585), who came from an aristocratic Roman family and served as an official of the Ostrogothic king Theodoric. The conflicts that erupted after the death of Theodoric led Cassiodorus to withdraw from public life and retire to his landed estates in southern Italy, where he wrote his final work, *Divine and Human Readings*. This was a compendium of the literature of both Christian and pagan antiquity. Cassiodorus accepted the advice of earlier Christian intellectuals to make use of Classical works while treasuring the Scriptures above all else.

Cassiodorus continued the tradition of late antiquity of classifying knowledge according to certain subjects. In assembling his compendium of authors, he followed the practice of late ancient authors in placing all secular knowledge into the categories of the seven **liberal arts**, which were divided into two major groups: the ***trivium***, consisting of grammar, rhetoric, and dialectic or logic, and the ***quadrivium***, consisting of the mathematical subjects of arithmetic, geometry, astronomy, and music. The seven liberal arts would become the cornerstone of Western education until the seventeenth century.

The Byzantine Empire

FOCUS QUESTION: How did the Byzantine Empire that had emerged by the eighth century differ from the empire of Justinian and from the Germanic kingdoms in the west?

As noted earlier, in the fourth century, the western and eastern parts of the Roman Empire began to go their separate ways. As the Germans moved into the western part of the empire and established various kingdoms over the course of the next hundred years, the Roman Empire in the east, centered on Constantinople, solidified and prospered.

The Reign of Justinian (527–565)

When he became emperor of the Eastern Roman Empire, Justinian was determined to reestablish the empire in the entire Mediterranean world. His army, commanded by Belisarius (bell-uh-SAH-ree-us), probably the best general of the late Roman period, sailed to North Africa and quickly destroyed the Vandals in two major battles. From North Africa, Belisarius led his forces onto the Italian peninsula and defeated the Ostrogoths. By 552, Justinian appeared to have achieved his goal. His reconstituted empire included Italy, part of Spain, North Africa, Asia Minor, Palestine, and Syria (see Map 7.4). But his success proved fleeting. Only three years after Justinian's death, the Lombards conquered much of Italy. Although the eastern empire maintained the fiction of Italy as a province, its forces were limited to southern and central Italy, Sicily, and some coastal areas.

Justinian's most important contribution was his codification of Roman law. The eastern empire had inherited a vast quantity of legal materials connected to the development of Roman law, which Justinian wished to simplify. The result was the *Corpus Iuris Civilis* (KOR-pus YOOR-iss SIV-i-liss) (Body of Civil Law), a codification of Roman law that remained in force in the Eastern Roman Empire until its end in 1453. And because it was written in Latin (it was in fact the last product of eastern Roman culture to be written in Latin, which was soon replaced by Greek), the *Corpus* was also eventually used in the west and ultimately became the basis of the legal systems of all of continental Europe.

LIFE IN CONSTANTINOPLE: TRADE AND THE EMPEROR'S BUILDING PROGRAM After riots destroyed much of Constantinople in 532, Emperor Justinian rebuilt the city and gave it the appearance it would keep for almost a thousand years. With a population estimated in the hundreds of thousands, Constantinople was the largest city in Europe during the Middle Ages. It viewed itself as the

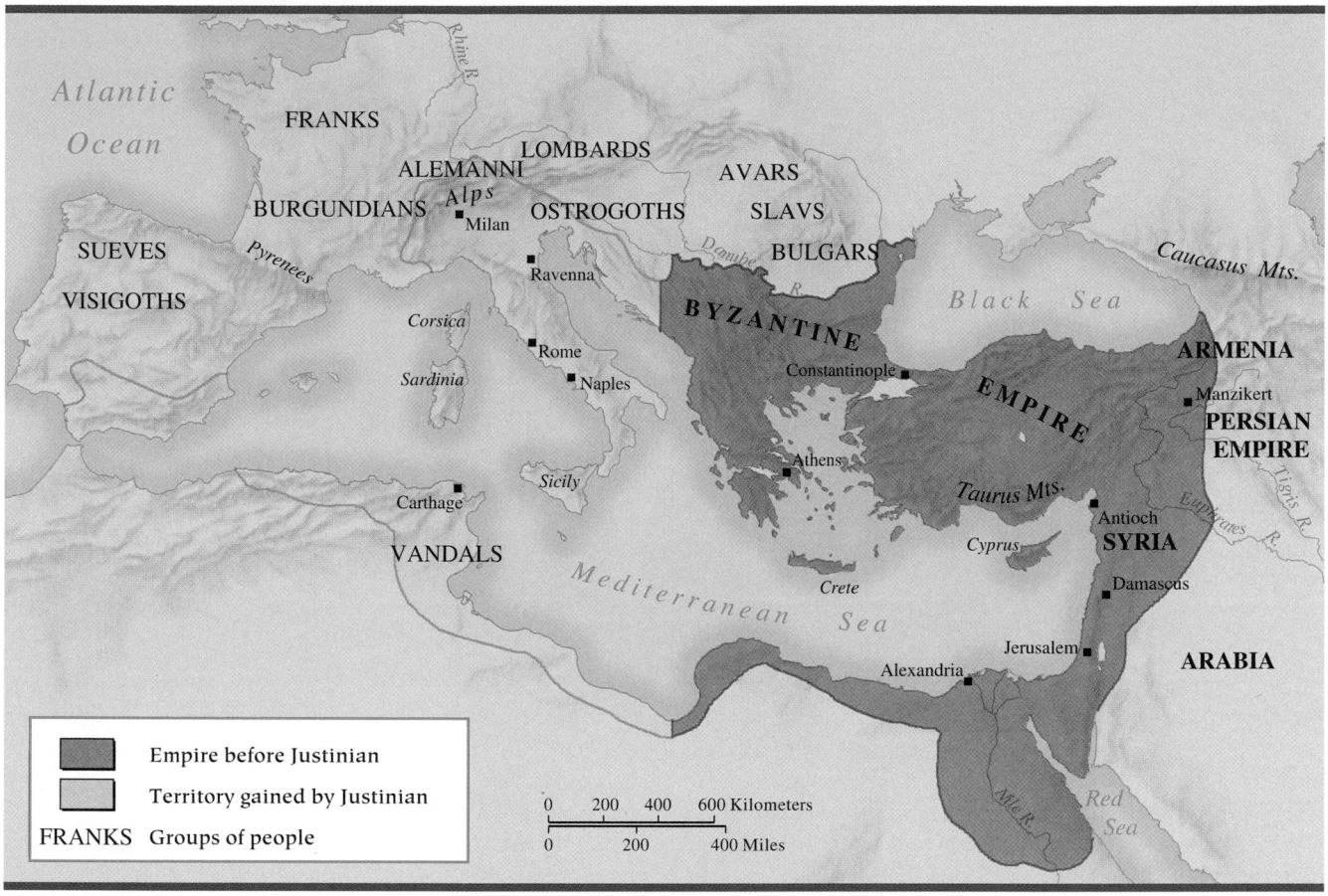

© Cengage Learning

MAP 7.4 The Byzantine Empire in the Time of Justinian. The Byzantine emperor Justinian briefly restored much of the Mediterranean portion of the old Roman Empire. His general Belisarius quickly conquered the Vandals in North Africa but wrested Italy from the Ostrogoths only after a long and devastating struggle.

Look back at Map 6.1. What former Roman territories lay outside Justinian's control?

center of an empire and a special Christian city. The Byzantines believed that the city was under the protection of God and the Virgin Mary. One thirteenth-century Byzantine said: "About our city you shall know: until the end she will fear no nation whatsoever, for no one will entrap or capture her, not by any means, for she has been given to the Mother of God and no one will snatch her out of Her hands. Many nations will break their horns against her walls and withdraw with shame."[8]

Until the twelfth century, Constantinople was Europe's greatest commercial center, the chief marketplace where western and eastern products were exchanged. Highly desired in Europe were the products of the East: silk from China, spices from Southeast Asia and India, jewelry and ivory from India (the latter used by artisans for church items), wheat and furs from southern Russia, and flax and honey from the Balkans. Many of these eastern goods were then shipped to the Mediterranean area and northern Europe. Moreover, imported raw materials were used in Constantinople for local industries. During Justinian's reign, two Christian monks smuggled silkworms from China to begin a Byzantine silk industry. The state controlled the production of silk cloth, and the workshops themselves were housed in Constantinople's royal palace complex. European demand for silk cloth made it the city's most lucrative product.

Much of Constantinople's appearance in the Middle Ages was due to Justinian's rebuilding program in the sixth century. The city was dominated by an immense palace complex, hundreds of churches, and a huge arena known as the Hippodrome. No residential district was particularly fashionable; palaces, tenements, and slums

S. Vitale, Ravenna, Italy/© Scala/Art Resource, NY

Justinian and His Court. Ravenna remained the center of the Byzantine presence in Italy for two hundred years. The Church of San Vitale at Ravenna contains some of the finest examples of sixth-century Byzantine mosaics (artworks created by cementing small pieces of colored glass or rock to a wall or floor). This mosaic depicts the emperor Justinian and his court dressed in their elaborate robes. Justinian is seen with soldiers, his staff, and members of the clergy.

ranged alongside one another. Justinian added many new buildings. His public works projects included roads, bridges, walls, public baths, law courts, and colossal underground reservoirs to hold the city's water supply. He also built hospitals, schools, monasteries, and churches. Churches were his special passion, and in Constantinople alone he built or rebuilt thirty-four of them. His greatest achievement was the famous Hagia Sophia, the Church of the Holy Wisdom, completed in 537. The center of Hagia Sophia consisted of four large piers crowned by an enormous dome, which seemed to be floating in space. In part this impression was created by ringing the base of the dome with forty-two windows, which allowed an incredible play of light within the cathedral. Light served to remind the worshipers of God. As darkness is illuminated by invisible light, so too, it was believed, is the world illuminated by an invisible spirit.

The Hippodrome was a huge amphitheater; constructed of brick covered by marble, it held between 40,000 and 60,000 spectators. Although gladiator fights were held there, the main events were the chariot races; twenty-four would usually be presented in one day. The citizens of Constantinople were passionate fans of chariot racing. Successful charioteers were acclaimed as heroes and honored with public statues.

From Eastern Roman to Byzantine Empire

Justinian's accomplishments had been spectacular, but when he died, he left the Eastern Roman Empire with serious problems: too much distant territory to protect, an empty treasury, a smaller population after an epidemic of plague, and renewed threats to its frontiers. In the first half of the seventh century, the empire faced attacks from the Persians to the east and the Slavs to the north.

The most serious challenge to the Eastern Roman Empire, however, came from the rise of Islam, which unified the Arab tribes and created a powerful new force that swept through the east (see the next section, "The Rise of Islam"). The empire lost the provinces of Syria and Palestine after the Arabs defeated an eastern Roman army at Yarmuk in 636. The Arabs also moved into the old Persian Empire and conquered it. Arabs and eastern Roman forces now faced each other along a frontier in southern Asia Minor.

Problems arose along the northern frontier as well, especially in the Balkans, where an Asiatic people known as the Bulgars had arrived earlier in the sixth century. In 679, the Bulgars defeated the eastern Roman forces and took possession of the lower Danube valley, establishing a strong Bulgarian kingdom.

By the beginning of the eighth century, the Eastern Roman Empire was greatly diminished in size. Consisting only of the eastern Balkans and Asia Minor, it was no longer a major eastern Mediterranean state. The external challenges had important internal repercussions as well. By the eighth century, the Eastern Roman Empire had been transformed into what historians call the Byzantine Empire, a civilization with its own unique character that would last until 1453 (Constantinople was built on the site of an older city named Byzantium—hence the term *Byzantine*).

© Robert Harding/Getty Images

Interior of Hagia Sophia. This view of the interior of the Church of the Holy Wisdom, constructed under Justinian by Anthemius of Tralles and Isidore of Miletus, gives an idea of how the windows around the base of the dome produced a special play of light within the cathedral. The pulpits and plaques bearing inscriptions from the Qur'an were introduced when the Turks converted this church to a mosque in the fifteenth century.

The Byzantine Empire was both a Greek and a Christian state. Increasingly, Latin fell into disuse as Greek became both the common and the official language of the empire. The Byzantine Empire was also built on a faith in Jesus that was shared by almost all of its citizens. An enormous amount of artistic talent was poured into the construction of churches, church ceremonies, and church decoration. Spiritual principles deeply permeated Byzantine art.

© Cengage Learning

The Byzantine Empire, c. 750

CHRONOLOGY The Byzantine Empire	
Reign of Justinian	527–565
Justinian codifies Roman law	529–533
Reconquest of Italy by the Byzantines	535–552
Completion of Hagia Sophia	537
Arab defeat of Byzantines at Yarmuk	636
Defeat by the Bulgars; losses in the Balkans	679

The emperor occupied a crucial position in the Byzantine state. Portrayed as chosen by God, the emperor was crowned in sacred ceremonies, and his subjects were expected to prostrate themselves in his presence. His power was considered absolute and was limited in practice only by deposition or assassination. Because the emperor appointed the head of the church (known as the patriarch), he also exercised control over both church and state. The Byzantines believed that God had commanded their state to preserve the true Christian faith. Emperor, clergy, and state officials were all bound together in service to this ideal. It can be said that spiritual values truly held the Byzantine state together.

By 750, it was apparent that two of Rome's heirs, the Germanic kingdoms and the Byzantine Empire, were moving in different directions. Nevertheless, Byzantine influence on the Western world was significant. The images of a Roman imperial state that continued to haunt the west lived on in Byzantium. The legal systems of the west owed much to Justinian's codification of Roman law. In addition, the Byzantine Empire served as a buffer state, protecting the west for a long time from incursions from the east. Although the Byzantine Empire would continue to influence the west until its demise in 1453, it went its own way. One of its bitterest enemies was the new power of Islam.

The Rise of Islam

FOCUS QUESTION: What was the basic message of Islam, and why was it able to expand so successfully?

The Arabs were a Semitic-speaking people of southwestern Asia with a long history. In Roman times, the Arabian peninsula came to be dominated by Bedouin nomads who moved constantly to find water and food for themselves and their animals. In early times, the Bedouins had supported themselves primarily by sheepherding or by raiding passing caravans, but after the domestication of the camel during the second millennium B.C.E., the Bedouins began to participate in the caravan trade themselves and became major carriers of goods between the Persian Gulf and the Mediterranean Sea.

Although these early Arabs were polytheistic, there was a supreme God named Allah (AH-lah) (Arabic for "God") who ruled over the other gods. Allah was symbolized by a sacred stone, and each tribe had its own stone. All tribes, however, worshiped a massive black meteorite—the Black Stone—which had been placed in a central shrine called the *Ka'ba* (KAH-buh) in the city of Mecca.

In the fifth and sixth centuries C.E., the Arabian peninsula took on new importance. As a result of political disorder in Mesopotamia and Egypt, the usual trade routes in the region began to change. A new trade route—from the Mediterranean through Mecca to Yemen and then by ship across the Arabian Sea and the Indian Ocean—became more popular, and communities in that part of the Arabian peninsula, including Mecca, began to prosper from this caravan trade. As a result, tensions arose between the Bedouins in the desert and the increasingly wealthy merchant classes in the towns. Into this intense world came Muhammad (moh-HAM-mud *or* moo-HAM-mud).

Muhammad

Born in Mecca to a merchant family, Muhammad (c. 570–632) was orphaned at the age of five. He grew up to become a caravan manager and eventually married a rich widow who was also his employer. In his middle years, he began to experience visions that he believed were inspired by Allah. Muhammad believed that although Allah had already revealed himself in part through Moses and Jesus—and thus through the Hebrew and Christian traditions—the final revelations were now being given to him. Out of these revelations, which were eventually written down, came the Qur'an (kuh-RAN *or* kuh-RAHN) or Koran, which contained the guidelines by which followers of Allah were to live. Muhammad's teachings formed the basis for the religion known as Islam, which means "submission to the will of Allah." Allah was the all-powerful being who had created the universe and everything in it. Humans must subject themselves to Allah if they wished to achieve everlasting life. Those who became his followers were called Muslims, meaning "practitioners of Islam."

After receiving the revelations, Muhammad set out to convince the people of Mecca that the revelations were true. At first, many thought he was insane, and others feared that his attacks on the corrupt society around him would upset the established social and political order. Discouraged by the failure of the Meccans to accept his message, in 622 Muhammad and some of his closest supporters left the city and moved north to the rival city of Yathrib, later renamed Medina ("city of the Prophet"). The year of the journey to Medina, known in history as the *Hegira* (hee-JY-ruh) ("departure"), became year 1 in the official calendar of Islam.

Muhammad, who had been invited to the town by a number of prominent residents, soon began to win support from people in Medina as well as from members of the Bedouin tribes in the surrounding countryside. From these groups, he formed the first Muslim community. Muslims saw no separation between political and religious authority; submission to the will of Allah meant submission to his Prophet, Muhammad. Muhammad soon became both a religious and a political leader. His political and military skills enabled him to put together a reliable military force, with which he returned to Mecca in 630, conquering the city and converting the townspeople to the new faith. From Mecca, Muhammad's ideas spread quickly across the Arabian peninsula and within a relatively short time had resulted in both the religious and the political unification of Arab society.

The Teachings of Islam

At the heart of Islam was its sacred book, the Qur'an, with the basic message that there is no God but Allah and Muhammad is his Prophet. Essentially, the Qur'an contains Muhammad's revelations of a heavenly book written down by secretaries. Consisting of 114 chapters, the Qur'an recorded the beliefs of the Muslims and served as their code of ethics and law.

Islam was a direct and simple faith, emphasizing the need to obey the will of Allah. This meant following a basic ethical code consisting of the **Five Pillars of Islam**: belief in Allah and Muhammad as his Prophet; standard prayer five times a day and public prayer on Friday at midday to worship Allah; observance of the holy month of Ramadan (the ninth month on the Muslim calendar) with fasting from dawn to sunset; making a pilgrimage—known as the *hajj* (HAJ)—to Mecca at least once in one's lifetime (see the box on p. 157); and giving alms to the poor and unfortunate. The faithful who observed the law were guaranteed a place in an eternal paradise.

Islam was not just a set of religious beliefs but a way of life as well. After the death of Muhammad, Muslim scholars drew up a law code, called the *Shari'a* (shah-REE-uh), to provide believers with a set of prescriptions to regulate their daily lives. Much of the *Shari'a* was drawn from the Qur'an. Believers' behavior was subject to strict guidelines. In addition to the Five Pillars, Muslims were forbidden to gamble, to eat pork, to drink alcoholic beverages, and to engage in dishonest behavior. Sexual practices were also strictly regulated. Marriages were to be arranged by

The Qur'an: The Pilgrimage

The Qur'an is the sacred book of the Muslims, comparable to the Bible in Christianity. This selection from Chapter 22, titled "Pilgrimage," discusses the importance of making a pilgrimage to Mecca, one of the Five Pillars of Islam. The pilgrim's final destination was the *Ka'ba* at Mecca, containing the Black Stone.

Qur'an, Chapter 22: "Pilgrimage"

Exhort all men to make the pilgrimage. They will come to you on foot and on the backs of swift camels from every distant quarter; they will come to avail themselves of many a benefit, and to pronounce on the appointed days the name of God over the cattle which He has given them for food. Eat of their flesh, and feed the poor and the unfortunate.

Then let the pilgrims tidy themselves, make their vows, and circle the Ancient House. Such is God's commandment. He that reveres the sacred rites of God shall fare better in the sight of his Lord.

The flesh of cattle is lawful for you, except for that which has been specified before. Guard yourselves against the filth of idols; and avoid the utterance of falsehoods.

Dedicate yourselves to God, and serve none besides Him. The man who serves other deities besides God is like him who falls from heaven and is snatched by the birds or carried away by the wind to some far-off region. Even such is he.

He that reveres the offerings made to God shows the piety of his heart. Your cattle are useful to you in many ways until the time of their slaughter. Then they are offered for sacrifice at the Ancient House.

For every community We have ordained a ritual, that they may pronounce the name of God over the cattle which He has given them for food. Your God is one God; to Him surrender yourselves. Give good news to the humble, whose hearts are filled with awe at the mention of God; who endure adversity with fortitude, attend to their prayers, and give in alms from what We gave them.

We have made the camels a part of God's rites. They are of much use to you. Pronounce over them the name of God as you draw them up in line and slaughter them; and when they have fallen to the ground eat of their flesh and feed the uncomplaining beggar and the demanding supplicant. Thus have We subjected them to your service, so that you may give thanks.

Their flesh and blood does not reach God; it is your piety that reaches Him. Thus has He subjected them to your service, so that you may give glory to God for guiding you.

Give good news to the righteous. God will ward off evil from true believers. God does not love the treacherous and the thankless.

Q What is the key purpose of undertaking a pilgrimage to Mecca? What is the historical importance of the sacred stone?

Source: From THE KORAN, translated by N. J. Dawood (Penguin Classics 1956, Fifth revised edition 1990). Copyright © N. J. Dawood, 1956, 1959, 1966, 1968, 1974, 1990, 1993, 1997, 1999, 2003. Reproduced by permission of Penguin Books Ltd.

parents, and contacts between unmarried men and women were discouraged. In accordance with Bedouin custom, males were permitted to have more than one wife, but Muhammad attempted to limit the practice by restricting the number of wives to four.

The Spread of Islam

The death of Muhammad presented his followers with a dilemma. Muhammad had never named a successor, and although he had several daughters, he left no sons. In a male-oriented society, who would lead the community of the faithful? Shortly after Muhammad's death, some of his closest followers selected Abu Bakr (ah boo BAHK ur), a wealthy merchant who was Muhammad's father-in-law, as **caliph** (KAY-luff), or temporal leader, of the Islamic community.

Muhammad and the early caliphs who succeeded him took up the Arabic tribal custom of the *razzia* or raid in the struggle against their enemies. Some have called this activity a *jihad* (ji-HAHD), which they misleadingly interpret as a "holy war." ***Jihad*** actually means "striving in the way of the Lord" to achieve personal betterment, although it can also mean a fair, defensive fight to preserve one's life and one's faith. Arab conquests were not carried out to convert others, because conversion to Islam was purely voluntary. Those who did not convert were required only to submit to Muslim rule and pay taxes.

The Byzantines and the Persians were the first to feel the strength of the newly united Arabs. At Yarmuk in 636, the Muslims defeated the Byzantine army, and by 640, they had taken possession of the province of Syria (see Map 7.5). To the east, the Arabs went on to conquer

© Bibliothèque Nationale (Ar 5847 f.19), Paris/The Bridgeman Art Library

Muslims Celebrating the End of Ramadan. During Ramadan, the holy month of Islam, all Muslims must fast each day from dawn to sunset. Observance of Ramadan is one of the Five Pillars of Islam. Muhammad instituted the fast during his stay at Medina. It was designed to replace the single Jewish Day of Atonement. This Persian miniature depicts Muslims on horseback celebrating the end of Ramadan.

the Persian Empire by 650. In the meantime, Egypt and other areas of northern Africa had been added to the new Muslim empire. Led by a series of brilliant generals, the Arabs had put together a large and highly motivated army, whose valor was enhanced by the belief that Muslim warriors were guaranteed a place in paradise if they died in battle.

Early caliphs, ruling from Medina, organized their newly conquered territories into taxpaying provinces. By the mid-seventh century, problems arose again over the succession to the Prophet until Ali, Muhammad's son-in-law, was assassinated and the general Muawiya (moo-AH-wee-yah), the governor of Syria and one of Ali's chief rivals, became caliph in 661. He was known for one outstanding virtue: he used force only when necessary. As he said, "I never use my sword when my whip will do, nor my whip when my tongue will do."[9] Muawiya moved quickly to make the caliphate hereditary in his own family, thus establishing the Umayyad (oo-MY-ad) dynasty. As one of its first actions, the Umayyad dynasty moved the capital of the Muslim empire from Medina to Damascus in Syria. This internal dissension over the caliphate created a split in Islam between the Shi'ites, or those who accepted only the descendants of Ali, Muhammad's son-in-law, as the true rulers, and the Sunnites, who claimed that the descendants of the Umayyads were the true caliphs. This seventh-century split in Islam has lasted to the present day.

Internal dissension, however, did not stop the expansion of Islam. After sweeping across North Africa, the Muslims crossed the Strait of Gibraltar and moved into Spain around 710. The Visigothic kingdom collapsed, and by 725, most of Spain had become a Muslim state with its center at Córdoba. In 732, a Muslim army, making a foray into southern France, was defeated at the Battle of Tours near Poitiers. Muslim expansion in Europe came to a halt.

Meanwhile, in 717, another Muslim force had launched a naval attack on Constantinople with the hope of destroying the Byzantine Empire. In the spring of 718, the Byzantines destroyed the Muslim fleet and saved the Byzantine Empire and indirectly Christian Europe, since the fall of Constantinople would no doubt have opened the door to Muslim invasion of eastern Europe. The Byzantine Empire and Islam now established an uneasy frontier in southern Asia Minor.

The Arab advance had finally come to an end, but not before the southern and eastern Mediterranean parts of the old Roman Empire had been conquered. Islam had become heir to much of the old Roman Empire. The Umayyad dynasty at Damascus now ruled an enormous empire. While expansion had conveyed untold wealth and new ethnic groups into the fold of Islam, it also brought contact with Byzantine and Persian civilization. As a result, the new Arab empire would be influenced by Greek culture as well as by the older civilizations of the ancient Near East.

CHRONOLOGY The Rise of Islam

Birth of Muhammad	c. 570
Muhammad's flight from Mecca *(Hegira)*	622
Death of Muhammad	632
Defeat of Byzantines at Yarmuk	636
Seizure of Byzantine provinces of Syria and Egypt	640–642
Defeat of Persians	650
Invasion of Spain	c. 710

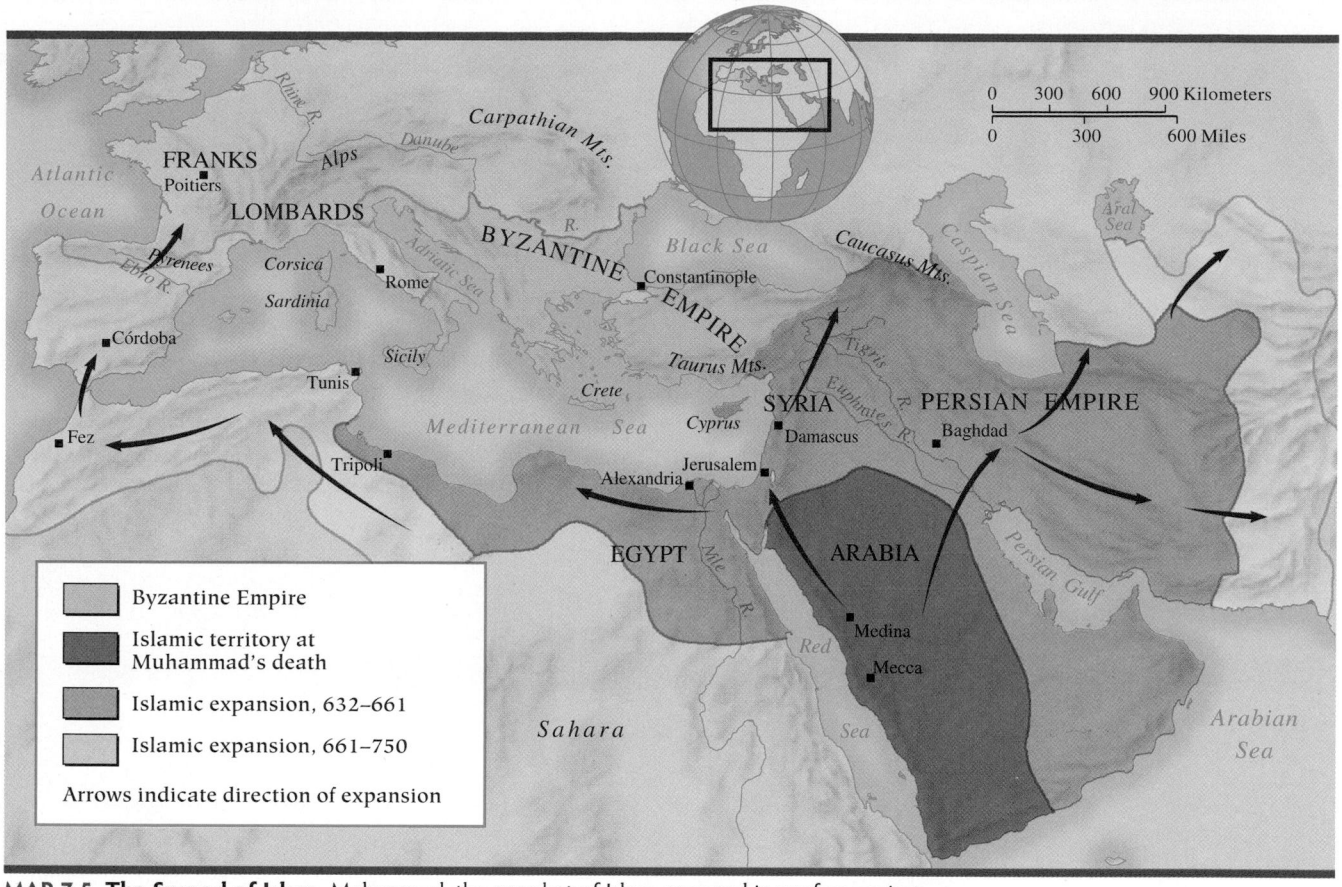

© Cengage Learning

MAP 7.5 The Spread of Islam. Muhammad, the prophet of Islam, engaged in warfare against neighboring tribes. Militaristic expansion continued with great zeal under the Prophet's successors. Islamic rule spread rapidly in the decades after Muhammad's death, until it was finally stopped by the Byzantine Empire and the Franks.

Q ***Why was the continuance of the Byzantine Empire a key factor in stopping the spread of Islam into Europe?***

CHAPTER SUMMARY

The period from the mid-third century to the mid-eighth century was both chaotic and creative. During late antiquity, the Roman world of the Mediterranean was gradually transformed. Diocletian and Constantine restored an aura of stability to the Late Empire by increasing the size of the bureaucracy and the army, establishing price controls, raising taxes, and making occupations hereditary. Nevertheless, even their efforts proved ultimately to be in vain as the empire stumbled along. With fewer resources and little resolve, the government was less able to repel the German migrants who moved into the western part of the empire. In 476, the last Roman emperor in the west was deposed.

As the western part of the Roman Empire disintegrated, a new civilization slowly emerged, formed by the coalescence of three major elements: the Germanic peoples who moved into the western part of the empire and established new kingdoms, the continuing attraction of the Greco-Roman cultural legacy, and the Christian church. Politically, the Roman Empire in the west was replaced by a new series of Germanic kingdoms, including the Ostrogothic kingdom in Italy, the Visigothic kingdom in Spain, several Anglo-Saxon kingdoms in Britain, and a Frankish kingdom in Gaul. Each of these kingdoms fused Roman and Germanic elements to create a new society.

In the fourth century, Christianity had become the official religion of the Roman Empire. The Christian church (or Roman Catholic Church, as it came to be called in the west) played a crucial role in the growth of a new civilization. The church developed an organized government under the leadership of the bishop of Rome, who became known as the pope. One of the most significant popes was Gregory I the Great, who established claims to both religious and political power. The church also assimilated the Classical tradition and through its clergy brought Christianized civilization to the Germanic tribes. Especially important were the monks and nuns who led the way in converting the Germanic peoples in Europe to Christianity.

But the Germanic kingdoms were not the only heir to Roman civilization. In the east, Greek and eastern elements of late antiquity were of more consequence as the Eastern Roman Empire was transformed into the Byzantine Empire. Although the Germanic kingdoms of the west and the Byzantine civilization of the east came to share a common bond in Christianity, it proved incapable of keeping them in harmony politically as the two civilizations continued to move apart.

The rise of Islam, Rome's third heir, resulted in the loss of the southern and eastern Mediterranean portions of the old Roman Empire to a religious power that was neither Roman nor Christian. The new Islamic empire forced Europe proper back upon itself, and slowly, a new civilization emerged that became the heart of what we know as Western civilization.

CHAPTER TIMELINE

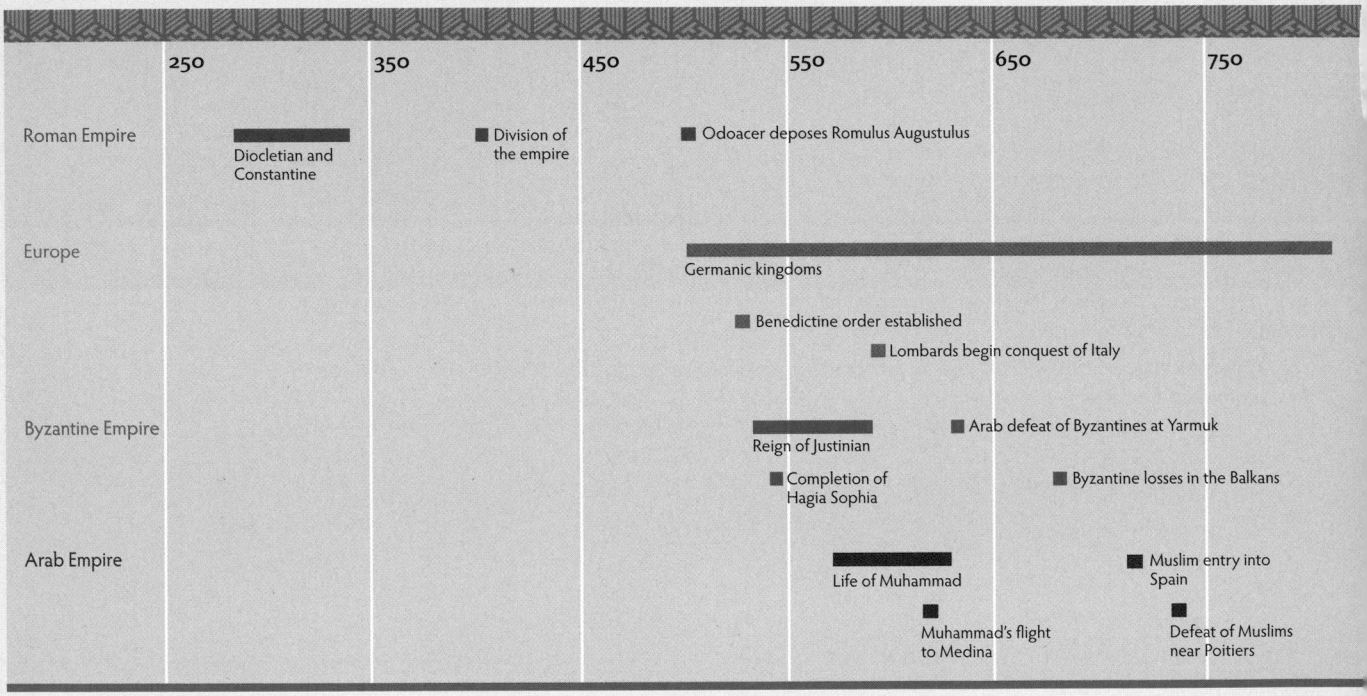

CHAPTER REVIEW

Upon Reflection

Q What role did monks and nuns play in early medieval society?

Q What contributions did the Germanic peoples make to the political, economic, and social conditions of early medieval society?

Q What impact did Christianity have on the intellectual life of early medieval society?

Key Terms

inflation (p. 138)
heresy (p. 140)
Arianism (p. 140)
wergeld (p. 145)
monk (p. 147)
monasticism (p. 147)
abbot (p. 148)
nuns (p. 148)
abbess (p. 150)
liberal arts (p. 152)
trivium (p. 152)
quadrivium (p. 152)
Five Pillars of Islam (p. 156)
caliph (p. 157)
jihad (p. 157)

Suggestions for Further Reading

GENERAL WORKS ON LATE ANTIQUITY For good introductions to late antiquity, see **P. Brown, *The World of Late Antiquity, A.D. 150–750*** (New York, 1989); **J. Moorhead, *The Roman Empire Divided, 400–700*** (London, 2001); and **J. J. O'Donnell, *The Ruin of the Roman Empire: A New History*** (New York, 2008).

LATE ROMAN EMPIRE On the Late Roman Empire, see **S. Mitchell, *History of the Later Roman Empire A.D. 284–641*** (Oxford, 2006). For new perspectives on the role of the Germans in the fall of the Western Roman Empire, see **P. Heather, *The Fall of the Roman Empire: A New History of Rome and the Barbarians*** (Oxford, 2006), and **B. Ward-Perkins, *The Fall of Rome and the End of Civilization*** (Oxford, 2005).

THE GERMANIC PEOPLES For a survey of the German tribes and their migrations, see **M. Todd, *The Early Germans,*** 2nd ed. (Oxford, 2004). On the relationship between the Romans and the Germans, see **T. S. Burns, *Rome and the Barbarians, 100 B.C.–A.D. 400*** (Baltimore, 2003), and **M. Kulikowski, *Rome's Gothic Wars*** (New York, 2007).

EARLY CHRISTIANITY For a superb introduction to early Christianity, see **P. Brown, *The Rise of Western Christendom: Triumph and Adversity A.D. 200–1000,*** 2nd ed. (Oxford, 2002). For a good account of early monasticism, see **C. H. Lawrence, *Medieval Monasticism,*** 3rd ed. (London, 2000). On Pope Gregory the Great, see **J. Moorhead, *Gregory the Great*** (London, 2005).

THE BYZANTINE EMPIRE Brief but good introductions to Byzantine history can be found in **A. Cameron, *The Byzantines*** (Oxford, 2006), and **W. Treadgold, *A Concise History of Byzantium*** (London, 2001). On Justinian, see **J. Moorhead, *Justinian*** (London, 1995). On Constantinople, see **J. Harris, *Constantinople: Capital of Byzantium*** (New York, 2007).

ISLAMIC MIDDLE EAST For a good brief survey of the Islamic Middle East, see **A. Goldschmidt Jr., *A Concise History of the Middle East,*** 8th ed. (Boulder, Colo., 2005). On the rise of Islam, see **F. E. Peters, *Muhammad and the Origins of Islam*** (Albany, N.Y, 1994).

Visit the CourseMate website at **www.cengagebrain.com** for additional study tools and review materials for this chapter.

CHAPTER 8

© The Art Archive/Bibliothèque Municipale Châteauroux (Ms 5 f. 133)/Kharbine-Tapabor/Collection Jean Vigne

A fifteenth-century French manuscript illustration of the coronation of Charlemagne by Pope Leo III

European Civilization in the Early Middle Ages, 750–1000

CHAPTER OUTLINE AND FOCUS QUESTIONS

The World of the Carolingians

Q What was the significance of Charlemagne's coronation as emperor? In what ways did the political, intellectual, and daily life in the Carolingian Empire represent a fusion of Gallo-Roman, Germanic, and Christian practices?

Disintegration of the Carolingian Empire

Q What impact did the Vikings have on the history and culture of medieval Europe?

The Emerging World of Lords and Vassals

Q What was fief-holding, and how was it related to manorialism?

The Zenith of Byzantine Civilization

Q What were the chief developments in the Byzantine Empire between 750 and 1000?

The Slavic Peoples of Central and Eastern Europe

Q What patterns of development occurred in central and eastern Europe as a result of the Slavic peoples?

The World of Islam

Q What were the chief developments in the Islamic world between 750 and 1000?

CRITICAL THINKING

Q Why can it be said that Islamic civilization was more advanced than the civilization of western Europe in the ninth and tenth centuries?

IN 800, CHARLEMAGNE, the king of the Franks, journeyed to Rome to help Pope Leo III, who was barely clinging to power in the face of rebellious Romans. On Christmas Day, Charlemagne and his family, attended by Romans, Franks, and even visitors from the Byzantine Empire, crowded into Saint Peter's Basilica to hear Mass. Quite unexpectedly, at least according to a Frankish writer, "as the king rose from praying before the tomb of the blessed apostle Peter, Pope Leo placed a golden crown on his head." In keeping with ancient tradition, the people in the church shouted, "Long life and victory to Charles Augustus, crowned by God the great and pacific Emperor of the Romans." Seemingly, the Roman Empire in the West had been reborn, and Charles had become the first western emperor since 476. But this "Roman emperor" was actually a German king, and he had been crowned by the head of the western Christian church. In truth, the coronation of Charlemagne was a sign not of the rebirth of the Roman Empire but of the emergence of a new European civilization.

By the year of Charlemagne's coronation, the contours of this new European civilization were beginning to emerge in western Europe. Increasingly, Europe would become the focus and center of Western civilization. Building on a fusion of Germanic, Greco-Roman, and Christian elements, the medieval European world first became visible in the Carolingian Empire of Charlemagne. The agrarian foundations of the eighth and ninth centuries proved inadequate to maintain a large monarchical system, however, and a new political and military order based on the decentralization of political power subsequently evolved to become an integral part of the political world of the Middle Ages.

European civilization began on a shaky and uncertain foundation, however. In the ninth century, Vikings, Magyars, and Muslims posed threats that could easily have stifled the new society. But European civilization absorbed the challenges. The Vikings and Magyars were assimilated, and recovery slowly began to set in. By 1000, European civilization was ready to embark on a period of dazzling vitality and expansion.

The World of the Carolingians

Q **Focus Questions:** What was the significance of Charlemagne's coronation as emperor? In what ways did the political, intellectual, and daily life in the Carolingian Empire represent a fusion of Gallo-Roman, Germanic, and Christian practices?

By the eighth century, the Merovingian dynasty was losing its control of the Frankish lands. Charles Martel, the mayor of the palace of Austrasia, became the virtual ruler of these territories. When Charles died in 741, his son, Pepin (PEP-in *or* pay-PAHN), deposed the Merovingians and assumed the kingship of the Frankish state for himself and his family. Pepin's actions, which were approved by the pope, created a new form of Frankish kingship. In imitation of an Old Testament practice, Pepin (751–768) was crowned and formally anointed with holy oil by a representative of the pope. The anointing not only symbolized that the king had been entrusted with a sacred office but also provided yet another example of how a Germanic institution fused with a Christian practice in the Early Middle Ages.

Charlemagne and the Carolingian Empire (768–814)

Pepin was succeeded on the throne of the Frankish kingdom by his son, a dynamic and powerful ruler known to history as Charles the Great, or Charlemagne (*Carolus magnus* in Latin—hence, our word *Carolingian*). Charlemagne was a determined and decisive man, intelligent and inquisitive. A fierce warrior, he was also a wise patron of learning and a resolute statesman (see the box on p. 164). He greatly expanded the territory of the Carolingian Empire during his lengthy rule.

EXPANSION OF THE CAROLINGIAN EMPIRE In the tradition of the Germanic kings, Charlemagne was a determined warrior who undertook fifty-four military campaigns. Even though the Frankish army was relatively small—only eight thousand men gathered each spring for campaigning—supplying it and transporting it to distant areas could still present serious problems. The Frankish army consisted mostly of infantry, with some cavalry armed with swords and spears.

Charlemagne's campaigns took him to many parts of Europe. In 773, Charlemagne led his army into Italy, crushed the Lombards, and took control of the Lombard state. Although his son was crowned king of Italy, Charlemagne was its real ruler. Four years after his invasion of Italy, Charlemagne moved his forces into northern Spain. This campaign proved disappointing: not only did the Basques harass his army as it crossed the Pyrenees on the way home, but they also ambushed and annihilated his rear guard.

Charlemagne was considerably more successful with his eastern campaigns into Germany, especially against the Saxons living between the Elbe River and the North Sea. As Einhard, Charlemagne's biographer, recounted it:

> No war ever undertaken by the Frank nation was carried on with such persistence and bitterness, or cost so much labor, because the Saxons, like almost all the tribes of Germany, were a fierce people, given to the worship of devils, and hostile to our religion, and did not consider it dishonorable to transgress and violate all law, human and divine.[1]

Charlemagne's insistence that the Saxons convert to Christianity simply fueled their resistance. Not until 804, after eighteen campaigns, was Saxony finally pacified and added to the Carolingian domain.

In southeastern Germany, Charlemagne invaded the land of the Bavarians in 787 and had incorporated them into his empire by the following year, an expansion that brought him into contact with the southern Slavs and the Avars. The latter disappeared from history after their utter devastation at the hands of Charlemagne's army. Now at its height, Charlemagne's empire covered much of

The Achievements of Charlemagne

Einhard, the biographer of Charlemagne, was born in the valley of the Main River in Germany about 775. Raised and educated in the monastery of Fulda, an important center of learning, he arrived at the court of Charlemagne in 791 or 792. Although he did not achieve high office under Charlemagne, he served as private secretary to Louis the Pious, Charlemagne's son and successor. Einhard's *Life of Charlemagne* was modeled on *Lives of the Caesars* by the Roman author Suetonius, especially his biography of Augustus. Einhard's work, written between 817 and 830, was the "first medieval biography of a lay figure." In this selection, he discusses some of Charlemagne's accomplishments.

Einhard, *Life of Charlemagne*

Such are the wars, most skillfully planned and successfully fought, which this most powerful king waged during the forty-seven years of his reign. He so largely increased the Frank kingdom, which was already great and strong when he received it at his father's hands, that more than double its former territory was added to it. . . . He subdued all the wild and barbarous tribes dwelling in Germany between the Rhine and the Vistula, the Ocean and the Danube, all of which speak very much the same language, but differ widely from one another in customs and dress. . . .

He added to the glory of his reign by gaining the good will of several kings and nations. . . . The Emperors of Constantinople [the Byzantine emperors] sought friendship and alliance with Charles by several embassies; and even when the Greeks [the Byzantines] suspected him of designing to take the empire from them, because of his assumption of the title Emperor, they made a close alliance with him, that he might have no cause of offense. In fact, the power of the Franks was always viewed with a jealous eye, whence the Greek proverb, "Have the Frank for your friend, but not for your neighbor."

This King, who showed himself so great in extending his empire and subduing foreign nations, and was constantly occupied with plans to that end, undertook also very many works calculated to adorn and benefit his kingdom, and brought several of them to completion. Among these, the most deserving of mention are the basilica of the Holy Mother of God at Aix-la-Chapelle [Aachen], built in the most admirable manner, and a bridge over the Rhine River at Mainz, half a mile long, the breadth of the river at this point. . . . Above all, sacred buildings were the object of his care throughout his whole kingdom; and whenever he found them falling to ruin from age, he commanded the priests and fathers who had charge of them to repair them, and made sure by commissioners that his instructions were obeyed. . . . Thus did Charles defend and increase as well as beautify his kingdom. . . .

He cherished with the greatest fervor and devotion the principles of the Christian religion, which had been instilled into him from infancy. Hence it was that he built the beautiful church at Aix-la-Chapelle, which he adorned with gold and silver and lamps, and with rails and doors of solid brass. He had the columns and marbles for this structure brought from Rome and Ravenna, for he could not find such as were suitable elsewhere. He was a constant worshiper at this church as long as his health permitted, going morning and evening, even after nightfall, besides attending mass. . . .

He was very forward in caring for the poor, so much so that he not only made a point of giving in his own country and his own kingdom, but when he discovered that there were Christians living in poverty in Syria, Egypt, and Africa, at Jerusalem, Alexandria, and Carthage, he had compassion on their wants, and used to send money over the seas to them. . . . He sent great and countless gifts to the popes, and throughout his whole reign the wish that he had nearest at heart was to reestablish the ancient authority of the city of Rome under his care and by his influence, and to defend and protect the Church of St. Peter, and to beautify and enrich it out of his own store above all other churches.

Q Based on Einhard's account, discuss the strengths and weaknesses of Charlemagne. Which characteristics help explain Charlemagne's success as a ruler? Does Einhard exaggerate Charlemagne's strengths? What might motivate him to do that?

Source: From Einhard, *The Life of Charlemagne*, translated by Samuel Epes Turner (New York: Harper & Brothers, 1880).

© Cengage Learning

MAP 8.1 The Carolingian Empire. Charlemagne inherited the Frankish kingdom from his father, Pepin. He expanded his territories in several directions, creating an empire that would not be rivaled in size until the conquests of Napoleon in the early nineteenth century.

Q ***How might Charlemagne's holdings in northern Italy have influenced his relationship with the pope?***

western and central Europe (see Map 8.1); not until the time of Napoleon in the nineteenth century would an empire of this size be seen again in Europe.

GOVERNING THE EMPIRE Charlemagne continued the efforts of his father in organizing the Carolingian kingdom. Because there was no system of public taxation, Charlemagne was dependent on the royal estates for the resources he needed to govern his empire. Food and goods derived from these lands provided support for the king, his household staff, and officials. To keep the nobles in his service, Charlemagne granted part of the royal lands as lifetime holdings to nobles who assisted him.

Besides the household staff, the administration of the empire depended on counts, who were the king's chief representatives in local areas. Counts were members of the nobility who had already existed under the Merovingians. They had come to control public services in their own lands and thus acted as judges, military leaders, and agents of the king. Gradually, as the rule of the Merovingian kings weakened, many counts had simply attached the royal lands and services performed on behalf of the king to their own family possessions.

In an effort to gain greater control over his kingdom, Charlemagne attempted to limit the power of the counts. They were required to serve outside their own family lands and were moved about periodically rather than being permitted to remain in a county for life. By making the offices appointive, Charlemagne tried to prevent the counts' children from automatically inheriting their offices. Moreover, as another check on the counts, Charlemagne instituted the *missi dominici* (MISS-ee doh-MIN-i-chee) ("messengers of the lord king"), a lay lord and a church official who were sent out to local districts to ensure that the counts were executing the king's wishes.

Nevertheless, the Carolingian system was glaringly inefficient. Great distances had to be covered on horseback, making it impossible for Charlemagne and his household staff to exercise much supervision over local affairs. The system was held together only by personal loyalty to the king, who was strong enough to ensure loyalty by force when necessary.

Charlemagne also realized that the Catholic Church could provide valuable assistance in governing his kingdom. By the end of the seventh century, the system of ecclesiastical government within the Christian church that had been created in the Late Roman Empire had largely disintegrated. Many church offices were not filled or were held by grossly unqualified relatives of the royal family. Both Pepin and his son Charlemagne took up the cause of church reform by creating new bishoprics and archbishoprics, restoring old ones, and seeing to it that the clergy accepted the orders of their superiors and executed their duties.

CHARLEMAGNE AS EMPEROR As Charlemagne's power grew, so did his prestige as the most powerful Christian ruler; one monk even wrote of his empire as the "kingdom of Europe." In 800, Charlemagne acquired a new title—emperor of the Romans—largely as a result of the ever-closer relationship between the papacy and the Frankish monarchs.

Louvre (OA 8260), Paris, France//© Réunion des Musées Nationaux/Art Resource, NY

Bronze Equestrian Statue of Charlemagne. This small bronze statue is believed to represent the emperor Charles the Great, although some scholars believe it is his grandson, Charles the Bald. The figure dates from the ninth century, but the horse is a sixteenth-century restoration. The attire on the figure accords with Einhard's account of how Charlemagne dressed. The imperial crown rests on his head, and in his left hand he grasps a globe, a symbol of world power and a reminder that the power of the Roman Empire had been renewed.

Already during the reign of Pepin, an alliance had emerged between the kingdom of the Franks and the papacy. The popes welcomed this support, and in the course of the second half of the eighth century, they increasingly severed their ties with the Byzantine Empire and drew closer to the Frankish kingdom. Charlemagne encouraged this development. In 799, after a rebellion against his authority, Pope Leo III (795–816) managed to escape from Rome and flee to safety at Charlemagne's court. Charlemagne offered assistance, and when he went to Rome in November 800 to settle affairs, he was received by the pope like an emperor. On Christmas Day in 800, Pope Leo placed a crown on Charlemagne's head and declared him emperor of the Romans.

THE SIGNIFICANCE OF CHARLEMAGNE The significance of this imperial coronation has been much debated by historians. We are not even sure whether the idea was discussed when Charlemagne and the pope met in the summer of 799 in Paderborn in German lands or whether Charlemagne was pleased or displeased. Charlemagne's biographer Einhard claimed that Charlemagne "at first had such an aversion that he declared that he would not have set foot in the Church the day that it was conferred, although it was a great feast-day, if he could have foreseen the design of the Pope."[2] But Charlemagne also perceived the usefulness of the imperial title; after all, he was now on a level of equality with the Byzantine emperor. Moreover, the papacy now had a defender of great stature, although later popes in the Middle Ages would become involved in fierce struggles with emperors over who possessed the higher power.

In any case, Charlemagne's coronation as Roman emperor demonstrated the strength, even after three hundred years, of the concept of an enduring Roman Empire. More important, it symbolized the fusion of Roman, Christian, and Germanic elements. Did this fusion constitute the foundation of European civilization? A Germanic king had been crowned emperor of the Romans by the spiritual leader of western Christendom. Charlemagne had created an empire that stretched from the North Sea in the north to Italy in the south and from France in western Europe to Vienna in central Europe. This empire differed significantly from the Roman Empire, which encompassed much of the Mediterranean world. Had a new civilization emerged? And should Charlemagne be seen, as one of his recent biographers has argued, as the "father of Europe"?[3]

The Carolingian Intellectual Renewal

Charlemagne had a strong desire to revive learning in his kingdom, an attitude that stemmed from his own intellectual curiosity as well as the need to provide educated clergy for the church and literate officials for the government. His efforts led to a revival of learning and culture that some historians have labeled the Carolingian Renaissance, or "rebirth" of learning.

For the most part, the revival of Classical studies and the efforts to preserve Latin culture took place in the monasteries, many of which had been established by the Irish and English missionaries of the seventh and eighth centuries. By the ninth century, the work required of Benedictine monks was the copying of manuscripts. Monasteries established **scriptoria** (skrip-TOR-ee-uh), or writing rooms, where monks copied not only the works of early Christianity, such as the Bible, but also the works of Classical Latin authors. The production of manuscripts in Carolingian monastic scriptoria was a crucial factor in the preservation of the ancient legacy. About eight thousand manuscripts survive from Carolingian times. Some 90 percent of the ancient Roman works that we have today exist because they were copied by Carolingian monks.

Charlemagne personally promoted learning by establishing a palace school and encouraging scholars from all over Europe to come to the Carolingian court. Best known was Alcuin (AL-kwin), from the famous school at York, founded as part of a great revival of learning in the Anglo-Saxon kingdom of Northumbria. From 782 to 796, while serving at Charlemagne's court as an adviser on ecclesiastical affairs, Alcuin also provided the leadership for the palace school. He concentrated on teaching Classical Latin and adopted Cassiodorus's sevenfold division of knowledge known as the liberal arts (see Chapter 7), which became the basis for all later medieval education.

Charlemagne's official seal carried the words "renewal of the Roman Empire." For Charlemagne, who had made a number of visits to Italy, this included a revival of the arts, which meant looking to Italy for inspiration. Charlemagne encouraged his own artists to look to the arts of ancient Rome and the Byzantine Empire. The chapel he built at Aachen was modeled after the Church of San Vitale in Ravenna, a church that had been built by the emperor Justinian after his reconquest of much of Italy (see Chapter 7). All in all, the Carolingian Renaissance played an important role in keeping the Classical heritage alive.

Life in the Carolingian World

In daily life as well as intellectual life, the Europe of the Carolingian era witnessed a fusion of Roman, Germanic, and Christian practices. The last in particular seem to have exercised an ever-increasing influence.

THE FAMILY AND MARRIAGE By Carolingian times, the Catholic Church had begun to influence Frankish family life and marital and sexual attitudes. Marriages in Frankish society were arranged by fathers or uncles to meet the needs of the extended family. Although wives were expected to be faithful to their husbands, Frankish aristocrats often kept concubines, either slave girls or free women from their estates. Even the "most Christian king" Charlemagne kept a number of concubines.

To limit such sexual license, the church increasingly emphasized its role in marriage and attempted to Christianize it. Although marriage was a civil arrangement, priests tried to add their blessings and strengthen the concept of a special marriage ceremony. To stabilize marriages, the church also began to emphasize **monogamy** and permanence. A Frankish church council in 789 stipulated that marriage was "indissoluble" and condemned the practice of concubinage and easy divorce, and during the reign of Emperor Louis the Pious (814–840), the church formally prohibited divorce. Now a man who married was expected to remain with his wife "even though she were sterile, deformed, old, dirty, drunken, a frequenter of bad company, lascivious, vain, greedy, unfaithful, quarrelsome, abusive . . ., for when that man was free, he freely engaged himself."[4]

The acceptance and spread of the Catholic Church's views on the indissolubility of marriage encouraged the development of the **nuclear family** at the expense of the extended family. Although kinship was still an influential social and political force, the conjugal unit came to be seen as the basic unit of society. The new practice of young couples establishing their own households brought a dynamic element to European society. It also had a significant impact on women. In the extended family, the eldest woman controlled all the other female members; in the nuclear family, the wife was still dominated by her husband, but at least she now had control of her own household and children.

CHRISTIANITY AND SEXUALITY The early church fathers had stressed that celibacy and complete abstinence from sexual activity constituted an ideal state superior to marriage. Subsequently, the early church gradually developed a case for clerical celibacy, although it proved impossible to enforce in the Early Middle Ages. The early fathers had also emphasized, however, that not all people had the self-discipline to remain celibate. It was thus permissible to marry, as Paul had indicated in his first epistle to the Corinthians:

> It is good for a man not to touch a woman. Nevertheless, to avoid fornication, let every man have his own wife, and let every woman have her own husband. . . . I say therefore to the unmarried and widows, it is good for them if they abide even as I. But if they cannot contain, let them marry: for it is better to marry than to burn.[5]

The church thus viewed marriage as the lesser of two evils; it was a concession to human weakness and fulfilled the need for companionship, sex, and children. The early medieval church generally accepted that marriage gave the right to indulge in sexual intercourse. Sex, then, was permissible within marriage, but only so long as it was used for the sole purpose of procreation and not for pleasure. The church condemned all forms of contraception and also strongly condemned abortion, although this prohibition failed to stop either practice. Various herbal potions were available to prevent conception or cause abortion. The Catholic Church accepted only one way to limit children: periodic or total abstinence from intercourse.

The Catholic Church's condemnation of sexual activity outside marriage also included homosexuality. Neither Roman religion nor Roman law had recognized any real difference between homosexual and heterosexual eroticism, and the Roman Empire had taken no legal measures against homosexual relations between adults. Later, in the Byzantine Empire, Emperor Justinian in 538 condemned homosexuality, emphasizing that such practices brought down the wrath of God ("we have provoked Him to anger") and endangered the welfare of the state. Justinian recommended that the guilty parties be punished by castration. Although the early medieval church similarly condemned homosexuality, it also pursued a flexible policy in its treatment of homosexuals. In the Early Middle Ages, homosexuals were treated less harshly than married couples who practiced contraception.

DIET For both rich and poor, the fundamental staple of the Carolingian diet was bread. The aristocratic classes, as well as monks and peasants, consumed it in large quantities. Ovens at the monastery of Saint Gall were able to bake a thousand loaves of bread. Sometimes a gruel made of barley and oats was substituted for bread in the peasant diet.

The upper classes in Carolingian society enjoyed a much more varied diet than the peasants. Pork was the primary meat. Domestic pigs, allowed to run wild in the forests to find their own food, were collected and slaughtered in the fall, then smoked and salted to be eaten during the winter months. Because Carolingian aristocrats were especially fond of roasted meat, hunting wild game became one of their favorite activities. They ate little beef and mutton, however, because cattle were kept as dairy cows and oxen to draw plows, and sheep were raised for wool.

Dairy products were also important in the Carolingian diet. Milk, which spoiled rapidly, was made into cheese and butter. Chickens were raised for their eggs. Vegetables also formed a crucial part of the diet of both the rich and the poor. These included legumes, such as beans, peas, and lentils, and roots, such as garlic, onions, and carrots.

Both gluttony and drunkenness were vices shared by many people in Carolingian society. Monastic rations were greatly enlarged in the eighth century to include a daily allotment of 3.7 pounds of bread (nuns were permitted only 3 pounds), 1.5 quarts of wine or ale, 2 to 3 ounces of cheese, and 8 ounces of vegetables (4 for nuns). These rations totaled 6,000 calories a day, and since only heavy and fatty foods—bread, milk, and cheese—were considered nourishing, we begin to understand why some Carolingians were known for their potbellies.

Everyone in Carolingian society, including abbots and monks, drank heavily and often to excess. Taverns became a regular feature of life and were found everywhere: in marketplaces, in pilgrimage centers, and on royal, episcopal, and monastic estates. Drinking contests were not unusual; one penitential stated, "Does drunken bravado encourage you to attempt to outdrink your friends? If so, thirty days' fast."

The aristocrats and monks favored wine above all other beverages, and much care was lavished on its production, especially by monasteries. Ale was especially popular in the northern and eastern parts of the Carolingian world. Water was also drunk as a beverage, but much care had to be taken to obtain pure sources from wells or clear streams.

HEALTH Medical practice in Carolingian times stressed the use of medicinal herbs and bleeding. Although the latter

© British Library (Add 42130, f.61), London, UK//HIP/Art Resource, NY

Bloodletting in Early Medieval Medicine. Bleeding was a regular part of medieval medical practice. It involved the withdrawing of blood from a person in the belief that doing so would bring balance to the body and thus heal a diseased condition. This fourteenth-century manuscript illustration shows a physician bleeding his patient through a cut in the arm. As the physician squeezes the arm, the blood spurts into a bowl; the patient seems to be quite anxious about the procedure.

was practiced regularly, moderation was frequently recommended. Some advised carefulness as well: "Who dares to undertake a bleeding should see to it that his hand does not tremble." Physicians were also available when people faced serious illnesses. Many were clerics, and monasteries trained their own. Monasteries kept medical manuscripts copied from ancient works and grew herbs to provide stocks of medicinal plants. Carolingian medical manuscripts contained descriptions of illnesses, recipes for medical potions, and even gynecological advice, although monks in particular expended little effort on female medical needs.

Physicians of the Early Middle Ages supplemented their medicines and natural practices with appeals for otherworldly help. Magical rites and influences were carried over from pagan times; Germanic tribes had used magical medicine for centuries. But as pagans were converted to Christianity, miraculous healing through the intervention of God, Jesus, or the saints soon replaced pagan practices. Medieval chronicles abound with accounts of people healed by touching a saint's body.

Disintegration of the Carolingian Empire

Q FOCUS QUESTION: What impact did the Vikings have on the history and culture of medieval Europe?

The Carolingian Empire began to disintegrate soon after Charlemagne's death. Charlemagne was succeeded by his son Louis the Pious, who was unable to control either the Frankish aristocracy or his own four sons, who fought continually. In 843, after their father's death, the three surviving brothers signed the Treaty of Verdun, which divided the Carolingian Empire among them: Charles the Bald (843–877) obtained the west Frankish lands, which formed the core of the eventual kingdom of France; Louis the German (843–876) took the eastern lands, which became Germany; and Lothair (840–855) received the title of emperor and a "Middle Kingdom" extending from the North Sea to Italy, including the Netherlands, the Rhineland, and northern Italy. The territories of the Middle Kingdom became a source of incessant struggle between the other two Frankish rulers and their heirs. Indeed, France and Germany would fight over the territories of the Middle Kingdom for centuries.

© Cengage Learning
Division of the Carolingian Empire by the Treaty of Verdun, 843

Although this division of the Carolingian Empire was made for political reasons (dividing landholdings among the male heirs was a traditional Frankish custom), two different cultures began to emerge. By the ninth century, inhabitants of the west Frankish area were speaking a Romance language derived from Latin that became French. Eastern Franks spoke a Germanic dialect. The later kingdoms of France and Germany did not yet exist, however. In the ninth century, the frequent struggles among the numerous heirs of the sons of Louis the Pious led to further disintegration of the Carolingian Empire. In the meantime, while powerful aristocrats acquired even more power in their own local territories at the expense of the squabbling Carolingian rulers, the process of disintegration was abetted by external attacks on various parts of the old Carolingian world.

Invasions of the Ninth and Tenth Centuries

In the ninth and tenth centuries, western Europe was beset by a wave of invasions of several non-Christian peoples—one old enemy, the Muslims, and two new ones, the Magyars (MAG-yarz) and Vikings (see Map 8.2). The Muslims began a new series of attacks in the Mediterranean in the ninth century. They raided the southern coasts of Europe, especially Italy; occupied Sicily; destroyed the Carolingian defenses in northern Spain; and conducted forays into southern France. The Magyars were a people from western Asia who moved into eastern and central Europe at the end of the ninth century. They established themselves on the plains of Hungary and from there made raids into western Europe. The Magyars were finally crushed at the Battle of Lechfeld in Germany in 955. At the end of the tenth century, they were converted to Christianity and settled down to establish the kingdom of Hungary.

THE VIKINGS By far the most devastating and far-reaching attacks of the time came from the Northmen or Norsemen of Scandinavia, also known as the Vikings. The Vikings were a Germanic people who had settled in Scandinavia. Why they invaded other areas of Europe is uncertain. Perhaps overpopulation and the emergence of more effective monarchs in Denmark, Norway, and Sweden caused some of the freedom-loving Scandinavians to seek escape from the growing order. The Vikings' great love of adventure and their search for booty and new avenues of trade may also have been important factors.

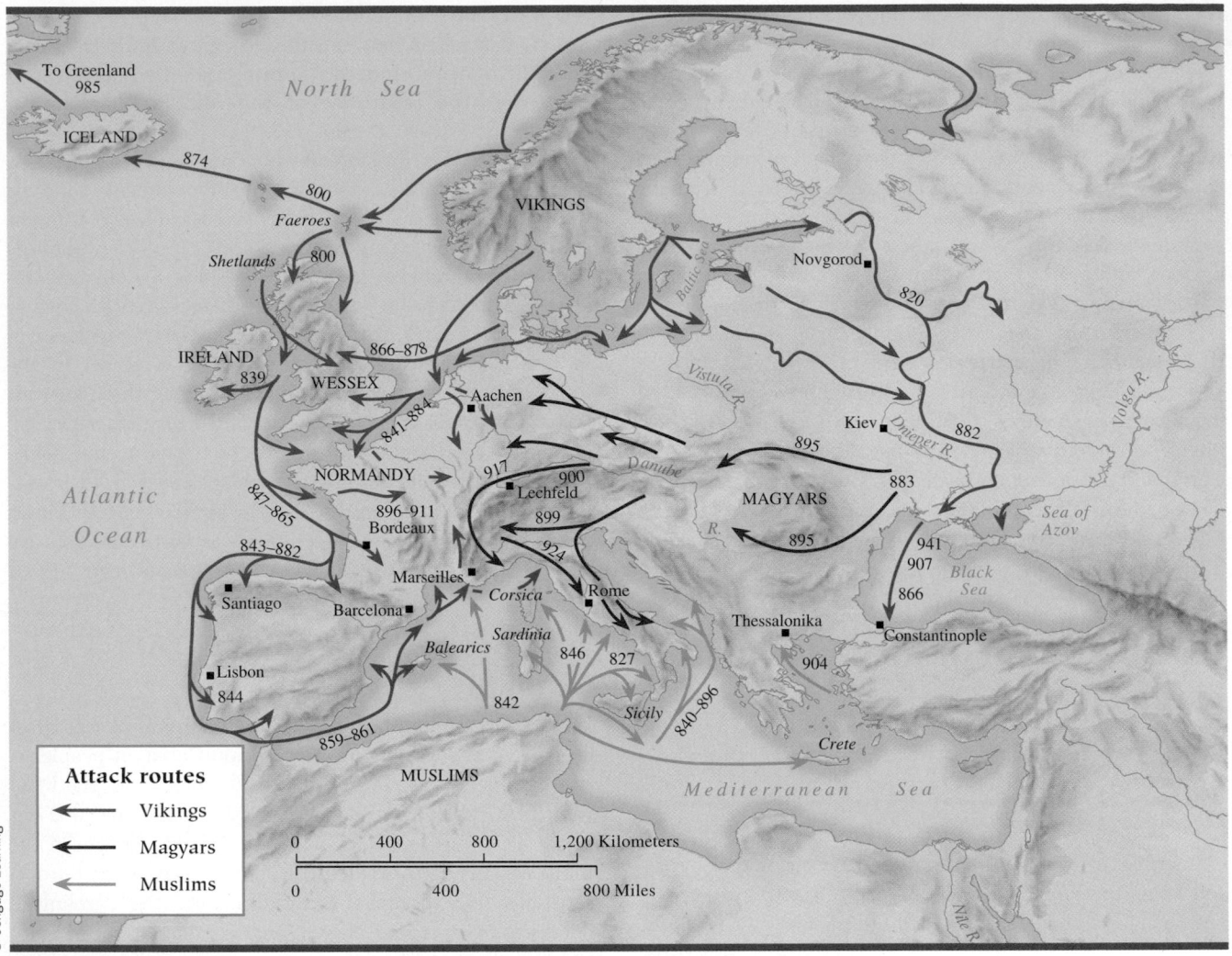

© Cengage Learning

MAP 8.2 Invasions of the Ninth and Tenth Centuries. Attacks by invading Vikings, Magyars, and Muslims terrorized much of Europe in the ninth and tenth centuries, disrupting the economy and spurring the development of fief-holding. The Vikings were the biggest problem, but they eventually formed settlements, converted to Christianity, and were assimilated.

Q ***Why was it important for the marauding Vikings to build sound boats and develop good seafaring skills?***

Two features of Viking society help explain what the Vikings accomplished. First, they were warriors. Second, they were superb shipbuilders and sailors. Their ships were the best of the period. Long and narrow with beautifully carved arched prows, the Viking "dragon ships" carried about fifty men. Their shallow draft enabled them to sail up European rivers and attack places at some distance inland. Vikings sacked villages and towns, destroyed churches, and easily defeated small local armies. Viking attacks frightened people and led many a clergyman to exhort his parishioners to change their behavior to appease God's anger, as in this sermon by an English archbishop in 1014:

> Things have not gone well now for a long time at home or abroad, but there has been devastation and persecution in every district again and again, and the English have been for a long time now completely defeated and too greatly disheartened through God's anger; and the pirates [Vikings] so strong with God's consent that often in battle one puts to flight ten, and sometimes less, sometimes more, all because of our sins. . . . We pay them continually and they humiliate us daily; they ravage and they burn, plunder, and rob and carry on

© The Pierpont Morgan Library (MS M.736, f.9v.), New York/Art Resource, NY

Vikings Attacking England. This illustration from an eleventh-century English manuscript depicts a group of armed Vikings invading England. Two ships have already reached the shore, and a few Vikings are shown walking down a long gangplank onto English soil.

> board; and lo, what else is there in all these events except God's anger clear and visible over this people?[6]

Because there were different groups of Scandinavians, Viking expansion varied a great deal. Norwegian Vikings moved into Ireland and western England, while the Danes attacked eastern England, Frisia, and the Rhineland and navigated rivers to enter western Frankish lands. Swedish Vikings dominated the Baltic Sea and progressed into the Slavic areas to the east. Moving into northwestern Russia, they went down the rivers to Novgorod and Kiev and established fortified ports throughout these territories.

Early Viking raids had been carried out largely in the summer, but by the mid-ninth century, the Northmen had begun to establish winter settlements in Europe from which they could make expeditions to conquer and settle new lands. By 850, groups of Norsemen had settled in Ireland, and the Danes occupied an area known as the Danelaw in northeastern England by 878. Beginning in 911, the ruler of the western Frankish lands gave one band of Vikings land at the mouth of the Seine River, a section of France that ultimately became known as Normandy. This policy of settling the Vikings and converting them to Christianity was a deliberate one, since the new inhabitants served as protectors against additional Viking attacks.

The Vikings were also daring explorers. After 860, they sailed westward in their long ships across the north Atlantic, reaching Iceland in 874. Erik the Red, a Viking exiled from Iceland, traveled even farther west and discovered Greenland in 985. A North American Viking site has been found in Newfoundland.

By the tenth century, Viking expansion was drawing to a close, but not before Viking settlements had been established in many parts of Europe. Like the Magyars, the Vikings were assimilated into European civilization. Once again, Christianity proved a decisive civilizing force, another indication that Europe and Christianity were becoming virtually synonymous.

The Viking raids and settlements also had important political repercussions. The inability of royal authorities to protect their peoples against these incursions caused local populations to turn instead to the local aristocrats who provided security for them. In the process, the landed aristocrats not only increased their strength and prestige but also assumed even more of the functions of local governments that had previously belonged to kings; over time these developments led to a new political and military order.

The Emerging World of Lords and Vassals

Q Focus Question: What was fief-holding, and how was it related to manorialism?

The renewed invasions and the disintegration of the Carolingian Empire led to the emergence of a new type of relationship between free individuals. When governments ceased to be able to defend their subjects, it became important to find some powerful lord who could offer protection in exchange for service. The contract sworn between a lord and his subordinate (known as a vassal) is the basis of a form of social organization that later generations of historians called *feudalism*. But feudalism was never a system, and many historians today prefer to avoid using the term.

Vassalage

The practice of **vassalage** was derived from Germanic society, in which warriors swore an oath of loyalty to their leader. They fought for their chief, and he in turn took care of their needs. By the eighth century, an individual who served a lord in a military capacity was known as a vassal. With the breakdown of governments, powerful nobles took control of large areas of land. Needing men to fight for them, they began to give grants of land to vassals who in return would fight for their lord. The Frankish army had originally consisted of foot soldiers, dressed in coats of mail and armed with swords. But in the eighth century, when larger horses and the stirrup were introduced, a military change began to occur. Previously, horsemen had been throwers of spears. Now they wore armored coats of mail (the larger horse could carry the weight) and wielded long lances that enabled them to act as battering rams (the stirrups kept them on their horses). For almost five hundred years, warfare in Europe was dominated by heavily armored cavalry, or knights, as they came to be called. The knights came to have the greatest social prestige and formed the backbone of the European aristocracy.

Musée Condé, Chantilly, France/©Lauros/Giraudon/The Bridgeman Art Library

A Knight's Equipment Showing Saddle and Stirrups. In return for his fighting skills, a knight received a piece of land from his lord that provided for his economic support. Pictured here is a charging knight with his equipment. The introduction of the high saddle, stirrup, and larger horses allowed horsemen to wear heavier armor and to wield long lances, vastly improving the fighting ability of the cavalry.

Of course, a horse, armor, and weapons were expensive to purchase and maintain, and learning to wield these instruments skillfully on horseback took much time and practice. Consequently, lords who wanted men to fight for them had to grant each vassal a piece of land that provided for the support of the vassal and his family. In return, the vassal provided fighting skills. In the Early Middle Ages, when trade was minimal and wealth was based primarily on landholdings, land became the most important gift a lord could give to a vassal in return for military service.

The relationship between lord and vassal was made official by a public ceremony. To become a vassal, a man performed an act of homage to his lord, as described in this passage from a medieval digest of law:

> The man should put his hands together as a sign of humility, and place them between the two hands of his lord as a token that he vows everything to him and promises faith to him; and the lord should receive him and promise to keep faith with him. Then the man should say: "Sir, I enter your homage and faith and become your man by mouth and hands [that is, by taking the oath and placing his hands between those of the lord], and I swear and promise to keep faith and loyalty to you against all others, and to guard your rights with all my strength."[7]

As in the earlier Germanic band, loyalty to one's lord was the chief virtue (see the box on p. 173).

Fief-Holding

The land or some other type of income granted to a vassal in return for military service came to be known as a **fief** (FEEF). In time, many vassals who held such grants of land came to exercise rights of jurisdiction or political and legal authority within their fiefs. As the Carolingian world disintegrated politically under the impact of internal dissension and invasions, an increasing number of powerful lords arose. Instead of a single government, many people were now responsible for keeping order.

Fief-holding also became increasingly complicated with the development of **subinfeudation**. The vassals of a king, who were themselves great lords, might also have vassals who would owe them military service in return for a grant of land from their estates. Those vassals, in turn, might likewise have vassals, who at this low level would be simple knights with barely enough land to provide their equipment. The lord-vassal relationship, then, bound together both greater and lesser landowners. At all levels, the lord-vassal relationship was always an honorable relationship between free men and did not imply any sense of servitude. Since kings could no longer provide security in the midst of the breakdown created by the invasions of

OPPOSING VIEWPOINTS

Lords and Vassals in Europe and Japan

When we use the word *feudalism*, we usually think of European knights on horseback clad in armor and armed with sword and lance. Indeed, a social order based on lords and vassals arose in Europe between 800 and 900 and flourished for the next four hundred years. But Europe was not the only part of the world where a form of social organization based on lords and vassals emerged. In Japan, a social order much like that found in Europe developed between 800 and 1500. The first selection is the classic statement by Bishop Fulbert of Chartres in 1020 on the mutual obligations between lord and vassals. The second selection is taken from *Tale of the Heike*, a Japanese tale written in the first half of the thirteenth century about military struggles that took place at the end of the twelfth century.

Bishop Fulbert of Chartres

Asked to write something concerning the form of fealty, I have noted briefly for you, on the authority of the books, the things which follow. He who swears fealty to his lord ought always to have these six things in memory: what is harmless, safe, honorable, useful, easy, practicable. *Harmless*, that is to say, that he should not injure his lord in his body; *safe*, that he should not injure him by betraying his secrets or the defenses upon which he relies for safety; *honorable*, that he should not injure him in his justice or in other matters that pertain to his honor; *useful*, that he should not injure him in his possessions; *easy* and *practicable*, that that good which his lord is able to do easily he make not difficult, nor that which is practicable he make not impossible to him.

That the faithful vassal should avoid these injuries is certainly proper, but not for this alone does he deserve his holding; for it is not sufficient to abstain from evil, unless what is good is done also. It remains, therefore, that in the same six things mentioned above he should faithfully counsel and aid his lord, if he wishes to be looked upon as worthy of his benefice [fief] and to be safe concerning the fealty which he has sworn.

The lord also ought to act toward his faithful vassal reciprocally in all these things. And if he does not do this, he will be justly considered guilty of bad faith, just as the former, if he should be detected in avoiding or consenting to the avoidance of his duties, would be perfidious and perjured.

Tale of the Heike

Recognizing each other, master and retainer spurred their horses to join each other. Seizing Kanehira's hands, Yoshinaka said: "I would have fought to the death on the banks of the Kamo at Rokujō. Simply because of you, however, I have galloped here through the enemy swarms."

"It was very kind of you, my lord," replied Kanehira. "I too would have fought to the death at Seta. But in fear of your uncertain fate, I have come this way."

"We are still tied by karma," said Yoshinaka. "There must be more of my men around here, for I have seen them scattered among the hills. Unroll the banner and raise it high!"

As soon as Kanehira unfurled the banner, many men who had been in flight from the capital and Seta saw it and rallied. They soon numbered more than three hundred.

"Since we still have so many men, let us try one last fight!" shouted Yoshinaka jubilantly. . . .

Shouting, Yoshinaka dashed ahead. That day he wore armor laced with twilled silk cords over a red battle robe. His helmet was decorated with long golden horns. At his side hung a great sword studded with gold. He carried his quiver a little higher than usual on his back. Some eagle-feathered arrows still remained. Gripping his rattan-bound bow, he rode his famous horse, Oniashige.

Rising high in his stirrups, he roared at the enemy: "You have often heard of me. Now take a good look at the captain of the Imperial Stables of the Left and governor of Iyo Province—Rising-Sun General Minamoto no Yoshinaka, that is who I am! I know that among you is Kai no Ichijōjirō Tadayori. We are fit opponents for each other. Cut off my head and show it to Yoritomo!"

At this challenge, Tadayori shouted to his men: "Now, hear this! He is the commander of our enemy. Let him not escape! All men—to the attack!"

Q According to Bishop Fulbert, what were the mutual obligations of lords and vassals? Why were these important in the practice of fief-holding? The lord-vassal relationship was based on loyalty. What differences and similarities do you see in the loyalty between lord and vassals in Europe and Japan? How did the weapons used by a European knight and a Japanese warrior differ?

Sources: Bishop Fulbert of Chartres. From *Readings in European History*, vol. 1, by James Harvey Robinson (Lexington, Mass.: Ginn and Co., 1904). *Tale of the Heike*. From Hiroski Kitagawa and Bruce T. Tsuchida, trans., THE TALE OF THE HEIKE (Tokyo: University of Tokyo Press, 1975), p. 520.

the ninth century, the practice of subinfeudation became ever more widespread. With their rights of jurisdiction, fiefs gave lords virtual possession of the rights of government.

The new practice of lordship was basically a product of the Carolingian world, but it also spread to England, Germany, central Europe, and in some form to Italy. Fief-holding came to be characterized by a set of practices that determined the relationship between a lord and his vassal. The major obligation of a vassal to his lord was to perform military service, usually about forty days a year. A vassal was also required to appear at his lord's court when summoned to give advice to the lord. He might also be asked to sit in judgment in a legal case because the important vassals of a lord were peers and only they could judge each other. Finally, vassals were also responsible for aids, or financial payments to the lord on a number of occasions, including the knighting of the lord's eldest son, the marriage of his eldest daughter, and the ransom of the lord's person in the event he was captured.

In turn, a lord had responsibilities toward his vassals. His major obligation was to protect his vassal, either by defending him militarily or by taking his side in a court of law if necessary. The lord was also responsible for the maintenance of the vassal, usually by granting him a fief.

The Manorial System

The landholding class of nobles and knights comprised a military elite whose ability to function as warriors depended on having the leisure time to pursue the arts of war. Landed estates, worked by a dependent peasant class, provided the economic sustenance that made this way of life possible. A **manor** (see Map 8.3) was simply an agricultural estate operated by a lord and worked by peasants.

Manorialism grew out of the unsettled circumstances of the Early Middle Ages, when small farmers often needed protection or food in a time of bad harvests. Free peasants gave up their freedom to the lords of large landed estates in return for protection and use of the lord's land. Although a large class of free peasants continued to exist, increasing numbers of free peasants became **serfs**—peasants bound to the land and required to provide labor services, pay rents, and be subject to the lord's jurisdiction. By the ninth century, probably 60 percent of the population of western Europe had become serfs.

Labor services consisted of working the lord's **demesne** (duh-MEEN *or* duh-MAYN), the land retained by the lord, which might encompass one-third to one-half of the cultivated lands scattered throughout the manor. The rest would be used by the peasants for themselves. Building barns and digging ditches were also part of the labor services. Serfs usually worked about three days a week for their lord.

The serfs paid rents by giving the lord a share of all the produce they raised. Moreover, serfs paid the lord for the use of the manor's common pasturelands, streams, ponds, and surrounding woodlands. For example, if a serf fished in the pond or stream on a manor, he turned over part of the catch to his lord. Peasants were also obliged to pay a tithe (a tenth of their produce) to their local village church.

Lords possessed various legal rights over their serfs as a result of their unfree status. Serfs were legally bound to the lord's lands and could not leave without his permission.

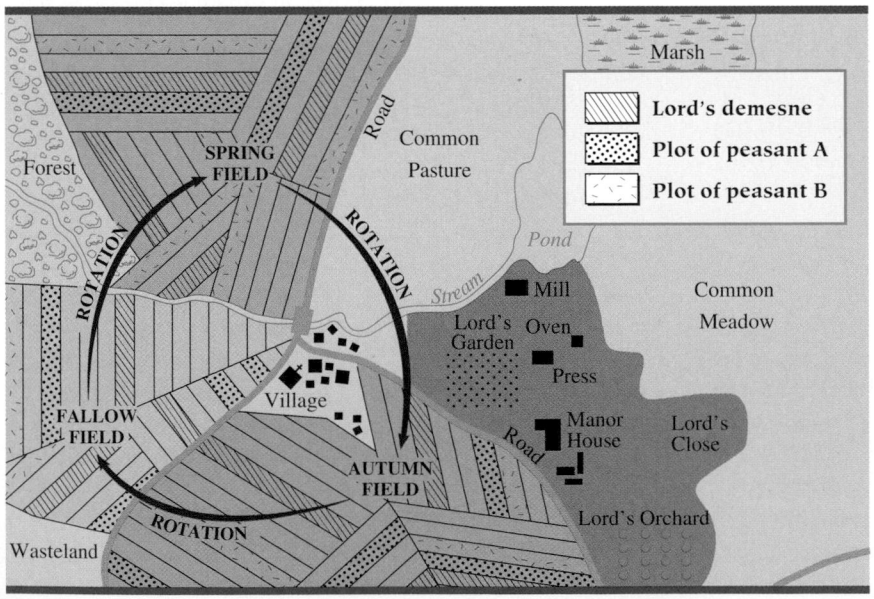

© Cengage Learning

MAP 8.3 A Typical Manor. The manorial system created small, tightly knit communities in which peasants were economically and physically bound to their lord. Crops were rotated, with roughly one-third of the fields lying fallow at any one time, which helped replenish soil nutrients (see Chapter 9).

Q *How does the area of the lord's manor house, other buildings, garden, and orchard compare with that of the peasant holdings in the village?*

© The Art Archive/British Library, London, UK

Peasants in the Manorial System. In the manorial system, peasants were required to provide labor services for their lord. This thirteenth-century illustration shows a group of English peasants harvesting grain, while a bailiff, or manager, supervises their work.

Although free to marry, serfs could not marry anyone outside their manor without the lord's approval. Moreover, lords sometimes exercised public rights or political authority on their lands. This gave a lord the right to try peasants in his own court. In fact, the lord's manorial court provided the only law that most peasants knew. Peasants also had to pay the lord for certain services; for example, they might be required to bring their grain to the lord's mill and pay a fee to have it ground into flour. Thus, the rights a lord possessed on his manor gave him virtual control over both the lives and the property of his serfs.

In the Early Middle Ages, whether free or unfree, the vast majority of men and women—possibly as many as 90 percent—worked the land. This period witnessed a precipitous decline in trade, although it never entirely disappeared. Overall, however, compared to the Byzantine Empire or Muslim caliphates, western Europe in the Early Middle Ages was an underdeveloped, predominantly agricultural society.

The Zenith of Byzantine Civilization

Focus Question: What were the chief developments in the Byzantine Empire between 750 and 1000?

In the seventh and eighth centuries, the Byzantine Empire had lost much of its territory to Slavs, Bulgars, and Muslims. By 750, the empire consisted only of Asia Minor, some lands in the Balkans, and the southern coast of Italy. Although Byzantium continued to be beset with internal dissension and invasions in the ninth century, it was able to deal with them and not only endured but even expanded, reaching its high point in the tenth century, which some historians have called the "golden age of Byzantine civilization."

During the reign of Michael III (842–867), the Byzantine Empire continued to be plagued by problems. The Bulgars mounted new attacks, and the Arabs continued to harass the empire. Moreover, a new church problem with political repercussions erupted over differences between the pope as leader of the western Christian church and the patriarch of Constantinople as leader of the eastern (or Orthodox) Christian church. Patriarch Photius (FOH-shuss) condemned the pope as a heretic for accepting a revised form of the Nicene Creed stating that the Holy Spirit proceeded from the Father and the Son instead of "the Holy Spirit, who proceeds from the Father." A council of eastern bishops followed Photius's wishes and excommunicated the pope, creating the so-called Photian schism. Although the differences were later papered over, this controversy served to further the rift between the eastern and western Christian churches.

The Macedonian Dynasty

The problems that arose during Michael's reign were effectively dealt with by the efforts of a new dynasty of Byzantine emperors, known as the Macedonians (867–1081). This dynastic line managed to repel the external enemies, go over to the offensive, and reestablish domestic order. Supported by the church, the emperors continued to think of the Byzantine Empire as a continuation of the Christian Roman Empire of late antiquity. Although for diplomatic reasons they occasionally recognized the imperial title of western emperors, such as Charlemagne, they still regarded them as little more than barbarian parvenus.

The Macedonian emperors could boast of a remarkable number of achievements in the late ninth and tenth centuries. They worked to strengthen the position of free farmers, who felt threatened by the attempts of landed aristocrats to expand their estates at the expense of the farmers. The emperors were well aware that the free farmers made up the rank and file of the Byzantine cavalry and provided the military strength of the empire. The

A Western View of the Byzantine Empire

Bishop Liudprand of Cremona undertook diplomatic missions to Constantinople on behalf of two western kings, Berengar of Italy and Otto I of Germany. This selection is taken from the bishop's description of his mission to the Byzantine emperor Constantine VII in 949 as an envoy for Berengar, king of Italy from 950 until his overthrow by Otto I of Germany in 964. Liudprand had mixed feelings about Byzantium: admiration but also envy and hostility because of its superior wealth.

Liudprand of Cremona, *Antapodosis*

Next to the imperial residence at Constantinople there is a palace of remarkable size and beauty which the Greeks called Magnavra . . . the name being equivalent to "fresh breeze." In order to receive some Spanish envoys, who had recently arrived, as well as myself . . ., Constantine gave orders that his palace should be got ready. . . .

Before the emperor's seat stood a tree, made of bronze gilded over, whose branches were filled with birds, also made of gilded bronze, which uttered different cries, each according to its varying species. The throne itself was so marvelously fashioned that at one moment it seemed a low structure, and at another it rose high into the air. It was of immense size and was guarded by lions, made either of bronze or of wood covered over with gold, who beat the ground with their tails and gave a dreadful roar with open mouth and quivering tongue. Leaning upon the shoulders of two eunuchs I was brought into the emperor's presence. At my approach the lions began to roar and the birds to cry out, each according to its kind; but I was neither terrified nor surprised, for I had previously made enquiry about all these things from people who were well acquainted with them. So after I had three times made obeisance to the emperor with my face upon the ground, I lifted my head, and behold! The man whom just before I had seen sitting on a moderately elevated seat had now changed his raiment and was sitting on the level of the ceiling. How it was done I could not imagine, unless perhaps he was lifted up by some such sort of device as we use for raising the timbers of a wine press. On that occasion he did not address me personally . . . but by the intermediary of a secretary he enquired about Berengar's doings and asked after his health. I made a fitting reply and then, at a nod from the interpreter, left his presence and retired to my lodging.

It would give me some pleasure also to record here what I did then for Berengar. . . . The Spanish envoys . . . had brought handsome gifts from their masters to the emperor Constantine. I for my part had brought nothing from Berengar except a letter and that was full of lies. I was very greatly disturbed and shamed at this and I began to consider anxiously what I had better do. In my doubt and perplexity it finally occurred to me that I might offer the gifts, which on my account I had brought for the emperor, as coming from Berengar, and trick out my humble present with fine words. I therefore presented him with nine excellent cuirasses, seven excellent shields with gilded bosses, two silver gilt cauldrons, some swords, spears and spits, and what was more precious to the emperor than anything, four *carzimasia*; that being the Greek name for young eunuchs who have had both their testicles and their penis removed. This operation is performed by traders at Verdun, who take the boys into Spain and make a huge profit.

Q What impressions of the Byzantine court do you receive from Liudprand of Cremona's account? What is the modern meaning of the word *Byzantine*? How does this account help explain the modern meaning of the word?

Source: From *The Works of Liudprand of Cremona*, trans. F. A. Wright, copyright © 1930 by Routledge and Sons. Reprinted with permission.

Macedonian emperors also fostered a burst of economic prosperity by expanding trade relations with western Europe, especially by selling silks and metalwork. Thanks to this prosperity, the city of Constantinople flourished. Foreign visitors continued to be astounded by its size, wealth, and physical surroundings. To western Europeans, it was the stuff of legends and fables (see the box above).

In the midst of this prosperity, Byzantine cultural influence expanded due to the active missionary efforts of eastern Byzantine Christians. Eastern Orthodox Christianity was spread to eastern European peoples, including the Bulgars and the Serbs. Perhaps the greatest missionary success occurred when the prince of Kiev in Russia converted to Christianity in 987.

The Byzantine Empire in 1025

Under the Macedonian rulers, Byzantium enjoyed a strong civil service, talented emperors, and successful military campaigns. In the tenth century, these competent emperors combined with a number of talented generals to mobilize the empire's military resources and take the offensive. The Bulgars were defeated, and both the eastern and western parts of Bulgaria were annexed to the empire. The Byzantines went on to add the islands of Crete and Cyprus to the empire and defeat the Muslim forces in Syria, expanding the empire to the upper Euphrates. By the end of the reign of Basil II (976–1025), the Byzantine Empire was the largest it had been since the beginning of the seventh century.

The Slavic Peoples of Central and Eastern Europe

Q FOCUS QUESTION: What patterns of development occurred in central and eastern Europe as a result of the Slavic peoples?

North of Byzantium and east of the Carolingian Empire lay a spacious plain through which a number of Asiatic nomads, including the Huns, Bulgars, Avars, and Magyars, had pushed their way westward, terrorizing and plundering the settled peasant communities. Eastern Europe was ravaged by these successive waves of invaders, who found it relatively easy to create large empires that were in turn overthrown by the next invaders. Over a period of time, the invaders themselves were largely assimilated with the native Slavic peoples of the area.

The Slavs were an Indo-European-speaking people who came to eastern Europe from the southeast. Originally a single people, the Slavs in late antiquity populated a large area in central and eastern Europe. Beginning in the sixth century, through mass migrations and nomadic invasions, they gradually divided into three major groups: the western, southern, and eastern Slavs (see Map 8.4).

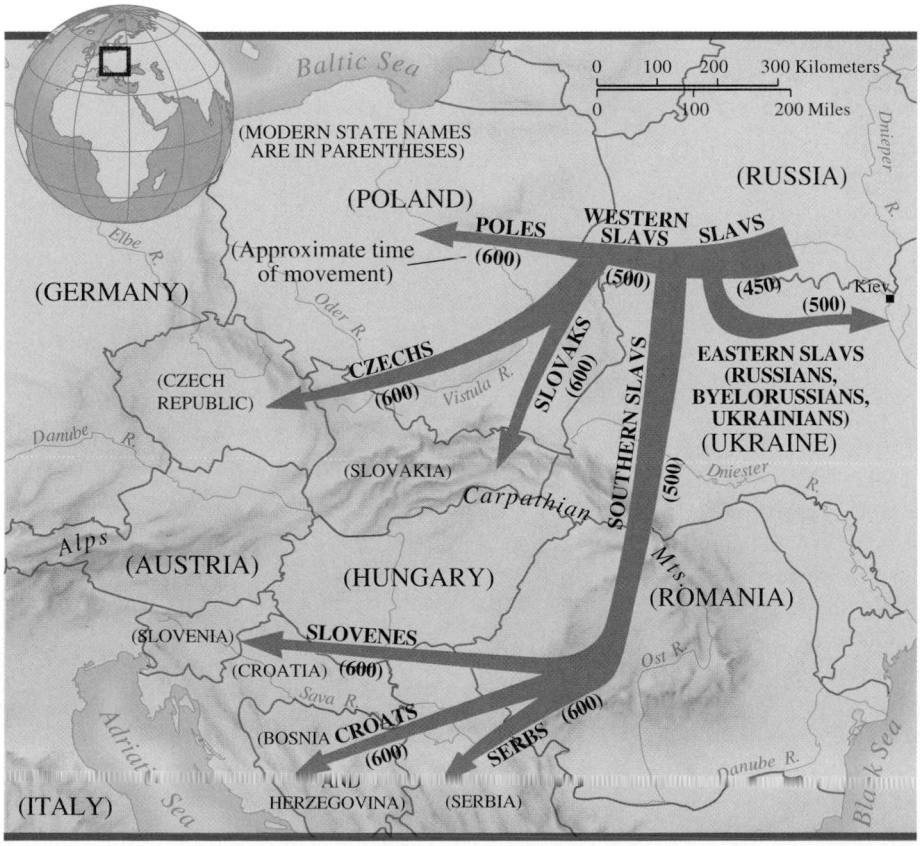

MAP 8.4 The Migrations of the Slavs. Originally from east-central Europe, the Slavic people broke into three groups. The western Slavs converted to Catholic Christianity, while the eastern Slavs and southern Slavs, under the influence of the Byzantine Empire, embraced the Eastern Orthodox faith.

Q ***What connections do these Slavic migrations have with what we today characterize as eastern Europe?***

© Cengage Learning

© Cengage Learning

A Muslim's Description of the Rus

Despite the difficulties that travel presented, some contact among the various cultures did occur through trade, diplomacy, and the conquest and migration of peoples. This document is a description of the Swedish Rus who eventually merged with the native Slavic peoples to form the principality of Kiev, commonly regarded as the first Russian state. This account was written by Ibn Fadlan, a Muslim diplomat sent from Baghdad in 921 to a settlement on the Volga River. His comments on the filthiness of the Rus reflect the Muslim preoccupation with cleanliness.

Ibn Fadlan, *Description of the Rus*

I saw the Rus folk when they arrived on their trading-mission and settled at the river Atul (Volga). Never had I seen people of more perfect physique. They are tall as date-palms, and reddish in color. They wear neither coat nor kaftan, but each man carried a cape which covers one half of his body, leaving one hand free. No one is ever parted from his axe, sword, and knife. Their swords are Frankish in design, broad, flat, and fluted. Each man has a number of trees, figures, and the like from the fingernails to the neck. Each woman carried on her bosom a container made of iron, silver, copper or gold—its size and substance depending on her man's wealth. . . .

They [the Rus] are the filthiest of God's creatures. They do not wash after discharging their natural functions, neither do they wash their hands after meals. They are as lousy as donkeys. They arrive from their distant river, and there they build big houses on its shores. Ten or twenty of them may live together in one house, and each of them has a couch of his own where he sits and diverts himself with the pretty slave girls whom he had brought along for sale. He will make love with one of them while a comrade looks on; sometimes they indulge in a communal orgy, and, if a customer should turn up to buy a girl, the Rus man will not let her go till he has finished with her.

They wash their hands and faces every day in incredibly filthy water. Every morning the girl brings her master a large bowl of water in which he washes his hands and face and hair, then blows his nose into it and spits into it. When he has finished the girl takes the bowl to his neighbor—who repeats the performance. Thus, the bowl goes the rounds of the entire household. . . .

If one of the Rus folk falls sick they put him in a tent by himself and leave bread and water for him. They do not visit him, however, or speak to him, especially if he is a serf. Should he recover he rejoins the others; if he dies they burn him. But if he happens to be a serf they leave him for the dogs and vultures to devour. If they catch a robber they hang him to a tree until he is torn to threads by wind and weather.

Q What was Ibn Fadlan's impression of the Rus? Why do you think he was so critical of their behavior?

Source: From THE VIKINGS by Johannes Brøndsted, translated by Kalle Skov (Penguin Books, 1965) copyright © Johannes Brøndsted, 1960, 1965. Reproduced by permission of Penguin Books Ltd.

Western Slavs

In the region east of the eastern Frankish or German kingdom emerged the Polish and Bohemian kingdoms of the western Slavs. The Germans assumed responsibility for the conversion of these Slavic peoples since some German emperors considered it their duty to spread Christianity to the barbarians. Of course, it also gave them the opportunity to extend their political authority. German missionaries had converted the Czechs in Bohemia by the end of the ninth century, and a bishopric eventually occupied by a Czech bishop was established at Prague in the tenth. The Slavs in Poland were not converted until the reign of Prince Mieszko (MYESH-koh) (c. 960–992). In 1000, an independent Polish archbishopric was set up at Gniezno by the pope. The non-Slavic kingdom of Hungary, which emerged when the Magyars settled down after their defeat at Lechfeld in 955, was also converted to Christianity by German missionaries. Saint Stephen, king of Hungary from 997 to 1038, facilitated the acceptance of Christianity by his people. The Poles, Czechs, and Hungarians all accepted Catholic or western Christianity and became closely tied to the Roman Catholic Church and its Latin culture.

Southern Slavs

The southern and eastern Slavic populations largely took a different path because of their proximity to the Byzantine Empire. The Slavic peoples of Moravia were converted to the Eastern Orthodox Christianity of the Byzantine Empire by two Byzantine missionary brothers, Cyril and Methodius, who began their activities in 863. They created a Slavonic (Cyrillic) alphabet, translated the Bible into Slavonic, and created Slavonic church services. While the southern Slavic peoples accepted Christianity, a split eventually developed between the Croats, who accepted the Roman church, and the Serbs, who remained loyal to eastern Christianity.

Although the Bulgars were originally an Asiatic people who conquered much of the Balkan peninsula, they were eventually absorbed by the larger native south Slavic population. Together, by the ninth century, they formed a largely Slavic Bulgarian kingdom. Although the conversion to Christianity of this state was complicated by the rivalry between the Roman Catholic and Eastern Orthodox Churches, the Bulgarians eventually accepted the latter. By the end of the ninth century, they embraced the Slavonic church services earlier developed by Cyril and Methodius. The acceptance of Eastern Orthodoxy by the southern Slavic peoples, the Serbs and Bulgarians, meant that their cultural life was also linked to the Byzantine state.

Eastern Slavs

The eastern Slavic peoples, from whom the modern Russians, White Russians (Belarusians), and Ukrainians are descended, had settled in the territory of present-day Ukraine and European Russia. There, beginning in the late eighth century, they began to contend with Viking invaders. Swedish Vikings, known to the eastern Slavs as Varangians, moved down the extensive network of rivers into the lands of the eastern Slavs in search of booty and new trade routes. After establishing commercial links with the Byzantine state, the Varangians built trading settlements, became involved in the civil wars among the Slavic peoples, and eventually came to dominate the native peoples, just as their fellow Vikings were doing in parts of western Europe. According to the traditional version of the story, the semilegendary Rurik secured his ruling dynasty in the Slavic settlement of Novgorod (NAHV-guh-rahd) in 862. Rurik (ROO-rik) and his fellow Vikings were called the Rus, from which Russia, the name eventually attached to the state they founded, is derived (see the box on p. 178). Although much about Rurik is unclear, it is certain that his follower Oleg (c. 873–913) took up residence in Kiev (KEE-eff) and established the Rus state, a union of east Slavic territories known as the principality of Kiev. Oleg's successors extended their control over the eastern Slavs and expanded the territory of Kiev until it encompassed the lands between the Baltic and Black Seas and the Danube and Volga Rivers. By marrying Slavic wives, the Viking ruling class was gradually assimilated into the Slavic population, a process confirmed by their assumption of Slavic names.

The growth of the principality of Kiev attracted religious missionaries, especially from the Byzantine Empire. One Rus ruler, Vladimir (c. 980–1015), married the Byzantine emperor's sister and officially accepted Christianity for himself and his people in 987. His primary motive was probably not a spiritual one. By all accounts, Vladimir was a cruel and vicious man who believed an established church would be helpful in the development of an organized state. From the end of the tenth century on, Byzantine Christianity became the model for Russian religious life, just as Byzantine imperial ideals came to influence the outward forms of Russian political life.

The World of Islam

Focus Question: What were the chief developments in the Islamic world between 750 and 1000?

The Umayyad dynasty of caliphs had established Damascus as the center of an Islamic empire created by Arab expansion in the seventh and eighth centuries. But Umayyad rule created resentment, and the Umayyads' corrupt behavior also helped bring about their own end. One caliph, for example, supposedly swam in a pool of wine and drank enough of it to lower the wine level considerably. Finally, in 750, Abu al-Abbas (uh-BOOL-uh-BUSS), a descendant of the uncle of Muhammad, brought an end to the Umayyad dynasty and established the Abbasid (uh-BAH-sid *or* AB-uh-sid) dynasty, which lasted until 1258.

The Abbasid rulers brought much change to the world of Islam. They tried to break down the distinctions between Arab and non-Arab Muslims. All Muslims, regardless of ethnic background, could now hold both civil and military offices. This helped open Islamic life to the influences of the civilizations they had conquered. Many Arabs now began to intermarry with the peoples they had conquered.

In 762, the Abbasids built a new capital city, Baghdad, on the Tigris River far to the east of Damascus. The new capital was well placed. It took advantage of river traffic to the Persian Gulf and was located on the caravan route from the Mediterranean to Central Asia. The move eastward allowed Persian influence to come to the fore, encouraging a new cultural orientation. Under the Abbasids, judges, merchants, and government officials, rather than warriors, were regarded as the ideal citizens.

The new Abbasid dynasty experienced a period of splendid rule well into the ninth century. Best known of

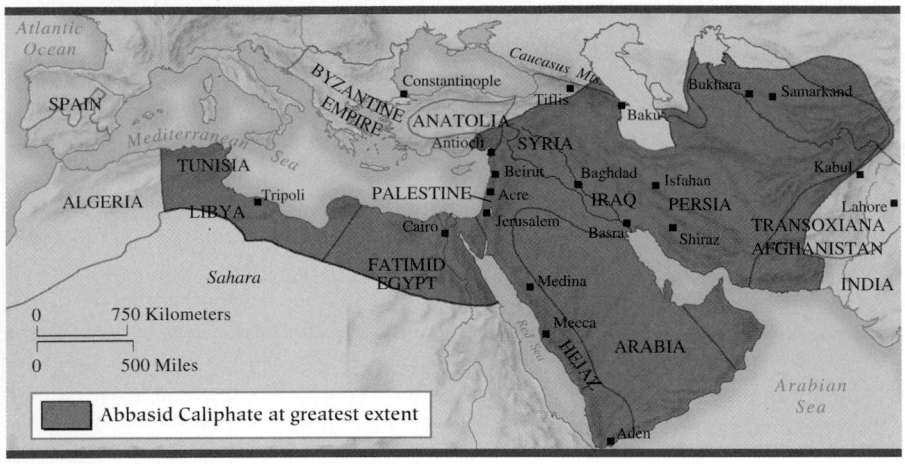

© Cengage Learning

The Abbasid Caliphate at the Height of Its Power

the caliphs of the time was Harun al-Rashid (huh-ROON al-rah-SHEED) (786–809), whose reign is often described as the golden age of the Abbasid caliphate. His son al-Ma'mun (al-muh-MOON) (813–833) was a great patron of learning. He founded an astronomical observatory and created a foundation for translating Classical Greek works. This was also a period of growing economic prosperity. The Arabs had conquered many of the richest provinces of the old Roman Empire, and they now controlled the trade routes to the east. Baghdad became the center of an enormous trade empire that extended into Europe, Asia, and Africa, greatly adding to the wealth of the Islamic world.

Despite the prosperity, all was not quite well in the empire of the Abbasids. There was much fighting over the succession to the caliphate. When Harun al-Rashid died, his two sons fought to succeed him in a struggle that almost destroyed the city of Baghdad. As the tenth-century Muslim historian al-Mas'udi wrote, "Mansions were destroyed, most remarkable monuments obliterated; prices soared. . . . Brother turned his sword against brother, son against father, as some fought for Amin, others for Ma'-mun. Houses and palaces fueled the flames; property was put to the sack."[8]

Vast wealth also gave rise to financial corruption. By awarding important positions to court favorites, the Abbasid caliphs began to undermine the foundations of their own power and become figureheads. Rulers of the provinces of the empire broke away from the control of the caliphs and established their own independent dynasties. In the eighth century, Spain had already established its own caliphate when Abd al-Rahman (ub-duh-rahkh-MAHN) of the Umayyad dynasty had fled there. In 756, he seized control of southern Spain and then expanded his power into the center of the peninsula. He took the title of *emir*, or commander, and set up the emirate of al-Andalus (the Arabic name for Spain), with its center at Córdoba (KOR-duh-buh). Under Abd al-Rahman's successors, a unique society developed in which all religions were tolerated. The court also supported writers and artists, creating a brilliant and flourishing culture.

The fragmentation of the Islamic empire accelerated in the tenth century. The Fatimid (FAT-i-mid) family established a caliphate in Egypt in 973, and an independent dynasty also operated in North Africa. Despite the political disunity of the Islamic world, however, the underlying Islamic civilization was unified by two common bonds: the Qur'an and the Arabic language.

CHRONOLOGY **Byzantium, the Slavs, and the Islamic World**

The Byzantine Empire	
Michael III	842–867
Macedonian dynasty	867–1081
Basil II	976–1025
The Slavs	
Establishment of Novgorod	c. 862
Cyril and Methodius begin conversion of Moravian Slavs	863
Founding of principality of Kiev	c. 873–913
Reign of Prince Mieszko; conversion of Slavs in Poland to Christianity	c. 960–992
Vladimir's conversion to Christianity	987
Saint Stephen, king of Hungary	997–1038
Islam	
Overthrow of Umayyad dynasty by Abbasids	750
Creation of emirate of al-Andalus	756
Harun al-Rashid	786–809
Establishment of Fatimid caliphate in Egypt	973

Islamic Civilization

From the beginning of their empire, Muslim Arabs had demonstrated a willingness to absorb the culture of their conquered territories. The Arabs were truly heirs to the

© Glen Allison/Photodisc/Getty Images

Mosque at Córdoba. The first Great Mosque of Córdoba was built by Abd al-Rahman, founder of the Umayyad dynasty of Spain, in the eighth century. The mosque was later enlarged in the tenth century. Shown here is the interior of the sanctuary, with its two levels of arches. Although the Umayyad caliphs of Damascus were overthrown and replaced by the Abbasid dynasty in the eighth century, the independent Umayyad dynasty in Spain lasted until the eleventh century.

remaining Greco-Roman culture of the Roman Empire. Just as readily, they assimilated Byzantine and Persian culture. In the eighth and ninth centuries, numerous Greek, Syrian, and Persian scientific and philosophical works were translated into Arabic. As the chief language in the southern Mediterranean and the Near East and the required language of Muslims, Arabic became a truly international tongue.

The Muslims created a brilliant urban culture at a time when western Europe was predominantly a world of small rural villages. This can be seen in such new cities as Baghdad and Cairo, but also in Córdoba, the capital of the Umayyad caliphate in Spain. With a population of possibly 100,000, Córdoba was Europe's largest city after Constantinople. It had seventy public libraries, and the number of manuscripts in the caliph's private library reached 400,000. One caliph collected books from different parts of the world and then had them translated into Arabic and Latin. These included works on geography that later proved valuable to Western sailors and merchants. Schools were also established, and the Great Mosque of Córdoba became a center for scholars from all over the Islamic world. Large numbers of women served as teachers and librarians in Córdoba.

During the first few centuries of the Arab empire, it was the Islamic world that saved and spread the scientific and philosophical works of ancient civilizations. At a time when the ancient Greek philosophers were largely unknown in Europe, key works by Plato and Aristotle were translated into Arabic. They were put in a library called the House of Wisdom in Baghdad, where they were read and studied by Muslim scholars. Texts on mathematics were brought from India. This process was aided by the use of paper. The making of paper was introduced from China in the eighth century, and by the end of the century, paper factories had been established in Baghdad. Booksellers and libraries soon followed. European universities later benefited from this scholarship when these works were translated from Arabic into Latin.

Although Islamic scholars are rightly praised for preserving much of Classical knowledge for the West, they also made considerable advances of their own. Nowhere is this more evident than in their contributions to mathematics and the natural sciences. The list of achievements in mathematics and astronomy alone is impressive. The Muslims adopted and passed on the numerical system of India, including the use of the zero. In Europe, it became known as the Arabic system. Al-Khwarizmi (al-KHWAR-iz-mee), a ninth-century Iranian mathematician, developed the mathematical discipline of algebra. In astronomy, the Muslims were aware that the earth was round, and they set up an observatory at Baghdad to study the stars, many of which they named. They also perfected the astrolabe, an instrument used by sailors to determine their location by observing the positions of heavenly bodies. It was the astrolabe that made it possible for Europeans to sail to the Americas.

Muslim scholars also made discoveries in chemistry and developed medicine as a field of scientific study. Especially renowned was Ibn Sina (ib-un SEE-nuh) (980–1037), known as Avicenna (av-i-SENN-uh) in the West, who wrote a medical encyclopedia that, among other things, stressed the contagious nature of certain diseases and showed how they could be spread by contaminated water supplies. After its translation into Latin, Avicenna's work became a basic medical textbook for medieval European university students. Avicenna was but one of many Arabic scholars whose work was translated into Latin and helped the development of intellectual life in Europe in the twelfth and thirteenth centuries.

CHAPTER SUMMARY

At the end of the eighth century, a new kingdom—the Carolingian Empire—came to control much of western and central Europe, especially during the reign of Charlemagne. The coronation of Charlemagne, descendant of a Germanic tribe converted to Christianity, as emperor of the Romans in 800 symbolized the fusion of the three chief components of a new European civilization: the German tribes, the Classical tradition, and Christianity. In the long run, the creation of a western empire fostered the idea of a distinct European identity and marked a shift of power from the south to the north. Italy and the Mediterranean had been the center of the Roman Empire. The lands north of the Alps now became the political center of Europe, and increasingly, Europe emerged as the focus and center of Western civilization.

The Carolingian Empire was well governed but was held together primarily by personal loyalty to a strong king. The economy of the eighth and ninth centuries was based almost entirely on farming, which proved inadequate to maintain a large monarchical system. As a result, a new political and military order, known as fief-holding, subsequently evolved to become an integral part of the political world of the Middle Ages. Fief-holding was characterized by a decentralization of political power, in which lords exercised legal, administrative, and military power. This transferred public power into many private hands and seemed to provide the security sorely lacking in a time of weak central government and invasions by Muslims, Magyars, and Vikings. In eastern Europe, the Slavic kingdoms of Poland and Bohemia were established; their peoples were converted to Christianity by Catholic missionaries, while the eastern and southern Slavs adopted Orthodox Christianity.

While Europe struggled, the Byzantine and Islamic worlds continued to prosper and flourish. The tenth century was the golden age of Byzantine civilization. Under the Macedonian dynasty, trade flourished, the Bulgars were defeated, Muslim armies were repelled, and Byzantine territory was increased.

The Umayyad dynasty of caliphs had established Damascus as the center of an Islamic empire created by Arab expansion in the seventh and eighth centuries. In the eighth century, the new Abbasid dynasty moved the capital east to Baghdad, where Persian influence was more pronounced. Greek and Persian scientific and philosophical writings were translated into Arabic, and the Muslims created a brilliant urban culture.

The brilliance of the urban cultures of both the Byzantine Empire and the Islamic world stood in marked contrast to the underdeveloped rural world of Europe. By 1000, however, that rural world had not only recovered but was beginning to expand in ways undreamed of by previous generations. Europe stood poised for a giant leap.

CHAPTER TIMELINE

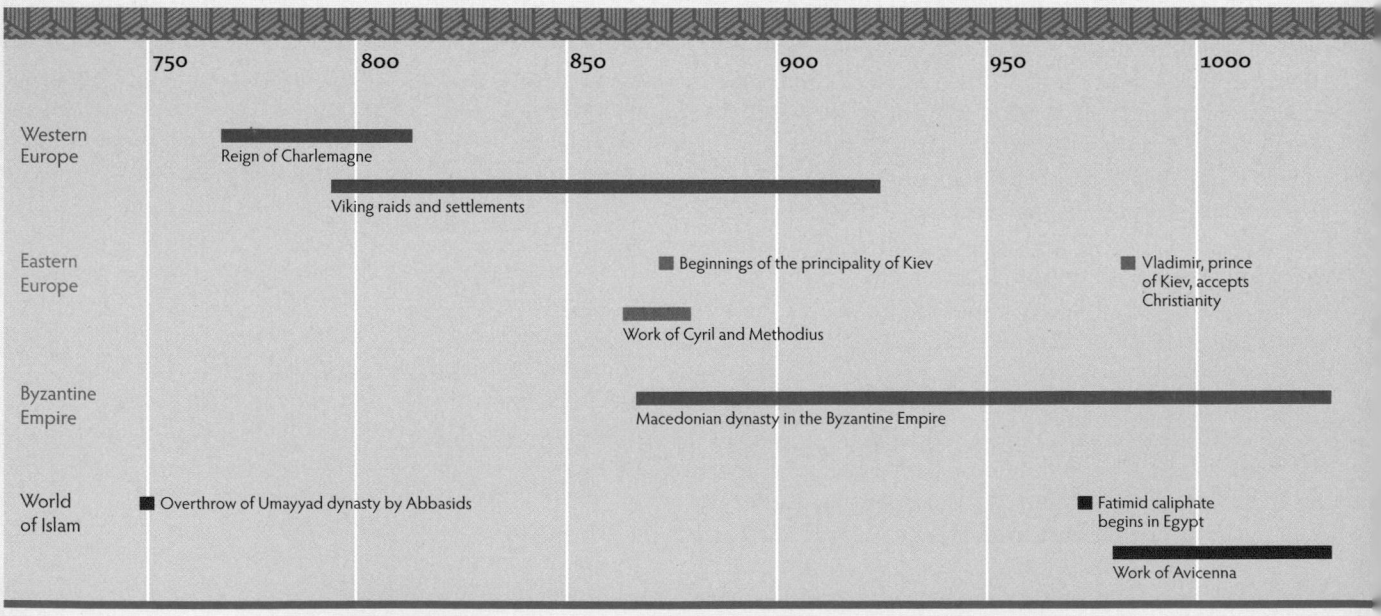

CHAPTER REVIEW

Upon Reflection

Q Of what significance was the Carolingian intellectual renaissance to western European civilization?

Q What role did the Vikings play in the history of medieval Europe?

Q Why does the author use the title, "The Zenith of Byzantine Civilization" to describe Byzantine civilization in the ninth and tenth centuries?

Key Terms

scriptoria (p. 166)
monogamy (p. 167)
nuclear family (p. 167)
vassalage (p. 171)
fief (p. 172)
subinfeudation (p. 172)
manor (p. 174)
serfs (p. 174)
demesne (p. 174)

Suggestions for Further Reading

GENERAL HISTORIES OF THE MIDDLE AGES A good general history of the entire medieval period can be found in **J. M. Riddle, *A History of the Middle Ages, 300–1500*** (Lanham, Md., 2008). For an excellent survey of the period covered in this chapter, see **C. Wickham, *The Inheritance of Rome: A History of Europe from 400 to 1000*** (New York, 2007). See also **L. Olson, *The Early Middle Ages*** (New York, 2007).

CAROLINGIAN EUROPE On Charlemagne, see **A. Barbero, *Charlemagne: Father of a Continent,*** trans. **A. Cameron** (Berkeley, Calif., 2004). On Carolingian culture, see ***History and Memory in the Carolingian World*** (Cambridge, 2004) by **R. McKitterick**.

CAROLINGIAN SOCIAL LIFE On one aspect of social life in the Carolingian world, see **L. Bitel, *Women in Early Medieval Europe, 400–1100*** (Cambridge, 2002). On attitudes toward sexuality in the early Christian church, see the important work by **P. Brown, *The Body and Society*** (New York, 1988).

THE VIKINGS The Vikings are examined in **M. Arnold, *The Vikings: Culture and Conquest*** (London, 2006), and **R. Hall, *The World of the Vikings*** (New York, 2007).

FIEF-HOLDING An introductory work on fief-holding is **J. R. Strayer, *Feudalism*** (Princeton, N.J., 1985). For an important revisionist view, see **S. Reynolds, *Fiefs and Vassals*** (Oxford, 1994).

ECONOMIC HISTORY For the economic history of the Early Middle Ages, see **A. E. Verhulst, *The Carolingian Economy*** (Cambridge, 2002).

BYZANTINE EMPIRE AND SLAVIC PEOPLES Byzantine civilization in this period is examined in **W. Treadgold, *The Byzantine Revival, 780–842*** (Stanford, Calif., 1988). On the Slavic peoples of eastern Europe, see **S. Franklin** and **J. Shepard, *The Emergence of Rus, 750–1200*** (New York, 1996).

WORLD OF ISLAM The world of Islam in this period is discussed in **H. Kennedy, *The Prophet and the Age of the Caliphates: The Islamic Near East from the Sixth to the Eleventh Century*** (London, 1986), and **J. Lassner, *The Shaping of Abbasid Rule*** (Princeton, N.J., 1980).

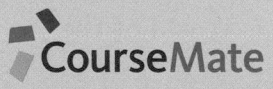

Visit the CourseMate website at **www.cengagebrain.com** for additional study tools and review materials for this chapter.

CHAPTER 9

© Mary Evans Picture Library/The Image Works

A street scene in a thirteenth-century English town

The Recovery and Growth of European Society in the High Middle Ages

CHAPTER OUTLINE AND FOCUS QUESTIONS

Land and People in the High Middle Ages

Q What new agricultural practices arose in the High Middle Ages? What roles did peasants and aristocrats play in the civilization of the High Middle Ages?

The New World of Trade and Cities

Q What developments contributed to the revival of trade during the High Middle Ages, and what areas were the primary beneficiaries of the revival? What were the major features of medieval cities?

The Intellectual and Artistic World of the High Middle Ages

Q What were the major intellectual and cultural achievements of European civilization in the High Middle Ages?

CRITICAL THINKING

Q What is the relationship between economic and social changes and intellectual and artistic developments in the High Middle Ages?

THE NEW EUROPEAN CIVILIZATION that had emerged in the ninth and tenth centuries began to come into its own in the eleventh and twelfth centuries as Europeans established new patterns that reached their zenith in the thirteenth century. The High Middle Ages (1000–1300) was a period of recovery and growth for Western civilization, characterized by a greater sense of security and a burst of energy and enthusiasm. New agricultural practices that increased the food supply helped spur a commercial and urban revival that, accompanied by a rising population, created new dynamic elements in a formerly static society.

Townspeople themselves were often great enthusiasts for their new way of life. In the twelfth century, William Fitz-Stephen spoke of London as one of the noble cities of the world: "It is happy in the healthiness of its air, in the Christian religion, in the strength of its defenses, the nature of its site, the honor of its citizens, the modesty of its women; pleasant in sports; fruitful of noble men." To Fitz-Stephen, London offered myriad opportunities and pleasures. Fairs and markets were held regularly, and "practically anything that man may need is brought daily not only into special places but even into the open squares." Any man, according to Fitz-Stephen, "if he is healthy and not a good-for-nothing, may earn his living expenses and esteem according to his station." Then, too, there are the happy inhabitants of the city: Where else has one "ever met such a wonderful show of people this side or the other side of the sea"? Sporting events and leisure activities are available in every season of the year: "In Easter holidays they fight battles on water." In summer, "the youths are exercised in leaping, dancing, shooting, wrestling, casting the stone; the maidens dance as long as they can well see." In winter, "when the great fen, or moor, which waters the walls of the city on the north side, is frozen, many young men play upon the ice; some, striding as wide as they may, do slide swiftly."[1] To Fitz-Stephen, "every convenience for human pleasure is known to be at hand" in London. One would hardly know from his cheerful description that medieval cities were overcrowded, smelled terrible from rotting garbage and raw sewage, and faced the constant challenges of epidemics and fires.

By the twelfth and thirteenth centuries, both the urban centers and the urban population of Europe were experiencing a dramatic expansion. New forms of cultural and intellectual expression also arose in this new urban world. Although European society in the High Middle Ages remained overwhelmingly agricultural, the growth of trade and cities along with the development of a money economy and new commercial practices and institutions constituted a veritable commercial revolution that affected most of Europe.

Land and People in the High Middle Ages

Focus Questions: What new agricultural practices arose in the High Middle Ages? What roles did peasants and aristocrats play in the civilization of the High Middle Ages?

In the Early Middle Ages, Europe was a sparsely populated expanse dotted with villages of farmers and warriors and covered with forests, which provided building and heating materials and food in the form of game. The climate began to improve around 700 after centuries of wetter and colder conditions, but natural disasters remained a threat. Drought or too much rain could mean bad harvests, famine, and dietary deficiencies that made people susceptible to a wide range of diseases. Life expectancy remained low.

The period from 1000 to 1300 witnessed continued improvement in climate as a small rise in temperature made for longer and better growing seasons. At the same time Europe experienced a dramatic increase in population, from 38.5 to 73.5 million people (see Table 9.1). This was physically evident in the growth of agricultural villages, towns, and cities and an increase in land under cultivation.

TABLE 9.1 Population Estimates (in millions), 1000 and 1340

Area	1000	1340
Mediterranean		
Greece and Balkans	5	6
Italy	5	10
Iberia	7	9
Total	17	25
Western and Central Europe		
France and Low Countries	6	19
British Isles	2	5
Germany and Scandinavia	4	11.5
Total	12	35.5
Eastern Europe		
Russia	6	8
Poland	2	3
Hungary	1.5	2
Total	9.5	13
Total	*38.5*	*73.5*

Source: J. C. Russell, *The Control of Late Ancient and Medieval Population* (Philadelphia: American Philosophical Society, 1985), p. 36. These are estimates; some figures, especially those for eastern Europe, could be radically revised by new research.

What accounted for this dramatic rise in population? For one thing, conditions in Europe were more settled and peaceful after the invasions of the Early Middle Ages had ended. Agricultural production also rose dramatically after 1000. Without this increase in food supplies, the greater population could never have been sustained.

The New Agriculture

During the High Middle Ages, significant changes occurred in the way Europeans farmed. In addition to the improved growing conditions, another factor contributing to the increased production of food was the expansion of arable land, achieved chiefly by clearing forested areas for cultivation (see the box on p. 186). Land-hungry peasants cut down trees and drained swamps. By the thirteenth century, the total acreage used for farming in Europe was greater than at any time before or since.

TECHNOLOGICAL CHANGES Technological changes also furthered the development of agriculture. Many of these depended on the use of iron, which was mined in various areas of Europe. Iron was in demand to make swords and armor as well as scythes, axheads, and hoes for use on farms and saws, hammers, and nails for use in building. Iron was crucial for making the *carruca* (kuh-ROO-kuh) a

The Elimination of Medieval Forests

One of the interesting environmental changes of the Middle Ages was the elimination of millions of acres of forest to create new areas of arable land and to meet the demand for timber. Timber was used as fuel and to build houses, mills of all kinds, bridges, fortresses, and ships. Incredible quantities of wood were burned to make charcoal for the iron forges. The clearing of the forests caused the price of wood to skyrocket by the thirteenth century. This document from 1140 illustrates the process. Suger, the abbot of Saint-Denis, needed 35-foot beams for the construction of a new church. His master carpenters told him that there were no longer any trees big enough in the area around Paris and that he would have to go far afield to find such tall trees. This selection recounts his efforts.

Suger's Search for Wooden Beams

On a certain night, when I had returned from celebrating Matins [a prayer service], I began to think in bed that I myself should go through all the forests of these parts. . . . Quickly disposing of all duties and hurrying up in the early morning, we hastened with our carpenters, and with the measurements of the beams, to the forest called Iveline. When we traversed our possession in the Valley of Chevreuse we summoned . . . the keepers of our own forests as well as men who know about the other woods, and questioned them under oath whether we would find there, no matter with how much trouble, any timbers of that measure. At this they smiled, or rather would have laughed at us if they had dared; they wondered whether we were quite ignorant of the fact that nothing of the kind could be found in the entire region, especially since Milon, the Castellan of Chevreuse, . . . had left nothing unimpaired or untouched that could be used for palisades and bulwarks while he was long subjected to wars both by our Lord the King and Amaury de Montfort. We however—scorning whatever they might say—began, with the courage of our faith as it were, to search through the woods; and toward the first hour we found one timber adequate to the measure. Why say more? By the ninth hour or sooner, we had, through the thickets, the depths of the forest and the dense, thorny tangles, marked down twelve timbers (for so many were necessary) to the astonishment of all.

Q What does Suger's search for wooden beams reveal about the environmental problems of the Middle Ages?

Source: From *Abbot Suger on the Abbey Church of St. Denis and its Art Treasures*, edited and translated by Erwin Panofsky. Copyright © 1946, renewed 1973 by Princeton University Press. Reprinted with permission of Dr. O. S. Panofsky.

heavy, wheeled plow strong enough to turn over the dense clay soil north of the Alps and allow for drainage.

Because the *carruca* was so heavy, six or eight oxen were needed to pull it, but oxen were slow. Two new inventions for the horse made it possible to plow faster. A new horse collar, which appeared in the tenth century, distributed the weight around the shoulders and chest, rather than along the throat, and could be used to hitch up a series of horses, enabling them to pull the heavy new plow faster and cultivate more land. The use of horseshoes, iron shoes nailed to a horse's hooves, provided better traction and more protection against the rocky and heavy clay soils of northern Europe.

The use of the heavy, wheeled plow also led to cooperative agricultural villages. Because iron was expensive, the plow had to be purchased by the entire community. Similarly, an individual family could not afford a team of animals, so villagers shared their beasts. Moreover, the plow's size and weight made it hard to maneuver, so land was cultivated in long strips to minimize the amount of turning that would have to be done.

People in the High Middle Ages also learned to harness the power of water and wind to do jobs formerly done by humans or animals. Mills, located along streams and powered by the rushing water, were used to grind grain and produce flour. Dams were built to increase the force of the water. The development of the cam enabled millwrights to mechanize entire industries; waterpower was used in certain phases of cloth production and to run trip-hammers for the working of metals. The Chinese had made use of the cam in operating trip-hammers for hulling rice by the third century C.E. but apparently had not extended its use to other industries.

Europeans also developed windmills to capture the power of the wind. Historians are uncertain whether windmills were imported into Europe (they were invented in Persia) or designed independently by Europeans. In either case, by the end of the twelfth century, they were beginning to dot the European landscape. The watermill and windmill were the most important devices for harnessing power before the invention of the steam engine in the eighteenth century, and their spread had revolutionary consequences for increasing the food supply.

THE THREE-FIELD SYSTEM The shift from a two-field to a three-field system of crop rotation also contributed to the increase in agricultural production. In the Early Middle Ages, farmers commonly planted one field while allowing another of equal size to lie fallow to regain its fertility. Now estates were divided into three parts. One field was planted in the fall with winter grains, such as rye and wheat, while spring grains, such as oats and barley, and vegetables, such as peas, beans, or lentils, were planted in the second field. The third was allowed to lie fallow. By rotating the fields, only one-third, rather than one-half, of the land lay fallow at any time. The rotation of crops also prevented the soil from being exhausted so quickly, and more crops could now be grown.

By the thirteenth century, the growing demand for agricultural produce in the towns and cities led to higher food prices. This encouraged lords to try to grow more food for profit. One way to do so was to lease their demesne land to their serfs. Labor services were then transformed into money payments or fixed rents, thereby converting many unfree serfs into free peasants. Although many peasants still remained economically dependent on their lords, they were no longer legally bound to the land. Lords, in turn, became collectors of rents rather than operators of manors with both political and legal privileges. The political and legal powers formerly exercised by lords were increasingly reclaimed by the monarchical states.

The Life of the Peasantry

Peasant activities were largely determined by the seasons of the year. Each season brought a new round of tasks appropriate for the time, although some periods were considerably more hectic than others, especially harvest time in August and September. A new cycle began in October, when the peasants prepared the ground for planting winter crops. In February and March, the land was plowed for spring crops. Early summer was a comparatively relaxed time, although there was still weeding and sheep-shearing to be done. In every season, serfs worked not only their own land but also the lord's demesne. They also tended the small gardens attached to their dwellings where they grew the vegetables that made up much of their diet.

Religious feast days, Sunday Mass, baptisms, marriages, and funerals all brought peasants into contact with the village church, a crucial part of manorial life. In the village church, the peasant was baptized as an infant, confirmed in his or her faith, sometimes married, and given the sacrament of Holy Communion as well as the last rites of the church before death. The village priest taught the peasants the basic elements of Christianity so that they might attain the Christian's ultimate goal—salvation.

The lifestyle of the peasants was very simple. Their cottages were built with wood frames with walls

Musée Condé (MS.340, f.303v), Chantilly, France)/© Réunion des Musées Nationaux (R.G. Ojeda)/ Art Resource, NY

Peasant Activities. The kind of work that peasants did was dictated by the month and the season of the year. This French calendar from 1460 shows a number of medieval farming activities, including sowing seeds, harvesting crops, pruning plants, shearing sheep, threshing, pressing grapes, and taking care of animals.

made of laths or sticks; the spaces between the laths were stuffed with straw and rubble and then plastered over with clay. Roofs were thatched. The houses of poorer peasants had only a single room, but others had at least two rooms—a main room for cooking, eating, and other activities and another room for sleeping. There was little privacy in a medieval peasant household.

Peasant women occupied a position in manorial society that was both important and difficult. They were expected to carry and bear children and at the same time fulfill their obligation to labor in the fields. Their ability to manage the household might determine whether their family would starve or survive in difficult times.

Though simple, a peasant's daily diet was nutritious when food was available. The basic staple of the peasant diet, and the medieval diet in general, was bread. After the women made the dough for the bread, the loaves were baked in community ovens, which were owned by the lord of the manor. Peasant bread generally contained not only wheat and rye but also barley, millet, and oats; it was dark and had a heavy, hard texture. Bread was supplemented by vegetables from the household gardens, cheese from cow's or goat's milk, nuts and berries from woodlands, and fruits such as apples, pears, and cherries. Chickens provided eggs and sometimes meat.

Grains were important not only for bread but also for making ale. In northern Europe, ale was the most common drink of the poor. If records are accurate, enormous quantities of it were consumed. A monastery in the twelfth century recorded a daily allotment of three gallons a day to each monk, far above the weekend consumption of many present-day college students. Peasants in the field undoubtedly consumed even more. This high consumption of alcohol might explain the large number of accidental deaths recorded in medieval court records.

The Aristocracy of the High Middle Ages

In the High Middle Ages, European society was dominated by a group of men whose chief preoccupation was warfare—the lords and vassals of medieval society. The lords were the kings, dukes, counts, barons, and viscounts (and even bishops and archbishops) who held extensive lands and considerable political power. They formed an **aristocracy** or nobility that held real political, economic, and social power. Nobles relied for military help on knights, mounted warriors who fought for them in return for weapons and daily sustenance. As warriors united by the institution of knighthood, lords and knights came to form a distinct group, albeit one with social divisions based on variations in wealth and landholdings.

Medieval theory maintained that the warlike qualities of the nobility were justified by their role as defenders of society, and the growth of the European nobility in the High Middle Ages was made visible by an increasing number of castles scattered across the landscape. Although castle architecture varied considerably, castles did possess two common features: they were permanent residences for the noble family, its retainers, and servants, and they were defensible fortifications. For defensive purposes, castles were surrounded by open areas and large stone walls. At the heart of the castle was the keep, a large, multistoried building that housed kitchens, stables, and storerooms; a great hall for visitors, dining, and administrative business; and numerous rooms for sleeping and living. The growing wealth of the High Middle Ages made it possible for the European nobility to build more complex castles with thicker walls and more elaborately decorated interiors. With their sturdier construction, castles were easier to defend and harder to seize by force.

THE WAY OF THE WARRIOR At the age of seven or eight, the sons of the nobility were sent either to a clerical school to pursue a religious career or to another nobleman's castle, where they prepared for the life of a noble. The chief lessons for those learning to be nobles were military; they learned how to joust, hunt, ride, and handle weapons properly. After his apprenticeship in knighthood, at about the age of twenty-one, a young man formally entered the adult world in a ceremony of "knighting." A sponsor girded a sword on the young candidate and struck him on the cheek or neck with an open hand (or later touched him three times on the shoulder with the blade of a sword), possibly signifying the passing of the sponsor's military valor to the new knight.

In the eleventh and twelfth centuries, under the influence of the church, an ideal of civilized behavior called **chivalry** gradually evolved among the nobility. Chivalry represented a code of ethics that knights were supposed to uphold. In addition to defending the church and the defenseless, knights were expected to treat captives as honored guests instead of putting them in dungeons. Chivalry also implied that knights should fight only for glory, but this account of a group of English knights by a medieval writer reveals another motive for battle: "The whole city was plundered to the last farthing, and then they proceeded to rob all the churches throughout the city, . . . and seizing gold and silver, cloth of all colors, gold rings, goblets, and precious stones . . . they all returned to their own lords rich men."[2] Apparently, not all chivalric ideals were taken seriously.

After his formal initiation into the world of warriors, a young man returned home to find himself once again subject to his parents' authority. Young men were discouraged

© British Library (Cott.Nero.D.IX. Folio No: 32v.Min.), London/HIP/Art Resource, NY

© Bibliothèque Municipale (Ms 527 f.5v), Dijon/The Bridgeman Art Library

The Joust and Tournament. The tournament arose as a socially acceptable alternative to the private warfare that plagued the nobility in the Middle Ages, and the joust eventually became the chief part of the tournament. The fifteenth-century English illustration at the top shows a joust between two heavily armored knights while a crowd of royal and noble onlookers watches. A wooden barrier separates the knights, whose lances have both been broken. The fifteenth-century French illustration below shows a group of knights being taught how to joust.

from marrying until their fathers died, at which time they could marry and become lords of the castle. Trained to be warriors but with no adult responsibilities, young knights had little to do but fight. As the church stepped up efforts to curb socially destructive fighting in the twelfth century, tournaments began to be organized. Initially, a tournament consisted of a melee, in which warriors on horseback fought with blunted weapons in free-for-all combat. By late in the century, the melee was preceded by a joust, individual combat between two knights. Gradually, jousts became the main part of the tournament. Knights saw tournaments as an excellent way to train for war. As one knight explained, "A knight cannot distinguish himself in [war] if he has not trained for it in tourneys. He must have seen his blood flow, heard his teeth crack under fist blows, felt his opponent's weight bear down upon him as he lay on the ground and, after being twenty times unhorsed, have risen twenty times to fight."[3]

ARISTOCRATIC WOMEN Although women could legally hold property, most women remained under the control of men—their fathers until they married (usually at the age of fifteen or sixteen) and their husbands after they married. Nevertheless, aristocratic women had numerous opportunities for playing important roles. Because the lord was often away at war, on a Crusade (see Chapter 10), or at court, the lady of the castle had to manage the estate, a considerable responsibility in view of the fact that households, even of lesser aristocrats, could include large numbers of officials and servants. The lady of the castle was also often responsible for overseeing the food supply and maintaining all other supplies for the smooth operation of the household.

Although women were expected to be subservient to their husbands (see the box on p. 190), there were many strong women who advised and sometimes even dominated their husbands. Perhaps the most famous was Eleanor of Aquitaine (c. 1122–1204), heiress to the duchy of Aquitaine in southwestern France. Married to King Louis VII of France (1137–1180), Eleanor accompanied her husband on a Crusade, but her alleged affair with her uncle during the Crusade led Louis to have their marriage annulled. Eleanor then married Henry, duke of Normandy and count of Anjou, who became King Henry II of England (1154–1189). She took an active role in politics, even assisting her sons in rebelling against Henry in 1173 and 1174.

Women in Medieval Thought

Whether a nun or the wife of an aristocrat, townsman, or peasant, a woman in the Middle Ages was considered inferior to a man and by nature subject to a man's authority. Although there are a number of examples of strong women who ignored such attitudes, church teachings reinforced these notions. The first selection from Gratian (GRAY-shun *or* GRAY-shee-un), the twelfth-century jurist who wrote the first systematic work on canon law (church law), supports this view. The second selection was written by a wealthy fifty-year-old merchant in Paris who wanted to instruct his fifteen-year-old bride on how to be a good wife.

Gratian, *Decretum*

Women should be subject to their men. The natural order for mankind is that women should serve men and children their parents, for it is just that the lesser serve the greater.

The image of God is in man and it is one. Women were drawn from man, who has God's jurisdiction as if he were God's vicar, because he has the image of one God. Therefore woman is not made in God's image.

Woman's authority is nil; let her in all things be subject to the rule of man. . . . And neither can she teach, nor be a witness, nor give a guarantee, nor sit in judgment.

Adam was beguiled by Eve, not she by him. It is right that he whom woman led into wrongdoing should have her under his direction, so that he may not fail a second time through female levity

A Merchant of Paris on Marriage

I entreat you to keep his linen clean, for this is up to you. Because the care of outside affairs is men's work, a husband must look after these things, and go and come, run here and there in rain, wind, snow, and hail—sometimes wet, sometimes dry, sometimes sweating, other times shivering, badly fed, badly housed, badly shod, badly bedded—and nothing harms him because he is cheered by the anticipation of the care his wife will take of him on his return—of the pleasures, joys, and comforts she will provide, or have provided for him in her presence: to have his shoes off before a good fire, to have his feet washed, to have clean shoes and hose, to be well fed, provided with good drink, well served, well honored, well bedded in white sheets and white nightcaps, well covered with good furs, and comforted with other joys and amusements, intimacies, affections, and secrets about which I am silent. And on the next day fresh linen and garments. . . .

Also keep peace with him. Remember the country proverb that says there are three things that drive a good man from his home: a house with a bad roof, a smoking chimney, and a quarrelsome woman. I beg you, in order to preserve your husband's love and good will, be loving, amiable, and sweet with him. . . . Thus protect and shield your husband from all troubles, give him all the comfort you can think of, wait on him, and have him waited on in your home. . . . If you do what is said here, he will always have his affection and his heart turned toward you and your service, and he will forsake all other homes, all other women, all other help, and all other households.

Q What do these two documents reveal about male attitudes toward women in the Middle Ages? How do the authors justify these attitudes?

Source: From *Not in God's Image: Women in History from the Greeks to Victorians* by Julia O'Faolain and Lauro Martines. Copyright © 1973 by Julia O'Faolain and Lauro Martines. Reprinted by permission of the authors.

Blanche of Castile (1188–1252) was another powerful medieval queen. She became regent while her son Louis IX was a boy and ruled France with a powerful hand during much of the 1220s and 1230s. She repelled the attempt of some rebellious French nobles to seize her son, the young king, and defeated Henry III of England when he tried to incite an uprising in France in an attempt to reconquer Normandy. Blanche's political sense was so astute that even when Louis IX came of age, he continued to rely on her as his chief adviser. One medieval chronicler gave her the highest compliment he could think of: "She ruled as a man."

The New World of Trade and Cities

Q **Focus Questions:** What developments contributed to the revival of trade during the High Middle Ages, and what areas were the primary beneficiaries of the revival? What were the major features of medieval cities?

Medieval Europe was an overwhelmingly agrarian society, with most people living in small villages. In the eleventh and twelfth centuries, however, new elements were introduced that began to transform the economic foundation of Western civilization: a revival of trade, considerable expansion in the circulation of money, the emergence of specialized craftspeople and artisans, and the growth and development of towns. These changes were made possible by the new agricultural practices and subsequent increase in food production, which freed some European families from the need to produce their own food. Merchants and artisans could now buy their necessities.

The Revival of Trade

The revival of commercial activity was a gradual process. During the chaotic conditions of the Early Middle Ages, large-scale trade had declined in western Europe except for Byzantine contacts with Italy and the Jewish traders who moved back and forth between the Muslim and Christian worlds. By the end of the tenth century, however, people with both the skills and the products for commercial activity were emerging in Europe.

Cities in Italy assumed a leading role in the revival of trade (see Map 9.1). By the end of the eighth century, Venice, on the northeastern coast, had emerged as a town with close trading ties to the Byzantine Empire. It developed a mercantile fleet and by the end of the tenth century had become the chief western trading center for Byzantine and Islamic commerce. Other coastal communities in western Italy, such as Genoa and Pisa, also opened new trade routes.

In the High Middle Ages, Italian merchants became even more daring in their trading activities. They established trading posts in Cairo, Damascus, and a number of Black Sea ports, where they acquired goods brought by Muslim merchants from India, China, and Southeast Asia. A few Italian merchants even journeyed to India and China in search of trade goods.

While the northern Italian cities were busy trading in the Mediterranean, the towns of Flanders were doing likewise in northern Europe. Flanders, the area along the coast of present-day Belgium and northern France, was known for the production of a much desired, high-quality woolen cloth. The location of Flanders made it a logical entrepôt for the traders of northern Europe. Merchants from England, Scandinavia, France, and Germany converged there to trade their wares for woolen cloth. Flanders prospered in the eleventh and twelfth centuries, and Flemish towns such as Bruges (BROOZH) and Ghent became centers for the trade and manufacture of woolen cloth.

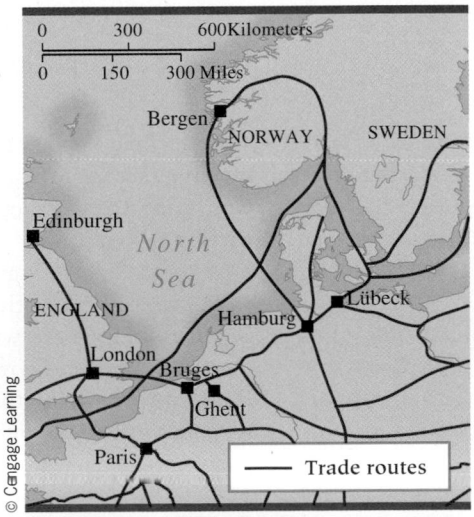

© Cengage Learning
Flanders as a Trade Center

By the twelfth century, it was almost inevitable that a regular exchange of goods would develop between Flanders and Italy. To encourage this trade, the counts of Champagne in northern France established a series of six fairs that were held annually in the chief towns of their territory. Northern merchants brought the furs, woolen cloth, tin, hemp, and honey of northern Europe to the fairs of Champagne and exchanged them for the cloth and swords of northern Italy and the silks, sugar, and spices of the East (see the box on p. 193).

As trade increased, both gold and silver came to be in demand at fairs and trading markets of all kinds. Slowly, a money economy began to emerge. New trading companies as well as banking firms were set up to manage the exchange and sale of goods. All of these new practices were part of the rise of **commercial capitalism**, an economic system in which people invested in trade and goods in order to make profits.

The Growth of Cities

The revival of trade led to a revival of cities. Merchants needed places where they could live and build warehouses to store their goods. Towns had greatly declined in the Early Middle Ages, especially in Europe north of the Alps. Old Roman cities continued to exist but had dwindled in size and population. With the revival of trade, merchants began to settle in these old cities; they were followed by craftworkers or artisans, people who had developed skills on manors or elsewhere and now perceived the opportunity to ply their trade producing objects that could be sold by the merchants. In the course of the eleventh and twelfth centuries, the old Roman cities came alive with new residents.

FOUNDING OF NEW CITIES AND TOWNS

Beginning in the late tenth century, many new cities and towns were founded, particularly in northern Europe. Usually, a group of merchants established a settlement near some fortified stronghold, such as a castle or monastery. The English *borough* or *burgh* and the German *Burg*, still evident in the names of many cities such as Edinburgh and Hamburg, originally meant a fortress or walled enclosure.

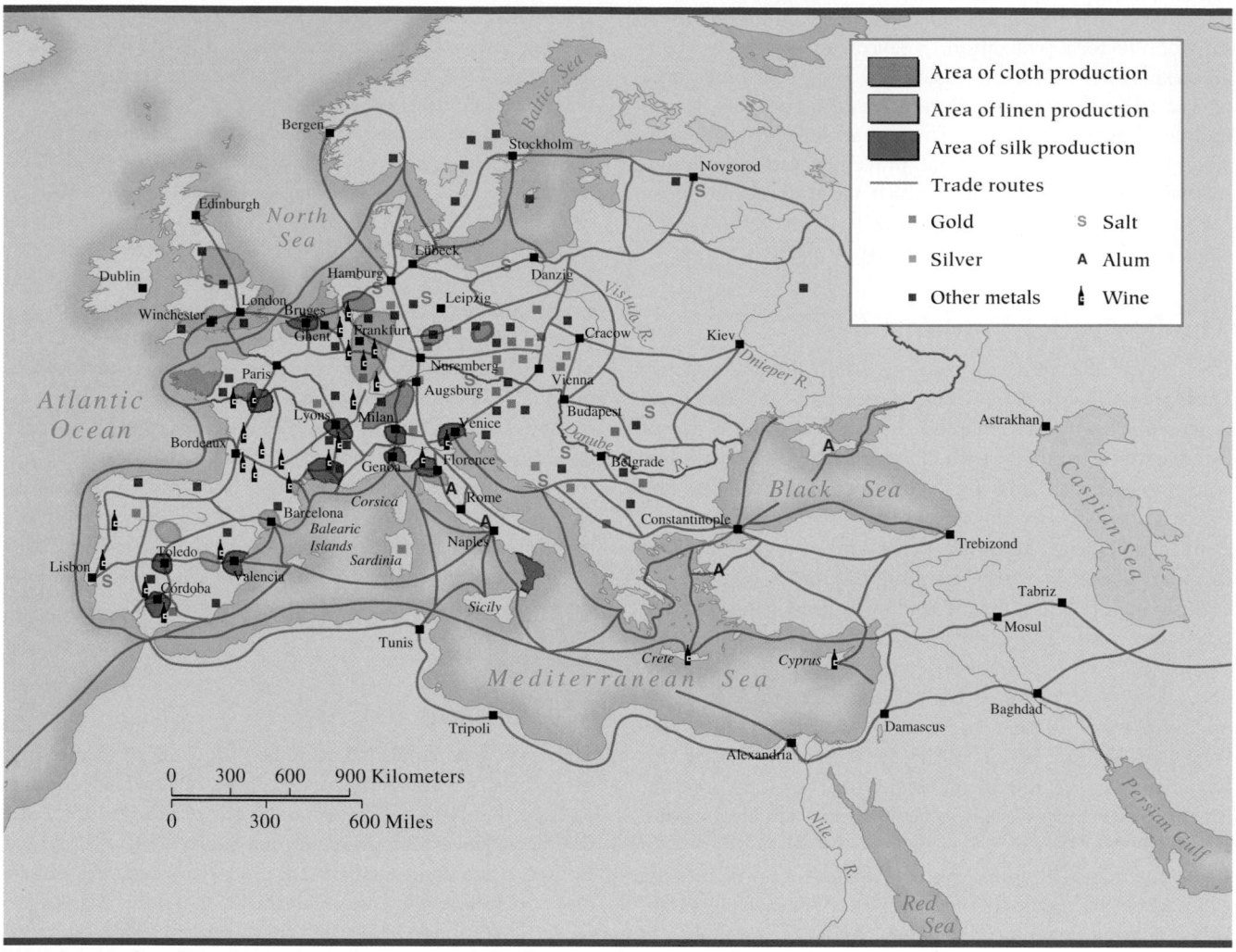

© Cengage Learning

MAP 9.1 Medieval Trade Routes. Italian cities and Flanders were the centers of gradually expanding trade in Europe. They fostered the exchange of goods from the Byzantine Empire and the Far East with those of various regions of Europe. The diminishing threats of violence over time greatly helped trade.

Q ***Look back at Map 6.2. In what areas had trade expanded since 200 C.E., and how can you account for this?***

Castles were particularly favored because they were usually located along major routes of transportation or at the intersection of two important trade routes; the lords of the castle also offered protection. As the settlement prospered and expanded outward, new walls were built to protect it.

Most towns were closely tied to their surrounding territories because they were dependent on the countryside for their food supplies. In addition, they were often part of the territory belonging to a lord and were subject to his jurisdiction. Although lords wanted to treat towns and townspeople as they would their vassals and serfs, cities had totally different needs and a different perspective. Townspeople needed mobility to trade. Consequently, the merchants and artisans of these boroughs and burghs, who came to be called burghers or **bourgeoisie**, constituted a revolutionary group who needed their own unique laws to meet their requirements. Since the townspeople were profiting from the growth of trade and sale of their products, they were willing to pay for the right to make their own laws and govern themselves. In many instances, lords and kings saw the potential for vast new sources of revenues and were willing to grant (or sell) to the townspeople the liberties they were beginning to demand. By 1100, burghers were obtaining charters of liberties from their territorial lords that granted them the privileges

OPPOSING VIEWPOINTS

Two Views of Trade and Merchants

The revival of trade in Europe was a gradual process, but by the High Middle Ages, it had begun to expand dramatically. During the medieval period, trade already flourished in other parts of the world, especially in the Islamic world and in China. Nevertheless, many people in these societies, including rulers, nobles, and religious leaders, had some reservations about the success of merchants. The first selection is taken from the life of Godric, a twelfth-century European merchant who became a saint. The second selection is from the *Prolegomena* (proh-li-GAHM-uh-nuh), the first part of a universal history written by Ibn Khaldun (ib-un khahl-DOON), a Muslim historian who traveled widely in the Muslim world in the fourteenth century.

Life of Saint Godric

At first, he lived as a peddler for four years in Lincolnshire, going on foot and carrying the smallest wares; then he traveled abroad, first to St. Andrews in Scotland and then for the first time to Rome. On his return, having formed a familiar friendship with certain other young men who were eager for merchandise, he began to launch upon bolder courses, and to coast frequently by sea to the foreign lands that lay around him. Thus, sailing often to and fro between Scotland and Britain, he traded in many divers wares and, amid these occupations, learned much worldly wisdom. . . .

Thus aspiring ever higher and higher, and yearning upward with his whole heart, at length his great labors and cares bore much fruit of worldly gain. For he labored not only as a merchant but also as a shipman . . . to Denmark and to Flanders and Scotland; in all which lands he found certain rare, and therefore more precious, wares, which he carried to other parts wherein he knew them to be least familiar, and coveted by the inhabitants beyond the price of gold itself; wherefore he exchanged these wares for others coveted by men of other lands; and thus he chaffered [traded] most freely and assiduously. Hence he made great profit in all his bargains, and gathered much wealth in the sweat of his brow; for he sold dear in one place the wares which he had bought elsewhere at a small price.

And now he had lived sixteen years as a merchant, and began to think of spending on charity, to God's honor and service, the goods which he had so laboriously acquired. He therefore took the cross as a pilgrim to Jerusalem [When he had returned to England] Godric, that he might follow Christ the more freely, sold all his possessions and distributed them among the poor [and began to live the life of a hermit].

Ibn Khaldun, *Prolegomena*

The manners of tradesmen are inferior to those of rulers, and far removed from manliness and uprightness. We have already stated that traders must buy and sell and seek profits. This necessitates flattery, and evasiveness, litigation and disputation, all of which are characteristic of this profession. And these qualities lead to a decrease and weakening in virtue and manliness. For acts inevitably affect the soul; thus good acts produce good and virtuous effects in the soul while evil or mean acts produce the opposite. Hence the effects of evil acts will strike root and strengthen themselves, if they should come early in life and repeat themselves; while if they come later they will efface the virtues by imprinting their evil effects on the soul; as is the case with all habits resulting from actions. . . .

As for Trade, although it be a natural means of livelihood, yet most of the methods it employs are tricks aimed at making a profit by securing the difference between the buying and selling prices, and by appropriating the surplus. This is why [religious] Law allows the use of such methods, which, although they come under the heading of gambling, yet do not constitute the taking without return of other people's goods. . . .

Should their standard of living, however, rise, so that they begin to enjoy more than the bare necessities, the effect will be to breed in them a desire for repose and tranquillity. They will therefore cooperate to secure superfluities; their food and clothing will increase in quantity and refinement; they will enlarge their houses and plan their towns for defense. A further improvement in their conditions will lead to habits of luxury, resulting in extreme refinement in cooking and the preparation of food; in choosing rich clothing of the finest silk; in raising

(Continued)

(Opposing Viewpoints continued)

lofty mansions and castles and furnishing them luxuriously, and so on. At this stage the crafts develop and reach their height. Lofty castles and mansions are built and decorated sumptuously, water is drawn to them and a great diversity takes place in the way of dress, furniture, vessels, and household equipment. Such are the townsmen, who earn their living in industry or trade.

Q What did the biographer of Godric and Ibn Khaldun see as valuable in mercantile activity? What reservations did they have about trade? How are the two perspectives alike? How are they different, and how do you explain the differences? What generalizations can you make about Christian and Muslim attitudes toward trade?

Sources: *Life of Saint Godric.* From Reginald of Durham, "Life of St. Godric," in G. G. Coulton, ed., *Social Life in Britain from the Conquest to the Reformation* (Cambridge: Cambridge University Press, 1918), pp. 415–20. Ibn Khaldun, *Prolegomena.* From *An Arab Philosophy of History.* Ed. and trans. by Charles Issawi. New York: Darwin Press, 1987. Reprinted by permission of the Darwin Press.

they wanted, including the right to bequeath goods and sell property, freedom from any military obligation to the lord, written urban law that guaranteed them their freedom, and the right to become a free person after residing a year and a day in the town. The last provision made it possible for a runaway serf who could avoid capture to become a free person in a city. Almost all new urban communities gained these elementary liberties, but some towns went further and obtained the right to govern themselves by choosing their own officials and administering their own courts of law.

CITY GOVERNMENTS Over time, medieval cities developed their own governments for running the affairs of the community. Citizens (males who had been born in the city or who had lived there for some time) elected members of a city council that ran the affairs of the city and also served as judges and magistrates. The electoral process was carefully engineered to ensure that only members of the wealthiest and most powerful families, who came to be called the patricians, were elected.

City governments kept close watch over the activities of their community. To care for the welfare of the community, a government might regulate air and water pollution; provide water barrels and delegate responsibility to people in every section of the town to fight fires, which were an ever-present danger; construct warehouses to stockpile grain in the event of food emergencies; and set the standards of weights and measures used in the various local industries. Urban crime was not a major problem in the towns of the High Middle Ages because their relatively small size made it difficult for criminals to operate openly. Nevertheless, medieval urban governments did organize town guards to patrol the streets by night and the city walls by day. People caught committing criminal acts were quickly tried for their offenses. Serious offenses, such as murder, were punished by execution, usually by hanging. Lesser crimes were punished by fines, flogging, or branding.

Medieval cities remained relatively small in comparison with either ancient or modern cities. A large trading city would have about 5,000 inhabitants. By 1300, London was the largest city in England, with 80,000 people or more. On the Continent north of the Alps, only a few great urban centers of commerce, such as Bruges and Ghent, had a population close to 40,000. Italian cities tended to be larger, with Venice, Florence, Genoa, Milan, and Naples numbering almost 100,000 inhabitants each. Even the largest European city, however, seemed insignificant alongside the Byzantine capital of Constantinople or the Arab cities of Damascus, Baghdad, and Cairo. For a long time to come, Europe remained predominantly rural, but in the long run, the rise of towns and the growth of trade laid the foundations for the eventual transformation of Europe from a rural agricultural society to an urban industrial one.

Life in the Medieval City

Medieval towns were surrounded by stone walls that were expensive to build, so the space within was precious and tightly filled. This gave medieval cities their characteristic appearance of narrow, winding streets with the houses crowded against each other and the second and third stories of the dwellings built out over the streets. Because buildings were constructed mostly of wood before the fourteenth century and candles and wood fires were used for light and heat, the danger of fire was great. Medieval cities burned rapidly once a fire started.

Most of the people who lived in cities were merchants involved in trade and artisans engaged in manufacturing of some kind (see Images of Everyday Life on p. 195). Generally, merchants and artisans had their own sections within a city. The merchant area included warehouses, inns, and taverns.

IMAGES OF EVERYDAY LIFE

Life in a Medieval Town

Bibliothèque de l'Arsenal, Paris//© Snark/Art Resource, NY

© Osterreichische Nationalbibliothek (f.74v), Vienna, Austria//Alinari/The Bridgeman Art Library

Most urban residents were merchants involved in trade and artisans who manufactured a wide variety of products. Master craftspeople had their workshops in the ground-level rooms of their houses. In the illustration at the left above, two well-dressed burghers are touring the shopping districts of a French town. Tailors, furriers, a barber, and a grocer (from left to right) are visible at work in their shops. Butchers were usually restricted to districts of the town that were downstream and downwind from where most people lived due to the smells from the waste products, many of which were often pitched into a nearby stream. Guild regulations forbade butchers from selling the meat of dogs, cats, and horses, and butchering places were routinely inspected to ensure that no spoiled meat was sold. The illustration at the right shows a medieval butcher shop in an Italian town. Although butchers wore aprons, they were relatively small, extending only below the waist, because medieval butchers were skilled individuals who wasted little of the animals they butchered. Even the blood was collected carefully in order to make a kind of sausage called blood pudding. Because violence was a common feature of medieval life, criminals, if apprehended, were punished quickly and severely, and public executions were considered a deterrent to crime. As one can surmise from the illustration at the right, executions were also a form of entertainment.

© British Library (Harl.4379, f.64), London, UK//HIP/Art Resource, NY

Artisan sections were usually divided along craft lines; each craft had its own street where its activity was pursued.

The physical environment of many medieval cities was not pleasant. They were often dirty and rife with smells from animal and human wastes deposited in backyard privies or on the streets. Air pollution was also a fact of life, not only from the ubiquitous wood fires but also from the burning of coal, a cheap fuel that was employed industrially by lime burners, brewers, and dyers, as well as by poor people who could not afford to purchase wood. Cities were also unable to stop water pollution, especially from the tanning and animal-slaughtering industries. Butchers dumped blood and waste products from their animals into the river, while tanners threw in tannic acids, dried blood, fat, hair, and wastes.

Because of the pollution, cities were not inclined to use the rivers for drinking water but relied instead on wells. Some communities repaired the aqueducts left over from Roman times, and some even constructed new ones. Private and public baths also existed in medieval towns. Paris, for example, had thirty-two public baths for men and women. City laws prohibited lepers and people with "bad reputations" from using them, but such measures did not prevent the public baths from being known for permissiveness. One contemporary commented on what occurred in public bathhouses: "Shameful things. Men make a point of staying all night in the public baths and women at the break of day come in and through 'ignorance' find themselves in the men's rooms."[4] Authorities came under increasing pressure to close the baths down, and the great plague of the fourteenth century sealed their fate.

There were considerably more men than women in medieval cities. Women, in addition to supervising the household, purchasing food and preparing meals, raising the children, and managing the family finances, were also often expected to help their husbands in their trades. Some women also developed their own trades, such as brewing ale or making glass, to earn extra money. Sometimes when master craftsmen died, their widows carried on their trades. Some women in medieval towns were thus able to lead lives of considerable independence.

Industry in Medieval Cities

The revival of trade enabled cities and towns to become important centers for manufacturing a wide range of products, such as cloth, metalwork, shoes, and leather goods. A host of crafts were carried on in houses along the narrow streets of the medieval cities. From the twelfth century on, artisans began to organize themselves into **guilds**, which came to play a leading role in the economic life of the cities.

By the thirteenth century, virtually every group of craftworkers, including tanners, carpenters, and bakers, had its own guild, and specialized groups of merchants, such as dealers in silk, spices, wool, or banking, had guilds as well. Craft guilds directed almost every aspect of the production process. They set standards for the articles produced, specified the methods of production to be used, and fixed the price at which the finished goods could be sold. Guilds also determined the number of men who could enter a specific trade and the procedure they must follow to do so.

A person who wanted to learn a trade first became an apprentice to a master craftsman, usually at around the age of ten. After five to seven years of service, in which they learned their craft, apprentices became journeymen (or journeywomen, although most were male), who then worked for wages for other masters. Journeymen aspired to become masters as well. To do so, they were expected to produce a "masterpiece," a finished piece in their craft that allowed the master craftsmen of the guild to judge whether the journeymen were qualified to become masters and join the guild.

The Intellectual and Artistic World of the High Middle Ages

Focus Question: What were the major intellectual and cultural achievements of European civilization in the High Middle Ages?

The High Middle Ages was a time of tremendous intellectual and artistic vitality. The period witnessed the growth of educational institutions, a rebirth of interest in ancient culture, a quickening of theological thought, the development of a vernacular literature, and a burst of activity in architecture. Although monks continued to play an important role in intellectual activity, the secular clergy, cities, and courts, whether of kings, princes, or high church officials, began to exert a newfound influence. Especially significant were the new cultural expressions that emerged in towns and cities.

The Rise of Universities

The university as we know it—with faculty, students, and degrees—was a product of the High Middle Ages. The word *university* is derived from the Latin word *universitas* (yoo-nee-VAYR-see-tahss), meaning a corporation or guild, and referred to either a guild of teachers or a guild of students. Medieval universities were educational guilds or corporations that produced educated and trained individuals.

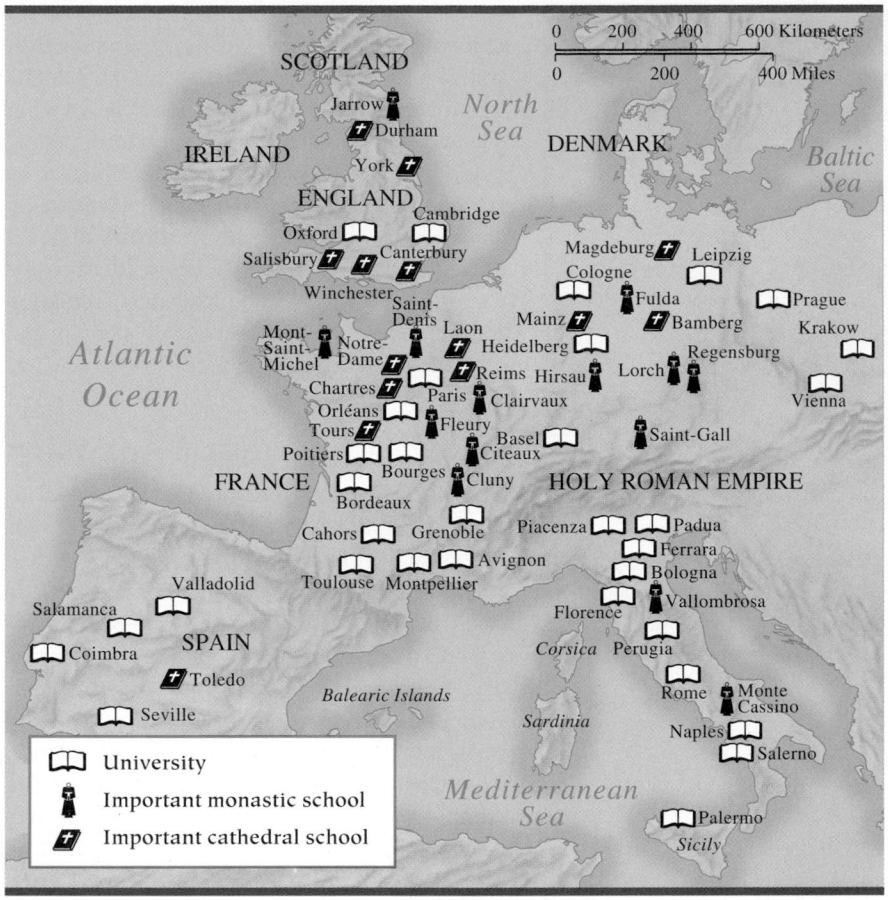

© Cengage Learning

MAP 9.2 Main Intellectual Centers of Medieval Europe. Education in the Early Middle Ages was provided primarily by the clergy, especially the monks. Although monastic schools were the centers of learning from the ninth century to the early eleventh, they were surpassed in the course of the eleventh century by the cathedral schools organized by the secular (nonmonastic) clergy. In the twelfth and thirteenth centuries, the universities surpassed both monastic and cathedral schools as intellectual centers.

Q *In what ways did France qualify as the intellectual capital of Europe?*

THE ORIGINS OF UNIVERSITIES The first European university was founded in Bologna, Italy, and coincided with the revival of interest in Roman law, especially the rediscovery of Justinian's *Body of Civil Law*. In the twelfth century, Irnerius (1088–1125), a great teacher of Roman law in Bologna (buh-LOHN-yuh), attracted students from all over Europe. Most of them were laymen, usually older individuals who served as administrators to kings and princes and were eager to learn more about law so they could apply it in their jobs. To protect themselves, students at Bologna formed a guild or *universitas*, which was recognized by Emperor Frederick Barbarossa and given a charter in 1158. Although the faculty members also organized themselves as a group, the *universitas* of students at Bologna was far more influential. It obtained a promise of freedom for students from local authorities, regulated the prices of books and lodging, and determined the curriculum, fees, and standards for their masters. Teachers were fined if they missed a class or began their lectures late.

In northern Europe, the University of Paris became the first recognized university. A number of teachers or masters who had received licenses to teach from the cathedral school of Notre-Dame in Paris began to take on extra students for a fee. By the end of the twelfth century, these masters teaching at Paris had formed a *universitas* or guild of masters. By 1200, the king of France, Philip Augustus, officially acknowledged the existence of the University of Paris. The University of Oxford in England, organized on the Paris model, appeared in 1208. A migration of scholars from Oxford led to the establishment of Cambridge University the following year. In the Late Middle Ages, kings, popes, and princes vied to found new universities. By the end of the Middle Ages, there were eighty universities in Europe, most of them located in England, France, Italy, and Germany (see Map 9.2).

TEACHERS AND STUDENTS IN THE MEDIEVAL UNIVERSITY A student's initial studies at a medieval university centered around the traditional liberal arts curriculum, which consisted of grammar, rhetoric, logic, arithmetic, geometry, astronomy, and music. All classes were conducted in Latin, which provided a common means of communication for students, regardless of their country of origin. Basically, medieval university instruction was done by the lecture method. The word *lecture* is derived from the Latin verb meaning "to read." Before the development of the printing press in the fifteenth century, books were expensive, and few students could afford them, so masters read from a text (such as a collection of laws if the subject was law) and then added their commentaries. No exams were given after a series of lectures, but when a student applied for a degree, he (women did not attend universities in the Middle Ages) was given a comprehensive oral examination by a committee of teachers. These exams were taken after a

Kupferstichkabinett (Min. 1233), Staatliche Museen zu Berlin, Germany//© Bildarchiv Preussischer Kulturbesitz (Jörg P. Anders)/Art Resource, NY

University Classroom. This illustration shows a university classroom in fourteenth-century Germany. As was customary in medieval classrooms, the master is reading from a text. The students vary considerably in age and in the amount of attention they are giving the lecturer.

four- or six-year period of study. The first degree a student could earn was the *artium baccalaureus* (ar-TEE-um bak-uh-LAR-ee-uss), or bachelor of arts; later he might receive an *artium magister* (ar-TEE-um muh-GISS-ter), or master of arts. All degrees were technically licenses to teach, although most students receiving them did not become teachers.

After completing the liberal arts curriculum, a student could go on to study law, medicine, or theology, which was the most highly regarded subject of the medieval curriculum. The study of law, medicine, or theology could take a decade or more. A student who passed his final oral examinations was granted a doctoral degree, which officially allowed him to teach his subject. Students who received degrees from medieval universities could also pursue other careers besides teaching that proved to be much more lucrative. A law degree was deemed essential for those who wished to serve as advisers to kings and princes. The growing administrative bureaucracies of popes and kings also demanded a supply of clerks with a university education who could keep records and draw up official documents. Medieval universities provided the teachers, administrators, lawyers, and doctors for medieval society.

Medieval universities shared in the violent atmosphere of the age. Records from courts of law reveal numerous instances of disturbances in European universities. One German professor was finally dismissed for stabbing one too many of his colleagues during faculty meetings. A student in Bologna was attacked in the classroom by another student armed with a sword. Oxford regulations attempted to dampen the violence by forbidding students to bring weapons to class. Not uncommonly, town-and-gown struggles ("gown" refers to the academic robe worn by teachers and students) escalated into bloody riots between townspeople and students (see the box on p. 199).

A Revival of Classical Antiquity

Another aspect of the intellectual revival of the High Middle Ages was a resurgence of interest in the works of Classical antiquity—the works of the Greeks and Romans. In the twelfth century, western Europe was introduced to a large number of Greek scientific and philosophical works, including those of Galen and Hippocrates on medicine, Ptolemy on astronomy, and Euclid on mathematics. Above all, the West now had available the complete works of Aristotle. During the second half of the twelfth century, all of Aristotle's scientific works were translated into Latin. This great influx of Aristotle's works had an overwhelming impact on the West. He came to be viewed as the "master of those who know," the man who seemed to have understood every field of knowledge.

The recovery of Greek scientific and philosophical works was not a simple process, however. Little knowledge of Greek had survived in Europe. It was through the Muslim world, especially in Spain, that the West recovered the works of Aristotle and other Greeks. The translation of Greek works into Arabic was one aspect of the brilliant Muslim civilization; in the twelfth century, these writings were translated from Arabic into Latin, making them available to the West.

The Islamic world had more to contribute intellectually to the West than translations, however. Scientific work in the ninth and tenth centuries had enabled Muslim scholars to forge far ahead of the Western world, and in the twelfth and thirteenth centuries, Arabic works on physics, mathematics, medicine, and optics became available to the West in Latin translations. Adelard of Bath (1090–1150) was one source of these works. Having traveled throughout the Mediterranean world, he later translated an Arabic version of Euclid's *Elements* (see Chapter 4) into Latin, as well as the mathematical works of al-Khwarizmi (see

University Students and Violence at Oxford

Medieval universities shared in the violent atmosphere of their age. Town-and-gown quarrels often resulted in bloody conflicts, especially during the universities' formative period. This selection is taken from an anonymous description of a student riot at Oxford at the end of the thirteenth century.

A Student Riot at Oxford

[The townsmen] seized and imprisoned all scholars on whom they could lay hands, invaded their inns [halls of residence], made havoc of their goods and trampled their books under foot. In the face of such provocation the Proctors [university officials] sent their assistants about the town, forbidding the students to leave their inns. But all commands and exhortations were in vain. By nine o'clock next morning, bands of scholars were parading the streets in martial array. If the Proctors failed to restrain them, the mayor was equally powerless to restrain his townsmen. The great bell of St. Martin's rang out an alarm; oxhorns were sounded in the streets; messengers were sent into the country to collect rustic allies. The clerks [students and teachers], who numbered three thousand in all, began their attack simultaneously in various quarters. They broke open warehouses in the Spicery, the Cutlery and elsewhere. Armed with bow and arrows, swords and bucklers, slings and stones, they fell upon their opponents. Three they slew, and wounded fifty or more. One band . . . took up a position in High Street between the Churches of St. Mary and All Saints', and attacked the house of a certain Edward Hales. This Hales was a longstanding enemy of the clerks. There were no half measures with him. He seized his crossbow, and from an upper chamber sent an unerring shaft into the eye of the pugnacious rector. The death of their valiant leader caused the clerks to lose heart. They fled, closely pursued by the townsmen and country-folk. Some were struck down in the streets, and others who had taken refuge in the churches were dragged out and driven mercilessly to prison, lashed with thongs and goaded with iron spikes.

Complaints of murder, violence and robbery were lodged straightway with the King by both parties. The townsmen claimed three thousand pounds' damage. The commissioners, however, appointed to decide the matter, condemned them to pay two hundred marks, removed the bailiffs, and banished twelve of the most turbulent citizens from Oxford.

Q Who do you think was responsible for this conflict between town and gown? Why? Why do you think the king supported the university?

Source: From *The Story of Oxford* by Cecil Headlam, 1907.

Chapter 8). Adelard also introduced Europeans to the astrolabe, an Arabic astronomical instrument of great value to sailors.

When Aristotle's works were brought into the West in the second half of the twelfth century, they were accompanied by commentaries written by outstanding Arabic and Jewish philosophers. One example was Ibn-Rushd (ib-un-RUSHT *or* ib-un-RUSH-ed), also known as Averroës (uh-VERR-oh-eez) (1126–1198), who lived in Córdoba and composed a systematic commentary on virtually all of Aristotle's surviving works.

The Revival of Roman Law

Another aspect of the revival of Classical antiquity was the rediscovery of the great work of Justinian, the *Body of Civil Law*, known to the medieval West before 1100 only at second hand. Initially, teachers of law, such as Irnerius of Bologna, were content merely to explain the meaning of Roman legal terms to their students. Gradually, they became more sophisticated so that by the mid-twelfth century, "doctors of law" had developed commentaries and systematic treatises on the legal texts. Italian cities, especially Pavia and Bologna, became prominent centers for the study of Roman law. By the thirteenth century, Italian jurists were systematizing the various professional commentaries on Roman law into a single commentary known as the ordinary gloss. Study of Roman law at the universities came to consist of learning the text of the law along with this gloss.

The training of students in Roman law at medieval universities led to further application of its principles as these students became judges, lawyers, scribes, and councillors for the towns and monarchies of western Europe. By the beginning of the thirteenth century, the old system of the ordeal was being replaced by a rational decision-making process based on the systematic collection and analysis of evidence, a clear indication of the impact of Roman law on the European legal system.

The Development of Scholasticism

The importance of Christianity in medieval society probably made it certain that theology would play a central role in the European intellectual world. Theology, the formal study of religion, was "queen of the sciences" in the new universities. Beginning in the eleventh century, the effort to apply reason or logical analysis to the church's basic doctrines had a significant impact on the study of theology. The philosophical and theological system of the medieval schools is known as **scholasticism**. A primary preoccupation of scholasticism was the attempt to reconcile faith and reason—to demonstrate that what was accepted on faith was in harmony with what could be learned by reason.

Scholasticism had its beginnings in the theological world of the eleventh and twelfth centuries but reached its high point in the thirteenth. The overriding task of scholasticism in the thirteenth century was to harmonize Christian revelation with the work of Aristotle. The great influx of Aristotle's works into the West in the High Middle Ages threw many theologians into consternation. Aristotle was so highly regarded that he was called simply "the Philosopher," yet he had arrived at his conclusions by rational thought—not revelation—and some of his doctrines, such as the mortality of the individual soul, contradicted the teachings of the church. The most famous attempt to reconcile Aristotle and the doctrines of Christianity was that of Saint Thomas Aquinas (uh-KWY-nuss).

Thomas Aquinas (1225–1274) studied theology at Cologne and Paris and taught at both Naples and Paris, and it was at the latter that he finished his famous *Summa Theologica* (SOO-muh tay-oh-LOG-jee-kuh) (*Summa of Theology*—a summa was a compendium that attempted to bring together all existing knowledge on a given subject). Aquinas's masterpiece was organized according to the dialectical method of the scholastics. Aquinas first posed a question, cited sources that offered opposing opinions on the question, and then resolved them by arriving at his own conclusions. In this fashion, Aquinas raised and discussed some six hundred articles or issues.

Aquinas's reputation derives from his masterful attempt to reconcile faith and reason. He took it for granted that there were truths derived by reason and truths derived by faith. He was certain, however, that the two truths could not be in conflict:

> The light of faith that is freely infused into us does not destroy the light of natural knowledge [reason] implanted in us naturally. For although the natural light of the human mind is insufficient to show us these things made manifest by faith, it is nevertheless impossible that these things which the divine principle gives us by faith are contrary to these implanted in us by nature [reason]. Indeed, were that the case, one or the other would have to be false, and, since both are given to us by God, God would have to be the author of untruth, which is impossible. . . . It is impossible that those things which are of philosophy can be contrary to those things which are of faith.[5]

The natural mind, unaided by faith, could arrive at truths concerning the physical universe. Without the help of God's grace, however, reason alone could not grasp spiritual truths, such as the Trinity (the belief that God, Jesus, and the Holy Spirit are three manifestations of the same unique deity) or the Incarnation (the belief that Jesus in his lifetime was God in human form).

Literature in the High Middle Ages

Latin was the universal language of medieval civilization. Used in the church and the schools, it enabled learned people to communicate anywhere in Europe. But in the twelfth century, much new literature was being written in the vernacular (the local language, such as Spanish, French, English, or German). A new market for vernacular literature appeared in the twelfth century when educated laypeople at court and in the new urban society sought fresh avenues of entertainment.

Perhaps the most popular vernacular literature of the twelfth century was troubadour poetry, which was chiefly the product of nobles and knights. This poetry focused on the love of a knight for a lady, generally a married noble lady, who inspires him to become a braver knight and a better poet. A good example is found in the laments of the crusading noble Jaufre Rudel (zhoh-FRAY roo-DEL), who cherished a dream lady from afar whom he said he would always love but feared he would never meet:

> *Most sad, most joyous shall I go away,*
> *Let me have seen her for a single day,*
> *My love afar,*
> *I shall not see her, for her land and mine*
> *Are sundered, and the ways are hard to find,*
> *So many ways, and I shall lose my way,*
> *So wills it God.*[6]

Although it originated in southern France, troubadour poetry also spread to northern France, Italy, and Germany.

Another type of vernacular literature was the ***chanson de geste*** (shahn-SAWNH duh ZHEST), or heroic epic. The earliest and finest example is *The Song of Roland*, which appeared around 1100 and was written in a dialect of

French, a language derived from Latin. The *chansons de geste* were written for a male-dominated society. The chief events described in these poems are battles and political contests. Their world is one of combat in which knights fight courageously for their kings and lords. Women play little or no role in this literary genre.

Romanesque Architecture: "A White Mantle of Churches"

The eleventh and twelfth centuries witnessed an explosion of building, both private and public. The construction of castles and churches absorbed most of the surplus resources of medieval society and at the same time reflected its basic preoccupations, God and warfare. The churches were by far the most conspicuous of the public buildings. A chronicler of the eleventh century commented:

> [After the] year of the millennium, which is now about three years past, people all over the world, but especially in Italy and France, began to rebuild their churches. Although most of them were well built and in little need of alterations, Christian nations were rivaling each other to have the most beautiful edifices. One might say the world was shaking herself, throwing off her old garments, and robing herself with a white mantle of churches. Then nearly all the cathedrals, the monasteries dedicated to different saints, and even the small village chapels were reconstructed more beautifully by the faithful.[7]

© The Art Archive/Gianni Dagli Orti

Barrel Vaulting. The eleventh and twelfth centuries witnessed an explosion of church construction. Using the basilica shape, master builders replaced flat wooden roofs with long, round stone vaults known as barrel vaults. As this illustration of a Romanesque church in Vienne, France, indicates, the barrel vault limited the size of the church and left little room for windows.

Hundreds of new cathedrals, abbeys, and pilgrimage churches, as well as thousands of parish churches in rural villages, were built in the eleventh and twelfth centuries. This building spree reflected a revived religious culture and the increased wealth of the period produced by agriculture, trade, and the growth of cities.

The cathedrals of the eleventh and twelfth centuries were built in the **Romanesque** style, a truly international style. The construction of churches required the services of a cadre of professional master builders whose employment throughout Europe guaranteed international unity in basic features.

Romanesque churches were normally built in the basilica shape used in the construction of churches in the Late Roman Empire. Basilicas were simply rectangular buildings with flat wooden roofs. Elaborating on this basic plan, Romanesque builders made a significant innovation by replacing the flat wooden roof with a long, round stone vault called a barrel vault or a cross vault where two barrel vaults intersected (a vault is simply a curved roof made of masonry). The barrel vault was used when a transept was added to create a church plan in the shape of a cross. Although barrel and cross vaults were technically difficult to construct, they were considered aesthetically pleasing and technically proficient. They also had fine acoustics.

Because stone roofs were extremely heavy, Romanesque churches required massive pillars and walls to hold them up. This left little space for windows, making Romanesque churches quite dark inside. The massive walls and pillars gave Romanesque churches a sense of solidity and a look reminiscent of a fortress.

The Gothic Cathedral

Begun in the twelfth century and brought to perfection in the thirteenth, the **Gothic** cathedral remains one of the great artistic triumphs of the High Middle Ages. Soaring skyward, as if to reach heaven, it was a fitting symbol for medieval people's preoccupation with God.

Two fundamental innovations of the twelfth century made Gothic cathedrals possible. The combination of ribbed vaults and pointed arches replaced the barrel vault of Romanesque churches and enabled builders to make Gothic churches higher than their Romanesque counterparts.

© Scala/Art Resource, NY

The Gothic Cathedral. The Gothic cathedral was one of the greatest artistic triumphs of the High Middle Ages. Shown here is the cathedral of Notre-Dame in Paris. Begun in 1163, it was not completed until the beginning of the fourteenth century.

© The Art Archive/Gianni Dagli Orti

Interior of a Gothic Cathedral. The use of ribbed vaults and pointed arches gave the Gothic cathedral a feeling of upward movement. Moreover, due to the flying buttress, the cathedral could have thin walls with stained-glass windows that filled the interior with light. The flying buttress was a heavy pier of stone built onto the outside of the walls to bear the brunt of the weight of the church's vaulted ceiling.

The use of pointed arches and ribbed vaults created an impression of upward movement, a sense of weightless upward thrust that implied the energy of God. Another technical innovation, the flying buttress, basically a heavy arched pier of stone built onto the outside of the walls, made it possible to distribute the weight of the church's vaulted ceilings outward and downward and thereby eliminate the thick, heavy walls used in Romanesque churches to hold the weight of the massive barrel vaults. Thus, Gothic cathedrals could be built with thinner walls that were filled with magnificent stained-glass windows, which created a play of light inside that varied with the sun at different times of the day. The preoccupation with colored light in Gothic cathedrals was inspired by the belief that natural light was a symbol of the divine light of God.

The first fully Gothic church was the abbey church of Saint-Denis (san-duh-NEE) near Paris, built between 1140 and 1150 at the inspiration of Suger (soo-ZHAYR), the monastery's famous abbot. A product of northern France, the Gothic style had spread by the mid-thirteenth century to England, Spain, Germany, and virtually all the rest of Europe. The most brilliant Gothic cathedrals were still to be found in France—in Paris (Notre-Dame), Reims, Amiens, and Chartres.

A Gothic cathedral was the work of an entire community. All classes of society contributed to its construction. Money was raised from wealthy townspeople, who had profited from the new trade and industries, as well as from kings and nobles. Master masons, who were both architects and engineers, designed the cathedrals. They drew up the plans and supervised the work of construction. Stonemasons and other craftspeople were paid a daily wage and provided the skilled labor to build the cathedrals. A Gothic cathedral symbolized the chief preoccupation of a medieval Christian community, its dedication to a spiritual ideal. As we have observed before, the largest buildings of an era reflect the values of its society. The Gothic cathedral, with its towers soaring toward heaven, gave witness to an age when a spiritual impulse still underlay most of existence.

CHAPTER SUMMARY

The new European civilization that had emerged in the ninth and tenth centuries began to come into its own in the eleventh and twelfth centuries, as Europeans established new patterns that reached their high point in the thirteenth century. The High Middle Ages (1000–1300) was a period of recovery and growth for Western civilization, characterized by a greater sense of security and a burst of energy and enthusiasm. Climatic improvements that produced better growing conditions, an expansion of cultivated land, and technological and agricultural changes combined to enable Europe's food supply to increase significantly after 1000. This increase in agricultural production helped sustain a dramatic rise in population that was physically apparent in the expansion of towns and cities.

The development of trade and the rise of cities added a dynamic new element to the civilization of the High Middle Ages. Trading activities flourished first in northern Italy and Flanders and then spread outward from these centers. In the late tenth and eleventh centuries, this renewal of commercial life led to a revival of cities. Old Roman cities came back to life, and new towns arose at major crossroads or natural harbors favorable to trading activities. By the twelfth and thirteenth centuries, both the urban centers and the urban population of Europe were experiencing a dramatic expansion. The revival of trade, the expansion of towns and cities, and the development of a money economy did not mean the end of a predominantly rural European society, but they did open the door to new ways to make a living and new opportunities for people to expand and enrich their lives. Eventually, they created the foundations for the development of a predominantly urban industrial society.

The High Middle Ages also gave birth to an intellectual and artistic revival. The intellectual revival led to a rediscovery of important aspects of the Classical heritage, including the works of Aristotle, who came to be viewed as the "master of those who know." New centers of learning emerged in the universities, where reason was used to systematize the study of theology and law. In addition to Latin literature, a vernacular literature emerged that appealed both to knights and to townspeople.

An artistic revival was especially evident in architecture, where Romanesque cathedrals, with their barrel vaults and massive pillars and walls with little space for windows, gave way in the twelfth century to Gothic cathedrals. Ribbed vaults and pointed arches made it possible to build higher cathedrals, and flying buttresses, by redistributing the weight, allowed them to have thinner walls and stained-glass windows. Construction of a cathedral took decades, but it was a community's act of faith in an age when a spiritual ideal still underlay most of existence.

CHAPTER TIMELINE

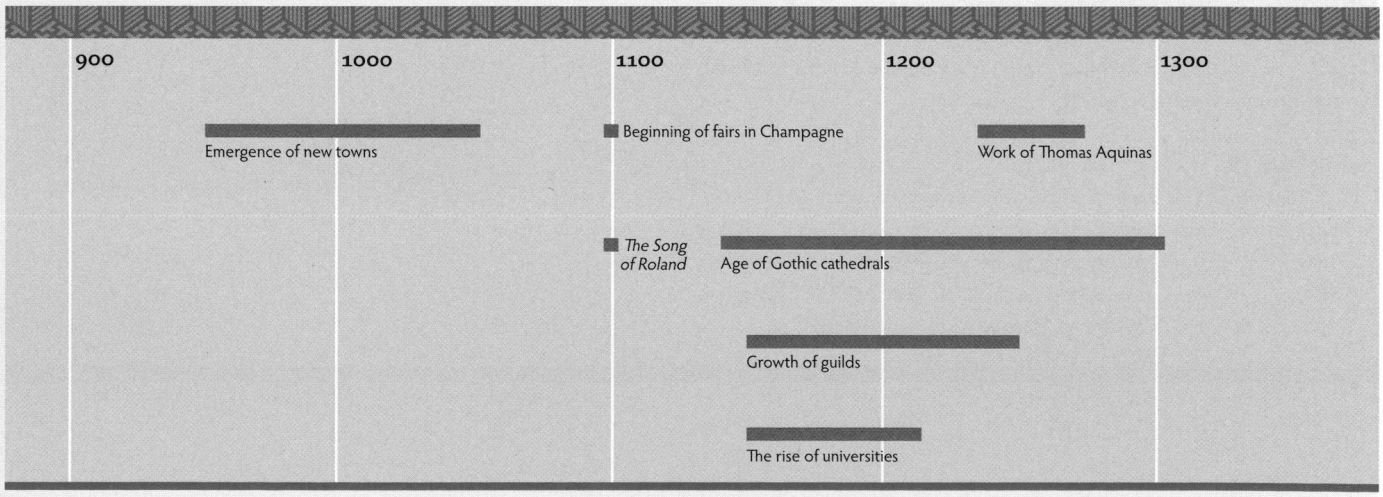

CHAPTER REVIEW

Upon Reflection

Q How did the revival of trade and cities affect the economy and society of Europe in the High Middle Ages?

Q What were the causes and the consequences of the development of the medieval universities?

Q In what ways did the artistic and literary culture of the High Middle Ages reflect the religious preoccupations and problems of medieval society?

Key Terms

aristocracy (p. 188)
chivalry (p. 188)
commercial capitalism (p. 191)
bourgeoisie (p. 192)
guilds (p. 196)
scholasticism (p. 200)
chanson de geste (p. 200)
Romanesque (p. 201)
Gothic (p. 201)

Suggestions for Further Reading

GENERAL HISTORIES For a good introduction to this period, see **W. C. Jordan, *Europe in the High Middle Ages*** (New York, 2003).

THE NEW AGRICULTURE On peasant life, see **R. Fossier, *Peasant Life in the Medieval West*** (New York, 1988). Technological changes are discussed in **J. Langdon, *Horses, Oxen, and Technological Innovation*** (New York, 1986).

THE ARISTOCRACY On the function and activities of the nobility in the High Middle Ages, see **S. Reynolds, *Kingdoms and Communities in Western Europe, 900–1300*** (Oxford, 1984). On tournaments, see **D. Crouch, *Tournament*** (London, 2005).

WOMEN IN THE HIGH MIDDLE AGES On women, see **J. Ward, *Women in Medieval Europe, 1200–1500*** (London, 2003). An excellent reference work is **M. C. Schaus, *Women and Gender in Medieval Europe: An Encyclopedia*** (London, 2006).

REVIVAL OF TRADE AND CITIES Urban history is covered in **D. Nicholas, *The Growth of the Medieval City: From Late Antiquity to the Early Fourteenth Century*** (New York, 1997). On daily life, see **C. Frugoi, *A Day in a Medieval City,*** trans. **W. McCuaig** (Chicago, 2006). On women in the cities, see **M. P. P. Cosman, *Women at Work in Medieval Europe*** (New York, 2001).

INTELLECTUAL LIFE A general work on medieval intellectual life is **M. L. Colish, *Medieval Foundations of the Western Intellectual Tradition, 400–1400*** (New Haven, Conn., 1997). The development of universities is covered in **S. Ferruolo, *The Origin of the University*** (Stanford, Calif., 1985). Various aspects of the intellectual and literary developments of the High Middle Ages are examined in **M. Haren, *Medieval Thought,*** 2nd ed. (London, 1992).

ART AND ARCHITECTURE A good introduction to Romanesque style is **A. Petzold, *Romanesque Art,*** rev. ed. (New York, 2003). On the Gothic movement, see **M. Camille, *Gothic Art: Glorious Visions,*** rev. ed. (New York, 2003).

Visit the CourseMate website at www.cengagebrain.com for additional study tools and review materials for this chapter.

© British Library (Harl.1498, f.76), London, UK//
HIP/Art Resource, NY

A medieval abbot and his monks

CHAPTER 10

The Rise of Kingdoms and the Growth of Church Power

CHAPTER OUTLINE AND FOCUS QUESTIONS

The Emergence and Growth of European Kingdoms, 1000–1300

Q What steps did the rulers of England and France take during the High Middle Ages to reverse the decentralizing tendencies of fief-holding? What were the major political and religious developments in Spain, the Holy Roman Empire, and northern and eastern Europe during the High Middle Ages?

The Recovery and Reform of the Catholic Church

Q What was at issue in the Investiture Controversy, and what effect did the controversy have on the church and on Germany?

Christianity and Medieval Civilization

Q What were the characteristics of the papal monarchy and the new religious orders of the High Middle Ages, and what role did women play in the religious life of the period? What was the church's attitude toward heretics and Jews during the High Middle Ages?

The Crusades

Q What were the reasons for the Crusades, and who or what benefited the most from the experience of the Crusades?

CRITICAL THINKING

Q What factors contributed to the development of centralized kingdoms in some parts of Europe but not in others?

THE RECOVERY AND GROWTH of European civilization in the High Middle Ages also affected the state and the church. Both lords and vassals and the Catholic Church recovered from the invasions and internal dissension of the Early Middle Ages. Although lords and vassals seemed forever mired in endless petty conflicts, some medieval kings began to exert a centralizing authority and inaugurated the process of developing new kinds of monarchical states. By the thirteenth century, European monarchs were solidifying their governmental institutions in pursuit of greater power.

The recovery of the Catholic Church produced a reform movement that led to exalted claims of papal authority. This increase in church power, coupled with the rise of monarchical states, made it almost inevitable that there would be conflicts between church and state. At the same time, vigorous papal leadership combined with new dimensions of religious life to make the Catholic Church a forceful presence in every area of life. The role of the church in the new European civilization was quite evident in the career of a man named Samson, who became abbot of the great English abbey of Bury Saint Edmunds in 1182. According to Jocelyn of Brakelond, a monk who assisted him, Abbot Samson was a devout man who wore "undergarments of horsehair and a horsehair shirt." He loved virtue and "abhorred liars, drunkards and talkative folk." His primary concern was the spiritual well-being of his monastery, but he spent much of his time working on problems in the world beyond the abbey walls. Since the monastery had fallen into debt under his predecessors, Abbot Samson toiled tirelessly to recoup the abbey's fortunes by carefully supervising its manors. He also rounded up murderers to stand trial in Saint Edmunds and provided knights for the king's army. But his actions were not always tolerant or beneficial. He was instrumental in driving the Jews from the town of Saint Edmunds and was not above improving the abbey's possessions at the expense of his neighbors: "He built up the bank of the fish-pond at Babwell so high, for the service of a new mill, that by the keeping back the water there is not a man, rich or poor, but has lost his garden and his orchards." The abbot's worldly cares weighed heavily on him, but he had little choice if his abbey were to flourish and fulfill its spiritual and secular functions. But he did have regrets; as he remarked to Jocelyn: "If he could have returned to the circumstances he had enjoyed before he became a monk, he would never have become a monk or an abbot."[1]

The Emergence and Growth of European Kingdoms, 1000–1300

Focus Questions: What steps did the rulers of England and France take during the High Middle Ages to reverse the decentralizing tendencies of fief-holding? What were the major political and religious developments in Spain, the Holy Roman Empire, and northern and eastern Europe during the High Middle Ages?

The domination of society by the nobility reached its apex in the High Middle Ages. During the same period, however, kings began the process of extending their power in more effective ways. Out of this growth in the monarchies would eventually come the European states that dominated much of later European history.

Kings possessed some sources of power that other lords did not. Usually, kings had greater opportunities to increase their lands through war and marriage alliances and then could use their new acquisitions to reward their followers and bind powerful nobles to them. In the High Middle Ages, kings found ways to strengthen governmental institutions and consequently to extend their powers. The growth of cities, the revival of commerce, and the emergence of a money economy enabled monarchs to hire soldiers and officials and to rely less on their vassals.

England in the High Middle Ages

In 1066, an army of heavily armed knights under William of Normandy landed on the southeastern coast of England and soundly defeated King Harold and his Anglo-Saxon foot soldiers at the Battle of Hastings on October 14. William (1066–1087) was crowned king of England at Christmastime in London and began the process of combining Anglo-Saxon and Norman institutions. Many of the Norman knights were given parcels of land that they held as fiefs from the new English king. William made all nobles swear an oath of loyalty to him and insisted that all people owed loyalty to the king rather than to their lords.

Gradually, fusion between the victorious Normans and the defeated Anglo-Saxons transformed England. Although the Norman ruling class spoke French, intermarriage of the Norman-French and the Anglo-Saxon nobility gradually blended the two cultures and vastly enriched the English language. The Normans also took over existing Anglo-Saxon institutions, such as the office of sheriff. William took a census and more fully developed the system of taxation and royal courts begun by the Anglo-Saxon kings of the tenth and eleventh centuries. All in all, William of Normandy created a strong, centralized monarchy.

The Norman conquest of England had other repercussions as well. Because the new king of England was still the duke of Normandy, he was both a king (of England) and at the same time a vassal to a king (of France), but a vassal who was now far more powerful than his lord. This connection with France kept England heavily involved in Continental affairs throughout the High Middle Ages.

HENRY II In the twelfth century, the power of the English monarchy was greatly expanded during the reign of Henry II (1154–1189), the founder of the Plantagenet (plan-TAJ-uh-net) dynasty (see the Film & History feature on p. 208). The king was particularly successful in strengthening the power of the royal courts. Henry increased the number of criminal cases tried in the king's court and also devised ways of taking

Musée de la Tapisserie, Bayeux, France/The Bridgeman Art Library

Norman Conquest of England. The Bayeux (by-YOO *or* bah-YURR) tapestry, which consists of woolen embroidery on a linen backing, was made by English needlewomen before 1082 for Bayeux Cathedral. It depicts scenes from the Norman invasion of England. This segment shows the Norman cavalry charging the shield wall of the Saxon infantry during the Battle of Hastings.

property cases from local courts to the royal courts. Henry's goals were clear: expanding the jurisdiction of royal courts extended the king's power and, of course, brought revenues into his coffers. Moreover, because the royal courts were now found throughout England, a body of **common law** (law that was common to the whole kingdom) began to replace the local law codes, which differed from place to place.

Henry was less successful at imposing royal control over the church. The king claimed the right to punish clergymen in royal courts, but Thomas à Becket, archbishop of Canterbury and therefore the highest-ranking English cleric, claimed that only church courts could try clerics. Attempts at compromise failed, and the angry king publicly expressed the desire to be rid of Becket: "Who will free me of this priest?" he screamed. Four knights took the challenge, went to Canterbury, and murdered the archbishop in the cathedral. Faced with public outrage, Henry was forced to allow the right of appeal from English church courts to the papal court.

KING JOHN AND MAGNA CARTA Many English nobles came to resent the continuing growth of the king's power and rose in rebellion during the reign of Henry's son, King John (1199–1216). Following in his father's footsteps, John continued the effort to strengthen royal power and proved particularly ingenious at finding novel ways to levy taxes. The barons of England came to resent him deeply. By 1205, John had lost Normandy, Maine, Anjou (AHN-zhoo), and Touraine to the French king, Philip Augustus; when John's attempt to reconquer the duchy ended in a devastating defeat, many of the English barons rose in rebellion. At Runnymede in 1215, John was forced to assent to Magna Carta, the "great charter" of feudal liberties. Much of Magna Carta was aimed at limiting government practices that affected the relations between the king and his vassals on the one hand and between the king and the church on the other (see the box on p. 209).

Despite later interpretations and efforts to broaden its principles, Magna Carta remains, above all, a feudal document. Feudal custom had always recognized that the relationship between king and vassals was based on mutual rights and obligations. Magna Carta gave written recognition to that fact and was used in subsequent years to underscore the concept that the monarch's power was limited rather than absolute.

EDWARD I AND THE EMERGENCE OF PARLIAMENT During the reign of Edward I (1272–1307), an institution of great importance in the development of representative government—the English Parliament—emerged. Originally, the word *parliament* was applied to meetings of the king's Great Council in which the greater barons and chief prelates of the church met with the king's judges and principal advisers to deal with judicial affairs. But in 1295, in need of money, Edward invited two knights from every county and two residents ("burgesses") from each town to meet with the Great Council to consent to new taxes. This was the first Parliament.

The English Parliament, then, came to be composed of two knights from every county and two burgesses from every town as well as the barons and eccelesiastical lords. Eventually, the barons and church lords formed the House of Lords; the knights and burgesses, the House of Commons. The Parliaments of Edward I granted taxes, discussed politics, passed laws, and handled judicial business. By the end of the thirteenth century, the law of the realm was being determined not by the king alone but by the king in consultation with representatives of various groups that constituted the community.

The Growth of the French Kingdom

In 843, the Carolingian Empire had been divided into three major sections. The west Frankish lands formed the

FILM & HISTORY

The Lion in Winter (1968)

Directed by Anthony Harvey, *The Lion in Winter* is based on a play by James Goldman, who also wrote the script for the movie and won an Oscar for best adapted screenplay for it. The action takes place in a castle in Chinon, France, over the Christmas holidays in 1183. The setting is realistic: medieval castles had dirt floors covered with rushes, under which lay, according to one observer, "an ancient collection of grease, fragments, bones, excrement of dogs and cats, and everything that is nasty." The powerful but world-weary King Henry II (Peter O'Toole), ruler of England and a number of French lands (the "Angevin Empire"), wants to establish his legacy and plans a Christmas gathering to decide which of his sons should succeed him. He favors his overindulged youngest son John (Nigel Terry), but he is opposed by his strong-willed and estranged wife, Eleanor of Aquitaine (Katharine Hepburn). She has been imprisoned by the king for leading a rebellion against him but has been temporarily freed for the holidays. Eleanor favors their son Richard (Anthony Hopkins), the most military minded of the brothers. The middle brother, Geoffrey (John Castle), is not a candidate but manipulates the other brothers to gain his own advantage. All three sons are portrayed as treacherous and traitorous, and Henry is distrustful of them. At one point, he threatens to imprison and even kill his sons; marry his mistress Alais (Jane Merrow), who is also the sister of the king of France; and have a new family to replace them.

In contemporary terms, Henry and Eleanor are a dysfunctional married couple, and their family is acutely dysfunctional. Sparks fly as family members plot against each other, using intentionally cruel comments and sarcastic responses in order to wound each other as much as possible—an aspect of the movie that reflected the use of verbal abuse that became fashionable in the 1960s in such plays and films as Edward Albee's *Who's Afraid of Virginia Woolf.* When Eleanor says to Henry, "What would you have me do? Give up? Give in?" he responds, "Give me a little peace." To which Eleanor replies, "A little? Why so modest? How about eternal peace? Now there's a thought." At one point, John responds to bad news about his chances for the throne with "Poor John. Who says poor John? Don't everybody sob at once? My God, if I went up in flames, there's not a living soul who'd pee on me to put the fire out." His brother Richard replies, "Let's strike a flint and see." Henry can also be cruel to his sons: "You're not mine! We're not connected! I deny you! None of you will get my crown. I leave you nothing, and I wish you plague!"

Avco Embassy/The Kobal Collection

Eleanor of Aquitaine (Katharine Hepburn) and Henry II (Peter O'Toole) at dinner at Henry's palace in Chinon, France.

In developing this well-written, imaginative re-creation of a royal family's Christmas gathering, James Goldman had a great deal of material to work with to fashion his story. Henry II was one of the most powerful monarchs of his day, and Eleanor of Aquitaine was one of the most powerful women. She had first been queen of France, but that marriage was annulled. Next she married Henry, who was then count of Anjou, and became queen of England when he became king in 1154. During their stormy marriage, Eleanor and Henry had five sons and three daughters. She is supposed to have murdered Rosamond, one of her husband's mistresses, and aided her sons in a rebellion against their father in 1173, causing Henry to distrust his sons ever after. But Henry struck back, imprisoning Eleanor for sixteen years. After his death, however, Eleanor returned to Aquitaine and lived on to play an influential role in the reigns of her two sons, Richard and John, who succeeded their father.

Magna Carta

After King John's dismal failure to reconquer Normandy from the French king, some of the English barons rebelled against their king. At Runnymede in 1215, King John agreed to seal Magna Carta, the Great Charter of liberties regulating the relationship between the king and his vassals. Although Magna Carta originated as a feudal document, its more general clauses defining rights and liberties were later interpreted in broader terms to make them applicable to all the English people.

Magna Carta

John, by the Grace of God, king of England, lord of Ireland, duke of Normandy and Aquitaine, count of Anjou, to the archbishops, bishops, abbots, earls, barons, justiciars, foresters, sheriffs, reeves, servants, and all bailiffs and his faithful people greeting.

1. In the first place we have granted to God, and by this our present charter confirmed, for us and our heirs forever, that the English church shall be free, and shall hold its rights entire and its liberties uninjured. . . . We have granted moreover to all free men of our kingdom for us and our heirs forever all the liberties written below, to be had and holden by themselves and their heirs from us and our heirs.
2. If any of our earls or barons, or others holding from us in chief by military service, shall have died, and when he had died his heir shall be of full age and owe relief, he shall have his inheritance by the ancient relief; that is to say, the heir or heirs of an earl for the whole barony of an earl a hundred pounds; the heir or heirs of a baron for a whole barony a hundred pounds; the heir or heirs of a knight, for a whole knight's fee, a hundred shillings at most; and who owes less let him give less according to the ancient custom of fiefs.
3. If moreover the heir of any one of such shall be under age, and shall be in wardship, when he comes of age he shall have his inheritance without relief and without a fine. . . .
12. No scutage [tax] or aid [tribute] shall be imposed in our kingdom except by the common council of our kingdom, except for the ransoming of our body, for the making of our oldest son a knight, and for once marrying our oldest daughter, and for these purposes it shall be only a reasonable aid. . . .
13. And the city of London shall have all its ancient liberties and free customs, as well by land as by water. Moreover, we will and grant that all other cities and boroughs and villages and ports shall have all their liberties and free customs.
14. And for holding a common council of the kingdom concerning the assessment of an aid otherwise than in the three cases mentioned above, or concerning the assessment of a scutage we shall cause to be summoned the archbishops, bishops, abbots, earls, and greater barons by our letters under seal; and besides we shall cause to be summoned generally, by our sheriffs and bailiffs all those who hold from us in chief, for a certain day, that is at the end of forty days at least, and for a certain place; and in all the letters of that summons, we will express the cause of the summons, and when the summons has thus been given the business shall proceed on the appointed day, on the advice of those who shall be present, even if not all of those who were summoned have come. . . .
39. No free man shall be taken or imprisoned or dispossessed, or outlawed, or banished, or in any way destroyed, nor will we go upon him, nor send upon him, except by the legal judgment of his peers or by the law of the land. . . .
60. Moreover, all those customs and franchises mentioned above which we have conceded in our kingdom, and which are to be fulfilled, as far as pertains to us, in respect to our men; all men of our kingdom as well as clergy as laymen, shall observe as far as pertains to them, in respect to their men.

Q What are the major principles of Magna Carta as seen in this excerpt? Why has Magna Carta been considered such an important historical document?

Source: From University of Pennsylvania Translation and Reprints, translated by E. P. Cheyney (Philadelphia, PA: University of Pennsylvania Press), 1897, Volume I, No. 6, pp. 6–16.

core of the eventual kingdom of France. In 987, after the death of the last Carolingian king, the west Frankish nobles chose Hugh Capet (YOO ka-PAY) (987–996) as the new king, thus establishing the Capetian (kuh-PEE-shun) dynasty of French kings. Although they carried the title of kings, the Capetians had little real power. They controlled as the royal domain (the lands of the king) only the lands around Paris known as the Île-de-France (EEL-de-fronhss).

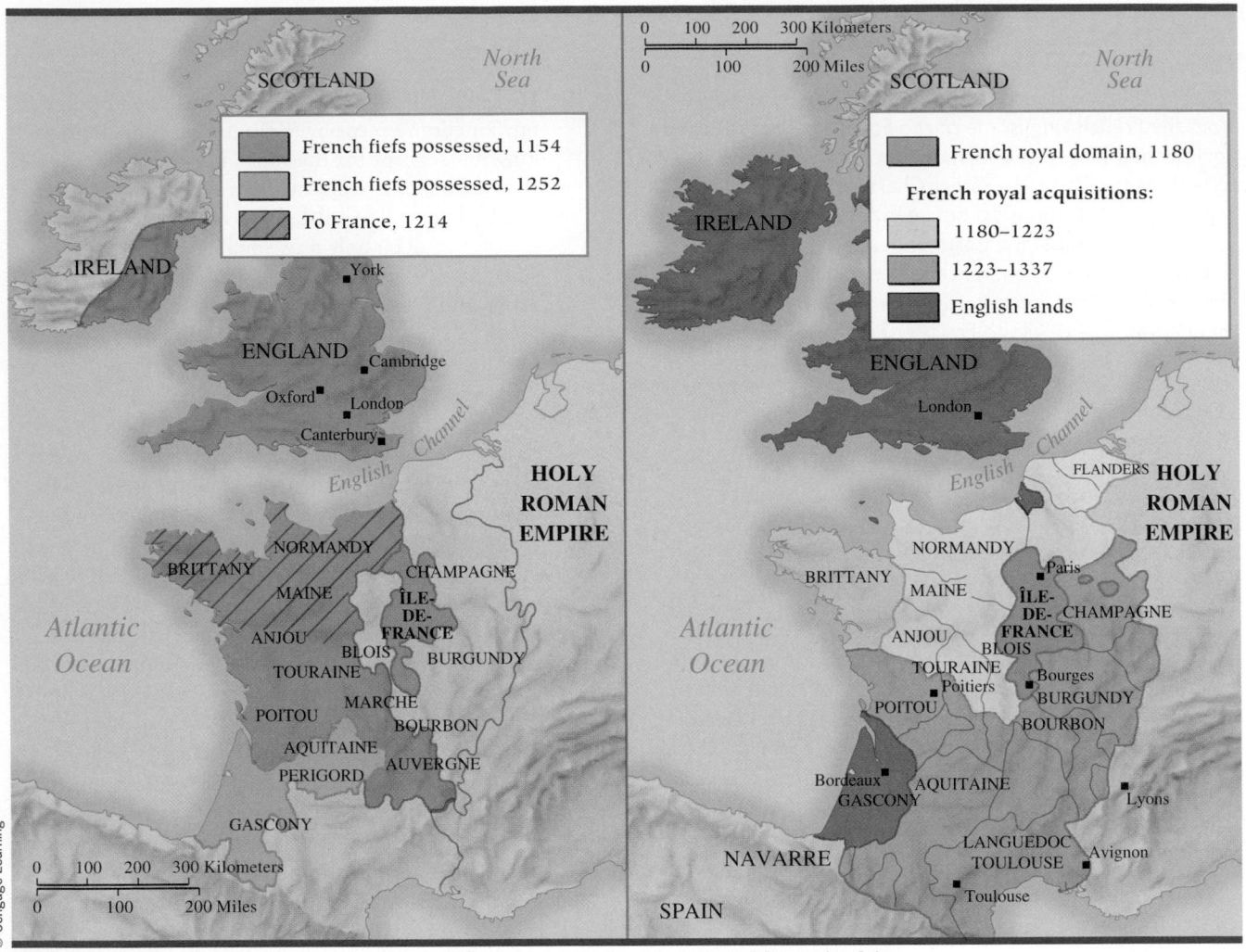

© Cengage Learning

MAP 10.1 England and France, 1154–1337: (*left*) England and Its French Holdings; (*right*) Growth of the French State. King Philip II Augustus of France greatly expanded the power of the Capetian royal family through his victories over the Plantagenet monarchy of England, which enabled Philip to gain control over much of north-central France.

How might the English Channel have made it more difficult for the English kings to rule their French possessions?

As kings of France, the Capetians were formally the overlords of the great lords of France, such as the dukes of Normandy, Brittany, Burgundy, and Aquitaine. In reality, however, many of the dukes were considerably more powerful than the Capetian kings. It would take the Capetian dynasty hundreds of years to create a truly centralized monarchical authority in France.

The reign of King Philip II Augustus (1180–1223) was an important turning point. Philip II waged war against the Plantagenet rulers of England, who also ruled the French territories of Normandy, Maine, Anjou, and Aquitaine, and was successful in gaining control of most of these territories (see Map 10.1). Through these conquests, Philip quadrupled the income of the French monarchy and greatly enlarged its power. To administer justice and collect royal revenues in his new territories, Philip appointed new royal officials, thus inaugurating a French royal bureaucracy.

Capetian rulers after Philip II continued to add lands to the royal domain. Although Philip had used military force, other kings used both purchase and marriage to achieve the same end. Much of the thirteenth century was dominated by Louis IX (1226–1270), one of the most celebrated of the medieval French kings. A deeply religious man, he was later canonized as a saint by the church, an unusual action regardless of the century. Louis was known for his attempts to bring justice to his people and ensure their rights. Sharing in the religious sentiments of his age, Louis played a major role in two of the later Crusades, but both were failures, and he met his death during an invasion of North Africa.

PHILIP IV AND THE ESTATES-GENERAL One of Louis's successors, Philip IV the Fair (1285–1314), was particularly effective in strengthening the French monarchy. The machinery of government became even more specialized. French kings going back to the early Capetians had possessed a household staff for running their affairs. Over time, however, this household staff was enlarged and divided into three groups to form three major branches of royal administration: a council for advice, a chamber of accounts for finances, and the *Parlement* (par-luh-MAHNH) or royal court (the French *Parlement* was not the same as the English Parliament). By the beginning of the fourteenth century, the Capetians had established an efficient royal bureaucracy.

Philip IV also brought a French parliament into being by summoning representatives of the three estates, or classes—the clergy (First Estate), the nobles (Second Estate), and the townspeople (Third Estate)—to meet with him. They did so in 1302, inaugurating the Estates-General, the first French parliament, although it had little real power. By the end of the thirteenth century, France was the largest, wealthiest, and best-governed monarchical state in Europe.

Christian Reconquest: The Spanish Kingdoms

Much of Spain had been part of the Islamic world since the eighth century. Muslim Spain had flourished in the Early Middle Ages. Córdoba became a major urban center with a population exceeding 300,000 people. Agriculture prospered, and Spain also became known for excellent leather, wool, silk, and paper. Beginning in the tenth century, however, the most noticeable feature of Spanish history was the weakening of Muslim power and the beginning of a Christian reconquest that lasted until the final expulsion of the Muslims at the end of the fifteenth century. The ***Reconquista*** (ray-con-KEES-tuh), as the Spaniards called it, became over a period of time a sacred mission to many of the Christian rulers and inhabitants of the peninsula.

By the eleventh century, a number of small Christian kingdoms in northern Spain were ready to take the offensive against the Muslims. Rodrigo Díaz de Vivar, known as El Cid ("The Master"), was the most famous military adventurer of the time. Unlike the Christian warriors of France, El Cid fought under either Christian or Muslim rulers. He carved out his own kingdom of Valencia in 1094 but failed to create a dynasty when it was reconquered by the Muslims after his death.

By the end of the twelfth century, the northern half of Spain had been consolidated into the Christian kingdoms of Castile, Navarre, Aragon, and Portugal, the last of which had emerged by 1179 as a separate kingdom (see Map 10.2). The southern half of Spain remained under the control of the Muslims.

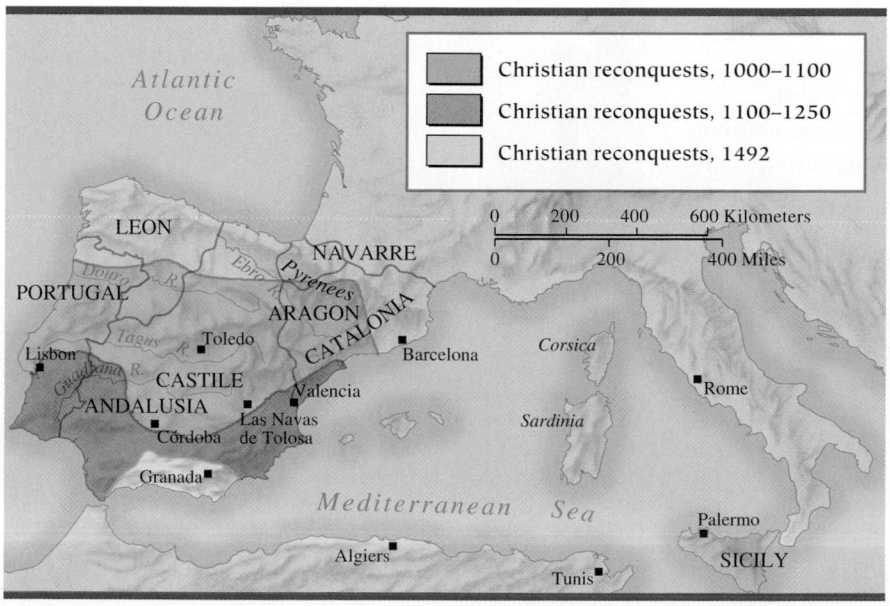

MAP 10.2 Christian Reconquests in the Western Mediterranean. Muslims seized most of Spain in the eighth century, near the end of the period of rapid Islamic expansion. In the eleventh century, small Christian kingdoms in the north began the *Reconquista*, finally conquering the last Moors near the end of the fifteenth century.

Q *How can you explain the roughly north-to-south conquest of the Muslim lands in Spain?*

© Cengage Learning

In the thirteenth century, Christian rulers took the offensive again in the reconquest of Muslim territory. Aragon and Castile had become the two strongest Spanish kingdoms, and Portugal had reached its modern boundaries. All three states made significant conquests of Muslim territory. Castile subdued most of Andalusia in the south, down to the Atlantic and the Mediterranean; at the same time, Aragon conquered Valencia. The crucial battle occurred in 1212 at Las Navas de Tolosa (lahss nah-vahss day tol-LOH-suh). Alfonso VIII of Castile (1155–1214) had amassed an army of 60,000 men and crushed the Muslim forces, leading to Christian victories over the next forty years. By the mid-thirteenth century, the Moors, as the Spanish Muslims were called, held only the kingdom of Granada, along the southeastern edge of the Iberian peninsula.

The Spanish kingdoms followed no consistent policy in the treatment of the conquered Muslim population. Muslim farmers continued to work the land but were forced to pay very high rents in Aragon. In Castile, King Alfonso X (1252–1284), who called himself the "King of Three Religions," encouraged the continued development of a cosmopolitan culture shared by Christians, Jews, and Muslims.

The Lands of the Holy Roman Empire: Germany and Italy

In the tenth century, the powerful dukes of Saxony became kings of the lands of the eastern Frankish kingdom (or Germany, as it came to be known). The best known of the Saxon kings of Germany was Otto I (936–973), who intervened in Italian politics and for his efforts was crowned emperor of the Romans by the pope in 962, reviving a title that had not been used since the time of Charlemagne. Otto's creation of a new "Roman Empire" in the hands of the eastern Franks (or Germans, as they came to be called) added a tremendous burden to the kings of Germany, who now took on the onerous task of ruling Italy as well.

In the eleventh century, German kings created a strong monarchy and a powerful empire by leading armies into Italy. To strengthen their power, German kings had come to rely on their ability to control the church and select bishops and abbots, whom they could then use as royal administrators. But the struggle between church and state during the reign of Henry IV (1056–1106) weakened the king's ability to use church officials in this way. The German kings also tried to bolster their power by using their position as emperors to exploit the resources of Italy. But this tended to backfire; many a German king lost armies in Italy in pursuit of a dream of empire, and no German dynasty demonstrates this better than the Hohenstaufens (hoh-en-SHTOW-fenz).

FREDERICK I Both Frederick I (1152–1190) and Frederick II (1212–1250), the two most famous members of the Hohenstaufen dynasty, tried to create a new kind of empire. Previous German kings had focused on building a strong German kingdom, to which Italy might be added as an appendage (see Map 10.3). Frederick I, known as Barbarossa (bar-buh-ROH-suh) (Redbeard) to the Italians, however, planned to get his chief revenues from Italy as the center of a "holy empire," as he called it (hence the name Holy Roman Empire). But his attempt to conquer northern Italy ran into severe difficulties. The pope opposed him, fearful that the emperor wanted to incorporate Rome and the Papal States into his empire. The cities of northern Italy, which had become used to their freedom, were also not willing to be Frederick's subjects. An alliance of these northern Italian cities called the Lombard League, with the support of the papacy, defeated the forces of Emperor Frederick at Legnano in 1176.

FREDERICK II Frederick II was the most brilliant of the Hohenstaufen rulers. King of Sicily in 1198, king of Germany in 1212, and crowned emperor in 1220, Frederick II

Musée Condé (Ms.722/1196, f.392r), Chantilly, France//© Bridgeman-Giraudon/Art Resource, NY

The Coronation of Frederick II. Shown here is the coronation of Frederick II of Germany as Holy Roman Emperor by Pope Honorius II in Rome on November 22, 1220. The pope agreed to the coronation after Frederick promised to lead a Crusade to the Holy Land, a promise that he took years to fulfill. This scene is taken from a fifteenth-century French manuscript on the monarchs of Europe.

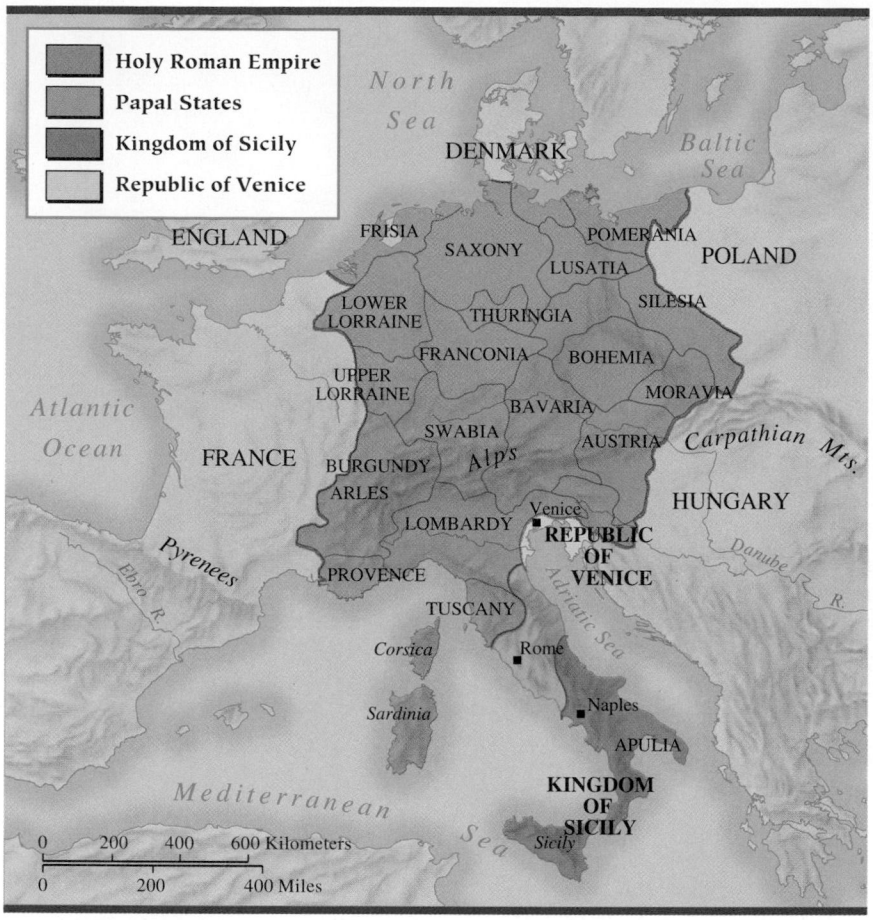

© Cengage Learning

MAP 10.3 The Holy Roman Empire in the Twelfth Century. The Hohenstaufen rulers Frederick I and Frederick II sought to expand the Holy Roman Empire to include all of Italy. Frederick II had only fleeting success: after his death, several independent city-states arose in northern Italy, while in Germany, the nobles had virtually free rein within their domains.

Q ***Why did the territorial conquests of the Holy Roman Empire cause alarm in the papacy?***

was a truly remarkable man who awed his contemporaries. Frederick had been raised in Sicily, with its diverse peoples, languages, and religions, and his court brought together a brilliant array of lawyers, poets, artists, and scientists. His main goal was to establish a strong centralized state in Italy dominated by his kingdom in Sicily. Frederick's major task was to gain control of northern Italy. In reaching to extend his power in Italy, he became involved in a deadly struggle with the popes, who realized that a single ruler of northern and southern Italy meant the end of papal secular power in central Italy. The northern Italian cities were also unwilling to give up their freedom. Frederick waged a bitter struggle in northern Italy, winning many battles but ultimately losing the war.

Frederick's preoccupation with the creation of an empire in Italy left Germany in confusion and chaos until 1273, when the major German princes, serving as electors, chose an insignificant German noble, Rudolf of Habsburg (HAPSburg), as the new German king. In choosing a weak king, the princes were ensuring that the German monarchy would remain impotent and incapable of reestablishing a centralized monarchical state. The failure of the Hohenstaufens had led to a situation in which his exalted majesty, the German king and Holy Roman Emperor, had no real power over either Germany or Italy. Unlike France, England, and even Spain, neither Germany nor Italy created a unified national monarchy in the Middle Ages. Both became geographic designations for loose confederations of hundreds of petty states under the vague direction of king or emperor. In fact, neither Germany nor Italy would become united until the nineteenth century.

Following the death of Frederick II, Italy fell into political confusion. While the papacy remained in control of much of central Italy, the defeat of imperial power left the cities and towns of northern Italy independent of any other authority. Gradually, the larger ones began to emerge as strong city-states. Florence assumed the leadership of Tuscany, and Milan, under the guidance of the Visconti family, took control of the Lombard region. With its great commercial wealth, the republic of Venice dominated the northeastern part of the peninsula.

New Kingdoms in Northern and Eastern Europe

The Scandinavian countries of northern Europe had little political organization before 1000, and it was not until around that time that the three Scandinavian kingdoms—Denmark, Norway, and Sweden (see Map 10.4)—emerged with a noticeable political structure. The three kingdoms were converted to Christianity by kings who believed that an organized church was a necessary accompaniment to an organized state. The adoption of Christianity, however, did not eliminate the warlike tendencies of the Scandinavians. Not only did the three kingdoms fight each other in the eleventh and twelfth centuries, but rival families were in regular conflict over the throne in each state. This period also witnessed the growth of a powerful noble landowning class. To the south, in eastern Europe, Hungary, which had been a Christian state since 1000, remained relatively stable throughout the High Middle Ages, but the history of Poland and Russia was far more turbulent. In the thirteenth century, eastern Europe was beset by two groups of invaders, the Teutonic Knights from the west and the Mongols from the east.

In the eleventh century, an independent Polish kingdom existed, but it had no natural frontiers. German settlers encroached on its territory on a regular basis, leading to considerable intermarriage between Slavs and Germans. During the thirteenth century, relations between the Germans and the Slavs of eastern Europe worsened due to the aggression of the Teutonic Knights. The Teutonic Knights had been founded near the end of the twelfth century to protect the Christian Holy Land. In the early thirteenth century, however, these Christian knights found greater opportunity to the east of Germany, where they attacked the pagan Slavs. East Prussia was given to the military order in 1226, and by the end of the thirteenth century, Prussia had become German and Christian as the pagan Slavs were forced to convert.

Central and eastern Europe had periodically been subject to invasions from fierce Asiatic nomads, including the Huns, Avars, Bulgars, and Magyars. In the thirteenth century, the Mongols burst onto the scene, causing far more disruption than earlier invaders.

© Cengage Learning

MAP 10.4 Northern and Eastern Europe, c. 1150. Acceptance of Christianity gave many northern and eastern European kingdoms greater control over their subjects. Warfare was common in the region: dynastic struggles occurred in Scandinavia, and the Teutonic Knights, based in East Prussia, attacked the pagan Slavs.

Q ***Which areas of northern and eastern Europe had large Slavic populations? (Look back at Map 8.4.)***

Impact of the Mongol Empire

The Mongols rose to power in Asia with stunning speed. They were a pastoral people in the region of modern-day Outer Mongolia organized loosely in clans and tribes, often warring with each other. This changed when one leader, Temuchin, unified the Mongol tribes and gained the title of Genghis Khan (c. 1162–1227), which means "universal ruler." From that time on, Genghis Khan created a powerful military force and devoted himself to fighting. "Man's highest joy," he remarked, "is in victory: to conquer one's enemies, to pursue them, to deprive them of their possessions, to make their beloved weep, to ride on their horses, and to embrace their wives and daughters."[2] Genghis Khan was succeeded by equally competent sons and grandsons.

In the thirteenth century, the Mongols exploded across the steppes of Asia. They advanced eastward, eventually conquering China and Korea. One of Genghis Khan's grandsons, Khubilai Khan (KOO-bluh KAHN), completed the conquest of China and established a new Chinese dynasty of rulers known as the Yuan. In 1279, Khubilai Khan moved the capital of China northward to Khanbaliq

© Cengage Learning

The Mongol Empire in the Thirteenth Century

(khahn-bah-LEEK) ("city of the Khan"), which would later be known by the Chinese name Beijing (bay-ZHING).

The Mongols also moved westward against the Islamic empire. Persia fell in 1233, and by 1258, the Mongols had conquered Baghdad and destroyed the Abbasid caliphate. In the 1230s, the Mongols also began moving into Europe. They conquered Russia, advanced into Poland and Hungary, and destroyed a force of Poles and Teutonic Knights in Silesia in 1241. At that point, the Mongol hordes turned back because of internal fighting; western and southern Europe thus escaped the wrath of the Mongols. Overall, the Mongols had little lasting impact in Europe, although their occupation of Russia had some residual effect.

The Development of Russia

The Kievan Rus state, which had formally become Christian in 987, prospered considerably afterward, reaching its high point in the first half of the eleventh century. Kievan society was dominated by a noble class of landowners known as the **boyars**. Kievan merchants maintained regular trade with Scandinavia to the north and the Islamic and Byzantine worlds to the south. But destructive civil wars and new invasions by Asiatic nomads caused the principality of Kiev to collapse, and the sack of Kiev by north Russian princes in 1169 brought an inglorious end to the first Russian state.

The fundamental civilizing and unifying force of early Russia was the Christian church. The Russian church imitated the liturgy and organization of the Byzantine Empire, whose Eastern Orthodox priests had converted the Kievan Rus to Christianity at the end of the tenth century. The Russian church became known for its rigid religious orthodoxy. Although Christianity provided a common bond between Russian and European civilization, Russia's religious development guaranteed an even closer affinity between the Russian and Byzantine civilizations.

In the thirteenth century, the Mongols conquered Russia and cut it off even more from western Europe. The Mongols were not numerous enough to settle the vast Russian lands but were content to rule directly an area along the lower Volga and north of the Caspian and Black Seas to Kiev and rule indirectly elsewhere. In the latter territories, Russian princes were required to pay tribute to the Mongol overlords.

One Russian prince soon emerged as more powerful than the others. Alexander Nevsky (NYEF-skee) (c. 1220–1263), prince of Novgorod, defeated a German invading army in northwestern Russia in 1242. His cooperation with the Mongols won him their favor. The khan, leader of the western part of the Mongol empire, rewarded Nevsky with the title of grand prince, enabling his descendants to become the princes of Moscow and eventually leaders of all Russia.

CHRONOLOGY Growth of the European Kingdoms

England	
Battle of Hastings	1066
William the Conqueror	1066–1087
Henry II, first of the Plantagenet dynasty	1154–1189
Murder of Thomas à Becket	1170
John	1199–1216
Magna Carta	1215
Edward I	1272–1307
First Parliament	1295
France	
Hugh Capet, first of the Capetian dynasty	987–996
Philip II Augustus	1180–1223
Louis IX	1226–1270
Philip IV	1285–1314
First Estates-General	1302
Spain	
El Cid in Valencia	1094–1099
Alfonso VIII of Castile	1155–1214
Establishment of Portugal	1179
Alfonso X of Castile	1252–1284
Germany, the Holy Roman Empire, and Italy	
Otto I	936–973
Henry IV	1056–1106
Frederick I Barbarossa	1152–1190
Lombard League defeats Frederick at Legnano	1176
Frederick II	1212–1250
Election of Rudolf of Habsburg as king of Germany	1273
Eastern Europe	
Alexander Nevsky, prince of Novgorod	c. 1220–1263
East Prussia given to the Teutonic Knights	1226
Mongol conquest of Russia	1230s

The Recovery and Reform of the Catholic Church

FOCUS QUESTION: What was at issue in the Investiture Controversy, and what effect did the controversy have on the church and on Germany?

In the Early Middle Ages, the Catholic Church had played a leading role in converting and civilizing first the Germanic invaders and later the Vikings and Magyars. Although highly successful, this effort brought challenges that undermined the spiritual life of the church itself.

The Problems of Decline

Since the eighth century, the popes had reigned supreme over the affairs of the Catholic Church. They had also come to exercise control over the territories in central Italy known as the Papal States; this kept the popes involved in political matters, often at the expense of their spiritual obligations. At the same time, the church became increasingly entangled in the evolving lord-vassal relationships. High officials of the church, such as bishops and abbots, came to hold their offices as fiefs from nobles. As vassals, they were obliged to carry out the usual duties, including military service. Of course, lords assumed the right to choose their vassals, even when those vassals included bishops and abbots. Because lords often selected their vassals from other noble families for political reasons, these bishops and abbots were often worldly figures who cared little about their spiritual responsibilities.

The monastic ideal had also suffered during the Early Middle Ages. Benedictine monasteries had sometimes been exemplary centers of Christian living and learning, but the invasions of Vikings, Magyars, and Muslims wreaked havoc with many monastic establishments. Discipline declined, and with it the monastic reputation for learning and holiness. At the same time, a growing number of monasteries fell under the control of local lords, as did much of the church. A number of people believed that the time for reform had come.

The Cluniac Reform Movement

Reform of the Catholic Church began in Burgundy in eastern France in 910 when Duke William of Aquitaine founded the abbey of Cluny. The monastery began with a renewed dedication to the highest spiritual ideals of the Benedictine rule and was fortunate in possessing a series of abbots in the tenth century who maintained these ideals. Cluny was deliberately kept independent from secular control. As Duke William stipulated in his original charter, "It has pleased us also to insert in this document that, from this day, those same monks there congregated shall be subject neither to our yoke, nor to that of our relatives, nor to the sway of the royal might, nor to that of any earthly power."[3]

The Cluniac reform movement sparked an enthusiastic response, first in France and eventually in all of western and central Europe. New monasteries were founded on Cluniac ideals, and existing monasteries rededicated themselves by adopting the Cluniac program. The movement also began to reach beyond monasticism and into the papacy itself, which was in dire need of help.

Reform of the Papacy

By the eleventh century, church leaders realized the need to free the church from the interference of lords in the appointment of church officials. This issue of **lay investiture**, the practice by which secular rulers both chose and invested their nominees to church offices with the symbols of their office, was dramatically taken up by the greatest of the reform popes of the eleventh century, Gregory VII (1073–1085).

Elected pope in 1073, Gregory was convinced that he had been chosen by God to reform the church. In pursuit of those aims, Gregory claimed that he, as pope, was God's "vicar on earth" and that the pope's authority extended over all Christians, including rulers. Gregory sought the elimination of lay investiture. Only then could the church regain its freedom, by which Gregory meant the right to appoint its own clergy and run its own affairs. If rulers did not accept these "divine" commands, they could be deposed by the pope in his capacity as the vicar of Christ.

Gregory VII soon found himself in conflict with King Henry IV of Germany over these claims. For many years, German kings had appointed high-ranking clerics, especially bishops, as their vassals in order to use them as administrators. Without them, the king could not hope to maintain his own power vis-à-vis the powerful German nobles. In 1075, Pope Gregory issued a decree forbidding important clerics from receiving their investiture from lay leaders: "We decree that no one of the clergy shall receive the investiture with a bishopric or abbey or church from the hand of an emperor or king or of any lay person."[4] Henry had no intention of obeying a decree that challenged the very heart of his administration.

The struggle between Henry IV and Gregory VII, which is known as the Investiture Controversy, was one of the great conflicts between church and state in the High Middle Ages. It dragged on until 1122, when a new German king and a new pope achieved a compromise in the Concordat of Worms (WURMZ *or* VORMPS). Under this agreement, a bishop in Germany was first elected by church officials. After his election, the nominee paid homage to the king as his lord, who in turn invested him with the symbols of temporal office. A representative of the pope then invested the new bishop with the symbols of his spiritual office.

Christianity and Medieval Civilization

Focus Questions: What were the characteristics of the papal monarchy and the new religious orders of the High Middle Ages, and what role did women play in the religious life of the period? What was the church's attitude toward heretics and Jews during the High Middle Ages?

Christianity was an integral part of the fabric of medieval European society and the consciousness of Europe. Papal directives affected the actions of kings and princes alike, while Christian teaching and practices touched the economic, social, intellectual, cultural, and daily lives of all Europeans.

Growth of the Papal Monarchy

The popes of the twelfth century did not abandon the reform ideals of Gregory VII, but they were less dogmatic and more inclined to consolidate their power and build a strong administrative system. By the twelfth century, the Catholic Church possessed a clearly organized hierarchical structure. The pope and **papal curia** (staffed by high church officials known as cardinals, the pope's major advisers and administrators) were at the center of the administrative structure. Below them were the bishops; all of Christendom was divided into dioceses under their direction. Archbishops were in principle more powerful than the bishops, but at this time they were unable to exercise any real control over the internal affairs of the bishops' dioceses. In the thirteenth century, the Catholic Church reached the height of its political, intellectual, and secular power. The papal monarchy extended its sway over both ecclesiastical and temporal affairs, as was especially evident during the pontificate of Pope Innocent III (1198–1216). At the beginning of his pontificate, in a letter to a priest, Innocent made a clear statement of his views on papal supremacy:

> As God, the creator of the universe, set two great lights in the firmament of heaven, the greater light to rule the day, and the lesser light to rule the night, so He set two great dignities in the firmament of the universal church, . . . the greater to rule the day, that is, souls, and the lesser to rule the night, that is, bodies. These dignities are the papal authority and the royal power. And just as the moon gets her light from the sun, and is inferior to the sun . . . so the royal power gets the splendor of its dignity from the papal authority.[5]

Sacro Speco (S. Scolastica), Subiaco, Italy//© Scala/Art Resource, NY

Pope Innocent III. Innocent III was an active and powerful pope during the High Middle Ages. He approved the creation of the Franciscan and Dominican religious orders and inaugurated the Fourth Crusade.

Innocent's actions were those of a man who believed that he, as pope, was the supreme judge of European affairs. He forced King Philip Augustus of France to take back his wife and queen after Philip had tried to have the marriage annulled. The pope intervened in German affairs and installed his candidate as emperor. He compelled King John of England to accept the papal choice for the position of archbishop of Canterbury. To achieve his political ends, Innocent did not hesitate to use the spiritual weapons at his command, especially the **interdict**, which forbade priests to dispense the **sacraments** of the church in the hope that the people, deprived of the comforts of religion, would exert pressure against their ruler. Pope Innocent's interdict was so effective that it caused Philip to restore his wife to her rightful place as queen of France.

New Religious Orders and Spiritual Ideals

In the second half of the eleventh century and the first half of the twelfth, a wave of religious enthusiasm seized Europe, leading to a spectacular growth in the number of

A Miracle of Saint Bernard

Saint Bernard of Clairvaux has been called the most widely respected holy man of the twelfth century. He was an outstanding preacher, wholly dedicated to the service of God. His reputation reportedly influenced many young men to join the Cistercian order. He also inspired a myriad of stories dealing with his miracles.

A Miracle of Saint Bernard

A certain monk, departing from his monastery . . . , threw off his habit and returned to the world at the persuasion of the Devil. . . . Because sin is punished with sin, the deserter from his Order lapsed into the vice of lechery. He took a concubine to live with him, as in fact is done by many, and by her he had children.

But as God is merciful and does not wish anyone to perish, it happened that many years after, the blessed abbot [Saint Bernard] was passing through the village in which this same monk was living, and went to stay at his house. The renegade monk recognized him, and received him very reverently, and waited on him devoutly . . . but as yet the abbot did not recognize him.

On the morrow, the holy man said Matins and prepared to be off. But as he could not speak to the priest, since he had got up and gone to the church for Matins, he said to the priest's son, "Go, give this message to your master." Now the boy had been born [mute]. He obeyed the command and feeling in himself the power of him who had given it, he ran to his father and uttered the words of the Holy Father clearly and exactly. His father, on hearing his son's voice for the first time, wept for joy, and made him repeat the same words . . . and he asked what the abbot had done to him. "He did nothing to me," said the boy, "except to say, 'Go and say this to your father.'"

At so evident a miracle the priest repented, and hastened after the holy man and fell at his feet saying, "My Lord and Father, I was your monk so-and-so, and at such-and-such a time I ran away from your monastery. I ask your Paternity to allow me to return with you to the monastery, for in your coming God has visited my heart." The saint replied unto him, "Wait for me here, and I will come back quickly when I have done my business, and I will take you with me." But the priest, fearing death (which he had not done before), answered, "Lord, I am afraid of dying before then." But the saint replied, "Know this for certain, that if you die in this condition, and in this resolve, you will find yourself a monk before God."

The saint [eventually] returned and heard that the priest had recently died and been buried. He ordered the tomb to be opened. And when they asked him what he wanted to do, he said, "I want to see if he is lying as a monk or a clerk in his tomb." "As a clerk," they said; "we buried him in his secular habit." But when they had dug up the earth, they found that he was not in the clothes in which they had buried him; but he appeared in all points, tonsure and habit, as a monk. And they all praised God.

Q What does this story illustrate about the nature of a medieval "holy man"?

Source: From *A History of Medieval Europe*, 2nd ed., by R. H. C. Davis (London: Longman Group, 1988) pp. 265–66. Copyright © 1957, 1988 by Longman Group UK Limited. Reprinted by permission of Pearson Education Ltd.

monasteries and the emergence of new monastic orders. Most important was the Cistercian (sis-TUR-shun) order, founded in 1098 by a group of monks dissatisfied with the lack of strict discipline at their Benedictine monastery. Cistercian monasticism spread rapidly from southern France into the rest of Europe.

The Cistercians were strict. They ate a simple diet and possessed only a single robe each. All decorations were eliminated from their churches and monastic buildings. More time for prayer and manual labor was provided by shortening the number of hours spent at religious services. The Cistercians played a major role in developing a new, activist spiritual model for twelfth-century Europe. A Benedictine monk often spent hours in prayer to honor God; the Cistercian ideal had a different emphasis: "Arise, soldier of Christ, arise! Get up off the ground and return to the battle from which you have fled! Fight more boldly after your flight, and triumph in glory!"[6] These were the words of Saint Bernard of Clairvaux (klair-VOH) (1090–1153), who more than any other person embodied the new spiritual ideal of Cistercian monasticism (see the box above).

© Musée de l'Université Catholique, Angers, Photo: Jean-Luc Ollivier, Paris, France/Archives Charmet/The Bridgeman Art Library

A Group of Nuns. Although still viewed by the medieval church as inferior to men, women were as susceptible to the spiritual fervor of the twelfth century as men, and female monasticism grew accordingly. This manuscript illustration shows at the left a group of nuns welcoming a novice (dressed in white) to their order. At the right, a nun receives a sick person on a stretcher for the order's hospital care.

WOMEN IN RELIGIOUS ORDERS Women were active participants in the spiritual movements of the age. The number of women joining religious houses increased perceptibly with the spread of the new orders of the twelfth century. In the High Middle Ages, most nuns were from the ranks of the landed aristocracy. Convents were convenient for families unable or unwilling to find husbands for their daughters and for aristocratic women who did not wish to marry. Female intellectuals found them a haven for their activities. Most of the learned women of the Middle Ages, especially in Germany, were nuns. One of the most distinguished was Hildegard of Bingen (HIL-duh-gard of BING-un) (1098–1179), who became abbess of a convent at Disibodenberg in western Germany.

Hildegard shared in the religious enthusiasm of the twelfth century. Soon after becoming abbess, she began to write an account of the mystical visions she had experienced for years. "A great flash of light from heaven pierced my brain and . . . in that instant my mind was imbued with the meaning of the sacred books,"[7] she wrote in a description typical of the world's mystical literature. Eventually, she produced three books based on her visions. Hildegard gained considerable renown as a mystic and prophet, and popes, emperors, kings, dukes, and bishops eagerly sought her advice.

LIVING THE GOSPEL LIFE In the thirteenth century, two new religious orders emerged that had a profound impact on the lives of ordinary people. The friars were particularly active in the cities, where, by their example, they strove to provide a more personal religious experience. Like their founder, Saint Francis of Assisi (1182–1226), the Franciscan friars lived among the people, preaching repentance and aiding the poor. Their calls for a return to the simplicity and poverty of the early church, reinforced by their own example, were especially effective and made them very popular.

The Dominicans arose out of the desire of a Spanish priest, Dominic de Guzmán (gooz-MAHN) (1170–1221), to defend church teachings from heresy. The spiritual revival of the High Middle Ages had also led to the emergence of heretical movements, which became especially widespread in southern France. Unlike Francis, Dominic was an intellectual, and he was appalled by the growth of heresy within the church. He believed that a new religious order of men who lived lives of poverty but were learned and capable of preaching effectively would best be able to attack heresy.

MONASTICISM AND SOCIAL SERVICES Monastic life in all of its different forms was the most important component of religious life in the Middle Ages. Monks and nuns performed a remarkable variety of tasks, including praying for themselves and others, copying manuscripts, maintaining libraries and schools, acting as missionaries to the heathen, preaching to the poor, and fighting heresy. But in an age when governments did not provide basic social services, monks and nuns also worked for society by performing a number of social welfare services that our govrnments provide today.

Monasteries often provided both food and clothing for the poor. Otto of Freising, a German writer of history in the twelfth century, declared, "There is always a pious, God-fearing friar sitting [at the gate] receiving all arriving guests, pilgrims, and poor people, as friendly and kind-hearted as Christ himself." Due to a shortage of inns, monasteries also provided refuge for pilgrims and other travelers. As the Rule of Saint Benedict noted, "All who arrive as guests are to be welcomed like Christ." Monks and nuns also took care of the sick. They planted herb gardens so that they could prepare the plant remedies that were commonly used in medieval medicine. In addition, monks and nuns ran hospitals, especially for poor people who could not receive care elsewhere. Unlike modern-day hospitals, medieval hospitals were primarily residences for the elderly, the terminally ill, or the blind. Separate quarters were provided for lepers. There were about two thousand leper houses in France in the thirteenth century, a good indication of the widespread nature of the disease.

Popular Religion in the High Middle Ages

We have witnessed the actions of popes, bishops, and monks. But what of ordinary clergy and laypeople? What were their religious hopes and fears? What were their spiritual aspirations?

The sacraments of the Catholic Church ensured that the church was an integral part of people's lives, from birth to death. There were (and still are) seven sacraments, administered only by the clergy. Sacraments—such as baptism and the **Eucharist** (the Lord's Supper)—were viewed as outward symbols of an inward grace (grace was God's freely given gift that enabled humans to be saved) and were considered imperative for a Christian's salvation. Therefore, the clergy were seen to have a key role in the attainment of salvation.

Other church practices were also important to ordinary people. Saints, it was believed, were men and women who, through their holiness, had achieved a special position in heaven, enabling them to act as intercessors before God. The saints' ability to protect poor souls enabled them to take on great importance at the popular level. Jesus's apostles were recognized throughout Europe as saints, but there were also numerous local saints who had special significance. New cults developed rapidly, particularly in the intense religious atmosphere of the eleventh and twelfth centuries. The English introduced Saint Nicholas, the patron saint of children, who remains instantly recognizable today through his identification with Santa Claus.

Of all the saints, the Virgin Mary, the mother of Jesus, occupied the foremost position in the High Middle Ages. Mary was viewed as the most important mediator with her son Jesus, the judge of all sinners. Moreover, from the eleventh century on, a fascination with Mary as Jesus's human mother became more evident. A sign of Mary's importance was the growing number of churches all over Europe that were dedicated to her in the twelfth and thirteenth centuries, including the cathedral of Notre-Dame in Paris.

Emphasis on the role of the saints was closely tied to the use of relics, which also increased noticeably in the High Middle Ages. **Relics** were usually the bones of saints or objects intimately connected to saints that were considered worthy of veneration by the faithful. A twelfth-century English monk began his description of the abbey's relics by saying, "There is kept there a thing more precious than gold, . . . the right arm of St. Oswald. . . . This we have seen with our own eyes and have kissed, and have handled with our own hands. . . . There are kept here also part of his ribs and of the soil on which he fell."[8] The monk went on to list additional relics possessed by the abbey, which were said to include two pieces of Jesus's swaddling clothes, pieces of Jesus's manger, and part of the five loaves of bread with which Jesus fed five thousand people. Because the holiness of the saint was considered to be inherent in his relics, these objects were believed to be capable of healing people or producing other miracles.

Voices of Protest and Intolerance

The desire for more personal and deeper religious experience, which characterized the spiritual revival of the High Middle Ages, also led people in directions hostile to the institutional church. From the twelfth century on, heresy—the holding of religious doctrines different from the orthodox teachings of the church as determined by church authorities—became a serious problem for the Catholic Church.

The best-known heresy of the twelfth and thirteenth centuries was Catharism (KA-thuh-riz-um). The Cathars (the word *Cathar* means "pure") were often called Albigensians (al-buh-JEN-see-unz) after the city of Albi, one of their strongholds in southern France. They believed in a dualist system in which good and evil were separate and distinct. Things of the spirit were good because they were created by God, the source of light; things of the world were evil because they were created by Satan, the prince of darkness. Humans, too, were enmeshed in dualism. Their souls, which were good, were trapped in material bodies, which were evil. According to the Cathars, the Catholic Church, itself a materialistic institution, had nothing to do with God and was essentially evil. There was no need to follow its teachings or recognize its authority. The Cathar movement gained valuable support from important nobles in southern France and northern Italy.

The spread of heresy in southern France alarmed the church authorities. Pope Innocent III appealed to the nobles of northern France for a **Crusade** (a military campaign in defense of Christianity) against the heretics. The Crusade against the Albigensians, which began in the summer of 1209 and lasted for almost two decades, was a bloody fight. Thousands of heretics (and innocents) were slaughtered, including entire populations of some towns. In Beziers, for example, seven thousand men, women, and children were massacred when they took refuge in the local church.

Southern France was devastated, but Catharism persisted, which caused the Catholic Church to devise a regular method for discovering and dealing with heretics. This

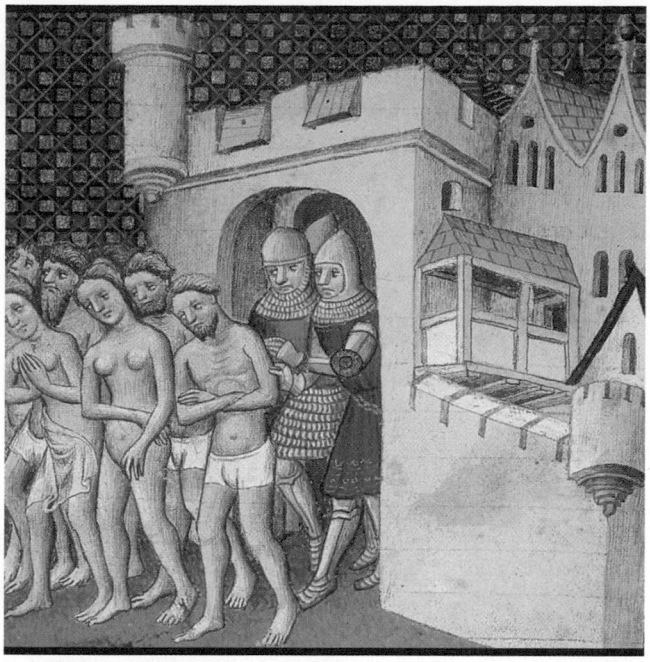

British Library Cotton Nero E II pt2 f.201, London/© British Library Board. All Rights Reserved/
The Bridgeman Art Library

Expulsion of Albigensian Heretics. In 1209, Pope Innocent III authorized a Crusade against the heretical Albigensians. In this medieval illustration, French knights are shown expelling Albigensian heretics from the town of Carcassonne near Albi, an Albigensian stronghold in southern France.

led to the emergence of the Holy Office, as the papal Inquisition was called, a formal court whose job it was to ferret out and try heretics. Anyone accused of heresy who refused to confess was considered guilty and was turned over to the secular authorities for execution. To the Christians of the thirteenth century, who believed that there was only one path to salvation, heresy was a crime against God and against humanity, and force was justified to save souls from damnation. The fanaticism and fear unleashed in the struggle against heretics were also used against others, especially the Jews.

PERSECUTION OF THE JEWS The Jews were the only religious minority in medieval Europe that was allowed to practice a non-Christian religion. But the religious enthusiasm of the High Middle Ages produced an outburst of intolerance against the supposed enemies of Christianity. After Crusades were launched against the Muslims starting in 1096, Christians took up the search for enemies at home, persecuting Jews in France and the Rhineland. Jews in Speyer, Worms, Mainz, and Cologne were all set upon by bands of Christian crusaders.

In the thirteenth century, in the supercharged atmosphere of fear created by the struggle with the heretics, Jews were persecuted more and more (see the box on p. 222). Friars urged action against these "murderers of Christ," contending that the Jews, having turned Jesus over to the Roman authorities, were responsible for his death, and organized the public burning of Jewish books. The Fourth Lateran Council in 1215 decreed that Jews must wear distinguishing marks, such as ribbons, yellow badges, and special veils and cloaks, to differentiate themselves from Christians. The same council encouraged the development of Jewish ghettos, neighborhoods built behind walled enclosures to isolate Jews from Christians. The persecutions and the new image of the hated Jew stimulated a tradition of anti-Semitism that proved to be one of Christian Europe's most insidious contributions to the Western heritage.

European kings, who had portrayed themselves as protectors of the Jews, had so fleeced the Jewish communities of their money by the end of the thirteenth century that they no longer had reason to resist the mob fury. Edward I expelled all Jews from England in 1290. The French followed suit in 1306. As the policy of expulsion spread into central Europe, most northern European Jews were driven into Poland.

INTOLERANCE AND HOMOSEXUALITY The climate of intolerance that characterized thirteenth-century attitudes toward Muslims, heretics, and Jews was also evident toward homosexuals. Although the church had condemned homosexuality in the Early Middle Ages, it had not been overly concerned with homosexual behavior, reflecting the attitude prevalent in the secular world. But by the thirteenth century, these tolerant attitudes had altered drastically. Some historians connect this change to the century's climate of fear and intolerance against any group that deviated from the standards of the now strictly Catholic majority. A favorite approach of the critics was to identify homosexuals with other detested groups. Homosexuality was portrayed as a regular practice of Muslims and such notorious heretics as the Albigensians. Between 1250 and 1300, what had been tolerated in most of Europe became a criminal act deserving of death.

CHRONOLOGY The Catholic Church in the High Middle Ages

Foundation of abbey of Cluny	910
Pope Gregory VII	1073–1085
Decree against lay investiture	1075
Pope Urban II	1088–1099
Founding of Cistercians	1098
Pope Innocent III	1198–1216
Start of Crusade against the Albigensians	1209
Fourth Lateran Council	1215

Treatment of the Jews

The development of new religious sensibilities in the High Middle Ages also had a negative side—the turning of Christians against their supposed enemies. Although the Crusades provide the most obvious example, Christians also turned on the "murderers of Christ," the Jews. As a result, Jews suffered increased persecution. These three documents show different sides of the picture. The first is Canon 68 of the decrees of the Fourth Lateran Council called by Pope Innocent III in 1215. The decree specifies the need for special dress, one of the ways Christians tried to separate Jews from their community. The second excerpt is a chronicler's account of the most absurd charge levied against the Jews—that they were guilty of the ritual murder of Christian children to obtain Christian blood for the Passover service (in which blood plays no part). This charge led to the murder of many Jews. The third document, taken from a list of regulations issued by the city of Avignon, France, illustrates the contempt Christian society held for the Jews.

Canon 68

In some provinces a difference in dress distinguishes the Jews or Saracens [Muslims] from the Christians, but in certain others such a confusion has grown up that they cannot be distinguished by any difference. Thus, it happens at times that through error Christians have relations with the women of Jews or Saracens, and Jews or Saracens with Christian women. Therefore, that they may not, under pretext of error of this sort, excuse themselves in the future for the excesses of such prohibited intercourse, we decree that such Jews and Saracens of both sexes in every Christian province and at all times shall be marked off in the eyes of the public from other peoples through the character of their dress. . . .

Moreover, during the last three days before Easter and especially on Good Friday, they shall not go forth in public at all, for the reason that some of them on these very days, as we hear, do not blush to go forth better dressed and are not afraid to mock the Christians who maintain the memory of the most holy Passion by wearing signs of mourning.

An Accusation of the Ritual Murder of a Christian Child by Jews

[The eight-year-old-boy] Harold, who is buried in the Church of St. Peter the Apostle, at Gloucester . . . , is said to have been carried away secretly by Jews, in the opinion of many, on Feb. 21, and by them hidden till March 16. On that night, on the sixth of the preceding feast, the Jews of all England coming together as if to circumcise a certain boy, pretend deceitfully that they are about to celebrate the feast [Passover] appointed by law in such case, and deceiving the citizens of Gloucester with the fraud, they tortured the lad placed before them with immense tortures. It is true no Christian was present, or saw or heard the deed, nor have we found that anything was betrayed by any Jew. But a little while after when the whole convent of monks of Gloucester and almost all the citizens of that city, and innumerable persons coming to the spectacle, saw the wounds of the dead body, scars of fire, the thorns fixed on his head, and liquid wax poured into the eyes and face, and touched it with the diligent examination of their hands, those tortures were believed or guessed to have been inflicted on him in that manner. It was clear that they had made him a glorious martyr to Christ, being slain without sin, and having bound his feet with his own girdle, threw him into the river Severn.

The Regulations of Avignon, 1243

We declare that Jews or whores shall not dare to touch with their hands either bread or fruit put out for sale, and that if they should do this they must buy what they have touched.

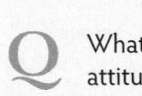

What do these documents reveal about Christian attitudes toward the Jews?

Source: From *The Jews of Angevin England*, Joseph Jacobs (London: David Nutt, 1893), p. 45.

The legislation against homosexuality commonly referred to it as a "sin against nature." This is precisely the argument developed by Thomas Aquinas (see Chapter 9), who formed Catholic opinion on the subject for centuries to come. In his *Summa Theologica*, Aquinas argued that because the purpose of sex was procreation, it could only legitimately take place in ways that did not exclude this possibility. Hence, homosexuality (like all other sexual practices that could not result in pregnancy) was "contrary to nature" and a deviation from the natural order established by God. This argument and laws prohibiting homosexual activity on pain of death remained the norm in Europe until the twentieth century.

The Crusades

Q FOCUS QUESTION: What were the reasons for the Crusades, and who or what benefited the most from the experience of the Crusades?

Another manifestation of the religious enthusiasm that seized Europe in the High Middle Ages was the series of Crusades mounted against the Muslims. These campaigns gave the revived papacy of the High Middle Ages yet another opportunity to demonstrate its influence over European society. The Crusades were a curious mix of God and warfare, two of the chief concerns of the Middle Ages.

Background to the Crusades

Although European civilization developed in relative isolation, it had never entirely lost contact with the lands and empires to the east. At the end of the eleventh century, that contact increased, in part because developments in the Islamic and Byzantine worlds prompted the first major attempt of the new European civilization to expand beyond Europe proper.

ISLAM AND THE SELJUK TURKS By the mid-tenth century the Islamic empire led by the Abbasid caliphate in Baghdad was in the process of disintegration. A Shi'ite dynasty known as the Fatimids had managed to conquer Egypt and establish the new city of Cairo as their capital. In establishing a Shi'ite caliphate, they became rivals to the Sunni caliphate of Baghdad, exacerbating the division in the Islamic world. Nevertheless, the Fatimid dynasty prospered and eventually surpassed the Abbasid caliphate as the dynamic center of the Islamic world. The Fatimids created a strong army by using nonnative peoples as mercenaries. One of these peoples, the Seljuk (SEL-jook) Turks, soon posed a threat to the Fatimids themselves.

The Seljuk Turks were a nomadic people from Central Asia who had been converted to Islam and flourished as military mercenaries for the Abbasid caliphate. Moving gradually into Persia and Armenia, they grew in number until by the eleventh century they were able to take over the eastern provinces of the Abbasid empire. In 1055, a Turkish leader captured Baghdad and assumed command of the Abbasid empire with the title of **sultan** ("holder of power"). By the second half of the eleventh century, the Seljuk Turks were exerting military pressure on Egypt and the Byzantine Empire. When the Byzantine emperor foolishly challenged the Turks, the latter routed the Byzantine army at Manzikert in 1071. In dire straits, the Byzantines turned to the west for help, setting in motion the papal pleas that led to the Crusades. To understand the complexities of the situation, however, we need to look first at the Byzantine Empire.

THE BYZANTINE EMPIRE The Macedonian dynasty of the tenth and eleventh centuries had restored much of the power of the Byzantine Empire; its incompetent successors, however, reversed most of the gains. After the Macedonian dynasty was extinguished in 1056, the empire was beset by internal struggles for power between ambitious military leaders and aristocratic families who attempted to buy the support of the great landowners of Anatolia by allowing them greater control over their peasants. This policy was self-destructive, however, because the peasant-warrior was the traditional backbone of the Byzantine state.

The growing division between the Catholic Church of the west and the Eastern Orthodox Church of the Byzantine Empire also weakened the Byzantine state. The Eastern Orthodox Church was unwilling to accept the pope's claim that he was the sole head of the church. This issue reached a climax when Pope Leo IX and the Patriarch Michael Cerularius (seer-oo-LAR-ee-uss), head of the Byzantine church, formally excommunicated each other in 1054, initiating a schism between the two great branches of Christianity that has not been healed to this day.

The Byzantine Empire faced external threats to its security as well. The greatest challenge came from the Seljuk Turks who had moved into Asia Minor, the heartland of the empire and its main source of food and manpower. After defeating Byzantine forces in 1071, the Turks advanced into Anatolia, where many peasants, already disgusted by their exploitation at the hands of Byzantine landowners, readily accepted Turkish control.

Another dynasty, however, soon breathed new life into the Byzantine Empire. The Comneni, under Alexius I Comnenus (kahm-NEE-nuss) (1081–1118), were victorious on the Greek Adriatic coast against the Normans, defeated the Pechenegs in the Balkans, and stopped the Turks in Anatolia. Lacking the resources to undertake additional campaigns against the Turks, Emperor Alexius I turned to the west for military assistance. The positive response to the emperor's request led to the Crusades. The Byzantine Empire lived to regret it.

The Early Crusades

The Crusades were based on the idea of a holy war against the infidel or unbeliever. The wrath of Christians was directed against the Muslims and had already found some expression in the attempt to reconquer Spain from the Muslims. At the end of the eleventh century, Christian Europe found itself with a glorious opportunity to attack the Muslims.

The immediate impetus for the Crusades came when the Byzantine emperor, Alexius I, asked Pope Urban II (1088–1099) for help against the Seljuk Turks. The pope saw a golden opportunity to provide papal leadership for a great cause: to rally the warriors of Europe for the liberation of Jerusalem and the Holy Land from the Muslim infidel. At the Council of Clermont in southern France near the end of 1095, Urban challenged Christians to take up their weapons against the infidel and join in a holy war to recover the Holy Land. The pope promised remission of sins: "All who die by the way, whether by land or by sea, or in battle against the pagans, shall have immediate remission of sins. This I grant them through the power of God with which I am invested."[9]

The initial response to Urban's speech reveals how appealing many people found this combined call to military arms and religious fervor. A self-appointed leader, Peter the Hermit, who preached of his visions of the Holy City of Jerusalem, convinced a large mob, most of them poor and many of them peasants, to undertake a Crusade to the east. One person who encountered Peter described him in these words: "Outdoors he wore a woolen tunic, which revealed his ankles, and above it a hood; he wore a cloak to cover his upper body, a bit of his arms, but his feet were bare. He drank wine and ate fish, but scarcely ever ate bread. This man, partly because of his reputation, partly because of his preaching, [assembled] a very large army."[10]

This so-called Peasants' Crusade or Crusade of the Poor comprised a ragtag rabble that moved through the Balkans, terrorizing natives and looting for their food and supplies. Their misplaced religious enthusiasm led to another tragic by-product as well, the persecution of the Jews, long depicted by the church as the murderers of Christ. As a contemporary chronicler described it, "They persecuted the hated race of the Jews wherever they were found." Two bands of peasant crusaders, led by Peter the Hermit, managed to reach Constantinople. Emperor Alexius wisely shipped them over to Asia Minor, where the Turks massacred the undisciplined and poorly armed mob.

THE FIRST CRUSADE Pope Urban II did not share the wishful thinking of the peasant crusaders but was more inclined to trust knights who had been well trained in the art of war. The warriors of western Europe, particularly France, formed the first "official" crusading armies. The knights who made up this first crusading host were motivated by religious fervor, but there were other attractions as well. Some sought adventure and welcomed a legitimate opportunity to pursue their favorite pastime—fighting. Others saw an opportunity to gain territory, riches, status, possibly a title, and even salvation—had the pope not offered a full remission of sins for those who participated in these "armed pilgrimages"? From the perspective of the pope and European monarchs, the Crusades offered a way to rid Europe of contentious young nobles who disturbed the peace and wasted lives and energy fighting each other. The Catholic Church had tried earlier to limit the ongoing bloodletting, but without a great deal of success. And merchants in many Italian cities relished the prospect of new trading opportunities in Muslim lands.

In the First Crusade, launched in 1096, three organized bands of noble warriors, most of them French, made their way to the east (see Map 10.5). This first crusading army probably numbered several thousand cavalry and as many as 10,000 foot soldiers. After the capture of Antioch in 1098, much of the crusading host proceeded down the coast of Palestine, evading the garrisoned coastal cities, and reached Jerusalem in June 1099. After a five-week siege, the Holy City was taken amid a horrible massacre of the inhabitants, men, women, and children (see the box on p. 226).

After further conquest of Palestinian lands, the crusaders ignored the wishes of the Byzantine emperor (who foolishly believed the crusaders were working on his behalf) and organized four crusader states (Edessa, Antioch, Tripoli, and Jerusalem). Because the crusader states were surrounded by Muslim enemies, they grew increasingly dependent on the Italian commercial cities for supplies from Europe. Some Italian cities, such as Genoa, Pisa, and especially Venice, became rich and powerful in the process.

THE SECOND CRUSADE The crusader states had a hard time maintaining themselves. Already by the 1120s, the Muslims had begun to strike back. In 1144, Edessa became the first of the four Latin states to be recaptured. Its fall led to renewed calls for another Crusade, especially from the monastic firebrand Saint Bernard of Clairvaux, who exclaimed, "Now, on account of our sins, the sacrilegious enemies of the cross have begun to show their faces. . . . What are you doing, you servants of the cross? Will you throw to the dogs that which is most holy? Will you cast pearls before swine?"[11] Bernard aimed his message at knights and even managed to enlist two powerful rulers, King Louis VII of France and Emperor Conrad III of Germany. Their Second Crusade, however, proved a total failure.

THE THIRD CRUSADE The Third Crusade was a reaction to the fall of the Holy City of Jerusalem in 1187 to Muslim forces under Saladin (SAL-uh-din). Now all of Christendom was ablaze with calls for a new Crusade in the east. Three major monarchs agreed to lead the crusading forces in person: Emperor Frederick Barbarossa of Germany, Richard I the Lionhearted of England (1189–1199), and Philip II

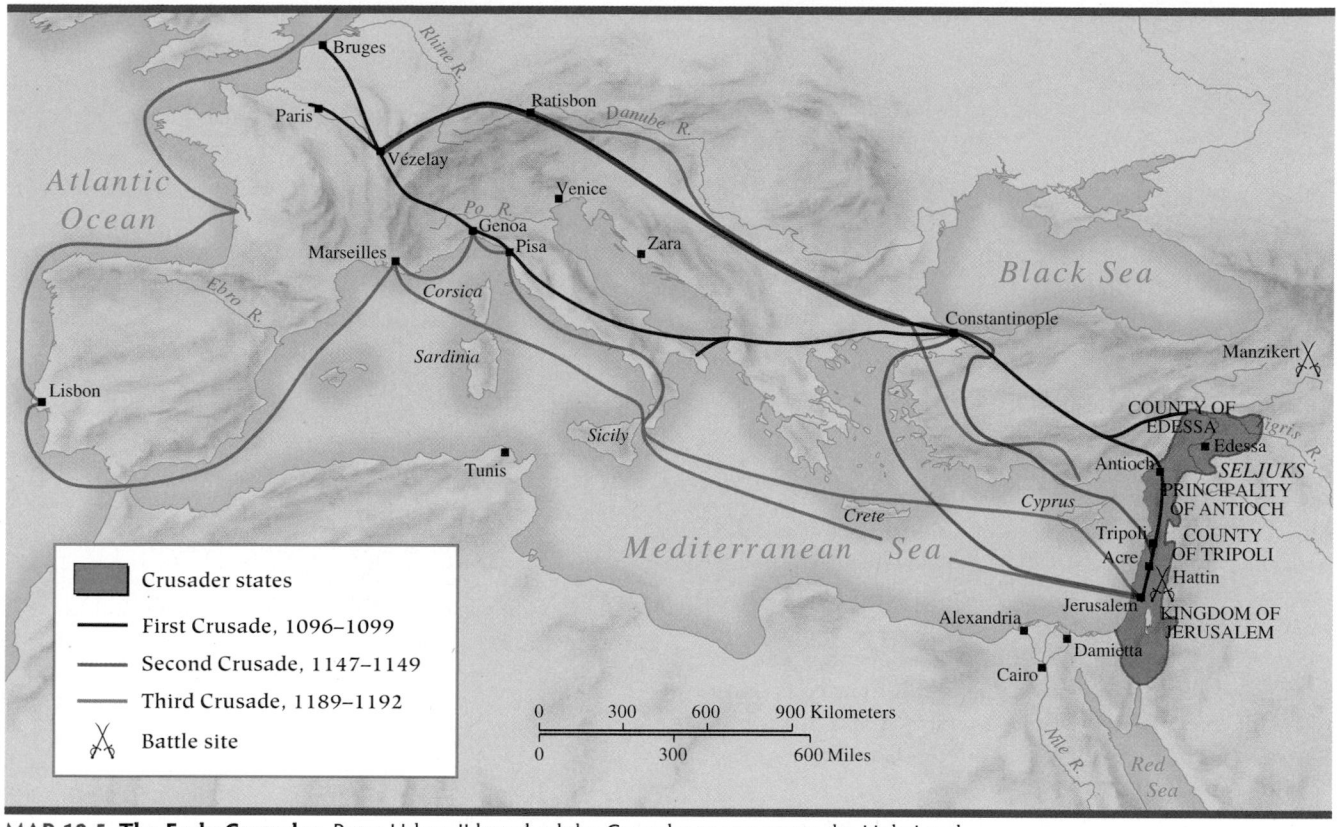

© Cengage Learning

MAP 10.5 The Early Crusades. Pope Urban II launched the Crusades to recapture the Holy Land from the "enemies of God," a call met with great enthusiasm in Europe. The fighters of the First Crusade massacred the inhabitants of Jerusalem and established four crusader states.

Q *In the Third Crusade, which countries sent crusaders by land and which by sea, and why would they choose these methods of travel?*

Bibliothèque de l'Arsenal, Paris/© Scala/Art Resource, NY

The First Crusade: The Capture of Jerusalem. Recruited from the noble class of western Europe, the first crusading army reached Constantinople in 1097. By 1098, the crusaders had taken Antioch. Working down the coast of Palestine, they captured Jerusalem in 1099. Shown here in a fifteenth-century French manuscript illustration is a fanciful re-creation of the capture and sack of Jerusalem. A crusader in the center is shown wearing the crusading cross on his back.

OPPOSING VIEWPOINTS

The Siege of Jerusalem: Christian and Muslim Perspectives

During the First Crusade, Christian knights laid siege to Jerusalem in June 1099. The first excerpt is taken from an account by Fulcher of Chartres, who accompanied the crusaders to the Holy Land. The second selection is from an account of the First Crusade by the Muslim historian Ibn al-Athir.

Fulcher of Chartres, *Chronicle of the First Crusade*

The Franks entered the city magnificently at the noonday hour on Friday, the day of the week when Christ redeemed the whole world on the cross. With trumpets sounding and with everything in an uproar, exclaiming: "Help, God!" they vigorously pushed into the city, and straightway raised the banner on the top of the wall. All the heathen, completely terrified, changed their boldness to swift flight through the narrow streets of the quarters. The more quickly they fled, the more quickly they put to flight.

Count Raymond and his men, who were bravely assailing the city in another section, did not perceive this until they saw the Saracens [Muslims] jumping from the top of the wall. Seeing this, they joyfully ran to the city as quickly as they could, and helped the others pursue and kill the wicked enemy.

Then some, both Arabs and Ethiopians, fled into the Tower of David; others shut themselves in the Temple of the Lord and of Solomon, where in the halls a very great attack was made on them. Nowhere was there a place where the Saracens could escape swordsmen.

On the top of Solomon's Temple, to which they had climbed in fleeing, many were shot to death with arrows and cast down headlong from the roof. Within this Temple, about ten thousand were beheaded. If you had been there, your feet would have been stained up to the ankles with the blood of the slain. What more shall I tell? Not one of them was allowed to live. They did not spare the women and children.

Account of Ibn al-Athir

In fact Jerusalem was taken from the north on the morning of Friday 22 Sha'ban 492/15 July 1099. The population was put to the sword by the Franks, who pillaged the area for a week. A band of Muslims barricaded themselves into the Oratory of David and fought on for several days. They were granted their lives in return for surrendering. The Franks honored their word, and the group left by night for Ascalon. In the Masjid al-Aqsa the Franks slaughtered more than 70,000 people, among them a large number of Imams and Muslim scholars, devout and ascetic men who had left their homelands to live lives of pious seclusion in the Holy Place. The Franks stripped the Dome of the Rock of more than forty silver candelabra, each of them weighing 3,600 drams, and a great silver lamp weighing forty-four Syrian pounds, as well as a hundred and fifty smaller candelabra and more than twenty gold ones, and a great deal more booty. Refugees from Syria reached Baghdad in Ramadan, among them the qadi Abu sa'd al-Harawi. They told the Caliph's ministers a story that wrung their hearts and brought tears to their eyes. On Friday they went to the Cathedral Mosque and begged for help, weeping so that their hearers wept with them as they described the sufferings of the Muslims in that Holy City: the men killed, the women and children taken prisoner, the homes pillaged. Because of the terrible hardships they had suffered, they were allowed to break the fast.

Q What happened to the inhabitants of Jerusalem when the Christian knights captured the city? How do you explain the extreme intolerance and brutality of the Christian knights? How do these two accounts differ, and how are they similar?

Sources: Fulcher of Chartres, *Chronicle of the First Crusade*. From *The First Crusade: The Chronicle of Fulcher of Chartres and Other Source Materials*, 2nd ed., ed. Edward Peters (University of Pennsylvania Press, 1998), pp. 90–91. Account of Ibn al-Athir. From *Arab Historians of the Crusades*, ed. and trans. E. J. Costello. Berkeley: University of California Press, 1969.

Augustus, king of France. The crusaders, who finally arrived in the east in 1189, encountered nothing but problems. Frederick Barbarossa drowned while swimming in a local river, and his army quickly fell apart. The English and French arrived by sea and met with success against the coastal cities, where they had the support of their fleets, but when they moved inland, they failed miserably. Eventually, after Philip went home, Richard negotiated a settlement whereby Saladin agreed to allow Christian pilgrims free access to Jerusalem.

The Crusades of the Thirteenth Century

After the death of Saladin in 1193, Pope Innocent III initiated the Fourth Crusade. On its way to the east, the crusading army became involved in a dispute over the succession to the Byzantine throne. The Venetian leaders of the Fourth Crusade saw an opportunity to neutralize their greatest commercial competitor, the Byzantine Empire. Diverted to Constantinople, the crusaders sacked that great capital city in 1204 and declared the new Latin Empire of Constantinople. Not until 1261 did a Byzantine army recapture Constantinople. The Byzantine Empire had been saved, but it was no longer a great Mediterranean power. The restored empire now consisted only of the city of Constantinople and its surrounding territory along with some lands in Asia Minor. Though reduced in size, the empire limped along for another 190 years until its weakened condition finally enabled the Ottoman Turks to conquer it in 1453.

Despite the failures, the crusading ideal was not yet completely lost. In Germany in 1212, a youth known as Nicholas of Cologne announced that God had inspired him to lead a Children's Crusade to the Holy Land. Thousands of young people joined Nicholas and made their way down the Rhine and across the Alps to Italy, where the pope told them to go home. Most tried to do so.

Four more Crusades of adult warriors over the next half-century were no more successful. Finally, Europe's Christians grudgingly accepted that they were not to be the guardians of the Holy Land.

Effects of the Crusades

Whether the Crusades had much effect on European civilization is debatable. The crusaders made little long-term impact in Asia Minor and the Middle East, where the only visible remnants of their conquests were the castles they erected. Some broadening of perspective may have come from the exchange between cultures, but the interaction of Christian Europe with the Muslim world was actually both more intense and more meaningful in Spain and Sicily than in the Holy Land.

CHRONOLOGY The Crusades

Pope Urban II calls for a Crusade	1095
First Crusade	1096–1099
Fall of Edessa	1144
Second Crusade	1147–1149
Saladin's conquest of Jerusalem	1187
Third Crusade	1189–1192
Fourth Crusade—sack of Constantinople	1204
Latin Empire of Constantinople	1204–1261
Children's Crusade	1212
Fifth Crusade	1219–1221
Frederick II occupies Jerusalem (Sixth Crusade)	1228
First Crusade of Louis IX (Seventh Crusade)	1248–1254
Second Crusade of Louis IX (Eighth Crusade)	1270
Surrender of Acre and end of Christian presence in the Holy Land	1291

Did the Crusades help stabilize European society by removing large numbers of young warriors who would have fought each other in Europe? Some historians think so and believe that western monarchs established their control more easily as a result. There is no doubt that the Italian seaports, especially Genoa, Pisa, and Venice, benefited economically from the Crusades, but even without them, Italian merchants would have pursued new trade contacts with the world to the east.

The Crusades prompted side effects that would haunt European society for generations. The first widespread attacks on the Jews began with the Crusades. As some Christians argued, to undertake holy wars against infidel Muslims while the "murderers of Christ" ran free at home was unthinkable. The massacre of Jews became a regular feature of medieval European life.

CHAPTER SUMMARY

During the High Middle Ages, European society was dominated by a landed aristocracy whose primary function was to fight. These nobles built innumerable castles that gave a distinctive look to the countryside. Although lords and vassals seemed forever mired in endless petty conflicts, over time medieval kings began to exert a centralizing authority and inaugurated the process of developing new kinds of monarchical states. By the thirteenth century, European monarchs were solidifying their governmental institutions in pursuit of greater power. The nobles, who rationalized their warlike attitudes by calling themselves the defenders of Christian society, continued to dominate the medieval world politically, economically, and socially. But quietly and surely, within this world of castles and private power, kings gradually began to extend their public powers and developed the machinery of government that would enable them to become the centers of political authority in Europe. The actions of these medieval monarchs laid the foundation for the European kingdoms that in one form or another have dominated the European political scene ever since.

The power of both nobles and kings, however, was often overshadowed by the authority of the Catholic Church, perhaps the dominant institution of the High Middle Ages. The church shared in the challenge of new growth by reforming itself and striking out on a path toward greater papal power, both within the church and over European society. The High Middle Ages also witnessed a spiritual renewal that led to numerous and even divergent paths: expanded papal leadership, especially evident in the reign of Pope Innocent III; the development of centralized administrative machinery within the church that buttressed papal authority; and new dimensions to the religious life of the clergy and laity. A wave of religious enthusiasm in the twelfth and thirteenth centuries led to the formation of new religious orders that worked to provide for the needs of the people, especially their concern for achieving salvation. But there were also seeds of discontent and change. Dissent from church teaching and practices grew, leading to a climate of fear and intolerance as the church responded with inquisitorial procedures to enforce conformity to its teachings.

At the same time, the spiritual renewal of the High Middle Ages also gave rise to the crusading "holy warrior" who killed for God, thereby creating an animosity between Christians and Muslims that still has repercussions to this day. The economic, political, and religious growth of the High Middle Ages had given European society a new confidence that enabled it to look beyond its borders to the lands and empires of the east. Only a confident Europe could have undertaken the Crusades, the military effort to recover the Holy Land of the Near East from the Muslims. The Crusades gave the revived papacy of the High Middle Ages yet another opportunity to demonstrate its influence over European society. And yet, the Crusades ended ignominiously with the fall of the last crusading foothold in the east in 1291. By that time, more and more signs of troubles were appearing. As we shall see in the next chapter, the fourteenth century would prove to be a time of crisis for European civilization.

CHAPTER TIMELINE

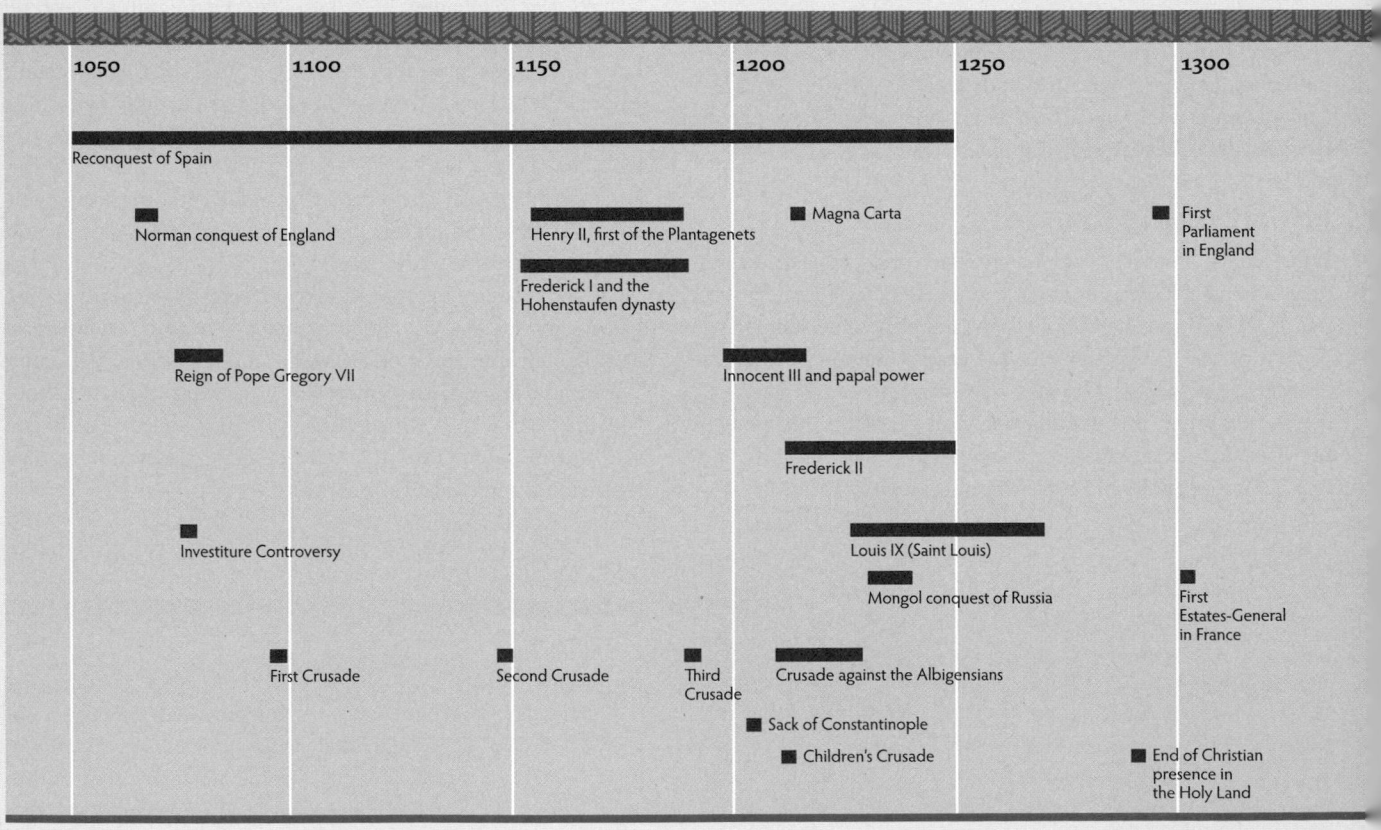

CHAPTER REVIEW

Upon Reflection

Q What are the similarities and dissimilarities in the development of England, France, and the German empire?

Q The medieval Catholic Church developed in the High Middle Ages at two levels, an institutional level and a popular religion level. What are the most important features of each level?

Q What were the motivations of the crusaders, and how successful were they?

Key Terms

common law (p. 207)
Reconquista (p. 211)
boyars (p. 215)
lay investiture (p. 216)
papal curia (p. 217)
interdict (p. 217)
sacraments (p. 217)
Eucharist (p. 220)
Relics (p. 220)
Crusade (p. 220)
sultan (p. 223)

Suggestions for Further Reading

THE MEDIEVAL STATES There are numerous works on the different medieval states. On England, see **R. Frame, *The Political Development of the British Isles, 1100–1400,*** 2nd ed. (Oxford, 1995). On France, see **M. Bull, *France in the Central Middle Ages, 900–1200*** (Oxford, 2003). On Germany, see **B. Arnold, *Princes and Territories in Medieval Germany,*** 2nd ed. (Cambridge, 2005). On Italy, see **P. Jones, *The Italian City-State: From Commune to Signoria*** (Oxford, 1997).

RELIGION IN MEDIEVAL EUROPE For good surveys of religion in medieval Europe, see **B. Hamilton, *Religion in the Medieval West,*** 2nd ed. (London, 2003), and **F. D. Logan, *A History of the Church in the Middle Ages*** (London, 2002).

THE PAPACY On the papacy in the High Middle Ages, see the general survey by **I. S. Robinson, *The Papacy*** (Cambridge, 1990). The papacy of Innocent III is covered in **J. C. Moore, *Pope Innocent III*** (New York, 2003).

MONASTICISM AND POPULAR RELIGION On monasticism, see **C. H. Lawrence, *Medieval Monasticism,*** 3rd ed. (London, 2000), a good general account. On Saint Francis, see **A. House, *Francis of Assisi: A Revolutionary Life*** (London, 2001). **S. Flanagan, *Hildegard of Bingen,*** 2nd ed. (London, 1998), is a good account of the twelfth-century mystic. For an introduction to popular religion in the eleventh and twelfth centuries, see **R. Brooke** and **C. N. L. Brooke, *Popular Religion in the Middle Ages*** (London, 1984).

DISSENT AND HERESY On dissent and heresy, see **M. Lambert, *Medieval Heresy,*** 3rd ed. (New York, 2002). The persecution of Jews in the thirteenth century can be examined in **R. Chazan, *The Jews of Medieval Western Christendom*** (Cambridge, 2006). The basic study on intolerance and homosexuality is **J. Boswell, *Christianity, Social Tolerance, and Homosexuality*** (Chicago, 1980).

THE CRUSADES For a detailed survey of the Crusades, see **C. Tyerman, *God's War: A New History of the Crusades*** (Cambridge, Mass., 2006). On the First Crusade, see **T. Asbridge, *The First Crusade: A New History*** (Oxford, 2004). The disastrous Fourth Crusade is examined in **J. Phillips, *The Fourth Crusade and the Sack of Constantinople*** (New York, 2004).

Visit the CourseMate website at www.cengagebrain.com for additional study tools and review materials for this chapter.

CHAPTER 11

© AAAC/Topham/The Image Works

A medieval illustration of Death as a reaper during the Black Death

The Later Middle Ages: Crisis and Disintegration in the Fourteenth Century

CHAPTER OUTLINE AND FOCUS QUESTIONS

A Time of Troubles: Black Death and Social Crisis

Q What impact did the Black Death have on the society and economy of Europe?

War and Political Instability

Q What major problems did European states face in the fourteenth century?

The Decline of the Church

Q How and why did the authority and prestige of the papacy decline in the fourteenth century?

Culture and Society in an Age of Adversity

Q What were the major developments in art and literature in the fourteenth century? How did the adversities of the fourteenth century affect urban life?

CRITICAL THINKING

Q Make an argument either for or against the idea that climate and disease played a major role in producing social, economic, and political changes in the fourteenth century.

AS A RESULT of their conquests in the thirteenth and fourteenth centuries, the Mongols created a vast empire stretching from Russia in the west to China in the east. Mongol rule brought stability to the Eurasian trade routes; increased trade brought prosperity but also created avenues for the spread of flea-infested rats that carried bubonic plague to both East Asia and Europe. The mid-fourteenth century witnessed one of the most destructive natural disasters in history—the Black Death. One contemporary observer named Henry Knighton, a canon of Saint Mary-of-the-Meadow Abbey in Leicester, England, was simply overwhelmed by the magnitude of the catastrophe. Knighton began his account of the great plague with these words: "In this year [1348] and in the following one there was a general mortality of people throughout the whole world." Few were left untouched; the plague struck even isolated monasteries: "At Montpellier, there remained out of a hundred and forty friars only seven." Knighton was also stunned by the economic and social consequences of the Black Death. Prices dropped: "And the price of everything was cheap, because of the fear of death; there were very few who took any care for their wealth, or for anything else." Meanwhile, laborers were scarce, so their wages increased: "In the following autumn, one could not hire a reaper at a lower wage than eight pence with food, or a mower at less than twelve pence with food. Because of this, much grain rotted in the fields for lack of harvesting." So many people died that some towns were deserted and some villages disappeared altogether: "Many small villages and hamlets were completely deserted; there was not one house left in them, but all those who had lived in them were dead." Some people thought the end of the world was at hand.

Plague was not the only disaster in the fourteenth century. Signs of disintegration were everywhere: famine, economic depression, war, social upheaval, a rise in crime and violence, and a decline in the power of the universal Catholic Church. Periods of disintegration, however, are often fertile ground for change and new developments. Out of the dissolution of medieval civilization came a rebirth of culture that has come to be known as the Renaissance.

A Time of Troubles: Black Death and Social Crisis

FOCUS QUESTION: What impact did the Black Death have on the society and economy of Europe?

Well into the thirteenth century, Europe had experienced good harvests and an expanding population. By the end of the century, however, a succession of disastrous events had begun.

For one thing, there were noticeable changes in weather patterns as Europe entered a "little ice age." Shortened growing seasons and miserable weather conditions, including heavy storms and constant rain, led to widespread famine and hunger. The great famine of 1315–1317 in northern Europe began an all-too-familiar pattern, as is evident in this scene described by a contemporary chronicler:

> We saw a larger number of both sexes, not only from nearby places but from as much as five leagues away, barefooted and maybe even, except for women, in a completely nude state, together with their priests coming in procession at the Church of the Holy Martyrs, their bones bulging out, devoutly carrying bodies of saints and other relics to be adorned hoping to get relief.[1]

Some historians have pointed out that famine may have led to chronic malnutrition, which in turn contributed to increased infant mortality, lower birthrates, and higher susceptibility to disease because malnourished people are less able to resist infection. This, they argue, helps explain the high mortality of the great plague known as the Black Death.

The Black Death: From Asia to Europe

In the mid-fourteenth century, the disaster known as the Black Death struck Asia, North Africa, and Europe. Although there were several types of plague, the most common and most important form in the diffusion of the Black Death was bubonic plague, which was spread by black rats infested with fleas that were host to the deadly bacterium *Yersinia pestis*.

ROLE OF THE MONGOLS This great plague originated in Asia. After disappearing from Europe and the Middle East earlier in the Middle Ages, bubonic plague continued to haunt areas of southwestern China. In the early 1300s, rats accompanying Mongol troops spread the plague into central China and by 1331 to northeastern China. Overall, China's population may have declined from 120 million in the mid-fourteenth century to 80 million by 1400.

In the thirteenth century, the Mongols had brought much of the Eurasian landmass under a single rule, which in turn facilitated long-distance trade, particularly along the Silk Road (see Chapter 6), now dominated by Muslim merchants from Central Asia. The movement of people and goods throughout this Eurasian landmass also facilitated the spread of the plague.

In the 1330s, there were outbreaks of plague in central Asia; by 1339, it had reached Samarkand, a caravan stop on the Silk Road. From Central Asia, trading caravans carried the plague westward, to Caffa, on the Black Sea, in 1346, and Constantinople by 1347. Its arrival in the Byzantine Empire was noted by Emperor John VI, who lost a son: "Upon arrival in Constantinople she [the empress] found Andronikos, the youngest born, dead from the invading plague, which . . . attacked almost all the seacoasts of the world and killed most of their people."[2] By 1348, the plague had spread to Egypt and also to Mecca and Damascus and other parts of the Middle East.

The Black Death in Europe

The **Black Death** of the mid-fourteenth century was the most devastating natural disaster in European history, ravaging Europe's population and causing economic, social, political, and cultural upheaval (see the box on p. 232). Contemporary chroniclers lamented that parents attempted to flee, abandoning their children; one related the words of a child left behind: "Oh father, why have you abandoned me? . . . Mother, where have you gone?"[3] People were horrified by an evil force they could not understand and by the subsequent breakdown of all normal human relations.

Symptoms of bubonic plague included high fever, aching joints, swelling of the lymph nodes, and dark blotches caused by bleeding beneath the skin. Bubonic plague was

OPPOSING VIEWPOINTS

Causes of the Black Death: Contemporary Views

The Black Death was the most terrifying natural calamity of the Middle Ages and affected wide areas of Europe, North Africa, and Asia. People were often baffled by the plague, especially by its causes, and gave widely different explanations. The first selection is taken from the preface to the *Decameron* by the fourteenth-century Italian writer Giovanni Boccaccio (joh-VAH-nee boh-KAH-choh). The other selections are from contemporary treatises that offered widely different explanations for the great plague.

Giovanni Boccaccio, *Decameron*

In the year of Our Lord 1348 the deadly plague broke out in the great city of Florence, most beautiful of Italian cities. Whether through the operation of the heavenly bodies or because of our own iniquities which the just wrath of God sought to correct, the plague had arisen in the East some years before, causing the death of countless human beings. It spread without stop from one place to another, until, unfortunately, it swept over the West. Neither knowledge nor human foresight availed against it, though the city was cleansed of much filth by chosen officers in charge and sick persons were forbidden to enter it, while advice was broadcast for the preservation of health. Nor did humble supplications serve. Not once but many times they were ordained in the form of processions and other ways for the propitiation of God by the faithful, but, in spite of everything, toward the spring of the year the plague began to show its ravages.

On Earthquakes as the Cause of Plague

There is a fourth opinion, which I consider more likely than the others, which is that insofar as the mortality arose from natural causes its immediate cause was a corrupt and poisonous earthy exhalation, which infected the air in various parts of the world and, when breathed in by people, suffocated them and suddenly snuffed them out. . . .

It is a matter of scientific fact that earthquakes are caused by the exhalation of fumes enclosed in the bowels of the earth. When the fumes batter against the sides of the earth, and cannot get out, the earth is shaken and moves. I say that it is the vapor and corrupted air which has been vented—or so to speak purged—in the earthquake which occurred on St Paul's day, 1347, along with the corrupted air vented in other earthquakes and eruptions, which has infected the air above the earth and killed people in various parts of the world; and I can bring various reasons in support of this conclusion.

Herman Gigas on Well Poisoning

In 1347 there was such a great pestilence and mortality throughout almost the whole world that in the opinion of well-informed men scarcely a tenth of mankind survived. . . . Some say that it was brought about by the corruption of the air; others that the Jews planned to wipe out all the Christians with poison and had poisoned wells and springs everywhere. And many Jews confessed as much under torture: that they had bred spiders and toads in pots and pans, and had obtained poison from overseas; and that not every Jew knew about this wickedness, only the more powerful ones, so that it would not be betrayed. As evidence of this heinous crime, men say that the bags full of poison were found in many wells and springs, and as a result, in cities, towns and villages throughout Germany, and in fields and woods too, almost all the wells and springs have been blocked up or built over, so that no one can drink from them or use the water for cooking, and men have to use rain or river water instead. God, the lord of vengeance, has not suffered the malice of the Jews to go unpunished. Throughout Germany, in all but a few places, they were burnt. For fear of that punishment many accepted baptism and their lives were spared. This action was taken against the Jews in 1349, and it still continues unabated, for in a number of regions many people, noble and humble alike, have laid plans against them and their defenders, which they will never abandon until the whole Jewish race has been destroyed.

Q What were the different explanations for the causes of the Black Death? How do you explain the differences, and what do these explanations tell you about the level of scientific knowledge in the Later Middle Ages? Why do you think Jews became scapegoats?

Sources: Giovanni Boccaccio, *Decameron*. From *The Decameron* by Giovanni Boccaccio, trans. by Frances Winwar, pp. xxii–xxiv, xxviii–xxix. Reprinted by permission of The Limited Editions Club. Geoffrey de Meaux on Astrological Causes and On Earthquakes as the Cause of Plague. Herman Gigas on Well-Poisoning. From *The Black Death*, by Horrox (Ed, & Trans), Manchester University Press, Manchester, UK. Reprinted with permission.

actually the least toxic form of plague but nevertheless killed 50 to 60 percent of its victims. In pneumonic plague, the bacterial infection spread to the lungs, resulting in severe coughing, bloody sputum, and the relatively easy spread of the bacillus from human to human by coughing.

The plague reached Europe in October 1347 when Genoese merchants brought it from Caffa to the island of Sicily off the coast of Italy. The plague spread quickly, reaching southern Italy and southern France and Spain by the end of 1347 (see Map 11.1). Usually, the diffusion of the Black Death followed commercial trade routes. In 1348, the plague spread through France and the Low Countries and into Germany. By the end of that year, it had moved to England, ravaging it in 1349. By the end of 1349, the plague had reached Scandinavia. Eastern Europe and Russia were affected by 1351, although mortality rates were never as high there as they were in western and central Europe.

Mortality figures for the Black Death were incredibly high. Italy was hit especially hard. Its crowded cities suffered losses of 50 to 60 percent. In northern France, farming villages suffered mortality rates of 30 percent, while cities such as Rouen experienced losses as high as 40 percent. In England and Germany, entire villages simply disappeared. In Germany, of approximately 170,000

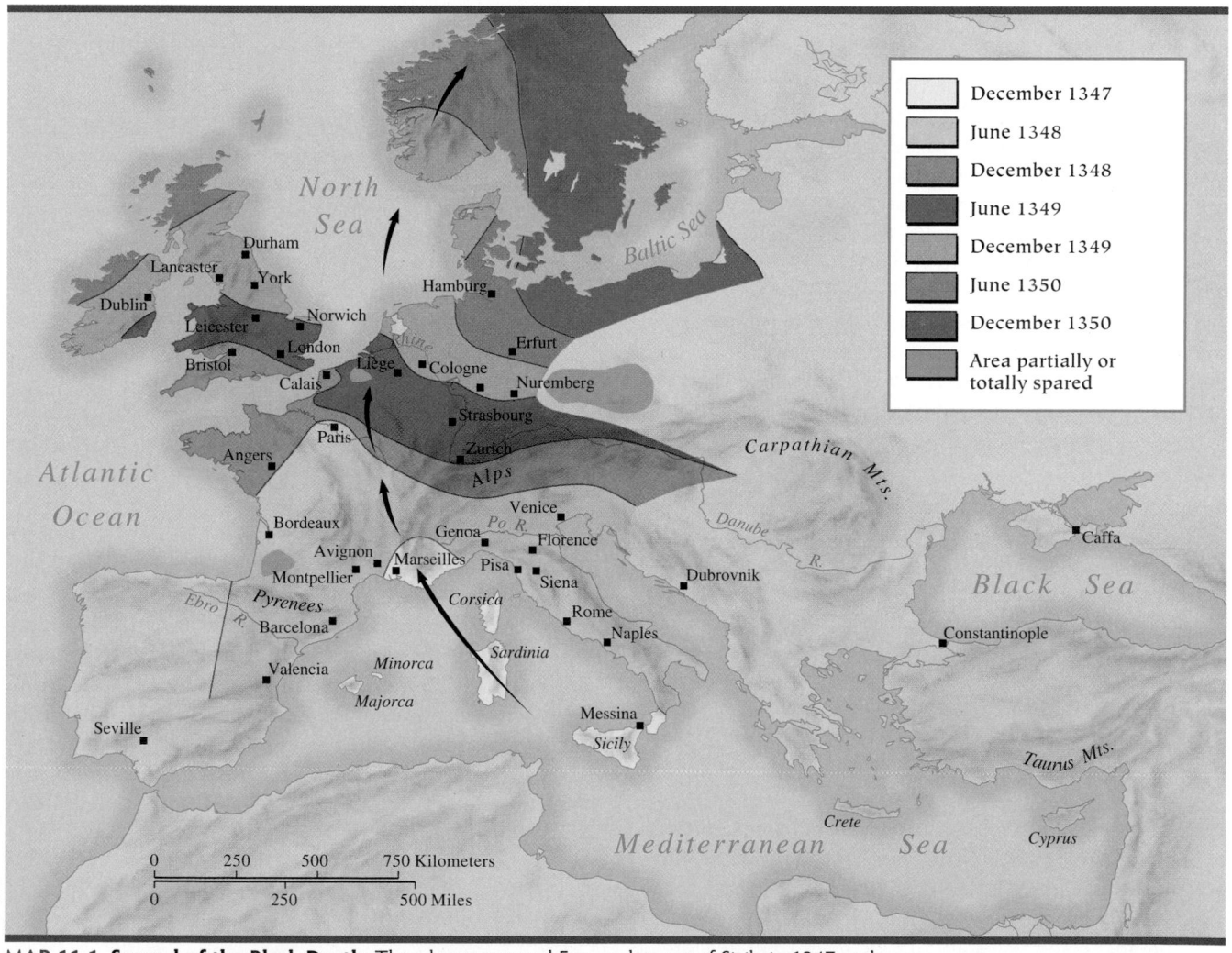

© Cengage Learning

MAP 11.1 Spread of the Black Death. The plague entered Europe by way of Sicily in 1347 and within four years had killed between one-quarter and one-half of the population. Outbreaks continued into the early eighteenth century, and the European population took two hundred years to return to the level it had reached before the Black Death.

Q *Is there a general pattern between distance from Sicily and the elapsed time before a region was infected with the plague?*

inhabited locations, 40,000 had disappeared by the end of the fourteenth century.

It has been estimated that the European population declined by 25 to 50 percent between 1347 and 1351. If we accept the recent scholarly assessment of a European population of 75 million in the early fourteenth century, this means a death toll of 19 to 38 million people in four years. And the plague did not end in 1351. There were major outbreaks again in 1361–1362 and 1369 and then recurrences every five or six to ten or twelve years, depending on climatic and ecological conditions, until the end of the fifteenth century. The European population thus did not begin to recover until around 1500 and took several generations after that to reattain thirteenth-century levels.

LIFE AND DEATH: REACTIONS TO THE PLAGUE The attempt to explain the Black Death and mitigate its harshness led to extreme sorts of behavior. To many people, the plague had either been sent by God as a punishment for humans' sins or been caused by the devil. Some resorted to extreme asceticism to cleanse themselves of sin and gain God's forgiveness. Such were the flagellants, whose movement became popular in 1348, especially in Germany. Groups of flagellants, both men and women, wandered from town to town, flogging each other with whips to win the forgiveness of God, whom they believed had sent the plague to punish humans for their sinful ways. One contemporary chronicler described a flagellant procession:

> The penitents went about, coming first out of Germany. They were men who did public penance and scourged themselves with whips of hard knotted leather with little iron spikes. Some made themselves bleed very badly between the shoulder blades and some foolish women had cloths ready to catch the blood and smear it on their eyes, saying it was miraculous blood. While they were doing penance, they sang very mournful songs about the nativity and the passion of Our Lord. The object of this penance was to put a stop to the mortality, for in that time . . . at least a third of all the people in the world died.[4]

The flagellants attracted attention and created mass hysteria wherever they went. The Catholic Church, however, became alarmed when flagellant groups began to kill Jews and attack clergy who opposed them. Pope Clement VI condemned the flagellants in October 1349 and urged the public authorities to crush them. By the end of 1350, most of the flagellant movement had been destroyed.

An outbreak of virulent **anti-Semitism** also accompanied the Black Death. Jews were accused of causing the plague by poisoning town wells. Although Jews were persecuted in Spain, the worst organized massacres, or

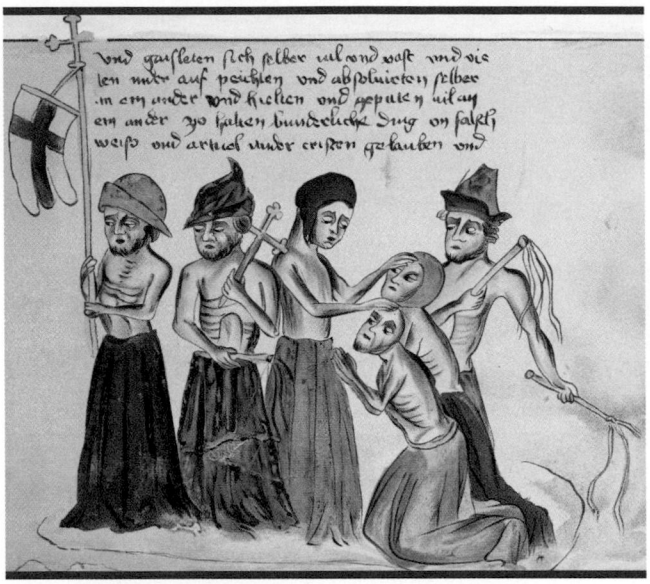

Bavarian State Library, Munich//© Interfoto/Alamy

The Flagellants. Reactions to the plague were extreme at times. Believing that asceticism could atone for humanity's sins and win God's forgiveness, flagellants wandered from town to town flogging themselves and each other with whips as in this illustration from a fifteenth-century German manuscript.

pogroms, against this helpless minority were carried out in Germany; more than sixty major Jewish communities in Germany had been exterminated by 1351. Many Jews fled eastward to Russia and especially to Poland, where the king offered them protection. Eastern Europe became home to large Jewish communities.

The prevalence of death because of the plague and its recurrences affected people in profound ways. Some survivors apparently came to treat life as something cheap and transient. Violence and violent death appeared to be more common after the plague than before. Postplague Europe also demonstrated a morbid preoccupation with death. In their sermons, priests reminded parishioners that each night's sleep might be their last. Tombstones were decorated with macabre scenes of naked corpses in various stages of decomposition with snakes entwined in their bones and their innards filled with worms.

Economic Dislocation and Social Upheaval

The population collapse of the fourteenth century had dire economic and social consequences. Economic dislocation was accompanied by social upheaval. Both peasants and noble landlords were affected by the demographic crisis of the fourteenth century. A serious labor shortage caused a dramatic rise in the price of labor. At Cuxham

Bibliothèque Nationale, Paris/© Art Media/HIP/The Image Works

Peasant Rebellion. The fourteenth century witnessed a number of revolts of the peasantry against noble landowners. Although the revolts often met with initial success, they were soon crushed. This fifteenth-century illustration shows nobles during the French *Jacquerie* of 1358 massacring the rebels in the town of Meaux, in northern France.

Manor in England, for example, a farm laborer who had received 2 shillings a week in 1347 was paid 7 in 1349 and almost 11 by 1350. At the same time, the decline in population depressed the demand for agricultural produce, resulting in falling prices for output. Because landlords were having to pay more for labor at the same time that their income from rents was declining, they began to experience considerable adversity and lower standards of living. In England, aristocratic incomes dropped more than 20 percent between 1347 and 1353.

Landed aristocrats responded by seeking to lower the wage rate. The English Parliament passed the Statute of Laborers (1351), which attempted to limit wages to preplague levels and to forbid the mobility of peasants as well. Although such laws proved largely unworkable, they did keep wages from rising as high as they might have in a free market. Overall, the position of landlords continued to deteriorate during the late fourteenth and early fifteenth centuries. At the same time, conditions for peasants improved, though not uniformly throughout Europe.

The decline in the number of peasants after the Black Death accelerated the process of converting labor services to rents, freeing peasants from the obligations of servile tenure and weakening the system of manorialism. But there were limits to how much the peasants could advance. Not only did they face the same economic hurdles as the lords, but the latter attempted to impose wage restrictions and reinstate old forms of labor service. New governmental taxes also hurt. Peasant complaints became widespread and soon gave rise to rural revolts.

PEASANT REVOLTS In 1358, a peasant revolt known as the *Jacquerie* (zhahk-REE) broke out in northern France. The destruction of normal order by the Black Death and the subsequent economic dislocation were important factors in causing the revolt, but the ravages created by the Hundred Years' War (see "War and Political Instability" later in this chapter) also affected the French peasantry. Both the French and English forces followed a deliberate policy of laying waste to peasants' fields while bands of mercenaries lived off the land by taking peasants' produce as well.

Peasant anger was also exacerbated by growing class tensions. Many aristocrats looked on peasants with utter contempt. One French aristocrat said, "Should peasants eat meat? Rather should they chew grass on the heath with the horned cattle and go naked on all fours." The peasants reciprocated this contempt for their so-called social superiors.

The outburst of peasant anger led to savage confrontations. Castles were burned and nobles murdered. Such atrocities did not go unanswered, however. The *Jacquerie* failed when the privileged classes closed ranks, savagely massacred the rebels, and ended the revolt.

The English Peasants' Revolt of 1381 was the most prominent of all. It was a product not of desperation but of rising expectations. After the Black Death, the condition of the English peasants had improved as they enjoyed greater freedom and higher wages or lower rents. Aristocratic landlords had fought back with legislation to depress wages and an attempt to reimpose old feudal dues. The most immediate cause of the revolt, however, was the monarchy's attempt to raise revenues by imposing a poll tax, a flat charge on each adult member of the population. Peasants in eastern England, the wealthiest part of the country, refused to pay the tax and expelled the collectors forcibly from their villages.

This action produced a widespread rebellion of both peasants and townspeople led by a well-to-do peasant called Wat Tyler and a preacher named John Ball. The latter preached an effective message against the noble class, as recounted by the French chronicler Jean Froissart (ZHAHNH frwah-SAR):

> Good people, things cannot go right in England and never will, until goods are held in common and there are no more peasants and gentlefolk, but we are all one and the same. In what way are those whom we call lords greater masters than ourselves? How have they deserved it? Why do they hold us in bondage? If we all spring from a single father and mother, Adam and Eve, how can they claim or prove that they are lords more than us, except by making us produce and grow the wealth which they spend?[5]

The revolt was initially successful as the rebels burned down the manor houses of aristocrats, lawyers, and government officers and murdered several important officials, including the archbishop of Canterbury. After the peasants marched on London, the young King Richard II (1377–1399) promised to accept the rebels' demands if they returned to their homes. They accepted the king's word and dispersed, but the king reneged and with the assistance of the aristocrats arrested hundreds of the rebels. The poll tax was eliminated, however, and in the end most of the rebels were pardoned.

REVOLTS IN THE CITIES Revolts also erupted in the cities. Commercial and industrial activity suffered almost immediately from the Black Death. Florence's woolen industry, one of the giants, produced 70,000 to 80,000 pieces of cloth in 1338; in 1378, it was yielding only 24,000 pieces. Bourgeois merchants and manufacturers responded to the decline in trade and production by attempting to restrict competition and resist the demands of the lower classes.

In urban areas, where capitalist industrialists paid low wages and managed to prevent workers from forming organizations to help themselves, industrial revolts broke out throughout Europe. Most famous was the revolt of the *ciompi* (CHAHM-pee) in Florence in 1378. In the 1370s, not only was the woolen industry depressed, but the wool workers saw their real wages decline when the coinage in which they were paid was debased. Their revolt won them some concessions from the municipal government, including the right to form guilds and be represented in the government. But their newly won rights were short-lived; authorities ended *ciompi* participation in the government by 1382.

Although the peasant and urban revolts sometimes resulted in short-term gains for the participants, the uprisings were quickly crushed and their gains lost. Accustomed to ruling, the established classes easily formed a united front and quashed dissent. Nevertheless, the rural and urban revolts of the fourteenth century ushered in an age of social conflict that characterized much of later European history.

War and Political Instability

FOCUS QUESTION: What major problems did European states face in the fourteenth century?

Famine, plague, economic turmoil, social upheaval, and violence were not the only problems of the fourteenth century. War and political instability must also be added to the list. And of all the struggles of the period, the most famous and the most violent was the Hundred Years' War (see Map 11.2).

The Hundred Years' War

In the thirteenth century, the English king still held one small possession in southwestern France, the duchy of Gascony. As duke of Gascony, the English king pledged loyalty as a vassal to the French king. But when King Philip VI (1328–1350) of France seized Gascony in 1337, the duke of Gascony—King Edward III (1327–1377) of England—declared war on Philip. The attack on Gascony was a convenient excuse; Edward had already laid claim to the throne of France after the senior branch of the Capetian dynasty had become extinct in 1328 and a cousin of the Capetians, the duke of Valois (val-WAH), had become king as Philip VI.

The war began in a burst of knightly enthusiasm. Trained to be warriors, knights viewed the clash of battle as the ultimate opportunity to demonstrate their fighting abilities. But this struggle would change the nature of warfare, for as it dragged on, the outcomes of battles were increasingly determined not by knights on horseback but by peasant foot soldiers. The French army of 1337, with its heavily armed noble cavalry, resembled its twelfth- and thirteenth-century forebears. Considering themselves the fighting elite, the mounted nobles looked with contempt on foot soldiers and crossbowmen because they were peasants or other social inferiors. The English army, however, had evolved differently and had included peasants as paid foot soldiers. Armed with pikes, many of these foot soldiers had also adopted the longbow, invented by the Welsh. The longbow had a more rapid speed of fire than the more powerful crossbow. Although the English also used heavily armed cavalry, they relied even more on large numbers of foot soldiers.

COURSE OF THE WAR Edward III's early campaigns in France were indecisive and achieved little. In 1346, Edward was forced to fight at Crécy (kray-SEE), just south of Flanders. The larger French army followed no battle plan but simply attacked the English lines in a disorderly fashion. The arrows of the English archers decimated the French cavalry. As the chronicler Froissart described it, "The English continued to shoot into the thickest part of the crowd, wasting none of their arrows. They impaled or wounded horses and riders, who fell to the ground in great distress, unable to get up again without the help of several men."[6] It was a stunning victory for the English.

The Battle of Crécy was not decisive, however. The English simply did not possess the resources to subjugate all France, and hostilities continued intermittently for another fifty years until a truce was negotiated in 1396, seemingly bringing an end to this protracted series of struggles between the French and English.

In 1415, however, the English king, Henry V (1413–1422), went back on the offensive at the very time the

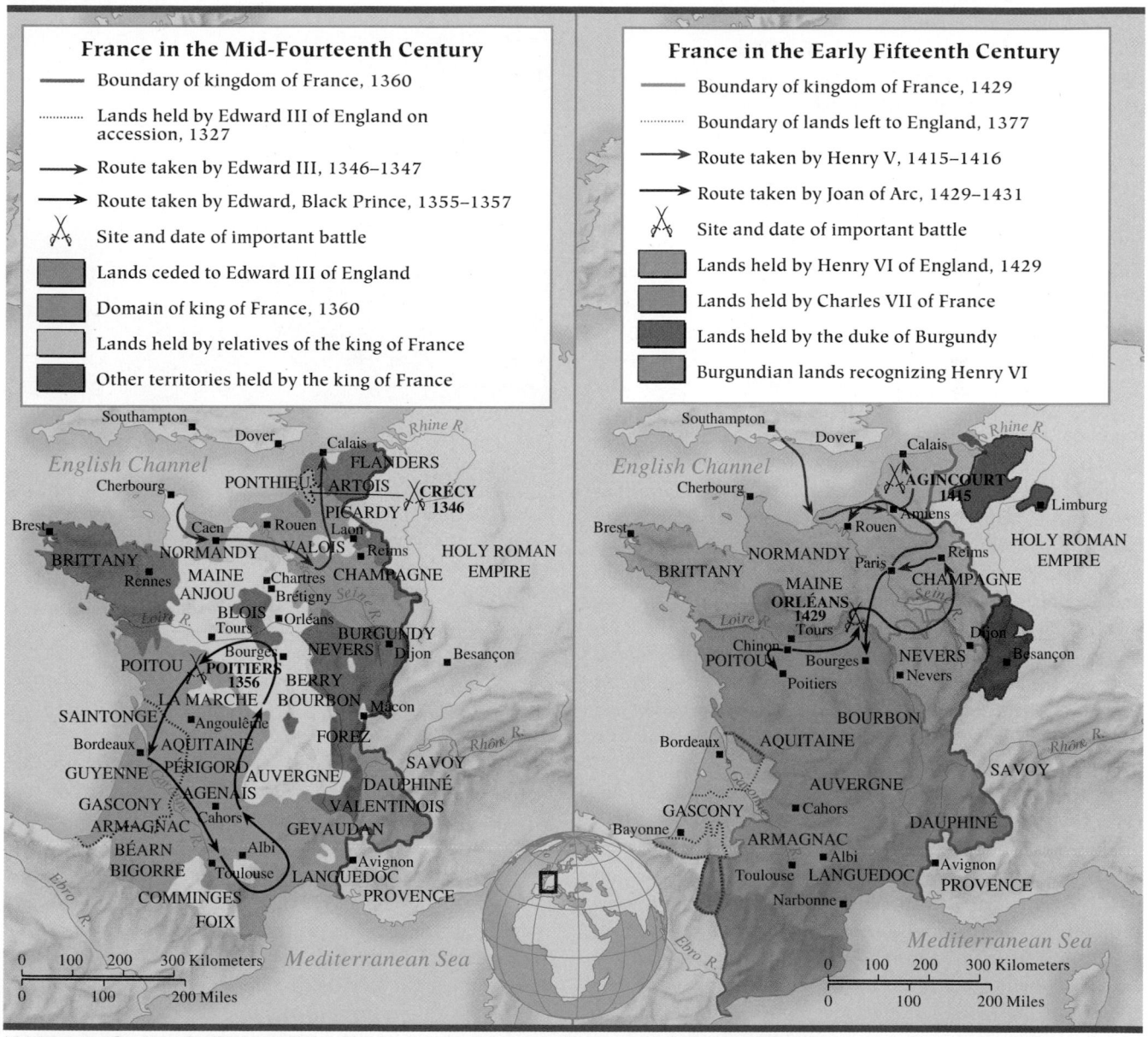

© Cengage Learning

MAP 11.2 The Hundred Years' War. This long, exhausting struggle began in 1337 and dragged on until 1453. The English initially gained substantial French territory, but in the later phases of the war, France turned the tide, eventually expelling the English from all Continental lands except the port of Calais.

Q ***What gains had the English made by 1429, and how do they correlate to proximity to England and the ocean?***

French were enduring a civil war as the dukes of Burgundy and Orléans (or-lay-AHN) competed to control the weak French king, Charles VI (1380–1422). In the summer of 1413, Paris exploded with bloody encounters. Taking advantage of the chaos, Henry V invaded France in 1415. At the Battle of Agincourt (AH-zhen-koor) (1415), the French suffered a disastrous defeat, and 1,500 French nobles died when the heavy, armor-plated French knights attempted to attack across a field turned to mud by heavy rain. Altogether, French losses were 6,000 dead; the English lost only three hundred men. Henry went on to reconquer Normandy and forge an alliance with the duke of Burgundy, making the English masters of northern France.

The seemingly hopeless French cause fell into the hands of Charles the dauphin (heir to the throne), the son of Charles VI. The dauphin (DOH-fen) governed the southern two-thirds of French lands from Bourges. Charles, weak and timid, was unable to rally the French against the English, who in 1428 had turned south and were besieging the city of Orléans to gain access to the valley of the Loire. The French monarch was saved, quite unexpectedly, by a French peasant woman.

JOAN OF ARC Joan of Arc was born in 1412 to well-to-do peasants in the village of Domrémy in Champagne. Deeply religious, Joan experienced visions and came to believe that her favorite saints had commanded her to free France and have the dauphin crowned king. In February 1429, Joan made her way to the dauphin's court, where her sincerity and simplicity persuaded Charles to allow her to accompany a French army to Orléans. Apparently inspired by the faith of the peasant girl, the French armies found new confidence in themselves and liberated Orléans, changing the course of the war. Within a few weeks, the entire Loire valley had been freed of the English. Joan had brought the war to a decisive turning point.

But she did not live to see the war concluded. Captured by the Burgundian allies of the English in 1430, Joan was turned over first to the English and then to the Inquisition on charges of witchcraft (see the box on p. 239). In the fifteenth century, spiritual visions were thought to be inspired either by God or the devil. Because Joan dressed in men's clothing, it was relatively easy to convince others that she was in league with the "prince of darkness." She was condemned to death as a heretic and burned at the stake in 1431. To the end, as the flames rose up around her, she declared "that her voices came from God and had not deceived her." Twenty-five years later, a new ecclesiastical court exonerated her of these charges, and five centuries later, in 1920, she was made a saint of the Roman Catholic Church (see the Film & History feature on p. 240). In the end, Joan of Arc's accomplishments proved decisive.

Musée de l'Histoire de France aux Archives Nationales, Paris, France/© Bridgeman-Giraudon/Art Resource, NY

Joan of Arc. Pictured here in a suit of armor, Joan of Arc is holding aloft a banner that shows Jesus and two angels. This portrait dates from the late fifteenth century; there are no portraits of Joan made from life.

END OF THE WAR Although the war dragged on for another two decades, defeats of English armies in Normandy and Aquitaine led to French victory. Important to the French success was the use of the cannon, a new weapon made possible by the invention of gunpowder. The Chinese had invented gunpowder in the eleventh century and devised a simple cannon by the thirteenth. The Mongols greatly improved this technology, developing more accurate cannons and cannonballs; both spread to the Middle East by the thirteenth century and to Europe by the fourteenth.

The death of England's best commanders and the instability of the English government under King Henry VI (1422–1461) also contributed to England's defeat. By 1453, the only part of France that was left in England's hands was the coastal town of Calais, which remained English for another century.

The Trial of Joan of Arc

Feared by the English and Burgundians, Joan of Arc was put on trial on charges of witchcraft and heresy after her capture. She was condemned for heresy and burned at the stake on May 30, 1431. This excerpt is taken from the records of Joan's trial, which presented a dramatic confrontation between the judges, trained in the complexities of legal questioning, and a nineteen-year-old woman who relied only on the "voices" of saints who gave her advice. In this selection, Joan describes what these voices told her to do.

The Trial of Joan of Arc

Afterward, she declared that at the age of thirteen she had a voice from God to help her and guide her. And the first time she was much afraid. And this voice came toward noon, in summer, in her father's garden. . . . She heard the voice on her right, in the direction of the church; and she seldom heard it without a light. This light came from the same side as the voice, and generally there was a great light. . . .

Asked what instruction this voice gave her for the salvation of her soul: she said it taught her to be good and to go to church often. . . . She said that the voice told her to come, and she could no longer stay where she was; and the voice told her again that she should raise the siege of the city of Orléans. She said moreover that the voice told her that she, Joan, should go to Robert de Baudricourt, in the town of Vaucouleurs of which he was captain, and he would provide an escort for her. And the said Joan answered that she was a poor maid, knowing nothing of riding or fighting. She said she went to an uncle of hers, and told him she wanted to stay with him for some time; and she stayed there about eight days. And she told her uncle she must go to the said town of Vaucouleurs, and so her uncle took her.

Then she said that when she reached Vaucouleurs she easily recognized Robert de Baudricourt, although she had never seen him before; and she knew him through her voice, for the voice had told her it was he. . . . The said Robert twice refused to hear her and repulsed her; the third time he listened to her and gave her an escort. And the voice had told her that it would be so.

How might you explain Joan's "voices"? How would you defend Joan against her judges?

Source: From *The Trial of Joan of Arc* translated by W. P. Barret. Copyright © 1932 by Gotham House, Inc.

Political Instability

The fourteenth century was a period of adversity for the internal political stability of European governments. Although government bureaucracies grew ever larger, at the same time the question of who should control the bureaucracies led to internal conflict and instability. Like the lord and serf relationship, the lord and vassal relationship based on land and military service was being replaced by a contract based on money. Especially after the Black Death, money payments called **scutage** were increasingly substituted for military service. Monarchs welcomed this development because they could now hire professional soldiers, who tended to be more reliable anyway. As lord and vassal relationships became less personal and less important, new relationships based on political advantage began to be formed, creating new avenues for political influence—and for corruption as well. Especially noticeable, as the landed aristocrats suffered declining rents and social uncertainties with the new relationships, was the formation of factions of nobles who looked for opportunities to advance their power and wealth at the expense of other noble factions and of their monarchs. Other nobles went to the royal courts, offering to serve the kings.

The kings had their own problems, however. By the mid-fifteenth century, reigning monarchs in many European

CHRONOLOGY The Hundred Years' War

Outbreak of hostilities	1337
Battle of Crécy	1346
Truce	1396
War renewed by Henry V	1415
Battle of Agincourt	1415
French recovery under Joan of Arc	1429–1431
End of the war	1453

FILM & HISTORY

JOAN OF ARC (1948)
THE MESSENGER: THE STORY OF JOAN OF ARC (1999)

Joan of Arc is one of history's best-known figures. Already by the time of her death she was a heroine, and in the nineteenth century, the French made her into an early nationalist. The Catholic Church recognized her as a saint in 1920, and a dozen films have been made about her short life. Born into a peasant family in Domrémy, France, Joan believed that, beginning at age thirteen, she had heard the voices of Saints Michael, Catherine, and Margaret telling her that she would play an important role in liberating France from the English invaders. Joan made her way to the court of the dauphin, the heir to the French throne, who agreed to let her accompany the royal army to Orléans, where she supposedly played a major role in the liberation of the city. In keeping with her prophecies, she then accompanied the dauphin to Reims, where he was crowned as King Charles VII. Although the king sought to end the war by negotiation, Joan continued to fight until she was captured by the Burgundians, allies of the English. Sold to the English, she was put on trail as a heretic in a French ecclesiastical court dominated by the English. Worn out by questioning, she renounced her voices but shortly afterward recanted and reaffirmed them. The English authorities then burned her at the stake as a relapsed heretic. Historians agree on many facts about Joan but differ in interpreting them; so too do movie producers.

Based on a play by Maxwell Anderson, the 1948 film version of Joan's story was directed by Victor Fleming. The movie follows the main historical facts that are known about Joan (played by Ingrid Bergman). Joan's voices are accepted as an important part of a spiritually determined young woman: "What I am commanded to do, I do." The film does deviate at times from the historical record: one member of the ecclesiastical court is shown opposing the trial, which did not happen. The dauphin (José Ferrer) is presented as a weak individual who nevertheless accepts Joan's offer of help. The movie ends in typical Hollywood fashion with a dramatic burning at the stake as Joan dies in a glorious blaze of heavenly sunbeams: "My victory is my martyrdom," she proclaims at the end.

Sierra Pictures/The Kobal Collection

Joan (Ingrid Bergman) prepares for battle.

Gaumont/The Kobal Collection/Jack English

Joan (Milia Jovovich) rides into battle.

(Continued)

(Film & History continued)

The Messenger, directed by Luc Besson, presents a more contemporary and fictionalized approach to Joan (Milia Jovovich). The brutality of war is rendered in realistically bloody detail. Joan's early life is reworked for the sake of the movie's theme. The movie introduces revenge as a possible motive by having Joan witness the rape and murder of her sister by an English mercenary—she must kill the English to avenge her sister's death. After this traumatic incident, her voices become more strident—God needs her for a higher calling, and she must answer that call. Joan becomes both a divinely and a madly driven person. Joan convinces the dauphin (John Malkovich) to support her, but after he is crowned, he is quite willing to have her captured by the enemy to get rid of her. After her capture, Joan is put on trial, which is one of the most accurate sequences of the film. But in another flight of fancy, the movie shows Joan wrestling mentally with a figure (Dustin Hoffman) who acts as her conscience. She is brought to the horrible recognition that perhaps she did not fight for God: "I fought out of revenge and despair." Besson raises issues that he does not resolve. Was Joan possibly mentally retarded or even insane? Were her visions a calling from God or a figment of her active imagination? Was she a devout, God-driven Christian or simply a paranoid schizophrenic? Nevertheless, whatever her motivations, she dies as heroically as Ingrid Bergman's Joan, although considerably more realistically, as the flames are shown igniting her body at the end of the movie.

countries were not the direct descendants of those ruling in 1300. The founders of these new dynasties had to struggle for position as factions of nobles vied to gain material advantages for themselves. As the fifteenth century began, there were two claimants to the throne of France, two aristocratic factions fighting for control of England, and three German princes struggling to be recognized as Holy Roman Emperor.

Fourteenth-century monarchs of old dynasties and new faced financial problems as well. The shift to using mercenary soldiers left monarchs perennially short of cash. Traditional revenues, especially rents from property, increasingly proved insufficient to meet their needs. Monarchs attempted to generate new sources of revenues, especially through taxes, which often meant going through parliaments. This opened the door for parliamentary bodies to gain more power by asking for favors first. Although unsuccessful in most cases, the parliaments simply added another element of uncertainty and confusion to fourteenth-century politics. Turning now to a survey of western and central European states (eastern Europe will be examined in Chapter 12), we can see how these disruptive factors worked.

Western Europe: England and France

In the fourteenth century, the fifty-year reign of Edward III (1327–1377) was important for the evolution of English political institutions. Parliament increased in prominence and developed its basic structure and functions during Edward's reign. Due to his constant need for money to fight the Hundred Years' War, Edward came to rely on Parliament to levy new taxes. In return for regular grants, Edward made several concessions, including a commitment to levy no direct tax without Parliament's consent and to allow committees of Parliament to examine the government accounts to ensure that the money was being spent properly. By the end of Edward's reign, Parliament had become an important component of the English governmental system.

During this same period, Parliament began to assume the organizational structure it has retained to this day. The Great Council of barons became the House of Lords and evolved into a body composed of the chief bishops and abbots of the realm and the aristocratic peers whose position in Parliament was hereditary. The representatives of the shires and boroughs, who were considered less important than the lay and ecclesiastical lords, held collective meetings to decide policy and soon came to be regarded as the House of Commons. Together, the House of Lords and the House of Commons constituted Parliament. Although the House of Commons did little beyond approving measures proposed by the Lords, during Edward's reign the Commons did begin the practice of drawing up petitions, which, if accepted by the Lords and king, became law.

After Edward III's death, England began to experience the internal instability of aristocratic factionalism that was racking other European countries. After Richard II was deposed and killed in 1399 by a baronial faction, the leader of the revolt, Henry of Lancaster, was made king. Although Henry IV (1399–1413) proved to be a competent ruler, factions of nobles rose to take advantage of the situation. England would soon be embroiled in a devastating series of civil wars known as the War of the Roses.

The Hundred Years' War left France prostrate. Depopulation, desolated farmlands, ruined commerce, and independent and unruly nobles made it difficult for the kings to assert their authority throughout the fourteenth century. In particular, the insanity of King Charles VI opened the door to rival factions of French nobles aspiring to power and wealth. The dukes of Burgundy and Orléans competed to control Charles and the French monarchy. Their struggles created chaos for the French government and the French people. Many nobles supported the Orléanist faction, while Paris and other towns favored the Burgundians. By the beginning of the fifteenth century, France seemed hopelessly mired in civil war.

The German Monarchy

England and France had developed strong national monarchies in the High Middle Ages. Nevertheless, by the end of the fourteenth century, they seemed in danger of disintegrating due to dynastic problems and the pressures generated by the Hundred Years' War. In contrast, the Holy Roman Empire, whose core consisted of the lands of Germany, had already begun to fall apart in the High Middle Ages. Northern Italy, which the German emperors had tried to include in their medieval empire, had been free from any real imperial control since the end of the Hohenstaufen dynasty in the thirteenth century. In Germany itself, the failure of the Hohenstaufens ended any chance of centralized monarchical authority, and Germany became a land of hundreds of states that varied in size and power. These included princely states, such as the duchies of Bavaria and Saxony; free imperial city-states (self-governing cities directly under the control of the Holy Roman Emperor rather than a German territorial prince), such as Nuremberg; modest territories of petty imperial knights; and ecclesiastical states, such as the archbishopric of Cologne. In the ecclesiastical states, a high church official, such as a bishop, archbishop, or abbot, served in a dual capacity as an administrative official of the Catholic Church and secular lord over the territories of the state. Although all of the rulers of these different states had some obligations to the German king and Holy Roman Emperor, more and more they acted independently.

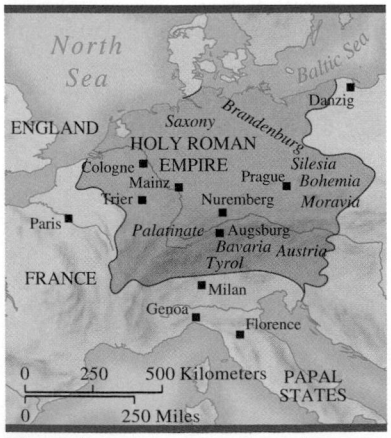

© Cengage Learning

The Holy Roman Empire in the Fourteenth Century

Because of its unique pattern of development in the High Middle Ages, the German monarchy had become established on an elective rather than a hereditary basis. This principle of election was standardized in 1356 by the Golden Bull issued by Emperor Charles IV (1346–1378). This edict stated that four lay princes and three ecclesiastical rulers would serve as electors with the legal power to elect the "king of the Romans and future emperor, to be ruler of the world and of the Christian people." "King of the Romans" was the official title of the German king; after his imperial coronation, he would also have the title of emperor.

In the fourteenth century, the electoral principle further ensured that kings of Germany were generally weak. Their ability to exercise effective power depended on the extent of their own family possessions. At the beginning of the fifteenth century, three emperors claimed the throne. Although the dispute was quickly settled, Germany entered the fifteenth century in a condition that verged on anarchy. Princes fought princes and leagues of cities. The emperors were virtually powerless to control any of them.

The States of Italy

By the fourteenth century, Italy, too, had failed to develop a centralized monarchical state. Papal opposition to the rule of the Hohenstaufen emperors in the thirteenth century had virtually guaranteed that. Moreover, southern Italy was divided into the kingdom of Naples, ruled by the house of Anjou, and Sicily, whose kings came from the Spanish house of Aragon. The center of the peninsula remained under the rather shaky control of the papacy. Lack of centralized authority had enabled numerous city-states in northern and central Italy to remain independent of any political authority.

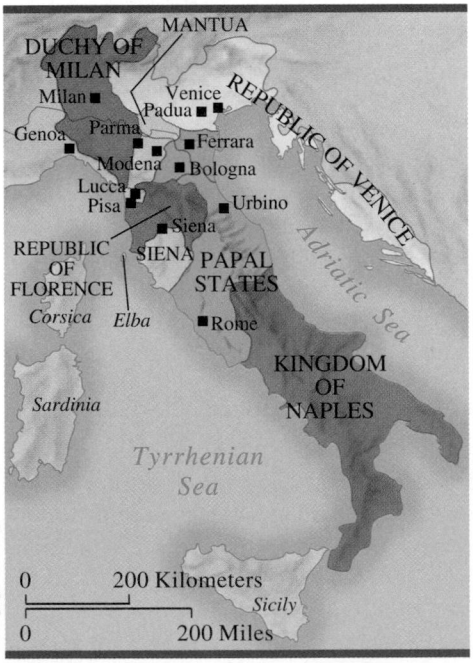

© Cengage Learning

The States of Italy in the Fourteenth Century

In the course of the fourteenth century, two general tendencies can be discerned in Italy: the replacement of republican governments by tyrants and the expansion of the larger city-states at the expense of the less powerful ones. Nearly all the cities of northern Italy began their existence as free communes with republican governments. But in the fourteenth century, intense internal strife led city-states to resort to temporary expedients, allowing rule by one man with dictatorial powers. Limited rule, however, soon became long-term despotism, as tyrants proved willing to use force to maintain power. Eventually, the tyrants tried to legitimize their power by purchasing titles from the emperor (still nominally ruler of northern Italy as Holy Roman Emperor). In this fashion, the Visconti became the dukes of Milan and the d'Este the dukes of Ferrara.

The other change of great significance was the development of regional entities as the larger states expanded at the expense of the smaller ones. By the beginning of the fifteenth century, three major states came to dominate northern Italy. Located in the fertile Po valley, where the chief trade routes from Italian coastal cities to the Alpine passes crossed, Milan was one of the richest city-states in Italy. Politically, it was also one of the most agitated until members of the Visconti family established themselves as hereditary dukes of Milan and extended their power over all of Lombardy. The republic of Florence dominated the region of Tuscany. In the course of the fourteenth century, a small but wealthy merchant oligarchy assumed control of the Florentine government, led the Florentines in a series of successful wars against their neighbors, and established Florence as a major territorial state in northern Italy. The other major northern Italian state was the maritime republic of Venice, which had grown rich from commercial activity in the eastern Mediterranean and northern Europe. Venice remained a stable political entity governed by a small oligarchy of merchant-aristocrats who had become extremely wealthy through their trading activities. Venice's commercial empire brought in enormous revenues and gave it the status of an international power. At the end of the fourteenth century, Venice embarked on the conquest of a territorial state in northern Italy to protect its food supply and its overland trade routes.

The Decline of the Church

Focus Question: How and why did the authority and prestige of the papacy decline in the fourteenth century?

The papacy of the Roman Catholic Church reached the height of its power in the thirteenth century. Theories of papal supremacy included a doctrine of "fullness of power" as the spiritual head of Christendom and claims to universal temporal authority over all secular rulers. But papal claims of temporal supremacy were increasingly out of step with the growing secular monarchies of Europe and ultimately brought the papacy into a conflict with the territorial states that it was unable to win.

Boniface VIII and the Conflict with the State

The struggle between the papacy and the secular monarchies began during the pontificate of Pope Boniface VIII (1294–1303). One major issue appeared to be at stake between the pope and King Philip IV (1285–1314) of France. Looking for a source of new revenues, Philip expressed the right to tax the French clergy. Boniface VIII claimed that the clergy of any state could not pay taxes to their secular ruler without the pope's consent. Underlying this issue, however, was a basic conflict between the claims of the papacy to universal authority over both church and state, which necessitated complete control over the clergy, and the claims of the king that all subjects, including the clergy, were under the jurisdiction of the crown and subject to the king's authority on matters of taxation and justice. In short, the fundamental issue was the universal sovereignty of the papacy versus the royal sovereignty of the monarch.

Boniface VIII asserted his position in a series of papal bulls or letters, the most important of which was *Unam Sanctam* (OO-nam SAHNK-tahm), issued in 1302. It was the strongest statement ever made by a pope on the supremacy of the spiritual authority over the temporal authority (see the box on p. 244). When it became apparent that the pope had decided to act on his principles by excommunicating Philip IV of France, the king sent a small contingent of French forces to capture Boniface and bring him back to France for trial. The pope was captured in Anagni, although Italian nobles from the surrounding countryside soon rescued him. The shock of this experience, however, soon led to the pope's death. Philip's strong-arm tactics had produced a clear victory for the national monarchy over the papacy—no later pope has dared renew the extravagant claims of Boniface VIII.

To ensure his position and avoid any future papal threat, Philip IV brought enough pressure on the college of cardinals to achieve the election of a Frenchman, Clement V (1305–1314), as pope. Using the excuse of turbulence in the city of Rome, the new pope took up residence in Avignon (ah-veen-YOHN), on the east bank of the Rhône River. Although Avignon was located in the Holy Roman Empire and was not a French possession, it lay just across the river from the possessions of King Philip IV and was French in culture.

Boniface VIII's Defense of Papal Supremacy

One of the most remarkable documents of the fourteenth century was the exaggerated statement of papal supremacy issued by Pope Boniface VIII in 1302 in the heat of his conflict with the French king Philip IV. Ironically, this strongest statement ever made of papal supremacy was issued at a time when the rising power of the secular monarchies made it increasingly difficult for its premises to be accepted. Not long after issuing it, Boniface was taken prisoner by the French. Although freed by his fellow Italians, the humiliation of his defeat led to his death a short time later.

Pope Boniface VIII, *Unam Sanctam*

We are compelled, our faith urging us, to believe and to hold—and we do firmly believe and simply confess—that there is one holy catholic and apostolic church, outside of which there is neither salvation nor remission of sins. . . . In this church there is one Lord, one faith and one baptism. . . . Therefore, of this one and only church there is one body and one head . . . Christ, namely, and the vicar of Christ, St. Peter, and the successor of Peter. For the Lord himself said to Peter, feed my sheep. . . .

We are told by the word of the gospel that in this His fold there are two swords—a spiritual, namely, and a temporal. . . . Both swords, the spiritual and the material, therefore, are in the power of the church; the one, indeed, to be wielded for the church, the other by the church; the one by the hand of the priest, the other by the hand of kings and knights, but at the will and sufferance of the priest. One sword, moreover, ought to be under the other, and the temporal authority to be subjected to the spiritual. . . .

Therefore if the earthly power err it shall be judged by the spiritual power; but if the lesser spiritual power err, by the greater. But if the greatest, it can be judged by God alone, not by man, the apostle bearing witness. A spiritual man judges all things, but he himself is judged by no one. This authority, moreover, even though it is given to man and exercised through man, is not human but rather divine, being given by divine lips to Peter and founded on a rock for him and his successors through Christ himself whom he has confessed; the Lord himself saying to Peter: "Whatsoever you shall bind, etc." Whoever, therefore, resists this power thus ordained by God, resists the ordination of God. . . .

Indeed, we declare, announce and define, that it is altogether necessary to salvation for every human creature to be subject to the Roman pontiff.

Q What claims did Boniface VIII make in *Unam Sanctam?* To what extent were these claims a logical continuation of the development of the papacy in the Middle Ages? If you were a monarch, why would you object to this papal bull?

Source: From *Select Historical Documents of the Middle Ages* by Ernest F. Henderson. London: George Bell & Sons, 1896.

© British Library (Ms Add 23923 f.2), London/The Bridgeman Art Library

Pope Boniface VIII. The conflict between church and state in the Middle Ages reached its height in the struggle between Pope Boniface VIII and Philip IV of France. This fourteenth-century miniature depicts Boniface VIII presiding over a gathering of cardinals.

The Papacy at Avignon (1305–1378)

The residency of the popes in Avignon for most of the fourteenth century led to a decline in papal prestige and growing antipapal sentiment. The city of Rome was the traditional capital of the universal church. The pope was the bishop of Rome, and his position was based on being the successor to the apostle Peter, the first bishop of Rome. It was unseemly that the head of the Catholic Church should reside outside of Rome. In the 1330s, the popes began to construct a stately palace in Avignon, a clear indication that they intended to stay for some time.

Other factors also contributed to the decline in papal prestige during the Avignonese residency. It was widely believed that the popes at Avignon were captives of the French monarchy. Although questionable, since Avignon did not belong to the French monarchy, it was easy to believe in view of Avignon's proximity to French lands. Moreover, during the seventy-three years of the Avignonese papacy, of the 134 new cardinals created by the popes, 113 of them were French.

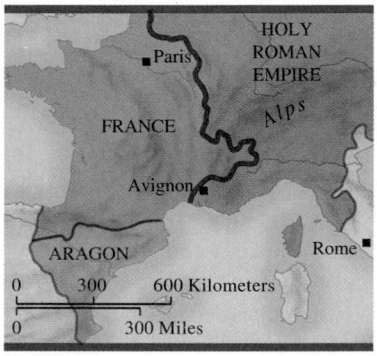

Avignon

© Cengage Learning

At the same time, the popes attempted to find new sources of revenue to compensate for their loss of revenue from the Papal States and began to impose new taxes on the clergy. Furthermore, the splendor in which the pope and cardinals were living in Avignon led to highly vocal criticism of both clergy and papacy in the fourteenth century. Avignon had become a powerful symbol of abuses within the church, and many people began to call for the pope's return to Rome.

One of the most prominent calls came from Catherine of Siena (c. 1347–1380), whose saintly demeanor and claims of visions from God led the city of Florence to send her on a mission to Pope Gregory XI (1370–1378) in Avignon. She told the pope, "Because God has given you authority and because you have accepted it, you ought to use your virtue and power; if you do not wish to use it, it might be better for you to resign what you have accepted; it would give more honor to God and health to your soul."[7]

The Great Schism

Catherine of Siena's admonition seemed to be heeded in 1377, when at long last Pope Gregory XI, perceiving the disastrous decline in papal prestige, returned to Rome. He died soon afterward, however, in the spring of 1378. When the college of cardinals met in conclave to elect a new pope, the citizens of Rome, fearful that the French majority would choose another Frenchman who would return the papacy to Avignon, threatened that the cardinals would not leave Rome alive unless they elected a Roman or at least an Italian as pope. Indeed, the guards of the conclave warned the cardinals that they "ran the risk of being torn in pieces" if they did not choose an Italian. The terrified cardinals duly elected the Italian archbishop of Bari, who was subsequently crowned as Pope Urban VI (1378–1389) on Easter Sunday.

Following his election, Urban VI made clear his plans to reform the papal curia and even to swamp the college of cardinals with enough new Italian cardinals to eliminate the French majority. After many of the cardinals (the French ones) withdrew from Rome in late summer and were finally free of the Roman mob, they issued a manifesto, saying that they had been coerced by the mob and that Urban's election was therefore null and void. The dissenting cardinals thereupon chose one of their number, a Frenchman, who took the title of Clement VII and promptly returned to Avignon. Since Urban remained in Rome, there were now two popes, initiating what has been called the **Great Schism** of the church.

Europe's loyalties soon became divided: France, Spain, Scotland, and southern Italy supported Clement, while England, Germany, Scandinavia, and most of Italy supported Urban. These divisions generally followed political lines. Because the French supported the Avignonese pope, so did their allies; their enemies, particularly England and its allies, supported the Roman pope.

The Great Schism badly damaged the faith of Christian believers. The pope was widely believed to be the leader of Christendom and, as Boniface VIII had pointed out, held the keys to the kingdom of heaven. Since each line of popes denounced the other as the Antichrist, such a spectacle could not help but undermine the institution that had become the very foundation of the church.

The Conciliar Movement

As dissatisfaction with the papacy grew, so did the calls for a revolutionary approach to solving the church's institutional problems. Final authority in spiritual matters must reside not with the popes, reformers claimed, but with a general church council representing all members. The Great Schism led large numbers of serious churchmen to take up this theory of **conciliarism** in the belief that only a general council of the church could end the schism

CHRONOLOGY The Decline of the Church	
Pope Boniface VIII	1294–1303
Unam Sanctam	1302
Papacy at Avignon	1305–1378
Pope Gregory XI's return to Rome	1377
Start of the Great Schism	1378
Pope Urban VI	1378–1389
Failure of Council of Pisa to end schism	1409
Council of Constance	1414–1418
End of schism; election of Martin V	1417

and bring reform to the church in its "head and members." In desperation, a group of cardinals from both lines of popes finally heeded these theoretical formulations and convened a general council. This Council of Pisa, which met in 1409, deposed the two rival popes and elected a new one. The council's action proved disastrous when the two deposed popes refused to step down. There were now three popes, and the church seemed more hopelessly divided than ever.

Leadership in convening a new council now passed to the Holy Roman Emperor, Sigismund. As a result of his efforts, a new ecumenical church council met at Constance from 1414 to 1418. It had three major objectives: to end the schism, to eradicate heresy, and to reform the church in "head and members." The ending of the schism proved to be the Council of Constance's easiest task. After the three competing popes either resigned or were deposed, a new conclave elected a Roman cardinal, a member of a prominent Roman family, as Pope Martin V (1417–1431). The council was much less successful in dealing with the problems of heresy and reform.

Culture and Society in an Age of Adversity

Focus Questions: What were the major developments in art and literature in the fourteenth century? How did the adversities of the fourteenth century affect urban life?

In the midst of disaster, the fourteenth century proved creative in its own way. The rapid growth of vernacular literature and new inventions made an impact on European life at the same time that the effects of plague were felt in many areas of medieval towns and cities.

The Development of Vernacular Literature

Although Latin remained the language of the church liturgy and the official documents of both church and state, the fourteenth century witnessed a surge in literature written in vernacular languages, especially in Italy. By the late fifteenth century, vernacular literary forms had become so celebrated that they could compete with and would eventually replace works in Latin.

Dante Alighieri (DAHN-tay al-ee-GYER-ee) (1265–1321) came from an old Florentine noble family that had fallen on hard times. His masterpiece in the Italian vernacular was the *Divine Comedy*, written between 1313 and 1321. Cast in a typical medieval framework, the *Divine Comedy* is basically the story of the soul's progression to salvation, a fundamental medieval preoccupation. The lengthy poem was divided into three major sections corresponding to the realms of the afterworld: hell, purgatory, and heaven or paradise. In the "Inferno" (see the box on p. 247), Dante is led by his guide, the Classical author Virgil, who is a symbol of human reason. But Virgil (or reason) can lead the poet only so far on his journey. At the end of "Purgatory," Beatrice (the true love of Dante's life), who represents revelation—which alone can explain the mysteries of heaven—becomes his guide into "Paradise." Here Beatrice presents Dante to Saint Bernard, a symbol of mystical contemplation. The saint turns Dante over to the Virgin Mary, since grace is necessary to achieve the final step of entering the presence of God, where one beholds "the love that moves the sun and the other stars."[8]

Geoffrey Chaucer (c. 1340–1400) brought a new level of sophistication to the English vernacular language in his famous work *The Canterbury Tales*. His beauty of expression and clear, forceful language were important in transforming his East Midland dialect into the chief ancestor of the modern English language. *The Canterbury Tales* is a collection of stories told by a group of twenty-nine pilgrims journeying from Southwark to the tomb of Saint Thomas à Becket at Canterbury. This format gave Chaucer the chance to portray an entire range of English society, from highborn to lowborn. The stories these pilgrims told to while away the time on the journey were just as varied as the storytellers themselves: knightly romances, fairy tales, saints' lives, sophisticated satires, and crude anecdotes.

One of the extraordinary vernacular writers of the age was Christine de Pizan (kris-TEEN duh pee-ZAHN) (c. 1364–1430). Because of her father's position at the court of Charles V of France, she received a good education. Her husband died when she was only twenty-five (they had been married for ten years), leaving her with little income and three small children and her mother to

Dante's Vision of Hell

The *Divine Comedy* of Dante Alighieri is regarded as one of the greatest literary works of all time. Many people consider it the supreme summary of medieval thought. It combines allegory with a remarkable amount of contemporary history. Indeed, forty-three of the seventy-nine people consigned to hell in the "Inferno" were Florentines. This excerpt is taken from canto 18 of the "Inferno," in which Dante and Virgil visit the eighth circle of hell, which is divided into ten trenches containing those who had committed malicious frauds upon their fellow human beings.

Dante, "Inferno," *Divine Comedy*

We had already come to where the walk
crosses the second bank, from which it lifts
another arch, spanning from rock to rock.

Here we heard people whine in the next chasm,
and knock and thump themselves with open palms,
and blubber through their snouts as if in a spasm.

Steaming from that pit, a vapor rose
over the banks, crusting them with a slime
that sickened my eyes and hammered at my nose.

That chasm sinks so deep we could not sight
its bottom anywhere until we climbed
along the rock arch to its greatest height.

Once there, I peered down; and I saw long lines
of people in a river of excrement
that seemed the overflow of the world's latrines.

I saw among the felons of that pit
one wraith who might or might not have been tonsured—
one could not tell, he was so smeared with shit.

He bellowed: "You there, why do you stare at me
more than at all the others in this stew?"
And I to him: "Because if memory

serves me, I knew you when your hair was dry.
You are Alessio Interminelli da Lucca.
That's why I pick you from this filthy fry."

And he then, beating himself on his clown's head:
"Down to this have the flatteries I sold
the living sunk me here among the dead."

And my Guide prompted then: "Lean forward a bit
and look beyond him, there—do you see that one
scratching herself with dungy nails, the strumpet

who fidgets to her feet, then to a crouch?
It is the whore Thaïs who told her lover
when he sent to ask her, 'Do you thank me much?'

'Much? Nay, past all believing!' And with this
Let us turn from the sight of this abyss."

Q How does Dante's vision of hell reflect medieval religious thought? Why were there Florentines in hell? What lessons do you think this work was intended to teach its readers?

Source: From THE DIVINE COMEDY by Dante Alighieri, translated by John Ciardi. Copyright 1954, 1957, 1959, 1960, 1961, 1965, 1967, 1970 by the Ciardi Family Publishing Trust. Used by permission of W. W. Norton & Company, Inc.

support. Christine took the unusual step of becoming a writer to earn her living. Her poems were soon in demand, and by 1400 she had achieved financial security.

Christine de Pizan is best known, however, for her French prose works written in defense of women. In *The Book of the City of Ladies*, written in 1404, she denounced the many male writers who had argued that women by their very nature were prone to evil, unable to learn, and easily swayed and consequently needed to be controlled by men. With the help of Reason, Righteousness, and Justice, who appear to her in a vision, Christine refutes these antifeminist attacks. Women, she argues, are not evil by nature and could learn as well as men if they were permitted to attend the same schools: "Should I also tell you whether a woman's nature is clever and quick enough to learn speculative sciences as well as to discover them, and likewise the manual arts? I assure you that women are equally well-suited and skilled to carry them out and to put them to sophisticated use once they have learned them."[9] She ends the book by encouraging women to defend themselves against the attacks of men, who are incapable of understanding women.

Art and the Black Death

The fourteenth century produced an artistic outburst in new directions as well as a large body of morbid work influenced by the Black Death and the recurrence of the plague. The city of Florence witnessed the first dramatic break with medieval tradition in the work of Giotto (JAH-toh) (1266–1337), often considered a forerunner of Italian Renaissance painting. Although he worked throughout Italy, Giotto's most famous works were done in Padua and Florence. Coming out of the formal Byzantine school, Giotto transcended it with a new kind of realism, a desire to imitate nature that Renaissance artists later identified as the basic component of Classical art. Giotto's figures were solid and rounded; placed realistically in relationship to each other and their background, they conveyed three-dimensional depth. The expressive faces and physically realistic bodies gave his sacred figures human qualities with which spectators could identify.

Scrovegni Chapel, Padua // © Scala/Art Resource, NY

Giotto, *Lamentation.* The work of Giotto marked the first clear innovation in fourteenth-century painting, making him a forerunner of the early Renaissance. This fresco was part of a series done on the walls of the Arena Chapel in Padua begun in 1305. Giotto painted thirty-eight scenes on three levels: the lives of Mary, the mother of Jesus, and her parents (top panel); the life and work of Jesus (middle panel); and his passion, crucifixion, and resurrection (bottom panel). Shown here from the bottom panel is the lamentation. A group of Jesus's followers, including his mother and Mary Magdalene, mourn over the body of Jesus before it is placed in its tomb. The solidity of Giotto's human figures gives them a three-dimensional quality. He also captured the grief and despair felt by the mourners.

The Black Death had a visible impact on art. For one thing, it wiped out entire guilds of artists. At the same time, survivors, including the newly rich who patronized artists, were no longer so optimistic. Some were more concerned about gaining salvation and felt guilty about enjoying life (see Images of Everyday Life on p. 249). Post-plague art began to concentrate on pain and death. A fairly large number of artistic works came to be based on the *ars moriendi* (AHRS moh-ree-EN-dee), the art of dying.

Changes in Urban Life

One immediate by-product of the Black Death was a greater regulation of urban activities by town governments. Authorities tried to keep cities cleaner by enacting new ordinances against waste products in the streets. Viewed as unhealthy places, bathhouses were closed down, leading to a noticeable decline in personal cleanliness.

The effects of plague were also felt in other areas of medieval urban life. The basic unit of the late medieval urban environment was the nuclear family of husband, wife, and children. Especially in wealthier families, there might also be servants, apprentices, and other relatives, including widowed mothers and the husband's illegitimate children.

Before the Black Death, late marriages were common for urban couples. It was not unusual for husbands to be in their late thirties or forties and wives in their early twenties. The expense of setting up a household probably necessitated the delay in marriage. But the situation changed dramatically after the plague, reflecting new economic opportunities for the survivors and a reluctance to postpone living in the presence of so much death.

The economic difficulties of the fourteenth century also had a tendency to strengthen the development of gender roles and to set new limits on employment opportunities for women. Based on the authority of Aristotle, Thomas Aquinas and other thirteenth-century scholastic theologians had maintained that according to the natural order, men were active and domineering while women were passive and submissive. As more and more lawyers, doctors, and priests, who had been trained in universities where these notions were taught, entered society, these ideas of man's and woman's different natures became widely acceptable. Increasingly, women were expected to forgo any active functions in society and remain subject to direction from males. A fourteenth-century Parisian provost commented that among glass cutters, "no master's widow who keeps working at his craft after her husband's death may take on apprentices, for the men of the craft do not believe that a woman can master it well enough to teach a child to master it, for the craft is a very

IMAGES OF EVERYDAY LIFE

Entertainment in the Middle Ages

Palazzo Borromeo, Milan//© Scala/Art Resource, NY

Medieval people engaged in a variety of activities for entertainment. City dwellers enjoyed feast days and holidays, when minstrels and jugglers amused people with their arts and tricks. Castle life had its courtly feasts, featuring tournaments accompanied by banquets, music, and dancing. Games were popular at all levels of society; castle dwellers played backgammon, checkers, and chess. The illustration at the left, from a fifteenth-century fresco, shows a group of ladies and gentlemen playing cards.

Like children in all eras, medieval children enjoyed playing a variety of games. A number of writers on children saw play as a basic symbol of childhood itself. In this series of illustrations from medieval manuscripts, we see children engaged in riding hobbyhorses (undoubtedly popular in a society dependent on horses), catching butterflies and playing with a spinning top, and playing a game of blind man's bluff.

© The Art Archive/Bodleian Library (Douce 276 folio 124v), Oxford, UK

© British Library (Roy 6 E VII f.67v), London, UK//
© British Library Board. All Rights Reserved/The Bridgeman Art Library

© The Art Archive/Bibliothèque Universitaire de Médecine, Montpellier/Gianni Dagli Orti

delicate one."[10] Although this statement suggests that some women were in fact running businesses, it also reveals that they were viewed as incapable of undertaking all of men's activities. Thus, fourteenth-century Europeans imposed a division of labor roles between men and women that continued until the Industrial Revolution of the eighteenth and nineteenth centuries.

In practice, however, some women benefited from the effects of the Black Death in the fourteenth century. The loss of so many male workers in cities opened up new jobs for women, including positions as metalworkers and stevedores. In clothmaking, women were allowed to assume better-paying jobs as weavers. Brewing became an all-female profession by 1450. Widows also occasionally carried on their husbands' shops or businesses.

Inventions and New Patterns

Despite its problems, the fourteenth century witnessed a continuation of the technological innovations that had characterized the High Middle Ages. The most extraordinary of these inventions, and one that had a major impact on European cities, was the clock. The mechanical clock was invented at the end of the thirteenth century but not perfected until the fourteenth. The time-telling clock was actually a by-product of a larger astronomical clock. The best-designed one was constructed by Giovanni di Dondi in the mid-fourteenth century. Dondi's clock contained the signs of the zodiac but also struck on the hour. Because clocks were expensive, they were usually installed only in the towers of churches or municipal buildings. The first clock striking equal hours was in a church in Milan; in 1335, a chronicler described it as "a wonderful clock, with a very large clapper which strikes a bell twenty-four hours of the day and night and thus at the first hour of the night gives one sound, at the second two strikes . . . and so distinguishes one hour from another, which is of greatest use to men of every degree."[11]

Clocks introduced a wholly new conception of time into the lives of Europeans; they revolutionized how people thought about and used time. Throughout most of the Middle Ages, time was determined by natural rhythms (daybreak and nightfall) or church bells that were rung at more or less regular three-hour intervals, corresponding to the ecclesiastical offices of the church. Clocks made it possible to plan one's day and organize one's activities around the regular striking of bells. This brought a new regularity into the lives of workers and merchants, defining urban existence and enabling merchants and bankers to see the value of time in a new way.

Invented earlier by the Chinese, gunpowder also made its appearance in the West in the fourteenth century. The use of gunpowder eventually brought drastic changes to European warfare. Its primary use was in cannons, although early cannons were prone to blow up, making them as dangerous to the people firing them as to the enemy. Even as late as 1460, an attack on a castle using the "Lion," an enormous Flemish cannon, proved disastrous for the Scottish king James II when the "Lion" blew up, killing the king and a number of his retainers. Continued improvement in the construction of cannons, however, soon made them extremely valuable in reducing both castles and city walls. Gunpowder made castles, city walls, and armored knights obsolete.

CHAPTER SUMMARY

In the eleventh, twelfth, and thirteenth centuries, European civilization developed many of its fundamental features. Territorial states, parliaments, capitalist trade and industry, banks, cities, and vernacular literature were all products of that fertile period. During the same time, the Catholic Church under the direction of the papacy reached its apogee.

Fourteenth-century European society, however, was challenged by an overwhelming number of crises that led to the disintegration of medieval civilization. At mid-century, one of the most destructive natural disasters in history erupted—the Black Death, a devastating plague that wiped out at least one-third of the European population, with even higher mortality rates in urban areas. Reactions varied. Some escaped into alcohol, sex, and crime. Others, such as the flagellants, believing the Black Death to be a punishment from God, attempted to atone for peoples' sins through self-inflicted pain. In many areas, the Jews became scapegoats. Economic crises and social upheavals, including a decline in trade and industry, bank failures, and peasant revolts pitting the lower classes against the upper classes, followed in the wake of the Black Death.

Political stability also declined, especially during the Hundred Years' War, a long, drawn-out conflict between the English and the French. Armored knights on horseback formed the backbone of medieval armies, but English peasants using the longbow began to change the face of war. After numerous defeats, the French cause was saved by Joan of Arc, a young peasant woman whose leadership inspired the French, who also began to rely on cannon and were victorious by 1453.

The Catholic Church, too, experienced a crisis. The confrontation between Pope Boniface VIII and Philip IV of France led to a loss of papal power and the removal of the papacy to Avignon on France's border in 1305. The absence of the popes from Rome created a new crisis, but the return of the papacy to Rome in 1377 only led to new problems. The Great Schism witnessed the spectacle of two competing popes condemning each other as the Antichrist. A new conciliar movement based on the belief that church councils, not popes, should rule the church finally ended the Great Schism in 1417.

All of these crises seemed to overpower Europeans in this calamitous fourteenth century. Not surprisingly, much of the art of the period depicted the Four Horsemen of the Apocalypse described in the New Testament Book of Revelation: Death, Famine, Pestilence, and War. No doubt, to some people, the last days of the world appeared to be at hand. European society, however, proved remarkably resilient. Already in the fourteenth century new ideas and practices were beginning to emerge, as often happens in periods of crisis. As we shall see in the next chapter, the pace of change began to quicken as Europe experienced a rebirth of Classical culture that some historians have called the Renaissance.

CHAPTER TIMELINE

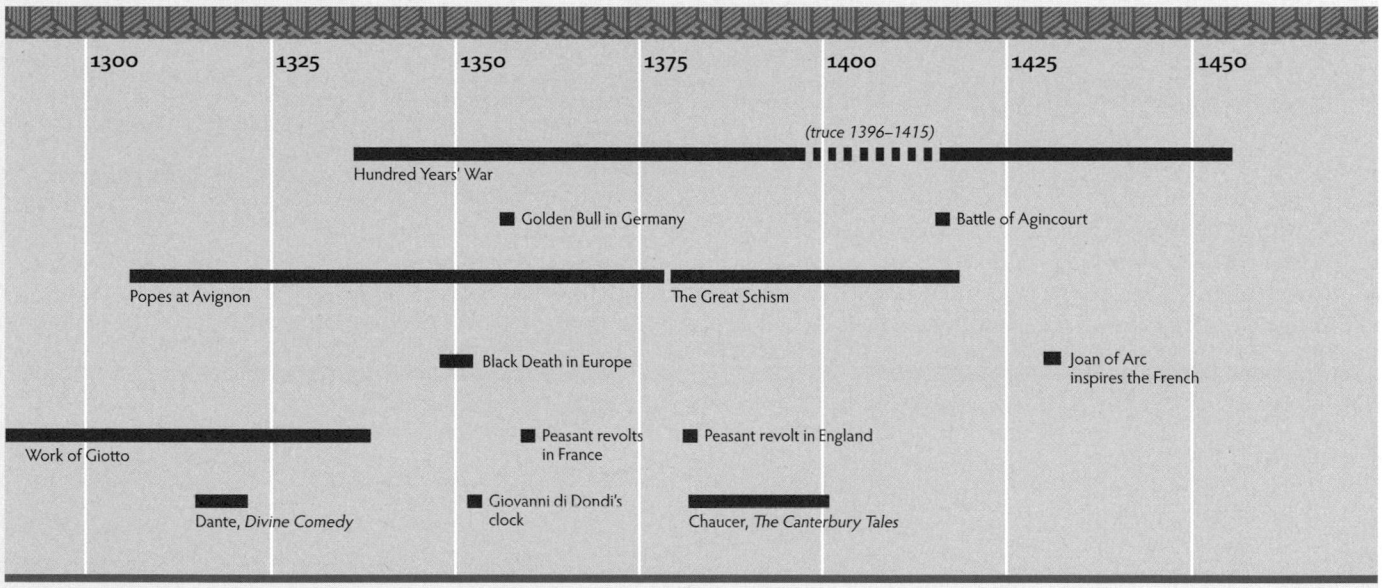

CHAPTER REVIEW

Upon Reflection

Q What were the chief factors that led to the urban and rural revolts of the fourteenth century?

Q What were the causes of the Hundred Years' War, and what were the results of the war in the fourteenth century for France and England?

Q What impact did the adversities of the fourteenth century have on the Catholic Church?

Key Terms

Black Death (p. 231)
anti-Semitism (p. 234)
pogroms (p. 234)
scutage (p. 239)
Great Schism (p. 245)
conciliarism (p. 245)

Suggestions for Further Reading

GENERAL WORKS For a general introduction to the fourteenth century, see **D. P. Waley** and **P. Denley, *Later Medieval Europe,*** 3rd ed. (London, 2001), and **J. Aberth, *From the Brink of the Apocalypse: Confronting Famine, War, Plague, and Death in the Later Middle Ages*** (London 2001).

THE BLACK DEATH On the Black Death, see **D. Herlihy, *The Black Death and the Transformation of the West,*** ed. **S. K. Cohn Jr.** (Cambridge, Mass., 1997), and **J. Kelly, *The Great Mortality*** (New York, 2005).

HUNDRED YEARS' WAR Good accounts of the Hundred Years' War include **A. Curry, *The Hundred Years' War,*** 2nd ed. (New York, 2004), and **R. H. Neillands, *The Hundred Years' War,*** 2nd ed. (New York, 2001). On Joan of Arc, see **M. Warner, *Joan of Arc: The Image of Female Heroism*** (New York, 1981).

POLITICAL HISTORY On the political history of the period, see **B. Guenee, *States and Rulers in Later Medieval Europe,*** trans. **J. Vale** (Oxford, 1985).

CATHOLIC CHURCH A good general study of the church in the fourteenth century can be found in **F. P. Oakley, *The Western Church in the Later Middle Ages*** (Ithaca, N.Y, 1980). See also **J. H. Lynch, *The Medieval Church: A Brief History*** (New York, 1992). On late medieval religious practices, see **R. N. Swanson, *Religion and Devotion in Europe, c. 1215–1515*** (Cambridge, 1995).

CULTURE A classic work on the life and thought of the Later Middle Ages is **J. Huizinga, *The Autumn of the Middle Ages,*** trans. **R. J. Payton** and **U. Mammitzsch** (Chicago, 1996). On Dante, see **B. Reynolds, *Dante: The Poet, the Political Thinker, the Man*** (London, 2006). The best work on Christine de Pizan is by **C. C. Willard, *Christine de Pizan: Her Life and Works*** (New York, 1984).

SOCIAL HISTORY On women in the Later Middle Ages, see **S. Shahar, *The Fourth Estate: A History of Women in the Middle Ages,*** trans. **C. Galai,** rev. ed. (London, 2003). The importance of inventions is discussed in **J. Gimpel, *The Medieval Machine*** (New York, 1976).

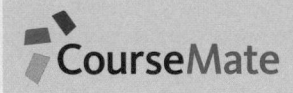

Visit the CourseMate website at www.cengagebrain.com for additional study tools and review materials for this chapter.

CHAPTER 12

Sistine Chapel, Vatican Palace, Vatican State // © Erich Lessing/Art Resource, NY

Michelangelo's Creation of Adam *on the Sistine Chapel ceiling*

Recovery and Rebirth: The Age of the Renaissance

CHAPTER OUTLINE AND FOCUS QUESTIONS

Characteristics of the Italian Renaissance

Q What characteristics distinguish the Renaissance from the Middle Ages?

The Making of Renaissance Society

Q What major social changes occurred during the Renaissance?

The Italian States in the Renaissance

Q How did Machiavelli's works reflect the political realities of Renaissance Italy?

The Intellectual Renaissance in Italy

Q What was humanism, and what effect did it have on philosophy, education, and attitudes toward politics?

The Artistic Renaissance

Q What were the chief characteristics of Renaissance art, and how did it differ in Italy and northern Europe?

The European State in the Renaissance

Q Why do historians sometimes refer to the monarchies of the late fifteenth century as "new monarchies" or "Renaissance states"?

The Church in the Renaissance

Q What were the policies of the Renaissance popes, and what impact did those policies have on the Roman Catholic Church?

CRITICAL THINKING

Q How did Renaissance art and the humanist movement reflect the political, economic, and social developments of the period?

WERE THE FOURTEENTH and fifteenth centuries a continuation of the Middle Ages or the beginning of a new era? Both positions can be defended. Although the disintegrative patterns of the fourteenth century continued into the fifteenth, at the same time there were elements of recovery that made the fifteenth century a period of significant political, economic, artistic, and intellectual change. The humanists or intellectuals of the age considered their period (from the mid-fourteenth to the mid-sixteenth century) an age of rebirth, believing that they had restored arts and letters to their former glory after they had been "neglected" or "dead" for centuries. The humanists also saw their age as one of accomplished individuals who dominated the landscape of their time. Michelangelo, the great Italian artist of the early sixteenth century, and Pope Julius II, the "warrior pope," were two such titans. The artist's temperament and the pope's temper led to many lengthy and often loud quarrels between the two. The pope had hired Michelangelo to paint the ceiling of the Sistine Chapel in Rome, a difficult task for a man long accustomed to being a sculptor. Michelangelo undertook the project but refused for a long time to allow anyone, including the pope, to see his work. Julius grew anxious, pestering Michelangelo on a regular basis about when the ceiling would be finished. Exasperated by the pope's requests, Michelangelo once replied, according to Giorgio Vasari, his contemporary biographer, that the ceiling would be completed "when it satisfies me as an artist." The pope responded, "And we want you to satisfy us and finish it soon," and then threatened that if Michelangelo did not "finish the ceiling quickly [the pope] would have him thrown down from the scaffolding." Fearing the pope's anger, Michelangelo "lost no time in doing all that was wanted" and quickly completed the ceiling, one of the great masterpieces in the history of Western art.

The humanists' view of their age as a rebirth of the Classical civilization of the Greeks and Romans ultimately led historians to use the French word *Renaissance* to identify this age. Although recent historians have emphasized the many elements of continuity between the Middle Ages and the Renaissance, the latter age was also distinguished by its own unique characteristics.

Characteristics of the Italian Renaissance

Q Focus Question: What characteristics distinguish the Renaissance from the Middle Ages?

Renaissance means "rebirth." Many people who lived in Italy between 1350 and 1550 believed that they were witnessing a rebirth of antiquity or Greco-Roman civilization, marking a new age. To them, the thousand or so years between the end of the Roman Empire and their own era was a middle period (the "Middle Ages"), characterized by darkness because of its lack of Classical culture. Historians of the nineteenth century later used similar terminology to describe this period in Italy. The Swiss historian and art critic Jacob Burckhardt (YAHK-ub BOORK-hart) created the modern concept of the **Renaissance** in his celebrated work *Civilization of the Renaissance in Italy*, published in 1860. He portrayed Italy in the fourteenth and fifteenth centuries as the birthplace of the modern world and saw the revival of antiquity, the "perfecting of the individual," and secularism ("worldliness of the Italians") as its distinguishing features. Burckhardt established the framework for all modern interpretations of the period. Although contemporary scholars do not believe that the Renaissance represents a sudden or dramatic cultural break with the Middle Ages (as Burckhardt argued)—there was, after all, much continuity between the two periods in economic, political, and social life—the Renaissance can still be viewed as a distinct period of European history that manifested itself first in Italy and then spread to the rest of Europe. What, then, are the characteristics of the Italian Renaissance?

Renaissance Italy was largely an urban society. The city-states, especially those of northern Italy, became the centers of Italian political, economic, and social life. In this new urban society, a secular spirit emerged as increasing wealth created new possibilities for the enjoyment of worldly things (see the box on p. 255).

Above all, the Renaissance was an age of recovery from the calamitous fourteenth century, a time for the slow process of recuperating from the effects of the Black Death, political disorder, and economic recession. This recovery was accompanied by a rediscovery of the culture of Classical antiquity. Increasingly aware of their own historical past, Italian intellectuals became intensely interested in the Greco-Roman culture of the ancient Mediterranean world. This revival of Classical antiquity (the Middle Ages had in fact preserved much of ancient Latin culture) affected activities as diverse as politics and art and led to new attempts to reconcile the pagan philosophy of the Greco-Roman world with Christian thought, as well as new ways of viewing human beings.

A revived emphasis on individual ability became a characteristic of the Italian Renaissance. As the fifteenth-century Florentine architect Leon Battista Alberti (al-BAYR-tee) expressed it, "Men can do all things if they will."[1] A high regard for human dignity and worth and a realization of individual potentiality created a new social ideal of the well-rounded personality or universal person—*l'uomo universale* (LWOH-moh OO-nee-ver-SAH-lay)—who was capable of achievements in many areas of life.

These general features of the Italian Renaissance were not characteristic of all Italians but were primarily the preserve of the wealthy upper classes, who constituted a small percentage of the total population. The achievements of the Italian Renaissance were the product of an elite group, and not a mass movement. Nevertheless, indirectly it did have some impact on ordinary people, especially in the cities, where so many of the intellectual and artistic accomplishments of the period were most apparent.

A Renaissance Banquet

Like the banquets of Greek and Roman society, a Renaissance banquet was an occasion for good food, interesting conversation, music, and dancing. In Renaissance society, a banquet was also a symbol of status and an opportunity to impress people with the power and wealth of one's family. Banquets were held to celebrate public and religious festivals, official visits, anniversaries, and weddings. The following menu lists the foods served at a grand banquet given by Pope Pius V in the sixteenth century.

A Sixteenth-Century Banquet

First Course:

Cold Delicacies from the Sideboard

Pieces of marzipan and marzipan balls
Neapolitan spice cakes
Malaga wine and Pisan biscuits
Fresh grapes
Prosciutto cooked in wine, served with capers and grape pulp
Salted pork tongues cooked in wine, sliced
Spit-roasted songbirds, cold, with their tongues sliced over them
Sweet mustard

Second Course:

Hot Foods from the Kitchen, Roasts

Fried veal sweetbreads and liver
Spit-roasted skylarks with lemon sauce
Spit-roasted quails with sliced eggplants
Stuffed spit-roasted pigeons with capers sprinkled over them
Spit-roasted rabbits, with sauce and crushed pine nuts
Partridges larded and spit-roasted, served with lemon
Heavily seasoned poultry with lemon slices
Slices of veal, spit-roasted with a sauce made from the juices
Leg of goat spit-roasted with a sauce made from the juices
Soup of almond paste, with the flesh of three pigeons to each serving

Third Course:

Hot Foods from the Kitchen, Boiled Meats and Stews

Stuffed fat geese, boiled Lombard style and covered with sliced almonds
Stuffed breast of veal, boiled, garnished with flowers
Very young calf, boiled, garnished with parsley
Almonds in garlic sauce
Turkish-style rice with milk, sprinkled with cinnamon
Stewed pigeons with mortadella sausage and whole onions
Cabbage soup with sausages
Poultry pie, two chickens to each pie
Fricasseed breast of goat dressed with fried onions
Pies filled with custard cream
Boiled calves' feet with cheese and egg

Fourth Course:

Delicacies from the Sideboard

Bean tarts
Quince pastries
Pear tarts, the pears wrapped in marzipan
Parmesan cheese and Riviera cheese
Fresh almonds on vine leaves
Chestnuts roasted over the coals and served with salt and pepper
Milk curds
Ring-shaped cakes
Wafers made from ground grain

Q What kinds of people would be present at a banquet where these foods would be served? What does this menu tell you about the material culture of the Renaissance and the association of food with social status?

Source: Reprinted from *Food in History* by Reay Tannahill, copyright © 1973, 1988 by Reay Tannahill.

The Making of Renaissance Society

Q **Focus Question:** What major social changes occurred during the Renaissance?

After the severe economic reversals and social upheavals of the fourteenth century, the European economy gradually recovered as the volume of manufacturing and trade increased.

Economic Recovery

By the fourteenth century, Italian merchants were carrying on a flourishing commerce throughout the Mediterranean and had also expanded their lines of trade north along the Atlantic seaboard. The great galleys of the Venetian Flanders Fleet maintained a direct sea route from Venice to England and the Netherlands, where Italian merchants came into contact with the increasingly powerful Hanseatic League of merchants. Hard hit by the plague, the Italians lost their commercial preeminence while the Hanseatic League continued to prosper.

EXPANSION OF TRADE As early as the thirteenth century, a number of north German coastal towns had formed a commercial and military alliance known as the Hansa or the Hanseatic League. By 1500, more than eighty cities belonged to the League, which established settlements and commercial bases in northern Europe and England. For almost two hundred years, the Hansa had a monopoly on northern European trade in timber, fish, grain, metals, honey, and wines. Its southern outlet in Flanders, the city of Bruges, became the economic crossroads of Europe in the fourteenth century because it served as the meeting place between Hanseatic merchants and the Flanders Fleet of Venice. In the fifteenth century, however, the Hanseatic League proved increasingly unable to compete with the developing larger territorial states.

Overall, trade recovered dramatically from the economic contraction of the fourteenth century. The Italians and especially the Venetians continued to maintain a wealthy commercial empire. Not until the sixteenth century, when overseas discoveries gave new importance to the states facing the Atlantic, did the petty Italian city-states begin to suffer from the competitive advantages of the ever-growing and more powerful national territorial states.

INDUSTRIES OLD AND NEW The economic depression of the fourteenth century also affected patterns of manufacturing. The woolen industries of Flanders and the northern Italian cities had been particularly devastated. By the beginning of the fifteenth century, however, the Florentine woolen industry began to recover. At the same time, the Italian cities began to develop and expand luxury industries, especially silk, glassware, and handworked items in metal and precious stones.

Other new industries, especially printing, mining, and metallurgy, began to rival the textile industry in importance in the fifteenth century. New machinery and techniques for digging deeper mines and for separating metals from ore and purifying them were devised, and entrepreneurs quickly developed large mining operations to produce copper, iron, and silver. Especially valuable were the rich mineral deposits in central Europe. Expanding iron production and new skills in metalworking in turn contributed to the development of firearms that were more effective than the crude weapons of the fourteenth century.

BANKING AND THE MEDICI The city of Florence regained its preeminence in banking in the fifteenth century, due primarily to the Medici family. In its best days (in the fifteenth century), the house of Medici was the greatest banking establishment in Europe, with branches in Venice, Milan, Rome, Avignon, Bruges, London, and Lyons. Moreover, the family had controlling interests in industrial enterprises for wool, silk, and the mining of alum, used in the dyeing of textiles. Despite its great success, the Medici bank suffered a sudden decline at the end of the fifteenth century due to poor leadership and a series of bad loans, especially uncollectible loans to rulers. In 1494, when the French expelled the Medici from Florence and confiscated their property, the Medici financial edifice collapsed.

Social Changes in the Renaissance

The Renaissance inherited its social structure from the Middle Ages. Society remained fundamentally divided into three **estates**: the First Estate, the clergy, whose preeminence was grounded in the belief that people should be guided to spiritual ends; the Second Estate, the nobility, whose privileges were based on the principle that the nobles provided security and justice for society; and the Third Estate, consisting of the peasants and inhabitants of the towns and cities. This social order experienced certain adaptations in the Renaissance, which we can see by examining the Second and Third Estates (the clergy will be examined in Chapter 13).

THE NOBILITY Throughout much of Europe, the landholding nobles faced declining real incomes during the greater part of the fourteenth and fifteenth centuries. Nevertheless, many members of the old nobility survived, and new blood infused their ranks. A reconstruction of the aristocracy was well under way by 1500. As a result of this reconstruction, the nobles, old and new, who constituted between 2 and 3 percent of the population in most countries, managed to dominate society as they had done in the Middle Ages, serving as military officers and holding important political posts as well as advising the king.

By 1500, certain ideals came to be expected of the noble or aristocrat. These ideals were best expressed in *The Book of the Courtier* by the Italian Baldassare Castiglione (bal-duh-SAH-ray ka-steel-YOH-nay) (1478–1529). First published in 1528, Castiglione's work soon became popular throughout Europe and remained a fundamental handbook for European aristocrats for centuries.

In his book, Castiglione described the three basic attributes of the perfect courtier. First, nobles should possess fundamental native endowments, such as impeccable character, grace, talents, and noble birth. The perfect courtier must also cultivate certain achievements. Primarily, he should participate in military and bodily exercises because the principal profession of a courtier was bearing arms. But unlike the medieval knight, who had been required only to have military skill, the Renaissance courtier was also expected to have a Classical education and to adorn his life with the arts by playing a musical instrument, drawing, and painting. In Castiglione's hands, the Renaissance ideal of the well-developed personality became a social ideal of the aristocracy. Finally, the aristocrat was expected to follow a certain standard of conduct. Nobles were expected to make a good impression; while remaining modest, they should not hide their accomplishments but show them with grace.

What was the purpose of these courtly standards? Castiglione said:

> I think that the aim of the perfect Courtier . . . is so to win for himself, by means of the accomplishments ascribed to him by these gentlemen, the favor and mind of the prince whom he serves that he may be able to tell him, and always will tell him, the truth about everything he needs to know, without fear or risk of displeasing him; and that when he sees the mind of his prince inclined to a wrong action, he may dare to oppose him . . . so as to dissuade him of every evil intent and bring him to the path of virtue.[2]

The aim of the perfect noble, then, was to serve his prince in an effective and honest way. Nobles would adhere to these principles for hundreds of years while they continued to dominate European life socially and politically.

PEASANTS AND TOWNSPEOPLE Peasants made up the overwhelming mass of the Third Estate and continued to constitute 85 to 90 percent of the European population, except in the highly urbanized areas of northern Italy and Flanders. The most noticeable trend produced by the economic crisis of the fourteenth century was the decline of the manorial system and the continuing elimination of serfdom. The contraction of the peasantry after the Black Death simply accelerated the process of converting servile labor dues into rents paid in money. By the end of the fifteenth century, serfdom was declining in western Europe, and more and more peasants were becoming legally free.

The remainder of the Third Estate centered around the inhabitants of towns and cities, originally the merchants and artisans who formed the bourgeoisie. The Renaissance town or city of the fifteenth century was home to a multitude of townspeople widely separated socially and economically.

At the top of urban society were the patricians, whose wealth from capitalistic enterprises in trade, industry, and banking enabled them to dominate their urban communities economically, socially, and politically. Below them were the petty burghers, the shopkeepers, artisans, guildmasters, and guild members who were largely concerned with providing goods and services for local consumption. Below these two groups were the propertyless workers earning pitiful wages and the unemployed, living squalid and miserable lives; these people constituted 30 to 40 percent of the population living in cities. In many places in Europe in the late fourteenth and fifteenth centuries, urban poverty increased dramatically. One rich merchant of Florence wrote:

> Those that are lazy and indolent in a way that does harm to the city, and who can offer no just reason for their condition, should either be forced to work or expelled from the Commune. The city would thus rid itself of that most harmful part of the poorest class. . . . If the lowest order of society earn enough food to keep them going from day to day, then they have enough.[3]

But even this large group of poor people was not at the bottom of the social scale; beneath them were a significant number of slaves, especially in the Italian cities.

The Family in Renaissance Italy

The family bond was a source of great security in the urban world of Renaissance Italy. To maintain the family, careful attention was given to marriages that were arranged by parents, often to strengthen business or family ties. Details were worked out well in advance, sometimes when children were only five or six years old, and reinforced by a legally binding marriage contract (see the box on p. 258). An important aspect of the contract was the size of the dowry, money presented by the wife's family to the husband upon marriage. The dowry could involve large sums of money and was expected of all families.

The father-husband was the center of the Italian family. He gave it his name, was responsible for it in all legal matters, managed all finances (his wife had no share in his wealth), and made the crucial decisions that determined his children's lives. A father's authority over his children was absolute until he died or formally freed his children. The age of emancipation varied from early teens to late twenties.

The wife managed the household, a position that gave women a certain degree of autonomy in their daily lives. Women of the upper and middle classes, however, were expected to remain at home. Moreover, most wives knew that their primary function was to bear children. Upper-class wives were frequently pregnant; Alessandra Strozzi (STRAWT-see) of Florence, for example, who had been married at the age of sixteen, bore eight children in ten years. Poor women did not conceive at the same rate because they nursed their own babies. Wealthy women gave their infants out to wet nurses, which enabled them to become pregnant more quickly after the birth of a child.

For women in the Renaissance, childbirth was a fearful occasion. Not only was it painful, but it could be deadly; possibly as many as 10 percent of mothers died in childbirth. In his memoirs, the Florentine merchant Gregorio Dati recalled that three of his four wives died in

Marriage Negotiations

Marriages were so important in maintaining families in Renaissance Italy that much energy was put into arranging them. Parents made the choices for their children, most often for considerations that had little to do with the modern notion of love. This selection is taken from the letters of a Florentine matron of the illustrious Strozzi family to her son Filippo in Naples. The family's position was complicated by the fact that the son was in exile.

Alessandra Strozzi to Her Son Filippo in Naples

[April 20, 1464] . . . Concerning the matter of a wife [for Filippo], it appears to me that if Francesco di Messer Tanagli wishes to give his daughter, that it would be a fine marriage. . . . Now I will speak with Marco [Parenti, Alessandra's son-in-law], to see if there are other prospects that would be better, and if there are none, then we will learn if he wishes to give her [in marriage]. . . . Francesco Tanagli has a good reputation, and he has held office, not the highest, but still he has been in office. You may ask: "Why should he give her to someone in exile?" There are three reasons. First, there aren't many young men of good family who have both virtue and property. Secondly, she has only a small dowry, 1,000 florins, which is the dowry of an artisan [although not a small sum, either—senior officials in the government bureaucracy earned 300 florins a year]. . . . Third, I believe that he will give her away, because he has a large family and he will need help to settle them. . . .

[July 26, 1465] . . . Francesco is a good friend of Marco and he trusts him. On [Saint] Jacopo's day, he spoke to him discreetly and persuasively, saying that for several months he had heard that we were interested in the girl and . . . that when we had made up our minds, she will come to us willingly. [He said that] you were a worthy man, and that his family had always made good marriages, but that he had only a small dowry to give her, and so he would prefer to send her outside of Florence to someone of worth, rather than to give her to someone here, from among those who were available, with little money. . . . We have information that she is affable and competent. She is responsible for a large family (there are twelve children, six boys and six girls), and the mother is always pregnant and isn't very competent. . . .

[August 31, 1465] . . . I have recently received some very favorable information [about the Tanagli girl] from two individuals. . . . They are in agreement that whoever gets her will be content. Concerning her beauty, they told me what I had already seen, that she is attractive and well-proportioned. Her face is long, but I couldn't look directly into her face, since she appeared to be aware that I was examining her . . . and so she turned away from me like the wind. . . . She reads quite well . . . and she can dance and sing. . . .

So yesterday I sent for Marco and told him what I had learned. And we talked about the matter for a while, and decided that he should say something to the father and give him a little hope, but not so much that we couldn't withdraw, and find out from him the amount of the dowry. . . . May God help us to choose what will contribute to our tranquility and to the consolation of us all.

[September 13, 1465] . . . Marco came to me and said that he had met with Francesco Tanagli, who had spoken very coldly, so that I understand that he had changed his mind. . . .

[Filippo Strozzi eventually married Fiametta di Donato Adimari in 1466.]

Q What were the most important considerations in marriage negotiations? Why were they so important?

Source: From *The Society of Renaissance Florence*, edited by Gene Brucker. Copyright © 1971 by Gene Brucker. Reprinted with permission of The Renaissance Society of America.

childbirth. His third wife, after delivering eleven children in fifteen years, "died in childbirth after lengthy suffering, which she bore with remarkable strength and patience."[4] Nor did the tragedies end with childbirth. Surviving mothers often faced the death of their children. In Florence in the fifteenth century, for example, almost half of the children born to merchant families died before the age of twenty. Given these mortality rates, many upper-class families sought to have as many children as possible to ensure that there would be a surviving male heir to the family fortune. This concern is evident in the Florentine humanist Leon Battista Alberti's treatise *On the Family*, where one of the characters remarks, "How many families do we see today in decadence and ruin! . . . Of all these

© Private Collection/The Bridgeman Art Library

Wedding Banquet. Parents arranged marriages in Renaissance Italy to strengthen business or family ties. A legally binding marriage contract was considered a necessary part of the marital arrangements. So was a wedding feast. This painting by Botticelli shows the wedding banquet in Florence that celebrated the marriage of Nastagio degli Onesti and the daughter of Paulo Traversaro.

families not only the magnificence and greatness but the very men, not only the men but the very names are shrunk away and gone. Their memory . . . is wiped out and obliterated."[5]

The Italian States in the Renaissance

Focus Question: How did Machiavelli's works reflect the political realities of Renaissance Italy?

By the fifteenth century, five major powers dominated the Italian peninsula: the duchy of Milan, Venice, Florence, the Papal States, and the kingdom of Naples (see Map 12.1). Northern Italy was divided between Milan and Venice. After the death of the last Visconti ruler of Milan in 1447, Francesco Sforza (frahn-CHESS-koh SFORT-sah), one of the era's leading ***condottieri*** (kahn-duh-TYAY-ree)—a *condottiere* was a leader of a mercenary band—turned on his Milanese employers, conquered the city, and became its new duke. Both the Visconti and Sforza rulers worked to create a highly centralized territorial state. They were especially successful in devising systems of taxation that generated enormous revenues for the government. The maritime republic of Venice remained an extremely stable political entity governed by a small oligarchy of merchant-aristocrats. Its commercial empire brought in enormous revenues and gave it the status of an international power.

The republic of Florence dominated the region of Tuscany. In 1434, Cosimo de' Medici (1434–1464) took control of the ruling oligarchy. Although the wealthy Medici family maintained republican forms of government for appearances' sake, it ran the government from behind the scenes. Through lavish patronage and careful courting of political allies, Cosimo and later his grandson Lorenzo the Magnificent (1469–1492) were successful in dominating the city at a time when Florence was the center of the cultural Renaissance.

The Papal States lay in central Italy. Although these lands were nominally under the political control of the popes, papal residence in Avignon and the Great Schism had enabled individual cities and territories, such as Urbino and Ferrara, to become independent of papal authority. The popes of the fifteenth century directed much of their energy toward reestablishing their control over the Papal States. The kingdom of Naples, which encompassed most of southern Italy and usually the island of Sicily, remained a backward monarchy that shared little in the cultural glories of the Renaissance.

Besides the five major states, there were a number of independent city-states under the control of powerful ruling families that became brilliant centers of Renaissance culture in the fifteenth century. Perhaps most famous was Urbino, ruled by the Montefeltro dynasty. Federigo da Montefeltro (fay-day-REE-goh dah mahn-tuh-FELL-troh), who ruled Urbino from 1444 to 1482, received a Classical

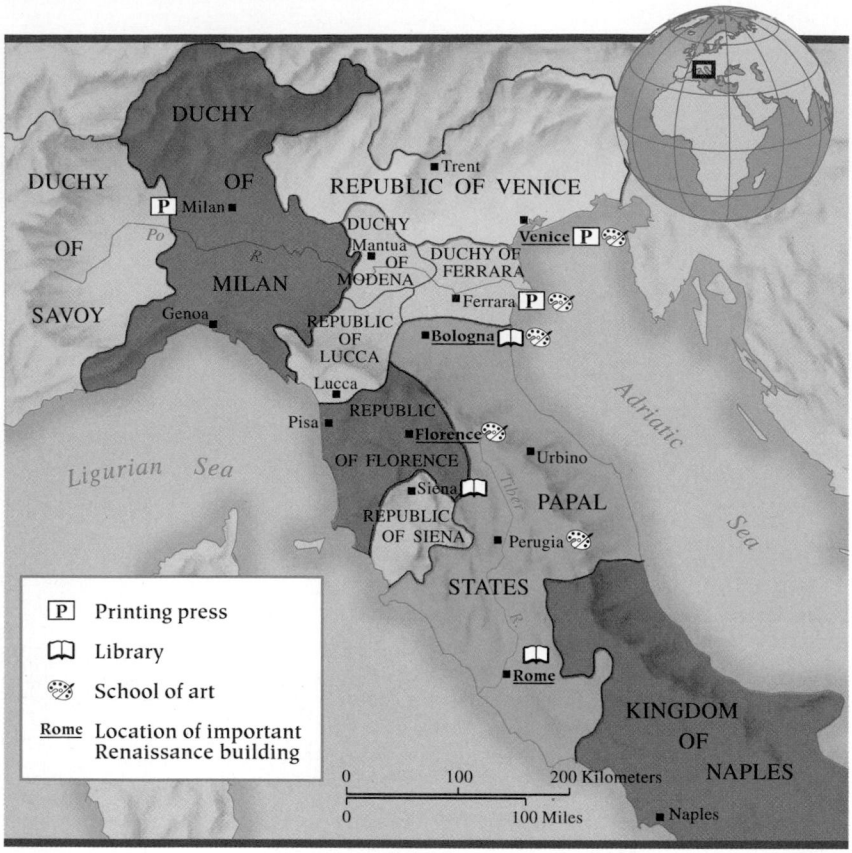

© Cengage Learning

MAP 12.1 Renaissance Italy. Italy in the late fourteenth century was a land of five major states and numerous independent city-states. Increased prosperity and a supportive intellectual climate helped create the atmosphere for the middle and upper classes to "rediscover" Greco-Roman culture. Modern diplomacy was also a product of Renaissance Italy.

Q ***Could the presence of several other powers within easy marching distance make it more likely that a ruler would recognize the importance of diplomacy?***

education. He had also learned the skills of fighting, since the Montefeltro family compensated for the poverty of Urbino by hiring themselves out as *condottieri*. Federigo was not only a good ruler but also a rather unusual *condottiere* by fifteenth-century standards. Although not a brilliant general, he was reliable and honest. At the same time, Duke Federigo was one of the greatest patrons of Renaissance culture. Under his direction, Urbino became a well-known cultural and intellectual center.

A noticeable feature of these smaller Italian courts was the important role played by women. The most famous of the Italian ruling women was Isabella d'Este (DESS-tay) (1474–1539), daughter of the duke of Ferrara, who married Francesco Gonzaga (gun-DZAH-gah), marquis of Mantua. Their court was another important center of art and learning in the Renaissance. Educated at the brilliant court of Ferrara, Isabella was known for her intelligence and political wisdom. Called the "first lady of the world," she attracted artists and intellectuals to the Mantuan court and was responsible for amassing one of the finest libraries in all of Italy. Her numerous letters to friends, family, princes, and artists all over Europe reveal her political acumen as well as a good sense of humor. Both before and after the death of her husband Francesco, she effectively ruled Mantua.

The growth of powerful monarchical states led to trouble for the Italians and brought an end to the independence of the Italian states. Attracted by the riches of Italy, the French king Charles VIII (1483–1498) led an army of 30,000 men into Italy in 1494 and occupied the kingdom of Naples. Other Italian states turned for help to the Spanish, who gladly complied. For the next thirty years, the French and Spanish competed to dominate Italy, which was merely a pawn for the two great powers, a convenient arena for fighting battles. The terrible sack of Rome in 1527 by the armies of the Spanish king Charles I brought a temporary end to the Italian wars. From then on, the Spaniards dominated Italy; the Renaissance in Italy was over.

CHRONOLOGY The Italian States in the Renaissance

Duchy of Milan	
Viscontis	1311–1447
Sforzas	1450–1494
Florence	
Cosimo de' Medici	1434–1464
Lorenzo de' Medici	1469–1492
Beginning of Italian wars—French invasion of Italy	1494
Sack of Rome	1527

Machiavelli and the New Statecraft

No one gave better expression to the Renaissance preoccupation with political power than Niccolò Machiavelli (nee-koh-LOH mahk-ee-uh-VEL-ee) (1469–1527). Although he served ably as a diplomat for Florence, he was eventually forced into exile. Embittered by this and forced to give up the great love of his life—politics—he wrote *The Prince*, one of the most famous treatises on political power in the Western world.

Machiavelli's ideas on politics stemmed from two major sources, his knowledge of ancient Rome and his preoccupation with Italy's political problems. As a result of his experiences, Machiavelli realized that the small Italian states were no match for Europe's large monarchical states and that Italy itself had become merely a battleground for the armies of foreign states. His major concerns in *The Prince* were the acquisition and expansion of political power as the means to restore and maintain order in his time. In the Middle Ages, many political theorists stressed the ethical side of a prince's activity—how a ruler ought to behave based on Christian moral principles. Machiavelli bluntly contradicted this approach:

> My hope is to write a book that will be useful, at least to those who read it intelligently, and so I thought it sensible to go straight to a discussion of how things are in real life and not waste time with a discussion of an imaginary world . . . for the gap between how people actually behave and how they ought to behave is so great that anyone who ignores everyday reality in order to live up to an ideal will soon discover he had been taught how to destroy himself, not how to preserve himself.[6]

Machiavelli considered his approach far more realistic than that of his medieval forebears.

In Machiavelli's view, a prince's attitude toward power must be based on an understanding of human nature, which he perceived as basically self-centered. He said, "For of men one can, in general, say this: They are ungrateful, fickle, deceptive and deceiving, avoiders of danger, eager to gain." Political activity, therefore, could not be restricted by moral considerations. The prince acts on behalf of the state and for the sake of the state must be willing to let his conscience sleep. As Machiavelli put it:

> You need to understand this: A ruler, and particularly a ruler who is new to power, cannot conform to all those rules that men who are thought good are expected to respect, for he is often obliged, in order to hold on to power, to break his word, to be uncharitable, inhumane, and irreligious. So he must be mentally prepared to act as circumstances and changes in fortune require. As I have said, he should do what is right if he can; but he must be prepared to do wrong if necessary.[7]

Machiavelli found a good example of the new Italian ruler in Cesare Borgia (CHE-zah-ray BOR-juh), the son of

© AKG/Photo Researchers, Inc.

Niccolò Machiavelli. In *The Prince*, Machiavelli gave concrete expression to the Renaissance preoccupation with political power. This slender volume remains one of the most famous Western treatises on politics. Machiavelli is seen here in a portrait by Santi di Tito.

Pope Alexander VI (popes were supposed to be celibate), who used ruthless measures to achieve his goal of carving out a new state in central Italy. As Machiavelli said, "Anyone who decides that the policy to follow when one has newly acquired power is to destroy one's enemies, to secure some allies, to win wars, whether by force or by fraud, to make oneself both loved and feared by one's subjects, . . . cannot hope to find, in the recent past, a better model to imitate than Cesare Borgia."[8] Machiavelli was among the first to abandon morality as the basis for the analysis of political activity (see the box on p. 262).

The Intellectual Renaissance in Italy

Q **Focus Question:** What was humanism, and what effect did it have on philosophy, education, and attitudes toward politics?

Individualism and **secularism**—two characteristics of the Italian Renaissance—were most noticeable in the intellectual and artistic realms. Italian culture had matured

OPPOSING VIEWPOINTS

The Renaissance Prince: The Views of Machiavelli and Erasmus

At the beginning of the sixteenth century, two writers produced very different views of political power and the proper way for a ruler to conduct the affairs of state. In 1513, Niccolò Machiavelli wrote a short treatise on political power that, justly or unjustly, has given him a reputation as a political opportunist. In this selection from Chapter 17 of *The Prince*, Machiavelli analyzes whether it is better for a ruler to be loved than to be feared. Three years later, the Dutch intellectual Erasmus, leader of the Christian humanists (see Chapter 13), also wrote a treatise on political power, titled *Education of a Christian Prince*. Following in the footsteps of medieval theorists on power, Erasmus insisted that a true prince should think only of his moral obligations to the people he rules, as is evident in this excerpt from his treatise.

Machiavelli, *The Prince* (1513)

This leads us to a question that is in dispute: Is it better to be loved than feared, or vice versa? My reply is one ought to be both loved and feared; but, since it is difficult to accomplish both at the same time, I maintain it is much safer to be feared than loved, if you have to do without one of the two. For of men one can, in general, say this: They are ungrateful, fickle, deceptive and deceiving, avoiders of danger, eager to gain. As long as you serve their interests, they are devoted to you. They promise you their blood, their possessions, their lives, and their children, as I said before, so long as you seem to have no need of them. But as soon as you need help, they turn against you. Any ruler who relies simply on their promises and makes no other preparations, will be destroyed. For you will find that those whose support you buy, who do not rally to you because they admire your strength of character and nobility of soul, these are people you pay for, but they are never yours, and in the end you cannot get the benefit of your investment. Men are less nervous of offending someone who makes himself lovable, than someone who makes himself frightening. For love attaches men by ties of obligation, which, since men are wicked, they break whenever their interests are at stake. But fear restrains men because they are afraid of punishment, and this fear never leaves them. Still, a ruler should make himself feared in such a way that, if he does not inspire love, at least he does not provoke hatred. For it is perfectly possible to be feared and not hated. You will only be hated if you seize the property or the women of your subjects and citizens. Whenever you have to kill someone, make sure that you have a suitable excuse and an obvious reason; but, above all else, keep your hands off other people's property; for men are quicker to forget the death of their father than the loss of their inheritance. Moreover, there are always reasons why you might want to seize people's property; and he who begins to live by plundering others will always find an excuse for seizing other people's possessions; but there are fewer reasons for killing people, and one killing need not lead to another.

When a ruler is at the head of his army and has a vast number of soldiers under his command, then it is absolutely essential to be prepared to be thought cruel; for it is impossible to keep an army united and ready for action without acquiring a reputation for cruelty.

Erasmus, *Education of a Christian Prince* (1516)

Follow the right, do violence to no one, plunder no one, sell no public office, be corrupted by no bribes. . . . As you would rather stand for an injury than avenge it at great loss to the state, perchance you will lose a little something of your empire. Bear that; consider that you have gained a great deal because you have brought hurt to fewer than you would otherwise have done. . . . If you cannot defend your realm without violating justice, without wanton loss of human life, without great loss to religion, give up and yield to the importunities of the age! . . .

A good prince . . . is a living likeness of God, who is at once good and powerful. His goodness makes him want to help all; his power makes him able to do so. On the other hand, an evil prince, who is like a plague to his country, is the incarnation of the devil, who has great power joined with his wickedness. All his resources to the very last, he uses for the undoing of the human race. . . .

[A good prince is one] who holds the life of each individual dearer than his own; who works and strives night and day for just one end—to be the best he can for everyone; with whom rewards are ready for all good men . . . for so much does he want to be of real help to his people, without thought of recompense, that if necessary

(Continued)

(Opposing Viewpoints continued)

he would not hesitate to look out for their welfare at great risk to himself; who considers his wealth to lie in the advantage of his country; who is ever on the watch so that everyone else may sleep deeply; who grants no leisure to himself so that he may spend his life in the peace of his country; who worries himself with continual cares so that his subjects may have peace and quiet. . . . He does everything and allows everything that will bring everlasting peace to his country, for he realizes that war is the source of all misfortunes to the state.

Q What does Machiavelli have to say about being loved rather than feared? How does this view contrast with that of Erasmus on the characteristics of a good ruler? Which viewpoint do you consider more modern? Why? Which viewpoint do you think is correct? Why?

Sources: Machiavelli, *The Prince* (1513). From *The Prince* by Machiavelli, translated by David Wootton, pp. 51–52. Copyright © 1995 by Hackett Publishing Company, Inc. Reprinted by permission of Hackett Publishing Company, Inc. All rights reserved. Erasmas, *Education of a Christian Prince* (1516). From *The Education of a Christian Prince*, by Erasmus, translated by L. K. Born. Copyright © 1936 by Columbia University Press. Reprinted with permission of the publisher.

by the fourteenth century. For the next two centuries, Italy was the cultural leader of Europe. This new Italian culture was primarily the product of a relatively wealthy, urban lay society. The most important literary movement associated with the Renaissance was **humanism**.

Italian Renaissance Humanism

Renaissance humanism was an intellectual movement based on the study of the Classical literary works of Greece and Rome. Humanists examined the *studia humanitatis* ("the studies of humanity")—grammar, rhetoric, poetry, moral philosophy or ethics, and history—all based on the writings of ancient Greek and Roman authors. These are the subjects we call the humanities.

Petrarch (1304–1374), often called the father of Italian Renaissance humanism, did more than any other individual in the fourteenth century to foster development of the movement. Petrarch's interest in the classics led him on a quest for forgotten Latin manuscripts and set in motion a ransacking of monastic libraries throughout Europe. In his preoccupation with the classics and their secular content, Petrarch doubted at times whether he was sufficiently attentive to spiritual ideals. His qualms, however, did not prevent him from inaugurating the humanist emphasis on the use of pure Classical Latin, making it fashionable for humanists to use Cicero as a model for prose and Virgil for poetry. Petrarch said, "Christ is my God; Cicero is the prince of the language."

In Florence, the humanist movement took a new direction at the beginning of the fifteenth century when it became closely tied to Florentine civic spirit and pride, giving rise to what one modern scholar has labeled **civic humanism**. Fourteenth-century humanists such as Petrarch had described the intellectual life as one of solitude. They rejected family and a life of action in the community. In the busy civic world of Florence, however, intellectuals began to take a new view of their role as intellectuals. The Classical Roman statesman and intellectual Cicero became their model. Leonardo Bruni (1370–1444), a humanist, Florentine patriot, and chancellor of the city, wrote a biography of Cicero titled the *New Cicero*, in which he waxed enthusiastic about the fusion of political action and literary creation in Cicero's life. From Bruni's time on, Cicero served as the inspiration for the Renaissance ideal that it was the duty of an intellectual to live an active life for one's state. An individual only "grows to maturity—both intellectually and morally—through participation" in the life of the state. Civic humanism reflected the values of the urban society of the Italian Renaissance. Humanists came to believe that their study of the humanities should be put to the service of the state. It is no accident that humanists served the state as chancellors, councillors, and advisers.

Also evident in the humanism of the first half of the fifteenth century was a growing interest in Classical Greek civilization. Bruni was one of the first Italian humanists to gain a thorough knowledge of Greek. He became an enthusiastic pupil of the Byzantine scholar Manuel Chrysoloras (kris-uh-LOR-uss), who taught in Florence from 1396 to 1400. Humanists eagerly perused the works of Plato as well as Greek poets, dramatists, historians, and orators, such as Thucydides, Euripides, and Sophocles, all of whom had been ignored by the scholastics of the High Middle Ages as irrelevant to the theological questions they were examining.

HUMANISM AND PHILOSOPHY In the second half of the fifteenth century, a dramatic upsurge of interest in the works of Plato occurred. Cosimo de' Medici, the de facto ruler of Florence, encouraged this development by commissioning a translation of Plato's dialogues by Marsilio Ficino (mar-SIL-yoh fee-CHEE-noh) (1433–1499), who dedicated his life to the translation of Plato and the exposition of the Platonic philosophy known as **Neoplatonism**.

In two major works, Ficino undertook the synthesis of Christianity and Platonism into a single system. His Neoplatonism was based on two primary ideas, the Neoplatonic hierarchy of substances and a theory of spiritual love. The former postulated the idea of a hierarchy of substances, or great chain of being, from the lowest form of physical matter (plants) to the purest spirit (God), in which humans occupied a central or middle position. They were the link between the material world (through the body) and the spiritual world (through the soul), and their highest duty was to ascend toward that union with God that was the true end of human existence. Ficino's theory of spiritual or Platonic love maintained that just as all people are bound together in their common humanity by love, so are all parts of the universe held together by bonds of sympathetic love.

RENAISSANCE HERMETICISM **Hermeticism** was another product of the Florentine intellectual environment of the late fifteenth century. At the request of Cosimo de' Medici, Ficino translated into Latin a Greek work titled *Corpus Hermeticum* (KOR-pus hur-MET-i-koom), which offered Renaissance intellectuals a new view of humankind. According to the Hermetic manuscripts, humans had been created as divine beings endowed with divine creative power but had freely chosen to enter the material world (nature). Humans could recover their divinity, however, through a regenerative experience or purification of the soul. Thus regenerated, they became true sages or magi, as the Renaissance called them, who had knowledge of God and of truth. In regaining their original divinity, they reacquired an intimate knowledge of nature and the ability to employ the powers of nature for beneficial purposes.

In Italy, the most prominent magi in the late fifteenth century were Ficino and his friend and pupil Giovanni Pico della Mirandola (PEE-koh DELL-uh mee-RAN-doh-lah) (1463–1494). Pico produced one of the most famous pieces of writing of the Renaissance, the *Oration on the Dignity of Man*. Pico combed diligently through the writings of many philosophers of different backgrounds for the common "nuggets of universal truth" that he believed were all part of God's revelation to humanity. In the *Oration*, Pico offered a ringing statement of unlimited human potential: "To him it is granted to have whatever he chooses, to be whatever he wills."[9] Like Ficino, Pico took an avid interest in Hermetic philosophy, accepting it as the "science of the Divine," which "embraces the deepest contemplation of the most secret things, and at last the knowledge of all nature."[10]

Education in the Renaissance

The humanist movement had a profound effect on education. Renaissance humanists believed that human beings could be dramatically changed by education, and as a result, they wrote treatises on education and opened schools based on their ideas. At the core of humanist schools were the "liberal studies." Humanists believed that the "liberal studies" (what we call the liberal arts) were the key to true freedom, enabling individuals to reach their full potential. The liberal studies included history, moral philosophy, eloquence (rhetoric), letters (grammar and logic), poetry, mathematics, astronomy, and music. The purpose of a liberal education was thus to produce individuals who followed a path of virtue and wisdom and possessed the rhetorical skills by which they could persuade others to do the same. Following the Greek precept of a sound mind in a sound body, humanist educators also stressed physical education. Pupils were taught the skills of javelin throwing, archery, and dancing and encouraged to run, wrestle, hunt, and swim.

The purpose of these humanist schools was to educate an elite, the ruling classes of their communities. Largely absent from such schools were females. The few female students who did attend humanist schools studied the classics and were encouraged to know some history and to ride, dance, sing, play the lute, and appreciate poetry. But they were told not to learn mathematics and rhetoric. Religion and morals were thought to hold first place in the education of Christian ladies and help prepare them for their roles as mothers and wives.

Nevertheless, some women in Italy who were educated in the humanist fashion went on to establish their own literary careers. Isotta Nogarola (ee-ZAHT-uh NOH-guh-roll-uh), born to a noble family in Verona, mastered Latin and wrote numerous letters and treatises that brought her praise from male Italian intellectuals. Laura Cereta (say-REE-tuh) was educated in Latin by her father, a physician from Brescia. Laura defended the ability of women to pursue scholarly pursuits (see the box on p. 265).

Humanist education was thought to be a practical preparation for life. Its aim was the creation not of a great scholar but of a complete citizen. As one humanist said, "Not everyone is obliged to excel in philosophy, medicine, or the law, nor are all equally favored by nature; but all are destined to live in society and to practice virtue."[11] Humanist schools, combining the classics and Christianity, provided the model for the basic education of the European ruling classes until the twentieth century.

The Impact of Printing

The Renaissance period witnessed the development of printing, one of the most important technological

A Woman's Defense of Learning

As a young woman, Laura Cereta was proud of her learning but condemned by a male world that found it unseemly for women to be scholars. One monk said to her father, "She gives herself to things unworthy of her—namely, the classics." Before being silenced, Laura Cereta wrote a series of letters, including one to a male critic who had argued that her work was so good it could not have been written by a woman.

Laura Cereta, *Defense of the Liberal Instruction of Women*

My ears are wearied by your carping. You brashly and publicly not merely wonder but indeed lament that I am said to possess as fine a mind as nature ever bestowed upon the most learned man. You seem to think that so learned a woman has scarcely before been seen in the world. You are wrong on both counts. . . .

I would have been silent. . . . But I cannot tolerate your having attacked my entire sex. For this reason my thirsty soul seeks revenge, my sleeping pen is aroused to literary struggle, raging anger stirs mental passions long chained by silence. With just cause I am moved to demonstrate how great a reputation for learning and virtue women have won by their inborn excellence, manifested in every age as knowledge. . . .

Only the question of the rarity of outstanding women remains to be addressed. The explanation is clear: women have been able by nature to be exceptional, but have chosen lesser goals. For some women are concerned with parting their hair correctly, adorning themselves with lovely dresses, or decorating their fingers with pearls and other gems. Others delight in mouthing carefully composed phrases, indulging in dancing, or managing spoiled puppies. Still others wish to gaze at lavish banquet tables, to rest in sleep, or, standing at mirrors, to smear their lovely faces. But those in whom a deeper integrity yearns for virtue, restrain from the start their youthful souls, reflect on higher things, harden the body with sobriety and trials, and curb their tongues, open their ears, compose their thoughts in wakeful hours, their minds in contemplation, to letters bonded to righteousness. For knowledge is not given as a gift, but [is gained] with diligence. The free mind, not shirking effort, always soars zealously toward the good, and the desire to know grows ever more wide and deep. It is because of no special holiness, therefore, that we [women] are rewarded by God the Giver with the gift of exceptional talent. Nature has generously lavished its gifts upon all people, opening to all the doors of choice through which reason sends envoys to the will, from which they learn and convey its desires. The will must choose to exercise the gift of reason. . . .

I have been praised too much; showing your contempt for women, you pretend that I alone am admirable because of the good fortune of my intellect. . . . Do you suppose, O most contemptible man on earth, that I think myself sprung [like Athena] from the head of Jove? I am a school girl, possessed of the sleeping embers of an ordinary mind. Indeed I am too hurt, and my mind, offended, too swayed by passions, sighs, tormenting itself, conscious of the obligation to defend my sex. For absolutely everything—that which is within us and that which is without—is made weak by association with my sex.

Q How did Cereta explain her intellectual interests and accomplishments? Why were Renaissance women rarely taken seriously when they sought educational opportunities and recognition for their intellectual talents? Were any of those factors unique to the Renaissance era?

Source: Laura Cereta, "Defense of the Liberal Instruction of Women," from *Her Immaculate Hand: Selected Works by and about the Women Humanists of Quattrocentro Italy*, ed. by Margaret King and Albert Rabil (Pegasus Press, Asheville, NC, 2000). Reprinted by permission.

innovations of Western civilization. The art of printing had an immediate impact on European intellectual life and thought. Printing from hand-carved wooden blocks had been done in the West since the twelfth century and in China even before that. What was new to Europe in the fifteenth century was repeatable printing with movable metal type. The development of printing from movable type was a gradual process that culminated between 1445 and 1450; Johannes Gutenberg (yoh-HAH-nuss GOO-ten-bayrk) of Mainz played an important role in bringing the process to completion. Gutenberg's Bible, completed in 1455 or 1456, was the first true book in the West produced from movable type.

The new printing capability spread rapidly throughout Europe in the second half of the fifteenth century. By 1500, there were more than a thousand printers in Europe who had published almost 40,000 titles (between 8 million and 10 million copies). Probably 50 percent of these books were religious—Bibles, books of devotion, and sermons. Next in importance were the Latin and Greek classics, medieval grammars, legal handbooks, works on philosophy, and an ever-growing number of popular romances.

Printing became one of the largest industries in Europe, and its effects were soon felt in many areas of European life. The printing of books encouraged the development of scholarly research and the desire to attain knowledge. Moreover, printing facilitated cooperation among scholars and helped produce standardized and definitive texts. Printing also stimulated the development of an ever-expanding lay reading public, a development that had an enormous impact on European society. Indeed, the new religious ideas of the Reformation would never have spread as rapidly as they did in the sixteenth century without the printing press.

The Artistic Renaissance

Q Focus Question: What were the chief characteristics of Renaissance art, and how did it differ in Italy and northern Europe?

Leonardo da Vinci, one of the great Italian Renaissance artists, once explained, "The painter will produce pictures of small merit if he takes for his standard the pictures of others, but if he will study from natural objects he will bear good fruit. . . . Those who take for their standard any one but nature . . . weary themselves in vain."[12] Renaissance artists considered the imitation of nature their primary goal. Their search for naturalism became an end in itself: to persuade onlookers of the reality of the object or event they were portraying. At the same time, the new artistic standards reflected a new attitude of mind as well, one in which human beings became the focus of attention, the "center and measure of all things," as one artist proclaimed.

Art in the Early Renaissance

The cycle of frescoes by Masaccio (muh-ZAH-choh) (1401–1428) in the Brancacci Chapel in Florence has long been regarded as the first masterpiece of Early Renaissance art. In his use of monumental figures, the demonstration of a more realistic relationship between figures and landscape, and the visual representation of the laws of perspective, a new realistic style of painting was born. Onlookers become aware of a world of reality that appears to be a continuation of their own world.

This new Renaissance style was absorbed and modified by other Florentine painters in the fifteenth century. Especially important was the development of an experimental trend that took two directions. One aspect emphasized the mathematical side of painting, the working out of the laws of perspective and the organization of outdoor

Brancacci Chapel, S. Maria del Carmine, Florence//© Scala/Art Resource, NY

Masaccio, *Tribute Money.* With the frescoes of Masaccio, regarded by many as the first great works of Early Renaissance art, a new realistic style of painting was born. *Tribute Money* is one of a series of frescoes that Masaccio painted in the Brancacci Chapel of the Church of Santa Maria del Carmine in Florence. In *Tribute Money,* Masaccio depicted the biblical story of Jesus's confrontation by a tax collector at the entrance to the town of Capernaum (seen at the center). Jesus sent Peter to collect a coin from the mouth of a fish from Lake Galilee (seen at the left); Peter then paid the tax collector (seen at the right). In illustrating this story from the Bible, Masaccio used a rational system of perspective to create a realistic relationship between the figures and their background; the figures themselves are also realistic. As one Renaissance observer said, "The works made before Masaccio's day can be said to be painted, while his are living, real, and natural."

Museo Nazionale del Bargello, Florence//© Scala/Art Resource, NY

Donatello, *David.* Donatello's *David* first stood in the courtyard of the Medici Palace. On its base was an inscription praising Florentine heroism and virtue, leading art historians to assume that the statue was meant to commemorate the victory of Florence over Milan in 1428. David's pose and appearance are reminiscent of the nude statues of antiquity.

space and light by geometry and perspective. The other aspect involved the investigation of movement and anatomical structure. Indeed, the realistic portrayal of the human nude became one of the foremost preoccupations of Italian Renaissance art. The fifteenth century, then, was a period of experimentation and technical mastery.

The revolutionary achievements of Florentine painters in the fifteenth century were matched by equally stunning advances in sculpture and architecture. Donato di Donatello (doh-NAH-toh dee doh-nuh-TELL-oh) (1386–1466) spent time in Rome, studying and copying the statues of antiquity. His subsequent work in Florence reveals how well he had mastered the essence of what he saw. Among his numerous works was a statue of David that was the first known life-size, freestanding bronze nude in European art since antiquity. Like Donatello's other statues, *David* radiated a simplicity and strength that reflected the dignity of humanity.

Filippo Brunelleschi (fee-LEE-poh BROO-nuh-LESS-kee) (1377–1446) was a friend of Donatello's who accompanied him to Rome. Brunelleschi drew much inspiration from the architectural monuments of Roman antiquity, and when he returned to Florence, the Medici commissioned him to design the Church of San Lorenzo. Inspired by Roman models, Brunelleschi created a church interior very different from that of the great medieval cathedrals. San Lorenzo's Classical columns, rounded arches, and coffered ceiling created an environment that did not overwhelm the worshiper, materially or psychologically, as Gothic cathedrals did, but comforted as a space created to fit human, not divine, measurements.

San Lorenzo, Florence//© Scala/Art Resource, NY

Filippo Brunelleschi, Interior of San Lorenzo. Cosimo de' Medici contributed massive amounts of money to the rebuilding of the Church of San Lorenzo. As seen in this view of the nave and choir of the church, Brunelleschi's architectural designs were based on the basilica plan borrowed by early Christians from pagan Rome. San Lorenzo's simplicity, evident in its rows of slender Corinthian columns, created a human-centered space.

The Artistic High Renaissance

By the end of the fifteenth century, Italian painters, sculptors, and architects had created a new artistic environment. Many artists had mastered the new techniques for a scientific observation of the world around them and were now ready to move into individualistic forms of creative expression. This final stage of Renaissance art, which flourished between 1480 and 1520, is called the High Renaissance. The shift to the High Renaissance was marked by the increasing importance of Rome as a new cultural center of the Renaissance.

The High Renaissance was dominated by the work of three artistic giants: Leonardo da Vinci (1452–1519), Raphael (1483–1520), and Michelangelo (1475–1564). Leonardo represents a transitional figure in the shift to High Renaissance principles. He stressed the need to advance beyond the mere realistic respresentation of nature and initiated the High Renaissance's preoccupation with the idealization of nature, or the attempt to generalize from realistic portrayal to an ideal form. Leonardo's *Last Supper*, painted in Milan, is a brilliant summary of fifteenth-century trends in its organization of space and use of perspective to depict subjects three-dimensionally. But it is also more. The figure of Philip is idealized, and there are profound psychological dimensions to the work. Jesus's words—"One of you shall betray me"—are experienced directly as each of the apostles reveals his personality and his relationship to the Savior. Through gestures and movement, Leonardo hoped to reveal a person's inner life.

Raphael (RAFF-ee-ul) blossomed as a painter at an early age; at twenty-five, he was already regarded as one of Italy's best painters. Raphael was acclaimed for his numerous madonnas (portraits of the Virgin Mary), in which he attempted to achieve an ideal of beauty far surpassing human standards. He is well known for his frescoes in the Vatican Palace; his *School of Athens* reveals a world of balance, harmony, and order—the underlying principles of the art of the Classical world of Greece and Rome.

Michelangelo (my-kuh-LAN-juh-loh), an accomplished painter, sculptor, and architect, was another giant of the High Renaissance. Fiercely driven by his desire to create, he worked with great passion and energy on a remarkable number of projects. Michelangelo was influenced by Neoplatonism, especially evident in his figures on the ceiling of the Sistine Chapel in Rome. In 1508, Pope Julius II had called Michelangelo to Rome and commissioned him to decorate the chapel ceiling. This colossal project was not completed until 1512. Michelangelo attempted to tell the story of the Fall of Man by depicting nine scenes from the biblical book of Genesis. In his *Creation of Adam* (reproduced at the start of this chapter), the well-proportioned figure of Adam awaits the divine spark. Adam, like the other muscular figures on the ceiling, reveals an ideal type of human being with perfect proportions. In good

S. Maria delle Grazie, Milan/© Scala/Ministero per i Beni e le Attività culturali/ Art Resource, NY

Leonardo da Vinci, *The Last Supper.* Leonardo da Vinci was the impetus behind the High Renaissance concern for the idealization of nature, moving from a realistic portrayal of the human figure to an idealized form. Evident in Leonardo's *Last Supper* is his effort to depict a person's character and inner nature by the use of gesture and movement. Unfortunately, Leonardo used an experimental technique in this fresco, which soon led to its physical deterioration.

Stanza della Segnatura, Stanze di Raffaello, Vatican Palace, Vatican State/ /© Erich Lessing/ Art Resource, NY

Raphael, *School of Athens.* Raphael arrived in Rome in 1508 and began to paint a series of frescoes commissioned by Pope Julius II for the papal apartments at the Vatican. In *School of Athens*, painted in 1510 or 1511, Raphael created an imaginary gathering of ancient philosophers. In the center stand Plato and Aristotle. At the left is Pythagoras, showing his system of proportions on a slate. At the right is the astronomer Ptolemy, holding a celestial globe.

Neoplatonic fashion, the beauty of these figures is meant to be a reflection of divine beauty—the more beautiful the body, the more God-like the figure.

Another manifestation of Michelangelo's search for ideal beauty was his *David*, a colossal marble statue commissioned by the Florentine government in 1501 and completed in 1504. Michelangelo maintained that the form of a statue already resided in the uncarved piece of stone: "I only take away the surplus; the statue is already there."[13] Out of a piece of marble that had remained unused for fifty years, Michelangelo created a 14-foot-high figure, the largest sculpture in Italy since Roman times. An awe-inspiring hero, Michelangelo's *David* proudly proclaims the beauty of the human body and the glory of human beings.

The Northern Artistic Renaissance

In trying to provide an exact portrayal of their world, the artists of the north (especially the Low Countries) and Italy took different approaches. In Italy, the human form became the primary vehicle of expression as Italian artists sought to master the technical skills that allowed them to portray humans in realistic settings. The large wall spaces of Italian churches had given rise to the art of fresco painting, but in the north, the prevalence of Gothic cathedrals with their stained-glass windows resulted in more emphasis on illuminated manuscripts and wooden panel painting for altarpieces. The space available in these works was limited, and great care was required to depict each object, leading northern painters to become masters at rendering details.

The most influential northern school of art in the fifteenth century was centered in Flanders. Jan van Eyck (YAHN vahn YK *or* van AYK) (c. 1380–1441) was among the first to use oil paint, a medium that enabled the artist to use a varied range of colors and create fine details. In the famous *Giovanni Arnolfini and His Bride*, van Eyck's attention to

Accademia, Florence//© Scala/Art Resource, NY

Michelangelo, *David.* This statue of David exalts the beauty of the human body and is a fitting symbol of the Italian Renaissance's affirmation of human power. Completed in 1504, *David* was moved by Florentine authorities to a special location in front of the Palazzo Vecchio, the seat of the Florentine government.

National Gallery, London//© Erich Lessing/Art Resource, NY

Jan van Eyck, *Giovanni Arnolfini and His Bride.* Northern painters took great care in depicting each object and became masters at rendering details. This emphasis on a realistic portrayal is clearly evident in this oil painting, said to be a portrait of Giovanni Arnolfini, an Italian merchant who had settled in Bruges, and his wife, Giovanna Cenami.

detail is staggering: precise portraits, a glittering chandelier, and a mirror reflecting the objects in the room. Although each detail was rendered as observed, it is evident that van Eyck's comprehension of perspective was still uncertain. His work is truly indicative of northern Renaissance painters, who, in their effort to imitate nature, did so not by mastery of the laws of perspective and proportion but by empirical observation of visual reality and the accurate portrayal of details. Moreover, northern painters placed great emphasis on the emotional intensity of religious feeling and created great works of devotional art, especially in their altarpieces. By the end of the fifteenth century, however, artists from the north began to study in Italy and were visually influenced by what artists were doing there.

One northern artist of this later period who was greatly influenced by the Italians was Albrecht Dürer (AHL-brekht DOO-rur) (1471–1528) from Nuremberg. Dürer made two trips to Italy and absorbed most of what the Italians could teach, as is evident in his mastery of the laws of perspective and Renaissance theories of proportion. He wrote detailed treatises on both subjects. At the same time, as in his famous *Adoration of the Magi*, Dürer did not reject the use of minute details characteristic of northern artists. He did try, however, to integrate those details more harmoniously into his works and, like the Italian artists of the High Renaissance, tried to achieve a standard of ideal beauty by a careful examination of the human form.

Galleria degli Uffizi, Florence/© Erich Lessing/Art Resource, NY

Albrecht Dürer, *Adoration of the Magi.* By the end of the fifteenth century, northern artists began studying in Italy and adopting many of the techniques used by Italian painters. As is evident in this painting, which was the central panel for an altarpiece done for Frederick the Wise in 1504, Albrecht Dürer masterfully incorporated the laws of perspective and the ideals of proportion into his works. At the same time, he did not abandon the preoccupation with detail typical of northern artists.

The European State in the Renaissance

Q Focus Question: Why do historians sometimes refer to the monarchies of the late fifteenth century as "new monarchies" or "Renaissance states"?

In the first half of the fifteenth century, European states continued the disintegrative patterns of the previous century. In the second half of the century, however, recovery set in, and attempts were made to reestablish the centralized power of monarchical governments. To characterize the results, some historians have used the label "Renaissance states"; others have spoken of the "**new monarchies**," especially those of France, England, and Spain at the end of the fifteenth century. Although monarchs in western Europe succeeded to varying degrees at extending their political authority, rulers in central and eastern Europe were often weak and unable to impose their will.

The Renaissance State in Western Europe

Although the Hundred Years' War (1337–1453; see Chapter 11) had made it difficult for French kings to assert their authority, the war had also developed a strong degree of French national feeling toward a common enemy that the kings could use to reestablish monarchical power. The process of developing a French territorial state was greatly advanced by King Louis XI (1461–1483), known as the Spider because of his devious ways. Louis strengthened the use of the *taille* (TY)—an annual direct tax, usually on land or property—as a tax imposed by royal authority, giving him a regular and reliable source of income. Louis repressed the French nobility and brought the provinces of Anjou, Maine, Bar, and Provence under royal control.

ENGLAND The Hundred Years' War had also strongly affected the other protagonist in that conflict. The cost of the war in its final years and the losses in manpower strained the English economy. Moreover, the end of the war brought even greater domestic turmoil to England when the War of the Roses broke out in the 1450s. This civil war pitted the ducal house of Lancaster, whose symbol was a red rose, against the ducal house of York, whose symbol was a white rose. Many aristocratic families of England were drawn into the conflict. Finally, in 1485, Henry Tudor, duke of Richmond, defeated the last Yorkist king, Richard III (1483–1485), at Bosworth Field and established the new Tudor dynasty.

As the first Tudor king, Henry VII (1485–1509) worked to reduce internal dissension and establish a strong monarchical government. The new king was particularly successful in obtaining sufficient income from the traditional financial resources of the English monarch, such as the crown lands, judicial fees and fines, and customs duties. By using diplomacy to avoid wars, which are always expensive, the king avoided having to call Parliament on any regular basis to grant him funds. By not overburdening the landed gentry and middle class with taxes, Henry won their favor, and they provided much support for his monarchy. Henry's policies enabled him to leave England with a stable and prosperous government and an enhanced status for the monarchy itself.

SPAIN Spain, too, experienced the growth of a strong national monarchy by the end of the fifteenth century. During the Middle Ages, several independent Christian kingdoms had emerged in the course of the long reconquest of the Iberian peninsula from the Muslims (see Map 12.2). Aragon and Castile were the strongest Spanish kingdoms; in the west was the independent monarchy of Portugal; in the north, the small kingdom of Navarre; and in the south, the Muslim kingdom of Granada.

A major step toward the unification of Spain was taken with the marriage of Isabella of Castile (1474–1504) and Ferdinand of Aragon (1479–1516) in 1469. This was a dynastic union of two rulers, not a political union. Both

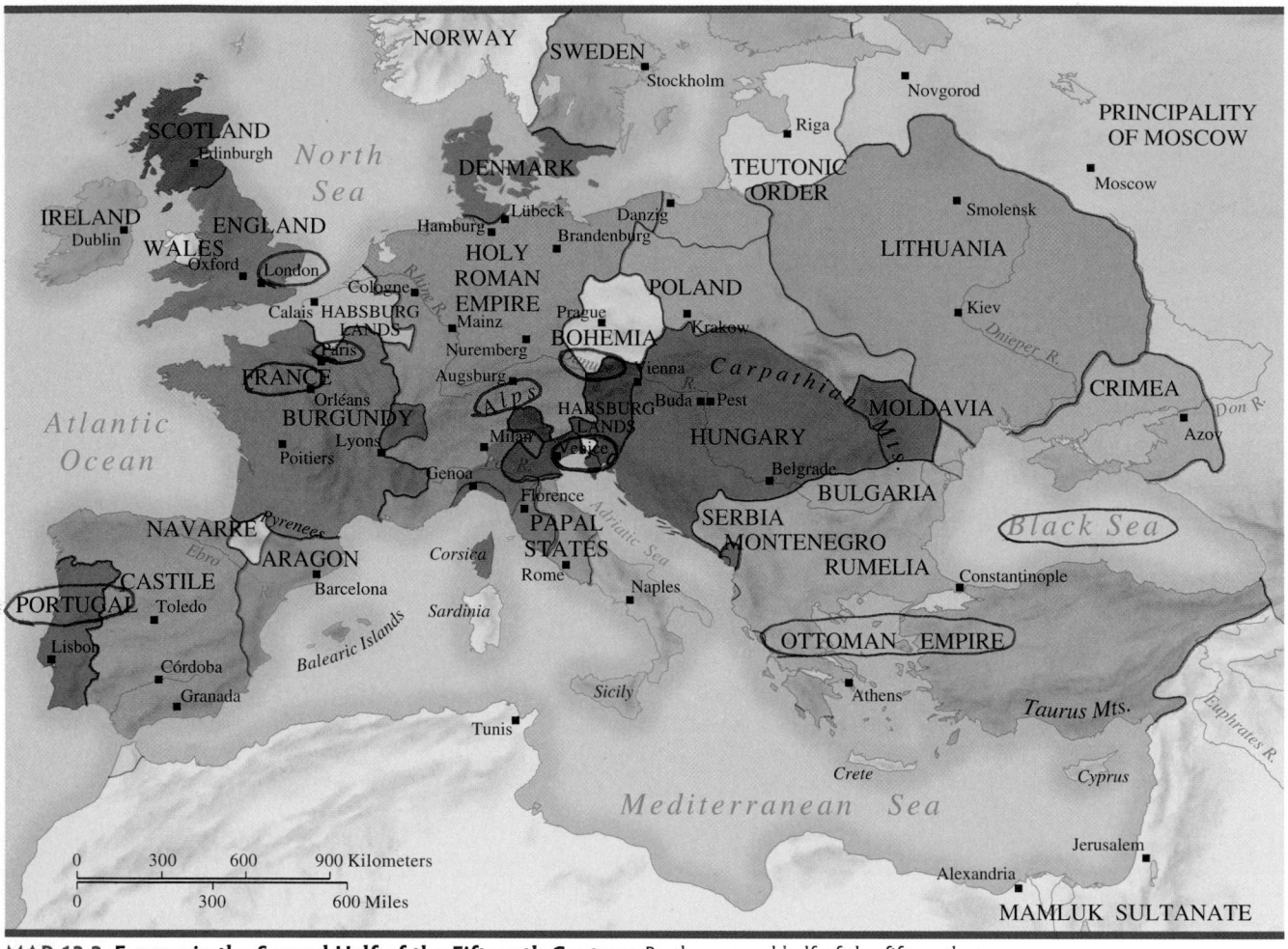

© Cengage Learning

MAP 12.2 Europe in the Second Half of the Fifteenth Century. By the second half of the fifteenth century, monarchs in western Europe, particularly in France, Spain, and England, had begun the process of modern state building. With varying success, they reined in the power of the church and nobles, increased the ability to levy taxes, and established effective government bureaucracies.

Q ***What aspects of Europe's political boundaries help explain why France and the Holy Roman Empire were often at war with each other?***

kingdoms maintained their own parliaments—each known as the Cortes (KOR-tez)—courts, laws, coinage, speech, customs, and political organs. Nevertheless, the two rulers worked to strengthen royal control of government, especially in Castile. The royal council, which was supposed to supervise local administration and oversee the implementation of government policies, was stripped of aristocrats and filled primarily with middle-class lawyers. Trained in the principles of Roman law, these officials operated on the belief that the monarchy embodied the power of the state.

Seeking to replace the undisciplined feudal levies they had inherited with a more professional royal army, Ferdinand and Isabella reorganized the military forces of Spain, The development of a strong infantry force as the heart of the new Spanish army made it the best in Europe by the sixteenth century, and Spain emerged as an important power in European affairs.

Because of its vast power and wealth, Ferdinand and Isabella recognized the importance of controlling the Catholic Church. They secured from the pope the right to select the most important church officials in Spain, virtually guaranteeing the foundation of a Spanish Catholic Church in which the clergy became an instrument for the extension of royal power. The monarchs also used their authority over the church to institute reform.

Ferdinand and Isabella also pursued a policy of strict religious uniformity. Of course, this served a political purpose as well: to create unity and further bolster royal power. Spain possessed two large religious minorities, Jews and Muslims; both had generally been tolerated in medieval Spain. Although anti-Semitism had become a fact of life in medieval Europe, Spain had largely remained tolerant. Increased persecution in the fourteenth century, however, led the majority of Spanish Jews to convert to Christianity. But complaints about the sincerity of these Jewish converts prompted Ferdinand and Isabella to ask the pope to introduce the Inquisition into Spain in 1478. Under royal control, the Inquisition worked with cruel efficiency to guarantee the orthodoxy of the converts but had no authority over practicing Jews. Consequently, in 1492, flush with the success of the conquest of Muslim Granada, Ferdinand and Isabella took the drastic step of expelling all professed Jews from Spain. It is estimated that 150,000 out of possibly 200,000 Jews fled.

Ferdinand and Isabella had also pursued a policy of battling the Muslims by attacking the kingdom of Granada. The war against this remaining Muslim kingdom lasted eleven years until the final bastion of the city of Granada fell in 1492. Muslims were now "encouraged" to convert to Christianity, and in 1502, Isabella issued a decree expelling all professed Muslims from her kingdom. To a very large degree, the "Most Catholic" monarchs had achieved their goal of absolute religious orthodoxy as a basic ingredient of the Spanish state. To be Spanish was to be Catholic, a policy of uniformity enforced by the Inquisition. It was no accident that Spain would be a staunch pillar of the Catholic Church in the sixteenth-century era of the Reformation (see Chapter 13).

Central Europe: The Holy Roman Empire

After 1438, the position of Holy Roman Emperor was in the hands of the Habsburg dynasty. Having gradually acquired a number of possessions along the Danube, known collectively as Austria, the house of Habsburg had become one of the wealthiest landholders in the empire and by the mid-fifteenth century began to play an important role in European affairs. Much of the Habsburg success in the fifteenth century was due not to military victories but to a well-executed policy of dynastic marriages.

Much was expected of the flamboyant Maximilian I (1493–1519) when he became emperor. Through the Reichstag, the imperial diet or parliament, Maximilian attempted to centralize the administration by creating new institutions common to the entire empire. Opposition from the German princes doomed these efforts, however. Maximilian's only real success lay in his marriage alliances, which led to his grandson, Charles V, inheriting the traditional lands of the Habsburg, Burgundian, and Spanish monarchical lines at the beginning of the sixteenth century, making him the leading monarch of his age (see Chapter 13).

The Struggle for Strong Monarchy in Eastern Europe

In eastern Europe, rulers struggled to achieve the centralization of their territorial states but faced serious obstacles. Although the population was mostly Slavic, there were islands of other ethnic groups that caused difficulties. Religious differences also troubled the area, as Roman Catholics, Greek Orthodox Christians, and pagans came into conflict.

Much of Polish history revolved around a bitter struggle between the crown and the landed nobility until the end of the fifteenth century, when the preoccupation of the Polish monarchy with problems in Bohemia and Hungary, as well as war with the Russians and Turks, enabled the aristocrats to reestablish their power. Through their control of the Sejm (SAYM) or national parliament, the magnates reduced the peasantry to serfdom by 1511 and established the right to elect their kings. The Polish kings proved unable to establish a strong royal authority.

Since the conversion of Hungary to Roman Catholicism by German missionaries, its history had been closely tied to that of central and western Europe. The church became a large and prosperous institution. Wealthy bishops, along with great territorial lords, became powerful, independent political figures. For a brief while, Hungary developed into an important European state, the dominant power in eastern Europe. King Matthias Corvinus (muh-THY-uss kor-VY-nuss) (1458–1490) broke the power of the wealthy lords and created a well-organized central administration. After his death, Hungary returned to weak rule, however, and the work of Corvinus was largely undone.

Since the thirteenth century, Russia had been under the domination of the Mongols. Gradually, the princes of Moscow rose to prominence by using their close relationship to the Mongol khans to increase their wealth and expand their possessions. In the reign of the great prince Ivan III (1462–1505), a new Russian state—the principality of Moscow—was born. Ivan III annexed other Russian principalities and took advantage of dissension among the Mongols to throw off their yoke by 1480.

The Ottoman Turks and the End of the Byzantine Empire

Eastern Europe was increasingly threatened by the steadily advancing Ottoman Turks. The Byzantine Empire had, of course, served as a buffer between the Muslim Middle

CHRONOLOGY The European State in the Renaissance	
France	
Louis XI the Spider	1461–1483
England	
War of the Roses	1450s–1485
Richard III	1483–1485
Henry VII	1485–1509
Spain	
Isabella of Castile	1474–1504
Ferdinand of Aragon	1479–1516
Marriage of Ferdinand and Isabella	1469
Introduction of the Inquisition	1478
Expulsion of Jews	1492
Expulsion of Muslims	1502
Holy Roman Empire	
Maximilian I	1493–1519
Eastern Europe	
Hungary: Matthias Corvinus	1458–1490
Russia: Ivan III	1462–1505
Fall of Constantinople and Byzantine Empire	1453

East and the Latin West for centuries, but it had been severely weakened by the sack of Constantinople in 1204 and its occupation by the West. Although the Paleologus dynasty (1260–1453) had tried to reestablish Byzantine power in the Balkans, the threat from the Turks finally doomed the long-lasting empire.

Beginning in northeastern Asia Minor in the thirteenth century, the Ottoman Turks spread rapidly, seizing the lands of the Seljuk Turks and the Byzantine Empire. In 1345, they bypassed Constantinople and moved into the Balkans. Under Sultan Murad (moo-RAHD), Ottoman forces moved through Bulgaria and into the lands of the Serbians, who provided a strong center of opposition under King Lazar (lah-ZAR). But in 1389, at the Battle of Kosovo (KAWSS-suh-voh), Ottoman forces defeated the Serbs; both King Lazar and Sultan Murad perished in the battle. Kosovo became a battlefield long revered and remembered by the Serbs. Not until 1480 were Bosnia, Albania, and the rest of Serbia added to the Ottoman Empire in the Balkans.

In the meantime, in 1453, the Ottomans also completed the demise of the Byzantine Empire. With 80,000 troops ranged against only 7,000 defenders, Sultan Mehmet II (meh-MET) laid siege to Constantinople. In their attack on the city, the Turks made use of massive cannons with 26-foot barrels that could launch stone balls weighing up to 1,200 pounds each. Finally, the walls were breached; the Byzantine emperor died in the final battle. Mehmet II, standing before the palace of the emperor, paused to reflect on the passing nature of human glory.

After their conquest of Constantinople, the Ottoman Turks tried to complete their conquest of the Balkans, where they had been established since the fourteenth century. Although they were successful in taking the Romanian territory of Wallachia (wah-LAY-kee-uh) in 1476, the resistance of the Hungarians initially kept the Turks from advancing up the Danube valley. Until the end of the fifteenth century, internal problems and the need to consolidate their eastern frontiers kept the Turks from any further attacks on Europe. But at the beginning of the sixteenth century, the Ottomans would renew their offensive against the West, challenging Hungary, Austria, Bohemia, and Poland and threatening to turn the Mediterranean into a Turkish lake.

The Church in the Renaissance

FOCUS QUESTION: What were the policies of the Renaissance popes, and what impact did those policies have on the Roman Catholic Church?

As a result of the efforts of the Council of Constance, the Great Schism of the Catholic Church had finally been brought to an end in 1417 (see Chapter 11). The ending of the schism proved to be the council's easiest task; it was much less successful in dealing with heresy and achieving reform.

Dealing with Heresy and Reform

Heresy was not a new problem, and in the thirteenth century, the church had developed inquisitorial machinery to deal with it. But two widespread movements in the fourteenth and early fifteenth centuries—Lollardy and Hussitism—posed new threats to the church.

WYCLIF AND LOLLARDY English Lollardy was a product of the Oxford theologian John Wyclif (WIK-lif) (c. 1328–1384), whose disgust with clerical corruption led him to a far-ranging attack on papal authority and medieval Christian beliefs and practices. Wyclif alleged that there was no basis in Scripture for papal claims of temporal authority and advocated that the popes be stripped of their authority and their property. Believing that the Bible should be a Christian's sole authority, Wyclif urged that it be made available in the vernacular languages so that every Christian could read it. Rejecting all practices not mentioned in Scripture, Wyclif condemned pilgrimages and the veneration of saints. Wyclif attracted a number of followers who came to be known as Lollards (literally, "mutterers").

HUS AND THE HUSSITES A marriage between the royal families of England and Bohemia enabled Lollard ideas to spread to Bohemia, where they reinforced the ideas of a group of Czech reformers led by the chancellor of the university at Prague, John Hus (1374–1415). In his call for reform, Hus urged the elimination of the worldliness and corruption of the clergy and attacked the excessive power of the papacy within the Catholic Church. Hus's objections fell on receptive ears, for the Catholic Church, as one of the largest landowners in Bohemia, was already widely criticized. Moreover, many clergymen were German, and the native Czechs' strong resentment of the Germans who dominated Bohemia also contributed to Hus's movement.

The Council of Constance attempted to deal with the growing problem of heresy by summoning Hus to appear before it. Granted safe conduct by Emperor Sigismund, Hus went in the hope of a free hearing of his ideas. Instead he was arrested, condemned as a heretic, and burned at the stake in 1415. This action turned the unrest in Bohemia into revolutionary upheaval, and the resulting Hussite wars racked the Holy Roman Empire until a truce was arranged in 1436.

REFORM OF THE CHURCH The reform of the church was even less successful than the attempt to eradicate heresy. The Council of Constance passed two reform decrees. One stated that a general council of the church received its authority from God; hence, every Christian, including the pope, was subject to its authority. The other decree provided for the regular holding of general councils to ensure that church reform would continue. Decrees alone, however, proved insufficient to reform the church. Councils could issue decrees, but popes had to execute them, and popes would not cooperate with councils that diminished their absolute authority. Beginning already in 1417, successive popes worked steadfastly for the next thirty years to defeat the conciliar movement (see Chapter 11).

By the mid-fifteenth century, the popes had reasserted their supremacy over the Roman Catholic Church. No longer, however, did they have any possibility of asserting supremacy over temporal governments as the medieval papacy had. Although the papal monarchy had been maintained, it had lost much moral prestige. In the fifteenth century, the Renaissance papacy contributed to an even further decline in the moral leadership of the popes.

The Renaissance Papacy

The Renaissance papacy encompasses the line of popes from the end of the Great Schism in 1417 to the beginning of the Reformation in the early sixteenth century. The primary concern of the papacy is governing the Catholic Church as its spiritual leader. But as heads of the church, popes had temporal preoccupations as well, and the story of the Renaissance papacy is really an account of how the latter came to overshadow the popes' spiritual functions.

The manner in which Renaissance popes pursued their interests in the Papal States and Italian politics, especially their use of intrigue and even bloodshed, seemed shocking. Of all the Renaissance popes, Julius II (1503–1513) was most involved in war and politics. The fiery "warrior pope" personally led armies against his enemies, much to the disgust of pious Christians, who viewed the pope as a spiritual leader. As one intellectual wrote at the beginning of the sixteenth century: "How, O bishop standing in the room of the Apostles [the pope], dare you teach the people the things that pertain to war?"

To further their territorial aims in the Papal States, the popes needed loyal servants. Because they were not

Galleria degli Uffizi, Florence//© Scala/Ministero per i Beni e le Attività culturali/Art Resource, NY

A Renaissance Pope: Leo X. The Renaissance popes allowed secular concerns to overshadow their spiritual duties. Shown here is the Medici pope Leo X. Raphael portrays the pope as a collector of books, looking up after examining an illuminated manuscript with a magnifying glass. At the left is the pope's cousin Guilio, a cardinal. Standing behind the pope is Luigi de' Rossi, another relative who had also been made a cardinal.

hereditary monarchs, popes could not build dynasties over several generations and came to rely on the practice of **nepotism** to promote their families' interests. Pope Sixtus IV (1471–1484), for example, made five of his nephews cardinals (the word *nepotism* is in fact derived from the Latin *nepos*, meaning "nephew") and gave them an abundance of church offices to build up their finances. Alexander VI (1492–1503), a member of the Borgia family who was known for his debauchery and sensuality, raised one son, one nephew, and the brother of one mistress to the cardinalate. Alexander scandalized the church by encouraging his son Cesare to carve a state out of the territories of the Papal States in central Italy.

The Renaissance popes were great patrons of Renaissance culture, and their efforts made Rome a cultural leader at the beginning of the sixteenth century. The warrior pope Julius II endeavored to add to the splendor of his pontificate by tearing down an old church and beginning construction of what was to be the greatest building in Christendom, Saint Peter's Basilica. Julius's successor, Leo X (1513–1521), was also a patron of Renaissance culture. A member of the Medici family, he was made a cardinal at the age of thirteen and acquired a refined taste in art, manners, and social life among the Florentine elite. He became pope at the age of thirty-seven, supposedly remarking to the Venetian ambassador, "Let us enjoy the papacy, since God has given it to us." Raphael was commissioned to do paintings, and the construction of Saint Peter's was accelerated as Rome became the literary and artistic center of the Renaissance.

CHAPTER SUMMARY

Beginning in Italy, the Renaissance was an era that rediscovered the culture of ancient Greece and Rome. It was also a time of recovery from the fourteenth century as well as a period of transition that witnessed a continuation of the economic, political, and social trends that had begun in the High Middle Ages.

The Renaissance was also a movement in which intellectuals and artists proclaimed a new vision of humankind and raised fundamental questions about the value and importance of the individual. The humanists or intellectuals of the age called their period (from the mid-fourteenth to the mid-sixteenth century) an age of rebirth, believing that they had restored arts and letters to their former glory. Humanism was an intellectual movement based on the study of the Classical literary works of Greece and Rome. The goal of a humanist education was to produce individuals of virtue and wisdom. Civic humanism posited that the ideal citizen was not only an intellectual but also an active participant in the life of the state.

The Renaissance is perhaps best known for its artistic brilliance. Renaissance artists in Italy sought not only to persuade onlookers of the reality of the object they were portraying, but also to focus attention on human beings as "the center and measure of all things." This new Renaissance style was developed, above all, in Florence, but by the end of the fifteenth century, Renaissance art moved into a new phase in which Rome became the new cultural center. In the works of Leonardo da Vinci, Raphael, and Michelangelo, the High Renaissance ideal of beauty was convincingly portrayed.

The Renaissance in Europe was also an era of "new monarchies," best seen in England, France, and Spain. Monarchs in these countries limited the private armies of the aristocracy, raised taxes, created professional armies, and in the process were able to reestablish the centralized power of monarchical governments. At the same time, the Renaissance popes became increasingly mired in political and temporal concerns that overshadowed their spiritual responsibilities.

Of course, the intellectuals and artists of the Renaissance wrote and painted for the upper classes, and the brilliant intellectual, cultural, and artistic accomplishments of the Renaissance were products of and for the elite. The ideas of the Renaissance did not have a broad base among the masses of the people. The Renaissance did, however, raise new questions about medieval traditions. In advocating a return to the early sources of Christianity and criticizing current religious practices, the humanists raised fundamental issues about the Catholic Church, which was still an important institution. In the sixteenth century, as we shall see in the next chapter, the intellectual revolution of the fifteenth century gave way to a religious renaissance that touched the lives of people, including the masses, in new and profound ways.

CHAPTER TIMELINE

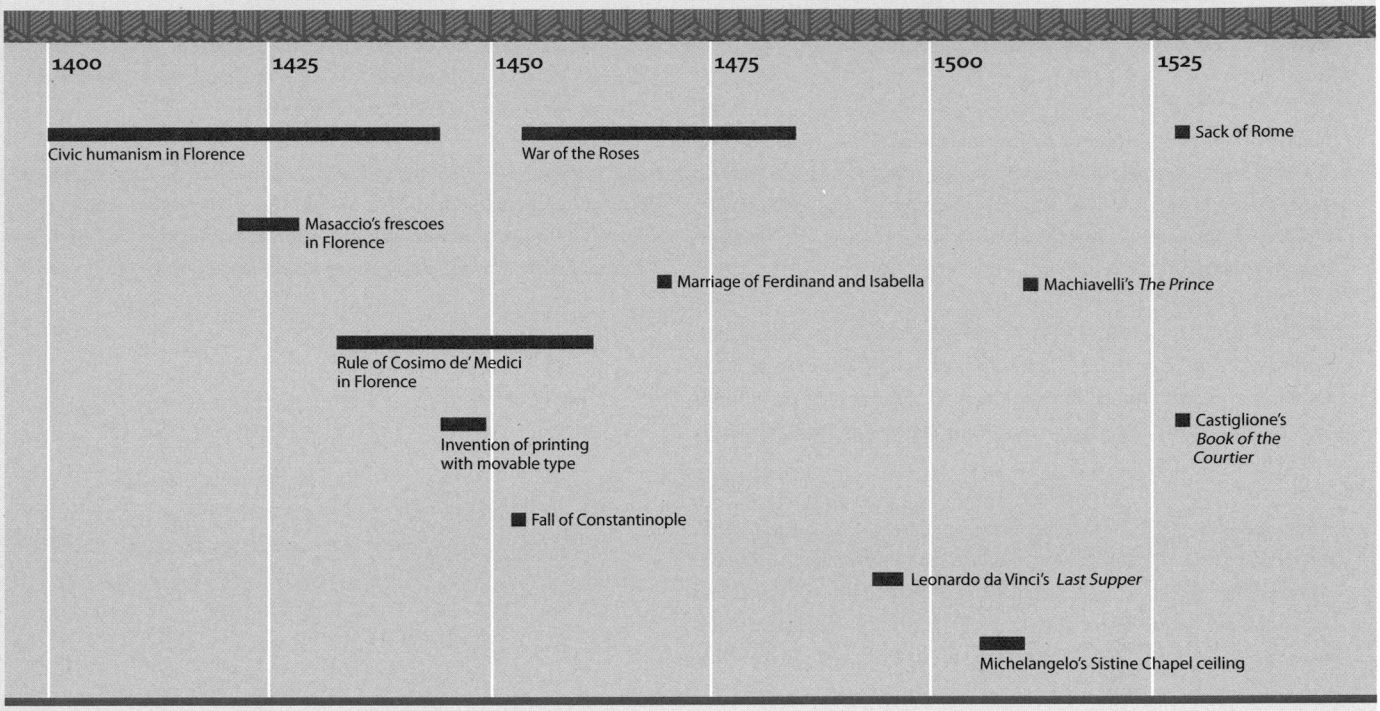

CHAPTER REVIEW

Upon Reflection

Q What was the pattern of political development in Italy? How was this pattern of political development reflected in the work of Machiavelli?

Q What was the relationship between Italian Renaissance humanism and Italian Renaissance art?

Q What impact did the policies of the Renaissance popes have on the Catholic Church?

Key Terms

Renaissance (p. 254)
estates (p. 256)
condottieri (p. 259)
individualism (p. 261)
secularism (p. 261)
humanism (p. 263)
civic humanism (p. 263)
Neoplatonism (p. 264)
Hermeticism (p. 264)
"new monarchies" (p. 271)
nepotism (p. 276)

Suggestions for Further Reading

GENERAL WORKS ON THE RENAISSANCE General works on the Renaissance in Europe include **M. L. King, *The Renaissance in Europe*** (New York, 2004), and **J. Hale, *The Civilization of Europe in the Renaissance*** (New York, 1994). Also valuable are **T. K. Rabb, *The Last Days of the Renaissance*** (New York, 2006), and **S. Sider, *Handbook to Life in Renaissance Europe*** (New York, 2005).

FAMILY AND MARRIAGE On family and marriage, see **C. Klapisch-Zuber, *Women, Family, and Ritual in Renaissance Italy*** (Chicago, 1985). On women, see **M. L. King, M. L. Brown,** and **K. B. McBride, *Women's Roles During the Renaissance*** (New York, 2005).

ITALIAN CITY-STATES On the Italian city-states, see **J. M. Najemy, *Italy in the Age of the Renaissance, 1300–1550*** (Oxford, 2004). There is an enormous literature on Renaissance Florence. A good introduction is **J. M. Najemy, *History of Florence, 1200–1575*** (London, 2006). Machiavelli's life can be examined in **Q. Skinner, *Machiavelli*** (Oxford, 2000).

RENAISSANCE HUMANISM A brief introduction to Renaissance humanism can be found in **C. G. Nauert Jr., *Humanism and the Culture of Renaissance Europe,*** 2nd ed. (Cambridge, 2006). See also **R. Mackenny, *Renaissances: The Cultures of Italy, c. 1300–c. 1600*** (New York, 2004).

RENAISSANCE ART Good surveys of Renaissance art include **J. T. Paoletti** and **G. M. Radke, *Art, Power, and Patronage in Renaissance Italy,*** 3rd ed. (Upper Saddle River, N.J., 2003); **C. Bucci** and **S. Buricchi, *Renaissance Art*** (New York, 2007); **R. Turner, *Renaissance Florence: The Invention of a New Art*** (New York, 1997); and **P. F. Brown, *Art and Life in Renaissance Venice*** (Upper Saddle River, N.J., 1997).

POLITICAL DEVELOPMENTS On the political development of Europe in the Renaissance, see **C. Mulgan, *The Renaissance Monarchies, 1469–1558*** (Cambridge, 1998).

THE CHURCH IN THE RENAISSANCE Aspects of the Renaissance papacy can be examined in **G. Noel, *The Renaissance Popes*** (New York, 2006). On Rome, see especially **P. Partner, *Renaissance Rome, 1500–1559: A Portrait of a Society*** (Berkeley, Calif., 1976).

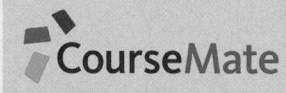

Visit the CourseMate website at **www.cengagebrain.com** for additional study tools and review materials for this chapter.

CHAPTER 13

© Bildarchiv Preussischer Kulturbesitz/Art Resource, NY

A nineteenth-century engraving showing Luther before the Diet of Worms

Reformation and Religious Warfare in the Sixteenth Century

CHAPTER OUTLINE AND FOCUS QUESTIONS

Prelude to Reformation

Q What were the chief ideas of the Christian humanists, and how did they differ from the ideas of the Protestant reformers?

Martin Luther and the Reformation in Germany

Q What were Martin Luther's main disagreements with the Roman Catholic Church, and what political, economic, and social conditions help explain why the movement he began spread so quickly across Europe?

The Spread of the Protestant Reformation

Q What were the main tenets of Lutheranism, Zwinglianism, Calvinism, and Anabaptism, and how did they differ from each other and from Catholicism? What impact did political, economic, and social conditions have on the development of these four reform movements?

The Social Impact of the Protestant Reformation

Q What impact did the Protestant Reformation have on society in the sixteenth century?

The Catholic Reformation

Q What measures did the Roman Catholic Church take to reform itself and to combat Protestantism in the sixteenth century?

Politics and the Wars of Religion in the Sixteenth Century

Q What role did politics, economic and social conditions, and religion play in the European wars of the sixteenth century?

CRITICAL THINKING

Q Where and how did the reform movements take hold, and how did the emergence of these reform movements affect the political and social realms where they were adopted?

ON APRIL 18, 1521, a lowly monk stood before the emperor and princes of the Holy Roman Empire in the city of Worms. He had been called before this august gathering to answer charges of heresy, charges that could threaten his very life. The monk was confronted with a pile of his books and asked if he wished to defend them all or reject a part. Courageously, Martin Luther defended them all and asked to be shown where any part was in error on the basis of "Scripture and plain reason." The emperor was outraged by Luther's response and made his own position clear the next day: "Not only I, but you of this noble German nation, would be forever disgraced if by our negligence not only heresy but the very suspicion of heresy were to survive. After having heard yesterday the obstinate defense of Luther, I regret that I have so long delayed in proceeding against him and his false teaching. I will have no more to do with him." Luther's appearance at Worms set the stage for a serious challenge to the authority of the Catholic Church. This was by no means the first crisis in the church's fifteen-hundred-year history, but its consequences were more far-reaching than anyone at Worms in 1521 could have imagined.

Throughout the Middle Ages, the Christian church continued to assert its primacy of position. It had overcome defiance of its temporal authority by emperors and kings while challenges to its doctrines had been crushed by the Inquisition and combated by new religious orders that carried its message of salvation to all the towns and villages of medieval Europe. The growth of the papacy had paralleled the growth of the church, but by the end of the Middle Ages, challenges to papal authority from the rising power of monarchical states had resulted in a loss of papal temporal authority. An even greater threat to papal authority and church unity arose in the sixteenth century when the unity of Christendom was shattered by the Reformation.

The movement begun by Martin Luther when he made his dramatic stand quickly spread across Europe, a clear indication of dissatisfaction with Catholic practices. Within a short time, new religious practices, doctrines, and organizations, including Zwinglianism, Calvinism, Anabaptism, and Anglicanism, were attracting adherents all over Europe. Although seemingly helpless to stop the new Protestant churches, the Catholic Church also underwent a reformation and managed to revive its fortunes by the mid-sixteenth century. All too soon, the doctrinal divisions between Protestants and Catholics led to a series of religious wars that dominated the history of western Europe in the second half of the sixteenth century.

Prelude to Reformation

Q FOCUS QUESTION: What were the chief ideas of the Christian humanists, and how did they differ from the ideas of the Protestant reformers?

Martin Luther's reform movement was by no means the first in sixteenth-century Europe. During the second half of the fifteenth century, the new Classical learning that was part of Italian Renaissance humanism spread to northern Europe and spawned a movement called **Christian** or **northern Renaissance humanism**, whose major goal was the reform of Christendom.

Christian or Northern Renaissance Humanism

The most important characteristic of northern Renaissance humanism was its reform program. Convinced of the ability of human beings to reason and improve themselves, the northern humanists thought that through education in the sources of Classical, and especially Christian, antiquity, they could instill a true inner piety or an inward religious feeling that would bring about a reform of the church and society. For this reason, Christian humanists supported schools, brought out new editions of the classics, and prepared new editions of the Bible and writings of the church fathers. In the preface to his edition of the Greek New Testament, the famous humanist Erasmus wrote:

> Indeed, I disagree very much with those who are unwilling that Holy Scripture, translated into the vulgar tongue, be read by the uneducated, as if Christ taught such intricate doctrines that they could scarcely be understood by very few theologians, or as if the strength of the Christian religion consisted in men's ignorance of it. . . . I would that even the lowliest women read the Gospels and the Pauline Epistles. And I would that they were translated into all languages so that they could be read and understood not only by Scots and Irish but also by Turks and Saracens [Arabs].[1]

Like later intellectuals, Christian humanists believed that to change society, they must first change the human beings who compose it.

ERASMUS The most influential of all the Christian humanists was the Dutch-born scholar Desiderius Erasmus (dez-i-DEER-ee-uss i-RAZZ-mus) (1466–1536). After withdrawing from a monastery, he wandered to France, England, Italy, Germany, and Switzerland, conversing everywhere in the Classical Latin that might be called his mother tongue. The *Handbook of the Christian Knight*, published in 1503, reflected his preoccupation with religion. He called his conception of religion "the philosophy of Christ," by which he meant that Christianity should be a guiding philosophy for the direction of daily life rather than the system of dogmatic beliefs and practices that the medieval church seemed to stress. In other words, he emphasized inner piety and de-emphasized the external forms of religion (such as the sacraments, pilgrimages, fasts, veneration of saints, and relics). To return to the simplicity of the early church, people needed to understand the original meaning of the Scriptures and early church fathers.

Louvre, Paris/© Scala/Art Resource, NY

Erasmus. Desiderius Erasmus was the most influential of the northern Renaissance humanists. He sought to restore Christianity to the early simplicity found in the teachings of Jesus. This portrait of Erasmus was painted in 1523 by Hans Holbein the Younger, who had formed a friendship with the great humanist when they both were in Basel.

To Erasmus, the reform of the church meant spreading an understanding of the philosophy of Jesus, providing enlightened education in the sources of early Christianity, and making commonsense criticism of the abuses in the church. This last is especially evident in *The Praise of Folly*, written in 1509, in which Erasmus engaged in humorous yet effective criticism of the most corrupt practices of his own society. He was especially harsh on the abuses within the ranks of the clergy:

> Many of [the monks] work so hard at protocol and at traditional fastidiousness that they think one heaven hardly a suitable reward for their labors; never recalling, however, that the time will come when Christ will demand a reckoning of that which he had prescribed, namely charity, and that he will hold their deeds of little account. One monk will then exhibit his belly filled with every kind of fish; another will profess a knowledge of over a hundred hymns. Still another will reveal a countless number of fasts that he has made, and will account for his large belly by explaining that his fasts have always been broken by a single large meal.[2]

Erasmus's program did not achieve the reform of the church that he so desired. His moderation and his emphasis on education were quickly overwhelmed by the passions of the Reformation. Undoubtedly, though, his work helped prepare the way for the Reformation; as contemporaries proclaimed, "Erasmus laid the egg that Luther hatched." Yet Erasmus eventually disapproved of Luther and the Protestant reformers. He had no intention of destroying the unity of the medieval Christian church; instead, his whole program was based on reform within the church.

Church and Religion on the Eve of the Reformation

Corruption in the Catholic Church was another factor that spurred people to want reform. No doubt the failure of the Renaissance popes to provide spiritual leadership had affected the spiritual life of all Christendom. The papal court's preoccupation with finances had an especially strong impact on the clergy. So did the economic changes of the fourteenth and fifteenth centuries. The highest positions among the clergy were increasingly held by nobles or wealthy members of the bourgeoisie. Moreover, to increase their revenues, high church officials (such as bishops, archbishops, and cardinals) took over more than one church office. This so-called **pluralism** led in turn to absenteeism: church officeholders ignored their duties and hired underlings who sometimes lacked the proper qualifications. There were widespread complaints about the ignorance and ineptness of parish priests.

While many of the leaders of the church were failing to meet their responsibilities, ordinary people were clamoring for meaningful religious expression and certainty of salvation. As a result, for some the salvation process became almost mechanical. As more and more people sought salvation through the veneration of relics, collections of such objects grew. Frederick the Wise, elector of Saxony and Martin Luther's prince, had amassed more than 19,000 relics to which were attached **indulgences** that could reduce one's time in purgatory by nearly 2 million years. (An indulgence is a remission, after death, of all or part of the punishment for sin.) Other people sought certainty of salvation in the popular mystical movement known as the Modern Devotion, which downplayed religious dogma and stressed the need to follow the teachings of Jesus. Thomas à Kempis, author of *The Imitation of Christ*, wrote that "truly, at the day of judgment we shall not be examined by what we have read, but what we have done; not how well we have spoken, but how religiously we have lived."

What is striking about the revival of religious piety in the fifteenth century—whether expressed through external forces such as the veneration of relics and the buying of indulgences or through the mystical path—was its adherence to the orthodox beliefs and practices of the Catholic Church. The agitation for certainty of salvation and spiritual peace was done within the framework of the "holy mother Church." But disillusionment grew as the devout experienced the clergy's inability to live up to their expectations. The deepening of religious life, especially in the second half of the fifteenth century, found little echo among the worldly-wise clergy, and this environment helps explain the tremendous and immediate impact of Luther's ideas.

Martin Luther and the Reformation in Germany

Focus Question: What were Martin Luther's main disagreements with the Roman Catholic Church, and what political, economic, and social conditions help explain why the movement he began spread so quickly across Europe?

The Protestant Reformation began with a typical medieval question: What must I do to be saved? Martin Luther, a deeply religious man, found an answer that did not fit within the traditional teachings of the late medieval church. Ultimately, he split with that church, destroying the religious unity of western Christendom.

The Early Luther

Martin Luther was born in Germany on November 10, 1483. His father wanted him to become a lawyer, so Luther enrolled at the University of Erfurt. In 1505, after becoming a master in the liberal arts, the young man began to study law. But Luther was not content, due in large part to his long-standing religious inclinations. That summer, while returning to Erfurt after a brief visit home, he was caught in a ferocious thunderstorm and vowed that if he survived unscathed, he would become a monk. He then entered the monastic order of the Augustinian Hermits in Erfurt, much to his father's disgust. In the monastery, Luther focused on his major concern, the assurance of salvation. The traditional beliefs and practices of the church seemed unable to relieve his obsession with this question. Luther threw himself into his monastic routine with a vengeance:

> I was indeed a good monk and kept my order so strictly that I could say that if ever a monk could get to heaven through monastic discipline, I was that monk. . . . And yet my conscience would not give me certainty, but I always doubted and said, "You didn't do that right. You weren't contrite enough. You left that out of your confession." The more I tried to remedy an uncertain, weak and troubled conscience with human traditions, the more I daily found it more uncertain, weaker and more troubled.[3]

Despite his herculean efforts, Luther achieved no certainty of salvation.

To help overcome his difficulties, his superiors recommended that he study theology. Luther received his doctorate in 1512 and then became a professor in the theological faculty at the University of Wittenberg, lecturing on the Bible. Sometime between 1513 and 1516, through his study of the Bible, he arrived at an answer to his problem.

Catholic doctrine emphasized that both faith and good works were required for a Christian to achieve personal salvation. In Luther's eyes, human beings, weak and powerless in the sight of an almighty God, could never do enough good works to merit salvation. Through his study of the Bible, especially his work on Paul's Epistle to the Romans, Luther discovered another way of viewing this problem. To Luther, humans are saved not through their good works but through faith in the promises of God, made possible by the sacrifice of Jesus on the cross. The doctrine of salvation or justification by grace through faith alone became the primary doctrine of the Protestant Reformation (**justification** is the act by which a person is made deserving of salvation). Because Luther had arrived at this doctrine from his study of the Bible, the Bible became for Luther, as for all other Protestants, the chief guide to religious truth. Justification by faith and the Bible as the sole authority in religious affairs were the twin pillars of the Protestant Reformation.

THE INDULGENCE CONTROVERSY Luther did not regard himself as either an innovator or a heretic, but his involvement in the indulgence controversy propelled him into an open confrontation with church officials and forced him to see the theological implications of justification by faith alone. In 1517, Pope Leo X had issued a special jubilee indulgence to finance the ongoing construction of Saint Peter's Basilica in Rome. Johann Tetzel, a rambunctious Dominican, hawked the indulgences with the slogan "As soon as the coin in the coffer [money box] rings, the soul from purgatory springs."

Luther was greatly distressed by the widespread selling of indulgences, certain that people who relied on these pieces of paper to assure themselves of salvation were guaranteeing their eternal damnation instead. Greatly angered, Luther issued a stunning indictment of the abuses in the sale of indulgences, known as the Ninety-Five Theses (see the box on p. 283). It is doubtful that Luther intended to break with the church over the issue

Luther and the Ninety-Five Theses

To most historians, the publication of Luther's Ninety-Five Theses marks the beginning of the Reformation. To Luther, they were simply a response to what he considered Johann Tetzel's blatant abuses in selling indulgences. Although written in Latin, Luther's statements were soon translated into German and disseminated widely across Germany. They made an immense impression on Germans already dissatisfied with the ecclesiastical and financial policies of the papacy.

Martin Luther, *Selections from the Ninety-Five Theses*

5. The Pope has neither the will nor the power to remit any penalties beyond those he has imposed either at his own discretion or by canon law.
20. Therefore the Pope, by his plenary remission of all penalties, does not mean "all" in the absolute sense, but only those imposed by himself.
21. Hence those preachers of Indulgences are wrong when they say that a man is absolved and saved from every penalty by the Pope's indulgences.
27. It is mere human talk to preach that the soul flies out [of purgatory] immediately the money clinks in the collection box.
28. It is certainly possible that when the money clinks in the collection box greed and avarice can increase; but the intercession of the Church depends on the will of God alone.
50. Christians should be taught that, if the Pope knew the exactions of the preachers of Indulgences, he would rather have the basilica of St. Peter reduced to ashes than built with the skin, flesh and bones of his sheep.
81. This wanton preaching of pardons makes it difficult even for learned men to redeem respect due to the Pope from the slanders or at least the shrewd questionings of the laity.
82. For example: "Why does not the Pope empty purgatory for the sake of most holy love and the supreme need of souls? This would be the most righteous of the reasons, if he can redeem innumerable souls for sordid money with which to build a basilica, the most trivial of reasons."
86. Again: "Since the Pope's wealth is larger than that of the crassest Crassi of our time, why does he not build this one basilica of St. Peter with his own money, rather than with that of the faithful poor?"
90. To suppress these most conscientious questionings of the laity by authority only, instead of refuting them by reason, is to expose the Church and the Pope to the ridicule of their enemies, and to make Christian people unhappy.
94. Christians should be exhorted to seek earnestly to follow Christ, their Head, through penalties, deaths, and hells.
95. And let them thus be more confident of entering heaven through many tribulations rather than through a false assurance of peace.

Q What were the major ideas of Luther's Ninety-Five Theses? Why did they have such a strong appeal in Germany?

Source: From *Martin Luther: Documents of Modern History* by E. G. Rupp and Benjamin Drewery. Palgrave Macmillan, 1970. Reproduced with permission of Palgrave Macmillan.

of indulgences. If the pope had clarified the use of indulgences, as Luther wished, Luther would probably have been satisfied. But Pope Leo X did not take the issue seriously and is even reported to have said that Luther was simply "some drunken German who will amend his ways when he sobers up." Thousands of copies of a German translation of the Ninety-Five Theses were quickly printed and were received sympathetically in a Germany that had a long tradition of dissatisfaction with papal policies and power.

THE QUICKENING REBELLION In three pamphlets published in 1520, Luther moved toward a more definite break with the Catholic Church. In *Address to the Nobility of the German Nation*, a political tract written in German, Luther called on the German princes to overthrow the papacy in Germany and establish a reformed German church. *The Babylonian Captivity of the Church* attacked the sacramental system as the means by which the pope and church had held the real meaning of the Gospel captive for a thousand years. Luther called for the reform of monasticism and for the clergy to marry. While virginity is good, he argued, marriage is better, and freedom of choice is best. *On the Freedom of a Christian Man* was a short treatise on the doctrine of salvation. It is faith alone, not good works, that justifies, frees, and brings salvation through Jesus. Being saved and freed by his faith in Jesus, however, does not free the Christian from doing good works. Rather, he performs good works out of gratitude to God: "Good works do not make a good man, but a good man does good works."[4]

Unable to accept Luther's forcefully worded dissent from traditional Catholic teachings, the church excommunicated him in January 1521. He was also summoned to appear before the Reichstag (RYKHSS-tahk), the imperial diet of the Holy Roman Empire, in Worms (WURMZ *or* VORMPS), convened by the recently elected Emperor Charles V (1519–1556). Expected to recant the heretical doctrines he had espoused, Luther refused and made the famous reply that became the battle cry of the Reformation:

> Since then Your Majesty and your lordships desire a simple reply, I will answer without horns and without teeth. Unless I am convicted by Scripture and plain reason—I do not accept the authority of popes and councils, for they have contradicted each other—my conscience is captive to the Word of God. I cannot and I will not recant anything, for to go against conscience is neither right nor safe. Here I stand, I cannot do otherwise. God help me. Amen.[5]

The young Emperor Charles was outraged at Luther's audacity and gave his opinion that "a single friar who goes counter to all Christianity for a thousand years must be wrong." By the Edict of Worms, Martin Luther was made an outlaw within the empire. His works were to be burned and Luther himself captured and delivered to the emperor. Instead, Luther's prince, the elector of Saxony sent him into hiding at the Wartburg (VART-bayrk) Castle, where he remained for nearly a year.

The Rise of Lutheranism

At the beginning of 1522, Luther returned to Wittenberg in Saxony and began to organize a reformed church. While at the Wartburg Castle, Luther's foremost achievement was his translation of the New Testament into German. Within twelve years, his German New Testament sold almost 200,000 copies. Lutheranism had wide appeal and spread rapidly, but not primarily through the written word, as only 4 to 5 percent of the people in Germany were literate at the time.

Instead, the primary means of disseminating Luther's ideas was the sermon. The preaching of evangelical sermons, based on a return to the original message of the Bible, found favor throughout Germany. Also useful to the spread of the Reformation were pamphlets illustrated with vivid woodcuts portraying the pope as a hideous Antichrist and titled with catchy phrases such as "I Wonder Why There Is No Money in the Land" (which, of course, was an attack on papal greed).

Kupferstichkabinett (Inv. 1170) Staatliche Museen zu Berlin//© Bildarchiv Preussischer Kulturbesitz (Jörg P. Anders)/Art Resource, NY

Woodcut: Luther Versus the Pope. In the 1520s, after Luther's return to Wittenberg, his teachings began to spread rapidly, resulting ultimately in a reform movement supported by state authorities. Pamphlets containing picturesque woodcuts were important in the spread of Luther's ideas. In the woodcut shown here, the crucified Jesus attends Luther's service on the left, while on the right the pope is at a table selling indulgences.

Luther was able to gain the support of his prince, the elector of Saxony, as well as other German rulers among the more than three hundred states that made up the Holy Roman Empire. Lutheranism spread to both princely and ecclesiastical states in northern and central Germany as well as to two-thirds of the free imperial cities, especially those of southern Germany, where prosperous burghers, for both religious and secular reasons, became committed to Luther's cause. At its outset, the Reformation in Germany was largely an urban phenomenon. Three-fourths of the early converts to the reform movement were from the clergy, many of them from the better-educated upper classes, which made it easier for them to work with the ruling elites in the cities.

A series of crises in the mid-1520s, however, made it apparent that spreading the word of God was not as easy as Luther had originally envisioned—the usual plight of most reformers. Luther experienced dissent within his own ranks in Wittenberg as well as defection from many Christian humanists who feared that Luther's movement threatened the unity of Christendom. The Peasants' War constituted Luther's greatest challenge, however. In June 1524, peasants in Germany rose in revolt against their lords and looked to Luther for support. But Luther, who knew how much his reformation of the church depended on the full support of the German princes and magistrates, supported the rulers, although he also blamed them for helping to cause the rebellion by their earlier harsh treatment of the peasants. To Luther, the state and its rulers were ordained by God and given the authority to maintain the peace and put down all revolts. By May 1525, the German princes had ruthlessly suppressed the peasant hordes. By this time, Luther found himself ever more dependent on state authorities for the growth and maintenance of his reformed church.

Organizing the Church

Justification by faith was the starting point for most of Protestantism's major doctrines. Since Luther downplayed the role of good works in salvation, the sacraments also had to be redefined. No longer regarded as merit-earning works, they were now viewed as divinely established signs signifying the promise of salvation. Luther kept only two of the Catholic Church's seven sacraments: baptism and the Lord's Supper (the Eucharist). Baptism signified rebirth through grace. Regarding the Lord's Supper, Luther denied the Catholic doctrine of **transubstantiation**, which taught that the substance of the bread and wine consumed in the rite is miraculously transformed into the body and blood of Jesus. Yet he continued to insist on the real presence of Jesus's body and blood in the bread and wine given as a testament to God's forgiveness of sin.

CHRONOLOGY Luther's Reform Movement	
Ninety-Five Theses	1517
Diet and Edict of Worms	1521
Peasants' War	1524–1525
Peace of Augsburg	1555

Luther took an active role in establishing a reformed church. Since the Catholic ecclesiastical hierarchy had been scrapped, Luther came to rely increasingly on the princes or state authorities to organize and guide the new Lutheran reformed churches. The Lutheran churches in Germany (and later in Scandinavia) quickly became territorial or state churches in which the state supervised and disciplined church members. As part of the development of these state-dominated churches, Luther also instituted new religious services to replace the Mass. These featured a worship service consisting of a German liturgy that focused on Bible reading, preaching the word of God, and song. Following his own denunciation of clerical celibacy, Luther married a former nun, Katherina von Bora (kat-uh-REE-nuh fun BOH-rah), in 1525. His union provided a model of married and family life for the new Protestant minister.

Germany and the Reformation: Religion and Politics

From its very beginning, the fate of Luther's movement was closely tied to political affairs. In 1519, Charles I, king of Spain and the grandson of the Emperor Maximilian, was elected Holy Roman Emperor as Charles V (1519–1556). Charles V ruled over an immense empire, consisting of Spain and its overseas possessions, the traditional Austrian Habsburg lands, Bohemia, Hungary, the Low Countries, and the kingdom of Naples in southern Italy (see Map 13.1). The extent of his possessions was reflected in the languages he used: "I speak Spanish to God, Italian to women, French to men, and German to my horse." Politically, Charles wanted to maintain his dynasty's control over his enormous empire; religiously, he hoped to preserve the unity of the Catholic faith throughout his empire. Despite Charles's strengths, his empire was overextended, and he spent a lifetime in futile pursuit of his goals. Four major problems—the French, the papacy, the Turks, and Germany's internal situation—cost him both his dream and his health. At the same time, the emperor's problems gave Luther's movement time to grow and organize before facing the concerted onslaught of the Catholic forces.

Charles V's chief political concern was his rivalry with the Valois king of France, Francis I (1515–1547).

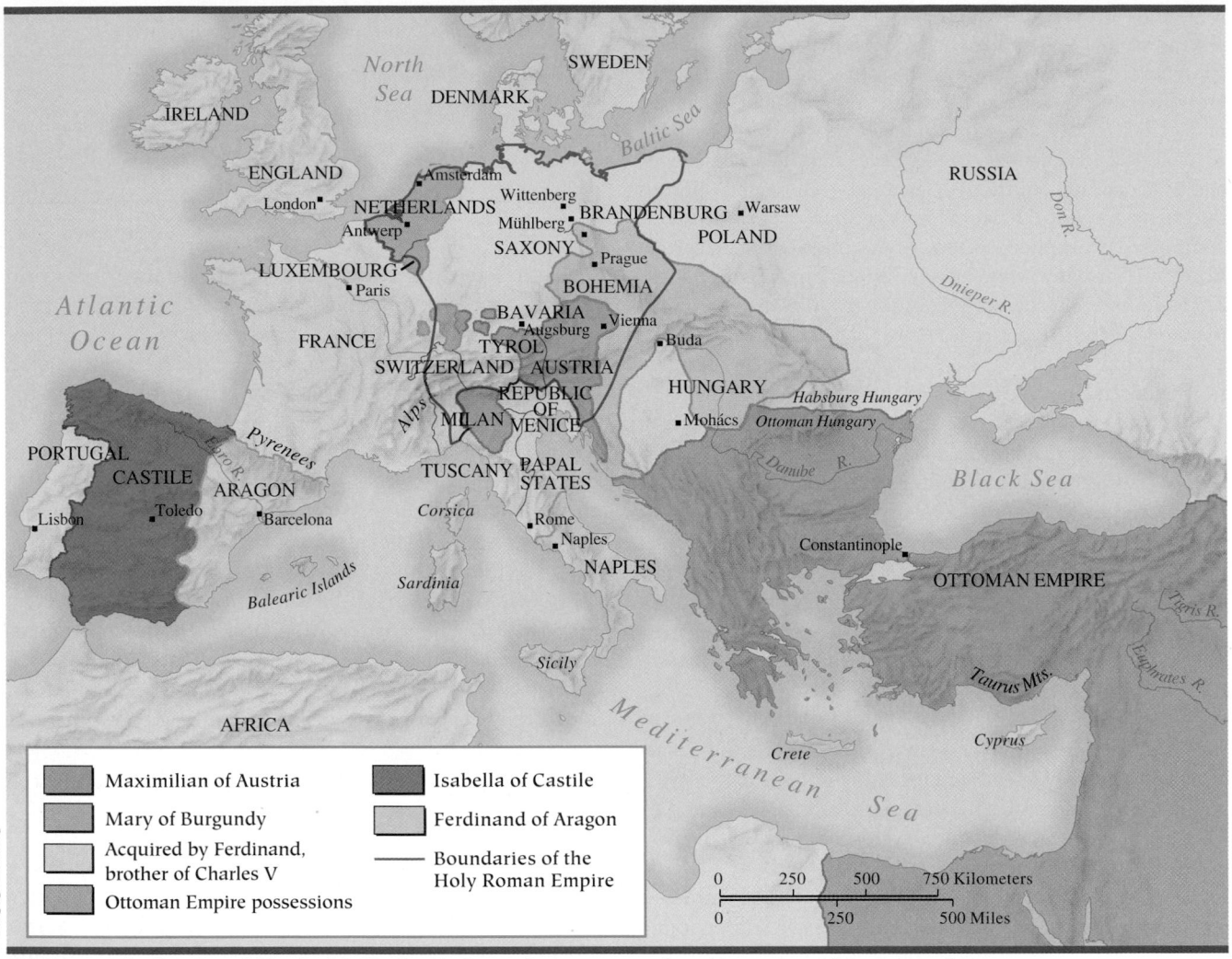

© Cengage Learning

MAP 13.1 The Empire of Charles V. Charles V inherited a vast empire from his ancestors (Maximilian of Austria, Mary of Burgundy, Isabella of Castile, and Ferdinand of Aragon). He spent much of his reign fighting wars in Italy, against France and the Ottoman Empire, and within the borders of the Holy Roman Empire. He failed in his main goal to secure Europe for Catholicism: the Peace of Augsburg in 1555 recognized the equality of Catholicism and Lutheranism and let each German prince choose his realm's religion.

Q *Why would France feel threatened by the empire of Charles V?*

Encircled by the possessions of the Habsburg empire, Francis became embroiled in conflict with Charles over disputed territories in southern France, the Netherlands, the Rhineland, northern Spain, and Italy. These conflicts, known as the Habsburg-Valois Wars, were fought intermittently for more than two decades (1521–1544), preventing Charles from concentrating on the Lutheran problem in Germany.

At the same time, Charles faced opposition from Pope Clement VII (1523–1534), who, guided by political considerations, joined the side of Francis I. The advance of the Ottoman Turks into the eastern part of Charles's empire forced the emperor to divert forces there as well. Under Suleiman (soo-lay-MAHN) the Magnificent (1520–1566), the Ottoman Turks overran most of Hungary, moved into Austria, and advanced as far as Vienna, where they were finally repulsed in 1529.

Finally, the internal political situation in the Holy Roman Empire was also not in Charles's favor. Germany was a land of several hundred territorial states—princely states, ecclesiastical principalities, and free imperial cities. Although all owed loyalty to the emperor, Germany's

Museo del Prado, Madrid/© Erich Lessing/Art Resource, NY

Charles V. Charles V sought to create religious unity throughout his vast empire by keeping all his subjects within the bounds of the Catholic Church. Due to his conflict with Francis I of France as well as his difficulties with the Turks, the papacy, and the German princes, Charles was never able to check the spread of Lutheranism. This portrait by the Venetian painter Titian shows Charles at the height of his power in 1547 after the defeat of the Lutherans at the Battle of Mühlberg.

medieval development had enabled these states to become quite independent of imperial authority. They had no desire to have a strong emperor. By the time Charles V was able to bring military forces to Germany in 1546, Lutheranism had become well established and the Lutheran princes were well organized. Unable to impose his will on Germany, Charles was forced to negotiate a truce. An end to religious warfare in Germany came in 1555 with the Peace of Augsburg, which marked an important turning point in the history of the Reformation. The division of Christianity was formally acknowledged, with Lutheranism granted equal legal standing with Catholicism. Moreover, the peace settlement accepted the right of each German ruler to determine the religion of his subjects (but not the right of the subjects to choose their religion). Charles's hope for a united empire had been completely dashed, and the ideal of medieval Christian unity was irretrievably lost. The rapid proliferation of new Protestant groups served to underscore that new reality.

The Spread of the Protestant Reformation

Focus Questions: What were the main tenets of Lutheranism, Zwinglianism, Calvinism, and Anabaptism, and how did they differ from each other and from Catholicism? What impact did political, economic, and social conditions have on the development of these four reform movements?

For both Catholics and Protestant reformers, Luther's heresy raised the question of how to determine what constituted the correct interpretation of the Bible. The inability to agree on this issue led not only to theological confrontations but also to bloody warfare as each Christian group was unwilling to admit that it could be wrong.

The Zwinglian Reformation

In the sixteenth century, the Swiss Confederation was a loose association of thirteen self-governing states called cantons. Theoretically part of the Holy Roman Empire, they had become virtually independent in 1499. The six forest cantons were democratic republics, while the seven urban cantons, which included Zürich, Bern, and Basel, were governed primarily by city councils controlled by narrow oligarchies of wealthy citizens.

Ulrich Zwingli (OOL-rikh TSFING-lee) (1484–1531) was ordained a priest in 1506 and accepted an appointment as a cathedral priest in the Great Minster of Zürich in 1518. Zwingli's preaching of the Gospel caused such unrest that the city council in 1523 held a public disputation or debate in the town hall. Zwingli's party was accorded the victory, and the council declared that "Mayor, Council and Great Council of Zürich, in order to do away with disturbance and discord, have upon due deliberation and consultation decided and resolved that Master Zwingli should continue as heretofore to proclaim the Gospel and the pure sacred Scriptures."[6]

Over the next two years, evangelical reforms were promulgated in Zürich by a city council strongly influenced by Zwingli. Relics and images were abolished; all paintings and decorations were removed from the churches and replaced by whitewashed walls. The Mass was replaced by a new liturgy consisting of Scripture reading, prayer, and sermons. Monasticism, pilgrimages, the veneration of saints, clerical celibacy, and the pope's authority were all abolished as remnants of papal Christianity.

As his movement began to spread to other cities in Switzerland, Zwingli sought an alliance with Martin Luther and the German reformers. Protestant political leaders attempted to promote an alliance of the Swiss and German reformed churches by persuading the leaders of both groups to attend a colloquy (conference) at Marburg to resolve their differences. Although both the German and Swiss reformers realized the need for unity to defend against the opposition of Catholic authorities, they were unable to agree on the interpretation of the Lord's Supper (see the box on p. 289). Zwingli believed that the scriptural words "This is my body" and "This is my blood" should be taken symbolically, not literally. To Zwingli, the Lord's Supper was only a meal of remembrance, and he refused to accept Luther's insistence on the real presence of the body and blood of Jesus "in, with, and under the bread and wine." The Marburg Colloquy of 1529 produced no agreement and no evangelical alliance. It was a foretaste of the issues that would divide one reform group from another and eventually lead to the creation of different Protestant groups.

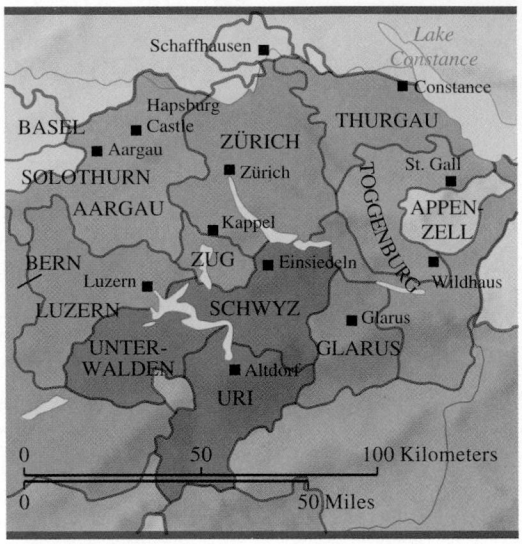

© Cengage Learning
Zwingli's Zürich

In October 1531, war erupted between the Swiss Protestant and Catholic cantons. Zürich's army was routed, and Zwingli was found wounded on the battlefield. His enemies killed him, cut up his body, burned it, and scattered the ashes. This Swiss civil war of 1531 provided an early indication of what religious passions would lead to in the sixteenth century. Unable to find peaceful ways to agree on the meaning of the Gospel, the disciples of Christianity resorted to violence and decision by force. When he heard of Zwingli's death, Martin Luther, who had not forgotten the confrontation at Marburg, is supposed to have remarked that Zwingli "got what he deserved."

The Radical Reformation: The Anabaptists

Although many reformers were ready to allow the state to play an important, if not dominant, role in church affairs, some people rejected this kind of magisterial reformation and favored a far more radical reform movement. Collectively called the Anabaptists, these radicals were actually members of a large variety of groups who had certain characteristics in common.

To the Anabaptists, the true Christian church was a voluntary association of believers who had undergone spiritual rebirth and had then been baptized into the church. Anabaptists advocated adult rather than infant baptism. No one, they believed, should be forced to accept the Bible as truth. They also tried to return literally to the practices and spirit of early Christianity. Adhering to the accounts of early Christian communities in the New Testament, they followed a strict sort of democracy in which all believers were considered equal. Each church chose its own minister, who might be any member of the community because all Christians were considered priests (though women were often excluded). Those chosen as ministers had the duty to lead services, which were very simple and contained nothing not found in the early church. Like early Christians, Anabaptists, who called themselves "Christians" or "Saints," accepted that they would have to suffer for their faith. Anabaptists rejected theological speculation in favor of simple Christian living according to what they believed was the pure word of God. The Lord's Supper was interpreted as a remembrance, a meal of fellowship celebrated in the evening in private houses according to Jesus's example.

Unlike the Catholics and other Protestants, most Anabaptists believed in the complete separation of church and state. Not only was government to be excluded from the realm of religion, but it was not even supposed to exercise political jurisdiction over true Christians. Human law had no power over those whom God had saved. Anabaptists refused to hold political office or bear arms because many took the commandment "Thou shall not kill" literally, although some Anabaptist groups did become quite violent. Their political beliefs as much as their religious beliefs caused the Anabaptists to be regarded as dangerous radicals who threatened the fabric of sixteenth-century society. Indeed, the chief thing Protestants and Catholics could agree on was the need to stamp out the Anabaptists.

One early group of Anabaptists known as the Swiss Brethren arose in Zürich. Their ideas frightened Zwingli, and they were expelled from the city in 1523. As their teachings spread through southern Germany, the Austrian Habsburg lands, and Switzerland, Anabaptists suffered ruthless persecution, especially after the Peasants' War of 1524–1525, when the upper classes resorted to repression. Virtually eliminated in Germany, Anabaptist survivors emerged in Moravia, Poland, and the Netherlands.

OPPOSING VIEWPOINTS

A Reformation Debate: Conflict at Marburg

Debates played a crucial role in the Reformation period. They were a primary instrument in introducing the Reformation into innumerable cities as well as a means of resolving differences among like-minded Protestant groups. This selection contains an excerpt from the vivacious and often brutal debate between Luther and Zwingli over the sacrament of the Lord's Supper at Marburg in 1529. The two protagonists failed to reach agreement.

The Marburg Colloquy, 1529

THE HESSIAN CHANCELLOR FEIGE: My gracious prince and lord [Landgrave Philip of Hesse] has summoned you for the express and urgent purpose of settling the dispute over the sacrament of the Lord's Supper. . . . Let everyone on both sides present his arguments in a spirit of moderation, as becomes such matters. . . . Now then, Doctor Luther, you may proceed.

LUTHER: Noble prince, gracious lord! Undoubtedly the colloquy is well intentioned. . . . Although I have no intention of changing my mind, which is firmly made up, I will nevertheless present the grounds of my belief and show where the others are in error. . . . Your basic contentions are these: In the last analysis you wish to prove that a body cannot be in two places at once, and you produce arguments about the unlimited body which are based on natural reason. I do not question how Christ can be God and man and how the two natures can be joined. For God is more powerful than all our ideas, and we must submit to his word.

Prove that Christ's body is not there where the Scripture says, "This is my body!" Rational proofs I will not listen to. God is beyond all mathematics and the words of God are to be revered and carried out in awe. It is God who commands, "Take, eat, this is my body." I request, therefore, valid scriptural proof to the contrary.

Luther writes on the table in chalk, "This is my body," and covers the words with a velvet cloth.

OECOLAMPADIUS [leader of the reform movement in Basel and a Zwinglian partisan]: The sixth chapter of John clarifies the other scriptural passages. Christ is not speaking there about a local presence. "The flesh is of no avail," he says. It is not my intention to employ rational, or geometrical, arguments—neither am I denying the power of God—but as long as I have the complete faith I will speak from that. For Christ is risen; he sits at the right hand of God; and so he cannot be present in the bread. Our view is neither new nor sacrilegious, but is based on faith and Scripture. . . .

ZWINGLI: I insist that the words of the Lord's Supper must be figurative. This is ever apparent, and even required by the article of faith: "taken up into heaven, seated at the right hand of the Father." Otherwise, it would be absurd to look for him in the Lord's Supper at the same time that Christ is telling us that he is in heaven. One and the same body cannot possibly be in different places

LUTHER: I call upon you as before: your basic contentions are shaky. Give way, and give glory to God!

ZWINGLI: And we call upon you to give glory to God and to quit begging the question! The issue at stake is this: Where is the proof of your position? I am willing to consider your words carefully—no harm meant! You're trying to outwit me. I stand by this passage in the sixth chapter of John, verse 63, and shall not be shaken from it. You'll have to sing another tune.

LUTHER: You're being obnoxious.

ZWINGLI: *(excitedly)* Don't you believe that Christ was attempting in John 6 to help those who did not understand?

LUTHER: You're trying to dominate things! You insist on passing judgment! Leave that to someone else! . . . It is your point that must be proved, not mine. But let us stop this sort of thing. It serves no purpose.

ZWINGLI: It certainly does! It is for you to prove that the passage in John 6 speaks of a physical repast.

LUTHER: You express yourself poorly and make about as much progress as a cane standing in a corner. You're going nowhere.

ZWINGLI: No, no, no! This is the passage that will break your neck!

(Continued)

(*Opposing Viewpoints continued*)

LUTHER: Don't be so sure of yourself. Necks don't break this way. You're in Hesse, not Switzerland.

Q How did the positions of Zwingli and Luther on the sacrament of the Lord's Supper differ? What was the purpose of this debate? Based on this example, why do you think Reformation debates led to further hostility rather than compromise and unity between religious and sectarian opponents? What implication did this have for the future of the Protestant Reformation?

Source: "The Marburg Colloquy," from GREAT DEBATES OF THE REFORMATION, edited by Donald Ziegler, copyright © 1969 by Donald Ziegler. Used by permission of Modern Library, a division of Random House, Inc.

Menno Simons (1496–1561) was the man most responsible for rejuvenating Dutch Anabaptism. A popular leader, Menno dedicated his life to the spread of a peaceful, evangelical Anabaptism that stressed separation from the world in order to truly emulate the life of Jesus. The Mennonites, as his followers were called, spread from the Netherlands into northwestern Germany and eventually into Poland and Lithuania as well as the New World. Both the Mennonites and Amish, who are also descended from the Anabaptists, maintain communities in the United States and Canada today.

The Reformation in England

The English Reformation was initiated by King Henry VIII (1509–1547), who wanted to divorce his first wife, Catherine of Aragon, because she had failed to produce a male heir. Furthermore, Henry had fallen in love with Anne Boleyn (BUH-lin *or* buh-LIN), a lady-in-waiting to Queen Catherine. Anne's unwillingness to be only the king's mistress and the king's desire to have a legitimate male heir made their marriage imperative, but the king's first marriage stood in the way.

Normally, church authorities might have been willing to grant the king an annulment of his marriage, but Pope Clement VII was dependent on the Holy Roman Emperor, Charles V, who happened to be Catherine's nephew. Impatient with the pope's inaction, Henry sought to obtain an annulment of his marriage in England's own ecclesiastical courts. As archbishop of Canterbury and head of the highest ecclesiastical court in England, Thomas Cranmer held official hearings on the king's case and ruled in May 1533 that the king's marriage to Catherine was "null and absolutely void." He then validated Henry's secret marriage to Anne, who had become pregnant. At the beginning of June, Anne was crowned queen. Three months later, a child was born. Much to the king's disappointment, the baby was a girl, who was named Elizabeth.

In 1534, at Henry's request, Parliament moved to finalize the Church of England's break with Rome. The Act of Supremacy of 1534 declared that the king was "taken, accepted, and reputed the only supreme head on earth of the Church of England," a position that gave him control of doctrine, clerical appointments, and discipline.

Although Henry VIII had broken with the papacy, little changed in matters of doctrine, theology, and ceremony. Some of his supporters, such as Archbishop Cranmer, sought a religious reformation as well as an administrative one, but Henry was unyielding. When Henry died in 1547, he was succeeded by his son, the underage and sickly Edward VI (1547–1553), the son of Henry's third wife, Jane Seymour. During Edward's reign, Cranmer and others inclined toward Protestant doctrines were able to move the Church of England (also known as the Anglican Church) in a more Protestant direction. New acts of Parliament instituted the right of the clergy to marry, the elimination of religious images, and the creation of a revised Protestant liturgy that was elaborated in a new prayer book known as the Book of Common Prayer. These rapid changes in doctrine and liturgy aroused much opposition and prepared the way for the reaction that occurred when Mary, Henry's daughter by Catherine of Aragon, came to the throne.

Mary (1553–1558) was a Catholic who fully intended to restore England to Roman Catholicism. But her restoration of Catholicism aroused much opposition. There was widespread antipathy to Mary's unfortunate marriage to Philip II, the son of Charles V and future king of Spain. Philip was strongly disliked in England, and Mary's foreign policy of alliance with Spain aroused further hostility. The burning of more than three hundred Protestant heretics aroused further ire against "bloody Mary." As a result of her policies, Mary managed to achieve the opposite of what she had intended: England was more Protestant by the end of her reign than it had been at the beginning. When she came to power, Protestantism had become identified with church destruction and religious anarchy. Now people identified it with English resistance to Spanish interference. Mary's death in 1558 ended the restoration of Catholicism in England.

John Calvin and the Development of Calvinism

Of the second generation of Protestant reformers, one stands out as the premier systematic theologian and organizer of the Protestant movement—John Calvin (1509–1564). Calvin was educated in his native France, but after his conversion to Protestantism, he was forced to flee to the safety of Switzerland. In 1536, he published the first edition of the *Institutes of the Christian Religion*, a masterful synthesis of Protestant thought that immediately secured Calvin's reputation as one of the new leaders of Protestantism.

CHRONOLOGY New Reform Movements

The Zwinglian Reformation	
Zwingli made cathedral priest at Zürich	1518
Reform adopted in Zürich	1523
Marburg Colloquy	1529
Death of Zwingli on the battlefield	1531
The Reformation in England	
Henry VIII	1509–1547
Act of Supremacy	1534
Edward VI	1547–1553
Mary	1553–1558
Calvin and Calvinism	
Institutes of the Christian Religion	1536
Calvin begins ministry in Geneva	1536

CALVIN'S IDEAS On most important doctrines, Calvin stood very close to Luther. He adhered to the doctrine of justification by faith alone to explain how humans achieved salvation. Calvin also placed much emphasis on the absolute sovereignty of God or the "power, grace and glory of God." One of the ideas derived from his emphasis on the absolute sovereignty of God—**predestination**—gave a unique cast to Calvin's teachings. This "eternal decree," as Calvin called it, meant that God had predestined some people to be saved (the elect) and others to be damned (the reprobate). According to Calvin, "He has once for all determined, both whom he would admit to salvation, and whom he would condemn to destruction."[7] Although Calvin stressed that there could be no absolute certainty of salvation, some of his followers did not always make this distinction. The practical psychological effect of predestination was to give some later Calvinists an unshakable conviction that they were doing God's work on earth. Thus, Calvinism became a dynamic and activist faith. It is no accident that Calvinism became the militant international form of Protestantism.

To Calvin, the church was a divine institution responsible for preaching the word of God and administering the sacraments. Calvin kept the same two sacraments as other Protestant reformers, baptism and the Lord's Supper. Baptism was a sign of the remission of sins. Calvin believed in the real presence of Jesus in the sacrament of the Lord's Supper, but only in a spiritual sense. Jesus's body is at the right hand of God and thus cannot be in the sacrament, but to the believer, Jesus is spiritually present in the Lord's Supper.

CALVIN'S GENEVA In 1536, Calvin began working to reform the city of Geneva. He established a church government that used both clergy and laymen in the service of the church. The Consistory, a special body for enforcing moral discipline, was set up as a court to oversee the moral life and doctrinal purity of Genevans. The Consistory had the right to punish people who deviated from the church's teachings and moral principles.

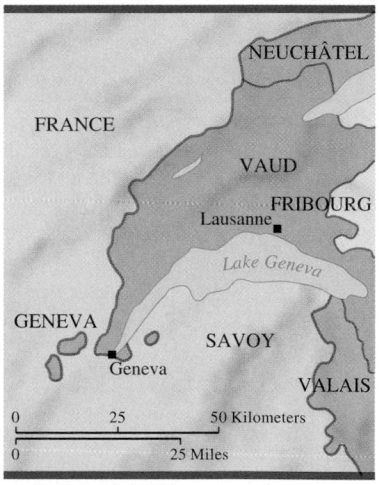

© Cengage Learning
Calvin's Geneva

Calvin's success in Geneva enabled the city to become a vibrant center of Protestantism. John Knox, the Calvinist reformer of Scotland, called Geneva "the most perfect school of Christ on earth." Following Calvin's lead, missionaries trained in Geneva were sent to all parts of Europe. Calvinism became established in France, the Netherlands, Scotland, and central and eastern Europe. By the mid-sixteenth century, Calvinism had replaced Lutheranism as the militant international form of Protestantism, and Calvin's Geneva stood as the fortress of the Reformation.

© The Art Archive/University Library, Geneva/Gianni Dagli Orti

John Calvin. After a conversion experience, John Calvin abandoned his life as a humanist and became a reformer. In 1536, Calvin began working to reform the city of Geneva, where he remained until his death in 1564. This sixteenth-century portrait of Calvin depicts him near the end of his life.

The Social Impact of the Protestant Reformation

FOCUS QUESTION: What impact did the Protestant Reformation have on society in the sixteenth century?

Because Christianity was such an integral part of European life, it was inevitable that the Reformation would have an impact on the family and popular religious practices.

The Family

For centuries, Catholicism had praised the family and sanctified its existence by making marriage a sacrament. But the Catholic Church's high regard for abstinence from sex as the surest way to holiness made the celibate state of the clergy preferable to marriage. Nevertheless, because not all men could remain chaste, marriage offered the best means to control sexual intercourse and give it a purpose, the procreation of children. To some extent, this attitude persisted among the Protestant reformers; Luther, for example, argued that sex in marriage allowed one to "make use of this sex in order to avoid sin," and Calvin advised that every man should "abstain from marriage only so long as he is fit to observe celibacy." If "his power to tame lust fails him," then he must marry.

But the Reformation did bring some change to the conception of the family. Both Catholic and Protestant clergy preached sermons advocating a more positive side to family relationships. The Protestants were especially important in developing this new view of the family. Because Protestantism had eliminated any idea of special holiness for celibacy, abolishing both monasticism and a celibate clergy, the family could be placed at the center of human life, and a new stress on "mutual love between man and wife" could be extolled. But were doctrine and reality the same? For more radical religious groups, at times they were. One Anabaptist wrote to his wife before his execution: "My faithful helper, my loyal friend. I praise God that he gave you to me, you who have sustained me in all my trial."[8] But more often reality reflected the traditional roles of husband as the ruler and wife as the obedient servant whose chief duty was to please her husband. Luther stated it clearly:

> The rule remains with the husband, and the wife is compelled to obey him by God's command. He rules the home and the state, wages war, defends his possessions, tills the soil, builds, plants, etc. The woman on the other hand is like a nail driven into the wall . . . so the wife should stay at home and look after the affairs of the household, as one who has been deprived of the ability of administering those affairs that are outside and that concern the state. She does not go beyond her most personal duties.[9]

Obedience to her husband was not a wife's only role; her other important duty was to bear children. To Calvin and Luther, this function of women was part of the divine plan. God punishes women for the sins of Eve by the burdens of procreation and feeding and nurturing their children, but, said Luther, "it is a gladsome punishment if you consider the hope of eternal life and the honor of motherhood which had been left to her."[10] Although the Protestant reformers sanctified this role of woman as mother and wife, viewing it as a holy vocation, Protestantism also left few alternatives for women. Because monasticism had been destroyed, that career avenue was no longer available; for most Protestant women, family life was their only destiny. At the same time, by emphasizing the father as "ruler" and hence the center of household religion, Protestantism even removed the woman from her traditional role as controller of religion in the home. Overall, the Protestant Reformation did not noticeably transform women's subordinate place in society.

Religious Practices and Popular Culture

The attacks of Protestant reformers on the Catholic Church led to radical changes in religious practices. The Protestant Reformation abolished or severely curtailed such customary practices as indulgences, the veneration of relics and saints, pilgrimages, monasticism, and clerical celibacy. The elimination of saints put an end to the numerous celebrations of religious holy days and changed a community's sense of time. Thus, in Protestant communities, religious ceremonies and imagery, such as processions and statues, tended to be replaced with individual private prayer, family worship, and collective prayer and worship at the same time each week on Sunday.

In addition to abolishing saints' days and religious carnivals, some Protestant reformers even tried to eliminate customary forms of entertainment. Puritans (as English Calvinists were called), for example, attempted to ban drinking in taverns, dramatic performances, and dancing. Dutch Calvinists denounced the tradition of giving small presents to children on the feast of Saint Nicholas in December. Many of these Protestant attacks on popular culture were unsuccessful, however. The importance of taverns in English social life made it impossible to eradicate them, and celebrating at Christmastime persisted in the Dutch Netherlands.

The Catholic Reformation

Q Focus Question: What measures did the Roman Catholic Church take to reform itself and to combat Protestantism in the sixteenth century?

By the mid-sixteenth century, Lutheranism had become established in Germany and Scandinavia and Calvinism in parts of Switzerland, France, the Netherlands, and eastern Europe (see Map 13.2). In England, the split from Rome had resulted in the creation of a national church. The situation in Europe did not look favorable for Roman Catholicism. But constructive, positive forces for reform were at work within the Catholic Church, and by the mid-sixteenth century, they came to be directed by a revived and reformed papacy, giving the church new strength. The revival of Roman Catholicism is often called the Catholic Reformation, although some historians prefer the term Counter-Reformation, especially for those elements of the Catholic Reformation that were directly aimed at stopping the spread of Protestantism. Eventually, in the course of the Catholic Reformation, the Catholic Church reaffirmed traditional Catholic teachings and practices while rejecting the principles and practices advocated by the Protestant reformers. Historians focus on three chief pillars of the Catholic Reformation: the development of the Jesuits, the creation of a reformed and revived papacy, and the Council of Trent.

The Society of Jesus

The Society of Jesus, whose members are known as Jesuits, was founded by a Spanish nobleman, Ignatius of Loyola (ig-NAY-shuss of loi-OH-luh) (1491–1556), whose injuries in battle cut short his military career. Loyola experienced a spiritual torment similar to Luther's but, unlike Luther, resolved his problems not by a new doctrine but by a decision to submit his will to the will of the church. Unable to be a real soldier, he vowed to be a soldier of God. Over a period of twelve years, Loyola prepared for his lifework by prayer, pilgrimages, going to school, and working out a spiritual program in his brief but powerful book, *The Spiritual Exercises*. This was a training manual for spiritual development emphasizing exercises by which the human will could be strengthened and made to follow the will of God as manifested through his instrument, the Catholic Church (see the box on p. 295).

Loyola gathered together a small group of individuals who were eventually recognized as a religious order, the Society of Jesus, by a papal bull in 1540. The new order was grounded on the principles of absolute obedience to the papacy, a strict hierarchical order for the society, the use of education to achieve its goals, and a dedication to engage in "conflict for God." Executive leadership was put in the hands of a general, who nominated all important positions in the order and was to be revered as the absolute head of the order. Loyola served as the first general of the order until his death in 1556. A special vow of absolute obedience to the pope made the Jesuits an important instrument for papal policy.

The Jesuits were active on behalf of the Catholic faith. They established well-disciplined schools, believing that thorough education of young people was crucial to combat the advance of Protestantism. Another prominent Jesuit activity was the propagation of the Catholic faith among non-Christians. Francis Xavier (ZAY-vee-ur) (1506–1552), one of the original members of the Society of Jesus, carried the message of Catholic Christianity to the East. After converting tens of thousands in India, he traveled to Malacca and the Moluccas before reaching Japan in 1549. He spoke highly of the Japanese: "They are a people of

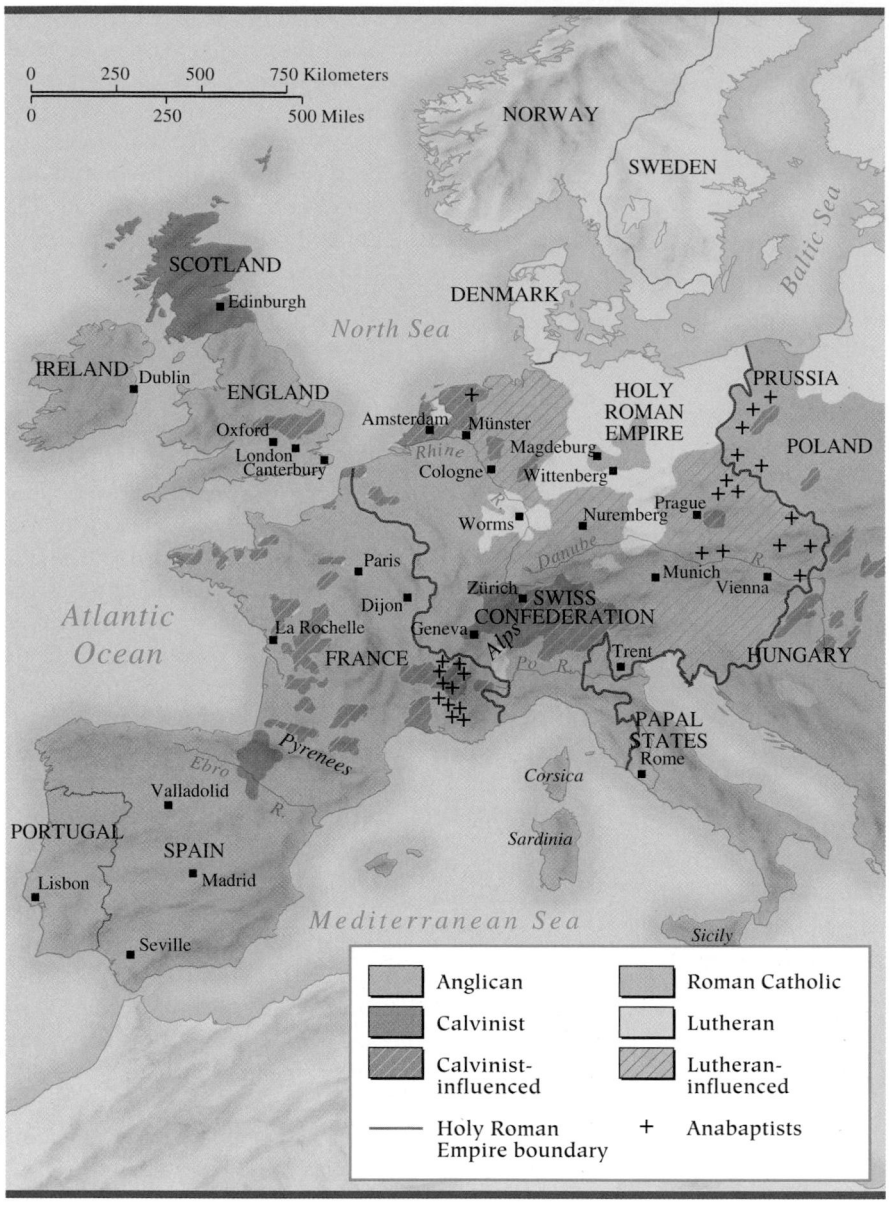

© Cengage Learning

MAP 13.2 Catholics and Protestants in Europe by 1560. The Reformation continued to evolve beyond the basic split of the Lutherans from the Catholics. Several Protestant sects broke away from the teachings of Martin Luther, each with a separate creed and different ways of worship. In England, Henry VIII broke with the Catholic Church for political and dynastic reasons.

Q ***Which areas of Europe were solidly Catholic, which were solidly Lutheran, and which were neither?***

excellent morals—good in general and not malicious."[11] Thousands of Japanese, especially in the southernmost islands, became Christians. In 1552, Xavier set out for China but died of a fever before he reached the mainland.

Although conversion efforts in Japan proved short-lived, Jesuit activity in China, especially that of the Italian Matteo Ricci (ma-TAY-oh REE-chee) (1552–1610), was more long-lasting. Recognizing the Chinese pride in their own culture, the Jesuits attempted to draw parallels between Christian and Confucian concepts and to show the similarities between Christian morality and Confucian ethics. For their part, the missionaries were impressed with many aspects of Chinese civilization, and reports of their experiences heightened European curiosity about this great society on the other side of the world.

The Jesuits were also determined to carry the Catholic banner and fight Protestantism. Jesuit missionaries succeeded in restoring Catholicism to parts of Germany and eastern Europe. Poland was largely won back for the Catholic Church through Jesuit efforts.

A Revived Papacy

A reformed papacy was another important factor in the development of the Catholic Reformation. The pontificate of Pope Paul III (1534–1549) proved to be a turning point in the reform of the papacy. Raised in the lap of luxury, Paul III continued Renaissance papal practices by appointing his nephews as cardinals, involving himself in politics, and patronizing arts and letters on a lavish scale. Nevertheless, he perceived the need for change and expressed it decisively. Advocates of reform, such as Gasparo Contarini (GAHS-puh-roh kahn-tuh-REE-nee) and Gian Pietro Caraffa (JAHN PYAY-troh kuh-RAH-fuh), were made cardinals. In 1535, Paul took the audacious step of appointing a commission to study the church's condition. The Reform Commission's report in 1537 blamed the church's problems on the corrupt policies of popes and cardinals. It was also Paul III who formally recognized the Jesuits and summoned the Council of Trent (see the next section).

Loyola and Obedience to "Our Holy Mother, the Hierarchical Church"

In his *Spiritual Exercises*, Ignatius of Loyola developed a systematic program for "the conquest of self and the regulation of one's life" for service to the hierarchical Catholic Church. Ignatius's supreme goal was the commitment of the Christian to active service in the Church of Christ (the Roman Catholic Church). In the final section of *The Spiritual Exercises*, Loyola explained the nature of that commitment in a series of "rules for thinking with the church."

Ignatius of Loyola, "Rules for Thinking with the Church"

The following rules should be observed to foster the true attitude of mind we ought to have in the Church militant.

1. We must put aside all judgment of our own, and keep the mind ever ready and prompt to obey in all things the true Spouse of Jesus Christ, our holy Mother, the hierarchical Church.
2. We should praise sacramental confession, the yearly reception of the Most Blessed Sacrament [the Lord's Supper], and praise more highly monthly reception, and still more weekly Communion. . . .
3. We ought to praise the frequent hearing of Mass, the singing of hymns, psalmody, and long prayers whether in the church or outside. . . .
4. We must praise highly religious life, virginity, and continency; and matrimony ought not be praised as much as any of these. . . .
6. We should show our esteem for the relics of the saints by venerating them and praying to the saints. We should praise visits to the Station Churches, pilgrimages, indulgences, jubilees, the lighting of candles in churches. . . .
8. We ought to praise not only the building and adornment of churches, but also images and veneration of them according to the subject they represent.
9. Finally, we must praise all the commandments of the Church, and be on the alert to find reasons to defend them, and by no means in order to criticize them.
10. We should be more ready to approve and praise the orders, recommendations, and way of acting of our superiors than to find fault with them. Though some of the orders, etc., may not have been praiseworthy, yet to speak against them, either when preaching in public or in speaking before the people, would rather be the cause of murmuring and scandal than of profit. As a consequence, the people would become angry with their superiors, whether secular or spiritual. But while it does harm in the absence of our superiors to speak evil of them before the people, it may be profitable to discuss their bad conduct with those who can apply a remedy.
13. If we wish to proceed securely in all things, we must hold fast to the following principle: What seems to me white, I will believe black if the hierarchical Church so defines. For I must be convinced that in Christ our Lord, the bridegroom, and in His spouse the Church, only one Spirit holds sway, which governs and rules for the salvation of souls.

Q What are the fundamental assumptions that inform Loyola's rules for "thinking with the church"? What do these assumptions tell you about the nature of the Catholic reform movement?

Source: Excerpt from *The Spiritual Exercises of St. Ignatius of Loyola* translated by Louis J. Puhl, S.J. (Newman Press 1951). Reprinted with permission of Loyola Press. To order copies of this book, call 1-800-621-1008 or visit www.loyolabooks.org.

A decisive turning point in the direction of the Catholic Reformation and the nature of papal reform came in the 1540s. In 1541, a colloquy had been held at Regensburg in a final attempt to settle the religious division peacefully. Here Catholic moderates, such as Cardinal Contarini, who favored concessions to Protestants in the hope of restoring Christian unity, reached a compromise with Protestant moderates on a number of doctrinal issues. When Contarini returned to Rome with these proposals, Cardinal Caraffa and other hard-liners, who regarded all

Il Gesu, Rome/© Scala/Art Resource, NY

Ignatius of Loyola. The Jesuits became the most important new religious order of the Catholic Reformation. Shown here in a sixteenth-century painting by an unknown artist is Ignatius of Loyola, founder of the Society of Jesus. Loyola is seen kneeling before Pope Paul III, who officially recognized the Jesuits in 1540.

compromise with Protestant innovations as heresy, accused him of selling out to the heretics. It soon became apparent that the conservative reformers were in the ascendancy when Caraffa was able to persuade Paul III to establish the Roman Inquisition or Holy Office in 1542 to ferret out doctrinal errors. There was to be no compromise with Protestantism.

When Cardinal Caraffa was chosen pope as Paul IV (1555–1559), he so increased the power of the Inquisition that even liberal cardinals were silenced. This "first true pope of the Catholic Counter-Reformation," as he has been called, also created the Index of Forbidden Books, a list of books that Catholics were not allowed to read. It included all the works of Protestant theologians. Any hope of restoring Christian unity by compromise was fading. The activities of the Council of Trent, the third major pillar of the Catholic Reformation, made compromise virtually impossible.

CHRONOLOGY The Catholic Reformation

Pope Paul III	1534–1549
Papal recognition of the Society of Jesus (Jesuits)	1540
Establishment of the Roman Inquisition (Holy Office)	1542
Council of Trent	1545–1563
Pope Paul IV	1555–1559

The Council of Trent

In March 1545, a group of cardinals, archbishops, bishops, abbots, and theologians met in the city of Trent on the border between Germany and Italy and initiated the Council of Trent, which met in three major sessions between 1545 and 1563. Moderate Catholic reformers hoped that compromises would be made in formulating doctrinal definitions that would encourage Protestants to return to the church. Conservatives, however, favored an uncompromising restatement of Catholic doctrines in strict opposition to Protestant positions. The latter group won, although not without a struggle.

The final doctrinal decrees of the Council of Trent reaffirmed traditional Catholic teachings in opposition to Protestant beliefs. Scripture and tradition were affirmed as equal authorities in religious matters; only the church could interpret Scripture. Both faith and good works were declared necessary for salvation. The seven sacraments, the Catholic doctrine of transubstantiation (rejected by the Protestant reformers), and clerical celibacy were all upheld. Belief in purgatory and in the efficacy of indulgences was strengthened, although the hawking of indulgences was prohibited.

After the Council of Trent, the Roman Catholic Church possessed a clear body of doctrine and a unified church under the acknowledged supremacy of the popes, who had triumphed over bishops and councils. The Roman Catholic Church had become one Christian denomination among many with an organizational framework and doctrinal pattern that would not be significantly altered for four hundred years. With renewed confidence, the Catholic Church entered a new phase of its history.

Politics and the Wars of Religion in the Sixteenth Century

Focus Question: What role did politics, economic and social conditions, and religion play in the European wars of the sixteenth century?

By the middle of the sixteenth century, Calvinism and Catholicism had become activist religions dedicated to spreading the word of God as they interpreted it. Although this struggle for the minds and hearts of

Europeans is at the core of the religious wars of the sixteenth century, economic, social, and political forces also played important roles in these conflicts. Of the sixteenth-century religious wars, none were more momentous or more shattering than the French civil wars known as the French Wars of Religion.

The French Wars of Religion (1562–1598)

Religion was the engine that drove the French civil wars of the sixteenth century. Concerned by the growth of Calvinism, the French kings tried to stop its spread by persecuting Calvinists but had little success. **Huguenots** (HYOO-guh-nots), as the French Calvinists were called, came from all layers of society: artisans and shopkeepers hurt by rising prices and a rigid guild system, merchants and lawyers in provincial towns whose local privileges were tenuous, and members of the nobility. Possibly 40 to 50 percent of the French nobility became Huguenots, including the house of Bourbon, which stood next to the Valois dynasty in the royal line of succession and ruled the southern French kingdom of Navarre (nuh-VAHR). The conversion of so many nobles made the Huguenots a potentially dangerous political threat to monarchical power. Though the Calvinists constituted only about 10 percent of the population, they were a strong-willed and well-organized minority.

The Catholic majority greatly outnumbered the Calvinist minority. The Valois monarchy was staunchly Catholic, and its control of the Catholic Church gave it little incentive to look favorably on Protestantism. At the same time, an extreme Catholic party—known as the Ultra-Catholics—favored strict opposition to the Huguenots and was led by the Guise (GEEZ) family. They received support abroad from the papacy and the Jesuits, who favored their uncompromising Catholic position.

But religion was not the only factor contributing to the French civil wars. Resentful of the growing power of monarchical centralization, towns and provinces were only too willing to join a revolt against the monarchy. This was also true of the nobility, and because so many of them were Calvinists, they formed an an important base of opposition to the crown. The French Wars of Religion, then, presented a major constitutional crisis for France and temporarily halted the development of the French centralized state. The claim of the state's ruling dynasty to a person's loyalties was temporarily superseded by loyalty to one's religious beliefs. For thirty years, battles raged in France between Catholic and Calvinist parties, who obviously considered the unity of France less important than religious truth. But there also emerged in France a group of public figures who placed politics before religion and believed that no religious truth was worth the ravages of civil war. These ***politiques*** (pul-lee-TEEKS) ultimately prevailed, but not until both sides had become exhausted by bloodshed.

Finally, in 1589, Henry of Navarre, the political leader of the Huguenots and a member of the Bourbon dynasty, succeeded to the throne as Henry IV (1589–1610). Realizing, however, that he would never be accepted by Catholic France, Henry took the logical way out and converted to Catholicism. With his coronation in 1594, the French Wars of Religion finally came to an end. The Edict of Nantes (NAHNT) in 1598 solved the religious problem by acknowledging Catholicism as the official religion of France while guaranteeing the Huguenots the right to worship and to enjoy all political privileges, including the holding of public offices.

Philip II and Militant Catholicism

The greatest advocate of militant Catholicism in the second half of the sixteenth century was King Philip II of Spain (1556–1598), the son and heir of Charles V. Philip's reign ushered in an age of Spanish greatness, both politically and culturally. Philip's first major goal was to consolidate and secure the lands he had inherited from his father. These included Spain, the Netherlands, and possessions in Italy and the New World. For Philip, this meant strict conformity to Catholicism and the establishment of strong monarchical authority. Establishing this authority was not an easy task because Philip had inherited a governmental structure in which each of the various states and territories of his empire stood in an individual relationship to the king.

Crucial to an understanding of Philip II is the importance of Catholicism to the Spanish people and their ruler. Driven by a heritage of crusading fervor, the Spanish had little difficulty seeing themselves as a nation divinely chosen to save Catholic Christianity from the Protestant heretics. Philip II, the "Most Catholic King," became the champion of Catholicism throughout Europe, a role that led him to spectacular victories and equally spectacular defeats. Spain's leadership of a "holy league" against Turkish encroachments in the Mediterranean resulted in a stunning victory over the Turkish fleet in the Battle of Lepanto in 1571. Philip's greatest misfortunes came from his attempts to crush the revolt in the Netherlands and his tortured relations with Queen Elizabeth of England.

Revolt of the Netherlands

As one of the richest parts of Philip's empire, the Spanish Netherlands was of great importance to the Most Catholic

CHRONOLOGY Wars of Religion in the Sixteenth Century	
The French Wars of Religion	1562–1598
Coronation of Henry IV	1594
Edict of Nantes	1598
Outbreak of revolt in the Netherlands	1566
Battle of Lepanto	1571
Spanish armada	1588
Twelve-year truce (Spain and the Netherlands)	1609
Independence of the United Provinces	1648

King. Philip's attempt to strengthen his control in the Netherlands, which consisted of seventeen provinces (modern Netherlands, Belgium, and Luxembourg), soon led to a revolt. The nobles, who stood to lose the most politically if their jealously guarded privileges and freedoms were weakened, strongly opposed Philip's efforts. Resentment against Philip was also aroused by his use of taxes collected in the Netherlands to further Spanish interests. Finally, religion became a major catalyst for rebellion when Philip attempted to crush Calvinism. Violence erupted in 1566 when Calvinists—many of them nobles—began to smash statues and stained-glass windows in Catholic churches. Philip responded by sending the duke of Alva with 10,000 veteran Spanish and Italian troops to crush the rebellion.

But the revolt became organized, especially in the seven northern provinces, where the Dutch, under the leadership of William of Nassau, the prince of Orange, offered growing resistance. The struggle dragged on until 1609, when a twelve-year truce ended the war, virtually recognizing the independence of the northern provinces. These seven northern provinces, which began to call themselves the United Provinces of the Netherlands in 1581, soon emerged as the Dutch Republic, although the Spanish did not formally recognize them as independent until 1648. The ten southern provinces remained a Spanish possession.

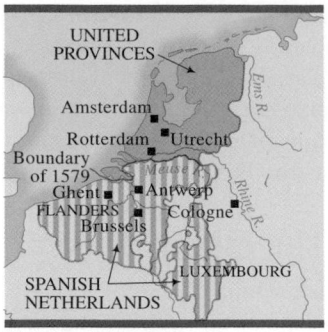

The Netherlands

© Cengage Learning

The England of Elizabeth

After the death of Queen Mary in 1558, her half-sister Elizabeth, the daughter of Henry VIII and Anne Boleyn, ascended the throne of England. During Elizabeth's reign, England rose to prominence as the relatively small island kingdom became the leader of the Protestant nations of Europe and laid the foundations for a world empire.

Intelligent, cautious, and self-confident, Elizabeth moved quickly to solve the difficult religious problem she inherited from her half-sister. Elizabeth's religious policy was based on moderation and compromise (see the box on p. 299). The Catholic laws of Mary's reign were repealed, and the new Act of Supremacy designated

© Stapleton Collection/CORBIS

Procession of Queen Elizabeth I. Intelligent and learned, Elizabeth was familiar with Latin and Greek and spoke several European languages. Served by able administrators, she ruled for nearly forty-five years and generally avoided open military action against any major power. Her participation in the revolt of the Netherlands, however, brought England into conflict with Spain. This picture, painted near the end of her reign, shows the queen in a ceremonial procession.

Queen Elizabeth Addresses Parliament (1601)

Queen Elizabeth I ruled England from 1558 to 1603 with a consummate skill that contemporaries considered remarkable in a woman. Though shrewd and paternalistic, Elizabeth, like other sixteenth-century monarchs, depended for her power on the favor of her people. This selection is taken from her speech to Parliament in 1601, when she had been forced to retreat on the issue of monopolies after vehement protest by members of Parliament. Although the speech was designed to make peace with Parliament, some historians feel that it nevertheless reflects a sincere expression of the rapport that existed between the queen and her subjects.

Queen Elizabeth I, "The Golden Speech"

I do assure you there is no prince that loves his subjects better, or whose love can countervail our love. There is no jewel, be it of never so rich a price, which I set before this jewel: I mean your love. For I do esteem it more than any treasure of riches. . . . And, though God has raised me high, yet this I count the glory of my crown, that I have reigned with your love. This makes me that I do not so much rejoice that God has made me to be a Queen, as to be a Queen over so thankful a people. . . .

Of myself I must say this: I never was any greedy, scraping grasper, nor a strait, fast-holding Prince, nor yet a waster. My heart was never set on any worldly goods, but only for my subjects' good. What you bestow on me, I will not hoard it up, but receive it to bestow on you again. Yea, mine own properties I account yours, to be expended for your good. . . .

I have ever used to set the Last-Judgment Day before mine eyes, and so to rule as I shall be judged to answer before a higher judge, to whose judgment seat I do appeal, that never thought was cherished in my heart that tended not unto my people's good. And now, if my kingly bounties have been abused, and my grants turned to the hurt of my people, contrary to my will and meaning, and if any in authority under me neglected or perverted what I have committed to them, I hope God will not lay their [crimes] and offenses to my charge; who, though there were danger in repealing our grants, yet what danger would I not rather incur for your good, than I would suffer them still to continue?

There will never [a] Queen sit in my seat with more zeal to my country, care for my subjects, . . . [or] with willingness venture her life for your good and safety, than myself. For it is my desire to live [and] reign no longer than my life and reign shall be for your good. And though you have had and may have many princes more mighty and wise sitting in this seat, yet you never had nor shall have any that will be more careful and loving.

Q What qualities evident in Elizabeth's speech would have endeared her to her listeners? How was her popularity connected to the events of the late sixteenth century? Would the members of Parliament have responded differently to a king? Why or why not?

Source: From *Elizabeth I and Her Parliaments* by John E. Neale. London: Jonathan Cape, 1953.

Elizabeth as "the only supreme governor" of both church and state. She used this title rather than "supreme head of the church," which had been used by both Henry VIII and Edward VI, because she did not want to upset Catholics, who considered the pope the supreme head, or radical Protestants, who thought that Christ alone was head of the church. The church service used during the reign of Edward VI was revised to make it more acceptable to Catholics. The Church of England under Elizabeth was basically Protestant, but of a moderate sort that kept most of the queen's subjects satisfied.

Caution, moderation, and expediency also dictated Elizabeth's foreign policy. Fearful of other countries' motives, Elizabeth realized that war could be disastrous for her island kingdom and her own rule. While encouraging English piracy and providing clandestine aid to French Huguenots and Dutch Calvinists to weaken France and Spain, Elizabeth pretended complete aloofness and avoided alliances that would force her into war with any major power (see the Film & History feature on p. 300). Gradually, however, Elizabeth was drawn into conflict with Spain. After years of resisting the idea of invading England as too impractical, Spain's Philip II was finally persuaded to do so by advisers who assured him that the people of England would rise against their queen when the Spaniards arrived. A successful invasion of England would mean the overthrow

FILM & HISTORY

Elizabeth (1998)

Directed by Shekhar Kapur, *Elizabeth* opens in 1554 with a scene of three Protestant heretics being burned alive as Queen Mary (Kathy Burke) pursues her dream of restoring Catholicism to England. Mary also contemplates signing a death warrant for her Protestant half-sister Elizabeth (Cate Blanchett) but refuses to do so before dying in 1558. Elizabeth becomes queen and is portrayed in her early years of rule as an uncertain monarch who "rules from the heart instead of the mind," as one adviser tells her. Elizabeth is also threatened by foreign rulers, the duke of Norfolk (Christopher Eccleston), and others who want a Catholic on the throne of England. A plot, which supposedly includes Robert Dudley (Joseph Fiennes), reputedly her former lover, is unraveled with the help of Francis Walsingham (Geoffrey Rush), a ruthless Machiavellian adviser whose primary goal is protecting Elizabeth. The queen avoids assassination, but the attempt nevertheless convinces Elizabeth that she must be a Virgin Queen who dedicates her life to England. As she tells Lord Burghley (Richard Attenborough), her closest adviser, during the procession that ends the film, "I am now married to England."

The strength of the movie, which contains numerous historical inaccuracies, is in the performance of Cate Blanchett, who captures some of the characteristics of Queen Elizabeth I. At one point, Elizabeth explains her reluctance to go to war: "I do not like wars. They have uncertain outcomes." After she rebuffs the efforts of her advisers to persuade her to marry a foreign prince for the sake of maintaining the throne, Elizabeth declares, "I will have one mistress here, and no master." Although the movie correctly emphasizes her intelligence and her clever handling of advisers and church officials, Elizabeth is shown inaccurately as weak and vacillating when she first comes to the throne. In fact, Elizabeth was already a practiced politician who knew how to use power. She was, as she reminds her advisers, her father's (Henry VIII) daughter.

In many other ways, the movie is not faithful to the historical record. It telescopes events that occurred over thirty years of Elizabeth's lengthy reign into the first five years of her reign and makes up other events altogether. Mary of Guise (Fanny Ardant) was not assassinated by Francis Walsingham, as the movie implies. Nor was Walsingham an important figure in the early years of Elizabeth's reign. Robert Dudley's marriage was well known in Elizabethan England, and there is no firm evidence that Elizabeth had a sexual relationship with him. The duke of Norfolk was not arrested until 1571, much later than in the film. The duc d'Anjou (Vincent Cassel) never came to England, nor would he, even if he had come, have addressed Elizabeth with the candid sexual words used in the film. It was the duc's younger brother, the duc d'Alençon, who was put forth as a possible husband for Elizabeth, although not until she was in her forties. And finally, Elizabeth's choice of career over family and personal happiness seems to reflect a feminist theme of our own times; it was not common in the sixteenth century when women were considered unfit to rule.

Polygram/The Kobal Collection

Queen Elizabeth I (Cate Blanchett) and the duke of Norfolk (Christopher Eccleston).

of heresy and the return of England to Catholicism, surely an act in accordance with the will of God. Philip therefore ordered preparations for an armada (fleet of warships) to spearhead the invasion of England in 1588.

The armada proved to be a disaster. The Spanish fleet that finally set sail had neither the ships nor the troops that Philip had planned to send. A conversation between a papal emissary and an officer of the Spanish fleet before the armada departed reveals the fundamental flaw:

> "And if you meet the English armada in the Channel, do you expect to win the battle?"
>
> "Of course," replied the Spaniard.
>
> "How can you be so sure?" [asked the emissary.]
>
> "It's very simple. It is well known that we fight in God's cause. So, when we meet the English, God will surely arrange matters so that we can grapple and board them, either by sending some strange streak of weather, or, more likely, just by depriving the English of their wits. If we can come to close quarters, Spanish valor and Spanish steel (and the great masses of soldiers we shall have on board) will make our victory certain. But unless God helps us by a miracle the English, who have faster and handier ships than ours, and many more long-range guns, and who know their advantage just as well as we do, will never close with us at all, but stand aloof and knock us to pieces with their culverins [cannons], without our being able to do them any serious hurt. So," concluded the captain, and one fancies a grim smile, "we are sailing against England in the confident hope of a miracle."[12]

The hoped-for miracle never materialized. The Spanish fleet, battered by a number of encounters with the English, sailed back to Spain by a northward route around Scotland and Ireland, where it was further ravaged by storms. Although the English and Spanish would continue their war for another sixteen years, the defeat of the Spanish armada guaranteed for the time being that England would remain a Protestant country. Although Spain made up for its losses within a year and a half, the defeat was a psychological blow to the Spaniards.

CHAPTER SUMMARY

When the Augustinian monk Martin Luther burst onto the scene with a series of theses on indulgences, few people suspected that his observations would eventually split all of Europe along religious lines. But the yearning for reform of the church and meaningful religious experiences caused a seemingly simple dispute to escalate into a powerful movement.

Martin Luther established the twin pillars of the Protestant Reformation: the doctrine of justification by faith alone and the Bible as the sole authority in religious affairs. Although Luther felt that his revival of Christianity based on his interpretation of the Bible should be acceptable to all, others soon appeared who also read the Bible but interpreted it in different ways. Protestantism fragmented into different sects—Zwinglianism, Calvinism, Anglicanism, Anabaptism—which, though united in their dislike of Catholicism, were themselves divided over the interpretation of the sacraments and religious practices. As reform ideas spread, religion and politics became ever more intertwined.

Although Lutheranism was legally acknowledged in the Holy Roman Empire by the Peace of Augsburg in 1555, it had lost much of its momentum and outside of Scandinavia had scant ability to attract new supporters. Its energy was largely replaced by the new Protestant form of Calvinism, which had a clarity of doctrine and a fervor that made it attractive to a whole new generation of Europeans. But while Calvinism's activism enabled it to spread across Europe, Catholicism was also experiencing its own revival. New religious orders based on reform, a revived and reformed papacy, and the Council of Trent, which reaffirmed traditional Catholic doctrine, gave the Catholic Church a renewed vitality.

By the middle of the sixteenth century, it was apparent that the religious passions of the Reformation era had brought an end to the religious unity of medieval Europe. The religious division (Catholics versus Protestant) was instrumental in beginning a series of religious wars that were complicated by economic, social, and political forces that also played a role. The French Wars of Religion, the revolt of the Netherlands against Philip II, and the conflict between Philip II of Spain and Elizabeth of England, which led to the failed attempt of the Spanish armada to invade England, were the major struggles in the sixteenth-century religious wars.

That people who were disciples of the Apostle of Peace would kill each other over their beliefs aroused skepticism about Christianity itself. As one German writer put it, "Lutheran, popish, and Calvinistic, we've got all these beliefs here, but there is some doubt about where Christianity has got."[13] It is surely no accident that the search for a stable, secular order of politics and for order in the universe through natural laws soon came to play important roles. Before we look at this search for order in the seventeenth century, however, we need first to look at the adventures that plunged Europe into its new role in the world.

CHAPTER TIMELINE

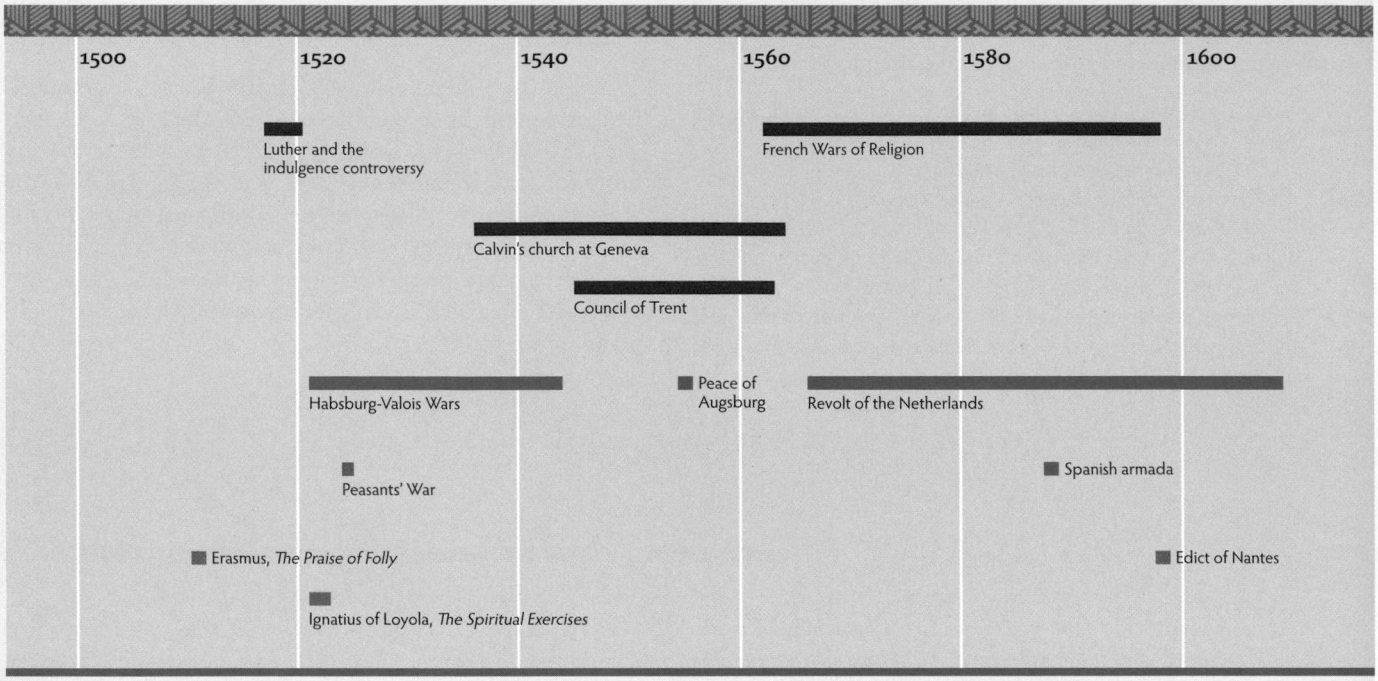

CHAPTER REVIEW

Upon Reflection

Q If attempts at reform of the Catholic Church were unsuccessful in the fifteenth century, why did they succeed in the sixteenth-century Reformation?

Q What role did politics play in the establishment of Lutheranism and Anglicanism?

Q Elizabeth of England and Philip II of Spain were two of Europe's most famous monarchs in the second half of the sixteenth century. Compare and contrast their methods of ruling and their foreign policy. Which was a more successful ruler? Why?

Key Terms

Christian (northern Renaissance) humanism (p. 280)
pluralism (p. 281)
indulgences (p. 281)
justification (p. 282)
transubstantiation (p. 285)
predestination (p. 291)
Huguenots (p. 297)
politiques (p. 297)

Suggestions for Further Reading

THE REFORMATION Basic surveys of the Reformation period include **J. D. Tracy, *Europe's Reformations, 1450–1650*** (Oxford, 1999), and **D. MacCulloch, *The Reformation*** (New York, 2003). See also the brief work by **P. Collinson, *The Reformation: A History*** (New York, 2006).

NORTHERN RENAISSANCE HUMANISM The development of humanism outside Italy is examined in **C. G. Nauert Jr., *Humanism and the Culture of Renaissance Europe,*** 2nd ed. (Cambridge, 2006).

LUTHER AND LUTHERANISM On Martin Luther's life, see **H. A. Oberman, *Luther*** (New York, 1992), and the brief biography by **M. Marty, *Martin Luther*** (New York, 2004). On the role of Charles V, see **W. Maltby, *The Reign of Charles V*** (New York, 2002).

SPREAD OF THE PROTESTANT REFORMATION The most comprehensive account of the various groups and individuals who are called Anabaptists is **G. H. Williams, *The Radical Reformation,*** 2nd ed. (Kirksville, Mo., 1992). On the English Reformation, see **N. L. Jones, *English Reformation: Religion and Cultural Adaptation*** (London, 2002). On Calvinism, see **W. G. Naphy, *Calvin and the Consolidation of the Genevan Reformation*** (Philadelphia, 2003).

SOCIAL IMPACT OF THE REFORMATION On the impact of the Reformation on the family, see **J. F. Harrington, *Reordering Marriage and Society in Reformation Germany*** (New York, 1995).

CATHOLIC REFORMATION A good introduction to the Catholic Reformation can be found in **M. A. Mullett, *The Catholic Reformation*** (London, 1999). Also valuable is **M. R. P. Hsia, *The World of Catholic Renewal, 1540–1770*** (Cambridge, 1998). **J. O'Malley, *The First Jesuits*** (Cambridge, Mass., 1995), offers a clear discussion of the founding of the Jesuits.

WARS OF RELIGION For a good introduction to the French Wars of Religion, see **R. J. Knecht, *The French Wars of Religion, 1559–1598,*** 2nd ed. (New York, 1996). On Philip II, see **G. Parker, *Philip II,*** 3rd ed. (Chicago, 1995). Elizabeth's reign can be examined in **C. Haigh, *Elizabeth I,*** 2nd ed. (New York, 1998).

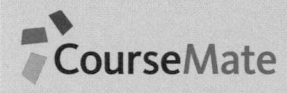

Visit the CourseMate website at www.cengagebrain.com for additional study tools and review materials for this chapter.

CHAPTER 14

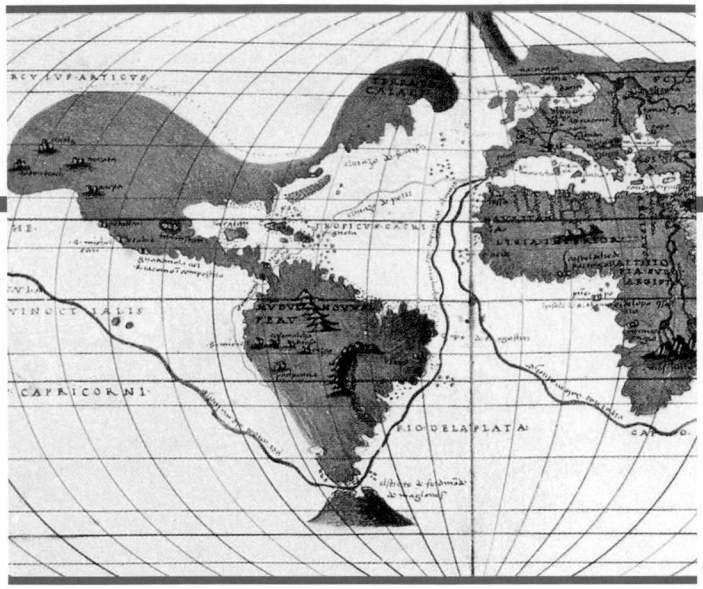

© Everett Collection

A 1536 Mercator projection map showing the route of Ferdinand Magellan's first circumnavigation of the world

Europe and the World: New Encounters, 1500–1800

CHAPTER OUTLINE AND FOCUS QUESTIONS

On the Brink of a New World

Q Why did Europeans begin to embark on voyages of discovery and expansion at the end of the fifteenth century?

New Horizons: The Portuguese and Spanish Empires

Q How did Portugal and Spain acquire their overseas empires, and how did their empires differ?

New Rivals on the World Stage

Q How did the arrival of the Dutch, British, and French on the world scene in the seventeenth and eighteenth centuries affect Africa, India, Southeast Asia, China, and Japan? What were the main features of the African slave trade, and what effects did it have on Africa?

The Impact of European Expansion

Q How did European expansion affect both the conquered and the conquerors?

Toward a World Economy

Q What was mercantilism, and what was its relationship to colonial empires?

CRITICAL THINKING

Q What was the relationship between European overseas expansion and political, economic, and social developments in Europe?

WHILE MANY EUROPEANS were occupied with the problems of dynastic expansion and religious reform, others were taking voyages that propelled Europeans far beyond the medieval walls in which they had been enclosed for almost a thousand years. One of these adventurers was the Portuguese explorer Ferdinand Magellan. Convinced that he could find a sea passage to Asia through America, Magellan persuaded the king of Spain to finance an exploratory voyage. On August 10, 1519, Magellan set sail on the Atlantic with five ships and a Spanish crew of 277 men. After a stormy and difficult crossing of the ocean, Magellan's fleet sailed down along the coast of South America, searching for the strait that would take him through. His Spanish ship captains thought he was crazy: "The fool is obsessed with his search for a strait," one remarked. "On the flame of his ambition he will crucify us all." At last, in October 1520, he found it, passing through a narrow waterway (later named the Strait of Magellan) and emerging into an unknown ocean that he called the Pacific Sea. Magellan reckoned that it would then be a short distance to the Spice Islands of the East, but he was badly mistaken. Week after week, he and his crew sailed on across the Pacific as their food supplies dwindled. According to one account, "When their last biscuit had gone, they scraped the maggots out of the casks, mashed them and served them as gruel. They made cakes out of sawdust soaked with the urine of rats—the rats themselves, as delicacies, had long since been hunted to extinction." At last they reached the islands that would later be called the Philippines (after King Philip II of Spain), where Magellan met his death at the hands of the local inhabitants. Although only one of his original fleet of five ships survived and returned to Spain, Magellan is still remembered as the first person to circumnavigate the world.

At the beginning of the sixteenth century, European adventurers like Magellan had begun launching small fleets into the vast reaches of the Atlantic Ocean. They were hardly aware that they were beginning a new era, not only for Europe, but for the peoples of Asia, Africa, and the Americas as well. Nevertheless, the voyages of these Europeans marked the beginning of a process that led to radical changes in the political, economic, and cultural life of the entire world.

Between 1500 and 1800, European power engulfed the globe. In the Americas, Europeans established colonies that spread their laws, religions, and cultures. In the island regions of Southeast Asia, Europeans firmly implanted their rule. In other parts of Asia and in Africa, their activities ranged from trading goods to trafficking in humans, permanently altering the lives of the local peoples. In all regions touched by European expansion, the indigenous peoples faced exposure to new diseases, alteration of their religions and customs, and the imposition of new laws.

On the Brink of a New World

Focus Question: Why did Europeans begin to embark on voyages of discovery and expansion at the end of the fifteenth century?

Nowhere has the dynamic and even ruthless energy of Western civilization been more apparent than in its expansion into the rest of the world. By the late sixteenth century, the Atlantic seaboard had become the center of a commercial activity that raised Portugal and Spain and later the Dutch Republic, England, and France to prominence. The age of expansion was a crucial factor in the European transition from the agrarian economy of the Middle Ages to a commercial and industrial capitalistic system. Expansion also brought Europeans into new and lasting contacts with non-European peoples that inaugurated a new age of world history in the sixteenth century.

The Motives for Expansion

Europeans had long been intrigued by lands outside Europe as a result of a large body of fantasy literature about "other worlds" that had blossomed in the Middle Ages. In the fourteenth century, the author of *The Travels of John Mandeville* spoke of realms (which he had never seen) filled with precious stones and gold. Other lands were more frightening and considerably less appealing. In one country, "the folk be great giants of twenty-eight foot long, or thirty foot long. . . . And they eat more gladly man's flesh than any other flesh." Farther north was a land inhabited by "cruel and evil women. And they have precious stones in their eyes. And they be of that kind that if they behold any man with wrath they slay him at once with the beholding."[1] Other writers attracted Europeans to the lure of foreign lands by describing mysterious Christian kingdoms: the magical kingdom of Prester John in Africa and a Christian community in southern India that was supposedly founded by Thomas, an apostle of Jesus.

Although Muslim control of Central Asia cut Europe off from the countries farther east, the Mongol conquests in the thirteenth century had reopened the doors. The most famous medieval travelers to the East were the Polos of Venice. Niccolò and Maffeo, merchants from Venice, accompanied by Niccolò's son Marco, undertook the lengthy journey to the court of the great Mongol ruler Khubilai Khan (1259–1294) in 1271. Marco's account of his experiences, the *Travels*, was the most informative of all the descriptions of Asia by medieval European travelers. Others followed the Polos, but in the fourteenth century, the conquests of the Ottoman Turks and then the breakup of the Mongol Empire reduced Western traffic to the East. With the closing of the overland routes, a number of people in Europe became interested in the possibility of reaching Asia by sea to gain access to the spices and other precious resources of the region. Christopher Columbus had a copy of Marco Polo's *Travels* in his possession when he began to envision his epoch-making voyage across the Atlantic Ocean.

An economic motive thus looms large in European expansion in the Renaissance. Merchants, adventurers, and government officials had high hopes of finding new areas of trade, especially more direct access to the spices of the East. In addition to the potential profits to be made from the spice trade, many European explorers and conquerors did not hesitate to express their desire for material gain in the form of gold and other precious metals. One Spanish conquistador said that he went to the New World to "serve God and His Majesty, to give light to those who were in darkness, and to grow rich, as all men desire to do."[2]

The conquistador's statement also expressed another major reason for the overseas voyages—religious zeal. Hernán Cortés (hayr-NAHN kor-TAYSS *or* kor-TEZ), the conqueror of Mexico, asked his Spanish rulers if it was not their duty to ensure that the native Mexicans "are introduced into and instructed in their holy Catholic faith."[3] Spiritual and secular affairs were closely intertwined in the sixteenth century. No doubt, the desire for grandeur and glory, as well as plain intellectual curiosity and a spirit of adventure also played some role in the European expansion.

The Means for Expansion

If "God, glory, and gold" were the primary motives, what made the voyages possible? First of all, the expansion of Europe was connected to the growth of centralized monarchies during the Renaissance. By the second half of the fifteenth century, European monarchies had increased both their authority and their resources and were in a position to turn their energies beyond their borders. At the same time, by the end of the fifteenth century, European states had achieved a level of wealth and technology that enabled them to make a regular series of voyages beyond Europe. Europeans had developed remarkably seaworthy ships and reliable navigational aids, such as the compass and astrolabe (an instrument used to determine the position of heavenly bodies).

One of the most important world maps available to Europeans at the end of the fifteenth century was that of Ptolemy, an astronomer of the second century C.E. Ptolemy's work, the *Geography*, had been known to Arab geographers as early as the eighth century, but it was not until the fifteenth century that a Latin translation was made of the work. Printed editions of Ptolemy's *Geography*, which contained his world map, first became available in 1477. Ptolemy's map showed the world as spherical with three major landmasses—Europe, Asia, and Africa—and only two oceans. In addition to showing the oceans as considerably smaller than the landmasses, Ptolemy had also dramatically underestimated the circumference of the earth, which led Columbus and other adventurers to believe that it would be feasible to sail west from Europe to Asia.

New Horizons: The Portuguese and Spanish Empires

FOCUS QUESTION: How did Portugal and Spain acquire their overseas empires, and how did their empires differ?

Portugal took the lead in the European age of expansion when it began to explore the coast of Africa under the sponsorship of Prince Henry the Navigator (1394–1460).

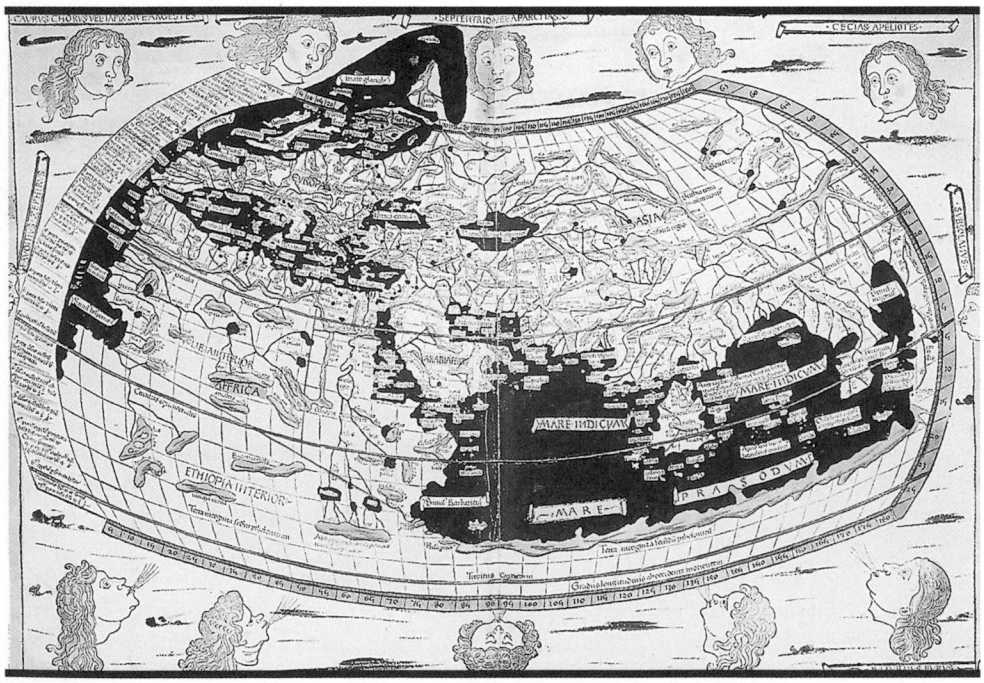

Ptolemy's World Map. Contained in the Latin translation of Ptolemy's *Geography* was this world map, which did not become available to Europeans until the late fifteenth century. Scholars quickly accepted it as the most accurate map of its time. The twelve "wind faces," meant to show wind currents around the earth, were a fifteenth-century addition to the ancient map.

© The Huntington Library, Art Collections and Botanical Gardens, San Marino, CA/SuperStock

His motives were a blend of seeking a Christian kingdom as an ally against the Muslims, acquiring trade opportunities for Portugal, and spreading Christianity.

The Development of a Portuguese Maritime Empire

In 1419, Portuguese fleets began probing southward along the western coast of Africa in search of gold. Exploration slowed after Prince Henry's death in 1460, but Portuguese ships gradually crept down the African coast until Bartholomeu Dias (bar-toh-loh-MAY-oo DEE-ush) (c. 1450–1500) finally rounded the Cape of Good Hope at the southern tip of Africa in 1488 (see Map 14.1). Ten years later, a fleet under the command of Vasco da Gama (VAHSH-koh dah GAHM-uh) rounded the cape and stopped at several ports controlled by Muslim merchants along the coast of East Africa. Da Gama's fleet then crossed the Arabian Sea and reached the port of Calicut, on the southwestern coast of India on May 18, 1498. On arriving in Calicut, da Gama announced to his surprised hosts that he had come in search of "Christians and spices." He found no Christians,

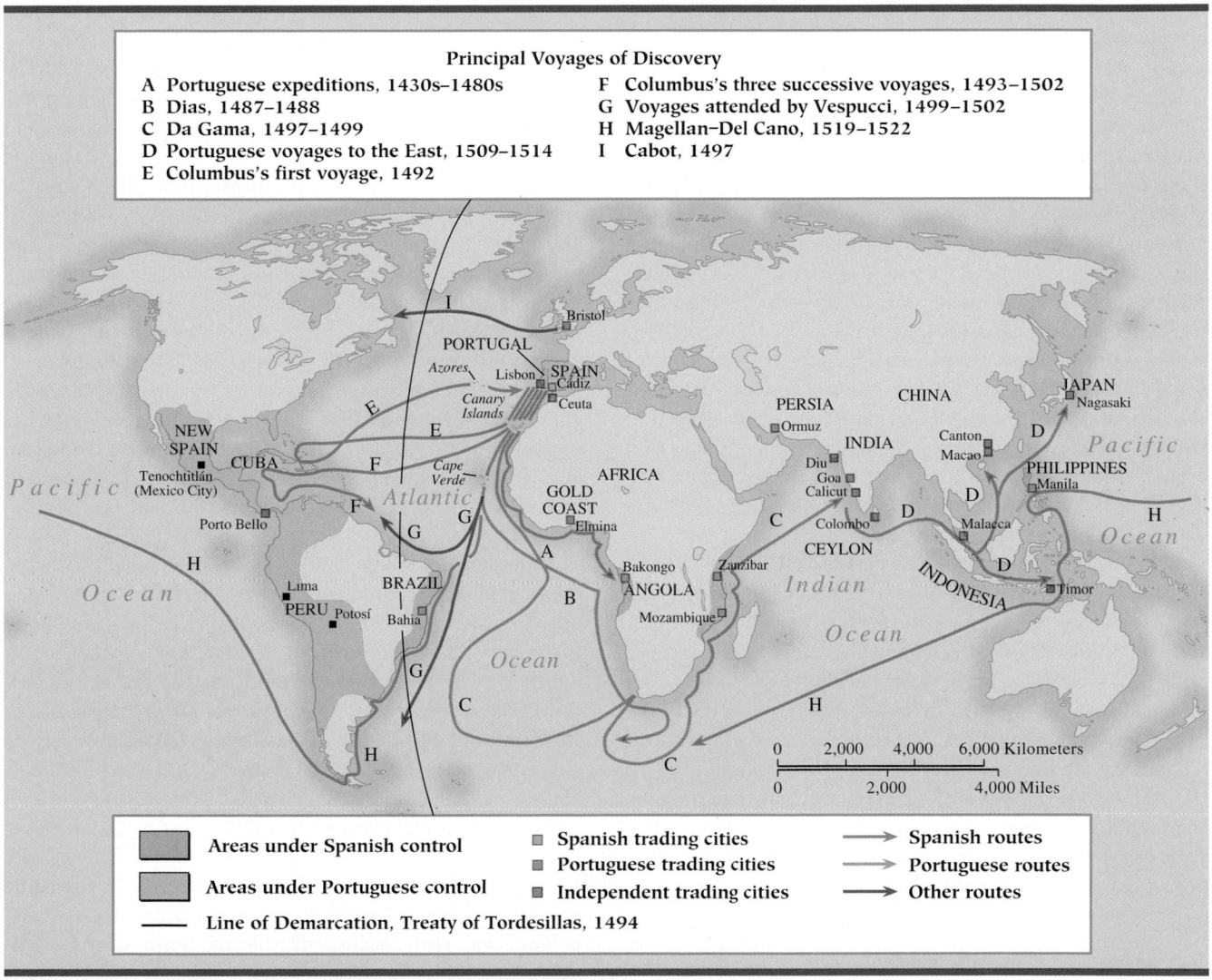

© Cengage Learning

MAP 14.1 European Discoveries and Possessions in the Fifteenth and Sixteenth Centuries. Desire for wealth was the main motivation of the early explorers, although spreading Christianity was also an important factor. Portugal under Prince Henry the Navigator initiated the first voyages in the early fifteenth century; Spain's explorations began at the century's end.

Q *Which regions of the globe were primarily explored by Portugal, and which were the main focus of Spain's voyages?*

but he did find the spices he sought. Although he lost two ships en route, da Gama's remaining vessels returned to Europe with their holds filled with ginger and cinnamon, a cargo that earned the investors a profit of several thousand percent.

Portuguese fleets returned annually to the area, seeking to destroy Arab shipping and establish a monopoly in the spice trade. In 1510, seeing the need for a land base in the area, admiral Afonso d'Albuquerque (ah-FAHN-soh day AL-buh-kur-kee) (c. 1462–1515), took the lead in establishing a ring of commercial-military bases on the western coast of India south of present-day Mumbai (Bombay). The port at Goa became the headquarters for operations throughout the entire region.

The Portuguese now began to range more widely in search of the source of the spice trade (see Images of Everyday Life on p. 309). Albuquerque sailed into the harbor of Malacca (muh-LAK-uh) on the Malay peninsula, and after a short but bloody battle, the Portuguese seized the city and massacred the local Arab population. From Malacca, the Portuguese launched expeditions farther east, to China and the Spice Islands. There they signed a treaty with a local ruler for the purchase and export of cloves to the European market. The new trading empire was now complete. Within a few years, the Portuguese had managed to seize control of the spice trade from Muslim traders and had garnered substantial profits for the Portuguese monarchy. Nevertheless, the Portuguese Empire remained limited, consisting only of trading posts on the coasts of India and China. The Portuguese lacked the power, the population, and the desire to colonize the Asian regions.

Why were the Portuguese so successful? Basically, their success was a matter of guns and seamanship. By the sixteenth century, Portuguese fleets were heavily armed and were able not only to intimidate but also to inflict severe defeats if necessary on local naval and land forces. The Portuguese by no means possessed a monopoly on the use of firearms and explosives, but their effective use of naval technology, their heavy guns that could be mounted in the hulls of of their sturdy vessels, and their tactics gave them military superiority over lightly armed rivals that they were able to exploit until the arrival of other European forces several decades later.

Voyages to the New World

While the Portuguese were seeking access to the spice trade of the Indies by sailing eastward through the Indian Ocean, the Spanish were attempting to reach the same destination by sailing westward across the Atlantic. Although the Spanish came to overseas discovery and exploration after the initial efforts of the Portuguese, their greater resources enabled them to establish a far grander and quite different overseas empire.

An important figure in the history of Spanish exploration was an Italian known as Christopher Columbus (1451–1506). Knowledgeable Europeans were aware that the world was round but had little understanding of its circumference or the extent of the continent of Asia. Convinced that the circumference of the earth was less than contemporaries believed and that Asia was larger than people thought, Columbus believed that Asia could be reached by sailing directly west instead of around Africa. After being rejected by the Portuguese, he persuaded Queen Isabella of Spain to finance his exploratory expedition.

With three ships, the *Santa María*, the *Niña*, and the *Pinta*, and a crew of ninety men, Columbus set sail on August 3, 1492. On October 12, he reached the Bahamas and then went on to explore the coastline of Cuba and the northern shores of Hispaniola (present-day Haiti and the Dominican Republic). Columbus believed that he had reached Asia, and in his reports to Queen Isabella and King Ferdinand upon his return to Spain, he assured them not only that he would eventually find gold but also that they had a golden opportunity to convert the indigenous peoples—whom Columbus persisted in calling "Indians"—to Christianity. In three subsequent voyages (1493, 1498, and 1502), Columbus sought in vain to find a route to the Asian mainland. In his four voyages, Columbus landed on all the major islands of the Caribbean and the mainland of Central America, still convinced that he had reached the Indies in Asia.

Although Columbus clung to his belief until his death, other explorers soon realized that he had discovered a new frontier altogether. State-sponsored explorers joined the race to the New World. A Venetian seaman, John Cabot, explored the New England coastline of the Americas under a license from King Henry VII of England. The continent of South America was discovered accidentally by the Portuguese sea captain Pedro Cabral (kuh-BRAL) in 1500. Amerigo Vespucci (ahm-ay-REE-goh vess-POO-chee), a Florentine, accompanied several voyages and wrote a series of letters describing the geography of the New World. The publication of these letters led to the use of the name "America" (after Amerigo) for the new lands.

The first two decades of the sixteenth century witnessed numerous overseas voyages that explored the eastern coasts of both North and South America. Perhaps the most dramatic of all these expeditions was the journey of Ferdinand Magellan (1480–1521) in 1519. After passing through the strait named after him at the southern tip of South America, he sailed across the Pacific Ocean. Although Magellan himself was killed in the Philippines

IMAGES OF EVERYDAY LIFE

Spices and World Trade

Pepper, cinnamon, nutmeg, and other spices from the East had long been a part of European life. The illustration at the top right from a fifteenth-century French manuscript shows pepper being harvested in Malabar, in southwestern India. Europeans' interest in finding a direct route to the Spice Islands intensified after the fall of Constantinople to the Ottoman Turks in 1453 caused the price for pepper to increase thirtyfold. The Venetians had played a dominant role in the spice trade via Constantinople, as is evident in the Venetian fresco shown at the bottom right. It depicts a spice seller's shop with a wide variety of spices for sale. Vasco de Gama's success in locating a route to the East by sailing around Africa shifted much of the control over the spice trade into Portuguese hands. Following the establishment in 1518 of a fort in Ceylon, the center of cinnamon production, the Portuguese were able to dominate Europe's cinnamon trade. The third illustration shows a portrait of da Gama from c. 1600. The artist depicted the explorer holding a large stick of cinnamon in his right hand, an indication of the significance of the spice to his legacy and its role in his expeditions. Without the desire for spices, men such as da Gama and Christopher Columbus might not have ventured around Africa or across the Atlantic Ocean, thereby opening and forever altering European trade.

Bibliothèque Nationale (Ms Fr 2810 f.84v), Paris/© Archives Charmet/ The Bridgeman Art Library

© The Art Archive/Marine Museum Lisbon/Gianni Dagli Orti

Castello d'Issogne, Val d'Aosta, Italy//© Scala/Art Resource, NY

© Museo Navale, Genova-Pegli/SuperStock

Christopher Columbus. Columbus was an Italian explorer who worked for the queen of Spain. He has become a symbol for two entirely different perspectives. To some, he was a great and heroic explorer who discovered the New World; to others, especially in Latin America, he was responsible for beginning a process of invasion that led to the destruction of an entire way of life. Because Columbus was never painted during his lifetime, the numerous portraits of him are more fanciful than accurate. The portrait shown here was probably done by the Italian painter Ridolfo Ghirlandaio.

and only one of his fleet of five ships completed the return voyage to Spain, his name is still associated with the first known circumnavigation of the earth.

The Europeans referred to the newly discovered territories as the New World, even though they held flourishing civilizations populated by millions of people. But the Americas were indeed new to the Europeans, who quickly saw opportunities for conquest and exploitation. The Spanish, in particular, were interested because in 1494 the Treaty of Tordesillas (tor-day-SEE-yass) had divided up the newly discovered world into separate Portuguese and Spanish spheres of influence, and it turned out that most of South America (except for the eastern hump) fell within the Spanish sphere. Hereafter the route east around the Cape of Good Hope was to be reserved for the Portuguese while the route across the Atlantic was assigned to Spain.

The Spanish Empire in the New World

The Spanish conquerors known as **conquistadors** were hardy individuals motivated by a typical sixteenth-century blend of glory, greed, and religious zeal. Although authorized by the Castilian crown, these groups were financed and outfitted privately, not by the government. Their superior weapons, organizational skills, and determination brought the conquistadors incredible success. They also benefited from rivalries among the native peoples and the decimation of the native populations by European diseases.

EARLY CIVILIZATIONS IN MESOAMERICA Before the Spaniards arrived in the New World, Mesoamerica (modern Mexico and Central America) had already hosted a number of flourishing civilizations. Beginning around 300 C.E., on the Yucatán peninsula a people known as the Maya (MY-uh) had developed one of the most sophisticated civilizations in the Americas. The Maya built splendid temples and pyramids, were accomplished artists, and developed a sophisticated calendar, as accurate as any in existence in the world at that time. The Maya were an agrarian people who cleared the dense rain forests, developed farming, and built a patchwork of city-states. Mayan civilization came to include much of Central America and southern Mexico. For unknown reasons, Mayan civilization began to decline around 800 and had collapsed less than a hundred years later.

© Cengage Learning

Lands of the Maya

Sometime during the early twelfth century C.E. a people known as the Aztecs began a long migration that brought them to the Valley of Mexico. They established their capital at Tenochtitlán (tay-nawch-teet-LAHN), on an island in the middle of Lake Texcoco (now the location of Mexico City). For the next hundred years, the Aztecs built their city, constructing temples, other public buildings, houses, and causeways of stone across Lake Texcoco to the north, south, and west, linking the many islands to the mainland.

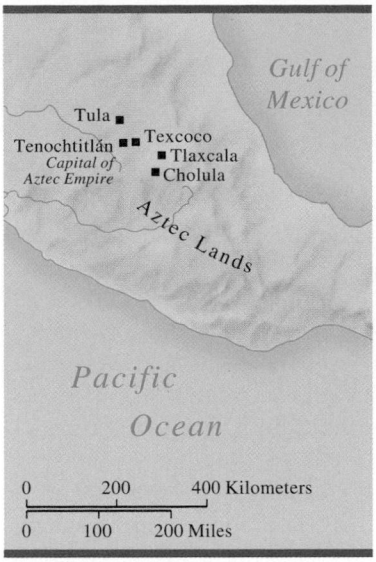

The Aztec Empire

The Aztecs were outstanding warriors, and while they were building their capital city, they also set out to bring the entire area around the city under their control. By the early fifteenth century, they had become the leading city-state in the lake region. For the remainder of the fifteenth century, the Aztecs consolidated their rule over much of what is modern Mexico, from the Atlantic to the Pacific Ocean and as far south as the Guatemalan border. The new kingdom was not a centralized state but a collection of semi-independent territories governed by local lords.

SPANISH CONQUEST OF THE AZTEC EMPIRE In 1519, a Spanish expedition under the command of Hernán Cortés (1485–1547) landed at Veracruz, on the Gulf of Mexico. He marched to the city of Tenochtitlán (see the box on p. 312) at the head of a small contingent of troops (550 soldiers and 16 horses); as he went, he made alliances with city-states that had tired of the oppressive rule of the Aztecs. Especially important was Tlaxcala (tuh-lah-SKAH-lah), a state that the Aztecs had not been able to conquer. In November, Cortés arrived at Tenochtitlán, where he received a friendly welcome from the Aztec monarch Moctezuma (mahk-tuh-ZOO-muh) (often called Montezuma). At first, Moctezuma believed that his visitor was a representative of Quetzalcoatl (KWET-sul-koh-AHT-ul), the god who had departed from his homeland centuries before and had promised someday to return.

But the Spaniards quickly wore out their welcome. They took Moctezuma hostage and proceeded to pillage the city. In the fall of 1520, one year after Cortés had arrived, the local population revolted and drove the invaders from the city. Many of the Spaniards were killed, but the Aztecs soon experienced new disasters. As one Aztec related, "At about the time that the Spaniards had fled from Mexico, there came a great sickness, a pestilence, the smallpox." With no natural immunity to the diseases of Europe, many Aztecs fell sick and died. Meanwhile, Cortés received fresh soldiers from his new allies; the state of Tlaxcala alone provided 50,000 warriors. After four months, the city capitulated. And then the destruction began. The pyramids, temples, and palaces were leveled, and the stones were used to build Spanish government buildings and churches. The rivers and canals were filled in. The mighty Aztec Empire on mainland Mexico was no more. Between 1531 and 1550, the Spanish gained control of northern Mexico.

THE INCA AND THE SPANISH In the late fourteenth century, the Inca were a small community in the area of Cuzco, a city located at an altitude of 10,000 feet in the mountains of southern Peru. In the 1440s, however, under the leadership of their powerful ruler Pachakuti (pah-chah-KOO-tee), the Inca launched a campaign of conquest that eventually brought the entire region under their control.

Pachakuti created a highly centralized state. Cuzco, the capital, was transformed from a city of mud and thatch into an imposing city of stone. Under Pachakuti and his immediate successors, Topa Inca and Huayna Inca (the word *inca* means "ruler"), the boundaries of the Inca Empire were extended as far as Ecuador, central Chile, and the edge of the Amazon basin. The empire included perhaps 12 million people.

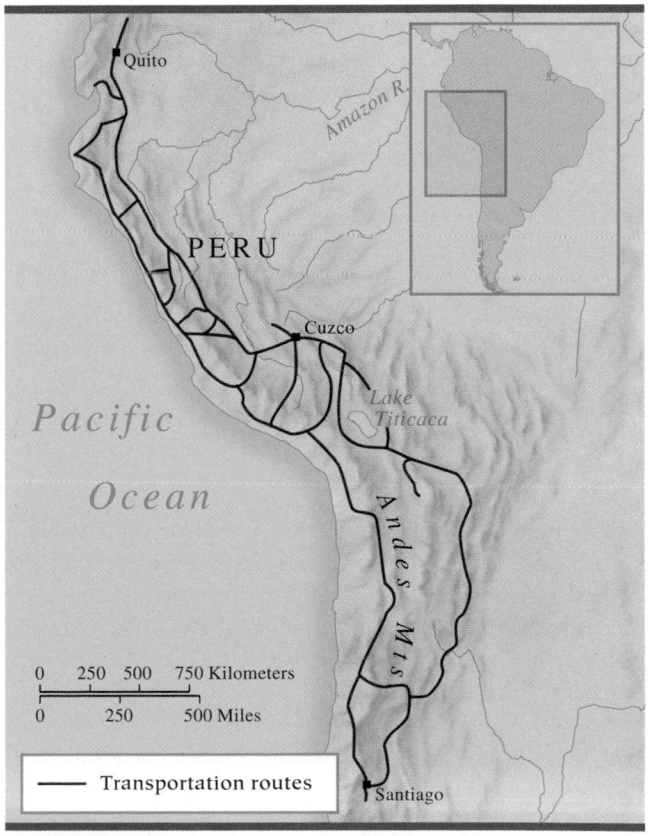

Lands of the Inca

© Cengage Learning

The Spanish Conquistador: Cortés and the Conquest of Mexico

Hernán Cortés was a minor Spanish nobleman who came to the New World in 1504 to seek his fortune. Contrary to his superior's orders, Cortés waged an independent campaign of conquest and overthrew the Aztec Empire in Mexico (1519–1521). Cortés wrote a series of five reports to Emperor Charles V to justify his action. The second report includes a description of Tenochtitlán, the capital of the Aztec Empire. The Spanish conquistador and his men were obviously impressed by this city, awesome in its architecture yet built by people who lacked European technology, such as wheeled vehicles and tools of hard metal.

Cortés's Description of Tenochtitlán

The great city Tenochtitlán is built in the midst of this salt lake, and it is two leagues [about 6 miles] from the heart of the city to any point on the mainland. Four causeways lead to it, all made by hand and some twelve feet wide. The city itself is as large as Seville or Córdoba. The principal streets are very broad and straight, the majority of them being of beaten earth, but a few and at least half the smaller thoroughfares are waterways along which they pass in their canoes. Moreover, even the principal streets have openings at regular distances so that the water can freely pass from one to another, and these openings which are very broad are spanned by great bridges of huge beams, very stoutly put together, so firm indeed that over many of them ten horsemen can ride at once. . . .

The city has many open squares in which markets are continuously held and the general business of buying and selling proceeds. One square in particular is twice as big as that of Salamanca and completely surrounded by arcades where there are daily more than sixty thousand folk buying and selling. Every kind of merchandise such as may be met with in every land is for sale there, whether of food and victuals, or ornaments of gold and silver, or lead, brass, copper, tin, precious stones, bones, shells, snails and feathers; limestone for building is likewise sold there, stone both rough and polished, bricks burnt and unburnt, wood of all kinds and in all stages of preparation. . . . There is a street of herb-sellers where there are all manner of roots and medicinal plants that are found in the land. There are houses as it were of apothecaries where they sell medicines made from these herbs, both for drinking and for use as ointments and salves. . . .

Finally, to avoid [excess] in telling all the wonders of this city, I will simply say that the manner of living among the people is very similar to that in Spain, and considering that this is a barbarous nation shut off from a knowledge of the true God or communication with enlightened nations, one may well marvel at the orderliness and good government which is everywhere maintained.

The actual service of Moctezuma and those things which call for admiration by the greatness and state would take so long to describe that I assure your Majesty I do not know where to begin with any hope of ending. For as I have already said, what could there be more astonishing than that a barbarous monarch such as he should have reproductions made in gold, silver, precious stones, and feathers of all things to be found in his land, and so perfectly reproduced that there is no goldsmith or silversmith in the world who could better them.

Q What did Cortés focus on in his description of this Aztec city? Why do you think he felt justified in overthrowing the Aztec Empire?

Source: From *The European Reconnaissance: Selected Documents* by John H. Parry. Copyright © 1968 by John H. Parry. Reprinted by permission Walker & Co.

The Inca were great builders. One major project was a system of 24,800 miles of roads that extended from the border of modern-day Colombia to a point south of modern-day Santiago, Chile. Two major roadways extended in a north-south direction, one through the Andes Mountains and the other along the coast, with connecting routes between them. Various types of bridges, including some of the finest examples of suspension bridges in premodern times, were built over ravines and waterways.

The Inca Empire was still flourishing when the first Spanish expeditions arrived in the area. In December 1530, Francisco Pizarro (frahn-CHESS-koh puh-ZAHR-oh) (c. 1475–1541) landed on the Pacific coast of South America with a band of about 180 men, but like Cortés, he had steel weapons, gunpowder, and horses, none of which were familiar to his hosts. Pizarro was also lucky because the Inca Empire had already succumbed to an epidemic of smallpox. Like the Aztecs, the Inca had no immunities to European diseases, and all too soon, smallpox was devastating entire villages. In another stroke of good fortune for Pizarro, even the Inca emperor was a victim. Upon the emperor's death, two sons claimed the throne, setting off a civil war. Pizarro took advantage of the situation by seizing Atahualpa (ah-tuh-WAHL-puh), whose forces had just defeated his brother's. Armed only with stones, arrows, and light spears, Incan soldiers were no match for the charging horses of the Spanish, let alone their guns and cannons. After executing Atahualpa, Pizarro and his soldiers, aided by their Incan allies, marched on Cuzco and captured the Incan capital. By 1535, Pizarro had established a capital at Lima for a new colony of the Spanish Empire.

ADMINISTRATION OF THE SPANISH EMPIRE Spanish policy toward the Indians of the New World was a combination of confusion, misguided paternalism, and cruel exploitation. Whereas the conquistadors made decisions based on expediency and their own interests, Queen Isabella declared the indigenous peoples to be subjects of Castile and instituted the Spanish ***encomienda*** (en-koh-MYEN-dah), an economic and social system that permitted the conquering Spaniards to collect tribute from the Indians and use them as laborers. In return, the holders of an *encomienda* were supposed to protect the Indians, pay them wages, and supervise their spiritual needs. In practice, this meant that the settlers were free to implement the paternalistic system of the government as they pleased. Three thousand miles from Spain, Spanish settlers largely ignored their government and brutally used the Indians to pursue their own economic interests. Indians were put to work on plantations and in the lucrative gold and silver mines. In Peru, the Spanish made use of the *mita*, a system that allowed authorities to draft native labor to work in the silver mines.

Forced labor, starvation, and especially disease took a fearful toll of Indian lives. With no natural resistance to European diseases, the Indians of America were ravaged not only by smallpox but also by the measles and typhus that came with the explorers and the conquistadors. Although scholarly estimates of native populations vary drastically, a reasonable guess is that 30 to 40 percent of the inhabitants died. On Hispaniola alone, out of an initial population of 100,000 when Columbus arrived in 1493, only 300 Indians survived by 1570.

In the New World, the Spanish developed an administrative system based on viceroys. Spanish possessions were initially divided into two major administrative units: New Spain (Mexico, Central America, and the Caribbean islands), with its center in Mexico City, and Peru (western South America), governed by a **viceroy** in Lima. Each viceroy served as the king's chief civil and military officer.

By papal agreement, the Catholic monarchs of Spain were given extensive rights over ecclesiastical affairs in the New World. They could appoint all bishops and clergy, build churches, collect fees, and supervise the affairs of the various religious orders that sought to convert the heathen. In the early years of the conquest, Catholic missionaries converted and baptized hundreds of thousands of Indians. Soon after the missionaries came the establishment of dioceses, parishes, cathedrals, schools, and hospitals—all the trappings of civilized European society.

CHRONOLOGY The Portuguese and Spanish Empires in the Sixteenth Century

Bartholomeu Dias sails around the tip of Africa	1488
Voyages of Columbus	1492–1502
Treaty of Tordesillas	1494
Vasco da Gama lands at Calicut in India	1498
Portuguese ships land in southern China	1514
Magellan's voyage around the world	1519–1522
Spanish conquest of Mexico	1519–1522
Pizarro's conquest of the Inca	1530–1535

New Rivals on the World Stage

FOCUS QUESTIONS: How did the arrival of the Dutch, British, and French on the world scene in the seventeenth and eighteenth centuries affect Africa, India, Southeast Asia, China, and Japan? What were the main features of the African slave trade, and what effects did it have on Africa?

Portugal and Spain had been the first Atlantic nations to take advantage of the age of exploration, starting in the late fifteenth century, and both had become great colonial powers. In the seventeenth century, however, their European neighbors to the north—first the Dutch and then the French and English—moved to replace the Portuguese and Spanish and create their own colonial empires. The new rivals and their rivalry soon had an impact on much of the rest of the world—in Africa, Asia, and the Americas.

Africa: The Slave Trade

Although the primary objective of the Portuguese in sailing around Africa was to find a sea route to the Spice Islands, they soon discovered that profits could be made in Africa itself. So did other Europeans.

Traffic in slaves was not new, and at first, the Portuguese simply replaced European slaves with African ones. During the second half of the fifteenth century, about a thousand slaves were taken to Portugal each year. Most wound up serving as domestic servants for affluent families in Europe. But the discovery of the Americas in the

1490s and the planting of sugarcane in South America and on the islands of the Caribbean changed the situation drastically.

Cane sugar had first been introduced to Europeans from the Middle East during the Crusades. During the sixteenth century, sugarcane plantations were set up along the eastern coast of Brazil and on several islands in the Caribbean. Because the growing of cane sugar demands both skill and large quantities of labor, the new plantations required more workers than could be provided by the small American Indian population in the New World, decimated by diseases imported from the Old World. Since the climate and soil of much of West Africa were not conducive to the cultivation of sugar, African slaves began to be shipped to Brazil and the Caribbean to work on the plantations. The first were sent from Portugal, but in 1518, a Spanish ship carried the first boatload of African slaves directly from Africa to the New World.

GROWTH IN THE SLAVE TRADE During the next two centuries, the trade in slaves grew dramatically and became part of the **triangular trade** connecting Europe, Africa, and the American continents that characterized the new Atlantic economy (see Map 14.2). European merchant ships (primarily those of England, France, Spain, Portugal, and the Dutch Republic) carried European manufactured goods, such as guns, gin, and cloth, to Africa, where they were traded for a cargo of slaves. The slaves were then shipped to the Americas and sold. European merchants then bought tobacco, molasses, sugar, rum, coffee, and raw cotton and shipped them back to Europe to be sold in European markets.

Bibliothèque des Arts Décoratifs, Paris/© Archives Charmet/The Bridgeman Art Library

The Sale of Slaves. The slave trade was one of the most profitable commercial enterprises of the eighteenth century. This painting shows a Western slave merchant negotiating with a local African leader over slaves at Gorée, Senegal, in West Africa in the late eighteenth century.

An estimated 275,000 enslaved Africans were exported to other countries during the sixteenth century, with 2,000 going annually to the Americas alone. The total climbed to over a million in the seventeenth century and jumped to 6 million in the eighteenth century, when the trade spread from West and Central Africa to East Africa. Altogether as many as 10 million African slaves were transported to the Americas between the early sixteenth and the nineteenth century.

One reason for the astonishing numbers of slaves, of course, was the high death rate. The journey of slaves from Africa to the Americas became known as the **Middle Passage**, the middle leg of the triangular trade route. African slaves were closely packed into cargo ships, 300 to 450 per ship, and chained in holds without sanitary facilities or room to stand up; there they remained during the voyage to America, which took at least 100 days (see the box on p. 316). Mortality rates averaged 10 percent; longer journeys due to storms or adverse winds resulted in even higher death rates. The Africans who survived the journey were subject to high death rates from diseases to which they had little or no immunity.

Before the coming of Europeans in the fifteenth century, most slaves in Africa were prisoners of war. When Europeans first began to take part in the slave trade, they bought slaves from local African merchants at slave markets in return for gold, guns, or other European goods such as textiles or copper or iron utensils.

At first, local slave traders obtained their supply from regions nearby, but as demand increased, they had to move farther inland to find their victims. In a few cases, local rulers became concerned about the impact of the slave trade on the well-being of their societies. In a letter to the king of Portugal in 1526, King Affonso of Congo (Bakongo) complained, "So great, Sire, is the corruption and licentiousness that our country is being completely depopulated."[4] But protests from Africans were generally ignored by Europeans as well as by other Africans.

EFFECTS OF THE SLAVE TRADE The effects of the slave trade varied from area to area. Of course, it had tragic

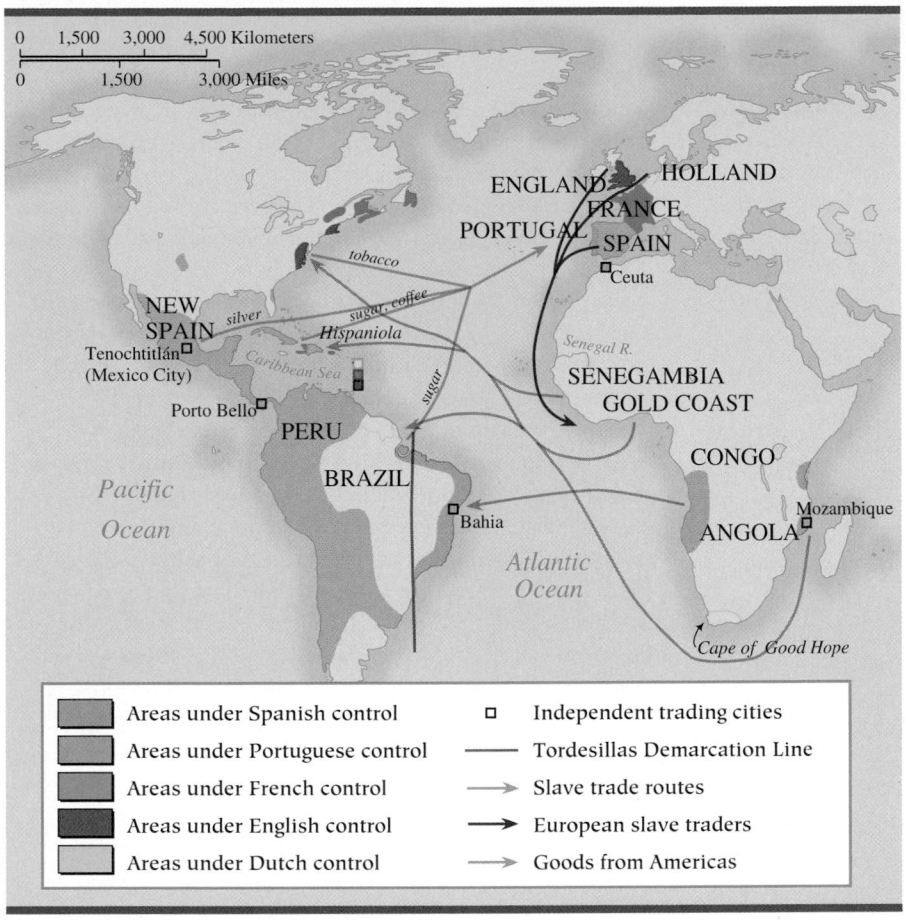

© Cengage Learning

MAP 14.2 Triangular Trade in the Atlantic Economy. As the trade in slaves grew, it became a part of the triangular trade route that characterized the Atlantic economy, involving the exchange of goods and slaves between the western coast of Europe, the slave depots on the African coast, and the ports of North and South America.

Q ***What were the important source regions for slaves, and where were most of the slaves taken?***

effects on the lives of the slaves and their families. There was also an economic price as the importation of cheap manufactured goods from Europe undermined local cottage industries and forced countless families into poverty. The slave trade also led to the depopulation of some areas and deprived many African communities of their youngest and strongest men and women.

The political effects of the slave trade were also devastating. The need to maintain a constant supply of slaves led to increased warfare and violence as African chiefs and their followers, armed with guns acquired from the trade in slaves, stepped up their raids and wars on neighboring peoples. A few Europeans lamented what they were doing to traditional African societies. One Dutch slave trader remarked, "From us they have learned strife, quarrelling, drunkenness, trickery, theft, unbridled desire for what is not one's own, misdeeds unknown to them before, and the accursed lust for gold."[5] Nevertheless, the slave trade continued unabated.

Despite a rising chorus of humanitarian sentiments from European intellectuals, the use of black slaves remained largely acceptable to Western society. Europeans continued to view blacks as inferior beings fit primarily for indentured labor. Not until the Society of Friends, known as the Quakers, began to criticize slavery in the 1770s and exclude from their church any member adhering to slave trafficking did European sentiment for the abolition of slavery begin to build. Even then, it was not until the radical stage of the French Revolution in the 1790s that the French abolished slavery. The British followed suit in 1807. Despite the elimination of the African source, slavery continued in the newly formed United States until the 1860s.

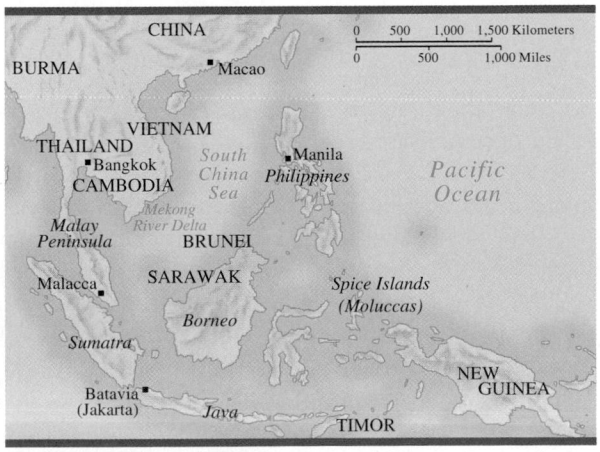

© Cengage Learning

Southeast Asia, c. 1700

The West in Southeast Asia

Portugal's efforts to dominate the trade of Southeast Asia were never totally successful. The Portuguese lacked both the numbers and the wealth to overcome local resistance and colonize the Asian regions. Portugal's empire was simply

The Atlantic Slave Trade

One of the most odious practices of early modern Western society was the Atlantic slave trade, which reached its height in the eighteenth century. Blacks were transported in densely packed cargo ships from the western coast of Africa to the Americas to work as slaves in the plantation economy. This excerpt presents a criticism of the slave trade from an anonymous French writer.

Diary of a Citizen

As soon as the ships have lowered their anchors off the coast of Guinea, the price at which the captains have decided to buy the captives is announced to the Negroes who buy prisoners from various princes and sell them to Europeans. Presents are sent to the sovereign who rules over that particular part of the coast, and permission to trade is given. Immediately the slaves are brought by inhuman brokers like so many victims dragged to a sacrifice. White men who covet that portion of the human race receive them in a little house they have erected on the shore, where they have entrenched themselves with two pieces of cannon and twenty guards. As soon as the bargain is concluded, the Negro is put in chains and led aboard the vessel, where he meets his fellow sufferers. . . .

The vessel sets sail for the Antilles, and the Negroes are chained in a hold of the ship, a kind of lugubrious prison where the light of day does not penetrate, but into which the air is introduced by means of a pump. Twice a day some disgusting food is distributed to them. Their consuming sorrow and the sad state to which they are reduced would make them commit suicide if they were not deprived of all the means for an attempt upon their lives. Without any kind of clothing it would be difficult to conceal from the watchful eyes of the sailors in charge any instrument apt to alleviate their despair. The fear of a revolt, such as sometimes happens on the voyage from Guinea, is the basis of a common concern and produces as many guards as there are men in the crew. The slightest noise or a secret conversation among two Negroes is punished with utmost severity. All in all, the voyage is made in a continuous state of alarm on the part of the white men, who fear a revolt, and in a cruel state of uncertainty on the part of the Negroes, who do not know the fate awaiting them.

When the vessel arrives at a port in the Antilles, they are taken to a warehouse where they are displayed, like any merchandise, to the eyes of buyers. The plantation owner pays according to the age, strength, and health of the Negro he is buying. He has him taken to his plantation, and there he is delivered to an overseer who then and there becomes his tormentor. In order to domesticate him, the Negro is granted a few days of rest in his new place, but soon he is given a hoe and a sickle and made to join a work gang. Then he ceases to wonder about his fate; he understands that only labor is demanded of him. But he does not know yet how excessive this labor will be. As a matter of fact, his work begins at dawn and does not end before nightfall; it is interrupted for only two hours at dinnertime. The food a full-grown Negro is given each week consists of two pounds of salt beef or cod and two pots of tapioca meal.

Q What does this account reveal about the nature of the slave trade and white attitudes toward blacks in the eighteenth century?

Source: From *European Society in the Eighteenth Century*, ed. Robert and Elborg Forster. New York: Walker & Co., 1969. Reprinted by permission of Walker & Co.

too large and Portugal too small to maintain it. By the end of the sixteenth century, new European rivals had entered the fray.

One of them was Spain. The Spanish had established themselves in the region when Magellan had landed in the Philippines. Although he was killed there, the Spanish were able to gain control over the Philippines, which eventually became a major Spanish base in the trade across the Pacific. Spanish ships carried silk and other luxury goods to Mexico in return for silver from the mines of Mexico.

The primary threat to the Portuguese Empire in Southeast Asia, however, came with the arrival of the Dutch and the English, who were better financed than the Portuguese. The shift in power began in the early seventeenth century when the Dutch seized a Portuguese fort in the Moluccas (muh-LUHK-uhz) and then gradually pushed the Portuguese out of the spice trade. During the next fifty years, the Dutch occupied most of the Portuguese coastal forts along the trade routes throughout the Indian Ocean, including the island of Ceylon (today's Sri Lanka) and seized Malacca in 1641. The aggressive Dutch drove the English traders out of the spice market as well.

The Dutch also began to consolidate their political and military control over the entire area. On the island of

Java, where they had established a fort at Batavia (buh-TAY-vee-uh) (modern Jakarta) in 1619, the Dutch found that it was necessary to bring the inland regions under their control to protect their position. On Java and the neighboring island of Sumatra, the Dutch East India Company, which had been founded in 1602, established pepper plantations, which soon became the source of massive profits for Dutch merchants in Amsterdam. By the end of the eighteenth century, the Dutch had succeeded in bringing almost the entire Indonesian archipelago under their control.

The arrival of the Europeans had less impact on mainland Southeast Asia, where strong monarchies in Burma (modern Myanmar), Siam (modern Thailand), and Vietnam resisted foreign encroachment. In the sixteenth century, the Portuguese established limited trade relations with several mainland states, including Siam, Burma, Vietnam, and the remnants of the old Angkor kingdom in Cambodia. By the early seventeenth century, other nations had followed and had begun to compete actively for trade and missionary privileges. In general, however, these states were able to unite and drive the Europeans out.

In Vietnam, the arrival of Western merchants and missionaries in the mid-seventeenth century coincided with a period of internal conflict among ruling groups in the country. The European powers began to take sides in local politics, with the Portuguese and the Dutch supporting rival factions. The Europeans also set up trading posts for their merchants, but by the end of the seventeenth century, when it became clear that economic opportunities were limited, most of them were abandoned. French missionaries attempted to remain, but their efforts were blocked by the authorities, who viewed converts to Catholicism as a threat to the prestige of the Vietnamese emperor (see the box on p. 318).

Europe in Asia. As Europeans began to move into parts of Asia, they reproduced many of the physical surroundings of their homeland in the port cities they built there. This is evident in comparing these two scenes. Below is a seventeenth-century view of Batavia, which the Dutch built as their headquarters on the northern coast of Java in 1619. The scene at the right is from a sixteenth-century engraving of Amsterdam. This Dutch city had become the financial and commercial capital of Europe. It was also the chief port for the ships of the Dutch East India Company, which carried the spices of the East to Europe.

© Private Collection/The Bridgeman Art Library

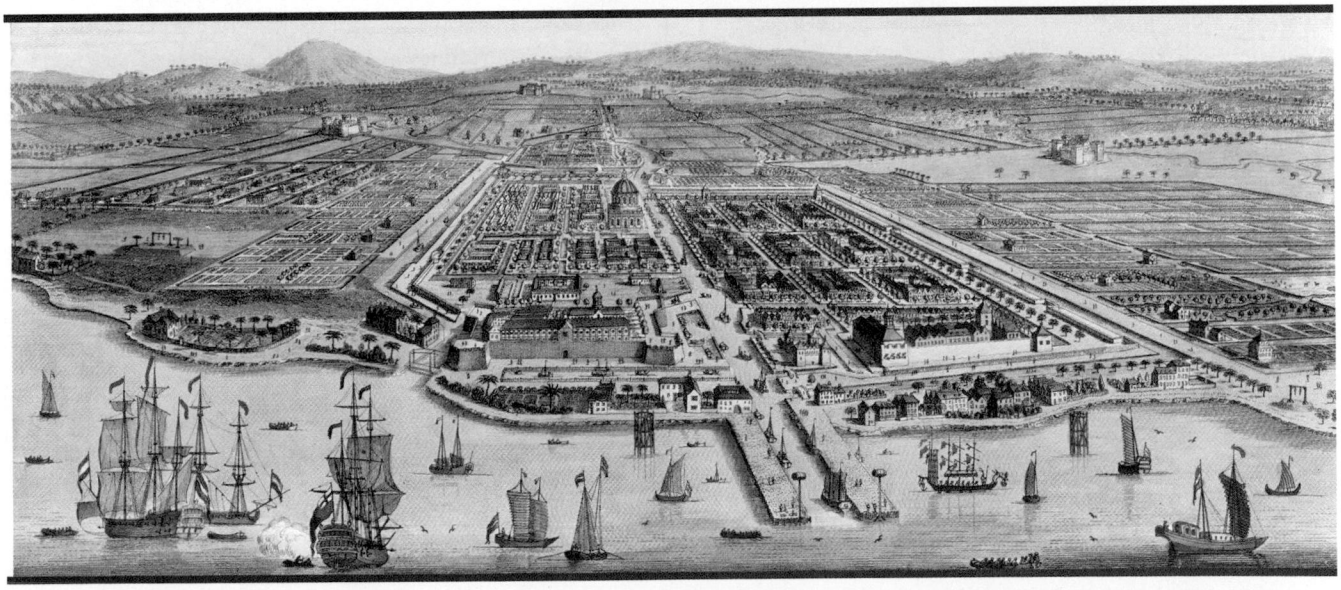

© The Art Archive

OPPOSING VIEWPOINTS

West Meets East: An Exchange of Royal Letters

Economic gain was not the only motivation of Western rulers who wished to establish a European presence in the East. In 1681, King Louis XIV of France wrote a letter to the king of Tonkin (the Trinh family head, then acting as viceroy to the Vietnamese emperor) asking permission for Christian missionaries to proselytize in Vietnam. The king of Tonkin politely declined the request.

A Letter to the King of Tonkin from Louis XIV

Most high, most excellent, most mighty and most magnanimous Prince, our very dear and good friend, may it please God to increase your greatness with a happy end!

We hear from our subjects who were in your Realm what protection you accorded them. We appreciate this all the more since we have for you all the esteem that one can have for a prince as illustrious through his military valor as he is commendable for the justice which he exercises in his Realm. We have even been informed that you have not been satisfied to extend this general protection to our subjects but, in particular, that you gave effective proofs of it to Messrs. Deydier and de Bourges. We would have wished that they might have been able to recognize all the favors they received from you by having presents worthy of you offered you; but since the war which we have had for several years, in which all of Europe had banded together against us, prevented our vessels from going to the Indies, at the present time, when we are at peace after having gained many victories and expanded our Realm through the conquest of several important places, we have immediately given orders to the Royal Company to establish itself in your kingdom as soon as possible, and have commanded Messrs. Deydier and de Bourges to remain with you in order to maintain a good relationship between our subjects and yours, also to warn us on occasions that might present themselves when we might be able to give you proofs of our esteem and of our wish to concur with your satisfaction as well as with your best interests.

By way of initial proof, we have given orders to have brought to you some presents which we believe might be agreeable to you. But the one thing in the world which we desire most, both for you and for your Realm, would be to obtain for your subjects who have already embraced the law of the only true God of heaven and earth, the freedom to profess it, since this law is the highest, the noblest, the most sacred and especially the most suitable to have kings reign absolutely over the people.

We are even quite convinced that, if you knew the truths and the maxims which it teaches, you would give first of all to your subjects the glorious example of embracing it. We wish you this incomparable blessing together with a long and happy reign, and we pray God that it may please Him to augment your greatness with the happiest of endings.

Written at Saint-Germain-en-Laye, the 10th day of January, 1681,

Your very dear and good friend, Louis

Answer from the King of Tonkin to Louis XIV

The King of Tonkin sends to the King of France a letter to express to him his best sentiments, saying that he was happy to learn that fidelity is a durable good of man and that justice is the most important of things. Consequently practicing of fidelity and justice cannot but yield good results. Indeed, though France and our Kingdom differ as to mountains, rivers, and boundaries, if fidelity and justice reign among our villages, our conduct will express all of our good feelings and contain precious gifts. Your communication, which comes from a country which is a thousand leagues away, and which proceeds from the heart as a testimony of your sincerity, merits repeated consideration and infinite praise. Politeness toward strangers is nothing unusual in our country. There is not a stranger who is not well received by us. How then could we refuse a man from France, which is the most celebrated among the kingdoms of the world and which for love of us wishes to frequent us and bring us merchandise? These feelings of fidelity and justice are truly worthy to be applauded. As regards your wish that we should cooperate in propagating your religion, we do not dare to permit it, for there is an ancient custom, introduced by edicts, which formally forbids it. Now, edicts are promulgated only to be carried out faithfully; without fidelity nothing is stable. How could we disdain a well-established custom to satisfy a private friendship? . . .

We beg you to understand well that this is our communication concerning our mutual acquaintance. This

(*Continued*)

(*Opposing Viewpoints continued*)

then is my letter. We send you herewith a modest gift, which we offer you with a glad heart.

This letter was written at the beginning of winter and on a beautiful day.

Q What are the underlying beliefs and approaches of these two rulers? How are they alike? How are they different? What is the significance of the way the two rulers date their letters?

Source: From *The World of Southeast Asia: Selected Historical Readings*, Harry J. Benda and John A. Larkin, eds. Copyright © 1967 by Harper & Row Publishers. Used with permission of John A. Larkin.

The French and British in India

When a Portuguese fleet arrived at the port of Calicut in the spring of 1498, the Indian subcontinent was divided into a number of Hindu and Muslim kingdoms. But it was on the verge of a new era of unity that would be brought about by a foreign dynasty called the Mughals (MOO-guls).

THE MUGHAL EMPIRE The founders of the Mughal Empire were not natives of India but came from the mountainous region north of the Ganges River valley. The founder of the dynasty, Babur (BAH-ber), had an illustrious background. His father was descended from the great Asian conqueror Tamerlane; his mother, from the Mongol conqueror Genghis Khan. It was Akbar (AK-bahr) (1556–1605), Babur's grandson, however, who brought Mughal rule to most of India, creating the greatest Indian empire since the Mauryan dynasty nearly two thousand years earlier.

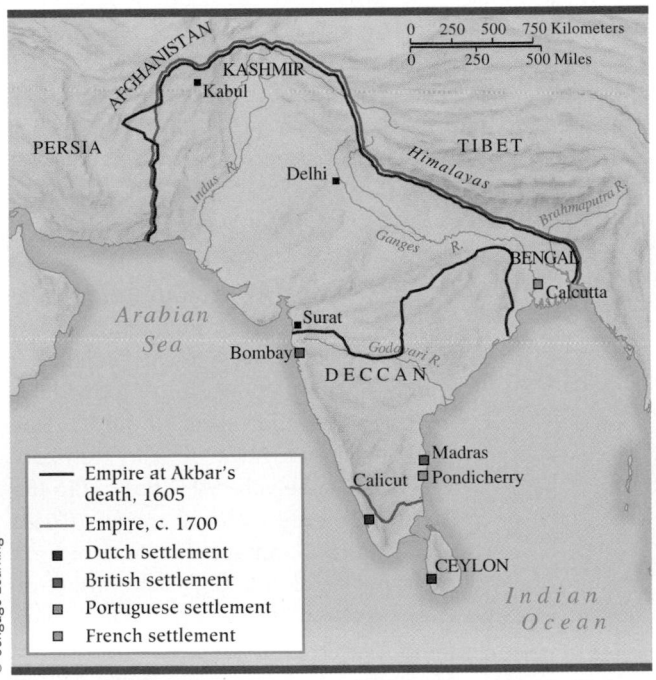

© Cengage Learning

The Mughal Empire

THE IMPACT OF THE WESTERN POWERS As we have seen, the first Europeans to arrive in India were the Portuguese. At first, Portugal dominated regional trade in the Indian Ocean, but at the end of the sixteenth century, the English and the Dutch arrived on the scene. Soon both powers were competing with Portugal, and with each other, for trading privileges in the region.

During the first half of the seventeenth century, the English presence in India steadily increased. By 1650, English trading posts had been established at Surat (a thriving port along the northwestern coast of India), Fort William (now the great city of Calcutta) near the Bay of Bengal, and Madras (now Chennai) on the southeastern coast. From Madras, English ships carried Indian-made cotton goods to the East Indies, where they were bartered for spices, which were shipped back to England.

English success in India attracted rivals, including the Dutch and the French. The Dutch abandoned their interests to concentrate on the spice trade in the middle of the seventeenth century, but the French were more persistent and established their own forts on the east coast. For a brief period, the French competed successfully with the British, even capturing the British fort at Madras.

But the British were saved by the military genius of Sir Robert Clive (1725–1774), an aggressive British empire-builder who eventually became the chief representative in India of the East India Company. (The East India Company had been founded as a joint-stock company in 1600.) Eventually, the French were restricted to the fort at Pondicherry (pon-di-CHER-ee) and a handful of small territories on the southeastern coast.

In the meantime, Clive began to consolidate British control in Bengal, where the local ruler had attacked Fort William and imprisoned the local British population in the "Black Hole of Calcutta" (an underground prison for holding the prisoners, many of whom died in captivity). In 1757, a small British force numbering about three thousand men defeated a Mughal-led army more than ten times its size in the Battle of Plassey (PLAH-see). As part of the spoils of victory, the British East India Company received from the now-decrepit Mughal court the authority to collect taxes from lands in the area surrounding Calcutta. During the Seven Years' War (1756–1763), the British forced the French to withdraw completely from India (see Chapter 18).

China

In 1514, a Portuguese fleet dropped anchor off the coast of China. At the time, the Chinese thought little of the event. China appeared to be at the height of its power as the most magnificent civilization on earth. Its empire stretched from the steppes of Central Asia to the China Sea, from the Gobi Desert to the tropical rain forests of Southeast Asia. From the lofty perspective of the imperial throne in Beijing, the Europeans could only be seen as an unusual form of barbarian. To the Chinese ruler, the rulers of all other countries were simply "younger brothers" of the Chinese emperor, who was regarded as the Son of Heaven.

By the time the Portuguese fleet arrived off the coast of China, the Ming dynasty, which ruled from 1369 to 1644, had already begun a new era of greatness in Chinese history. Under a series of strong rulers, China extended its rule into Mongolia and Central Asia. The Ming even briefly reconquered Vietnam. Along the northern frontier, they strengthened the Great Wall and made peace with the nomadic tribesmen who had troubled China for centuries.

But the days of the Ming dynasty were numbered. After a period of prosperity and growth, the Ming gradually began to decline. During the late sixteenth century, a series of weak rulers led to a period of government corruption. Internal problems went hand in hand with unrest along the northern frontier. The Ming had tried to come to terms with the frontier tribes by making alliances with them. One of the alliances was with the Manchus, who lived northeast of the Great Wall in the area known today as Manchuria. In 1644, the Manchus overthrew the last Ming emperor and declared the creation of a new dynasty with the reign title of the Qing (Ch'ing, "Pure"). The Qing (CHING) were blessed with a series of strong early rulers who pacified the country, corrected the most serious social and economic ills, and restored peace and prosperity. Two Qing monarchs, Kangxi (GANG-zhee) and Qianlong (CHAN-lung), ruled China for well over a century, from the middle of the seventeenth century to the end of the eighteenth. They were responsible for much of the greatness of Manchu China.

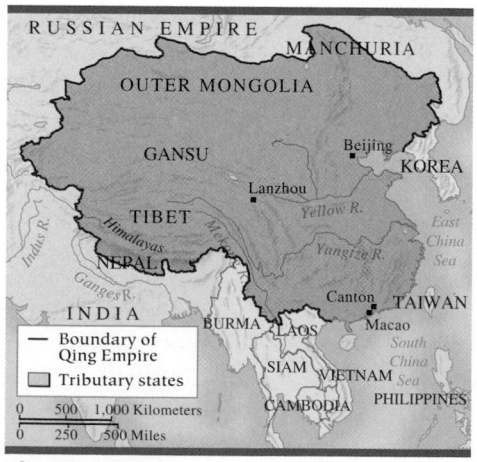

© Cengage Learning

The Qing Empire

WESTERN INROADS Although China was at the height of its power and glory in the mid-eighteenth century, the first signs of internal decay in the Manchu dynasty were beginning to appear. Unfortunately for China, the decline of the Qing dynasty occurred just as Europe was increasing pressure for more trade. The first conflict had come from the north, where Russian traders sought skins and furs. Formal diplomatic relations between China and Russia were established in 1689 and provided for regular trade between the two countries.

Dealing with the foreigners who arrived by sea was more difficult. By the end of the seventeenth century, the English had replaced the Portuguese as the dominant force in European trade. Operating through the East India Company, which served as both a trading unit and the administrator of English territories in Asia, the English established their first trading post at Canton (modern Guangzhou) in 1699. Over the next decades, trade with China, notably the export of tea and silk to England, increased rapidly. To limit contacts between Europeans and Chinese, the Qing government confined all European traders to a small island just outside the city walls of Canton and permitted them to reside there only from October through March.

By the end of the eighteenth century, some British traders had begun to demand access to other cities along the Chinese coast and insist that the country be opened to British manufactured goods. In 1793, a British mission under Lord Macartney visited Beijing to press for liberalization of trade restrictions. But Emperor Qianlong expressed no interest in British products. The Chinese would later pay for their rejection of the British request (see Chapter 24).

Japan

At the end of the fifteenth century, Japan was at a point of near anarchy, but in the course of the sixteenth century, a number of powerful individuals achieved the unification of Japan. One of them, Tokugawa Ieyasu (toh-koo-GAH-wah ee-yeh-YAH-soo) (1543–1616), took the title of shogun ("general") in 1603, an act that initiated the most powerful and longest-lasting of all the Japanese shogunates. The Tokugawa rulers completed the restoration of central authority and remained in power until 1868.

Musée des Arts Asiatiques-Guimet (MG 18653), Paris// © Réunion des Musées Nationaux (Arnaudet)/Art Resource, NY

Arrival of the Portuguese at Nagasaki. Portuguese traders landed accidentally in Japan in 1543. In a few years, they arrived regularly, taking part in a regional trade network involving Japan, China, and Southeast Asia. In these panels, done in black lacquer and gold leaf, we see a late-sixteenth-century Japanese interpretation of the first Portuguese landing at Nagasaki.

OPENING TO THE WEST Portuguese traders had landed on the islands of Japan in 1543, and in a few years, Portuguese ships began stopping at Japanese ports on a regular basis to take part in the regional trade between Japan, China, and Southeast Asia. The first Jesuit missionary, Francis Xavier, arrived in 1549 and had some success in converting the local population to Christianity.

Initially, the visitors were welcomed. The curious Japanese were fascinated by tobacco, clocks, eyeglasses, and other European goods, and local nobles were interested in purchasing all types of European weapons and armaments. Japanese rulers found the new firearms especially helpful in defeating their enemies and unifying the islands.

The success of the Catholic missionaries, however, provoked a strong reaction against the Westerners. When the missionaries interfered in local politics, Tokugawa Ieyasu, newly come to power, expelled all missionaries. Japanese Christians were now persecuted.

The European merchants were the next to go. The government closed the two major foreign trading posts on the island of Hirado and at Nagasaki. Only a small Dutch community in Nagasaki was allowed to remain in Japan. The Dutch, unlike the Spanish and Portuguese, had not allowed missionary activities to interfere with their trade interests. But the conditions for staying were strict. Dutch ships were allowed to dock at Nagasaki harbor once a year and could remain for only two to three months.

The Americas

In the sixteenth century, Spain and Portugal had established large colonial empires in the Americas. Portugal continued to profit from its empire in Brazil. The Spanish also maintained an enormous South American empire, but Spain's importance as a commercial power declined rapidly in the seventeenth century because of a drop in the output of the silver mines and the poverty of the Spanish monarchy. As the seventeenth century began, both Portugal and Spain found themselves facing new challenges to their American empires from the Dutch, English, and French, who increasingly sought to create their own colonial empires in the New World.

THE WEST INDIES Both the French and English colonial empires in the New World included large parts of the West Indies. The English held Barbados, Jamaica, and Bermuda, and the French possessed Saint-Domingue, Martinique, and Guadeloupe.

On these tropical islands, both the English and the French had developed plantation economies, worked by African slaves, which produced tobacco, cotton, coffee, and sugar, all products increasingly in demand in Europe.

The "sugar factories," as the sugar plantations in the Caribbean were called, played an especially prominent role. By the last two decades of the eighteenth century, the British colony of Jamaica, one of Britain's most important, was producing 50,000 tons of sugar annually with the slave labor of 200,000 blacks. The French colony of Saint-Domingue (later Haiti) had 500,000 slaves working on three thousand plantations at the same time. This colony produced 100,000 tons of sugar a year, but at the expense of a high death rate from the brutal treatment of the slaves.

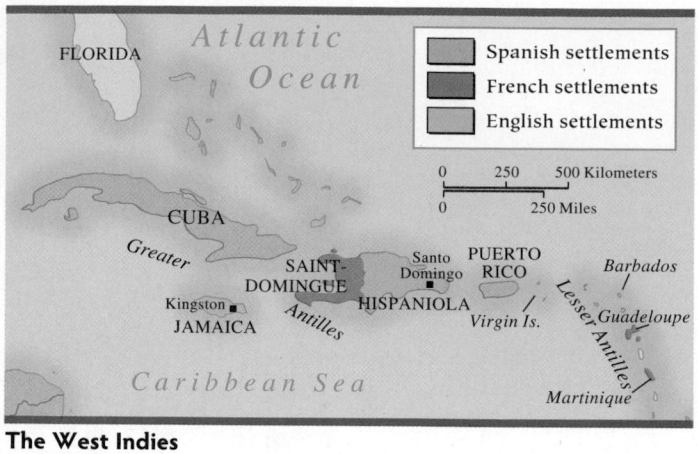

© Cengage Learning

The West Indies

BRITISH NORTH AMERICA The Dutch were among the first to establish settlements on the North American continent after Henry Hudson, an English explorer hired by the Dutch, discovered the river that bears his name in 1609. Within a few years, the Dutch had established the mainland colony of New Netherland, which stretched from the mouth of the Hudson River as far north as Albany, New York. In the second half of the seventeenth century, competition from the English and French and years of warfare with those rivals led to the decline of the Dutch commercial empire. In 1664, the English seized the colony of New Netherland and renamed it New York.

In the meantime, the English had begun to establish their own colonies in North America. The first permanent English settlement in America was Jamestown, founded in 1607 in modern Virginia. It barely survived, making it evident that the colonizing of American lands was not necessarily conducive to quick profits. But the desire to practice one's own religion, combined with economic interests, could lead to successful colonization, as the Massachusetts Bay Company demonstrated. The Massachusetts colony had 4,000 settlers in its early years but by 1660 had swelled to 40,000. By the end of the seventeenth century, the English had established control over most of the eastern seaboard of the present United States.

British North America came to consist of thirteen colonies. They were thickly populated, containing about 1.5 million people by 1750, and were also prosperous. Supposedly run by the British Board of Trade, the Royal Council, and Parliament, these thirteen colonies had legislatures that tended to act independently. Merchants in such port cities as Boston, Philadelphia, New York, and Charleston resented and resisted regulation by the British government.

FRENCH NORTH AMERICA The French also established a colonial empire in North America. In 1663, Canada was made the property of the French crown and administered by a French governor like a French province.

French North America was run autocratically as a vast trading area, where valuable furs, leather, fish, and timber were acquired. The French government was unable to get people to emigrate to its Canadian possessions, however, so they remained thinly populated. By the mid-eighteenth century, there were only about 15,000 French Canadians, most of whom were hunters, trappers, missionaries, and explorers. The French failed to provide adequate men or money, allowing their European wars to take precedence over the conquest of the North American continent.

CHRONOLOGY New Rivals on the World Stage

Portuguese traders land in Japan	1543
British East India Company formed	1600
Dutch East India Company formed	1602
English settlement at Jamestown	1607
Dutch fort established at Batavia	1619
Dutch seize Malacca from the Portuguese	1641
English seize New Netherland	1664
English establish trading post at Canton	1699
Battle of Plassey	1757
British mission to China	1793

The Impact of European Expansion

FOCUS QUESTION: How did European expansion affect both the conquered and the conquerors?

Between 1500 and 1800, the Atlantic nations of Europe moved into all parts of the world. The first had been Spain and Portugal, the two great colonial powers of the sixteenth century, followed by the Dutch, who built their colonial empire in the seventeenth century as Portugal and Spain declined. The Dutch were soon challenged by the British and French, who outstripped the others in the eighteenth century while becoming involved in a bitter rivalry. By the end of the eighteenth century, it appeared that Britain would become the great European imperial power. European expansion made a great impact on both the conquered and the conquerors.

The Conquered

Different regions experienced different effects from the European expansion. The native American civilizations, which had their own unique qualities and a degree of sophistication not much appreciated by the Europeans, were virtually destroyed. In addition to devastating losses of population from European diseases, ancient social and political structures were ripped up and replaced by European institutions, religion, language, and culture. In Africa, the real demographic impact of the slave trade is uncertain due to a lack of records; however, estimates of the population in West Africa suggest that the slave trade negated any population growth, rather than causing a decline. Politically and socially, the slave trade encouraged the growth of territories in West Africa, such as Dahomey and Benin, where the leaders waged internal wars to secure more slaves to trade for guns and gunpowder. Without the slave trade in the nineteenth century, these territories became susceptible to European control. In Asia, the Portuguese trading posts had little impact on native Asian civilizations, although Dutch control of the Indonesian archipelago was more intrusive. China and Japan were still little affected by Westerners, although India was subject to ever-growing British encroachment.

In Central and South America, a new civilization arose that we have come to call Latin America. It was a multiracial society. Spanish and Portuguese settlers who arrived in the Western Hemisphere were few in number relative to the native Indians; many of the newcomers were males who not only used local females for their sexual pleasure but married them as well. Already by 1501, Spanish rulers had authorized intermarriage between Europeans and native American Indians, whose offspring became known as mestizos (mess-TEE-zohs). Another group of people brought to Latin America were the Africans. Over a period of three centuries, possibly as many as 8 million slaves were brought to Spanish and Portuguese America to work the plantations. Africans also contributed to Latin America's multiracial character. Mulattoes (muh-LAH-tohs)—the offspring of Africans and whites—joined mestizos and descendants of whites, Africans, and native Indians to produce a unique society in Latin America. Unlike both Europe and British North America, which remained a largely white offshoot of Europe, Latin America developed a multiracial society with less rigid attitudes about race.

The ecology of the conquered areas was also affected by the European presence. Europeans brought horses and cattle to the Americas, which revolutionized the life of the Indians. Cattle farming supplanted the Indian agricultural practice of growing maize (Indian corn), eventually leading to the development of large estates for raising cattle. South America would later become a great exporter of beef. Europeans also brought new crops, such as wheat and cane sugar, to be cultivated on large plantations by native or imported slave labor. In their trips to other parts of the world, Europeans also carried New World plants with them. Thus, Europeans introduced sweet potatoes and maize to Africa in the sixteenth century.

CATHOLIC MISSIONARIES Although there were some Protestant missionaries in the world outside Europe, Catholic missionaries were far more active in spreading Christianity. From the beginning of their conquest of the New World, Spanish and Portuguese rulers were determined to Christianize the native peoples. This policy gave the Catholic Church an important role to play in the New World, one that added considerably to church power. Catholic missionaries—especially the Dominicans, Franciscans, and Jesuits—fanned out to different parts of the Spanish Empire.

To facilitate their efforts, missionaries brought Indians together into villages, where they could be converted, taught trades, and encouraged to grow crops. These missions enabled the missionaries to control the lives of the Indians and helped ensure that they would remain docile members of the empire (see the box on p. 324 and the Film & History feature on p. 325). Basically, the missions benefited the missionaries more than the Indians. In frontier districts such as California and Texas, missions also served as military barriers to foreign encroachment.

The Catholic Church constructed hospitals, orphanages, and schools. Monastic schools instructed Indian students in the rudiments of reading, writing, and arithmetic. The church also provided outlets for women other than marriage. Nunneries were places of prayer and quiet contemplation, but women in religious orders, many of them of aristocratic background, often lived well and worked outside their establishments by running schools and hospitals. Indeed, one of these nuns, Sor Juana Inés de la Cruz (SAWR HWAH-nuh ee-NAYSS day lah KROOZ) (1651–1695), was one of seventeenth-century Latin America's best-known literary figures. She wrote poetry and prose and urged that women be educated.

Christian missionaries also made the long voyage to China on European merchant ships. The Jesuits were among the most active and the most effective. Many of the early Jesuit missionaries to China were highly educated men who were familiar with European philosophical and scientific developments. They brought along clocks

The Mission

In 1609, two Jesuit priests embarked on a missionary calling with the Guaraní Indians in eastern Paraguay. Eventually, the Jesuits established more than thirty missions in the region. This description of a Jesuit mission in Paraguay was written by Félix de Azara, a Spanish soldier and scientist.

Félix de Azara, *Description and History of Paraguay and Rio de la Plata*

Having spoken of the towns founded by the Jesuit fathers, and of the manner in which they were founded, I shall discuss the government which they established in them. . . . In each town resided two priests, a curate and a subcurate, who had certain assigned functions. The subcurate was charged with all the spiritual tasks, and the curate with every kind of temporal responsibility. . . .

The curate allowed no one to work for personal gain; he compelled everyone, without distinction of age or sex, to work for the community, and he himself saw to it that all were equally fed and dressed. For this purpose the curates placed in storehouses all the fruits of agriculture and the products of industry, selling in the Spanish towns their surplus of cotton, cloth, tobacco, vegetables, skins, and wood, transporting them in their own boats down the nearest rivers, and returning with implements and whatever else was required.

From the foregoing one may infer that the curate disposed of the surplus funds of the Indian towns, and that no Indian could aspire to own private property. This deprived them of any incentive to use reason or talent, since the most industrious, able, and worthy person had the same food, clothing, and pleasures as the most wicked, dull, and indolent. It also follows that although this form of government was well designed to enrich the communities it also caused the Indian to work at a languid pace, since the wealth of his community was of no concern to him.

It must be said that although the Jesuit fathers were supreme in all respects, they employed their authority with a mildness and a restraint that command admiration. They supplied everyone with abundant food and clothing. They compelled the men to work only half a day, and did not drive them to produce more. Even their labor was given a festive air, for they went in procession to the fields, to the sound of music . . . and the music did not cease until they had returned in the same way they had set out. They gave them many holidays, dances, and tournaments, dressing the actors and the members of the municipal councils in gold or silver tissue and the most costly European garments, but they permitted the women to act only as spectators.

They likewise forbade the women to sew; this occupation was restricted to the musicians, sacristans, and acolytes. But they made them spin cotton; and the cloth that the Indians wove, after satisfying their own needs, they sold together with the surplus cotton in the Spanish towns, as they did with the tobacco, vegetables, wood, and skins. The curate and his companion, or subcurate, had their own plain dwellings, and they never left them except to take the air in the great enclosed yard of their college. They never walked through the streets of the town or entered the house of any Indian or let themselves be seen by any woman—or indeed, by any man, except for those indispensable few through whom they issued their orders.

Q How were the missions organized to enable missionaries to control many aspects of the Indians' lives? Why was this deemed necessary?

Source: Excerpt from *Latin American Civilization* by Benjamin Keen, ed. (Boston: Houghton Mifflin, 1974), Vol. I, pp. 223–224. Reprinted by permission of the estate of Benjamin Keen.

and various other instruments that impressed Chinese officials and made them more open to Western ideas.

The Jesuits used this openness to promote Christianity. To make it easier for the Chinese to accept Christianity, the Jesuits pointed to similarities between Christian morality and Confucian ethics. The efforts of the Christian missionaries reached their height in the early eighteenth century. Several hundred Chinese officials became Catholics, as did an estimated 300,000 ordinary Chinese. But ultimately the Christian effort was undermined by squabbling among the religious orders themselves. To make it easier for the Chinese to convert, the Jesuits had allowed the new Catholics to continue the practice of ancestor worship. Jealous Dominicans and Franciscans complained to the pope, who condemned the practice. Soon Chinese authorities began to suppress Christian activities throughout China.

The Jesuits also had some success in Japan, where they converted a number of local nobles. By the end of the

FILM & HISTORY

The Mission (1986)

Directed by Roland Joffé, *The Mission* examines religion, politics, and colonialism in Europe and South America in the mid-eighteenth century. The movie begins with a flashback as Cardinal Altamirano (Ray McAnally) is dictating a letter to the pope to discuss the fate of the Jesuit missions in Paraguay. He begins by describing the establishment of a new Jesuit mission (San Carlos) in Spanish territory in the borderlands of Paraguay and Brazil. Father Gabriel (Jeremy Irons) has been able to win over the Guaraní Indians and create a community based on communal livelihood and property (private property has been abolished). The mission includes dwellings for the Guaraní and a church where they can practice their new faith by learning the Gospel and singing hymns. This small band of Jesuits is joined by Rodrigo Mendozo (Robert De Niro), who has been a slave trader dealing in Indians and now seeks to atone for killing his brother in a fit of jealous rage by joining the community at San Carlos. Won over to Father Gabriel's perspective, he also becomes a member of the Jesuit order.

The Jesuit missionary Father Gabriel (Jeremy Irons) with the Guaraní Indians of Paraguay before their slaughter by Portuguese troops.

© Warner Brothers/Courtesy Everett Collection

Cardinal Altamirano now travels to the New World, sent by a pope anxious to appease the Portuguese monarch over the activities of the Jesuits. Portuguese settlers in Brazil are eager to use the native people as slaves and to confiscate their communal lands and property. In 1750, when Spain agrees to turn over the Guaraní territory in Paraguay to Portugal, they seize their opportunity. Although the cardinal visits a number of missions, including that of San Carlos, and obviously approves of their accomplishments, his hands are tied by the Portuguese king who is threatening to disband the Jesuit order if the missions are not closed. The cardinal acquiesces, and Portuguese troops are sent to take over the missions. Although Rodrigo and the other Jesuits join the natives in fighting the Portuguese while Father Gabriel refuses to fight, all are massacred. The cardinal returns to Europe, dismayed by the murderous activities of the Portuguese but hopeful that the Jesuit order will be spared. All is in vain, however, as the Catholic monarchs of Europe expel the Jesuits from their countries and pressure Pope Clement XIV into disbanding the Jesuit order in 1733.

In its approach to the destruction of the Jesuit missions, *The Mission* clearly exalts the dedication of the Jesuit order and praises the missionaries' devotion to the welfare of the Indians. The movie ends with a small group of Guaraní children, now all orphans, picking up a few remnants of debris left in their destroyed mission and moving off down the river back into the wilderness to escape enslavement. The final words on the screen illuminate the movie's message about the activities of the Europeans who destroyed the native civilizations in their conquest of the Americas: "The Indians of South America are still engaged in a struggle to defend their land and their culture. Many of the priests who, inspired by faith and love, continue to support the rights of the Indians, do so with their lives," a reference to the ongoing struggle in Latin America against the regimes that continue to oppress the landless masses.

sixteenth century, thousands of Japanese on the southernmost islands of Kyushu and Shikoku had become Christians. But the Jesuit practice of destroying local idols and shrines and turning some temples into Christian schools or churches caused a severe reaction. When a new group of Spanish Franciscans continued the same policies, the government ordered the execution of nine missionaries and a number of their Japanese converts.

The Conquerors

For some Europeans, expansion abroad brought the possibility of obtaining land, riches, and social advancement. One Spaniard commented in 1572 that many "poor young men" had left Spain for Mexico, where they hoped to acquire landed estates and call themselves "gentlemen." Although some wives accompanied their husbands abroad, many ordinary European women found new opportunities for marriage in the New World because of the lack of white women. Indeed, as one commentator bluntly put it, even "a whore, if handsome, [can] make a wife for some rich planter."[6] In the violence-prone world of early Spanish America, a number of women also found themselves rich after their husbands were killed unexpectedly. In one area of Central America, women owned about 25 percent of the landed estates by 1700.

European expansion also had other economic effects on the conquerors. Wherever they went in the New World, Europeans looked for sources of gold and silver. One Aztec commented that the Spanish conquerors "longed and lusted for gold. Their bodies swelled with greed, and their hunger was ravenous; they hungered like pigs for that gold."[7] Rich silver deposits were found and exploited in Mexico and southern Peru (modern Bolivia). When the mines at Potosí in Peru were opened in 1545, the value of precious metals imported into Europe quadrupled. Between 1503 and 1650, more than 35 million pounds of silver and 400,000 pounds of gold entered the port of Seville and set off a price revolution that affected the Spanish economy.

But gold and silver were only two of the products that became part of the exchange between the New World and the Old. Historians refer to the reciprocal importation and exportation of plants and animals between Europe and the Americas as the **Columbian Exchange**. While Europeans were bringing horses, cattle, and wheat to the New World, they were taking new agricultural products such as potatoes, chocolate, corn, tomatoes, and tobacco back to Europe. Potatoes became especially popular as a basic dietary staple in some areas of Europe. High in carbohydrates and rich in vitamins A and C, potatoes could be easily stored for winter use and soon enabled more people to survive on smaller plots of land. This improvement in nutrition was soon reflected in a rapid increase in population.

The European lifestyle was greatly affected by new products from abroad. In addition to new foods, new drinks also appeared in Europe. Chocolate, which had been brought to Spain from Aztec Mexico, became a common drink by 1700. The first coffee and tea houses opened in London in the 1650s and spread rapidly to other parts of Europe. In the eighteenth century, a craze for Chinese furniture and porcelain spread among the upper classes. Chinese ideas would also make an impact on intellectual attitudes (see Chapter 17).

European expansion, which was in part a product of European rivalries, also deepened that competition and increased the tensions among European states. Bitter conflicts arose over the cargoes coming from the New World and Asia. The Anglo-Dutch trade wars and the British-French rivalry over India and North America became part of a new pattern of worldwide warfare in the eighteenth century (see Chapter 18). Bitter rivalries also led to state-sponsored piracy in which governments authorized private captains to attack enemy shipping and keep part of the proceeds for themselves.

In the course of their expansion, Europeans also came to have a new view of the world. When the travels began in the fifteenth century, Europeans were dependent on maps that were often fanciful and inaccurate. Their explorations helped them create new maps that gave a more realistic portrayal of the world, as well as new techniques called map projections that allowed them to represent the round surface of a sphere on a flat piece of paper. The most famous of these is the Mercator projection, the work of a Flemish cartographer, Gerardus Mercator (juh-RAHR-dus mur-KAY-tur) (1512–1594). A Mercator projection is what mapmakers call a conformal projection. It tries to show the true shape of landmasses, but only in a limited area. On the Mercator projection, the shapes of lands near the equator are quite accurate, but the farther away from the equator they lie, the more exaggerated their size becomes. Nevertheless, the Mercator projection was valuable to ship captains. Every straight line on a Mercator projection is a line of true direction, whether north, south, east, or west. For four centuries, ship captains were very grateful to Mercator.

The psychological impact of colonization on the colonizers is awkward to evaluate but hard to deny. Europeans were initially startled by the discovery of new peoples in the Americas. Some deemed them inhuman and thus fit to be exploited for labor. Others, however, found them to be refreshingly natural and as yet untouched by European corruption. But even the latter group still believed that the Indians should be converted—if not forcefully, at least peacefully—to Christianity. Overall, Europeans' relatively easy success in dominating native peoples (whether Africans or Indians) reinforced Christian Europe's belief in the inherent superiority of European civilization and religion. The Scientific Revolution of the seventeenth century (see Chapter 16), the Enlightenment of the eighteenth (see Chapter 17), and the imperialism of the nineteenth (see Chapter 24) would all bolster this

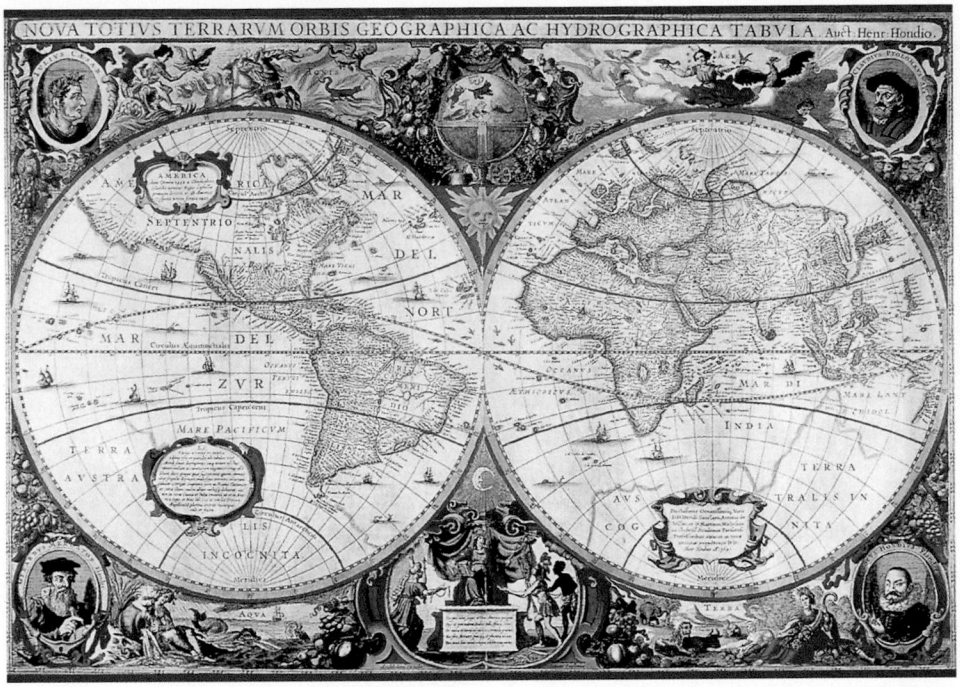

© The Huntington Library, Art Collections and Botanical Gardens, San Marino, CA/SuperStock

A Seventeenth-Century World Map. This beautiful map was prepared in 1630 by Henricus Hondius. The portraits in the corners are of Caesar, the Roman statesman; Ptolemy, the second-century astronomer; Mercator, the Flemish cartographer whose map projection Hondius followed; and Hondius himself. By comparing this map with the map created by Ptolemy on page 306, one can see how much Europeans had learned about the shape of the world by the seventeenth century.

Eurocentric perspective, which has pervaded Western civilization's relations with the rest of the world.

Toward a World Economy

Focus Question: What was mercantilism, and what was its relationship to colonial empires?

During the High Middle Ages, Europeans had experienced a commercial revolution that created new opportunities for townspeople in a basically agrarian economy. Although this commercial growth was slowed by the crises of the fourteenth century, Europe's discovery of the world outside in the fifteenth century led to an even greater burst of commercial activity and the inception of a world market.

Economic Conditions in the Sixteenth Century

Inflation was a major economic problem in the sixteenth and early seventeenth centuries. This so-called **price revolution** was a Europe-wide phenomenon, although different areas were affected at different times. Foodstuffs were most subject to price increases. But wages failed to keep up with the rising prices. Wage earners, especially agricultural laborers and salaried workers in urban areas, saw their standard of living drop. At the same time, landed aristocrats, who could raise rents, managed to prosper. Commercial and industrial entrepreneurs also benefited from the price revolution because of rising prices, expanding markets, and relatively cheaper labor costs. Some historians regard this profit inflation as a valuable stimulus to investment and the growth of capitalism, helping to explain the economic expansion and prosperity of the sixteenth century. Governments were likewise affected by inflation. They borrowed heavily from bankers and imposed new tax burdens on their subjects, often arousing additional discontent.

The Growth of Commercial Capitalism

The flourishing European trade of the sixteenth century revolved around three major areas: the Mediterranean in the south, the Low Countries and the Baltic region in the north, and central Europe, whose inland trade depended on the Rhine and Danube Rivers. As overseas trade expanded, however, the Atlantic seaboard began to play a more important role, linking the Mediterranean, Baltic, and central European trading areas together and making the whole of Europe into a more integrated market that was all the more vulnerable to price shifts.

The commercial expansion of the sixteenth and seventeenth centuries was made easier by new forms of commercial organization, especially the **joint-stock company**. Individuals bought shares in a company and received dividends on their investment while a board of directors ran the company and made the important business decisions. The return on investments could be spectacular. During its first ten years, investors received 30 percent on their money from the Dutch East India Company, which opened the Spice Islands and Southeast Asia to Dutch activity. The joint-stock company made it easier to raise large amounts of capital for world trading ventures.

By the seventeenth century, the traditional family banking firms were no longer able to supply the numerous services needed for the expanding commercial capitalism. New institutions arose to take their place. The city of Amsterdam created the Bank of Amsterdam in 1609 as both a deposit and a transfer institution and the Amsterdam Bourse, or Exchange, where the trading of stocks replaced the exchange of goods. In the first half of the seventeenth century, the Amsterdam Exchange became the hub of the European business world, just as Amsterdam itself had replaced Antwerp as the greatest commercial and banking center of Europe.

Despite the growth of commercial capitalism, most of the European economy still depended on an agricultural system that had experienced few changes since the thirteenth century. At least 80 percent of Europeans still worked the land. Almost all of the peasants of western Europe were free of serfdom, although many still owed a variety of feudal dues to the nobility. Despite the expanding markets and rising prices, European peasants saw little or no improvement in their lot as they faced increased rents and fees and higher taxes imposed by the state.

Mercantilism

Mercantilism is the name historians use to identify a set of economic tendencies that came to dominate economic practices in the seventeenth century. Fundamental to mercantilism was the belief that the total volume of trade was unchangeable. Therefore, states protected their economies by following certain principles: hoarding precious metals, implementing protectionist trade policies, promoting colonial development, increasing shipbuilding, supporting trading companies, and encouraging the manufacturing of products to be used in trade.

According to the mercantilists, a nation's prosperity depended on a plentiful supply of bullion (gold and silver). For this reason, it was desirable to achieve a favorable balance of trade in which goods exported were of greater value than those imported, promoting an influx of gold and silver payments that would increase the quantity of bullion. Furthermore, to encourage exports, governments should stimulate and protect export industries and trade by granting trade monopolies, encouraging investment in new industries through subsidies, importing foreign artisans, and improving transportation systems by building roads, bridges, and canals. By imposing high tariffs on foreign goods, they could be kept out of the country and prevented from competing with domestic products. Colonies were also deemed valuable as sources of raw materials and markets for finished goods.

The mercantilists also focused on the role of the state, believing that state intervention in some aspects of the economy was desirable for the sake of the national good. Government regulations to ensure the superiority of export goods, the construction of roads and canals, and the granting of subsidies to create trade companies were all predicated on government involvement in economic affairs.

Overseas Trade and Colonies: Movement Toward Globalization

Mercantilist theory on the role of colonies was matched in practice by Europe's overseas expansion. With the development of colonies and trading posts in the Americas and the East, Europeans embarked on an adventure in international commerce in the seventeenth century. Although some historians speak of a nascent world economy, we should remember that local, regional, and intra-European trade still predominated. About one-tenth of English and Dutch exports were shipped across the Atlantic; slightly more went to the East. What made the transoceanic trade rewarding, however, was not the volume but the value of its goods. Dutch, English, and French merchants were bringing back products that were still consumed largely by the wealthy but were beginning to make their way into the lives of artisans and merchants. Pepper and spices from the Indies, West Indian and Brazilian sugar, and Asian coffee and tea were becoming more readily available to European consumers.

Trade within Europe remained strong throughout the eighteenth century, although this trade increased only slightly while overseas trade boomed. From 1716 to 1789, total French exports quadrupled; intra-European trade, which constituted 75 percent of these exports in 1716, accounted for only 50 percent of the total in 1789. This increase in overseas trade has led some historians to proclaim the emergence of a truly global economy in the eighteenth century. Trade patterns now interlocked Europe, Africa, the East, and the Americas.

CHAPTER SUMMARY

At the end of the fifteenth century, Europeans sailed out into the world in all directions. Beginning in the mid-fifteenth century with the handful of Portuguese ships that ventured southward along the West African coast, bringing back slaves and gold, the process of European expansion accelerated with the epochal voyages of Christopher Columbus to the Americas and Vasco da Gama to the Indian Ocean in the 1490s. The Portuguese Empire was based on trade; Portugal's population was too small for it to establish large colonies. But Spain had greater resources. Spanish conquistadors overthrew both the Aztec and Inca Empires, and Spain created two major administrative units in New Spain and Peru that subjected the native population to Spanish control. Catholic missionaries, under the control of the Spanish crown, brought Christianity, including cathedrals and schools.

Soon a number of other European peoples, including the Dutch, British, and French, had joined in the process of expansion, and by the end of the eighteenth century, they had created a global trade network dominated by Western ships and Western power. Although originally less prized than gold and spices, slaves became a major object of trade, and by the nineteenth century 10 million African slaves had been shipped to the Americas. Slavery was common in Africa, and the African terminus of the trade was in the hands of the Africans, but the insatiable demand for slaves led to increased warfare on that unfortunate continent. It was not until the late 1700s that slavery came under harsh criticism in Europe.

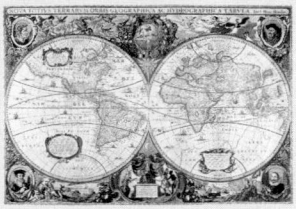

In less than three hundred years, the European age of exploration had changed the shape of the world. In some areas, such as the Americas and the Spice Islands in Asia, it led to the destruction of indigenous civilizations and the establishment of European colonies. In others, such as Africa, India, and mainland Southeast Asia, it left native regimes intact but had a strong impact on local societies and regional trade patterns. Japan and China were least affected.

At the time, many European observers viewed the process in a favorable light. They believed that it not only expanded wealth through world trade and the exchange of crops and discoveries between the Old World and the New, but also introduced "heathen peoples" to the message of Jesus. No doubt, the conquest of the Americas and expansion into the rest of the world brought out the worst and some of the best of European civilization. The greedy plundering of resources and the brutal repression and enslavement were hardly balanced by attempts to create new institutions, convert the natives to Christianity, and foster the rights of the indigenous peoples. In any event, Europeans had begun to change the face of the world and increasingly saw their culture, with its religion, languages, and technology, as a coherent force to be exported to all corners of the world.

CHAPTER TIMELINE

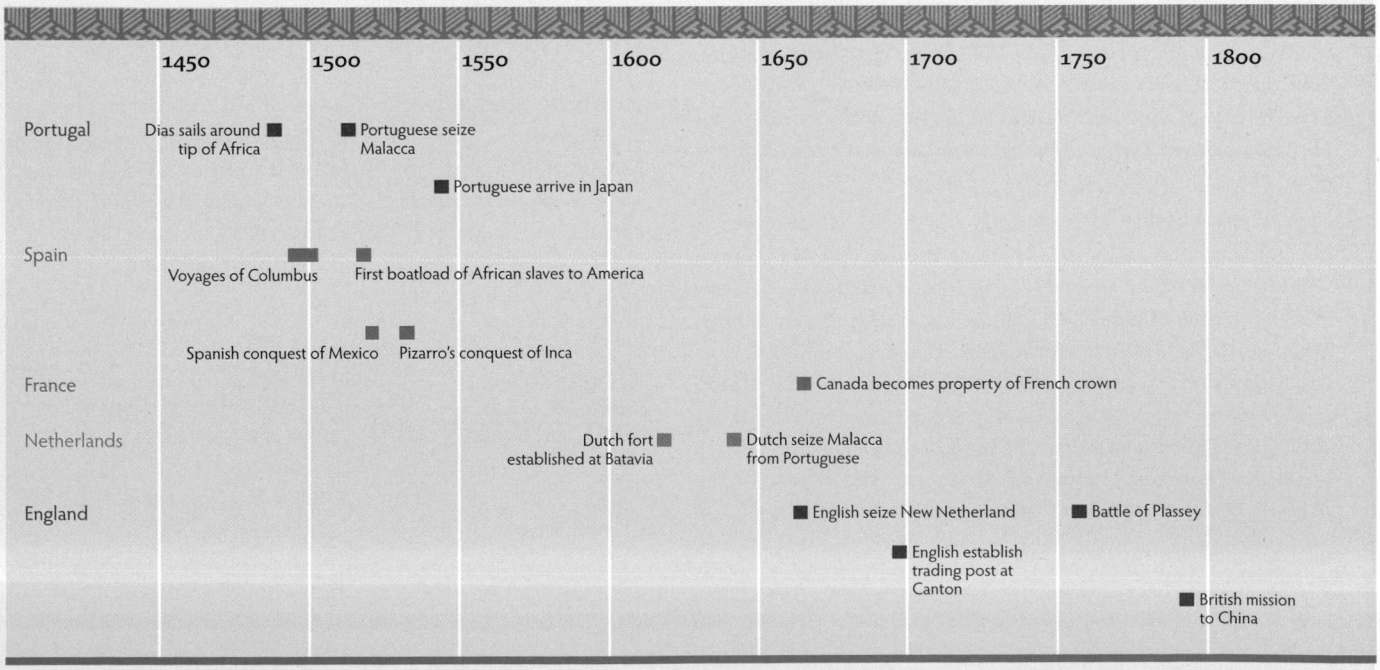

CHAPTER REVIEW

Upon Reflection

Q How did the experiences of the Spanish and Portuguese during the age of exploration differ from those of their French, Dutch and English counterparts?

Q What role did religion play as a motivation in the age of exploration? Was it as important as the economic motive? Why or why not?

Q Why and how did Japan succeed in keeping Europeans largely away from its territory in the seventeenth century?

Key Terms

conquistadors (p. 310)
encomienda (p. 313)
viceroy (p. 313)
triangular trade (p. 314)
Middle Passage (p. 314)
Columbian Exchange (p. 326)
price revolution (p. 327)
joint-stock company (p. 327)
mercantilism (p. 328)

Suggestions for Further Reading

GENERAL WORKS For general accounts of European discovery and expansion, see **G. V. Scammell, *The First Imperial Age: European Overseas Expansion, c. 1400–1715*** (London, 1989); **D. Arnold, *Age of Discovery,*** 2nd ed. (London, 2002); and **G. J. Ames, *The Globe Encompassed: The Age of European Discovery, 1500–1700*** (Upper Saddle River, N.J., 2007).

PORTUGUESE AND SPANISH EXPANSION On Portuguese expansion, see **M. Newitt, *A History of Portuguese Overseas Expansion*** (London, 2004). On Columbus, see **W. D. Phillips** and **C. R. Phillips, *The Worlds of Christopher Columbus*** (Cambridge, 1992). On the Spanish Empire in the New World, see **H. Kamen, *Empire: How Spain Became a World Power, 1492–1763*** (New York, 2003). For a revisionist view of the Spanish conquest of the Americas, see **M. Restall, *Seven Myths of the Spanish Conquest*** (Oxford, 2003).

MERCANTILE EMPIRES AND WORLDWIDE TRADE The subject of mercantile empires and worldwide trade is covered in **J. D. Tracy, *The Rise of Merchant Empires: Long-Distance Trade in the Early Modern World, 1350–1750*** (Cambridge, 1990); **J. H. Elliott, *Empires of the Atlantic World*** (New Haven, Conn., 2006); and **M. J. Seymour, *Transformation of the North Atlantic World, 1492–1763*** (Westport, Conn., 2004). On the African slave trade, see **M. Rediker, *The Slave Ship: A Human History*** (New York, 2007), and **J. K. Thornton, *Africa and Africans in the Making of the Atlantic World, 1400–1800*** (Cambridge, 1998).

IMPACT OF EXPANSION The impact of expansion on European consciousness is explored in **A. Pagden, *European Encounters with the New World: From Renaissance to Romanticism*** (New Haven, Conn., 1993). On the impact of disease, see **N. D. Cook, *Born to Die: Disease and the New World*** (New York, 1998). The human and ecological effects of the interaction of New World and Old World cultures are examined thoughtfully in **A. W. Crosby, *Ecological Imperialism: The Biological Expansion of Europe*** (New York, 1986). The native American female experience with the European encounter is presented in **R. Gutierrez, *When Jesus Came the Corn Mother Went Away: Marriage, Sexuality, and Power in New Mexico, 1500–1846*** (Stanford, Calif., 1991).

ECONOMIC DIMENSIONS OF EXPANSION On mercantilism, see **L. Magnusson, *Mercantilism: The Shaping of an Economic Language*** (New York, 1994). On the concept of a world economy, see **A. K. Smith, *Creating a World Economy: Merchant Capital, Colonialism, and World Trade, 1400–1825*** (Boulder, Colo., 1991).

Visit the CourseMate website at www.cengagebrain.com for additional study tools and review materials for this chapter.

CHAPTER 15

Versailles/© Reunion des Musees Nationaux (Gérard Blot)/Art Resource, NY

Nicolas-René Jollain the Elder's portrait of Louis XIV captures the king's sense of royal grandeur.

State Building and the Search for Order in the Seventeenth Century

CHAPTER OUTLINE AND FOCUS QUESTIONS

Social Crises, War, and Rebellions

Q What economic, social, and political crises did Europe experience in the first half of the seventeenth century?

The Practice of Absolutism: Western Europe

Q What was absolutism in theory, and how did its actual practice in France reflect or differ from the theory?

Absolutism in Central and Eastern Europe

Q What developments enabled Brandenburg-Prussia, Austria, and Russia to emerge as major powers in the seventeenth century?

Limited Monarchy: The Dutch Republic and England

Q What were the main issues in the struggle between king and Parliament in seventeenth-century England, and how were they resolved?

The Flourishing of European Culture

Q How did the artistic and literary achievements of this era reflect the political and economic developments of the period?

CRITICAL THINKING

Q What theories of government were proposed by Thomas Hobbes and John Locke, and how did their respective theories reflect the concerns of the seventeenth century?

BY THE END of the sixteenth century, Europe was beginning to experience a decline in religious passions and a growing secularization that affected both the political and intellectual worlds (for the intellectual effect, see Chapter 16). Some historians like to speak of the seventeenth century as a turning point in the evolution of the modern state system in Europe. The ideal of a united Christian Europe gave way to the practical realities of a system of secular entities in which matters of state took precedence over the salvation of subjects' souls. By the seventeenth century, the credibility of Christianity had been so weakened through religious wars that more and more Europeans came to think of politics in secular terms.

One of the responses to the religious wars and other crises of the time was a yearning for order. As the internal social and political rebellions and revolts died down, it became apparent that the privileged classes of society—the aristocrats—remained in control, although the various states exhibited important differences in political forms. The most general trend saw an extension of monarchical power as a stabilizing force. This development, which historians have called absolute monarchy or absolutism, was most evident in France during the flamboyant reign of Louis XIV, regarded by some as the perfect embodiment of an absolute monarch. In his memoirs, the duc de Saint-Simon, who had firsthand experience of French court life, said that Louis was "the very figure of a hero, so imbued with a natural but most imposing majesty that it appeared even in his most insignificant gestures and movements." The king's natural grace gave him a special charm as well: "He was as dignified and majestic in his dressing gown as when dressed in robes of state, or on horseback at the head of his troops." His life was orderly: "Nothing could be regulated with greater exactitude than were his days and hours." His self-control was impeccable: "He did not lose control of himself ten times in his whole life, and then only with inferior persons." But even absolute monarchs had imperfections, and Saint-Simon had the courage to point them out: "Louis XIV's vanity was without limit or restraint," which led to his "distaste for all merit, intelligence, education, and, most of all, for all independence of character and sentiment in others," as well as "to mistakes of judgment in matters of importance."

But absolutism was not the only response to the search for order in the seventeenth century. Other states, such as England, reacted differently to domestic crisis, and another very different system emerged in which monarchs were limited by the power of their representative assemblies. Absolute and limited monarchy were the two poles of seventeenth-century state building.

Social Crises, War, and Rebellions

Q FOCUS QUESTION: What economic, social, and political crises did Europe experience in the first half of the seventeenth century?

The inflation-fueled prosperity of the sixteenth century showed signs of slackening by the beginning of the seventeenth. Economic contraction was evident in some parts of Europe by the 1620s. In the 1630s and 1640s, as imports of silver from the Americas declined, economic recession intensified, especially in the Mediterranean area. Once the industrial and financial center of Europe in the Renaissance, Italy was now becoming an economic backwater. Spain's economy was also seriously failing by the 1640s.

Population trends of the sixteenth and seventeenth centuries also reveal Europe's worsening conditions. The sixteenth century was a period of expanding population, possibly related to a warmer climate and increased food supplies. It has been estimated that the population of Europe increased from 60 million in 1500 to 85 million by 1600, the first major recovery of European population since the devastation of the Black Death in the mid-fourteenth century. Records also indicate a leveling off of the population by 1620, however, and even a decline by 1650, especially in central and southern Europe.

Only the Dutch, English, and French grew in number in the first half of the seventeenth century. Europe's long-time adversaries—war, famine, and plague—continued to affect population levels, and another "little ice age," when average temperatures fell, affected harvests and gave rise to famines. These problems created social tensions that came to a boil in the witchcraft craze.

The Witchcraft Craze

Hysteria over witchcraft affected the lives of many Europeans in the sixteenth and seventeenth centuries. Witchcraft trials were held in England, Scotland, Switzerland, Germany, some parts of France and the Low Countries, and even New England in America.

Witchcraft was not a new phenomenon. Its practice had been part of traditional village culture for centuries, but it came to be viewed as both sinister and dangerous when the medieval church began to connect witches to the activities of the devil, thereby transforming witchcraft into a heresy that had to be wiped out. After the establishment of the Inquisition in the thirteenth century, some people were accused of a variety of witchcraft practices and, following the biblical injunction "Thou shalt not suffer a witch to live," were turned over to secular authorities for burning at the stake or, in England, hanging.

THE SPREAD OF WITCHCRAFT What distinguished witchcraft in the sixteenth and seventeenth centuries from these previous developments was the increased number of trials and executions of presumed witches. Perhaps more than 100,000 people were prosecuted throughout Europe on charges of witchcraft. Although larger cities were affected first, the trials spread to smaller towns and rural areas as the hysteria persisted well into the seventeenth century (see the box on p. 333).

The accused witches usually confessed to a number of practices, most often after intense torture. Many said that they had sworn allegiance to the devil and attended sabbats or nocturnal gatherings where they feasted, danced, and even copulated with the devil in sexual orgies. More common, however, were admissions of using evil incantations and special ointments and powders to wreak havoc on neighbors by killing their livestock, injuring their children, or raising storms to destroy their crops.

A Witchcraft Trial in France

Persecutions for witchcraft reached their high point in the sixteenth and seventeenth centuries when tens of thousands of people were brought to trial. In this excerpt from the minutes of a trial in France in 1652, we can see why the accused witch stood little chance of exonerating herself.

The Trial of Suzanne Gaudry

28 May, 1652. . . . Interrogation of Suzanne Gaudry, prisoner at the court of Rieux. . . . [During interrogations on May 28 and May 29, the prisoner confessed to a number of activities involving the devil.]

Deliberation of the Court—June 3, 1652

The undersigned advocates of the Court have seen these interrogations and answers. They say that the aforementioned Suzanne Gaudry confesses that she is a witch, that she had given herself to the devil, that she had renounced God, Lent, and baptism, that she has been marked on the shoulder, that she has cohabited with the devil and that she has been to the dances, confessing only to have cast a spell upon and caused to die a beast of Philippe Cornie. . . .

Third Interrogation—June 27

The prisoner being led into the chamber, she was examined to know if things were not as she had said and confessed at the beginning of her imprisonment.

—Answers no, and that what she has said was done so by force.

Pressed to say the truth, that otherwise she would be subjected to torture, having pointed out to her that her aunt was burned for this same subject.

—Answers that she is not a witch. . . .

She was placed in the hands of the officer in charge of torture, throwing herself on her knees, struggling to cry, uttering several exclamations, without being able, nevertheless, to shed a tear. Saying at every moment that she is not a witch.

The Torture

On this same day, being at the place of torture.

This prisoner, before being strapped down, was admonished to maintain herself in her first confessions and to renounce her lover.

—Says that she denies everything she has said, and that she has no lover. Feeling herself being strapped down, says that she is not a witch, while struggling to cry . . . and upon being asked why she confessed to being one, said that she was forced to say it.

Told that she was not forced, that on the contrary she declared herself to be a witch without any threat.

—Says that she confessed it and that she is not a witch, and being a little stretched [on the rack] screams ceaselessly that she is not a witch. . . .

Asked if she did not confess that she had been a witch for twenty-six years.

—Says that she said it, that she retracts it, crying that she is not a witch.

Asked if she did not make Philippe Cornie's horse die, as she confessed.

—Answers no, crying Jesus-Maria, that she is not a witch.

The mark having been probed by the officer, in the presence of Doctor Bouchain, it was adjudged by the aforesaid doctor and officer truly to be the mark of the devil.

Being more tightly stretched upon the torture-rack, urged to maintain her confessions.

—Said that it was true that she is a witch and that she would maintain what she had said.

Asked how long she has been in subjugation to the devil.

—Answers that it was twenty years ago that the devil appeared to her, being in her lodgings in the form of a man dressed in a little cow-hide and black breeches. . . .

Verdict

July 9, 1652. In the light of the interrogations, answers and investigations made into the charge against Suzanne Gaudry, . . . seeing by her own confessions that she is said to have made a pact with the devil, received the mark from him, . . . and that following this, she had renounced God, Lent, and baptism and had let herself be known carnally by him, in which she received satisfaction. Also, seeing that she is said to have been a part of nocturnal carols and dances.

For expiation of which the advice of the undersigned is that the office of Rieux can legitimately condemn the aforesaid Suzanne Gaudry to death, tying her to a gallows, and strangling her to death, then burning her body and burying it here in the environs of the woods.

Q Why were women, particularly older women, especially vulnerable to accusations of witchcraft? What "proofs" are offered here that Suzanne Gaudry had consorted with the devil? What does this account tell us about the spread of witchcraft persecutions in the seventeenth century?

Source: From *Witchcraft in Europe, 1100–1700: A Documentary History* edited by Alan C. Kors and Edward Peters. Copyright © 1972 University of Pennsylvania Press. Reprinted with permission of the University of Pennsylvania Press.

A number of contributing factors have been suggested to explain why the witchcraft frenzy became so widespread in the sixteenth and seventeenth centuries. Religious uncertainties clearly played some part. Many witchcraft trials occurred in areas where Protestantism had been recently victorious or in regions, such as southwestern Germany, where Protestant-Catholic controversies still raged. As religious passions became inflamed, accusations of being in league with the devil became common on both sides.

Recently, however, historians have emphasized the importance of social conditions, especially the problems of a society in turmoil, in explaining the witchcraft hysteria. At a time when the old communal values that stressed working together for the good of the community were disintegrating before the onslaught of a new economic ethic that emphasized looking out for oneself, property owners became more fearful of the growing numbers of poor in their midst and transformed them psychologically into agents of the devil. Old women were particularly susceptible to suspicion. When problems arose—and there were many in this crisis-laden period—these people were handy scapegoats.

That women should be the chief victims of witchcraft trials was hardly accidental. Nicholas Rémy, a witchcraft judge in France in the 1590s, found it "not unreasonable that this scum of humanity [witches] should be drawn chiefly from the feminine sex."[1] To another judge, it came as no surprise that witches would confess to sexual experiences with Satan: "The Devil uses them so, because he knows that women love carnal pleasures, and he means to bind them to his allegiance by such agreeable provocations."[2] Of course, witch hunters were not the only ones who held women in such low esteem. Most theologians, lawyers, and philosophers in early modern Europe believed in the natural inferiority of women and thus would have found it plausible that women would be more susceptible to witchcraft.

DECLINE By the mid-seventeenth century, the witchcraft hysteria began to subside. The destruction caused by the religious wars had forced people to accept at least a grudging toleration, tempering religious passions. Moreover, as governments began to stabilize after the period of crisis, fewer magistrates were willing to accept the unsettling and divisive conditions generated by the trials of witches. Finally, by the turn of the eighteenth century, more and more people were questioning traditional attitudes toward religion and finding it contrary to reason to believe in the old view of a world haunted by evil spirits.

The Thirty Years' War

Although many Europeans responded to the upheavals of the second half of the sixteenth century with a desire for peace and order, the first fifty years of the seventeenth century continued to be plagued by crises. A devastating war that affected much of Europe and rebellions seemingly everywhere protracted the atmosphere of disorder and violence.

Religion, especially the struggle between militant Catholicism and militant Calvinism, played an important role in the outbreak of the Thirty Years' War (1618–1648), often called the "last of the religious wars." As the war progressed, however, it became increasingly clear that secular, dynastic-nationalist considerations were far more important.

The Thirty Years' War began in the Germanic lands of the Holy Roman Empire as a struggle between Catholic forces, led by the Habsburg Holy Roman Emperors, and Protestant—primarily Calvinist—nobles in Bohemia who rebelled against Habsburg authority. What began as a struggle over religious issues soon became a wider conflict determined by political motivations as both minor and major European powers—Denmark, Sweden, France, and Spain—made the war a Europe-wide struggle (see Map 15.1). The struggle for European leadership between the Bourbon dynasty of France and the Habsburg dynasties of Spain and the Holy Roman Empire was an especially important factor. Nevertheless, most of the battles were fought on German soil, with devastating results for the German people.

The war in Germany was officially ended by the Peace of Westphalia in 1648, which ensured that all German states, including the Calvinist ones, were free to determine their own religion. The major contenders gained new territories, and one of them, France, emerged as the dominant nation in Europe. The more than three hundred states that made up the Holy Roman Empire were recognized as virtually independent, each with the power to conduct its own foreign policy. The Habsburg emperor had been reduced to a figurehead. The Peace of Westphalia also made it clear that religion and politics were now separate in the Holy Roman Empire. Political motives became the guiding forces in public affairs as religion moved closer to becoming primarily a matter of personal conviction and individual choice. Some historians also argue that the Peace of Westphalia marks the beginning of a modern international order in which sovereign states began to operate as equals within a secular framework.

The economic and social effects of the Thirty Years' War on Germany are still debated. Some areas of Germany were completely devastated, but others remained relatively untouched. The most recent work pictures a damaged economy and a population decline of 15 to 20 percent in the Holy Roman Empire. Although historians may debate the degree of devastation, many people in

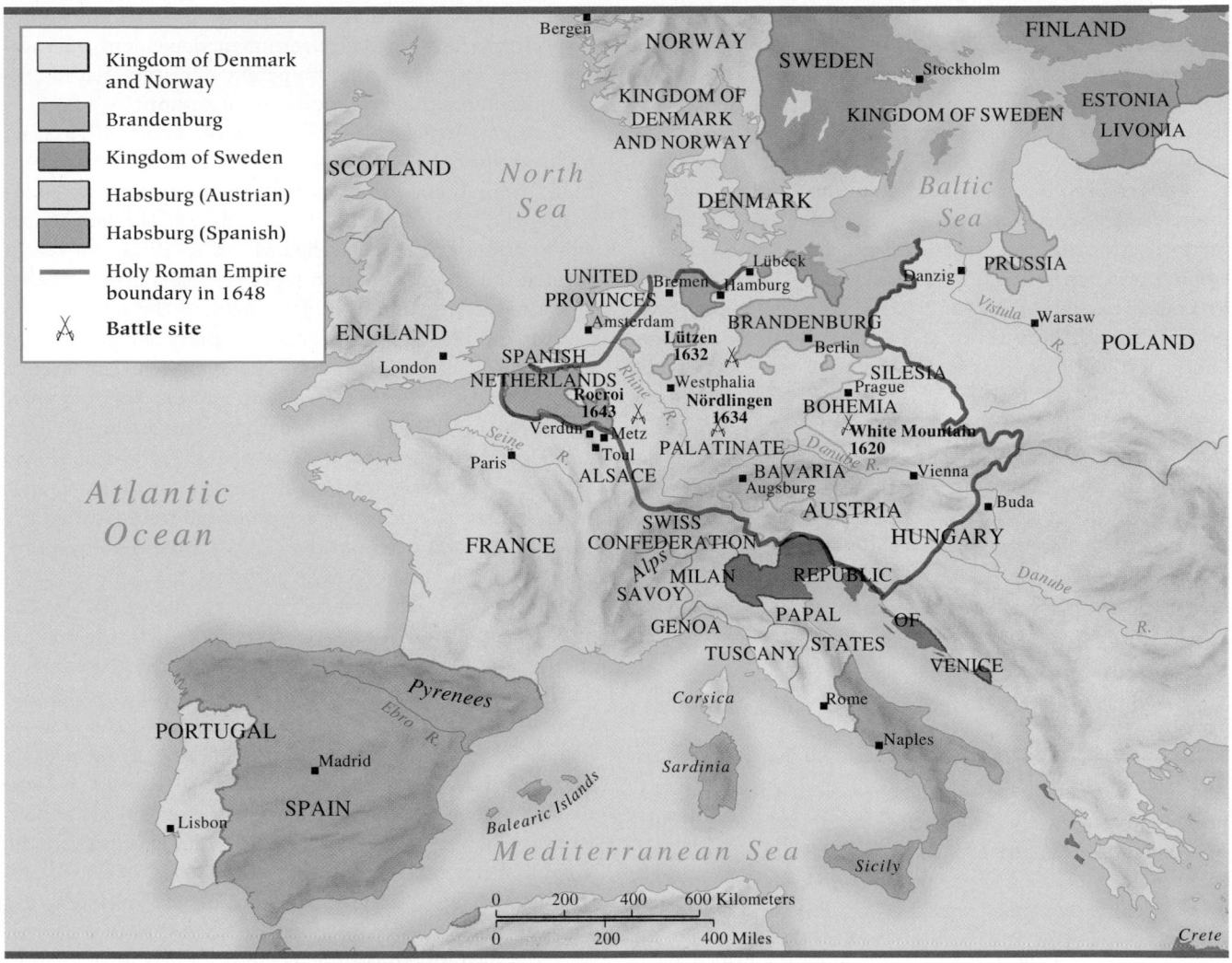

© Cengage Learning

MAP 15.1 The Thirty Years' War. The conflict began in the German states as Europe's major powers backed either the northern Protestant Union or the southern Catholic League. As the war progressed, religion receded in importance, replaced by a dynastic struggle between the French Bourbons and the Spanish and Austrian Habsburgs.

Compare this map with Map 13.2. Which countries engaged in the war were predominantly Protestant, which were predominantly Catholic, and which were mixed?

Germany would have understood this description by a traveler journeying along the Main River in 1636:

> [We] came to a wretched little village called Neukirchen, which we found quite uninhabited yet with one house on fire. Here, since it was now late, we were obliged to stay all night, for the nearest town was four miles away; but we spent that night walking up and down with guns in our hands, and listening fearfully to the sound of shots in the woods around us. . . . Early next morning, His Excellency went to inspect the church and found it had been plundered and that the pictures and the altar had been desecrated. In the churchyard we saw a dead body, scraped out of the grave, while outside the churchyard we found another dead body.[3]

The Thirty Years' War was undoubtedly the most destructive conflict Europeans had yet experienced.

Rebellions

Before, during, and after the Thirty Years' War, a series of rebellions and civil wars stemming from the discontent of both nobles and commoners rocked the domestic stability of many European governments. To strengthen their power, monarchs attempted to extend their authority at the expense of traditional powerful elements who resisted the rulers' efforts. At the same time, to fight their battles, governments increased taxes and caused such hardships that common people also rose in opposition.

Between 1590 and 1640, peasant and lower-class revolts occurred in central and southern France, Austria, and Hungary. Portugal and Catalonia rebelled against the Spanish government in 1640. Russia, too, was rocked by urban uprisings in 1641, 1645, and 1648. Nobles rebelled in France from 1648 to 1652 to halt the growth of royal power. The northern states of Sweden, Denmark, and the United Provinces were also not immune from upheavals involving clergy, nobles, and mercantile groups. The most famous and widest-ranging struggle, however, was the civil war and rebellion in England, commonly known as the English Revolution (discussed later in this chapter).

The Practice of Absolutism: Western Europe

Focus Question: What was absolutism in theory, and how did its actual practice in France reflect or differ from the theory?

Absolute monarchy or **absolutism** meant that the sovereign power or ultimate authority in the state rested in the hands of a king who claimed to rule by divine right—that kings received their power from God and were responsible to no one (including parliaments) except God. But what did sovereignty mean? The late-sixteenth-century political theorist Jean Bodin (ZHAHN boh-DAN) believed that sovereign power consisted of the authority to make laws, tax, administer justice, control the state's administrative system, and determine foreign policy. These powers made a ruler sovereign.

France: Foundations of Absolutism

France during the reign of Louis XIV (1643–1715) has traditionally been regarded as the best example of the practice of absolute monarchy in the seventeenth century. French culture, language, and manners reached into all levels of European society. French diplomacy and wars shaped the political affairs of western and central Europe. Of course, the stability of Louis's reign was magnified by the instability that had preceded it.

The half century of French history before Louis XIV came to power was a time in which royal and ministerial governments struggled to avoid the breakdown of the state. The situation was complicated by the fact that both Louis XIII (1610–1643) and Louis XIV were only boys when they succeeded to the throne in 1610 and 1643, respectively, leaving the government dependent on royal ministers. Two especially competent ministers played crucial roles in maintaining monarchical authority.

Cardinal Richelieu (REESH-uh-lyoo), Louis XIII's chief minister from 1624 to 1642, initiated policies that eventually strengthened the power of the monarchy. By eliminating the political and military rights of the Huguenots while preserving their religious ones, Richelieu transformed the Huguenots into more reliable subjects. Richelieu acted more cautiously in "humbling the pride of the great men," the important French nobility. He understood the influential role played by the nobles in the French state. The dangerous ones were those who asserted their territorial independence when they were excluded from participating in the central government. Proceeding slowly but determinedly, Richelieu developed an efficient network of spies to uncover noble plots and then crushed the conspiracies and executed the conspirators, thereby eliminating a major threat to royal authority.

When Louis XIV succeeded to the throne in 1643 at the age of four, Cardinal Mazarin (maz-uh-RANH), the trained successor of Cardinal Richelieu, dominated the government. An Italian who had come to France as a papal legate and then become naturalized, Mazarin attempted to carry on Richelieu's policies. The most important event during Mazarin's rule was the Fronde (FROHND), a revolt led primarily by nobles who wished to curb the centralized administrative power being built up at the expense of the provincial nobility. The Fronde was crushed by 1652, and with its end, a vast number of French people concluded that the best hope for stability in France lay in the crown. When Mazarin died in 1661, the greatest of the seventeenth-century monarchs, Louis XIV, took over supreme power.

The Reign of Louis XIV (1643–1715)

The day after Cardinal Mazarin's death, Louis XIV, age twenty-three, expressed his determination to be a real king and the sole ruler of France:

> Up to this moment I have been pleased to entrust the government of my affairs to the late Cardinal. It is now time that I govern them myself. You [secretaries and ministers of state] will assist me with your counsels when I ask for them. I request and order you to seal no orders except by my command. . . . I order you not to sign anything, not even a passport . . . without my command; to render account to me personally each day and to favor no one.[4]

His mother, who was well aware of Louis's proclivity for fun and games and getting into the beds of the maids in the royal palace, laughed aloud at these words. But Louis was quite serious.

Louis proved willing to pay the price of being a strong ruler. He established a conscientious routine from which he seldom deviated. Eager for glory (in the French sense of achieving what was expected of one in an important position), Louis created a grand and majestic spectacle at the court of Versailles (vayr-SY). Consequently, Louis and his court came to set the standard for monarchies and aristocracies all over Europe.

Although Louis may have believed in the theory of absolute monarchy and consciously fostered the myth of himself as the Sun King, the source of light for all of his people, historians are quick to point out that the realities fell far short of the aspirations. Despite the centralizing efforts of Cardinals Richelieu and Mazarin, seventeenth-century France still possessed a bewildering system of overlapping authorities. Provinces had their own regional courts, their own local Estates (parliaments), and their own sets of laws. Members of the high nobility, with their huge estates and clients among the lesser nobility, still exercised much authority. Both towns and provinces possessed privileges and powers seemingly from time immemorial that they would not easily relinquish.

ADMINISTRATION OF THE GOVERNMENT One of the keys to Louis's power was that he was able to restructure the central policy-making machinery of government because it was part of his own court and household. The royal court located at Versailles was an elaborate structure that served different purposes: it was the personal household of the king, the location of central governmental machinery, and the place where powerful subjects came to find favors and offices for themselves and their clients as well as the main arena where rival aristocratic factions jostled for power. The greatest danger to Louis's personal rule came from the very high nobles and "princes of the blood" (the royal princes) who considered it their natural function to assert the policy-making role of royal ministers. Louis eliminated this threat by removing them from the royal council, the chief administrative body of the king and overseer of the central machinery of government, and enticing them to his court, where he could keep them preoccupied with court life and out of politics. Instead of the high nobility and royal princes, Louis relied for his ministers on other nobles. His ministers were expected to be subservient; said Louis, "I had no intention of sharing my authority with them."

Louis's domination of his ministers and secretaries gave him control of the central policy-making machinery of government and thus authority over the traditional areas of monarchical power: the formulation of foreign policy, the making of war and peace, the assertion of the secular power of the crown against any religious authority, and the ability to levy taxes to fulfill these functions. Louis had considerably less success with the internal administration of the kingdom, however. The traditional groups and institutions of French society—the nobles, officials, town councils, guilds, and representative Estates in some provinces—were simply too powerful for the king to have direct control over the lives of his subjects. Consequently, control of the provinces and the people was achieved largely by bribing the individuals responsible for executing the king's policies.

RELIGIOUS POLICY The maintenance of religious harmony had long been considered an area of monarchical power. The desire to keep it led Louis to pursue an anti-Protestant policy, aimed at converting the Huguenots to Catholicism. In October 1685, Louis issued the Edict of Fontainebleau (fawnh-ten-BLOH). In addition to revoking the Edict of Nantes, the new edict provided for the destruction of the Huguenots' churches and the closing of Protestant schools.

FINANCIAL ISSUES The cost of building Versailles and other palaces, maintaining his court, and pursuing his wars made finances a crucial issue for Louis XIV. He was most fortunate in having the services of Jean-Baptiste Colbert (ZHAHNH-bah-TEEST kohl-BAYR) (1619–1683) as controller-general of finances. Colbert was an avid practitioner of mercantilism. To decrease the need for imports and increase exports, he founded new luxury industries and granted special privileges, including tax exemptions, loans, and subsidies, to individuals who established new industries. To improve communications and the transportation of goods internally, he built roads and canals. To decrease imports directly, Colbert raised tariffs on foreign manufactured goods and created a merchant marine to carry French goods.

THE WARS OF LOUIS XIV Both the increase in royal power that Louis pursued and his desire for military glory led the king to develop a professional army numbering 100,000 men in peacetime and 400,000 in time of war. Louis made war an almost incessant activity of his reign. To achieve the prestige and military glory befitting the Sun King as well as to ensure the domination of his Bourbon dynasty over European affairs, Louis waged four wars between 1667 and 1713. His ambitions roused much of Europe to form coalitions to prevent the destruction of the European balance of power that Bourbon hegemony would cause. Although Louis added some territory to France's northeastern frontier and established a member

Chateaux de Versailles et de Trianon, Versailles,//© Réunion des Musées Nationaux/Art Resource, NY

Interior of Versailles: The Hall of Mirrors. Louis XIV spent untold sums of money on the construction of a new royal residence at Versailles. As the largest royal residence in Europe, the enormous palace (it was more than a quarter of a mile long) impressed foreigners and became a source of envy for other rulers. Pictured here is the exquisite Hall of Mirrors at Versailles. Located on the second floor, the hall overlooks the park below. Three hundred and fifty-seven mirrors were placed on the wall opposite the windows in order to create an illusion of even greater width. Careful planning went into every detail of the interior decoration. Even the doorknobs were specially designed to reflect the magnificence of Versailles. This photo shows the Hall of Mirrors after the restoration work that was completed in June 2007, a project that took three years, cost 12 million euros (more than $16 million), and included the restoration of the Bohemian crystal chandeliers.

of his own Bourbon dynasty on the throne of Spain, he also left France impoverished and surrounded by enemies.

The Decline of Spain

At the beginning of the seventeenth century, Spain possessed the most populous empire in the world, controlling almost all of South America and a number of settlements in Asia and Africa. To most Europeans, Spain still seemed the greatest power of the age, but the reality was quite different. The treasury was empty; Philip II went bankrupt in 1596 from excessive expenditures on war, and his successor did the same in 1607 by spending a fortune on his court. The armed forces were out-of-date, the government was inefficient, and the commercial class was weak in the midst of a suppressed peasantry, a luxury-loving class of nobles, and an oversupply of priests and monks.

During the reign of Philip III (1598–1621), many of Spain's weaknesses became apparent. Interested only in court luxury and miracle-working relics, Philip III allowed his first minister, the greedy duke of Lerma, to run the country. The aristocratic Lerma's primary interest was accumulating power and wealth for himself and his family. As important offices were filled with his relatives, crucial problems went unsolved.

The reign of Philip IV (1621–1665) seemed to offer hope for a revival of Spain's energies, especially in the capable hands of his chief minister, Gaspar de Guzmán (gahs-PAR day goos-MAHN), the count of Olivares (oh-lee-BAH-rayss). This clever, hardworking, and power-hungry statesman worked to revive the interests of the monarchy. A flurry of domestic reform decrees, aimed at curtailing the power of the Catholic Church and the landed aristocracy, was soon followed by a political reform program aimed at further centralizing the government of Spain and its possessions in monarchical hands. All of these efforts met with little real success, however, because both the number (estimated at one-fifth of the population) and power of the Spanish aristocrats made them too strong to curtail in any significant fashion.

At the same time, most of the efforts of Olivares and Philip were undermined by their desire to pursue Spain's imperial glory and by a series of internal revolts. Spain's involvement in the Thirty Years' War led to a series of frightfully expensive military campaigns that incited internal revolts and years of civil war. Unfortunately for Spain, the campaigns also failed to produce victory. As Olivares wrote to King Philip IV, "God wants us to make peace; for He is depriving us visibly and absolutely of all the means of war."[5]

The defeats in Europe and the internal revolts of the 1640s ended any illusions about Spain's greatness. The actual extent of Spain's economic difficulties is still debated, but there is no question about its foreign losses. Dutch independence was formally recognized by the Peace of Westphalia in 1648, and the Peace of the Pyrenees with France in 1659 meant the surrender of some border regions to France.

CHRONOLOGY Absolutism in Western Europe

France	
Louis XIII	1610–1643
Cardinal Richelieu as chief minister	1624–1642
Ministry of Cardinal Mazarin	1642–1661
Fronde	1648–1652
Louis XIV	1643–1715
Edict of Fontainebleau	1685
Spain	
Philip III	1598–1621
Philip IV	1621–1665

Absolutism in Central and Eastern Europe

FOCUS QUESTION: What developments enabled Brandenburg-Prussia, Austria, and Russia to emerge as major powers in the seventeenth century?

During the seventeenth century, a development of great importance for the modern Western world took place in central and eastern Europe, as three new powers made their appearance: Prussia, Austria, and Russia.

The German States

The Peace of Westphalia, which officially ended the Thirty Years' War in 1648, left each of the states in the Holy Roman Empire virtually autonomous and sovereign. Properly speaking, there was no longer a German state but rather more than three hundred little Germanies. Of these, two emerged as great European powers in the seventeenth and eighteenth centuries.

THE RISE OF BRANDENBURG-PRUSSIA The evolution of Brandenburg into a powerful state was largely the work of the Hohenzollern (hoh-en-TSULL-urn) dynasty. By the seventeenth century, the dominions of the house of Hohenzollern, now called Brandenburg-Prussia, consisted of three disconnected masses in western, central, and eastern Germany (see Map 15.2).

The foundation for the Prussian state was laid by Frederick William the Great Elector (1640–1688). Realizing that Brandenburg-Prussia was a small, open territory with no natural frontiers for defense, Frederick William built an army of 40,000 men, the fourth largest in Europe. To sustain the army and his own power, Frederick William established the General War Commissariat to levy taxes to support the army and oversee its growth and training. The Commissariat soon evolved into an agency for civil government as well. Directly responsible to the elector, the new bureaucratic machine became his chief instrument for governing the state. Many of its officials were members of the Prussian landed aristocracy, the Junkers (YOONG-kers), who also served as officers in the all-important army.

Frederick William was succeeded by his son Frederick III (1688–1713), who made one significant contribution to the development of Prussia. In return for aiding the Holy Roman Emperor in a war against Spain, he was officially granted the title of king-in-Prussia in 1701. Thus was Elector Frederick III transformed into King Frederick I, and Brandenburg-Prussia became simply Prussia. In the eighteenth century, Prussia emerged as a great power on the European stage.

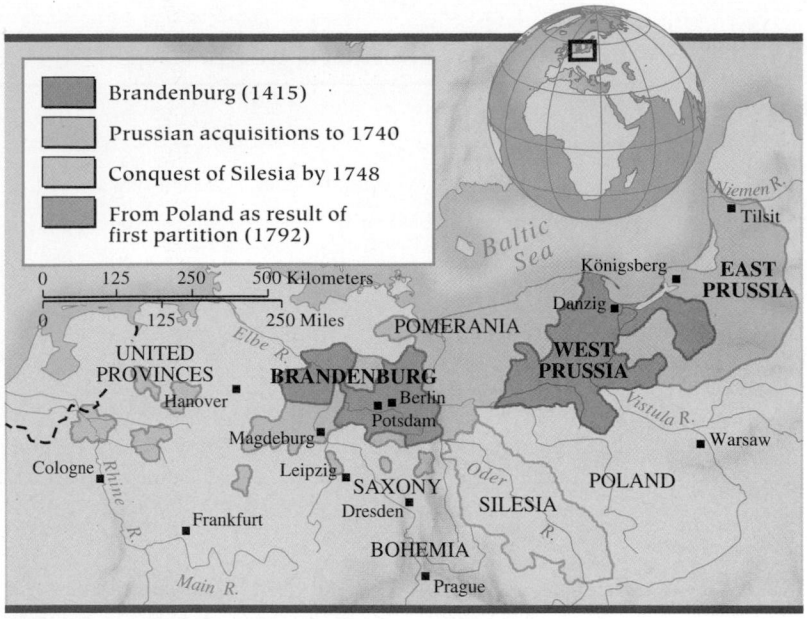

MAP 15.2 The Growth of Brandenburg-Prussia. Frederick William the Great Elector laid the foundation for a powerful state when he increased the size and efficiency of the army, raised taxes and created an efficient bureaucracy to collect them, and gained the support of the landed aristocracy. Later rulers added more territory.

Q ***Why were the acquisitions of Pomerania and West Prussia important for the continued rise in power of Brandenburg-Prussia?***

© Cengage Learning

The Emergence of Austria

The Austrian Habsburgs had long played a significant role in European politics as Holy Roman Emperors, but by the end of the Thirty Years' War, the Habsburg hopes of creating an empire in Germany had been dashed. In the seventeenth century, the house of Austria assembled a new empire in eastern and southeastern Europe.

The nucleus of the new Austrian Empire remained the traditional Austrian hereditary possessions: Lower and Upper Austria, Carinthia, Carniola, Styria, and Tyrol (see Map 15.3). To these had been added the kingdom of Bohemia and parts of northwestern Hungary in the sixteenth century. In the seventeenth century, Leopold I (1658–1705) encouraged the eastward movement of the Austrian Empire, but he was sorely challenged by the revival of Ottoman power. The Ottomans eventually pushed westward and laid siege to Vienna in 1683. A European army, led by the Austrians, counterattacked and decisively defeated the Ottomans in 1687. Austria took control of Hungary, Transylvania, Croatia, and Slovenia, thus extending its empire in southeastern Europe. By the beginning of the eighteenth century, the house of Austria had acquired an empire of considerable size.

The Austrian monarchy, however, never became a highly centralized, absolutist state, primarily because it contained so many different national groups. The Austrian Empire remained a collection of territories held together by a personal union. The Habsburg emperor was archduke of Austria, king of Bohemia, and king of Hungary. Each of these areas, however, had its own laws, Estates-General, and political life.

Russia: From Fledgling Principality to Major Power

A new Russian state had emerged in the fifteenth century under the leadership of the principality of Moscow and its grand dukes. In the sixteenth century, Ivan IV the Terrible (1533–1584), the first ruler to take the title of tsar ("Caesar"), expanded the territories of Russia eastward. Ivan also extended the autocracy of the tsar by crushing the power of the Russian nobility, known as the **boyars**. Ivan's dynasty came to an end in 1598 and was followed by a resurgence of aristocratic power in a period of anarchy known as the Time of Troubles. It did not end until 1613 when the Zemsky Sobor (ZEM-skee suh-BOR), or national assembly, chose Michael Romanov (1613–1645) as the new tsar, beginning a dynasty that lasted until 1917.

In the seventeenth century, Muscovite society was highly stratified. At the top was the tsar, who claimed to be a divinely ordained autocratic ruler. Russian society was dominated by an upper class of landed aristocrats who, in the course of the seventeenth century, managed to bind their peasants to the land. Townspeople were also controlled. Many merchants were not allowed to move from their cities without government permission or to sell their businesses to anyone outside their class. In the seventeenth century, merchant and peasant revolts as well as a schism in the Russian Orthodox Church created very unsettled conditions. In the midst of these political and religious upheavals, Russia was experiencing more frequent contacts with the West, and Western ideas were beginning to penetrate a few Russian circles. Nevertheless, Russia remained largely outside the framework of the West: the Renaissance, the Reformation, and the geographic discoveries of the sixteenth and seventeenth centuries made little impact on Russia. At the end of the seventeenth century, Peter the Great (1689–1725) noticeably accelerated the westernizing process.

© Cengage Learning

MAP 15.3 The Growth of the Austrian Empire. The Habsburgs had hoped to establish a German empire, but the results of the Thirty Years' War crushed that dream. So Austria expanded to the east and the south, primarily at the expense of the Ottoman Empire, and also gained the Spanish Netherlands and former Spanish territories in Italy.

Q *In which areas did the Austrian Empire have access to the Mediterranean Sea, and why would that potentially be important?*

THE REIGN OF PETER THE GREAT (1689–1725) Peter the Great was an unusual character. A strong man, towering 6 feet 9 inches tall, Peter enjoyed a low kind of humor—belching contests and crude jokes—and vicious punishments including flogging, impalings, and roastings. He gained a firsthand view of the West when he made a trip there in 1697–1698 and returned to Russia with a firm determination to westernize or Europeanize his realm. He admired European technology and gadgets and desired to transplant these to Russia. Only this kind of modernization could give him the army and navy he needed to make Russia a great power.

As could be expected, one of his first priorities was the reorganization of the army and the creation of a navy. Employing both Russians and Europeans as officers, he conscripted peasants for twenty-five-year stints of service to build a standing army of 210,000 men. Peter has also been given credit for forming the first Russian navy.

Peter reorganized the central government, partly along Western lines. To impose the rule of the central government more effectively throughout the land, he divided Russia into eight provinces and later, in 1719, into fifty. Although he hoped to create a "police state," by which he meant a well-ordered community governed in accordance with law, few of his bureaucrats shared his concept of honest service and duty to the state. Peter hoped for a sense of civic duty, but his own forceful personality created an atmosphere of fear that prevented it.

Peter also sought to gain state control of the Russian Orthodox Church. In 1721, he abolished the position of patriarch and created a body called the Holy Synod to make decisions for the church. At its head stood a **procurator**, a layman who represented the interests of the tsar and assured Peter of effective domination of the church.

Shortly after his return from the West in 1698, Peter had begun to introduce Western customs, practices, and manners into Russia. He ordered the preparation of the first Russian book of etiquette to teach Western manners. Among other things, it pointed out that it was not polite to spit on the floor or scratch oneself at dinner. Because Europeans at that time did not wear beards or traditional long-skirted coats, Russian beards had to be shaved and coats shortened, a reform Peter personally enforced at court by shaving off his nobles' beards and cutting their coats at the knees with his own hands. Outside the court, barbers and tailors planted at town gates enforced the edicts by cutting the beards and cloaks of those who entered or left.

One group of Russians benefited greatly from Peter's cultural reforms—women. Having watched women mixing freely with men in Western courts, Peter shattered the seclusion of upper-class Russian women and demanded that they remove the traditional veils that covered their faces. Peter also decreed that social gatherings be held three times a week in the large houses of Saint Petersburg where men and women could mix for conversation, card games, and dancing, which Peter had learned in the West. The tsar also now insisted that women could marry of their own free will.

The object of Peter's domestic reforms was to make Russia into a great state and a military power. His primary goal was to "open a window to the West," meaning a port easily accessible to Europe. This could only be achieved on the Baltic, but at that time the Baltic coast was controlled by Sweden, the most important power in northern Europe. Desirous of these lands, Peter attacked Sweden in the summer of 1700, believing that its young king, Charles XII (1697–1718), could easily be defeated. Charles, however, proved to be a brilliant general and, with a well-disciplined force of only 8,000 men, routed the Russian army of 40,000 at the Battle of Narva (1700). The Great Northern War (1701–1721) soon ensued.

But Peter fought back. He reorganized his army along Western lines and at the Battle of Poltava (pul-TAH-vuh) in 1709 decisively defeated Charles's army. Although the war dragged on for another twelve years, the Peace of Nystadt (NEE-shtaht) in 1721 gave formal recognition to what Peter had already achieved: the acquisition of Estonia, Livonia, and Karelia (see Map 15.4). Sweden had become a second-rate power, and Russia was now the great European state Peter had envisioned. Already in 1703, Peter had begun the construction of a new city on the Baltic, Saint Petersburg, his window to the West and a symbol that Russia was looking toward Europe. Peter realized his dream: by the time of his death in 1725, Russia had become a great military power and an important actor on the European stage.

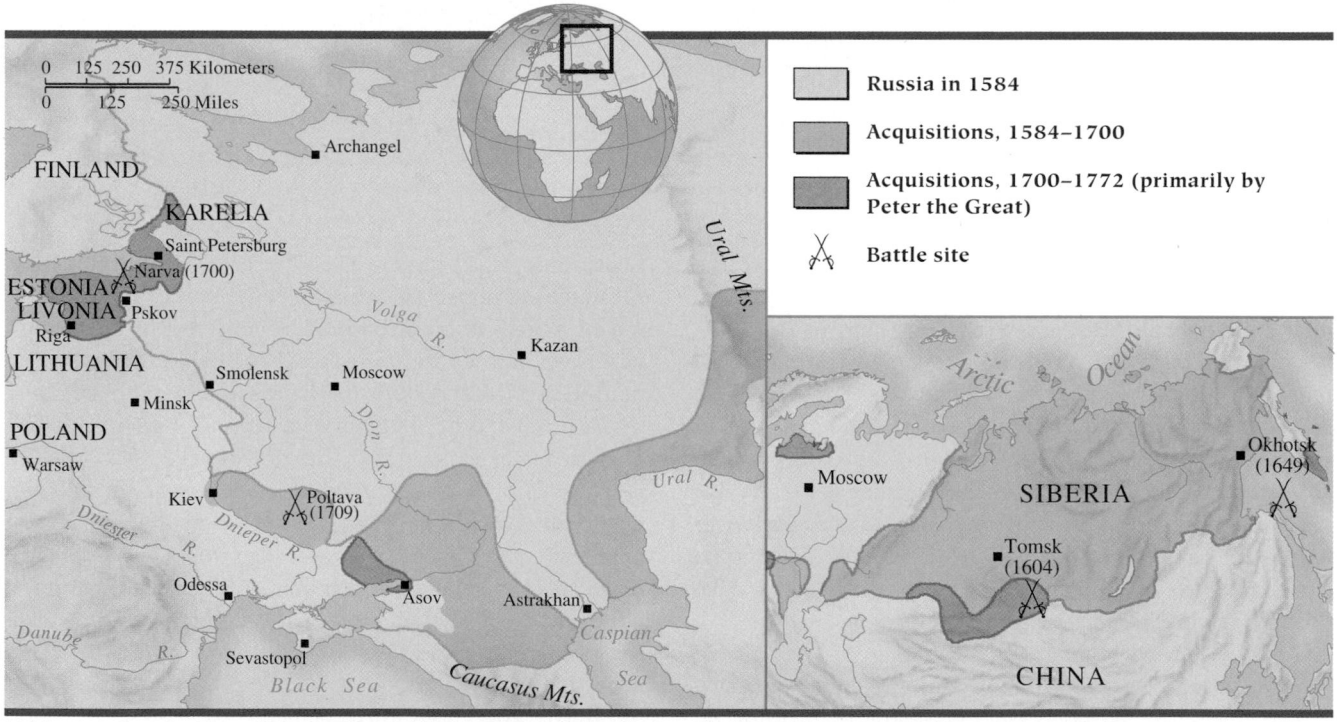

© Cengage Learning

MAP 15.4 Russia: From Principality to Nation-State. Russia had swelled in size since its emergence in the fifteenth century. Peter the Great, however, modernized the country, instituting bureaucratic and taxation reforms and building up the military. He won territory on the Baltic from Sweden, giving Russia a port at Saint Petersburg.

Q ***Why would the westward expansion of Russia during Peter's reign affect the international balance of power in Europe?***

The Ottoman Empire

After conquering Constantinople in 1453, the Ottoman Turks tried but failed to complete their conquest of the Balkans, where they had been established since the fourteenth century (see Map 15.3). The reign of Sultan Suleiman (soo-lay-MAHN) I the Magnificent (1520–1566), however, brought the Ottomans back to Europe's attention. Advancing up the Danube, the Ottomans seized Belgrade in 1521 and Hungary by 1526, although their attempts to conquer Vienna in 1529 were repulsed. At the same time, the Ottomans extended their power into the western Mediterranean, threatening to turn it into an Ottoman lake until a large Ottoman fleet was destroyed by the Spanish at Lepanto (in modern-day Greece) in 1571. Despite the defeat, the Ottomans continued to hold nominal control over the southern shores of the Mediterranean.

Although Europeans frequently spoke of new Christian Crusades against the "infidel" Ottomans, by the beginning of the seventeenth century, the Ottoman Empire was being treated like any other European power by European rulers seeking alliances and trade concessions. In the first half of the century, the empire was a "sleeping giant." Occupied by domestic bloodletting and severely threatened by a challenge from Persia, the Ottomans were content with the status quo in eastern Europe. But under a new line of grand viziers in the second half of the seventeenth century, the Ottoman Empire again took the offensive. By 1683, the Ottomans had marched through the Hungarian plain and laid siege to Vienna. Repulsed by a mixed army of Austrians, Poles, Bavarians, and Saxons, the Ottomans retreated and were pushed out of Hungary by a new European coalition. Although they retained the core of their empire, the Ottoman Turks would never again be a threat to Europe.

The Limits of Absolutism

In recent decades, historical studies of local institutions have challenged the traditional picture of absolute monarchs. We now recognize that their power was far from absolute, and it is misleading to think that they actually controlled the lives of their subjects. In 1700, government for most people still meant the local institutions that affected their lives: local courts, local tax collectors, and local organizers of armed forces. Kings and ministers might determine policies and issue guidelines, but they still had to function through local agents and had no guarantee that their wishes would be carried out. A mass of urban and provincial privileges, liberties, and exemptions (including from taxation) and a whole host of corporate bodies and interest groups—provincial and national Estates, clerical officials, officeholders who had bought or inherited their positions, and provincial nobles—limited what monarchs could achieve. The most successful rulers were not those who tried to destroy the old system but rather those like Louis XIV who knew how to use the old system to their advantage. Above all other considerations stood the landholding nobility. Everywhere in the seventeenth century, the landed aristocracy played an important role in the European monarchical system. As military officers, judges, officeholders, and landowners in control of vast, untaxed estates, their power remained immense. In some places, their strength even put severe limits on how effectively monarchs could rule.

CHRONOLOGY Absolutism in Central and Eastern Europe

Brandenburg-Prussia	
Frederick William the Great Elector	1640–1688
Elector Frederick III (King Frederick I)	1688–1713
Austrian Empire	
Leopold I	1658–1705
Ottoman siege of Vienna	1683
Russia	
Ivan IV the Terrible	1533–1584
Time of Troubles	1598–1613
Michael Romanov	1613–1645
Peter the Great	1689–1725
First trip to the West	1697–1698
Great Northern War	1701–1721
Founding of Saint Petersburg	1703
Battle of Poltava	1709
Holy Synod	1721
Ottoman Empire	
Suleiman I the Magnificent	1520–1566
Battle of Lepanto	1571
Ottoman defeat at Vienna	1683

Limited Monarchy: The Dutch Republic and England

Focus Question: What were the main issues in the struggle between king and Parliament in seventeenth-century England, and how were they resolved?

Almost everywhere in Europe in the seventeenth century, kings and their ministers were in control of central governments. But not all European states followed the pattern of absolute monarchy. In western Europe, two great states—the Dutch Republic and England—successfully resisted the power of hereditary monarchs.

The Golden Age of the Dutch Republic

The seventeenth century has often been called the golden age of the Dutch Republic as the United Provinces held center stage as one of Europe's great powers. Like France and England, the United Provinces was an Atlantic power, underlining the importance of the shift of political and economic power in the seventeenth century from the Mediterranean basin to the countries on the Atlantic seaboard. As a result of the sixteenth-century revolt of the Netherlands, the seven northern provinces, which began to call themselves the United Provinces of the Netherlands in 1581, became the core of the modern Dutch state. The new state was officially recognized by the Peace of Westphalia in 1648.

With independence came internal dissension. There were two chief centers of political power in the new state. Each province had an official known as a stadholder (STAD-hohl-dur) who was responsible for leading the army and maintaining order. Beginning with William of Orange and his heirs, the house of Orange occupied the stadholderate in most provinces and favored the development of a centralized government with themselves as hereditary monarchs. The States General, an assembly of representatives from every province, opposed the Orangist ambitions and advocated a decentralized or republican form of government. For much of the seventeenth century, the republican forces were in control. But in 1672, burdened with war against both France and England, the United Provinces allowed William III (1672–1702) of the house of Orange to establish a monarchical regime. But his death in 1702 without direct heirs enabled the republican forces to gain control once more, although the struggle persisted throughout the eighteenth century.

Underlying Dutch prominence in the seventeenth century was economic prosperity, fueled by the role of the Dutch as carriers of European trade (see Images of Everyday Life on p. 345). But warfare proved disastrous to the Dutch Republic. Wars with France and England placed heavy burdens on Dutch finances and manpower. English shipping began to challenge what had been Dutch commercial supremacy, and by 1715, the Dutch were experiencing a serious economic decline.

England and the Emergence of Constitutional Monarchy

One of the most prominent examples of resistance to absolute monarchy came in seventeenth-century England, where king and Parliament struggled to determine the role each should play in governing the nation.

KING JAMES I AND PARLIAMENT On the death of Queen Elizabeth in 1603, the Tudor dynasty became extinct, and the Stuart line of rulers was inaugurated with the accession to the throne of Elizabeth's cousin, King James VI of Scotland (son of Mary, Queen of Scots), who became James I (1603–1625) of England. James espoused the divine right of kings, a viewpoint that alienated Parliament, which had grown accustomed under the Tudors to act on the premise that monarch and Parliament together ruled England as a "balanced polity." Parliament expressed its displeasure with James's claims by refusing his requests for additional monies needed by the king to meet the increased cost of government. Parliament's power of the purse proved to be its trump card in its relationship with the king.

Some members of Parliament were also alienated by James's religious policy. The Puritans—Protestants in the Anglican Church inspired by Calvinist theology—wanted James to eliminate the episcopal system of church organization used in the Church of England (in which the bishop or *episcopos* played the major administrative role) in favor of a Presbyterian model (used in Scotland and patterned after Calvin's church organization in Geneva, where ministers and elders—also called presbyters—played an important governing role). James refused because he realized that the Anglican Church, with its bishops appointed by the crown, was a major supporter of monarchical authority. But the Puritans were not easily cowed and added to the rising chorus of opposition to the king. Many of England's **gentry**, mostly well-to-do landowners below the level of the nobility, had become Puritans, and these Puritan gentry not only formed an important and substantial part of the House of Commons, the lower house of Parliament, but also held important positions locally as justices of the peace and sheriffs. It was not wise to alienate them.

CHARLES I AND THE MOVE TOWARD REVOLUTION The conflict that had begun during the reign of James came to a head during the reign of his son, Charles I (1625–1649). In 1628, Parliament passed the Petition of Right, which the king was supposed to accept before being granted any tax revenues. This petition prohibited levying taxes without Parliament's consent, arbitrary imprisonment, the quartering of soldiers in private houses, and the declaration of martial law in peacetime. Although he initially accepted it, Charles later reneged on the agreement because of its limitations on royal power. In 1629, Charles decided that since he could not work with Parliament, he would not summon it to meet. From 1629 to 1640, Charles pursued a course of

IMAGES OF EVERYDAY LIFE

Dutch Domesticity

During the golden age of the Dutch Republic, Dutch painters delighted in painting scenes of domestic life, especially the lives of the wealthy burghers who prospered from trade, finance, and manufacturing. The Dutch painter Pieter de Hooch (pee-TUR duh HOHKH) specialized in painting pictures of Dutch interiors, as can be seen in three of his paintings. In *The Mother* (below left), de Hooch portrays a tranquil scene of a mother with her infant and small daughter. The spotless, polished floors reflect the sunlight streaming in through the open door. The rooms are clean and in good order. Household manuals, such as *The Experienced and Knowledgeable Hollands Householder*, provided detailed outlines of the cleaning tasks that should be performed each day of the week. In *The Linen Cupboard* (below right), a Dutch mother, assisted by her daughter, is shown storing her clean sheets in an elegant cupboard in another well-polished Dutch room. The Chinese porcelain on top of the cupboard and the antique statue indicate that this is the residence of a wealthy family. In *Two Women Teach a Child to Walk* (at the right), the artist again shows a nicely furnished and spotless interior. A small girl is learning to walk, assisted by a servant holding straps attached to a band around the girl's head to keep her from falling.

Museum der Bildenden Kuenste (Inv. 1558), Leipzig/© Erich Lessing/Art Resource, NY

Gemäldegalerie (Inv. 820 B), Staatliche Museen zu Berlin/© Bildarchiv Preussischer Kulturbesitz (Jörg P. Anders)/Art Resource, NY

Rijksmuseum, Amsterdam/© Alinari/Art Resource, NY

personal rule, which forced him to find ways to collect taxes without the cooperation of Parliament. These expedients aroused opposition from middle-class merchants and landed gentry, who objected to the king's attempts to tax without Parliament's consent.

The king's religious policy also proved disastrous. His attempt to impose more ritual on the Anglican Church struck the Puritans as a return to Catholic popery. Charles's efforts to force them to conform to his religious policies infuriated the Puritans, thousands of whom abandoned England for the "howling wildernesses" of America.

CIVIL WAR AND A NEW GOVERNMENT Grievances mounted until England finally slipped into a civil war (1642–1648) that was won by the parliamentary forces. Most important to Parliament's success was the creation of the New Model Army, one of whose leaders was Oliver Cromwell (1599–1658), the only real military genius of the war. The New Model Army was composed primarily of more extreme Puritans known as the Independents, who, in typical Calvinist fashion, believed they were doing battle for the Lord. As Cromwell wrote in one of his military reports, "Sir, this is none other but the hand of God; and to Him alone belongs the glory."

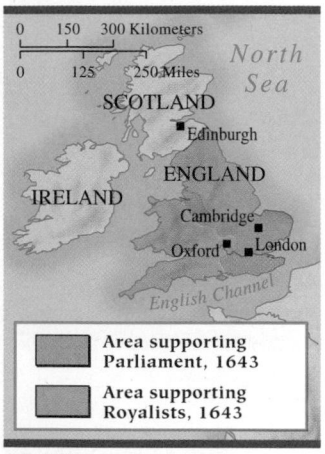

© Cengage Learning

Civil War in England

Between 1648 and 1660, England faced a trying situation. After the execution of Charles I on January 30, 1649, Parliament abolished the monarchy and the House of Lords and proclaimed England a republic or commonwealth. But Cromwell and his army, unable to work effectively with Parliament, dispersed it by force. As the members of Parliament departed in April 1653, Cromwell shouted after them, "It's you that have forced me to do this, for I have sought the Lord night and day that He would slay me rather than put upon me the doing of this work." With the certainty of one who is convinced he is right, Cromwell had destroyed both king and Parliament (see the box on p. 347). Finally, Cromwell dissolved Parliament and divided the country into eleven regions, each ruled by a major general who served as a military governor. Unable to establish a constitutional basis for a working government, Cromwell had resorted to military force to maintain the rule of the Independents.

© National Portrait Gallery, London/SuperStock

Oliver Cromwell. Oliver Cromwell was a dedicated Puritan who formed the New Model Army and defeated the forces supporting King Charles I. Unable to work with Parliament, he came to rely on military force to rule England. Cromwell is pictured here in 1649, on the eve of his military campaign in Ireland.

Oliver Cromwell died in 1658. After floundering for eighteen months, the military government decided that arbitrary rule by the army was no longer feasible and reestablished the monarchy in the person of Charles II (1660–1685), the son of Charles I. The restoration of the Stuart monarchy ended England's time of troubles, but it was not long before yet another constitutional crisis arose.

RESTORATION AND A GLORIOUS REVOLUTION Charles was sympathetic to and perhaps even inclined to Catholicism. Moreover, Charles's brother James, heir to the throne, did not hide the fact that he was a Catholic. Parliament's suspicions were therefore aroused in 1672 when Charles took the audacious step of issuing the Declaration of Indulgence, which suspended the laws that Parliament had passed against Catholics and Puritans after the restoration of the Anglican Church as the official church of England. Parliament would have none of it and induced the king to suspend the declaration. Propelled by a strong anti-Catholic sentiment, Parliament then passed the Test

OPPOSING VIEWPOINTS

Oliver Cromwell: Three Perspectives

Oliver Cromwell was a strong leader with firm religious convictions. The first selection below, taken from a letter written after the defeat of the king's forces at Naseby in 1645, reveals Cromwell's feelings about the reasons for his military victory. The next selection, also by Cromwell, is taken from his comments after his army's massacre of Catholic forces at Drogheda in Catholic Ireland. The third selection is by Edmund Ludlow, a general on Cromwell's side who broke with Cromwell after the latter dispersed Parliament in 1653. The final selection by Edward Hyde, the first earl of Clarendon, a supporter of King Charles I and later Charles II, presents a royalist view of Cromwell.

Oliver Cromwell on the Victory at Naseby

Sir, this is none other but the hand of God; and to Him alone belongs the glory, wherein none are to share with Him. The general [Fairfax] served you with all faithfulness and honor: and the best commendations I can give him is, that I dare say he attributes all to God, and would rather perish than assume to himself.

Cromwell on the Massacre at Drogheda

The next day, the other two towers were summoned, in one of which was about six or seven score; but they refused to yield themselves, and we knowing that hunger must compel them, set only good guards to secure them from running away until their stomachs were come down. From one of the said towers, notwithstanding their condition, they killed and wounded some of our men. When they submitted, their officers were knocked on the head, and every tenth man of the soldiers killed, and the rest shipped for the Barbados. The soldiers in the other tower were all spared, as to their lives only, and shipped likewise for the Barbados.

I am persuaded that this is a righteous judgment of God upon these barbarous wretches, who have imbrued their hands in so much innocent blood; and that it will tend to prevent the effusion of blood for the future.

Edmund Ludlow, *Memoirs*

Then I drew near to the council-table, where Cromwell charged me with dispersing treasonable books in Ireland, and with endeavoring to render the officers of the army disaffected, by discoursing to them concerning new models of Government. . . .

"You do well," said he, "to reflect on our fears. . . . I now require you to give assurance not to act against the Government." I desired to be excused in that particular, reminding him of the reasons I had formerly given him for my refusal, adding, that I was in his power, and that he might use me as he thought fit. "Pray then," said he, "what is it that you would have? May not every man be as good as he will? What can you desire more than you have?" "It were easy," said I, "to tell what we would have." "What is that, I pray?" said he. "That which we fought for," said I, "that the nation might be governed by its own consent." "I am," said he, "as much for a government by consent as any man; but where shall we find that consent? Amongst the Prelatical, Presbyterian, Independent, Anabaptist, or Leveling Parties?" I answered, "Amongst those of all sorts who had acted with fidelity and affection to the public."

Lord Clarendon, *The History of the Rebellion and Civil Wars in England*

He was one of those men, . . . whom his very enemies could not condemn without commending him at the same time: for he could never have done half that mischief without great parts of courage, industry, and judgment. He must have had a wonderful understanding in the natures and humors of men, and as great a dexterity in applying them; who, from a private and obscure birth (though of a good family), without interest or estate, alliance or friendship, could raise himself to such a height. . . . What [a Roman writer] said of Cinna [a Roman politician] may very justly be said of him: he attempted those things which no good man dared have ventured on; and achieved those in which none but a valiant and great man could have succeeded. Without doubt, no man with more wickedness ever attempted any

(Continued)

(Opposing Viewpoints continued)

thing, or brought to pass what he desired more wickedly, more in the face and contempt of religion, and moral honesty; yet wickedness as great as his could never have accomplished those trophies, without the assistance of a great spirit, an admirable circumspection and sagacity, and a most magnanimous resolution.

Q What motivated Cromwell's political and military actions? What was Edmund Ludlow's criticism of Cromwell, and how did Cromwell respond? In what ways did Edward Hyde see both good and bad features in Cromwell? How do you explain the differences in these three perspectives?

Sources: Oliver Cromwell on the Victory at Naseby. Oliver Cromwell on the Massacre at Drogheda. From Thomas Carlyle, ed., THE LETTERS AND SPEECHES OF OLIVER CROMWELL, 3 vols. (New York: G.P. Putnam's Sons, 1904), Vol. I, p. 204, Vol II, p. 15. Edmund Ludlow, *Memoirs*. From C.H. Firth, THE MEMOIRS OF EDMUND LUDLOW (Oxford: Oxford University Press, 1894), Vol. 2, pp. 10–11. Lord Clarendon, *The History of the Rebellion and Civil Wars in England*. From Lord Clarendon, THE HISTORY OF THE REBELLION AND CIVIL WARS IN ENGLAND (Oxford: Oxford University Press, 1839), Vol. 6, pp. 349–350.

Act of 1673, specifying that only Anglicans could hold military and civil offices.

The accession of James II (1685–1688) virtually guaranteed a new constitutional crisis for England. An open and devout Catholic, his attempt to further Catholic interests made religion once more a primary cause of conflict between king and Parliament. In 1687, James issued a new Declaration of Indulgence, which suspended all laws that excluded Catholics and Puritans from office. Parliamentary outcries against James's policies stopped short of rebellion because members knew that he was an old man and his successors were his Protestant daughters Mary and Anne, born to his first wife. But on June 10, 1688, a son was born to James II's second wife, also a Catholic. Suddenly, the specter of a Catholic hereditary monarchy loomed large.

A group of prominent English noblemen invited the Dutch chief executive, William of Orange, husband of James's daughter Mary, to invade England. William and Mary raised an army and invaded England while James, his wife, and their infant son fled to France. With almost no bloodshed, England had embarked on a "Glorious Revolution," not over the issue of whether there would be monarchy but rather over who would be monarch.

In January 1689, Parliament offered the throne to William and Mary, who accepted it along with the provisions of a bill of rights (see the box on p. 349). The Bill of Rights affirmed Parliament's right to make laws and levy taxes and made it impossible for kings to oppose or do without Parliament by stipulating that standing armies could be raised only with the consent of Parliament. The rights of citizens to petition the sovereign, keep arms, have a jury trial, and not be subject to excessive bail were also confirmed. The Bill of Rights helped fashion a system of government based on the rule of law and a freely elected Parliament, thus laying the foundation for a constitutional monarchy.

The Bill of Rights did not settle the religious questions that had played such a large role in England's troubles in the seventeenth century. The Toleration Act of 1689 granted Puritan Dissenters the right of free public worship (Catholics were still excluded). Although the Toleration Act did not mean complete religious freedom and equality, it marked a departure in English history in that few people would ever again be persecuted for religious reasons.

CHRONOLOGY Limited Monarchy and Republics

United Provinces of the Netherlands	
Official recognition	1648
House of Orange: William III	1672–1702
England	
James I	1603–1625
Charles I	1625–1649
Petition of Right	1628
Civil War	1642–1648
Commonwealth	1649–1653
Death of Cromwell	1658
Restoration of monarchy	1660
Charles II	1660–1685
Declaration of Indulgence	1672
Test Act	1673
James II	1685–1688
Declaration of Indulgence	1687
Glorious Revolution	1688
Bill of Rights	1689

The Bill of Rights

In 1688, the English experienced yet another revolution, a bloodless one in which the Stuart king James II was replaced by Mary, James's daughter, and her husband, William of Orange. After William and Mary had assumed power, Parliament passed a bill of rights that specified the rights of Parliament and laid the foundation for a constitutional monarchy.

The Bill of Rights

Whereas the said late King James II having abdicated the government, and the throne being thereby vacant, his Highness the prince of Orange (whom it has pleased Almighty God to make the glorious instrument of delivering this kingdom from popery and arbitrary power) did (by the device of the lords spiritual and temporal, and diverse principal persons of the Commons) cause letters to be written to the lords spiritual and temporal, being Protestants, and other letters to the several counties, cities, universities, boroughs, and Cinque Ports, for the choosing of such persons to represent them, as were of right to be sent to parliament, to meet and sit at Westminster upon the two and twentieth day of January, in this year 1689, in order to such an establishment as that their religion, laws, and liberties might not again be in danger of being subverted; upon which letters elections have been accordingly made.

And thereupon the said lords spiritual and temporal and Commons, pursuant to their respective letters and elections, being now assembled in a full and free representation of this nation, taking into their most serious consideration the best means for attaining the ends aforesaid, do in the first place (as their ancestors in like case have usually done), for the vindication and assertion of their ancient rights and liberties, declare:

1. That the pretended power of suspending laws, or the execution of laws, by regal authority, without consent of parliament is illegal.
2. That the pretended power of dispensing with the laws, or the execution of law by regal authority, as it has been assumed and exercised of late, is illegal.
3. That the commission for erecting the late court of commissioners for ecclesiastical causes, and all other commissions and courts of like nature, are illegal and pernicious.
4. That levying money for or to the use of the crown by pretense of prerogative, without grant of parliament, for longer time or in other manner than the same is or shall be granted, is illegal.
5. That it is the right of the subjects to petition the king, and all commitments and prosecutions for such petitioning are illegal.
6. That the raising or keeping a standing army within the kingdom in time of peace, unless it be with consent of parliament, is against law.
7. That the subjects which are Protestants may have arms for their defense suitable to their conditions, and as allowed by law.
8. That election of members of parliament ought to be free.
9. That the freedom of speech, and debates or proceedings in parliament, ought not to be impeached or questioned in any court or place out of parliament.
10. That excessive bail ought not to be required, nor excessive fines imposed, nor cruel and unusual punishments inflicted.
11. That jurors ought to be duly impaneled and returned, and jurors which pass upon men in trials for high treason ought to be freeholders.
12. That all grants and promises of fines and forfeitures of particular persons before conviction are illegal and void.
13. And that for redress of all grievances, and for the amending, strengthening, and preserving of the laws, parliament ought to be held frequently.

Q How did the Bill of Rights lay the foundation for a constitutional monarchy in England? What key aspects of this document testify to the exceptional nature of English state politics in the seventeenth century?

Source: From *The Statutes: Revised Edition* (London: Eyre and Spottiswoode, 1871), Vol. 2, pp. 10–12.

Many historians have viewed the Glorious Revolution as the end of the seventeenth-century struggle between king and Parliament. By deposing one king and establishing another, Parliament had demolished the divine-right theory of kingship (William was, after all, king by grace of Parliament, not God) and confirmed its right to participate in the government. Parliament did not have complete control of the government, but it now had an unquestioned role in affairs of state. Over the next century, it would gradually prove to be the real authority in the English system of constitutional monarchy.

RESPONSES TO REVOLUTION The English revolutions of the seventeenth century prompted very different responses from two English political thinkers—Thomas Hobbes and John Locke. Thomas Hobbes (1588–1679), who lived during the English Civil War, was alarmed by the revolutionary upheavals in his contemporary England. His name has since been associated with the state's claim to absolute authority over its subjects, a topic that he elaborated in his major treatise on political thought known as the *Leviathan* (luh-VY-uh-thun), published in 1651.

Hobbes claimed that in the state of nature, before society was organized, human life was "solitary, poor, nasty, brutish, and short." Humans were guided not by reason and moral ideals but by animalistic instincts and a ruthless struggle for self-preservation. To save themselves from destroying each other (the "war of every man against every man"), people contracted to form a commonwealth, which Hobbes called "that great Leviathan (or rather, to speak more reverently, that mortal god) to which we owe our peace and defense." This commonwealth placed its collective power into the hands of a sovereign authority, preferably a single ruler, who served as executor, legislator, and judge. This absolute ruler possessed unlimited power. In Hobbes's view, subjects may not rebel; if they do, they must be suppressed.

John Locke (1632–1704), author of a political work called *Two Treatises of Government*, viewed the exercise of political power quite differently from Hobbes and argued against the absolute rule of one man. Like Hobbes, Locke began with the state of nature before human existence became organized socially. But unlike Hobbes, Locke believed that humans lived then in a state of equality and freedom rather than a state of war. In this state of nature, humans had certain inalienable natural rights—to life, liberty, and property. Like Hobbes, Locke did not believe that all was well in the state of nature, and people found it difficult to protect these rights. So they mutually agreed to establish a government to ensure the protection of their rights. This agreement established mutual obligations: government would protect the rights of people, and the people would act reasonably toward their government. But if a government broke this agreement—if a king, for example, failed to live up to his obligation to protect the people's rights or claimed absolute authority and made laws without the consent of the community—the people might form a new government. For Locke, however, the community of people was primarily the landholding aristocracy who were represented in Parliament, not the landless masses. Locke was hardly an advocate of political democracy, but his ideas proved important to both the Americans and the French in the eighteenth century and were used to support demands for constitutional government, the rule of law, and the protection of rights.

The Flourishing of European Culture

FOCUS QUESTION: How did the artistic and literary achievements of this era reflect the political and economic developments of the period?

In the midst of religious wars and the growth of absolutism, European culture continued to flourish. The era was blessed with a number of prominent artists and writers.

The Changing Faces of Art

After the Renaissance, European art passed through a number of stylistic stages. The artistic Renaissance came to an end when a new movement called Mannerism emerged in Italy in the 1520s and 1530s.

MANNERISM The Reformation's revival of religious values brought much political turmoil. Especially in Italy, the worldly enthusiasm of the Renaissance gave way to anxiety, uncertainty, suffering, and a yearning for spiritual experience. **Mannerism** reflected this environment in its deliberate attempt to break down the High Renaissance principles of balance, harmony, and moderation. Italian Mannerist painters deliberately distorted the rules of proportion by portraying elongated figures that conveyed a sense of suffering and a strong emotional atmosphere filled with anxiety and confusion.

THE BAROQUE Mannerism was eventually replaced by a new movement—the **Baroque**—that began in Italy in the last quarter of the sixteenth century and spread to the rest of Europe. The style was most wholeheartedly embraced by the Catholic reform movement, as is evident at the Catholic courts, especially those of the Habsburgs in Madrid, Prague, Vienna, and Brussels. Although it was resisted in France, England, and the Netherlands, eventually the Baroque style spread to all of Europe and Latin America.

Baroque artists sought to bring together the Classical ideals of Renaissance art and the spiritual feelings of the sixteenth-century religious revival. In large part, though, Baroque art and architecture reflected the search for power that was such a large part of the seventeenth-century ethos. Baroque churches and palaces were magnificent and richly detailed. Kings and princes wanted other kings and princes as well as their subjects to be in awe of their power. The Catholic Church, which commissioned many new churches, wanted people to see the triumphant power of the Catholic faith.

Baroque painting was known for its use of dramatic effects to heighten emotional intensity. This style was especially evident in the works of the Flemish painter Peter Paul Rubens (1577–1640), a prolific artist and an important figure in the spread of the Baroque from Italy to other parts of Europe. In his artistic masterpieces, bodies in vigorous motion, heavily fleshed nudes, a dramatic use of light and shadow, and rich, sensuous pigments converge to express intense emotions. The restless forms and constant movement blend into a dynamic unity.

Perhaps the greatest figure of the Baroque was the Italian architect and sculptor Gian Lorenzo Bernini (ZHAHN loh-RENT-zoh bur-NEE-nee) (1598–1680), who completed Saint Peter's Basilica at the Vatican and designed the vast colonnade enclosing the piazza in front of it. Action, exuberance, profusion, and dramatic effects mark the work of Bernini in the interior of Saint Peter's, where his *Throne of Saint Peter* hovers in midair, held by the hands of the four great doctors of the Catholic Church.

Less well known than the male artists who dominated the art world of the seventeenth century in Italy but prominent in her own right was Artemisia Gentileschi (ar-tuh-MEE-zhuh jen-tuh-LESS-kee) (1593–1653). Born in Rome, she studied painting under her father's direction. In 1616, she moved to Florence and began a successful career as a painter. At the age of twenty-three, she became the first woman to be elected to the Florentine Academy of Design. Although she was known internationally in her day as a portrait painter, her fame now rests on a series of pictures of heroines from the Old Testament, including Judith, Esther, and Bathsheba. Most famous is *Judith Beheading Holofernes*, a dramatic rendering of the biblical scene in which Judith slays the Assyrian general Holofernes to save her besieged town from the Assyrian army.

Louvre (Inv. 1774), Paris/© Réunion des Musées Nationaux (Jean Lewandowski)/Art Resource, NY

Peter Paul Rubens, *The Landing of Marie de' Medici at Marseilles.* The Flemish artist Peter Paul Rubens played a key role in spreading the Baroque style from Italy to other parts of Europe. In *The Landing of Marie de' Medici at Marseilles,* Rubens made dramatic use of light and color, bodies in motion, and luxurious nudes to heighten the emotional intensity of the scene. This was one of a cycle of twenty-one paintings dedicated to the queen mother of France.

FRENCH CLASSICISM AND DUTCH REALISM In the second half of the seventeenth century, France replaced Italy as the cultural leader of Europe. Rejecting the Baroque style as showy and overly passionate, the French remained committed to the Classical values of the High Renaissance. French late Classicism, with its emphasis on clarity, simplicity, balance, and harmony of design, was a rather austere version of the High Renaissance style. Its triumph reflected the shift in seventeenth-century French society from chaos to order. Though it rejected the emotionalism and high drama of the Baroque, French Classicism continued the Baroque's conception of grandeur in the portrayal of noble subjects, especially those from Classical antiquity.

The supremacy of Dutch commerce in the seventeenth century was paralleled by a brilliant flowering of Dutch painting. Wealthy patricians and burghers of Dutch urban society commissioned works of art for their guild halls, town halls, and private dwellings. The interests of this burgher society were reflected in the subject matter of many Dutch paintings: portraits of themselves, landscapes, seascapes, genre scenes, still lifes, and the interiors

Galleria degli Uffizi, Florence/© Alinari/Art Resource, NY

Artemisia Gentileschi, *Judith Beheading Holofernes.* Artemisia Gentileschi painted a series of pictures portraying scenes from the lives of courageous Old Testament women. In this painting, a determined Judith, armed with her victim's sword, struggles to saw off the head of Holofernes. Gentileschi realistically and dramatically shows the gruesome nature of Judith's act.

of their residences. Neither Classical nor Baroque, Dutch painters were primarily interested in the realistic portrayal of secular everyday life.

The finest product of the golden age of Dutch painting was Rembrandt van Rijn (REM-brant vahn RYN) (1606–1669). Although Rembrandt shared the Dutch predilection for realistic portraits, he became more introspective as he grew older. He refused to follow his contemporaries, whose pictures were largely secular; half of his own paintings depicted scenes from biblical tales. Since the Protestant tradition of hostility to religious pictures had discouraged artistic expression, Rembrandt stands out as the one great Protestant painter of the seventeenth century.

A Wondrous Age of Theater

In England and Spain, writing reached new heights between 1580 and 1640. The greatest age of English literature is often called the Elizabethan era because much of this English cultural flowering of the late sixteenth and early seventeenth centuries occurred during the reign of Queen Elizabeth I. Elizabethan literature exhibits the exuberance and pride associated with England's international exploits at the time. Of all the forms of Elizabethan literature, none expressed the energy and intellectual versatility of the era better than drama. And of all the dramatists, none is more famous than William Shakespeare (1564–1616).

WILLIAM SHAKESPEARE Shakespeare was the son of a prosperous glovemaker from Stratford-upon-Avon. When he appeared in London in 1592, Elizabethans were already addicted to the stage. In Greater London, as many as six theaters were open six afternoons a week. London theaters ranged from the Globe, which was a circular unroofed structure holding three thousand spectators, to the Blackfriars, which was roofed and held only five hundred. In the former, the admission charge of only a penny or two enabled even the lower classes to attend; the higher prices in the latter ensured an audience of the well-to-do. Elizabethan audiences varied greatly, putting pressure on playwrights to write works that pleased nobles, lawyers, merchants, and even vagabonds.

William Shakespeare was a "complete man of the theater." Although best known for writing plays, he was also an actor and a shareholder in the chief company of the time, the Lord Chamberlain's Company, which played in theaters as diverse as the Globe and the Blackfriars. Shakespeare has long been recognized as a universal genius. A master of the English language, he was instrumental in codifying a language that was still in transition. This technical proficiency was matched by an incredible insight into human psychology. In both tragedies and comedies, Shakespeare exhibited a remarkable understanding of the human condition (see the box on p. 354).

SPAIN'S GOLDEN CENTURY The theater was also one of the most creative forms of expression during Spain's golden century. The first professional theaters founded in Seville and Madrid in the 1570s were run by actors' companies, as in England. Soon a public playhouse could be found in every large town, including Mexico City in the New World. Touring companies brought the latest Spanish plays to all parts of the Spanish Empire.

Beginning in the 1580s, the agenda for playwrights was set by Lope de Vega (LOH-pay day VAY-guh) (1562–1635). Like Shakespeare, he was from a middle-class background. He was an incredibly prolific writer; almost one-third of his fifteen hundred plays survive. They have been

© Rijksmuseum, Amsterdam/SuperStock

Rembrandt van Rijn, *Syndics of the Cloth Guild.* The Dutch experienced a golden age of painting during the seventeenth century. The burghers and patricians of Dutch urban society commissioned works of art, and these quite naturally reflected the burghers' interests, as this painting by Rembrandt illustrates.

characterized as witty, charming, action packed, and realistic. Lope de Vega made no apologies for the fact that he wrote his plays to please his audiences. In a treatise on drama written in 1609, he stated that the foremost duty of the playwright was to satisfy public demand. He remarked that if anyone thought he had written his plays for fame, "undeceive him and tell him that I wrote them for money."

FRENCH DRAMA As the great age of theater in England and Spain was drawing to a close around 1630, a new dramatic era began to dawn in France that lasted into the 1680s. Unlike Shakespeare in England and Lope de Vega in Spain, French playwrights wrote more for an elite audience and were forced to depend on royal patronage. Louis XIV used theater as he did art and architecture—to attract attention to his monarchy. French dramatists cultivated a style that emphasized the clever, polished, and correct over the emotional and imaginative. Many of the French works of this period derived their themes and plots from Greek and Roman sources.

Jean-Baptiste Molière (ZHAHNH bah-TEEST mohl-YAYR) (1622–1673) enjoyed the favor of the French court and benefited from the patronage of the Sun King. Molière wrote, produced, and acted in a series of comedies that often satirized the religious and social world of his time. In *Tartuffe*, he ridiculed religious hypocrisy. Molière's satires, however, sometimes got him into trouble. The Parisian clergy did not find *Tartuffe* funny and had it banned for five years. Only the protection of Louis XIV saved Molière from more severe harassment.

William Shakespeare: In Praise of England

William Shakespeare is one of the most famous playwrights of the Western world. He was a universal genius, outclassing all others in his psychological insights, depth of characterization, imaginative skills, and versatility. His historical plays reflected the patriotic enthusiasm of the English in the Elizabethan era, as this excerpt from *Richard II* illustrates.

William Shakespeare, *Richard II*

This royal throne of kings, this sceptered isle,
This earth of majesty, this seat of Mars,
This other Eden, demi-Paradise,
This fortress built by Nature for herself
Against infection and the hand of war,
This happy breed of men, this little world,
This precious stone set in the silver sea,
Which serves it in the office of a wall
Or as a moat defensive to a house
Against the envy of less happier lands—
This blessed plot, this earth, this realm, this England,
This nurse, this teeming womb of royal kings,
Feared by their breed and famous by their birth,
Renowned for their deeds as far from home,
For Christian service and true chivalry,
As is the sepulcher in stubborn Jewry [the Holy Sepulcher in Jerusalem]
Of the world's ransom, blessed Mary's Son—
This land of such dear souls, this dear dear land,
Dear for her reputation through the world,
Is now leased out, I die pronouncing it,
Like a tenement or pelting farm.
England, bound in with the triumphant sea,
Whose rocky shore beats back the envious siege
Of watery Neptune, is now bound in with shame,
With inky blots and rotten parchment bonds.
That England, what was wont to conquer others,
Hath made a shameful conquest of itself.
Ah, would the scandal vanish with my life,
How happy then were my ensuing death!

Q Why is William Shakespeare aptly described as not merely a playwright but a "complete man of the theater"? Which countries might Shakespeare have meant to suggest by the phrase "the envy of less happier lands"?

Source: Excerpt from *Richard II in Shakespeare, The Complete Works*, edited by G. B. Harrison (New York: Harcourt Brace & World, 1952).

CHAPTER SUMMARY

To many historians, the seventeenth century has assumed extraordinary proportions. The divisive effects of the Reformation had been assimilated, and the concept of a united Christendom, held as an ideal since the Middle Ages, had been irrevocably destroyed by the religious wars, making possible the emergence of a system of nation-states in which power politics took on an increasing significance. The growth of political thought focusing on the secular origins of state power reflected the changes that were going on in seventeenth-century society.

Within those states, there slowly emerged some of the machinery that made possible a growing centralization of power. In those states called absolutist, strong monarchs with the assistance of their aristocracies took the lead in providing the leadership for greater centralization. In this so-called age of absolutism, Louis XIV, the Sun King of France, was the model for other rulers. His palace of Versailles, where the nobles were entertained and controlled by ceremony and etiquette, symbolized his authority. Louis revoked his grandfather's Edict of Nantes and fought four costly wars, mainly to acquire lands on France's eastern borders. Strong monarchy also prevailed in central and eastern Europe, where three new powers made their appearance: Prussia, Austria, and Russia. Russia's Peter the Great attempted to westernize Russia, especially militarily, and built Saint Petersburg, a new capital city, as his window on the West.

But not all European states followed the pattern of absolute monarchy. Especially important were developments in England, where a series of struggles between king and Parliament took place in the seventeenth century. The conflict between the Stuart kings, who were advocates of divine-right monarchy, and Parliament led to civil war and the creation of a republic and then a military dictatorship under Oliver Cromwell. After his death, the Stuart monarchy was restored, but a new conflict led to the overthrow of James II and the establishment of a new order. The landed aristocracy gained power at the expense of the monarchs, thus laying the foundations for a constitutional government in which Parliament provided the focus for the institutions of centralized power. In all the major European states, a growing concern for power and dynamic expansion led to larger armies and greater conflict. War remained an endemic feature of Western civilization.

But the search for order and harmony continued, evident in art and literature. At the same time, religious preoccupations and values were losing ground to secular considerations. The seventeenth century was a period of transition toward the more secular spirit that has characterized modern Western civilization to the present. No stronger foundation for this spirit could be found than in the new view of the universe that was ushered in by the Scientific Revolution of the seventeenth century, and it is to that story that we turn in the next chapter.

CHAPTER TIMELINE

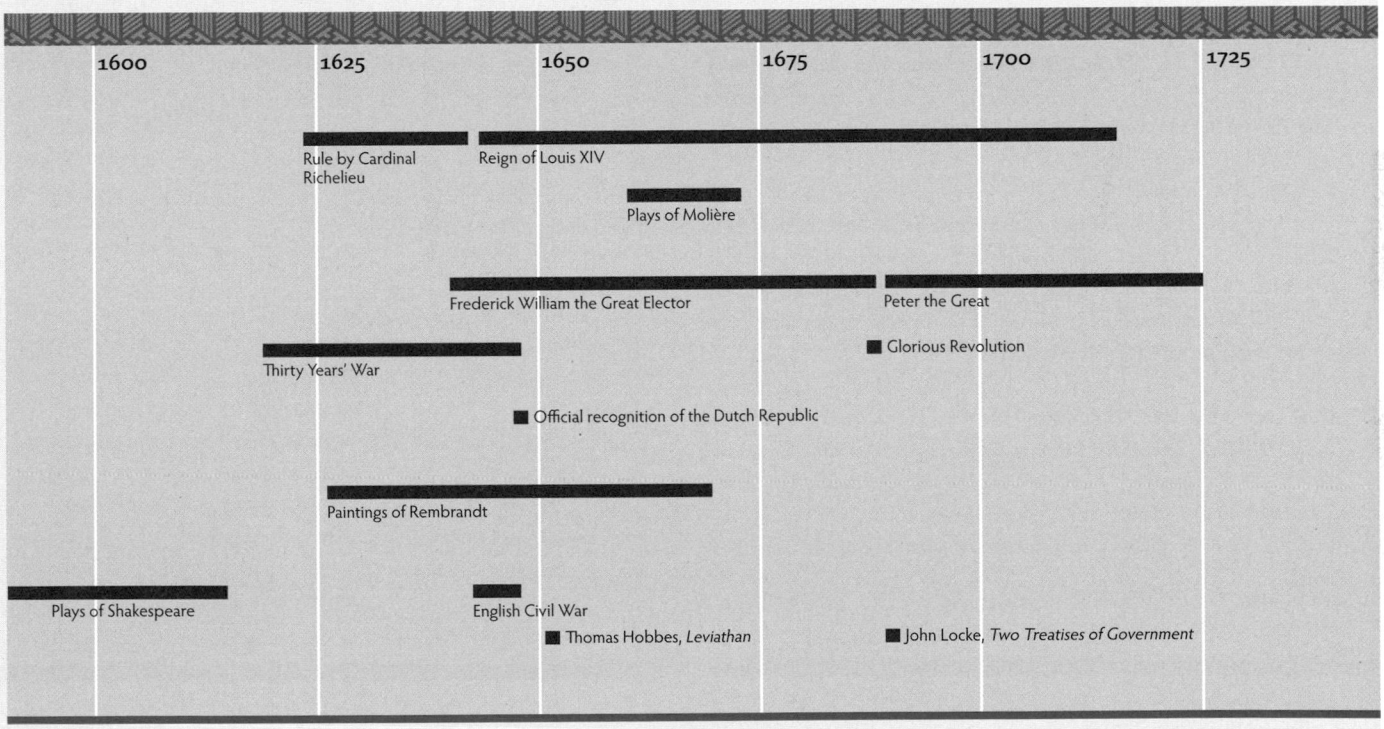

CHAPTER REVIEW

Upon Reflection

Q What does the witchcraft craze tell us about European society in the sixteenth and seventeenth centuries?

Q What did Louis XIV hope to accomplish in his domestic and foreign policies? To what extent did he succeed?

Q What role did the nobility play in England?

Key Terms

absolutism (p. 336)
boyars (p. 340)
procurator (p. 341)
gentry (p. 344)
Mannerism (p. 350)
Baroque (p. 350)

Suggestions for Further Reading

GENERAL WORKS For general works on the seventeenth century, see **T. Munck, *Seventeenth-Century Europe, 1598–1700,*** 2nd ed. (London, 2005); **Q. Deakin, *Expansion, War, and Rebellion, 1598–1661*** (Cambridge, 2000); and **J. Bergin, *Seventeenth-Century Europe, 1598–1715*** (Oxford, 2001).

WITCHCRAFT HYSTERIA The story of the witchcraft frenzy can be examined in **R. Briggs, *Witches and Neighbors: The Social and Cultural Context of European Witchcraft,*** 2nd ed. (Oxford, 2002).

THIRTY YEARS' WAR The fundamental study on the Thirty Years' War is **P. H. Wilson, *The Thirty Years War: Europe's Tragedy*** (Cambridge, Mass., 2009). For a brief study, see **R. Bonney, *The Thirty Years' War, 1618–1648*** (Oxford, 2002).

FRANCE AND SPAIN For a succinct account of seventeenth-century French history, see **R. Briggs, *Early Modern France, 1560–1715,*** 2nd ed. (Oxford, 1998). A solid and very readable biography of Louis XIV is **A. Levi, *Louis XIV*** (New York, 2004). A good general work on seventeenth-century Spanish history is **J. Lynch, *Spain Under the Habsburgs,*** 2nd ed. (New York, 1981).

CENTRAL AND EASTERN EUROPE On the German states, see **P. H. Wilson, *The Holy Roman Empire, 1495–1806*** (New York, 1999). On the creation of Austria, see **P. S. Fichtner, *The Habsburg Monarchy, 1490–1848*** (New York, 2003). On Austria and Prussia, see **P. H. Wilson, *Absolutism in Central Europe*** (New York, 2000).

RUSSIA On Peter the Great, see **P. Bushkovitz, *Peter the Great*** (Oxford, 2001).

ENGLISH REVOLUTIONS Good general works on the period of the English Revolution include **M. A. Kishlansky, *A Monarchy Transformed*** (London, 1996), and **D. Purkiss, *The English Civil War*** (New York, 2006). On Oliver Cromwell, see **P. Gaunt, *Oliver Cromwell*** (Cambridge, Mass., 1996).

UNITED PROVINCES On the United Provinces, **J. Israel, *The Dutch Republic: Its Rise, Greatness, and Fall*** (New York, 1995), is a valuable but lengthy study.

EUROPEAN CULTURE For an introduction to Baroque culture, see **F. C. Marchetti et al., *Baroque, 1600–1770*** (New York, 2005). For a biography of Shakespeare, see **A. L. Rowse, *The Life of Shakespeare*** (New York, 1963).

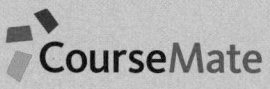

Visit the CourseMate website at www.cengagebrain.com for additional study tools and review materials for this chapter.

CHAPTER 16

Louvre (RF 567), Paris//© Erich Lessing/Art Resource, NY

A nineteenth-century painting of Galileo before the Holy Office in the Vatican in 1633

Toward a New Heaven and a New Earth: The Scientific Revolution and the Emergence of Modern Science

CHAPTER OUTLINE AND FOCUS QUESTIONS

Background to the Scientific Revolution

Q What developments during the Middle Ages and the Renaissance contributed to the Scientific Revolution of the seventeenth century?

Toward a New Heaven: A Revolution in Astronomy

Q What did Copernicus, Kepler, Galileo, and Newton contribute to a new vision of the universe, and how did it differ from the Ptolemaic conception of the universe?

Advances in Medicine and Chemistry

Q What did Vesalius, Harvey, Boyle, and Lavoisier contribute to a scientific view of medicine and chemistry?

Women in the Origins of Modern Science

Q What role did women play in the Scientific Revolution?

Toward a New Earth: Descartes, Rationalism, and a New View of Humankind

Q Why is Descartes considered the "founder of modern rationalism"?

The Spread of Scientific Knowledge

Q How were the ideas of the Scientific Revolution spread, and what impact did they have on society and religion?

CRITICAL THINKING

Q In what ways were the intellectual, political, social, and religious developments of the seventeenth century related?

IN ADDITION TO the political, economic, social, and international crises of the seventeenth century, we need to add an intellectual one. The Scientific Revolution questioned and ultimately challenged conceptions and beliefs about the nature of the external world and reality that had crystallized into a rather strict orthodoxy by the Later Middle Ages. Derived from the works of ancient Greeks and Romans and grounded in Christian thought, the medieval worldview had become formidable. But the breakdown of Christian unity during the Reformation and the subsequent religious wars had created an environment in which Europeans became more comfortable with challenging both the ecclesiastical and the political realms. Should it surprise us that a challenge to intellectual authority soon followed?

The Scientific Revolution taught Europeans to view the universe and their place in it in a new way. The shift from an earth-centered to a sun-centered cosmos had an emotional as well as an intellectual effect on those who understood it. Thus, the Scientific Revolution, popularized in the eighteenth-century Enlightenment, stands as the major force in the transition to the largely secular, rational, and materialistic perspective that has defined the modern Western mentality since its full acceptance in the nineteenth and twentieth centuries.

The transition to a new worldview was far from easy, however. In the seventeenth century, the Italian scientist Galileo Galilei (gal-li-LAY-oh GAL-li-lay), an outspoken advocate of the new worldview, found that his ideas were strongly opposed by the authorities of the Catholic Church. Galileo's position was clear: "I hold the sun to be situated motionless in the center of the revolution of the celestial bodies, while the earth rotates on its axis and revolves about the sun." Moreover, "nothing physical that sense-experience sets before our eyes . . . ought to be called in question (much less condemned) upon the testimony of biblical passages." But the church had a different view, and in 1633, Galileo, now sixty-eight and in ill health, was called before the dreaded Inquisition in Rome. He was kept waiting for two months before he was tried and found guilty of heresy and disobedience. Completely shattered by the experience, he denounced his errors: "With a sincere heart and unfeigned faith I curse and detest the said errors and heresies contrary to the Holy Church." Legend holds that when he left the trial room, Galileo muttered to himself: "And yet it does move!" In any case, Galileo had been silenced, but his writings remained, and they spread through Europe. The Inquisition had failed to stop the new ideas of the Scientific Revolution.

In one sense, the Scientific Revolution was not a revolution. It was not characterized by the explosive change and rapid overthrow of traditional authority that we normally associate with the word *revolution*. The Scientific Revolution did overturn centuries of authority, but only in a gradual and piecemeal fashion. Nevertheless, its results were truly revolutionary. The Scientific Revolution was a key factor in setting Western civilization along its modern secular and material path.

Background to the Scientific Revolution

Focus Question: What developments during the Middle Ages and the Renaissance contributed to the Scientific Revolution of the seventeenth century?

To say that the **Scientific Revolution** brought about a dissolution of the medieval worldview is not to say that the Middle Ages was a period of scientific ignorance. Many educated Europeans took an intense interest in the world around them since it was, after all, "God's handiwork" and therefore an appropriate subject for study. Late medieval scholastic philosophers had advanced mathematical and physical thinking in many ways, but the subjection of these thinkers to a strict theological framework and their unquestioning reliance on a few ancient authorities, especially Aristotle and Galen, limited where they could go. Many "natural philosophers," as medieval scientists were called, preferred refined logical analysis to systematic observations of the natural world. A number of changes and advances in the fifteenth and sixteenth centuries may have played a major role in helping the "natural philosophers" abandon their old views and develop new ones.

Ancient Authors and Renaissance Artists

The Renaissance humanists mastered both Greek and Latin and made available new works of Ptolemy and Archimedes as well as Plato. These writings made it apparent that even the unquestioned authorities of the Middle Ages, Aristotle and Galen, had been contradicted by other thinkers. The desire to discover which school of thought was correct stimulated new scientific work that sometimes led to a complete rejection of the Classical authorities.

Renaissance artists have also been credited with making an impact on scientific study. Their desire to imitate nature led them to rely on a close observation of nature. Their accurate renderings of rocks, plants, animals, and human anatomy established new standards for the study of natural phenomena. At the same time, the "scientific" study of the problems of perspective and correct anatomical proportions led to new insights. "No painter," one Renaissance artist declared, "can paint well without a thorough knowledge of geometry."[1]

Technological Innovations and Mathematics

Technical problems such as accurately calculating the tonnage of ships also stimulated scientific activity because they required careful observation and precise measurements. Then, too, the invention of new instruments and machines, such as the telescope and microscope, often made new scientific discoveries possible. The printing press had an indirect but crucial role in spreading innovative ideas quickly and easily.

Mathematics, so fundamental to the scientific achievements of the sixteenth and seventeenth centuries, was promoted in the Renaissance by the rediscovery of the works of ancient mathematicians and the influence of Plato, who had emphasized the importance of mathematics in explaining the universe. Applauded as the key to navigation, military science, and geography, mathematics was also regarded as the key to understanding the nature of things. According to Leonardo da Vinci, since God eternally geometrizes, nature is inherently mathematical: "Proportion is not only found in numbers and measurements but also in sounds, weights, times, positions, and in whatsoever power there may be."[2] Copernicus, Kepler, Galileo, and Newton were all great mathematicians who believed that the secrets of nature were written in the language of mathematics.

Renaissance Magic

Another factor in the Scientific Revolution may have been magic. Renaissance magic was the preserve of an intellectual elite from all of Europe. By the end of the sixteenth century, Hermetic magic had become fused with alchemical thought into a single intellectual framework. This tradition believed that the world was a living embodiment of divinity. Humans, who it was believed also had that spark of divinity within, could use magic, especially mathematical magic, to understand and dominate the world of nature or employ the powers of nature for beneficial purposes. Was it Hermeticism, then, that inaugurated the shift in consciousness that made the Scientific Revolution possible, since the desire to control and dominate the natural world was a crucial motivating force in the Scientific Revolution? Scholars debate the issue, but histories of the Scientific Revolution frequently overlook the fact that the great names we associate with the revolution in cosmology—Copernicus, Kepler, Galileo, and Newton—all had a serious interest in Hermetic ideas and the fields of astrology and alchemy. The mention of these names also reminds us of one final consideration in the origins of the Scientific Revolution: it resulted largely from the work of a handful of great intellectuals.

Toward a New Heaven: A Revolution in Astronomy

Focus Question: What did Copernicus, Kepler, Galileo, and Newton contribute to a new vision of the universe, and how did it differ from the Ptolemaic conception of the universe?

The cosmological views of the Later Middle Ages had been built on a synthesis of the ideas of Aristotle, Ptolemy (the greatest astronomer of antiquity, who lived in the second century C.E.), and Christian theology. In the resulting Ptolemaic (tahl-uh-MAY-ik) or **geocentric** (earth-centered) **conception**, the universe was seen as a series of concentric spheres with a fixed or motionless earth at its center. Composed of material substance, the earth was imperfect and constantly changing. The spheres that surrounded the earth were made of a crystalline, transparent substance and moved in circular orbits around the earth. Circular movement, according to Aristotle, was the most "perfect" kind of motion and hence appropriate for the "perfect" heavenly bodies thought to consist of a nonmaterial, incorruptible "quintessence." These heavenly bodies, pure orbs of light, were embedded in the moving, concentric spheres, which in 1500 were believed to number ten. Working outward from the earth, the first eight spheres contained the moon, Mercury, Venus, the sun, Mars, Jupiter, Saturn, and the fixed stars. The ninth sphere imparted to the eighth sphere of the fixed stars its motion, and the tenth sphere was frequently described as the prime mover that moved itself and imparted motion to the other spheres. Beyond the tenth sphere was the Empyrean Heaven—the location of God and all the saved souls. This Christianized Ptolemaic universe, then, was finite. It had a fixed outer boundary in harmony with Christian thought and expectations. God and the saved souls were at one end of the universe, and humans were at the center. They had been given power over the earth, but their real purpose was to achieve salvation.

Copernicus

Shortly before his death, Nicolaus Copernicus (nee-koh-LOW-uss kuh-PURR-nuh-kuss) (1473–1543), who had studied mathematics and astronomy first at Krakow in his native Poland and later at the Italian universities of Bologna and Padua, published his famous book *On the Revolutions of the Heavenly Spheres*. Copernicus was not an accomplished observational astronomer and relied for his data on the records of his predecessors. But he was a mathematician who felt that Ptolemy's geocentric system was too complicated and failed to accord with the observed motions of the heavenly bodies (see the box on p. 362). Copernicus hoped that his **heliocentric** (sun-centered) **conception** would offer a more accurate explanation.

Copernicus argued that the universe consisted of eight spheres with the sun motionless at the center and the sphere of the fixed stars at rest in the eighth sphere. The planets revolved around the sun in the order of Mercury, Venus, the earth, Mars, Jupiter, and Saturn. The moon, however, revolved around the earth. Moreover, according to Copernicus, what appeared to be the movement of the sun and the fixed stars around the earth was really explained by the daily rotation of the earth on its axis and the journey of the earth around the sun each year.

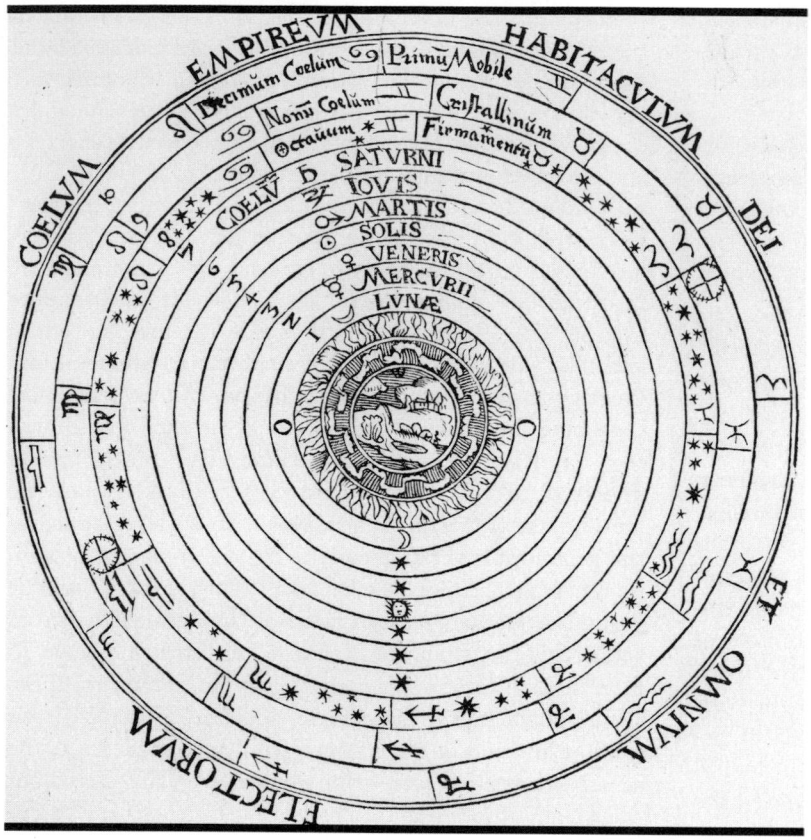

© Image Select/Art Resource, NY

Medieval Conception of the Universe. As this sixteenth-century illustration shows, the medieval cosmological view placed the earth at the center of the universe, surrounded by a series of concentric spheres. The earth was imperfect and constantly changing, whereas the heavenly bodies that surrounded it were perfect and incorruptible. Beyond the tenth and final sphere was heaven, where God and all the saved souls were located. (The circles read, from the center outward: 1. Moon, 2. Mercury, 3. Venus, 4. Sun, 5. Mars, 6. Jupiter, 7. Saturn, 8. Firmament (of the Stars), 9. Crystalline Sphere, 10. Prime Mover; and around the outside, Empyrean Heaven—Home of God and All the Elect, that is, saved souls.)

The heliocentric theory had little immediate impact; most people were not yet ready to accept Copernicus's thinking. But doubts about the Ptolemaic system were growing. The next step in destroying the geocentric conception and supporting the Copernican system was taken by the German scientist Johannes Kepler.

Kepler

The work of Johannes Kepler (1571–1630) illustrates the narrow line that often separated magic and science in the early Scientific Revolution. An avid astrologer, Kepler possessed a keen interest in Hermetic thought and mathematical magic. In a book written in 1596, he elaborated on his theory that the universe was constructed on the basis of geometric figures, such as the pyramid and the cube. Believing that the harmony of the human soul (a divine attribute) was mirrored in the numerical relationships existing between the planets, he focused much of his attention on discovering the "music of the spheres." Kepler was also a brilliant mathematician and astronomer who took a post as imperial mathematician to Emperor Rudolf II. Using the detailed astronomical data compiled by his predecessor, Kepler derived laws of planetary motion that confirmed the heliocentric theory. In his first law, he contradicted Copernicus by showing that the orbits of the planets around the sun were not circular but elliptical, with the sun at one focus of the ellipse rather than at the center

Kepler's work effectively eliminated the idea of uniform circular motion as well as the idea of crystalline spheres revolving in circular orbits. The basic structure of the traditional Ptolemaic system had been disproved, and people had been freed to think in new ways of the paths of planets revolving around the sun. By the end of Kepler's life, the Ptolemaic system was rapidly losing ground to the new ideas. Important questions remained unanswered, however. What were the planets made of? And how could motion in the universe be explained? It was an Italian scientist who achieved the next important breakthrough to a new cosmology by answering the first question.

Galileo

Galileo Galilei (1564–1642) taught mathematics, first at Pisa and later at Padua, one of the most prestigious universities in Europe. Galileo was the first European to make systematic observations of the heavens by means of a telescope, thereby inaugurating a new age in astronomy. He had heard of a Flemish lens grinder who had created a "spyglass" that magnified objects seen at a distance and soon constructed his own. Instead of peering at terrestrial objects, Galileo turned his telescope to the skies and made a remarkable series of discoveries: mountains and craters on the moon, four moons revolving around Jupiter, the phases of Venus, and sunspots. Galileo's observations demolished yet another aspect of the traditional cosmology in that the universe seemed to be composed of a

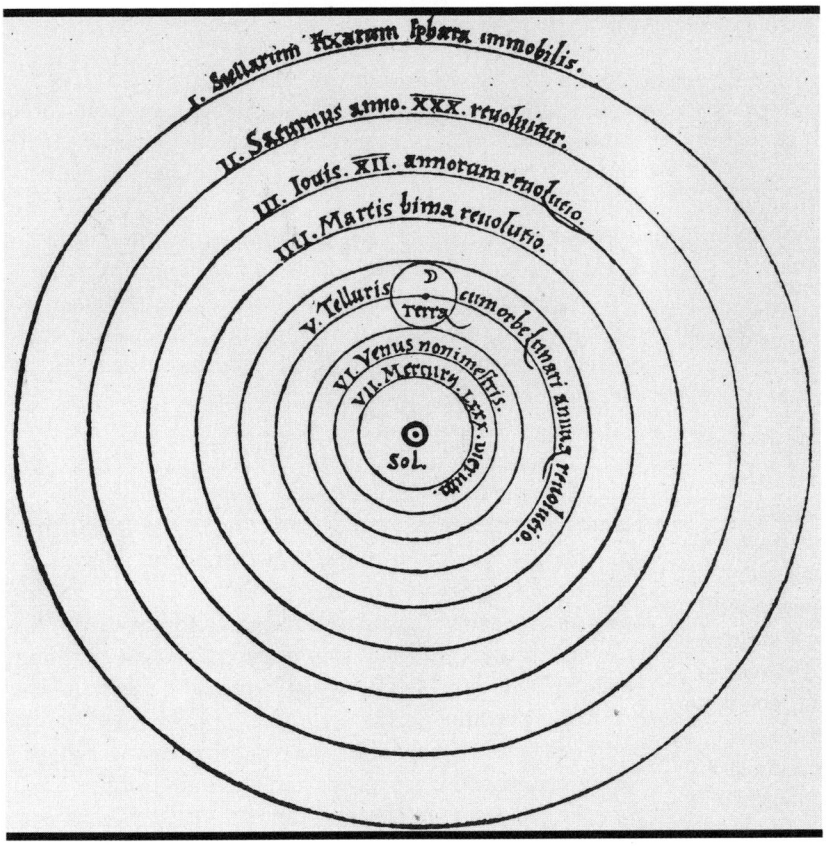

© Image Select/Art Resource, NY

The Copernican System. The Copernican system was presented in *On the Revolutions of the Heavenly Spheres*, published in 1543 shortly before Copernicus's death. As shown in this illustration from the first edition of the book, Copernicus maintained that the sun was at the center of the universe and that the planets, including the earth, revolved around it. Moreover, the earth rotated daily on its axis. (The circles read, from the center outward: 1. Sun; 2. Mercury, orbit of 80 days; 3. Venus; 4. Earth, with the moon, orbit of one year; 5. Mars, orbit of 2 years; 6. Jupiter, orbit of 12 years; 7. Saturn, orbit of 30 years; 8. Immobile Sphere of the Fixed Stars.)

material substance similar to that of earth rather than ethereal or perfect and unchanging substances.

Galileo's revelations, published in *The Starry Messenger* in 1610, stunned his contemporaries and probably did more to make Europeans aware of the new picture of the universe than the mathematical theories of Copernicus and Kepler. But his newfound acclaim brought Galileo under the increasing scrutiny of the Catholic Church. The Roman Inquisition (or Holy Office) of the church condemned Copernicanism and ordered Galileo to reject the Copernican thesis. The Inquisition's report insisted that "the doctrine that the sun was the center of the world and immovable was false and absurd, formally heretical and contrary to Scripture, whereas the doctrine that the earth was not the center of the world but moved, and has further a daily motion, was philosophically false and absurd and theologically at least erroneous."[3] Thus, the church attacked the Copernican system because it threatened not only Scripture but also the entire prevailing conception of the universe (see the box on p. 363). The heavens were no longer a spiritual world but a world of matter. Humans were no longer at the center, and God was no longer in a specific place. All this the church found intolerable. In 1633, Galileo was found guilty of teaching the condemned Copernican system and was forced to recant his "errors."

The condemnation of Galileo by the Inquisition, coming at a time of economic decline, seriously undermined further scientific work in Italy, which had been at the forefront of scientific innovation. Leadership in science now passed to the northern countries, especially England, France, and the Dutch Netherlands. By the 1630s and 1640s, no reasonable astronomer could overlook that Galileo's discoveries, combined with Kepler's mathematical laws, had made nonsense of the Ptolemaic-Aristotelian world system and clearly established the reasonableness of the Copernican model. Nevertheless, the problem of explaining motion in the universe and tying together the ideas of Copernicus, Galileo, and Kepler had not yet been solved. This would be the work of an Englishman who has long been considered the greatest genius of the Scientific Revolution.

Newton

Born in the English village of Woolsthorpe, Isaac Newton (1642–1727) showed little promise until he attended Cambridge University. In 1669, he accepted a chair in mathematics at the university. During an intense period of creativity from 1684 to 1686, he wrote his major work, *Mathematical Principles of Natural Philosophy*, known simply as the *Principia* (prin-SIP-ee-uh), from the first word of its Latin title. In this work, Newton spelled out the mathematical proofs demonstrating his universal law of gravitation. Newton's work was the culmination of the theories of Copernicus, Kepler, and Galileo. Though each had undermined some part of the Ptolemaic-Aristotelian

On the Revolutions of the Heavenly Spheres

Nicolaus Copernicus began a revolution in astronomy when he argued that the sun and not the earth was at the center of the universe. Expecting controversy and scorn, Copernicus hesitated to publish the work in which he put forth his heliocentric theory. He finally relented, however, and managed to see a copy of it just before he died.

Nicolaus Copernicus, *On the Revolutions of the Heavenly Spheres*

For a long time, then, I reflected on this confusion in the astronomical traditions concerning the derivation of the motions of the universe's spheres. I began to be annoyed that the movements of the world machine, created for our sake by the best and most systematic Artisan of all, were not understood with greater certainty by the philosophers, who otherwise examined so precisely the most insignificant trifles of this world. For this reason I undertook the task of rereading the works of all the philosophers which I could obtain to learn whether anyone had ever proposed other motions of the universe's spheres than those expounded by the teachers of astronomy in the schools. And in fact first I found in Cicero that Hicetas supposed the earth to move. Later I also discovered in Plutarch that certain others were of this opinion. I have decided to set his words down here, so that they may be available to everybody:

> Some think that the earth remains at rest. But Philolaus the Pythagorean believes that, like the sun and moon, it revolves around the fire in an oblique circle. Heraclides of Pontus and Ecphantus the Pythagorean make the earth move, not in a progressive motion, but like a wheel in a rotation from the west to east about its own center.

Therefore, having obtained the opportunity from these sources, I too began to consider the mobility of the earth. And even though the idea seemed absurd, nevertheless I know that others before me had been granted the freedom to imagine any circles whatever for the purpose of explaining the heavenly phenomena. Hence I thought that I too would be readily permitted to ascertain whether explanations sounder than those of my predecessors could be found for the revolution of the celestial spheres on the assumption of some motion of the earth.

Having thus assumed the motions which I ascribe to the earth later on in the volume, by long and intense study I finally found that if the motions of the other planets are correlated with the orbiting of the earth, and are computed for the revolution of each planet, not only do their phenomena follow therefrom but also the order and size of all the planets and spheres, and heaven itself is so linked together that in no portion of it can anything be shifted without disrupting the remaining parts and the universe as a whole. . . .

Hence I feel no shame in asserting that this whole region engirdled by the moon, and the center of the earth, traverse this grand circle amid the rest of the planets in an annual revolution around the sun. Near the sun is the center of the universe. Moreover, since the sun remains stationary, whatever appears as a motion of the sun is really due rather to the motion of the earth.

Q What major new ideas did Copernicus discuss in this excerpt? What was the source of these ideas? Why might one say that European astronomers finally destroyed the Middle Ages?

Source: From *The Collected Works* by Copernicus, translated by Edward Rosen. Rev. ed. published 1978 by Palgrave Macmillan. Reproduced with permission of Palgrave Macmillan.

cosmology, no one until Newton had pieced together a coherent synthesis for a new cosmology.

In the first book of the *Principia*, Newton defined the basic concepts of mechanics by elaborating the three laws of motion: every object continues in a state of rest or uniform motion in a straight line unless deflected by a force; the rate of change of motion of an object is proportional to the force acting on it; and to every action there is always an equal and opposite reaction. In book 3, Newton applied his theories of mechanics to the problems of astronomy by demonstrating that these three laws of motion govern the planetary bodies as well as terrestrial objects. Integral to his whole argument was the universal law of gravitation, which explained why the planetary bodies did not go off in straight lines but continued in elliptical orbits about the sun. In mathematical terms,

OPPOSING VIEWPOINTS

A New Heaven? Faith Versus Reason

In 1614, Galileo wrote a letter to the Grand Duchess Christina of Tuscany in which he explained why his theory that the earth rotated around the sun was not necessarily contrary to Scripture. To Galileo, it made little sense for the church to determine the nature of physical reality on the basis of biblical texts that were subject to different interpretations. One year later, Cardinal Robert Bellarmine, a Jesuit and now a member of the church's Inquisition, wrote a letter to one of Galileo's followers that laid out the Roman Catholic Church's approach to the issue of Galileo's theory.

Galileo, Letter to the Grand Duchess Christina, 1614

Some years ago, as Your Serene Highness well knows, I discovered in the heavens many things that had not been seen before our own age. The novelty of these things, as well as some consequences which followed from them in contradiction to the physical notions commonly held among academic philosophers, stirred up against me no small number of professors—as if I had placed these things in the sky with my own hands in order to upset nature and overturn the sciences. . . .

Contrary to the sense of the Bible and the intention of the holy Fathers, if I am not mistaken, they would extend such authorities until even in purely physical matters—where faith is not involved—they would have us altogether abandon reason and the evidence of our senses in favor of some biblical passage, though under the surface meaning of its words this passage may contain a different sense. . . .

The reason produced for condemning the opinion that the earth moves and the sun stands still is that in many places in the Bible one may read that the sun moves and the earth stands still. Since the Bible cannot err, it follows as a necessary consequence that anyone takes an erroneous and heretical position who maintains that the sun is inherently motionless and the earth movable.

With regard to this argument, I think in the first place that it is very pious to say and prudent to affirm that the holy Bible can never speak untruth—whenever its true meaning is understood. But I believe nobody will deny that it is often very abstruse, and may say things which are quite different from what its bare words signify. . . . For the sake of those who deserve to be separated from the herd, it is necessary that wise expositors should produce the true senses of such passages, together with the special reasons for which they were set down in these words. . . .

This being granted, I think that in discussions of physical problems we ought to begin not from the authority of scriptural passages, but from sense-experiences and necessary demonstrations. . . . For that reason it appears that nothing physical which sense-experience sets before our eyes, or which necessary demonstrations prove to us, ought to be called in question (much less condemned) upon the testimony of biblical passages which may have some different meaning beneath their words.

Robert Bellarmine, Letter to Paolo Foscarini, 1615

First, I say that it seems to me that Your Reverence and Galileo did prudently to content yourself with speaking hypothetically, and not absolutely, as I have always believed that Copernicus spoke. For to say that, assuming the earth moves and the sun stands still, all the appearances are saved better than with eccentrics and epicycles, is to speak well; there is no danger in this, and it is sufficient for mathematicians. But to want to affirm that the sun really is fixed in the center of the heavens and only revolves around itself (i.e., turns upon its axis) without traveling from east to west, and that the earth is situated in the third sphere and revolves with great speed around the sun, is a very dangerous thing, not only by irritating all the philosophers and scholastic theologians, but also by injuring our holy faith and rendering the Holy Scriptures false. . . .

Second, I say that, as you know, the Council [of Trent] prohibits expounding the Scriptures contrary to the common agreement of the holy Fathers. And if Your Reverence would read not only the Fathers but also the commentaries of modern writers on Genesis, Psalms, Ecclesiastes and Josue, you would find that all agree in explaining literally (*ad litteram*) that the sun is in the heavens and moves swiftly around the earth, and that the earth is far from the heavens and stands immobile in the

(Continued)

(Opposing Viewpoints continued)

center of the universe. Now consider whether in all prudence the Church could encourage giving to Scripture a sense contrary to the holy Fathers and all the Latin and Greek commentators. . . . Third, I say that if there were a true demonstration that the sun was in the center of the universe and the earth in the third sphere, and that the sun did not travel around the earth but the earth circled the sun, then it would be necessary to proceed with great caution in explaining the passages of Scripture which seemed contrary, and we would rather have to say that we did not understand them than to say that something was false which has been demonstrated. But I do not believe that there is any such demonstration; none has been shown to me.

Q What did Galileo think was the difference between knowledge about the natural world and knowledge about the spiritual world? What did Galileo suggest that his opponents should do before dismissing his ideas? In what ways did Cardinal Bellarmine attempt to refute Galileo's ideas? Why did Galileo's ideas represent a threat to the Catholic Church?

Sources: Galileo, Letter to the Grand Duchess Christina, 1614. From DISCOVERIES AND OPINIONS OF GALILEO by Galileo Galilei, translated by Stillman Drake, copyright © 1957 by Stillman Drake. Used by permission of Doubleday, a division of Random House, Inc. Robert Bellarmine, Letter to Paolo Foscarini, 1615. From *Galileo, Science, and the Church* by Jerome J. Langford (New York: Desclee, 1966).

© National Portrait Gallery, London/The Bridgeman Art Library

Isaac Newton. With a single law, that of universal gravitation, Isaac Newton was able to explain all motion in the universe. His great synthesis of the work of his predecessors created a new picture of the universe, one in which the universe was viewed as a great machine operating according to natural laws. Enoch Seeman painted this portrait of Newton one year before his death.

Newton explained that every object in the universe was attracted to every other object with a force (gravity) that is directly proportional to the product of their masses and inversely proportional to the square of the distances between them.

The implications of Newton's universal law of gravitation were enormous, even though another century would pass before they were widely recognized. Newton had demonstrated that one universal law, mathematically proved, could explain all motion in the universe. At the same time, the Newtonian synthesis created a new cosmology in which the world was seen largely in mechanistic terms. The universe was one huge, regulated, and uniform machine that operated according to natural laws in absolute time, space, and motion. Although Newton believed that God was "everywhere present" and acted as the force that moved all bodies on the basis of the laws he had discovered, later generations dropped his spiritual assumptions. Newton's **world-machine**, conceived as operating absolutely in space, time, and motion, dominated the modern worldview until the twentieth century, when the Einsteinian revolution, based on the concept of relativity, superseded the Newtonian mechanistic concept.

Newton's ideas were soon accepted in England but were resisted on the Continent, and it took much of the eighteenth century before they were generally accepted everywhere in Europe. They were also reinforced by developments in other fields, especially medicine.

Advances in Medicine and Chemistry

Focus Question: What did Vesalius, Harvey, Boyle, and Lavoisier contribute to a scientific view of medicine and chemistry?

Although the Scientific Revolution of the sixteenth and seventeenth centuries is associated primarily with the dramatic changes in astronomy and mechanics that precipitated a new perception of the universe, a third field that had been dominated by Greek thought in the Later Middle Ages, that of medicine, also experienced a transformation. Late medieval medicine was dominated by the teachings of the Greek physician Galen, who had lived in the second century C.E.

Galen's influence on the medieval medical world was pervasive in anatomy, physiology, and disease. Galen had relied on animal, rather than human, dissection to arrive at a picture of human anatomy that was quite inaccurate in many instances. Even when Europeans began to practice human dissection in the Later Middle Ages, instruction in anatomy still relied on Galen. While a professor read a text of Galen, an assistant dissected a cadaver for illustrative purposes. Physiology, or the functioning of the body, was also dominated by Galenic hypotheses, including the belief that there were two separate blood systems. One controlled muscular activities and contained bright red blood moving upward and downward through the arteries; the other governed the digestive functions and contained dark red blood that ebbed and flowed in the veins.

Vesalius

Two major figures are associated with the changes in medicine in the sixteenth and seventeenth centuries: Andreas Vesalius and William Harvey. The new anatomy of the sixteenth century was the work of the Belgian Andreas Vesalius (ahn-DRAY-ahs vi-SAY-lee-uss) (1514–1564). After receiving a doctorate in medicine at the University of Padua in 1536, Vesalius accepted a position there as professor of surgery. In 1543, he published his masterpiece, *On the Fabric of the Human Body*. This book was based on his Paduan lectures, in which he deviated from traditional practice by personally dissecting a body to illustrate what he was discussing. Vesalius's anatomical treatise presented a careful examination of the individual organs and general structure of the human body. The book would not have been feasible without the artistic advances of the Renaissance and the technical developments in the art of printing. Together, they made possible the creation of illustrations superior to any hitherto produced.

Vesalius's hands-on approach to teaching anatomy enabled him to rectify some of Galen's most glaring errors. He did not hesitate, for example, to correct Galen's assertion that the great blood vessels originated from the liver since his own observations made it apparent that they came from the heart. Nevertheless, Vesalius still clung to a number of Galen's erroneous assertions, including the Greek physician's ideas on the ebb and flow of two kinds of blood in the veins and arteries. It was not until William Harvey's work on the circulation of the blood nearly a century later that this Galenic misperception was corrected.

Harvey

The Englishman William Harvey (1578–1657) attended Cambridge University and later Padua, where he earned a doctorate in medicine in 1602. His reputation rests on his book *On the Motion of the Heart and Blood*, published in 1628. Although questions had been raised in the sixteenth century about Galen's physiological principles, no major challenge to his system had emerged. Harvey's work, based on meticulous observations and experiments, led him to demolish the ancient Greek's contentions. Harvey demonstrated that the heart was the beginning point of the circulation of blood in the body, that the same blood flows in both veins and arteries, and that the blood makes a complete circuit as it passes through the body. Although Harvey's work dealt a severe blow to Galen's theories, his ideas did not begin to achieve general recognition until the 1660s, when the capillaries, which explained how the blood passed from the arteries to the veins, were discovered. Harvey's theory of the circulation of the blood laid the foundation for modern physiology.

Chemistry

In the seventeenth and eighteenth centuries, a science of chemistry emerged. Robert Boyle (1627–1691) was one of the first scientists to conduct controlled experiments. His pioneering work on the properties of gases led to Boyle's law, which states that the volume of a gas varies with the pressure exerted on it. Boyle also rejected the medieval belief that all matter consisted of the same components in favor of the view that matter is composed of atoms, which he called "little particles of all shapes and sizes" and which would later be known as the chemical elements.

In the eighteenth century, the Frenchman Antoine Lavoisier (AHN-twahn lah-vwah-ZYAY) (1743–1794) invented a system of naming the chemical elements, much of which is still used today. In helping to show that water is a compound of oxygen and hydrogen, he demonstrated the fundamental rules of chemical combination. He is regarded by many as the founder of modern chemistry. Lavoisier's wife, Marie-Anne, was her husband's scientific collaborator. She learned English in order to translate the work of British chemists for her husband and made engravings to illustrate his scientific experiments. Marie-Anne Lavoisier is a reminder that women too played a role in the Scientific Revolution.

Women in the Origins of Modern Science

FOCUS QUESTION: What role did women play in the Scientific Revolution?

During the Middle Ages, except for members of religious orders, women who sought a life of learning were severely hampered by the traditional attitude that a woman's proper role was as a daughter, wife, and mother. But in the late fourteenth and early fifteenth centuries, new opportunities for elite women emerged as enthusiasm for the new secular learning called humanism led Europe's privileged and learned men to encourage women to read and study Classical and Christian texts. The ideal of a humanist education for some of the daughters of Europe's elite persisted into the seventeenth century, but only for some privileged women.

Margaret Cavendish

Much as they were drawn to humanism, women were also attracted to the Scientific Revolution. Unlike girls educated formally in humanist schools, women interested in science had to obtain a largely informal education. European nobles had the leisure and resources that gave them easy access to the world of learning. This door was also open to noblewomen, who could participate in the informal scientific networks of their fathers and brothers.

One of the most prominent female scientists of the seventeenth century, Margaret Cavendish (KAV-un-dish) (1623–1673) came from an aristocratic background. Cavendish was not a popularizer of science for women but a participant in the crucial scientific debates of her time. Despite her achievements, however, she was excluded from membership in the Royal Society (see "The Spread of Scientific Knowledge" later in this chapter), although she was once allowed to attend a meeting. She wrote a number of works on scientific matters, including *Observations upon Experimental Philosophy* and *Grounds of Natural Philosophy*. In these works, she did not hesitate to attack what she considered the defects of the rationalist and empiricist approaches to scientific knowledge and was especially critical of the growing belief that humans through science were the masters of nature: "We have no power at all over natural causes and effects . . . for man is but a small part. . . . His powers are but particular actions of Nature, and he cannot have a supreme and absolute power."[4]

As an aristocrat, Cavendish, the duchess of Newcastle, was a good example of the women in France and England

© Bettmann/CORBIS

Margaret Cavendish. Shown in this portrait is Margaret Cavendish, the duchess of Newcastle. Her husband, who was thirty years her senior, encouraged her to pursue her literary interests. In addition to scientific works, she wrote plays, an autobiography, and a biography of her husband titled *The Life of the Thrice Noble, High and Puissant Prince William Cavendish, Duke, Marquess and Earl of Newcastle.* The autobiography and biography led one male literary critic to call her "a mad, conceited and ridiculous woman."

CHRONOLOGY Important Works of the Scientific Revolution

Copernicus, *On the Revolutions of the Heavenly Spheres*	1543
Vesalius, *On the Fabric of the Human Body*	1543
Galileo, *The Starry Messenger*	1610
Harvey, *On the Motion of the Heart and Blood*	1628
Cavendish, *Grounds of Natural Philosophy*	1668
Newton, *Principia*	1687

who worked in science. Women interested in science who lived in Germany came from a different background. There the tradition of female participation in craft production enabled some women to become involved in observational science, especially astronomy. Between 1650 and 1710, one in every seven German astronomers was a woman.

Maria Winkelmann

The most famous of the female astronomers in Germany was Maria Winkelmann (VINK-ul-mahn) (1670–1720). She was educated by her father and uncle and received advanced training from a local self-taught astronomer. When she married Gottfried Kirch, Germany's foremost astronomer, she became his assistant at the astronomical observatory operated in Berlin by the Academy of Science. She made some original contributions, including a hitherto undiscovered comet, as her husband related:

> Early in the morning (about 2:00 A.M.) the sky was clear and starry. Some nights before, I had observed a variable star, and my wife (as I slept) wanted to find and see it for herself. In so doing, she found a comet in the sky. At which time she woke me, and I found that it was indeed a comet. . . . I was surprised that I had not seen it the night before.[5]

When her husband died in 1710, she applied for a position as assistant astronomer for which she was highly qualified. As a woman—with no university degree—she was denied the post by the Berlin Academy, which feared that it would establish a precedent if it hired a woman ("mouths would gape").

Winkelmann's difficulties with the Berlin Academy reflect the obstacles women faced in being accepted in scientific work, which was considered a male preserve. Although no formal statutes excluded women from membership in the new scientific societies, no woman was invited to join either the Royal Society of England or the French Academy of Sciences until the twentieth century. All of these women scientists were exceptional, since a life devoted to any kind of scholarship was still viewed as being at odds with the domestic duties women were expected to perform.

Debates on the Nature of Women

The nature and value of women had been the subject of an ongoing, centuries-long debate. Male opinions in the debate were largely a carryover from medieval times and were not favorable. Women were portrayed as inherently base, prone to vice, easily swayed, and "sexually insatiable." Hence, men needed to control them. Learned women were viewed as having overcome female liabilities to become like men. One man in praise of a woman scholar remarked that her writings were so good that you "would hardly believe they were done by a woman at all."

In the seventeenth century, women joined this debate by arguing against these male images of women. They argued that women also had rational minds and could grow from education. Further, since most women were pious, chaste, and temperate, there was no need for male authority over them. These female defenders of women emphasized education as the key to women's ability to move into the world. How, then, did the Scientific Revolution affect this debate over the nature of women? As this was an era of intellectual revolution in which traditional authorities were being overthrown, we might expect significant change in men's views of women. But by and large, instead of becoming an instrument for liberation, science was used to find new support for the old, stereotypical views about a woman's "true place" in the scheme of things.

An important project in the new anatomy of the sixteenth and seventeenth centuries was the attempt to illustrate the human body and skeleton. For Vesalius, the physical differences between males and females were limited to external bodily form (the outlines of the body) and the sexual organs. Vesalius saw no differences in male and female skeletons and portrayed them as being the same. It was not until the eighteenth century, in fact, that a new anatomy finally prevailed. Drawings of female skeletons between 1730 and 1790 varied, but females tended to have a larger pelvic area, and in some instances, female skulls were portrayed as smaller than those of males. Eighteenth-century studies on the anatomy and physiology of sexual differences provided "scientific evidence" to reaffirm the traditional inferiority of women. The larger pelvic area "proved" that women were meant to be childbearers, and men's larger skulls "demonstrated" the superiority of the male mind. Male-dominated science had been used to "prove" male social dominance.

Overall, the Scientific Revolution reaffirmed traditional ideas about women. Male scientists used the new science to spread the view that women were inferior by nature, subordinate to men, and suited by nature to play a domestic role as nurturing mothers (see the box on p. 368). The widespread distribution of books—written primarily by men, of course—ensured the continuation of these ideas. Jean de La Bruyère (ZHAHNH du lah broo-YARE), the seventeenth-century French moralist, was typical when he remarked that an educated woman was like a collector's item "which one shows to the curious, but which has no use at all, any more than a carousel horse."[6]

The "Natural" Inferiority of Women

Despite the shattering of old views and the emergence of a new worldview in the Scientific Revolution of the seventeenth century, attitudes toward women remained tied to traditional perspectives. In this selection, the philosopher Benedict de Spinoza argues for the "natural" inferiority of women to men.

Benedict de Spinoza, *A Political Treatise*

But, perhaps, someone will ask, whether women are under men's authority by nature or institution. For if it has been by mere institution, then we had no reason compelling us to exclude women from government. But if we consult experience itself, we shall find that the origin of it is in their weakness. For there has never been a case of men and women reigning together, but wherever on the earth men are found, there we see that men rule, and women are ruled, and that on this plan, both sexes live in harmony. But on the other hand, the Amazons, who are reported to have held rule of old, did not suffer men to stop in their country, but reared only their female children, killing males to whom they gave birth. But if by nature women were equal to men, and were equally distinguished by force of character and ability, in which human power and therefore human right chiefly consist; surely among nations so many and different some would be found, where both sexes rule alike, and others, where men are ruled by women, and so brought up, that they can make less use of their abilities. And since this is nowhere the case, one may assert with perfect propriety, that women have not by nature equal right with men: but that they necessarily give way to men, and that thus it cannot happen, that both sexes should rule alike, much less that men should be ruled by women. But if we further reflect upon human passions, how men, in fact, generally love women merely from the passion of lust, and esteem their cleverness and wisdom in proportion to the excellence of their beauty, and also how very ill-disposed men are to suffer the women they love to show any sort of favor to others, and other facts of this kind, we shall easily see that men and women cannot rule alike without greater hurt to peace.

Q What arguments did Spinoza use to support the idea of female inferiority? What was the effect of this line of reasoning on the roles women could play?

Source: From *A Political Treatise*, Benedict de Spinoza, copyright 1895 by George Routledge & Sons.

Toward a New Earth: Descartes, Rationalism, and a New View of Humankind

Q **Focus Question:** Why is Descartes considered the "founder of modern rationalism"?

The fundamentally new conception of the universe contained in the cosmological revolution of the sixteenth and seventeenth centuries inevitably had an impact on the Western view of humankind. Nowhere is this more evident than in the work of the Frenchman René Descartes (ruh-NAY day-KART) (1596–1650), an extremely important figure in Western history. Descartes began by reflecting the doubt and uncertainty that seemed pervasive in the confusion of the seventeenth century and ended with a philosophy that dominated Western thought until the twentieth century.

The starting point for Descartes's new system was doubt, as he explained at the beginning of his most famous work, *Discourse on Method*, written in 1637:

> From my childhood I have been familiar with letters; and as I was given to believe that by their means a clear and assured knowledge can be acquired of all that is useful in life, I was extremely eager for instruction in them. As soon, however, as I had completed the course of study, at the close of which it is customary to be admitted into the order of the learned, I entirely changed my opinion. For I found myself entangled in so many doubts and errors that, as it seemed to me, the endeavor to instruct myself had served only to disclose to me more and more of my ignorance.[7]

Descartes decided to set aside all that he had learned and begin again. One fact seemed beyond doubt—his own existence:

> But I immediately became aware that while I was thus disposed to think that all was false, it was absolutely necessary

> that I who thus thought should be something; and noting that this truth *I think, therefore I am*, was so steadfast and so assured that the suppositions of the skeptics, to whatever extreme they might all be carried, could not avail to shake it, I concluded that I might without scruple accept it as being the first principle of the philosophy I was seeking.[8]

With this emphasis on the mind, Descartes asserted that he would accept only things that his reason said were true.

From his first postulate, Descartes deduced an additional principle, the separation of mind and matter. Descartes argued that since "the mind cannot be doubted but the body and material world can, the two must be radically different." From this came an absolute duality between mind and matter that has been called **Cartesian dualism**. Using mind or human reason, the path to certain knowledge, and its best instrument, mathematics, humans can understand the material world because it is pure mechanism, a machine that is governed by its own physical laws because it was created by God—the great geometrician.

Louvre (Inv.1317 photo: G. Blot/C. Jean), Paris//© Réunion des Musées Nationaux/Art Resource, NY

René Descartes. René Descartes was one of the primary figures in the Scientific Revolution. Claiming to use reason as his sole guide to truth, Descartes posited a sharp distinction between mind and matter. He is shown here in a portrait by Frans Hals, one of the painters of the Dutch golden age who was famous for his portraits, especially that of Descartes.

Descartes's conclusions about the nature of the universe and human beings had important implications. His separation of mind and matter allowed scientists to view matter as dead or inert, as something that was totally separate from themselves and could be investigated independently by reason. The split between mind and body led Westerners to equate their identity with mind and reason rather than with the whole organism. Descartes has rightly been called the father of modern **rationalism**. The radical Cartesian split between mind and matter, and between mind and body, had devastating implications not only for traditional religious views of the universe but also for how Westerners viewed themselves.

The Spread of Scientific Knowledge

Focus Question: How were the ideas of the Scientific Revolution spread, and what impact did they have on society and religion?

During the seventeenth century, scientific learning and investigation began to increase dramatically. Major universities in Europe established new chairs of science, especially in medicine. Royal and princely patronage of individual scientists became an international phenomenon. Of greater importance to the work of science, however, was the creation of a scientific method and new learned societies that enabled the new scientists to communicate their ideas to each other and to disseminate them to a wider, literate public.

The Scientific Method

In the course of the Scientific Revolution, attention was paid to the problem of establishing the proper means to examine and understand the physical realm. The development of a **scientific method** was crucial to the evolution of science in the modern world. Curiously enough, it was an Englishman with few scientific credentials who attempted to put forth a new method of acquiring knowledge that made an impact on English scientists in the seventeenth century and other European scientists in the eighteenth century. Francis Bacon (1561–1626), a lawyer and lord chancellor, rejected Copernicus and Kepler and misunderstood Galileo. And yet in his unfinished work *The Great Instauration (The Great Restoration)*, he called for his contemporaries "to commence a total reconstruction of sciences, arts, and all human knowledge, raised upon the proper foundations." Bacon did not doubt humans' ability to know the natural world, but he believed that they had proceeded incorrectly: "The entire fabric of human reason which we employ in the inquisition of nature is badly put together and built up, and like some magnificent structure without foundation."[9]

Bacon's new foundation—a correct scientific method—was to be built on inductive principles. Rather than beginning with assumed first principles from which logical conclusions could be deduced, he urged scientists to proceed from the particular to the general. From carefully organized experiments and systematic, thorough observations, correct generalizations could be developed. Bacon was clear about what he believed his method could accomplish. His concern was for practical results rather than for pure science. He stated that "the true and lawful goal of the sciences is none other than this: that human life be endowed with new discoveries and power." He wanted science to contribute to the "mechanical arts" by creating devices that would benefit industry, agriculture, and trade. Bacon was prophetic when he said that "I am laboring to lay the foundation, not of any sect or doctrine, but of human utility and power." And how would this "human power" be used? To "conquer nature in action."[10] The control and domination of nature became a central proposition of modern science and the technology that accompanied it. Only in the twentieth century did some scientists ask whether this assumption might not be at the heart of the earth's ecological crisis.

René Descartes proposed a different approach to scientific methodology by emphasizing deduction and mathematical logic. Descartes believed that one could start with self-evident truths, comparable to geometrical axioms, and deduce more complex conclusions. His emphasis on deduction and mathematical order complemented Bacon's stress on experiment and induction. It was Isaac Newton who synthesized the two approaches into a single scientific methodology by uniting Bacon's **empiricism** with Descartes's rationalism. This scientific method began with systematic observations and experiments, which were used to arrive at general concepts. New deductions derived from these general concepts could then be tested and verified by precise experiments.

The Scientific Societies

The first of the scientific societies appeared in Italy, but those of England and France were ultimately of more significance. The English Royal Society evolved out of informal gatherings of scientists at London and Oxford in the 1640s, although it did not receive a formal charter from King Charles II until 1662. The French Royal Academy of Sciences also arose out of informal scientific meetings in Paris during the 1650s. In 1666, Louis XIV formally recognized the group. The French Academy received abundant state support and remained under government control; its members were appointed and paid salaries by the state. In contrast, the Royal Society of England received little government encouragement, and its fellows simply co-opted new members.

Early on, both the English and French scientific societies formally emphasized the practical value of scientific

Chateaux de Versailles et de Trianon, Versailles//© Réunion des Musées Nationaux (Gérard Blot)/Art Resource, NY

Louis XIV and Colbert Visit the Academy of Sciences. In the seventeenth century, individual scientists received royal and princely patronage, and a number of learned societies were established. In France, Louis XIV, urged on by his minister Colbert, gave formal recognition to the French Academy in 1666. In this painting by Henri Testelin, Louis XIV is shown seated, surrounded by Colbert and members of the French Royal Academy of Sciences.

research. The Royal Society created a committee to investigate technological improvements for industry; the French Academy collected tools and machines. This concern with the practical benefits of science proved short-lived, however, as both societies came to focus their primary interest on theoretical work in mechanics and astronomy. The construction of observatories at Paris in 1667 and at Greenwich, England, in 1675 greatly facilitated research in astronomy by both groups. Although both the English and French societies made useful contributions to scientific knowledge in the second half of the seventeenth century, their true significance was that they demonstrated the benefits of science proceeding as a cooperative venture.

Science and Society

The importance of science in the history of modern Western civilization is usually taken for granted. But how did science become such an integral part of Western culture in the seventeenth and early eighteenth centuries? Recent research has stressed that one cannot simply assert that people perceived that science was a rationally superior system. An important social factor, however, might help explain the relatively rapid acceptance of the new science.

It has been argued that the literate mercantile and propertied elites of Europe were attracted to the new science because it offered new ways to exploit resources for profit. Some of the early scientists made it easier for these groups to accept the new ideas by showing how they could be applied directly to specific industrial and technological needs. Galileo, for example, consciously sought an alliance between science and the material interests of the educated elite when he assured his listeners that the science of mechanics would be quite useful "when it becomes necessary to build bridges or other structures over water, something occurring mainly in affairs of great importance." At the same time, Galileo stressed that science was fit for the "minds of the wise" and not for "the shallow minds of the common people." This made science part of the high culture of Europe's wealthy elites at a time when that culture was being increasingly separated from the popular culture of the lower classes (see Chapter 17).

At the same time, princes and kings who were providing patronage for scientists were doing so not only for prestige but also for practical reasons, especially the military applications of the mathematical sciences. The use of gunpowder, for example, gave new importance to ballistics and metallurgy. Rulers, especially absolute ones, were also concerned about matters of belief in their realms and recognized the need to control and manage the scientific body of knowledge, as occurred with the French Academy. In appointing its members and paying their salaries, Louis XIV was also ensuring that the scientists and their work would be under his control.

Science and Religion

In Galileo's struggle with the inquisitorial Holy Office of the Catholic Church, we see the beginning of the conflict between science and religion that has marked the history of modern Western civilization. Since time immemorial, theology had seemed to be the queen of the sciences. It was natural that the churches would continue to believe that religion was the final measure of all things. The emerging scientists, however, tried to draw lines between the knowledge of religion and the knowledge of "natural philosophy" or nature. Galileo had clearly felt that it was unnecessary to pit science against religion when he wrote:

> In discussions of physical problems we ought to begin not from the authority of scriptural passages, but from sense-experiences and necessary demonstrations; for the holy Bible and the phenomena of nature proceed alike from the divine word, the former as the dictate of the Holy Ghost and the latter as the observant executrix of God's commands. It is necessary for the Bible, in order to be accommodated to the understanding of every man, to speak many things which appear to differ from the absolute truth so far as the bare meaning of the words is concerned. But Nature, on the other hand, is inexorable and immutable; she never transgresses the laws imposed upon her, or cares a whit whether her abstruse reasons and methods of operation are understandable to men.[11]

To Galileo, it made little sense for the church to determine the nature of physical reality on the basis of biblical texts that were subject to radically divergent interpretations. The church, however, decided otherwise in Galileo's case and lent its great authority to one scientific theory, the Ptolemaic-Aristotelian cosmology, no doubt because it fit so well with its own philosophical views of reality. But the church's decision had tremendous consequences. For educated individuals, it established a dichotomy between scientific investigations and religious beliefs. As the scientific beliefs triumphed, it became almost inevitable that religious beliefs would suffer, leading to a growing secularization in European intellectual life. Many seventeenth-century intellectuals were both religious and scientific and believed that the implications of this split would be tragic. Some believed that the split was largely unnecessary, while others felt the need to combine God, humans, and a mechanistic universe into a new philosophical synthesis.

PASCAL Blaise Pascal (BLEZ pass-KAHL) (1623–1662) was a Frenchman who sought to keep science and religion united. An accomplished scientist and a brilliant mathematician,

Pascal: "What Is a Man in the Infinite?"

Perhaps no intellectual in the seventeenth century gave greater expression to the uncertainties generated by the cosmological revolution than Blaise Pascal, himself a scientist. Pascal's mystical vision of God's presence caused him to pursue religious truths with a passion. His work, the *Pensées*, consisted of notes for a larger, unfinished work justifying the Christian religion. In this selection, Pascal presents his musings on the human place in an infinite world.

Blaise Pascal, *Pensées*

Let man then contemplate the whole of nature in her full and exalted majesty. Let him turn his eyes from the lowly objects which surround him. Let him gaze on that brilliant light set like an eternal lamp to illumine the Universe; let the earth seem to him a dot compared with the vast orbit described by the sun, and let him wonder at the fact that this vast orbit itself is no more than a very small dot compared with that described by the stars in their revolutions around the firmament. But if our vision stops here, let the imagination pass on; it will exhaust its powers of thinking long before nature ceases to supply it with material for thought. All this visible world is no more than an imperceptible speck in nature's ample bosom. No idea approaches it. We may extend our conceptions beyond all imaginable space; yet produce only atoms in comparison with the reality of things. It is an infinite sphere, the center of which is everywhere, the circumference nowhere. In short, it is the greatest perceptible mark of God's almighty power that our imagination should lose itself in that thought.

Returning to himself, let man consider what he is compared with all existence; let him think of himself as lost in his remote corner of nature; and from this little dungeon in which he finds himself lodged—I mean the Universe—let him learn to set a true value on the earth, its kingdoms, and cities, and upon himself. What is a man in the infinite? . . .

For, after all, what is a man in nature? A nothing in comparison with the infinite, an absolute in comparison with nothing, a central point between nothing and all. Infinitely far from understanding these extremes, the end of things and their beginning are hopelessly hidden from him in an impenetrable secret. He is equally incapable of seeing the nothingness from which he came, and the infinite in which he is engulfed. What else then will he perceive but some appearance of the middle of things, in an eternal despair of knowing either their principle or their purpose? All things emerge from nothing and are borne onward to infinity. Who can follow this marvelous process? The Author of these wonders understands them. None but He can.

Q Why did Pascal question whether human beings could achieve scientific certainty? What is the significance of Pascal's thoughts for modern science?

Source: From PENSÉES by Blaise Pascal, translated with an introduction by A. J. Krailsheimer (Penguin Classics, 1966). Copyright © A. J. Krailsheimer, 1966. Reproduced by permission of Penguin Books Ltd.

Pascal excelled at both the practical, by inventing a calculating machine, and the abstract, by devising a theory of chance or probability and doing work on conic sections. After a profound mystical vision on the night of November 23, 1654, which assured him that God cared for the human soul, he devoted the rest of his life to religious matters. He planned to write an "apology for the Christian religion" but died before he could do so. He did leave a set of notes for the larger work, however, which in published form became known as the *Pensées* (pahn-SAY) (*Thoughts*).

In the *Pensées,* Pascal tried to convert rationalists to Christianity by appealing to both their reason and their emotions. Humans were, he argued, frail creatures, often deceived by their senses, misled by reason, and battered by their emotions. And yet they were beings whose very nature involved thinking: "Man is but a reed, the weakest in nature; but he is a thinking reed."[12]

Pascal was determined to show that the Christian religion was not contrary to reason: "If we violate the principles of reason, our religion will be absurd, and it will be laughed at."[13] To a Christian, a human being was both fallen and at the same time God's special creation. But it was not necessary to emphasize one at the expense of the other—to view humans as only rational or only hopeless. Pascal even had an answer for skeptics in his famous wager: God is a reasonable bet; it is worthwhile to assume that God exists. If he does, then we win all; if he does not, we lose nothing. Despite his own background as a scientist and mathematician, Pascal refused to rely on the scientist's world of order and rationality to attract people to God: "If we submit everything to reason, there will be no mystery and no supernatural element in our religion." In the new cosmology of the seventeenth century, "finite man," Pascal believed, was lost in the new infinite world, a realization that frightened him: "The eternal silence of those infinite spaces strikes me with terror" (see the box on p. 372).

For Pascal, then, the world of nature could never reveal God: "Because they have failed to contemplate these infinites, men have rashly plunged into the examination of nature, as though they bore some proportion to her. . . . Their assumption is as infinite as their object." A Christian could only rely on a God who through Jesus cared for human beings. In the final analysis, after providing reasonable arguments for Christianity, Pascal came to rest on faith. Reason, he believed, could take people only so far: "The heart has its reasons of which the reason knows nothing." As a Christian, faith was the final step: "The heart feels God, not the reason. This is what constitutes faith: God experienced by the heart, not by the reason."[14]

CHAPTER SUMMARY

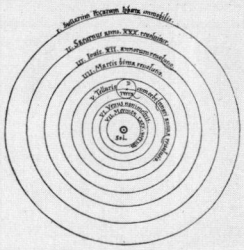

The Scientific Revolution represents a major turning point in modern Western civilization. In the Scientific Revolution, the Western world overthrew the medieval, Ptolemaic-Aristotelian worldview and geocentric universe and arrived at a new conception of the universe: the sun at the center, the planets as material bodies revolving around the sun in elliptical orbits, and an infinite rather than finite world. This new conception of the heavens was the work of a number of brilliant individuals: Nicolaus Copernicus, who theorized a heliocentric or sun-centered universe; Johannes Kepler, who discovered that planetary orbits were elliptical; Galileo Galilei, who, by using a telescope and observing the moon and sunspots, discovered that the universe seemed to be composed of material substance; and Isaac Newton, who tied together all of these ideas with his universal law of gravitation. The contributions of each individual built on the contributions of the others, thus establishing one of the basic principles of the new science—cooperation in the pursuit of new knowledge.

With the changes in the conception of "heaven" came changes in the conception of "earth." The work of Bacon and Descartes left Europeans with the separation of mind and matter and the belief that by using only reason they could in fact understand and dominate the world of nature. The development of a scientific methodology furthered the work of the scientists, and the creation of scientific societies and learned journals spread its results. The Scientific Revolution was more than merely intellectual theories. It also appealed to nonscientific elites because of its practical implications for economic progress and for maintaining the social order, including the waging of war.

Although traditional churches stubbornly resisted the new ideas and a few intellectuals pointed to some inherent flaws, nothing was able to halt the replacement of the traditional ways of thinking by new ways of thinking that created a more fundamental break with the past than that represented by the breakup of Christianity in the Reformation.

The Scientific Revolution forced Europeans to change their conception of themselves. At first, some were appalled and even frightened by its implications. Formerly, humans on earth had viewed themselves as being at the center of the universe. Now the earth was only a tiny planet revolving around a sun that was itself only a speck in a boundless universe. Most people remained optimistic despite the apparent blow to human dignity. After all, had Newton not demonstrated that the universe was a great machine governed by natural laws? Newton had found one—the universal law of gravitation. Could others not find other laws? Were there not natural laws governing every aspect of human endeavor that could be found by the new scientific method? Thus, as we shall see in the next chapter, the Scientific Revolution leads us logically to the Enlightenment in the eighteenth century.

CHAPTER TIMELINE

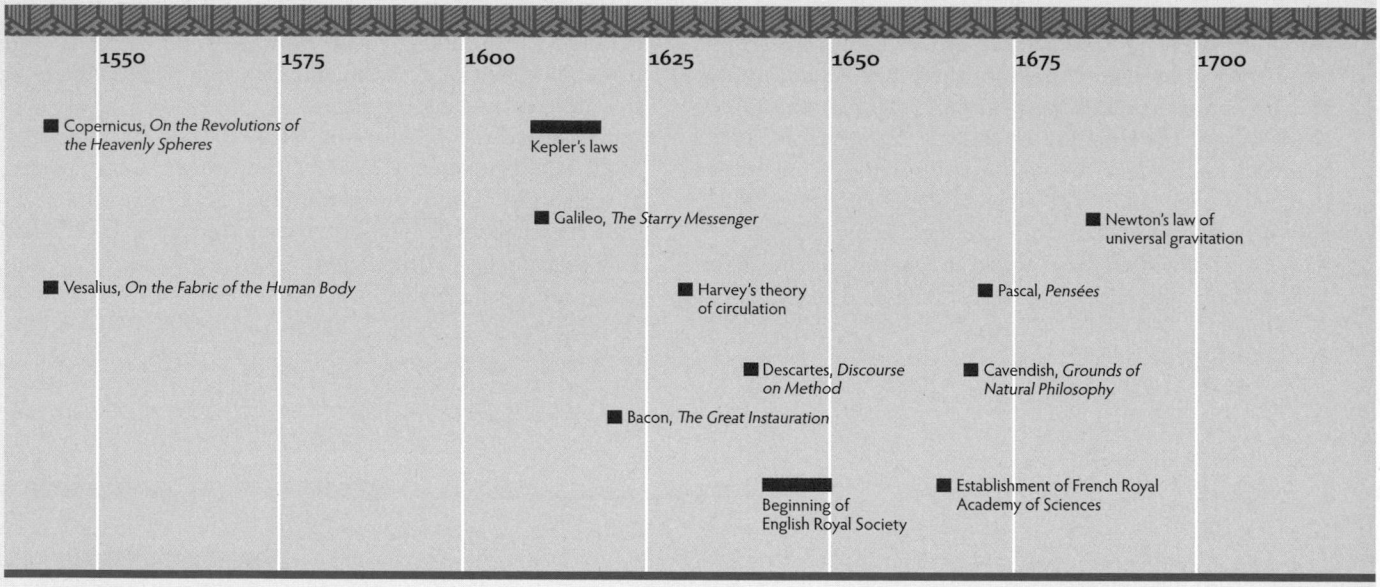

CHAPTER REVIEW

Upon Reflection

Q How do you explain the emergence of the Scientific Revolution?

Q What do we mean by the "Newtonian world-machine," and what is its significance?

Q Compare the methods used by Bacon and Descartes. Would Pascal agree with the methods and interests of these men? Why or why not?

Key Terms

Scientific Revolution (p. 358)
geocentric conception (p. 359)
heliocentric conception (p. 359)
world-machine (p. 364)
Cartesian dualism (p. 369)
rationalism (p. 369)
scientific method (p. 369)
empiricism (p. 370)

Suggestions for Further Reading

GENERAL WORKS General surveys of the entire Scientific Revolution include **J. Henry, *The Scientific Revolution and the Origins of Modem Science,*** 2nd ed. (London, 2002), and **J. R. Jacob, *The Scientific Revolution: Aspirations and Achievements, 1500–1700*** (Atlantic Highlands, N.J., 1998). See also **P. Dear, *Revolutionizing the Sciences: European Knowledge and Its Ambitions, 1500–1700*** (Princeton, N.J., 2001). On the relationship of magic to the beginnings of the Scientific Revolution, see the pioneering work by **F. Yates, *The Rosicrucian Enlightenment*** (London, 1975). On the importance of mathematics, see **P. Dear, *Discipline and Experience: The Mathematical Way in the Scientific Revolution*** (Chicago, 1995). On the relationship between Renaissance artists and the Scientific Revolution, see **P. H. Smith, *Body of the Artisan: Art and Experience in the Scientific Revolution*** (Chicago, 2006).

A REVOLUTION IN ASTRONOMY On the important figures of the revolution in astronomy, see **H. Margolis, *It Started with Copernicus: How Turning the World Inside Out Led to the Scientific Revolution*** (New York, 2002); **M. Sharratt, *Galileo: Decisive***

Innovator (Oxford, 1994); **M. Casper, *Johannes Kepler,*** trans. **C. D. Hellman** (London, 1959), the standard biography; **R. S. Westfall, *The Life of Isaac Newton*** (New York, 1993); and **P. Fara, *Newton: The Making of Genius*** (New York, 2004).

THE IMPACT OF SCIENCE The importance of Francis Bacon in the early development of science is underscored in **P. Zagorin, *Francis Bacon*** (Princeton, N.J., 1998). A good introduction to the work of Descartes can be found in **G. Radis-Lewis, *Descartes: A Biography*** (Ithaca, N.Y., 1998).

WOMEN AND SCIENCE On the subject of women and early modern science, see the comprehensive and highly informative work by **L. Schiebinger, *The Mind Has No Sex? Women in the Origins of Modern Science*** (Cambridge, Mass., 1989).

SCIENCE AND SOCIETY The social and political context for the triumph of science in the seventeenth and eighteenth centuries is examined in **M. C. Jacob, *The Cultural Meaning of the Scientific Revolution*** (New York, 1988). On the relationship of science and industry, see **M. C. Jacob, *Scientific Culture and the Making of the Industrial West*** (Oxford, 1997).

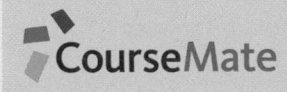

Visit the CourseMate website at www.cengagebrain.com for additional study tools and review materials for this chapter.

GLOSSARY

abbess the head of a convent or monastery for women.
abbot the head of a monastery.
absolutism a form of government in which the sovereign power or ultimate authority rested in the hands of a monarch who claimed to rule by divine right and was therefore responsible only to God.
aediles Roman officials who supervised the public games and the grain supply of the city of Rome.
Agricultural (Neolithic) Revolution *see* Neolithic Revolution.
anti-Semitism hostility toward or discrimination against Jews.
Arianism a Christian heresy that taught that Jesus was inferior to God. Though condemned by the Council of Nicaea in 325, Arianism was adopted by many of the Germanic peoples who entered the Roman Empire over the next centuries.
aristocracy a class of hereditary nobility in medieval Europe; a warrior class who shared a distinctive lifestyle based on the institution of knighthood, although there were social divisions within the group based on extremes of wealth.

Baroque an artistic movement of the seventeenth century in Europe that used dramatic effects to arouse the emotions and reflected the search for power that was a large part of the seventeenth-century ethos.
Black Death the outbreak of plague (mostly bubonic) in the mid-fourteenth century that killed from 25 to 50 percent of Europe's population.
bourgeoisie (burghers) inhabitants (merchants and artisans) of boroughs and burghs (towns).
boyars the Russian nobility.
Bronze Age the period from around 3000 to 1200 B.C.E. It was characterized by the widespread use of bronze for making tools and weapons.

caliph the secular leader of the Islamic community.
Cartesian dualism Descartes's principle of the separation of mind and matter (and mind and body) that enabled scientists to view matter as something separate from themselves that could be investigated by reason.
centuriate assembly the chief popular assembly of the Roman Republic. It passed laws and elected the chief magistrates.
chansons de geste a form of vernacular literature in the High Middle Ages that consisted of heroic epics focusing on the deeds of warriors.
chivalry the ideal of civilized behavior that emerged among the nobility in the eleventh and twelfth centuries under the influence of the church; a code of ethics knights were expected to uphold.
Christian (northern) humanism an intellectual movement in northern Europe in the late fifteenth and early sixteenth centuries that combined the interest in the classics of the Italian Renaissance with an interest in the sources of early Christianity, including the New Testament and the writings of the church fathers.
civic humanism an intellectual movement of the Italian Renaissance that saw Cicero, who was both an intellectual and a statesman, as the ideal and held that humanists should be involved in government and use their rhetorical training in the service of the state.
civilization a complex culture in which large numbers of humans share a variety of common elements, including cities; religious, political, military, and social structures; writing; and significant artistic and intellectual activity.
Columbian Exchange the reciprocal importation and exportation of plants and animals between Europe and the Americas.
commercial capitalism beginning in the Middle Ages, an economic system in which people invested in trade and goods in order to make profits.
common law law common to the entire kingdom of England; imposed by the king's courts beginning in the twelfth century to replace the customary law used in county and feudal courts that varied from place to place.
conciliarism a movement in fourteenth- and fifteenth-century Europe that held that final authority in spiritual matters resided with a general church council, not the pope. It emerged in response to the Avignon papacy and the Great Schism and was used to justify the summoning of the Council of Constance (1414–1418).
condottieri leaders of bands of mercenary soldiers in Renaissance Italy who sold their services to the highest bidder.
conquistadors "conquerors." Leaders in the Spanish conquests in the Americas, especially Mexico and Peru, in the sixteenth century.
consuls the chief executive officers of the Roman Republic. Two were chosen annually to administer the government and lead the army in battle.
council of the plebs a council only for plebeians. After 287 B.C.E., however, its resolutions were binding on all Romans.
Crusade in the Middle Ages, a military campaign in defense of Christendom.
cuneiform "wedge-shaped." A system of writing developed by the Sumerians that consisted of wedge-shaped impressions made by a reed stylus on clay tablets.

demesne the part of a manor retained under the direct control of the lord and worked by the serfs as part of their labor services.
divination the practice of seeking to foretell future events by interpreting divine signs, which could appear in various forms, such as in entrails of animals, in patterns in smoke, or in dreams.

empiricism the practice of relying on observation and experiment.
encomienda in Spanish America, a form of economic and social organization in which a Spaniard was given a royal grant that enabled the holder of the grant to collect tribute from the Indians and use them as laborers.

Epicureanism a philosophy founded by Epicurus in the fourth century B.C.E. that taught that happiness (freedom from emotional turmoil) could be achieved through the pursuit of pleasure (intellectual rather than sensual pleasure).

equestrian order a group of extremely wealthy men in the late Roman Republic who were effectively barred from high office but sought political power commensurate with their wealth; called equestrians because many had gotten their start as cavalry officers (*equites*).

estates (orders) the traditional tripartite division of European society based on heredity and quality rather than wealth or economic standing, first established in the Middle Ages and continuing into the eighteenth century; traditionally consisted of those who pray (the clergy), those who fight (the nobility), and those who work (all the rest).

Eucharist a Christian sacrament in which consecrated bread and wine are consumed in celebration of Jesus's Last Supper; also called the Lord's Supper or communion.

fief a landed estate granted to a vassal in exchange for military services.

Five Pillars of Islam the core requirements of the faith, observation of which would lead to paradise: belief in Allah and his Prophet Muhammad; prescribed prayers; observation of Ramadan; pilgrimage to Mecca; and giving alms (charitable contributions) to the poor.

gentry well-to-do English landowners below the level of the nobility. They played an important role in the English Civil War of the seventeenth century.

geocentric conception the belief that the earth was at the center of the universe and that the sun and other celestial objects revolved around the earth.

good emperors the five emperors who ruled from 96 to 180 (Nerva, Trajan, Hadrian, Antoninus Pius, and Marcus Aurelius), a period of peace and prosperity for the Roman Empire.

Gothic a term used to describe the art and especially architecture of Europe in the twelfth, thirteenth, and fourteenth centuries.

Great Schism the crisis in the late medieval church when there were first two and then three popes; ended by the Council of Constance (1414–1418).

guild an association of people with common interests and concerns, especially people working in the same craft. In medieval Europe, guilds came to control much of the production process and to restrict entry into various trades.

heliocentric conception the belief that the sun, not the earth, is at the center of the universe.

Hellenistic literally, "imitating the Greeks"; the era after the death of Alexander the Great when Greek culture spread into the Near East and blended with the culture of that region.

helots serfs in ancient Sparta who were permanently bound to the land that they worked for their Spartan masters.

heresy the holding of religious doctrines different from the official teachings of the church.

Hermeticism an intellectual movement beginning in the fifteenth century that taught that divinity is embodied in all aspects of nature. It included works on alchemy and magic as well as theology and philosophy. The tradition continued into the seventeenth century and influenced many of the leading figures of the Scientific Revolution.

hieroglyphics a pictorial system of writing used in ancient Egypt.

hoplites heavily armed infantry soldiers in ancient Greece who entered battle in a phalanx formation.

Huguenots French Calvinists.

humanism an intellectual movement in Renaissance Italy based on the study of the Greek and Roman classics.

imperium in the Roman Republic, the right to command troops that belonged to the chief executive officers (consuls and praetors). A military commander was known as an *imperator*. In the Roman Empire, the title *imperator* (emperor) came to be used for the ruler.

individualism emphasis on and interest in the unique traits of each person.

indulgence in Christian theology, the remission of part or all of the temporal punishment in purgatory due to sin; granted for charitable contributions and other good deeds. Indulgences became a regular practice of the Catholic Church in the High Middle Ages, and their abuse was instrumental in sparking Luther's reform movement in the sixteenth century.

inflation a sustained rise in the price level.

intendants royal officials in seventeenth-century France who were sent into the provinces to execute the orders of the central government.

interdict in the Catholic Church, a censure by which a region or country is deprived of receiving the sacraments.

jihad "striving in the way of the Lord." In Islam, the attempt to achieve personal betterment, although it can also mean fair, defensive fighting to preserve one's life and one's faith.

joint-stock company a company or association that raises capital by selling shares to individuals who receive dividends on their investment while a board of directors runs the company.

justification the primary doctrine of the Protestant Reformation, teaching that humans are saved not through good works but by the grace of God, bestowed freely through the sacrifice of Jesus.

latifundia large landed estates in the Roman Empire (singular: *latifundium*).

lay investiture the practice in which someone other than a member of the clergy chose a bishop and invested him with the symbols of both his temporal office and his spiritual office; led to the Investiture Controversy, which was ended by compromise in the Concordat of Worms in 1122.

liberal arts the seven areas of study that formed the basis of education in medieval and early modern Europe. Following Boethius and other late Roman authors, they consisted of grammar, rhetoric, and dialectic or logic (the *trivium*) and arithmetic, geometry, astronomy, and music (the *quadrivium*).

Mannerism a sixteenth-century artistic movement in Europe that deliberately broke down the High Renaissance principles of balance, harmony, and moderation.

manor an agricultural estate operated by a lord and worked by peasants who performed labor services and paid various rents and fees to the lord in exchange for protection and sustenance.

mercantilism an economic theory that held that a nation's prosperity depended on its supply of gold and silver and that the total volume of trade is unchangeable. Its adherents therefore advocated that the government play an active role in the economy by encouraging exports and discouraging imports, especially through the use of tariffs.

Middle Passage the journey of slaves from Africa to the Americas as the middle leg of the triangular trade.

monasticism a movement that began in early Christianity whose purpose was to create communities of men and women who practiced a communal life dedicated to God as a moral example to the world around them.

monk a man who chooses to live a communal life divorced from the world in order to dedicate himself totally to the will of God.

monogamy the practice of being married to one person at a time.

monotheism the doctrine or belief that there is only one God.

mystery religions religions that involve initiation into secret rites that promise intense emotional involvement with spiritual forces and a greater chance of individual immortality.

Neolithic Revolution the shift from hunting animals and gathering plants for sustenance to producing food by systematic agriculture that occurred gradually between 10,000 and 4000 B.C.E. (the Neolithic or "New Stone" Age).

Neoplatonism a revival of Platonic philosophy in the third century C.E., associated with Plotinus; a similar revival in the Italian Renaissance, associated with Marsilio Ficino, who attempted to synthesize Christianity and Platonism.

nepotism the appointment of family members to important political positions; derived from the regular appointment of nephews (Latin, *nepos*) by Renaissance popes.

new monarchies the governments of France, England, and Spain at the end of the fifteenth century, whose rulers succeeded in reestablishing or extending centralized royal authority, suppressing the nobility, controlling the church, and insisting on the loyalty of all people living in their territories.

nobiles "nobles." The small group of families from both patrician and plebeian origins who produced most of the men who were elected to office in the late Roman Republic.

nuclear family a family group consisting only of a father, a mother, and one or more children.

nuns women who withdrew from the world and joined a religious community; the female equivalent of monks.

oligarchy rule by a few.

optimates "best men." Aristocratic leaders in the late Roman Republic who generally came from senatorial families and wished to retain their oligarchical privileges.

orders *see* estates.

Paleolithic Age the period of human history when humans used simple stone tools (c. 2,500,000–10,000 B.C.E.).

papal curia the administrative staff of the Catholic Church, composed of cardinals who assist the pope in running the church.

paterfamilias the dominant male in a Roman family whose powers over his wife and children were theoretically unlimited, though they were sometimes circumvented in practice.

patricians great landowners who became the ruling class in the Roman Republic.

Pax Romana "Roman peace." A term used to refer to the stability and prosperity that Roman rule brought to the Mediterranean world and much of western Europe during the first and second centuries C.E.

perioikoi in ancient Sparta, free inhabitants but not citizens who were required to pay taxes and perform military service.

plebeians the class of Roman citizens that included nonpatrician landowners, craftspeople, merchants, and small farmers in the Roman Republic. Their struggle for equal rights with the patricians dominated much of the Republic's history.

plebiscita laws passed by the council of the plebs during the Roman Republic.

pluralism the practice of holding several church offices simultaneously; a problem of the late medieval church.

pogroms organized massacres of Jews.

polis an ancient Greek city-state encompassing both an urban area and its surrounding countryside; a small but autonomous political unit where all major political and social activities were carried out centrally.

politiques a group who emerged during the French Wars of Religion in the sixteenth century, placed politics above religion, and believed that no religious truth was worth the ravages of civil war.

polytheistic believing in or worshiping more than one god.

populares "favoring the people." Aristocratic leaders in the late Roman Republic who tended to use the people's assemblies in an effort to break the stranglehold of the *nobiles* on political offices.

praetor a Roman executive official responsible for the administration of the law.

praetorian guard the military unit that served as the personal bodyguard of the Roman emperors.

predestination the belief, associated with Calvinism, that God, as a consequence of his foreknowledge of all events, has predetermined those who will be saved (the elect) and those who will be damned.

price revolution the dramatic rise in prices (inflation) that occurred throughout Europe in the sixteenth and early seventeenth centuries.

principate the form of government established by Augustus for the Roman Empire. It continued the constitutional forms of the Republic and consisted of the *princeps* ("first citizen") and the senate, although the *princeps* was clearly the dominant partner.

procurator the head of the Holy Synod, the chief decision-making body for the Russian Orthodox Church.

Puritans English Protestants inspired by Calvinist theology who wished to remove all traces of Catholicism from the Church of England.

quadrivium arithmetic, geometry, astronomy, and music; four of the seven liberal arts (the others made up the *trivium*) that formed the basis of medieval and early modern education.

quaestors Roman officials responsible for the administration of financial affairs.

Ramadan the holy month of Islam, during which believers fast from dawn to sunset. Since the Islamic calendar is lunar, Ramadan migrates through the seasons.

rationalism a system of thought based on the belief that human reason and experience are the chief sources of knowledge.

Reconquista in Spain, the reconquest of Muslim lands by Christian rulers and their armies.

relics the bones of Christian saints or objects intimately associated with saints that were considered worthy of veneration.

Renaissance the "rebirth" of Classical culture that occurred in Italy between c. 1350 and c. 1550; also, the earlier revivals of Classical culture that occurred under Charlemagne and in the twelfth century.

rhetoric the art of persuasive speaking; in the Middle Ages, one of the seven liberal arts.

Romanesque a term used to describe the art and especially architecture of Europe in the eleventh and twelfth centuries.

sacraments rites considered imperative for a Christian's salvation. By the thirteenth century, these consisted of the Eucharist or Lord's Supper, baptism, marriage, penance, extreme unction, holy orders, and confirmation of children; Protestant reformers of the sixteenth century generally recognized only two—baptism and communion (the Lord's Supper).

satrap a governor with both civil and military duties in the ancient Persian Empire, which was divided into satrapies, or provinces, each administered by a satrap.

scholasticism the philosophical and theological system of the medieval schools, which emphasized rigorous analysis of contradictory authorities; often used to try to reconcile faith and reason.

scientific method a method of seeking knowledge through inductive principles, using experiments and observations to develop generalizations.

Scientific Revolution the transition from the medieval worldview to a largely secular, rational, and materialistic perspective that began in the seventeenth century and was popularized in the eighteenth.

scriptoria writing rooms for the copying of manuscripts in medieval monasteries.

scutage in the fourteenth century, a money payment for military service that replaced the obligation of military service in the lord-vassal relationship.

secularism the process of becoming more concerned with material, worldly, temporal things and less with spiritual and religious things.

senate the leading council of the Roman Republic; composed of about three hundred men (senators) who served for life and dominated much of the political life of the Republic.

serf a peasant who is bound to the land and obliged to provide labor services and pay various rents and fees to the lord; considered unfree but not a slave because serfs could not be bought and sold.

Shari'a a law code, originally drawn up by Muslim scholars shortly after the death of Muhammad, that provides believers with a set of prescriptions to regulate their daily lives.

Socratic method a form of teaching that uses a question-and-answer format to enable students to reach conclusions by using their own reasoning.

Sophists wandering scholars and professional teachers in ancient Greece who stressed the importance of rhetoric and tended toward skepticism and relativism.

Stoicism a philosophy founded by Zeno in the fourth century B.C.E. that taught that happiness could be obtained by accepting one's lot and living in harmony with the will of God, thereby achieving inner peace.

subinfeudation the practice whereby a lord's greatest vassals subdivided their fiefs and had vassals of their own, who in turn subdivided their fiefs, and so on down to simple knights, whose fiefs were too small to subdivide.

sultan "holder of power." A title taken by Turkish leaders who took command of the Abbasid Empire in 1055.

syncretism the combining of different forms of belief or practice, as, for example, when two gods are regarded as different forms of the same underlying divine force and are fused together.

theocracy a government ruled by a divine authority.

three-field system in medieval agriculture, the practice of dividing the arable land into three fields so that one could lie fallow while the others were planted in winter grains and spring crops.

tithe a portion of one's harvest or income, paid by medieval peasants to the village church.

transubstantiation a doctrine of the Roman Catholic Church that during the Eucharist, the substance of the bread and wine is miraculously transformed into the body and blood of Jesus.

triangular trade a pattern of trade in early modern Europe that connected Europe, Africa, and the Americas in an Atlantic economy.

tribunes of the plebs beginning in 494 B.C.E., Roman officials who were given the power to protect plebeians against arrest by patrician magistrates.

trivium grammar, rhetoric, and dialectic or logic; three of the seven liberal arts (the others made up the *quadrivium*) that were the basis of medieval and early modern education.

tyrant in an ancient Greek *polis* (or an Italian city-state during the Renaissance), a ruler who came to power in an unconstitutional way and ruled without being subject to the law.

umma the Muslim community, as a whole.

vassalage the granting of a fief, or landed estate, in exchange for providing military services to the lord and fulfilling certain other obligations such as appearing at the lord's court when summoned and making a payment on the knighting of the lord's eldest son.

viceroy the administrative head of the provinces of New Spain and Peru in the Americas.

wergeld "money for a man." In early Germanic law, a person's value in monetary terms, paid by a wrongdoer to the family of the person who had been injured or killed.

world-machine Newton's conception of the universe as one huge, regulated, and uniform machine that operated according to natural laws in absolute time, space, and motion.

ziggurat a massive stepped tower on which a temple dedicated to the chief god or goddess of a Sumerian city was built.

Zoroastrianism a religion founded by the Persian Zoroaster in the seventh century B.C.E., characterized by worship of a supreme god, Ahuramazda, who represents the good against the evil spirit, identified as Ahriman.

NOTES

CHAPTER 1

1. J.-M. Chauvet et al., *Dawn of Art: The Chauvet Cave* (New York, 1996), pp. 49–50.
2. Quoted in A. Kuhrt, *The Ancient Near East, c. 3000–330 B.C.* (London, 1995), vol. 1, p. 68.
3. Quoted in M. van de Mieroop, *A History of the Ancient Near East, ca. 3000–323 B.C.* (Oxford, 2004), p. 106.
4. T. Jacobsen, "Mesopotamia," in H. Frankfort et al., *Before Philosophy* (Baltimore, 1949), p. 139.
5. J. B. Pritchard, *Ancient Near Eastern Texts*, 3rd ed. (Princeton, N.J., 1969), p. 372.
6. Quoted in M. Covensky, *The Ancient Near Eastern Tradition* (New York, 1966), p. 51.
7. Quoted in B. G. Trigger, B. J. Kemp, D. O'Connor, and A. B. Lloyd, *Ancient Egypt: A Social History* (Cambridge, 1983), p. 74.
8. Pritchard, *Ancient Near Eastern Texts*, p. 34.
9. Ibid., p. 36.
10. Quoted in R.-M. Hagen and R. Hagen, *Egypt: People, Gods, Pharaohs* (Cologne, 2002), p. 148.
11. Pritchard, *Ancient Near Eastern Texts*, p. 413.
12. Ibid., p. 420.

CHAPTER 2

1. 2 Samuel 8:2.
2. Psalms 137:1, 4–6.
3. Psalms 145:8–9.
4. Psalms 121:2–3.
5. Exodus 20:13–15.
6. Isaiah 2:4.
7. Quoted in H. W. F. Saggs, *The Might That Was Assyria* (London, 1984), p. 261.
8. Ibid., p. 262.
9. J. C. Rolfe, trans., *Quintus Curtius I* (Cambridge, Mass., 1971), pp. 337–339.
10. Quoted in J. M. Cook, *The Persian Empire* (New York, 1983), p. 32.
11. Herodotus, *The Persian Wars*, trans. G. Rawlinson (New York, 1942), p. 257.
12. Isaiah 44:28, 45:1.
13. Quoted in A. T. Olmstead, *History of the Persian Empire* (Chicago, 1948), p. 168.
14. Quoted in Cook, *The Persian Empire*, p. 76.
15. Yasna 44:3–4, 7, as quoted in A. C. Bouquet, *Sacred Books of the World* (Harmondsworth, England, 1954), pp. 111–112.

CHAPTER 3

1. H. D. F. Kitto, *The Greeks* (Harmondsworth, England, 1951), p. 64.
2. Homer, *Odyssey*, trans. E. V. Rieu (Harmondsworth, England, 1946), p. 337.
3. Xenophon, *Symposium*, trans. O. J. Todd (Cambridge, Mass., 1968), III, 5.
4. Homer, *Odyssey*, pp. 290–291.
5. Quoted in T. R. Martin, *Ancient Greece* (New Haven, Conn., 1996), p. 62.
6. Quoted in V. D. Hanson, *The Wars of the Ancient Greeks*, rev. ed. (London, 2006), p. 14.
7. Plutarch, quoted in E. Fantham et al., *Women in the Classical World* (New York, 1994), p. 64.
8. Herodotus, *The Persian Wars*, trans. G. Rawlinson (New York, 1942), p. 3.
9. Thucydides, *History of the Peloponnesian War*, trans. R. Warner (Harmondsworth, England, 1954), p. 24.
10. Sophocles, *Oedipus the King*, trans. D. Grene (Chicago, 1959), pp. 68–69.
11. Sophocles, *Antigone*, trans. D. Taylor (London, 1986), p. 146.
12. Plato, *The Republic*, trans. F. M. Cornford (New York, 1945), pp. 178–179.
13. Aristotle, quoted in S. Blundell, *Women in Ancient Greece* (Cambridge, Mass., 1995), p. 106.
14. Ibid., p. 186.

CHAPTER 4

1. Quoted in S. B. Pomeroy, S. M. Burstein, W. Donlan, and J. T. Roberts, *Ancient Greece: A Political, Social, and Cultural History* (Oxford, 1999), p. 390.
2. Quoted in G. Shipley, *The Greek World After Alexander, 323–30 B.C.* (London, 2000), p. 53.
3. Quoted in M. B. Fant and M. R. Lefkowitz, *Women's Life in Greece and Rome: A Source Book in Translation* (Baltimore, 1992), no. 208.
4. Plutarch, *Life of Marcellus*, trans. J. Dryden (New York, n.d.), p. 378.
5. *Epicurus: The Extant Remains*, trans. C. Bailey (Oxford, 1926), pp. 89–90.
6. Ibid.
7. Quoted in W. W. Tarn, *Hellenistic Civilization* (London, 1930), p. 324.

CHAPTER 5

1. Quoted in C. Starr, *Past and Future in Ancient History* (Lanham, Md., 1987), pp. 38–39.
2. *The Poems of Catullus*, trans. C. Martin (Baltimore, 1990), p. 109.
3. Quoted in A. Everitt, *Cicero* (New York, 2001), p. 181.
4. Quoted in Adrian Goldsworthy, *Caesar: Life of a Colossus* (New Haven, Conn., 2006), p. 358.
5. Florus, *Epitome of Roman History*, trans. E. S. Forster (Cambridge, Mass., 1961), IV, ii, 149–151.

CHAPTER 6

1. Livy, *The Early History of Rome*, trans. A. de Sélincourt (Harmondsworth, England, 1960), p. 35.
2. Tacitus, *The Annals of Imperial Rome*, trans. M. Grant (Harmondsworth, England, 1956), p. 30.
3. Ibid., p. 37.
4. Ibid., p. 31.
5. Tacitus, *The Histories*, trans. K. Wellesley (Harmondsworth, England, 1964), p. 23.
6. Virgil, *The Aeneid*, trans. C. Day Lewis (Garden City, N.Y., 1952), p. 154.
7. Horace, *Satires*, in *The Complete Works of Horace*, trans. Lord Dunsany and M. Oakley (London, 1961), 1.1, p. 139; 1.3, p. 151.
8. Livy, *Early History of Rome*, p. 18.
9. Seneca, *Letters from a Stoic*, trans. R. Campbell (Harmondsworth, England, 1969), let. 5.
10. Tacitus, *Annals of Imperial Rome*, p. 147.
11. Juvenal, *The Sixteen Satires*, trans. P. Green (Harmondsworth, England, 1967), sat. 10, p. 207.
12. Tacitus, *A Dialogue on Oratory*, in *The Complete Works of Tacitus*, trans. A. Church and W. Brodribb (New York, 1942), 29, p. 758.
13. Matthew 5:17.
14. Matthew 7:12.
15. Mark 12:30–31.
16. John 18:36.
17. Colossians 3:10–11.

CHAPTER 7

1. "The Creed of Nicaea," in H. Bettenson, ed., *Documents of the Christian Church* (London, 1963), p. 35.
2. E. F. Henderson, *Select Historical Documents of the Middle Ages* (London, 1892), p. 181.
3. N. F. Cantor, ed., *The Medieval World, 300–1300* (New York, 1963), p. 104.
4. Ibid., p. 103.
5. Bede, *A History of the English Church and People*, trans. L. Sherley-Price (Harmondsworth, England, 1968), pp. 86–87.
6. Quoted in P. Brown, *The Rise of Western Christendom: Triumph and Adversity, A.D. 200–1000* (Oxford, 1997), p. 98.
7. Tertullian, "The Prescriptions Against the Heretics," in *The Library of Christian Classics*, vol. 5, *Early Latin Theology*, ed. and trans. S. L. Greenslade (Philadelphia, 1956), p. 36.
8. Quoted in Jonathan Harris, *Constantinople: Capital of Byzantium* (New York, 2007), p. 40.
9. Quoted in A. Goldschmidt Jr., *A Concise History of the Middle East*, 7th ed. (Boulder, Colo., 2001), p. 60.

CHAPTER 8

1. Einhard, *The Life of Charlemagne*, trans. S. Turner (Ann Arbor, Mich., 1960), p. 30.
2. Ibid., p. 57.
3. A. Barbero, *Charlemagne: Father of a Continent*, trans. A. Cameron (Berkeley, Calif., 2004), p. 4.
4. Quoted in P. Riché, *Daily Life in the World of Charlemagne*, trans. J. A. McNamara (Philadelphia, 1978), p. 56.
5. 1 Corinthians 7:1–2, 8–9.
6. Quoted in S. Keynes, "The Vikings in England, c. 790–1016," in P. Sawyer, ed., *The Oxford Illustrated History of the Vikings* (Oxford, 1997), p. 81.
7. Quoted in O. Thatcher and E. McNeal, eds., *A Source Book for Medieval History* (New York, 1905), p. 363.
8. al-Mas'sudi, *The Meadows of Gold: The Abbasids*, ed. P. Lunde and C. Stone (London, 1989), p. 151.

CHAPTER 9

1. Quoted in N. F. Cantor, ed., *The Medieval Reader* (New York, 1994), pp. 69–70.
2. Quoted in J. Gies and F. Gies, *Life in a Medieval Castle* (New York, 1974), p. 175.
3. Quoted in R. Delort, *Life in the Middle Ages*, trans. R. Allen (New York, 1972), p. 218.
4. Quoted in J. Gimpel, *The Medieval Machine* (Harmondsworth, England, 1977), p. 92.
5. Quoted in J. Mundy, *Europe in the High Middle Ages, 1150–1309* (New York, 1973), pp. 474–475.
6. Quoted in H. Waddell, *The Wandering Scholars* (New York, 1961), p. 222.
7. Quoted in J. W. Baldwin, *The Scholastic Cult of the Middle Ages, 1000–1300* (Lexington, Mass., 1971), p. 15.

CHAPTER 10

1. Quoted in N. F. Cantor, ed., *The Medieval Reader* (New York, 1994), pp. 42–47.
2. Quoted in J. K. Fairbank, E. O. Reischauer, and A. M. Craig, *East Asia: Tradition and Transformation* (Boston, 1973), p. 164.
3. E. F. Henderson, ed., *Selected Historical Documents of the Middle Ages* (London, 1892), p. 332.
4. Ibid., p. 365.
5. O. J. Thatcher and E. H. McNeal, eds., *A Source Book for Medieval History* (New York, 1905), p. 208.
6. Quoted in R. H. C. Davis, *A History of Medieval Europe from Constantine to Saint Louis*, 2nd ed. (New York, 1988), p. 252.
7. Hildegard of Bingen, *The Book of Divine Works* (Santa Fe, N.M., 1987), 1:1.

8. Quoted in R. Brooke and C. N. L. Brooke, *Popular Religion in the Middle Ages* (London, 1984), p. 19.
9. Thatcher and McNeal, *Source Book for Medieval History*, p. 517.
10. Quoted in Thomas Asbridge, *The First Crusade: A New History* (Oxford, 2004), pp. 79–80.
11. Quoted in H. E. Mayer, *The Crusades*, trans. J. Gillingham (New York, 1972), pp. 99–100.

CHAPTER 11

1. Quoted in H. S. Lucas, "The Great European Famine of 1315, 1316, and 1317," *Speculum* 5 (1930): 359.
2. Quoted in Christos S. Bartsocas, "Two Fourteenth-Century Descriptions of the 'Black Death,'" *Journal of the History of Medicine* (October 1966): 395.
3. Quoted in D. Herlihy, *The Black Death and the Transformation of the West*, ed. S. K. Cohn Jr. (Cambridge, Mass., 1997), p. 9.
4. J. Froissart, *Chronicles*, ed. and trans. G. Brereton (Harmondsworth, England, 1968), p. 111.
5. Ibid., p. 212.
6. Ibid., p. 89.
7. Quoted in R. Coogan, *Babylon on the Rhône: A Translation of Letters by Dante, Petrarch, and Catherine of Siena* (Washington, D.C., 1983), p. 115.
8. Dante, *Divine Comedy*, trans. D. Sayers (New York, 1962), "Paradise," canto 33, line 145.
9. Christine de Pizan, *The Book of the City of Ladies*, trans. E. J. Richards (New York, 1982), pp. 83–84.
10. Quoted in S. Stuard, "Dominion of Gender: Women's Fortunes in the High Middle Ages," in R. Bridenthal, C. Koonz, and S. Stuard, eds., *Becoming Visible: Women in European History*, 2nd ed. (Boston, 1987), p. 169.
11. Quoted in J. Gimpel, *The Medieval Machine* (New York, 1976), p. 168.

CHAPTER 12

1. Quoted in J. Burckhardt, *The Civilization of the Renaissance in Italy*, trans. S. G. C. Middlemore (London, 1960), p. 81.
2. B. Castiglione, *The Book of the Courtier*, trans. C. S. Singleton (Garden City, N.Y., 1959), pp. 288–289.
3. Quoted in D. L. Jensen, *Renaissance Europe* (Lexington, Mass., 1981), p. 94.
4. G. Brucker, ed., *Two Memoirs of Renaissance Florence* (New York, 1967), p. 132.
5. Quoted in M. L. King, *Women of the Renaissance* (Chicago, 1991), p. 3.
6. N. Machiavelli, *The Prince*, trans. D. Wootton (Indianapolis, 1995), p. 48.
7. Ibid., p. 55.
8. Ibid., p. 27.
9. G. Pico della Mirandola, *Oration on the Dignity of Man*, in E. Cassirer, P. O. Kristeller, and J. H. Randall Jr., eds., *The Renaissance Philosophy of Man* (Chicago, 1948), p. 225.
10. Ibid., pp. 247–249.
11. Quoted in I. Origo, *The Light of the Past* (New York, 1959), p. 136.
12. Quoted in E. G. Holt, ed., *A Documentary History of Art* (Garden City, N.Y., 1959), vol. 1, p. 286.
13. Quoted in R. M. Letts, *The Cambridge Introduction to Art: The Renaissance* (Cambridge, 1981), p. 86.

CHAPTER 13

1. D. Erasmus, *The Paraclesis*, in J. Olin, ed., *Christian Humanism and the Reformation: Selected Writings of Erasmus*, 3rd ed. (New York, 1987), p. 101.
2. J. P. Dolan, ed., *The Essential Erasmus* (New York, 1964), p. 149.
3. Quoted in A. E. McGrath, *Reformation Thought: An Introduction* (Oxford, 1988), p. 72.
4. Quoted in E. G. Rupp and B. Drewery, eds., *Martin Luther* (New York, 1970), p. 50.
5. Quoted in R. Bainton, *Here I Stand: A Life of Martin Luther* (New York, 1950), p. 144.
6. Quoted in D. L. Jensen, *Reformation Europe* (Lexington, Mass., 1981), p. 83.
7. J. Calvin, *Institutes of the Christian Religion*, trans. J. Allen (Philadelphia, 1936), vol. 1, p. 228; vol. 2, p. 181.
8. Quoted in R. Bainton, *Women of the Reformation in Germany and Italy* (Boston, 1971), p. 154.
9. Quoted in B. S. Anderson and J. P. Zinsser, *A History of Their Own: Women in Europe from Prehistory to the Present* (New York, 1988), vol. 1, p. 259.
10. Quoted in J. A. Phillips, *Eve: The History of an Idea* (New York, 1984), p. 105.
11. Quoted in J. O'Malley, *The First Jesuits* (Cambridge, Mass., 1993), p. 76.
12. Quoted in G. Mattingly, *The Armada* (Boston, 1959), pp. 216–217.
13. Quoted in T. Schieder, *Handbuch der Europäischen Geschichte* (Stuttgart, 1979), vol. 3, p. 579.

CHAPTER 14

1. Quoted in J. R. Hale, *Renaissance Exploration* (New York, 1968), p. 32.
2. Quoted in J. H. Parry, *The Age of Reconnaissance: Discovery, Exploration, and Settlement, 1450 to 1640* (New York, 1963), p. 33.
3. Quoted in R. B. Reed, "The Expansion of Europe," in R. De Molen, ed., *The Meaning of the Renaissance and Reformation* (Boston, 1974), p. 308.
4. Quoted in B. Davidson, *Africa in History: Themes and Outlines*, rev. ed. (New York, 1991), p. 213.
5. Quoted in ibid., p. 198.
6. Quoted in G. V. Scammell, *The First Imperial Age: European Overseas Expansion, c. 1400–1715* (London, 1989), p. 62.
7. M. Leon-Portilla, ed., *The Broken Spears: The Aztec Account of the Conquest of Mexico* (Boston, 1969), p. 51.

CHAPTER 15

1. Quoted in J. Klaits, *Servants of Satan: The Age of the Witch Hunts* (Bloomington, Ind., 1985), p. 68.
2. Quoted in ibid., p. 68.

3. Quoted in Peter H. Wilson, *The Thirty Years War: Europe's Tragedy* (Cambridge, Mass., 2009), p. 783.
4. Quoted in J. B. Wolf, *Louis XIV* (New York, 1968), p. 134.
5. Quoted in J. H. Elliot, *Imperial Spain, 1469–1716* (New York, 1963), p. 306.

CHAPTER 16

1. Quoted in A. G. R. Smith, *Science and Society in the Sixteenth and Seventeenth Centuries* (London, 1972), p. 59.
2. Quoted in E. MacCurdy, *The Notebooks of Leonardo da Vinci* (London, 1948), vol. 1, p. 634.
3. Quoted in J. H. Randall, *The Making of the Modern Mind* (Boston, 1926), p. 234.
4. Quoted in L. Schiebinger, *The Mind Has No Sex? Women in the Origins of Modern Science* (Cambridge, Mass., 1989), pp. 52–53.
5. Quoted in ibid., p. 85.
6. Quoted in P. Stock, *Better than Rubies: A History of Women's Education* (New York, 1978), p. 16.
7. R. Descartes, *Philosophical Writings*, ed. and trans. N. K. Smith (New York, 1958), p. 95.
8. Ibid., pp. 118–119.
9. F. Bacon, *The Great Instauration*, trans. J. Weinberger (Arlington Heights, Ill., 1989), pp. 2, 8.
10. Ibid., pp. 2, 16, 21.
11. S. Drake, ed. and trans., *Discoveries and Opinions of Galileo* (New York, 1957), p. 182.
12. B. Pascal, *Pensées*, trans. J. M. Cohen (Harmondsworth, England, 1961), p. 100.
13. Ibid., p. 31.
14. Ibid., pp. 52–53, 164, 165.

INDEX

Italicized page numbers show the locations of illustrations.

Aachen, 167
Abbasid caliphate, 179, 180 (map), 215
Abbess/abbot, 148, 150, 216
Abd al-Rahman (Umayyad), 180
Abortion: Catholic Church on, 167
Absolutism, 332, 336; in Austria, 340; in central and eastern Europe, 339–43; in France, 336–38; in German states, 339; limits of, 343; in Ottoman Empire, 343–44; in Prussia, 339; in Russia, 340–42; in Spain, 338–39; in Western Europe, 336–39
Abu al-Abbas (Abbasid), 179
Abu Bakr (Muslim caliph), 157
Academy: Platonic (Athens), 62
Academy of Science (Berlin), 367
Academy of Sciences (France), 367, 370, *370*
Account of the Court of Attila the Hun, The (Priscus), 142–43
"Accusation of the Ritual Murder of a Christian Child by Jews," 222
Achaemenid dynasty (Persia), 38
Achilles (Greek hero), *48*, 48–49
Acropolis, 50; in Athens, *60*
Actium, Battle of, 109
Act of Supremacy (England, 1534), 290, 298
Address to Philip (Isocrates), 71
Address to the Nobility of the German Nation (Luther), 283
Adelard of Bath, 198
Administration. *See* Government
Adoration of the Magi (Dürer), 270, *271*
Adrianople, Battle of, 141
Adultery: in Egypt, 23; in Frankish society, 145
Aediles (Rome), 93
Aegospotami, Battle of, 58
Aelius Spartianus, 113–14
Aeneid, The (Virgil), 123–24
Aeolian Greeks, 48
Aequi people, 93
Aeschylus, 59
Affonso of Congo (Bakongo), 314
Afghanistan: Greek culture in, 79
Africa: Carthage as, 97; Egyptian civilization and, 13–14; gold in, 308, 315; Greek settlements in, 51; humans in, 2–3; Rome and, 119; slavery and, 313–15, 323
Against Celsus (Origen), 133–34
Agamemnon (Mycenae), 48, 49, 59
Agincourt, Battle of, 238
Agora, 50
Agricultural revolution: Neolithic, 4, 5
Agriculture, 4–5, 27, 130; Assyrian, 37; in Athens, 63–64; Columbian Exchange and, 326; in Egypt, 14, 16; in Middle Ages, 185–87; Roman, 90, 121–22, 139. *See also* Irrigation; Manors and manorialism
Agrippina (Rome), 126
Ahuramazda (god), 42, 130
Ain Ghazal, statue from, *4*
Akbar (Mughals), 319
Akhenaten (Egypt), 19; *Hymn to Aten,* 21
Akhetaten, Egypt. *See* Tell el-Amarna
Akkad and Akkadians, 9
Alaric (Visigoths), 141
Albania: Ottomans and, 274
Alberti, Leon Battista, 254, 258–59
Albigensians, 220, *221*
Albuquerque, Afonso de, 308
Alcuin, 167
Alemanni people, 138, 141
Alexander (movie), 75, *75*
Alexander VI (Pope), 261, 276
Alexander the Great, 22, *69,* 69–76, *72, 73;* conquests by, 72, 73 (map), 74; in India, 69, 72, 74; legacy of, 74–76
Alexandria, Egypt, 72, 78, 79, 81
Alexius I Comnenus (Byzantine), 223, 224
Alfonso VIII (Castile), 212
Algebra, 181
Ali (Muhammad's son-in-law), 158
Allah, 156
Alphabet: Greek, 34, *34,* 48; Latin (Roman), 34, *34*; Phoenician, 34, *34,* 48. *See also* Languages; Writing
Amazon River region: Inca and, 311
Amenhotep IV. *See* Akhenaten (Egypt)
America(s): Columbian Exchange and, 326; Columbus in, 305, *307,* 308, *310;* Europeans and, 305–6, 313, 321–22, 323; gold/silver in, 314, 316, 321, 326; naming of, 308. *See also* Colonies and colonization
American Indians, 308, 323
Ammianus Marcellinus: *Later Roman Empire, The,* 142
Amores (Ovid), 124
Amorites, 9
Amos (prophet), 32
Amsterdam: Exchange in, 328
An (god), 12
Anabaptists, 288–90
Anatolia, 28, 223. *See also* Turkey
al-Andalus (Andalusia, Spain), 180
Angkor kingdom, 317
Anglican Church. *See* Church of England
Anglo-Dutch trade wars, 326
Anglo-Saxons, in England, 145, 149, 206
Anjou, 207, 242, 271
Anne (England), 348
Anthemius of Tralles, *155*
Anthony (Saint), 147–48
Antigone (Sophocles), 59
Antigonid dynasty (Macedonia), 76
Antigonus Gonatus, 76
Antioch, Syria, 224, *225*
Antiochus IV (Seleucid), 85–86, 97
Anti-Semitism, 221, 234. *See also* Jews and Judaism
Antonine dynasty (Rome), *129*
Antoninus Pius (Rome), 117
Antony, Mark, 105, 109
Antwerp, 328
Apennine Mountains, 90
Aphrodite (goddess), 63
Apollo (god), 63
Appian Way, *95*
Appius Claudius (Rome), *95*
Aqueducts: in Rome, 105
Aquinas, Thomas (Saint), 200, 222–23, 248
Aquitaine, 210, 238
Arab Empire. *See* Arabs and Arab world
Arabian peninsula, 117, 155
Arabic language, 181, 198
Arabic numbers, 181
Arabs and Arab world: Byzantine Empire and, 154; cities of, 194; commentaries on Aristotle, 199; Islam and, 156–59; trade in, 180. *See also* Islam; Israel; Muslims Aragon, 212, 242, 271
Archaic Age (Greece), 49–50, 55
Archelaus (Macedonia), 70
Archimedean screw, 83
Archimedes of Syracuse, 82–83, 358
Architecture: of churches, *201,* 201–2, *202*; in Greece, 60–61; Hellenistic, 82; Roman, 105, 126
Arete (excellence), 49
Arian Christians, 140, 141–43
Aristarchus of Samos, 82
Aristocracy: in 17th century, 331–32; Aristotle on, 62; in Athens, 55; Junkers as, 339; in Middle Ages, 188–90; in Rome, 93, 106; in Russia, 340; in Spain, 339; women of, 189–90. *See also* Nobility
Aristophanes, 60
Aristotle, 51, 62, 181, 359; on gender roles, 248; medieval translation of, 198, 199; *Politics,* 62, 65; scholasticism and, 200
Armada (Spain), 301
Arretium, 121
Arrian (historian): on Alexander the Great, 74
Art(s): Black Death and, 248; as characteristic of civilization, 5; Egyptian, 18; in Europe, 350–52; in Greece, 60–61; Hellenistic, 82; Mesopotamian, 13; Paleolithic cave art and, 3; in Renaissance, *266,* 266–71, *267, 268, 269, 270, 271,* 358; Roman, 105. *See also* Culture; specific artists
Artisans, 16, 64; medieval, 194–96, *195*
Art of Love, The (Ovid), 124, 125
Ashur (god), 37
Ashurbanipal (Assyria), 34, 36, *37*
Ashurnasirpal II (Assyria), 35
Asia, 2, 98, 119, 177; Black Death and, 231; Catholic missionaries in, 293–94; Europeans and, 308, 315–21, *317,* 323; Mongols in, 214–15; Southeast, 315–21
Asia Minor, 28, 34, 39, 158; Alexander the Great in, 72; Pergamum control over, *78*
Asinoë II (Egypt), 81, *81*
Assemblies: in Athens, 55, 56; in Rome, 93; in Sparta, 53

Assyrian Empire, 34–37, 35 (map); Hebrews and, 30, *30*
Astrolabe, 181, 306
Astronomy: megalithic structures and, 27; Mesopotamian, 13; Muslim, 181; observatories and, 371; in Scientific Revolution, 359–64; women in, 367. *See also* Geocentric conception; Heliocentric conception
Atahualpa (Inca), 313
Aten (god), 19
Athanasius, 140
Athena (goddess), 59, 61, 63
Athenaeus (Greek historian), 41
Athens, 39, 46, 51, 53–55, 58, 70; democracy in, 55, 56–57; economy in, 54–55; empire of, 56–58; lifestyle in, 63–64; Peloponnesian War and, 45–46, 58; Persian Wars and, 39, 56; women in, 65–66
Attalid dynasty, 76
Attalus I (Pergamum), *78*
Attica, 46, 51, 53, 55
Atum (god), 17
Augsburg, Peace of, 286 (map), 287
Augustine of Canterbury (Saint), 149
Augustine of Hippo (Saint), 151–52
Augustus (Octavian, Rome), 105, 109, 113, *114*, 114–17, 118 (map), 130; Age of, 117, 123–24, 125; *Res Gestae*, 115
Aurelian (Rome), 129–30
Australopithecines, 2
Austrasia, 144
Austria/Austrian Empire, 341 (map); absolutism in, 340; Ottomans and, 274, 286; revolts in, 336
Avars, 163, 177, 214
Averroës, 199
Avicenna, 181
Avignon: papacy in, 243, 245
Azara, Félix de, 324
Aztecs, 310–11, 311 (map), *312*

Babur (Mughals), 319
Babylon and Babylonia, 34, 72 ; Chaldeans and, 38; Hammurabi in, 9–11; Hanging Gardens of, 38; Persians and, 38 39
Babylonian captivity, of Judaeans, 29, 30
Babylonian Captivity of the Church, The (Luther), 283
Bacchae, The (Euripides), 59
Bacon, Francis, 369–70
Baghdad, 179, 180, 194, 215, 223
Balkan region, 116, 129, 179; Byzantine Empire and, 223; Ottomans in, 274
Ball, John, 236
Baltic region, 179, 327; Russia and, 342, 342 (map)
Banking, 256, 328
Banquets: in Renaissance, 255, *259*
Bar (province), 271
Baroque style, 350–51
Barrel vault, 201, *201*
Basel, 287
Basil II (Byzantine Empire), 177
Basilicas, *201*, 201–2
Basques, 163
Batavia (Jakarta), 316–17
Baths: Roman, *119*
Bavaria, 163
Bayeux tapestry, *207*
Becket, Thomas à, 207
Bedouins, 155–56
Belgium, 191, 298
Belgrade: Ottomans and, 343
Belisarius (Byzantine general), 152
Bellarmine, Robert, 363–64
Belorussians, 179
Benedictine monasticism, 216
Benedict of Nursia (Saint), 148
Bengal, 319
Benin, 323
Berlin Academy: Winkelmann and, 367
Bern, 287
Bernard of Clairvaux (Saint), 218, 224
Bernini, Gian Lorenzo, 351
Beziers, France, 220
Bible, 151, 179; Gutenberg, 265; Vulgate, 152. *See also* Hebrew Bible; New Testament
Bill of Rights: in England, 348, 349
Birth control: Catholic Church on, 167
Bischofsheim: German convent at, 150
Bishops, 147, 216
Bithynia, 97
Black Death (plague), 230, 231–34, 233 (map); arts and, 248
Blackfriars (London), 352
Black Hole of Calcutta, 319
Black Sea region, 52, 141, 179
Blanche of Castile, 190
Boccaccio, Giovanni: on Black Death, 232
Bodin, Jean, 336
Body of Civil Law (Justinian), 152, 197, 199
Boeotia, 46, 58
Boğazkale, Turkey, 28
Bohemia, 273; in Austrian Empire, 340; Czechs in, 178; in Holy Roman Empire, 285; Hussites and, 275; Ottomans and, 274; in Thirty Years' War, 334
Boleyn, Anne, 290, 298
Bolivia: silver in, 326
Bologna: law school in, 197, 198
Bombay (Mumbai), 308
Boniface (Saint), 150
Boniface VIII (Pope), 243, 244, *244*, 245
Book of Common Prayer, 290
Book of Exodus, 31
Book of Kells, The, 150
Book of the City of Ladies, The (Christine de Pizan), 247
Book of the Courtier, The (Castiglione), 256–57
Book of the Dead (Egypt), 18
Books: printing and, 265–66
Bora, Katherina von, 285
Borgia family: Alexander VI of, 261, 276; Cesare, 261
Boroughs: in England, 191
Bosnia, 274
Bosporus, 51
Bourbon dynasty (France), 297, 337–38; in Spain, 338; Thirty Years' War and, 334
Bourgeoisie, 192
Boyars (Russian nobles), 215, 340
Boyle, Robert, 365
Brandenburg-Prussia, 339, 340 (map)
Brazil, 313, 321
Britain. *See* England (Britain)
British East India Company, 319–20
Britons: Celtic, 145
Brittany, 210
Bronze Age, 5
Bruges, 191, 194
Brunelleschi, Filippo, 267, *267*
Bruni, Leonardo, 263
Bubonic plague. *See* Black Death; Plague
Buddha: portrayals of, *83*
Bulgaria: Slavic, 179
Bulgars, 175, 177, 179, 214
Burckhardt, Jacob: on Renaissance, 254
Burg: in Germany, 191
Burgesses: in England, 207
Burgundians, 138, 141
Burgundy, 144, 210; dukes of, 238, 242
Burma (Myanmar), 317
Bury Saint Edmonds (abbey), 206
Byblos, 33
Byzantine Empire, 231; Arabs and, 154, 157; Crusades and, 223, 227; golden age of, 175–77; under Justinian, 144, 152–54, 153 (map); Macedonian dynasty in, 175–77; Ottoman conquest of, 227, 273–74; Seljuk Turks and, 223; silk industry in, 152; Venetian trade with, 144, 155 (map), 177 (map), 191. *See also* Eastern Roman Empire; Roman Empire
Byzantium, 51, 139–40, 154. *See also* Constantinople

Cabot, John, 308
Cabral, Pedro, 308
Caesar, Julius, 100, 107, *107*; *Civil Wars, The*, 108
Caffa, 231
Cairo, 180, 194; Fatimids in, 223
Calais, 238
Calendar: Mayan, 310; Mesopotamian, 13
Calicut (Kozhikode), 307
Caliphs and caliphates, 157, 158, 223; Abbasid, 179–80, 180 (map); Umayyad, 179
Calvin, John, and Calvinism, 291, 291 (map), *292*, 296; Church of England and, 299, 344; French Wars of Religion and, 297; Netherlands and, 298; Thirty Years' War and, 334
Cam (China), 186
Cambodia, 317
Cambridge University, 197
Cambyses (Persia), 39
Campania, 90
Canaan, 27, 28, 33, 34; Egypt and, 19, 22; Israel and, 29
Canada: France and, 322
Cannae, Battle of 97, 98
Canterbury, archbishop of, 207, 290
Canterbury Tales, The (Chaucer), 246
Canton (Guangzhou), China, 320
Cape of Good Hope, 307 310
Capetian dynasty (France), 209–11, 210 (map), 236
Capua, *95*, 121
Caracalla (Rome), 118, 120, *129*
Caraffa, Gian Pietro (Paul IV), 294, 295–96
Caral (city), 6
Cardinals, 217, 243, 245
Carinthia, 340
Carniola, 340
Carolingian Empire, 163–71, 165 (map); disintegration of, 169–75; division of, 169 (map)
Carolingian Renaissance, 166–67
Carruca (plow), 185–86
Carthage, 34, 96; Roman conquest of, 96–97
Caspian Sea region, 38
Cassiodorus, 152
Castiglione, Baldassare, 256–57
Castile, 212, 271
Castles: medieval, 188
Çatal Hüyük, 4
Catalonia: revolts in, 336
Catharism, 220
Cathedrals: Gothic, 201–2, *202*

Catherine of Aragon, 290
Catherine of Siena, 245
Catholic Church, 140, 143, 273; in Americas, 313, 323; on Arianism, 143; in Carolingian Empire, 165, 167; decline of, 216, 243–46; in Early Middle Ages, *147*; Eastern Orthodox Christianity and, 223; England and, 290–91, 346–48; in Europe (by 1560), 294 (map); in France, 297; Galileo and, 361; Great Schism in, 245–46, 274, 275; heresies in, 220; in High Middle Ages, 205–6, 216–27; Protestant Reformation and, 280, 281–82; reforms of, 216–17, 275; in Renaissance, 274–76; in Spain, 272, 273; Thirty Years' War and, 334; in Vietnam, 317; western Slavs and, 178. *See also* Catholic Reformation; Inquisition; Reformation
Catholic League, 335 (map)
Catholic Reformation, 293–96
Cato the Elder, 101, 102
Catullus, 103
Cavendish, Margaret, *366*, 366–67
Celtic languages, 28
Celtic peoples, 76–77, *78*, 106
Central America, 308, 323 *See also* Latin America
Central Asia: civilization of, 6, 6 (map), 114, 231, 305
Centuriate assembly (Rome), 93
Cereta, Laura, 264, 265
Ceylon (Sri Lanka), 309, 316
Chaeronea, Battle of, 70
Chaldeans, 30, 34, 38
Champagne: trade fairs in, 191
Chandragupta Maurya (India), 76
Chanson de geste, 200–201
Chariots, 19, 100, 154
Charlemagne, 162–63, *166*; achievements of, 165–68; coronation of, 162, *162*, 166
Charles I (England), 344–46
Charles II (England), 346, 370
Charles IV (Holy Roman Empire), 242
Charles V (Holy Roman Empire), 260, 273, 284, 285–87, 286 (map), *287*, 290
Charles VI (France), 238, 242
Charles VII (France), 238, 240
Charles VIII (France), 260
Charles XII (Sweden), 342
Charles Martel, 163
Charles the Bald (Frankish kingdom), *166*, 169
Charters of liberties, 192–94
Chaucer, Geoffrey, 246
Chauvet Cave, 3
Chemistry: Muslim, 181; in Scientific Revolution, 365–66
Children's Crusade, 227
China, 6, 121, 186; bubonic plague in, 231 Christian missionaries in, 323–24; Han Empire in, 114, 118; Portugal and, 308, 320; Russia and, 320
Chivalry, 188
Christian (northern Renaissance) humanism, 280–81
Christianity, 42, 85, 130; in Americas, 323; in Britain, 149–50; in Byzantine Empire, 155; in China, 323–24; in Germanic kingdoms, 141–43, 150, 163; intellectual thought and, 151–52; in Japan, 293–94; Jewish background of, 130–31; of Magyars, 169; medieval civilization and, 217–23; origins and early development of, 130–34, 137, 140; in Prussia, 214; in Russia, 176, 179, 215; in Scandinavia, 213–14; secularism and, 331; sexuality and, 167–68; Slavic, 178–79; in Spain, 211–12; spread and growth of, 147–52, 151 (map); Viking conversion to, 171; women and, 134, 148, 150–51. *See also* Papacy; Popes; Reformation; specific groups
Christine de Pizan, 246–47
Chronicle of the First Crusade (Fulcher of Chartres), 226
Chrysoloras, Manuel, 263
Church of England, 290, 299, 344
Cicero, 100, 103, 263; *Letter to Atticus*, 108–9
Cincinnatus, 94
Ciompi revolt: in Florence, 236
Circus Maximus, 100, 127
Cistercian order, 218
Cities and towns: in Arab world, 194; Assyrian, 37; as characteristic of civilization, 5; governments of, 194; Hellenistic, 78–79; in Middle Ages, 185, 191–96, *195*; Neolithic, 4–5; in North America, 322; revolts in, 236; in Roman Empire, 119, 121; Sumerian, 7–8
City of God, The (Augustine of Hippo), 151–52
City-states: Greek, 45–46, 47 (map), 49–55, 58; Italian, 213, 213 (map), 242–43, 259–60; Mesopotamian, 9, 11
Civic humanism, 263
Civilization: characteristics of, 5. *See also* specific civilizations
Civilization of the Renaissance in Italy (Burckhardt), 254
Civil Wars, The (Caesar), 108
Clarendon, Lord, 347–48
Classes. *See* Estates (social orders); Society
Classical culture: in Carolingian Renaissance, 166–67; Christianity and, 152; in Greece, 46, 47 (map), 58–66; Islamic scholars and, 181; medieval revival of, 198–99; Renaissance and, 254, 263–64
Classicism: in arts, 351
Cleanthes, 84
Cleisthenes (Athens), 55
Clement VII (Pope), 286, 290
Cleopatra VII (Egypt), 76, 109
Clergy: in Catholic Church, 216, 281; celibacy and, 150–51, 167, 283, 285, 292, 296; in England, 150, 290; Erasmus on, 281; heresy and, 275; sacraments administered by, 220; taxation of, 243. *See also* First Estate
Clermont, Council of, 224
Climate: "little ice age" and, 231, 332; plague and, 234
Clive, Robert, 319
Clocks: invention of, 250
Clotilde (Burgundians), 138
Clouds, The (Aristophanes), 60
Clovis (Franks), *137*, 138, 143
Cluniac reform movement, 216
Cluny: abbey at, 216
Code of Hammurabi, 9–11
Colbert, Jean-Baptiste, 337, *370*
Colleges. *See* Universities and colleges
Colloquy of Regensburg, 295–96
Cologne, Germany, 221
Colonies and colonization, 107, 305, 326; in Americas, 321–22; Greek, 46, 51–52, 78, 90; Phoenician, 33 (map), 34
Colosseum (Rome), *127*
Columba (Saint), 148–49
Columbian Exchange, 326
Columbus, Christopher, 305, *307*, 308, *310*
Columns: Greek, *60*
Comedy (drama): Greek, 60; New Comedy, 81
Commerce: in Constantinople, 153; Dutch, 322; expansion of, 305–6; Hellenistic, 79; international, 328; Minoan, 46; price revolution and, 327. *See also* Trade
Commercial capitalism, 191, 327–28
Common law (England), 207
Commonwealth: England as, 346
Comneni dynasty (Byzantine Empire), 223
Compass, 306
Compurgation, 145
Conciliarism, 245–46
Concordat of Worms, 216
Condottieri (mercenaries), 259, 260
Conquistadors, 306, 310
Conrad III (Germany), 224
Consistory, 291
Constance, Council of, 246, 274, 275
Constantine (Rome), 137, 139–41, *140*
Constantinople, 139–40, 152, 194, 231; Byzantium as, 51; fall of (1453), 309; Latin Empire of, 227; lifestyle in, 152–54; Muslim attack on (717), 158; Ottoman Turks and, 274; sack of, 227
Constitutional monarchy: in England, 344–50
Constitution of the Spartans (Xenophon), 65
Consuls (Rome), 92, 93, 106
Contarini, Gasparo, 294, 295
Convents, 150. *See also* Monks and monasticism; Nuns; Religious orders
Copernicus, Nicolaus, 359–60, 361, *361*, 362
Copper, 5
Córdoba, 158, 180; Great Mosque of, 181, *181*
Corinth, 46, 98
Corinthian League, 70
Corinthian order (columns), *60*
Corn. *See* Maize (corn)
Cornwall, 145
Corpus Hermeticum, 264
Corpus Iuris Civilis (Justinian), 152
Corsica, 27, 96
Cortes (Spanish parliament), 272
Cortés, Hernán, 306, 311, 312
Cosimo de' Medici. *See* Medici family
Council of Five Hundred (Athens), 55
Council of the plebs (Rome), 93
Councils (Christian), 245–46; of Clermont, 224; of Constance, 246, 274, 275; of Nicaea, 140; of Pisa, 246; of Trent, 294, 296
Counter-Reformation, 293, 296. *See also* Catholic Reformation
Counts: in Carolingian Empire, 165
Covenant: Hebrew, 31–32
Cranmer, Thomas, 290
Crassus (Rome), 107
Creation of Adam (Michelangelo), *253*, 253–54
Crécy, Battle of, 236–37
Crete, 16, 177; Minoan civilization of, 46–47, 48 (map)
Croatia: Austrian Empire and, 340
Croesus (Lydia), 63
Cromwell, Oliver, 346, *346*, 347–48
Crossbow, 236
Crusader states, 224
Crusades, 189, 220, 221, 223–27; 1st, 224, *225*, 225 (map); 2nd, 224, 225 (map); 3rd, 224–26, 225 (map); 4th, 227; of 13th century, 227; against Albigensians, 220; Children's, 227; Frederick II (Holy Roman Empire) and, *212*; Louis IX and, 211; Peasants', 224
Cruz, Juana Inés de la, 323
Culture: Assyrian, 37; Byzantine, 176; civilization as, 5; Egyptian, 17–19; European, 350–53, 354; of Frankish lands, 169; Greek, 46, 47

(map), 51–52, 58–66, 69–70, 138; Hellenistic, 70, 76, 78–79, 81–85; in High Middle Ages, 196–202; Hittite, 28; Islamic, 180–81; in Later Middle Ages, 246–48; Mesopotamian, 11–13; Phoenicians as transmitters of, 34; popular, 293; Renaissance, 261–66, 276; Roman, 103–5, 119, 123–25, 138; science and, 371. *See also* Intellectual thought; Society
Cumberland (region), 145
Cummean (Irish abbot): Penitential of, 149
Cuneiform writing, *12*, 13
Cuxham Manor, England, 234–35
Cuzco, Peru, 311, 313
Cyaxares (Medes), 38
Cyprus, 177
Cyril (missionary), 179
Cyrillic alphabet, 179
Cyrus Cylinder, 36
Cyrus the Great (Persia), 36, 38–39
Czech people, 178, 275

Dacia (Romania), 117
Da Gama, Vasco, 307–8, 309, *309*
Dahomey, 323
Daily life. *See* Lifestyle
Damascus, 158, 179, 194
Danelaw, 171
Dante Alighieri, 246, 247
Dardanelles. *See* Hellespont
Darius III (Persia), 72, *73*
Dark Age, in Greece, 48–49
Dati, Gregorio, 257–58
David (Donatello), 267, *267*
David (Israel), 29
David (Michelangelo), 269, *270*
Dead Sea Scrolls, 131
Death rates. *See* Mortality rates
Decameron (Boccaccio), 232
Declaration of Indulgence (England), 346, 348
Decretum (Gratian), 190
Defense of the Liberal Instruction of Women (Cereta), 265
De Hooch, Pieter, 345, *345*
Deir el Bahri (Egypt): temple at, 23
Delian League, 56, 57, 64
Delphi, oracle at, 63
Demes (Attica villages and townships), 55
Demesne, 174
Democracy: in Athens, 55, 56–57
Demosthenes (Athens): on Philip II (Macedonia), 71
Denmark, 145, 213, 336; in Thirty Years' War, 334; Vikings and, 169, 170 (map)
Descartes, René, 368–69, *369*, 370
Description and History of Paraguay and Rio de la Plata (Azara), 324
Description of the Rus (Ibn Fadlan), 178
D'Este family: dukes of, 243; Isabella, 260
"Diary of a Citizen," 316
Dias, Bartolomeu, 307
Díaz de Vivar, Rodrigo. *See* El Cid
Dictators: in Rome, 94, 106–7
Diet of Worms, *284*
Diet (food): Athenian, 64; in Carolingian Empire, 168; in Egypt, *20*; in Islam, 156; of medieval peasants, 188. *See also* Food
Diocletian (Rome), 134, 137, 138
Dionysus (god), 59
Diplomacy, 320, Roman, 95–96
Discourse on Method (Descartes), 368–69
Diseases: European in Americas, 311, 312, 313. *See also* Black Death
Disibodenberg: convent at, 219
Divination, 12
Divine and Human Readings (Cassiodorus), 152
Divine Comedy (Dante), 246, 247
Divine-right theory: England and, 350
Divorce: Code of Hammurabi on, 11; in Egypt, 23; in Frankish society, 145
Dominican Republic, 308
Dominicans, 219, 323, 324
Dominic de Guzmán (Saint), 219
Donatello, Donati de, 267
Dondi, Giovanni di, 250
Dorian Greeks, 48
Doric order (columns), *61*
Doryphoros (statue), 61, *61*
Dowry: in Hammurabi's Code, 10–11; in Renaissance, 257
Drama: English, 352, 354; French, 353; Greek, 59–60; Hellenistic, 81; Roman, 103; Spanish, 352–53
Drogheda, massacre at, 347
Dualism: Cartesian, 369
Dürer, Albrecht, 270, *271*
Dutch, 332; in Americas, 322; domesticity of, 345, *345*; in Indonesia, 317; in Japan, 321; painting, 351–52; Republic, 298, 305, 344; Scientific Revolution and, 361; in Southeast Asia, 316–17, *316–17*; Spain and, 298. *See also* Netherlands
Dutch East India Company, 317, *317*, 328

Early History of Rome (Livy), 94
Early Middle Ages: Catholic Church in, *147*; Europe in, 162–82; lords and vassals in, 171–75; medicine in, *168*, 168–69; monasticism during, 216. *See also* Middle Ages
Early Roman Empire. *See* Roman Empire
Earth-centered view. *See* Geocentric conception
East Africa, 2, 314
Eastern Europe, 214 (map); absolutism in, 340–42; Jews in, 234; monarchs in, 273; Slavic peoples of, 177–79. *See also* Europe
Eastern Orthodox Christianity, 176; in Byzantine Empire, 175, 223; in Russia, 215; of southern Slavs, 179
Eastern Roman Empire, 140–41, 143, 152; transition to Byzantine Empire, 154–55. *See also* Byzantine Empire
Eastern Slavs, 179
East India Company. *See* British East India Company; Dutch East India Company
East Prussia, 214
Economy: in Athens, 54–55; Black Death and, 234–35, 248; Byzantine, 176; in Carolingian Empire, 165; as characteristic of civilization, 5; commercial capitalism and, 191, 327–28; in Egypt, 16; European expansion and, 326; global, 327–28; in Greece, 63–64; Hellenistic, 79; Islamic, 180; mercantilism and, 328; price revolution and, 327; in Roman Empire, 120–22, 130, 138–39; in Sumer, 8–9; Thirty Years' War and, 334–35; worldwide, 327–28. *See also* Trade
Edessa, 224
Edict of Fontainebleau, 337
Edict of Nantes, 297
Edict of Worms, 284
Education: Islamic, 181; Mesopotamian, 13; in Renaissance, 264; for women, 80, 101. *See also* Universities and colleges
Education of a Christian Prince (Erasmus), 262–63
Edward I (England), 207
Edward III (England), 236–37
Edward VI (England), 290, 299
Egypt, 2, 5, 6; agriculture in, 14, 16; Alexander the Great and, 22, 72; Antony and Cleopatra in, 109; Assyrians in, 34; burials in, 18, *19*; culture of, 17–19; diet (food) in, *20*; dynasties in, 19, 22; economy in, 14, 16; expansion of, 19; Fatimid conquest of, 223; geography of, 13–14; government of, 15–16; Hebrew Exodus from, 28; historical periods in, 16; Hyksos people in, 19; invasions of, 22; Jews in, 86; lifestyle in, 22–23; Middle Kingdom in, 16; New Kingdom in, 15; Old Kingdom in, 15–16; Persians and, 22, 39; pharaohs in, 15, 16, 22, 76, 81; Ptolemaic dynasty in, 76; pyramids in, 18, *19*; religion in, *17*, 17–18, 19, 85; Rome and, 22; society in, 16; wise sayings from, 22, 23; women in, 22–23, 81, *81*; writing in, 19
Einhard: on Charlemagne, 163, 164, 166
El Cid (Spain), 211
Eleanor of Aquitaine, 189, 208, *208*
Electors of Saxony, 284, 285
Elements (Euclid), 82, 198
Eleusis, 85
Elizabeth (movie), 300, *300*
Elizabeth I (England), 290, *298*, 298–301; address to Parliament (1601), 299
Elizabethan literature, 352
Empires: of Alexander the Great, 72–76, 73 (map); of Charlemagne, 166; in Mesoamerica, 310–11; in Mesopotamia, 9–11, 9 (map); Mongol, 230; in Near East, 27; in South America, 311–12; trading, 308. *See also* specific empires
Empiricism, 370
Encomienda system, 313
England (Britain), 27, 210 (map); Anglo-Saxon, 145; Christianity in, 148–49; civil war in, 346; colonies of, 321–22; as commonwealth, 346; constitutional monarchy in, 344–50; drama in, 352, 354; under Elizabeth I, 290, *298*, 298–301; exploration by, 305, 308; foreign policy in, 299–301; France and, 206, 326; gentry in, 271; after Hundred Years' War, 271; India and, 319–20; monarchy in, 206–7, 344–50; Peasants' Revolt in (1381), 235; plague in, 233; population in 17th century, 332; Protestant Reformation in, 290–91; restoration of monarchy in, 346–48; revolt in, 336; Rome and, 114; Scientific Revolution and, 361; taxation in, 344–46; Vikings in, *171*; West Indies colonies of, 321; Wyclif in, 274
English Revolution, 336
Enki (god), 11
Enlil (god), 11
Enuma Elish (Babylonian creation epic), 11
Epaminondas (Thebes), 58
Ephors: in Sparta, 53
Epic of Gilgamesh, The, 11, 13, 14
Epicureanism, 83–84
Epicurus, 83
Epidemics. *See* Black Death; Diseases
Epistle to the Colossians (Paul), 134
Equestrian order (Rome), 106, 116
Erasmus, Desiderius, 262–63, 280–81, *281*
Eratosthenes, 82
Eridu, Mesopotamia, 7
Erik the Red, 171

Essenes, 131
Estates (parliaments): in France, 337
Estates (social orders), 256; in France, 211; in Renaissance, 256
Estonia, 342
Ethelbert (England), 149
Etruria, 91
Etruscans, 89, 90, 90 (map), 91, 91 (map), *92*, 93, 95
Eucharist, 220, 285
Euclid, 82, 198
Euphrates River, 6
Euripides, 59, 263
Eurocentric perspective, 326–27
Europe, 2, 28, 162–63, 215; in 15th century, 272 (map); Americas and, 305–6, 321–22, 326; Asia and, 315–21, *317*; Black Death in, 231–34, 233 (map); Crusades and, 227; culture in, 350–53, 354; in Early Middle Ages, 162–82; exploration and expansion by, 304–28; in High Middle Ages, 184–203, 205–28; India and, 319–20; lords and vassals in, 173; megalithic structures in, 27; Mongols and, 215; recession in 17th century, 332; state building in, 331–53; trade of, 328. *See also* Eastern Europe; Western Europe; specific locations
Evans, Arthur, 46
"Exchange Between Pliny and Trajan, An," 133
Excommunication: of Luther, 284; of Phillip IV (France), 243; of pope and patriarch, 223
Exodus: Book of, 31; of Hebrews, 28
Exports: Hellenistic, 79; mercantilism and, 328

Families: in Athens, 64; Black Death and, 248; in Carolingian Empire, 167; in Code of Hammurabi, 10; in Egypt, 22–23; Frankish, 145; Germanic, 145; Protestantism and, 292–93; in Renaissance Italy, 257–59; in Rome, 100, 101, 125–26
Fatimid dynasty, 180, 223
Ferdinand of Aragon (Spain), 271–72
Ferrara, 260
Fertile Crescent, 4, 6
Feudalism, 171, 173
Ficino, Marsilio, 264
Fiefs: in Europe, 172–74
Fire, 3
Firearms. *See* Weapons
First Crusade, 224
First Estate (clergy), 211, 256
First Punic War, 97
First Triumvirate (Rome), 107, *107*
Fitz-Stephen, William, 184–85
Five good emperors (Rome), 117
Five Pillars of Islam, 156, 157
Flagellants, Black Death and, 234, *234*
Flanders: trade in, 191, 191 (map), 256
Flavian dynasty (Rome), 117
Flood(s): in *Epic of Gilgamesh*, 14; by Nile, 13–14
Florence, 194, 213, 243, 258; *ciompi* revolt in, 236; cultural Renaissance in, 259; Medici in, 256; painting in, 248
Florus (historian), 109
Flying buttress, 202, *202*
Fontainebleau, Edict of, 337
Food: in Athens, 64; human survival and, 5; medieval prices of, 187; Neolithic, 5; of Paleolithic peoples, 3; production of, 4. *See also* Agriculture; Diet (food);
Forests: destruction of medieval, 186
Fort William (Calcutta), 319
Forum (Rome), 117
Foscarini Paolo: Bellarmine's letter to, 363–64
Fourth Crusade, 227
Fourth Lateran Council: on Jews, 221, 222
France, 51, 169, 337; in 14th century, 237 (map); in 15th century, 237 (map); absolutism in, 336–38; Albigensian Crusade in, 220; Avignon papacy and, 243, 245; Capetian dynasty in, 209–11; classicism in, 351; Crusades and, 224; drama in, 353; England and, 206, 210 (map), 326; exploration by, 305; Habsburg-Valois Wars and, 286; Huguenots in, 297, 336; Hundred Years' War and, 271; India and, 319–20; intellectual thought in, 197; Italian states occupied by, 260; *Jacquerie* in, 235; kingdom of, 207–11; Middle Kingdom territories and, 169; North American colonies of, 322; plague in, 233; population in 17th century, 332; religion in, 297, 336; revolts in, 336; Scientific Revolution and, 361; Spain and, 339; in Thirty Years' War, 334; trade and, 191; Vietnam and, 317; Vikings in, 171; West Indies colonies of, 321; witchcraft trial in, 333
Francis I (France), 285–86
Franciscans, 219, 323, 324, 325
Francis of Assisi (Saint), 219
Francis Xavier, 293–94, 321
Franks, 129, 138; kingdom of (Frankish kingdom), 143–45, 169, 171
Frederick I ("Barbarossa," Holy Roman Empire), 197, 212, 213 (map), 224, 226
Frederick I (Prussia), 339
Frederick II (Holy Roman Empire), *212*, 212–13, 213 (map)
Frederick the Wise (elector of Saxony), *271*, 281
Frederick William (Great Elector, Brandenburg-Prussia), 339, 340 (map)
French language, 169, 201
Friars. *See* Monks and monasticism
Frisia/Frisians, 150, 170
Froissart, Jean (chronicler), 236, 237
Fronde, 336
Fulbert of Chartres: on lords and vassals, 173

Gaius Gracchus (Rome), 106
Galen (Greek physician), 198, 365
Galilei, Galileo, 358, 359, 360–61; on science vs. religion, 363, 371
Gallo-Roman peoples, 144
Gandhara: Greek sculpture and, 82
Ganges River region, 319
Gascony, 236
Gasga people, 28
Gaudry, Suzanne, witchcraft trial of, 333
Gaugamela, Battle of, 72
Gaul: Caesar in, 107; Frankish, 129, 143–45; Rome and, 107, 116, 119, 129–30
Gedrosian Desert, 72
Gender: Neolithic agriculture and, 5; roles after Black Death, 248; in Roman society, 101. *See also* Women
General War Commissariat (Prussia), 339
Geneva, Calvin in, 291, 291 (map)
Genghis Khan (Mongols), 214, 319
Genoa, 194, 233; in Crusades, 224, 227
Gentiles: Paul and, 132
Gentileschi, Artemisia, 351, *352*
Gentry: in England, 271, 344
Geocentric conception, 82, 358, 359, 360
Geography: Assyrian, 37; Egyptian, 13–14; of Greece, 46; of Italy, 90
Geography (Ptolemy), 306, *306*
Geometry: Euclid on, 82; Mesopotamian, 13
Germania (Tacitus), 125
Germanic kingdoms, 141–46, 155; Christianity in, 141–43, 144 (map), 163
Germanic languages, 28
Germanic peoples, 169, 216; kingdoms of, 137–38; Rome and, 116, 129, 130, 141
German language, 169
Germany, 3, 150, 163; after Carolingian Empire, 169; Habsburgs and, 340; in Holy Roman Empire, 212–13; Jews in, 234; Lutheranism in, 285–87; Middle Kingdom territories and, 169; monarchy in, 242; nobility in, 213 (map); Peasants' War in, 285; plague in, 233–34; Protestant Reformation in, 285–87; Roman Empire and, *119*; in Thirty Years' War, 334, 339; trade and, 191; tribes from, 145; witchcraft trials in, 334. *See also* Brandenburg-Prussia
Geta (Rome), *129*
Ghent, 191, 194
Gigas, Herman, 232
Gilgamesh (legendary king), 11, 13, 14
Giotto, *248*
Giovanni Arnolfini and His Bride (Van Eyck), 269–70, *271*
Giza, pyramids of, 18, *19*
Gladiator (movie), 128, *128*
Gladiators, 100, 127, 154
Globalization: of economy, 327–28; of trade, 328
Globe theater (London), 352
Glorious Revolution (England), 348–50
Goa: Portugal and, 308
Godric, 193
Gods and goddesses: Assyrian, 37; Egyptian, *17*, 17–18, 85; Greek, 60, 63, 85; Jewish, 30–32; Mesopotamian, 11–13; Roman, 99–100; Sumerian, 8. *See also* Religion
Gold: in Africa, 308; in Americas, 314, 326; 326; mercantilists and, 328
Golden Bull, 242
"Golden Speech, The" (Elizabeth I, England), 299
Good emperors (Rome), 117
Gospels (Christian), 132, 147, 219
Gothic architecture, 201–2, *202*
Goths, 129
Government: in 14th century, 239–41; Aristotle on, 62; of Assyrian Empire, 34–35; of Athens, 56–57; Augustine of Hippo on, 152; of Carolingian Empire, 165–66; in central Europe, 273; as characteristic of civilization, 5; in eastern Europe, 273; of Egypt, 15–16; of England, 241; of Greek *polis*, 52; Hittite, 28; Hobbes and Locke on, 350; lord-vassal relationships and, 172–74; of Medes, 38; of medieval cities and towns, 194; of Ostrogothic Italy, 143; of Persian Empire, 38, 40–42; Plato on, 62; in Renaissance, 271–74; of Rome, 92–93, 114–16, 138; of Russia, 341; of Spanish Empire, 313; in Sparta, 53; of Sumer, 8. *See also* Law codes; Monarchs and monarchies
Gracchi (Rome): reforms by, 106
Granada, 271, 273
Granicus River, Battle of, 72
Gratian: *Decretum*, 190
Great Britain. *See* England (Britain)
Great Council of barons (England), 241
Great Instauration, The (Bacon), 369
Great Mosque: of Córdoba, 181, *181*
Great Northern War, 342
Great Pyramid (Giza), 18, *19*
Great Schism, in Catholic Church, 245–46, 274, 275

Great Wall (China), 320
Greco-Macedonian society, 76, 78
Greco-Roman civilization, 99–100; Christians and, 132, 151; in Italian Renaissance, 254. *See also* Greece; Roman Empire
Greece, 45–46, 47 (map); Antigonids and, 76; Archaic Age in, 49–50, 55; architecture in, 60–61; city-states in, 49–55; Classical culture of, 46, 47 (map), 58–66, 198–99; colonization and trade in, 46, 51–52; Dark Age in, 48; drama in, 59–60; economy in, 63–64; geography of, 46; Homeric, 48–49; Ionia and, 39, 48; Italy and, 90, 91; lifestyle in, 63–64; migration from, 48, 78; military in, 51; Minoan Crete and, 46–47, 48 (map); Mycenaean, 47–48, 48 (map); Persian Empire and, 39, 55–56; Philip II and conquest of, 46, 70; philosophy in, 61–63; religion in, 60, 63, 85; Rome and, 90, 91, 95, 97–98, 99, 101; society in, 63–64; tyranny in, 52. *See also* Athens; Hellenistic world; *Polis* (Greek city-state); Sparta
Greek language, 28; alphabet of, *34*; in Byzantine Empire, 155; New Testament in, 151; in Renaissance, 263; in Roman provinces, 118, 119
Greenland: Vikings in, 171
Greenwich, England: observatory in, 371
Gregory I ("the Great," Pope), 147, *147*, 149–50
Gregory VII (Pope), 216
Gregory XI (Pope), 245
Gregory of Tours, 138, 146
Guadeloupe, 321
Guangzhou, China, 320
Guaraní Indians, 324
Guilds, 248; in medieval cities, 196; in universities, 196
Guise family (France), 297
Gunpowder, 238, 250, 274
Gutenberg, Johannes, 265
Guzman, Gaspar de (Spain), 339

Habsburg dynasty, 213, 334, 340; Holy Roman Empire and, 273, 285
Habsburg-Valois Wars, 286
Hadrian (Rome), 113, *113*, 117
Hagia Sophia (Constantinople), 154, *155*
Haiti, 308, 321, 322
Hajj (pilgrimage), 156
Hall of Mirrors (Versailles), *338*
Hammurabi, 9–11, 9 (map)
Handbook of the Christian Knight (Erasmus), 280
Han Empire (China), 114, 118
Hanging Gardens of Babylon, 38
Hannibal (Carthage), 97
Hanseatic League, 255, 256
Hanukkah, 86
Harappa (city), 5, 6 (map)
Harold (England), 206
Harun al-Rashid (Abbasid), 180
Harvey, William, 365
Hastati (Roman spearmen), 98
Hastings, Battle of, 206, *207*
Hatshepsut (Egyptian queen), 23
Hattusha, 28
Hebrew Bible, 28, 132; Psalm 104 of, 21; translation of, 152; on united kingdom of Israel, 29
Hebrews, 27, 28–33; Assyria and, 30; laws of, 31–32, *33*; in Persian Empire, 39; prophets of, 32–33. *See also* Israel; Jews and Judaism
Hegira, 156
Heliocentric conception, 82, 359
Hellenic languages, 28
Hellenistic world, 70, 73 (map), 75–76, 77 (map); Celtic threat in, 76–77; cities in, 78–79; culture in, 81–85; economy in, 79; intellectual thought in, 81–85; Jews in, 85–86; monarchies in, 76; religion in, 85–86; Rome and, 97–98; science in, 82–83; women in, 79–81
Hellespont, 51, 58
Helots, 53
Henry II (England), 189, 206–7, 208, *208*
Henry III (England), 190
Henry IV (England), 241
Henry IV (France), 216, 297
Henry IV (Germany), 212
Henry V (England), 237–38
Henry VI (England), 238
Henry VII (England), 271, 308
Henry VIII (England), 290, 294 (map), 298
Henry the Navigator (Portugal), 306–7, 307 (map)
Heracleion, Greece, 46
Heresy, 140; Albigensian, 220; Catholic Church and, 140, 219, 220–21, 275
Hermes (god), 100
Hermeticism, 264, 359
Herodotus (historian), 18, 58–59
Hibernia: Ireland as, *150*
Hiberno-Saxon works, *150*
Hieroglyphics: Egyptian, 19. *See also* Writing
High Middle Ages, 184–203; aristocracy of, 188–90; arts in, *201*, 201–2, *202*; Catholic Church in, 205–6, 216–27; church-state conflict during, 216–17; cities and towns in, 191–96, *195*; culture of, 198–202; Holy Roman Empire in, 242; industry in, 196; intellectual thought in, 196–202, 197 (map), *198*; inventions in, 250; Jews in, 221, 222; literature in, 200–201; nobility in, 206; nuns in, 219; popular religion in, 220; trade and cities in, 190–96. *See also* Crusades; Middle Ages
High Renaissance: in arts, 268–69
Hilda of Whitby (Saint), 150
Hildegard of Bingen, 219
Hindus and Hinduism: in India, 319
Hippias (Athens), 55
Hippocrates, 198
Hippodrome (Constantinople), 153, 154
Hispaniola, 308, 313
Hispano-Roman peoples, 143
History and historical writing: about Egypt, 15, 18; in Greece, 41, 58–59; Hellenistic, 81–82; about Rome, 94, 98, 108–9, 117, 124, 127
History of Rome (Livy), 102, 124–25
History of the Peloponnesian War (Thucydides), 58, 59
History of the Rebellion and Civil Wars in England, The (Clarendon), 347–48
Hittites, 28
Hobbes, Thomas, 350
Hohenstaufen family, 212, 242
Hohenzollern dynasty, 339
Holbein, Hans (the Younger), *281*
Holland. *See* Netherlands
Holy Land: in Crusades, 224; Teutonic Knights and, 214. *See also* Crusades; Jerusalem
Holy league, Spanish leadership of, 297
Holy Office. *See* Inquisition
Holy Roman Empire, 212–13, 213 (map), 242 (map), 286 (map); in Central Europe, 273; Council of Constance and, 246; Habsburg-Valois Wars and, 286; Luther, Lutheranism, and, 284, 285, 287; Ottoman Turks in, 286; politics in, 286–87, 334; religion in, 334; Thirty Years' War and, 334, 339
Holy Synod (Russia), 341
Homer and Homeric Greece, 48–49, 50
Hominids, 2–3
Homo: erectus, 22; *sapiens*, 2; *sapiens sapiens*, 2 (map), 3
Homosexuality: in Athens, 64; Catholic Church on, 168; medieval attitude toward, 221–23
Hondius, Henricus: map by, *327*
Hoplites, in Greece, 51, *56*
Horace (poet), 99, 124
Horatius (legendary hero), *89*, 89–90
Horses, 323; in Early Middle Ages, 172, *172*
Horus (god), 17, 85
House of Commons (England), 207, 241
House of Lords (England), 207, 241
House of Wisdom (Baghdad), 181
Housing, 3, 5, 6; in Constantinople, 153–54; in medieval castles, 188; of medieval peasants, 187–88; in Rome, 126
Huayna Inca, 311
Hudson, Henry, 322
Hugh Capet (France), 209
Huguenots, 297, 336, 337
Humanism, 253, 254, 263; Christian (northern Renaissance), 280–81; education and, 264; Italian Renaissance, 263–64 Hundred Years' War, 235, 236–38, *238*, 239, 241–42
Hungarians, 178. *See also* Magyars
Hungary, 214, 273; Austrian Empire and, 340; Christianity in, 178; in Holy Roman Empire, 285; Magyars in, 169; Mongols in, 215; Ottomans and, 274, 286, 343
Huns, 141, 177, 214; perceptions of, 142–43
Hunter-gatherers, 2, 3
Hus, John, and Hussites, 275
Hydaspes River, Battle of the, 72, 74
Hyksos people, Egypt and, 19
Hymn to Aten (Akhenaten), 21

Ibn al-Athir: on siege of Jerusalem, 226
Ibn Fadlan: *Description of the Rus*, 178
Ibn Khaldun: *Prolegomena*, 193–94
Ibn-Rushd. *See* Averroës
Ibn Sina. *See* Avicenna
Ice ages. *See* "Little ice age"
Ignatius of Loyola. *See* Loyola, Ignatius of
Île-de-France, 209
Iliad (Homer), 48–49, *49*, 50
Imitation of Christ (Thomas à Kempis), 281
Imperator (Rome), 116
Imperium (Rome), 92
Inca Empire, 311–13, 311 (map)
Incarnation, 200
Index of Forbidden Books, 296
India, 5, 6; Alexander the Great and, 69, 72, 74; England and, 319–20; France and, 319–20; West and, 319–20, 323
Indo-European languages, 28
Indo-Europeans, 27–28, 48
Indo-Iranian languages, 28
Indonesia: Dutch in, 317
Indulgences, 281, 282–83, 296
Indus River region: civilization in, 5–6
Industry: in Constantinople, 153; Hellenistic, 79; in medieval cities, 196; in Renaissance, 256; in Rome, 121
"Inferno" (*Divine Comedy*, Dante), 246, 247
Inflation: in price revolution, 327; in Roman Empire, 138–39; in Western Europe, 332

Innocent III (Pope), 217, 227
Inquisition, 296; Roman, 221, 361, 371; Scientific Revolution and, 358
Institutes of the Christian Religion (Calvin), 291
Instruction of the Vizier Ptah-hotep, The, 22
Insulae (Roman apartment blocks), 126
Intellectual thought: in Carolingian Empire, 166–67; Christianity and, 151–52; Hellenistic, 81–85; in High Middle Ages, 196–201, 197 (map); in Irish monasteries, 149; Islamic, 180–81; in Muslim Spain, 180; in Renaissance Italy, 261–66; scholasticism and, 200. *See also* Art(s); Literature; Science; Scientific Revolution
Interdict, 217
Intermediate Periods (Egypt), 15
Intolerance: of homosexuals, 221–23; of Jews, 221
Investiture Controversy, 216–17
Iona: monastic community in, 149
Ionia and Ionians, 39, 48, 55. *See also* Greece
Ionic order (columns), *60*
Iran, 34, 38. *See also* Persia; Persian Empire
Ireland, *150,* 170; monasticism in, 148–49
Irnerius (teacher), 197
Iron and iron industry, 5, 256; agriculture and, 185–86; Assyrians and, 34
Isabella d'Este. *See* d'Este family
Isabella of Castile (Spain), 271–72, 308, 313
Isaiah (prophet), 32, 33
Isidore of Miletus, *155*
Isis (goddess), 17; cult of, 85
Islam, 154, 179–81, 215; civilization of, 180–81; intellectual thought in, 198–99; law code of, 156–57; rise and spread of, 155–58, 159 (map); Seljuk Turks and, 223; teachings of, 156–57
Isocrates (Athens), 71
Israel/Israelites, 26–27, 29–34, 29 (map), 33 (map). *See also* Hebrews; Jews and Judaism
Issus, Battle of, 72, *73*
Istanbul. *See* Constantinople
Italic languages, 28
Italy, 90, 91 (map); in 14th century, 242 (map); in 17th century, 332; banking in, 256; Byzantine conquest of, 143, 152; Charlemagne and, 163, 167; cities in, 194; in Crusades, 224; family in Renaissance, 257–59; after Frederick II, 213; geography of, 90; Germany and, 242; Greeks in, 51, 90, 91; Habsburg-Valois Wars and, 286; in Holy Roman Empire, 212–13; intellectual thought in, 197, 261–66; law in, 199–200; Lombards in, 152; Ostrogoths in, 141, 143; papacy and, 242; Papal States in, 212, 213 (map), 216; plague in, 233; Renaissance in, 254, 255–69, 260 (map); Romans and, 93–96; states of, 242–43; trade in, 191. *See also* Holy Roman Empire; Roman Empire; Roman Republic; Rome
Ivan III (Russia), 273
Ivan IV ("the Terrible," Russia), 340

Jacquerie uprising, 235, *235*
Jamaica, 321
James I (England), 344
James II (England), 346–48, 349
James II (Scotland), 250
Jamestown, 322
Japan: Catholic missionaries in, 293–94, 324–25; lords and vassals in, 173; West and, 320–21, 323
Java: Dutch colonialism in, 316–17
Jerome (Saint), 152
Jerusalem, 29; Chaldean conquest of, 30; in Crusades, 224, 225, *225,* 226
Jesuits, 293–94, *296,* 323; in China, 323–24; in Japan, 293–94
Jesus of Nazareth, *131,* 131–32, 140, 156. *See also* Christianity
Jews and Judaism, 38; Black Death and, 234; Christianity and, 130–31; commentaries on Aristotle, 199; Crusades and, 224, 227; in Hellenistic world, 85–86; Inquisition and, 221; medieval treatment of, 221, 222; monotheism of, 30–32; persecution of, 221; in Spain, 212, 273. *See also* Hebrews
Jihad, 157
Joan of Arc, 238, *238,* 239
Joan of Arc (movie), *240,* 240–41
Jocelyn of Brakeland (monk), 206
John (England), 207, 209, 217
John (Saint): Gospel of, 132
John VI (Byzantine Empire), '231
Joint-stock company, 319, 327–28
Jollain, Nicolas-René, the Elder, *331*
Journeymen crafts workers, 196
Jousts, 189, *189*
Juana Inés de la Cruz (Sor), 323
Judaea, 85–86, 131
Judah, kingdom of, *29,* 29–30
Judaism. *See* Hebrews; Jews and Judaism
Judith Beheading Holofernes (Gentileschi), 351, *352*
Julia (Augustus's daughter), 116
Julio-Claudians (Rome), 117
Julius II (Pope), *269,* 275, 276
Junkers (Prussia), 339
Juno (goddess), 99
Jupiter Optimus Maximus (god), 99, 100
Justification by faith, 282, 285
Justinian (Byzantine Empire), 143, 152–55, *154,* 153 (map), 168; law codification by, 152, 197, 199
Juvenal (poet), 127–27

Ka (Egypt), 18
Ka'ba (Mecca), 156, 157
Kangxi (China), 320
Karelia, 342
Kassites, 9
Kent (kingdom), 145, 149
Kepler, Johannes, 350, 360
Khanbaliq, 215
Khorsabad, Assyria, 37
Khubilai Khan (Mongols), 214–15, 305
Khufu (Egypt), 18, *19*
al-Khwarizmi (mathematician), 181, 198–99
Kiev, 171, 179, 215
Kievan Rus: Christianity in, 176, 215
Kirch, Gottfried, 367
Knighton, Henry, 230
Knights, 172, *172,* 174, 188–89, *189;* gunpowder and, 250; Hundred Years' War and, 236; Teutonic, 214
Knossus, 46, 47
Knox, John, 291
Koran. *See* Qur'an
Kosovo: Battle of (1389), 274
Kyushu, 325

La Bruyère, Jean de, 367
Lachish, Judah, *30*
Laconia, 53
Lagash, Mesopotamia, 7
Lamentation (Giotto), *248*
Lancaster, House of (England), 241, 271
Landing of Marie de' Medici at Marseilles, The (Rubens), *351*
Languages: Greek, 28, 118, 119; Indo-European, 28; in Roman provinces, 118; Slavonic, 179; vernacular, 200, 246–47. *See also* Alphabet; Writing
Las Navas de Tolosa, Battle of, 212
Last Supper, The (Leonardo da Vinci), 268, *268*
Later Middle Ages, 241–43; culture and society of, 231–36
Later Roman Empire, The (Ammianus Marcellinus), 142
Latifundia (estates), 101, 106, 121
Latin alphabet, *34*
Latin Empire of Constantinople, 227
Latin Fathers of Catholic Church, 151
Latin language, 28, 118, 119; Arabic works in, 181; in Byzantine Empire, 155; in Carolingian Empire, 167; literature in, 103, 123–25; New Testament in, 132; in Renaissance, 263; translation of works into, 198; vernacular and, 246
Latin people: in Rome, 94, 95
Latin Vulgate, 152
Latium, 90, 91, 94–95
Laureti, Tommaso, *89*
Lavoisier, Antoine, 365–66
Lavoisier, Marie-Anne, 366
Law(s): English common law, 207; Germanic, 145, 146; Hebrew, 31–32, *33;* Islamic, 156–57; of Justinian, 152, 155; Roman, 93, 101–2, 119–20, 199–200; in Spain, 143, 272; study of, 197, 198
Law codes: of Hammurabi, 9–11; of Justinian, 152; Twelve Tables (Rome), 101–2, 104
Law of nations (Rome), 103
Law of nature (Rome), 102
Lay investiture, 216
Lazar (Serbians), 274
Lechfeld, Battle of, 169
Lecture: origins of term, 197
Legions (Rome), 98, *99,* 116
Legnano, Battle of, 212
Leo III (Pope), 162, *162,* 166
Leo IX (Pope), 223
Leo X (Pope), *275,* 276, 282, 283
Leoba (nun), 150
Leonardo da Vinci, 268, *268,* 359
Leonidas (Sparta), 56
Leopold I (Austria), 340
Lepanto, Battle of, 297, 343
Lerma (duke of, Spain), 338
Lesbia (Clodia), 103
Lesbos, 48
"Letter from Isias to Hephaistion," 80
"Letter from Ktesikles to King Ptolemy," 80
Letter to Atticus (Cicero), 108–9
"Letter to Fuscus Salinator" (Pliny), 123
Leuctra, Battle of, 58
Levers: Archimedes and, 83
Leviathan (Hobbes), 350
Liberal arts curriculum, 152, 167, 264
Liberty(ies): charters of, 192–94
Libraries: in Alexandria, 81; Islamic, 181
Life of Charlemagne (Einhard), 164
Life of Saint Godric, 193
Lifestyle, 3–5; in Athens, 63–64; after Black Death, 248–50; in Byzantine Empire, 152–54; in Carolingian Empire, 167; in Constantinople, 152–54; Dutch domestic, 345, *345;* in Egypt, 22–23; European, 326; in Greek city-states, 49–55; in medieval

cities, 184–85, 194–96, *195*; peasant, *187*, 187–88; in Roman Empire, 123, 126–27; Spartan, 53. *See also* Society
Lima, Peru, 313
Limited (constitutional) monarchy, 332, 343–50; in Dutch Republic, 344; in England, 344–50
Lion in Winter, The (movie), 208, *208*
Literature: Classical, 152; Egyptian, 19; Hellenistic, 81–82; heroic, 48–49; in High Middle Ages, 200–201; historical writing and, 58–59; in Rome, 99, 103, 123–25; vernacular, 246–47
"Little ice age," 231, 332
Lives of the Caesars (Suetonius), 164
Livia (Rome), 117, 126
Livonia, 342
Livy (historian), 94, 102, 124
Locke, John, 350
Loftus, William, 1
Lollards (England), 274
Lombard League, 212
Lombards, 143, 152, 163
Lombardy, 213, 243
London: in High Middle Ages, 184–85; population of, 194
Longbow, 236
Lope de Vega, 352
Lord's Supper, 220, 285, 288, 291
Lord-vassal relationship, 171–72
Lorenzo the Magnificent. *See* Medici family
Lothair, 169
Louis VII (France), 189, 224
Louis IX (Saint Louis, France), 190, 210–11
Louis XI ("Spider," France), 271
Louis XIII (France), 336
Louis XIV (France), *331*, *336*, 336–38; Academy of Sciences and, *370*; Tonkin king and, 318–19; wars of, 337–38
Louis the German (Germany), 169
Louis the Pious (Carolingian Empire), 167, 169
Low Countries: commerce in, 327; in Holy Roman Empire, 285; plague in, 233. *See also* Belgium; Luxembourg; Netherlands
Lower Austria, 340
Lower Egypt, 14, 15
Loyola, Ignatius of (Saint), 293, *295*, *296*
Ludlow, Edmund, 347
Luke (Saint): Gospel of, 132
Luther, Martin, and Lutheranism, 279–80, 282–87, *293*; Bible translation and, 284; marriage and, 283, 285, 292; Ninety-Five Theses of, 282–83; Peasants' War and, 285; pope and, *284*; Zwingli and, 287–88, 289–90
Luxembourg, 298
Lycurgus (Plutarch), 54, 65–66
Lydia, 39, 63
Lysistrata (Aristophanes), 60

Ma'at principle (Egypt), 16
Macartney (Lord), 320
Maccabaeus, Judas, 86
Macedonia, 22, 39, 46, 70; Alexander the Great and, 69–70, 74; Antigonid dynasty in, 76; Hellenistic kingdoms and, 77–78; Rome and, 97, 98
Macedonian dynasty (Byzantine), 175–77, 223
Machiavelli, Niccolò, 261, *261*, 262
Madras (Chennai), India, 319
Magellan, Ferdinand, 304–5, 308–9
Magi (sages), 261
Magic: in Renaissance, 359
Magna Carta (England), 207, 209
Magyars (Hungarians), 169, 177, 214, 216
Maine, France, 207, 271
Mainz: Jews in, 221
Maize (corn), 323
Malacca, 308, *316*
Malta: megaliths in, 27
al-Ma'mun (Abbasid), 180
Manchu Empire (Qing China), 320, 320 (map)
Manchuria, 320
Manetho (Egypt), 15
Mannerism, 350
Manors and manorialism, *174*, 174–75, *175*
Mantinea, Battle of, 58
Manzikert, Battle of, 223
Maps: by Hondius, *327*; Mercator projection and, 326; Ptolemy's world map, 306, *306*
Marathon, Battle of, 39, 56
Marburg Colloquy, 288 289–90
Marcella (Rome), 151
Marcus Aurelius (Rome), 117, 128
Marduk (god), 11
Marius (Rome), 98, 106
Mark (Saint): Gospel of, 132
Marriage: Aristotle on, 62; Black Death and, 248; in Carolingian Empire, 167; in Christianity, 167; in Code of Hammurabi, 10; dynastic, 273; in Egypt, 23; Frankish, 145–46; in Islam, 156; Luther and, 283, 285, 292; of medieval women, 189; Protestantism and, 292–93; in Renaissance Italy, 257, 258, 259; in Rome, 93, 101–2
Mars (god), 99
Martin V (Pope), 246
Martinique, 321
Mary. *See* Virgin Mary
Mary I (England), 290–91, 298
Mary II (England). *See* William and Mary
Mary, Queen of Scots, 344
Masaccio, 266, *266*
Massachusetts colony, 322
al-Mas'udi (historian), 180
Mathematical Principles of Natural Philosophy. See Principia (Newton)
Mathematics: Hellenistic, 82–83; Mesopotamian, 13; Muslim, 181; Scientific Revolution and, 358–59
Matthew (Saint): Gospel of, 132
Matthias Corvinus (Hungary), 273
Mauryan Empire (India), 76, 319
Maximilian I (Holy Roman Empire), 273
Maya civilization, 310, 310 (map)
Mazarin (Cardinal), 336
Mecca, 156
Medes/Media, 34, 38
Medici family, *256*; Cosimo de', 259, 263–64; Lorenzo the Magnificent, 259
Medicine: medieval, *168*, 168–69, 198; Muslim studies of, 181; in Scientific Revolution, 365. *See also* Diseases
Medina, 156, 158
Meditations (Marcus Aurelius), 128
Mediterranean region, 13, 14, 327; Christian reconquests in, 211 (map); Greeks in, 46, 51; Ottomans and, 343; Phoenicians and, 33–34; Roman expansion in, 92, 96–98, 96 (map)
Megalithic structures, in Europe, 27
Mehmet II (Ottomans), 274
Memoirs (Ludlow), 347
Memphis, Egypt, 15, 39
Menander, 81
Menes (Egypt), 15
Menkaure (Egypt): pyramid of, *19*
Mennonites, 290
Mercantilism, 328
Mercator, Gerardus, 326
Merchant of Paris on Marriage, A, 190
Merchants: Dutch, 317; in Egypt, 16; European in Japan, 321; in medieval cities, 194–96, *195*; views of, 193–94. *See also* Trade
Mercury (god), 100
Merovingian dynasty, 143–44, 163
Mesoamerica: civilizations of, 310–11, 310 (map), 311 (map)
Mesopotamia, 72, 117; Assyria and, 34, 37; civilization of, 6–13
Messenger, The: The Story of Joan of Arc (movie), *240*, 241
Messenia, 53
Messiah, 131
Mestizos, 323
Methodius (missionary), 179
Metropolis, 51
Mexico, 326; Cortés in, 306, 311
Mexico City, 310
Micah (prophet), 32
Michael III (Byzantine), 175
Michael Cerularius (Patriarch), 223
Michelangelo, *253*, 253–54, 268, 269, *270*
Microscope, 358
Middle Ages: Christianity and civilization in, 217–23; cities and towns in, 185; Constantinople during, 152–53; entertainment in, *249*; homosexuality in, 221–23; intellectual thought in, 196–201, 197 (map); Jews in, 221, 222; lords and vassals in, 171–75; religious orders in, 217–18; Renaissance and, 253; trade and trade routes in, 191, 192 (map). *See also* Early Middle Ages; High Middle Ages; Later Middle Ages
Middle Kingdom: in Egypt, 16; in medieval Europe, 169
Middle Passage, 314
Mieszko (Poland), 178
Migration: Celtic, 76–77; Greek, 48, 51, 78; of Slavs, 177–79, 177 (map)
Milan, 194, 213; duchy of, 243
Military: of Alexander the Great, 72, 74; Assyrian, 35; in Athens, 55–56; in Brandenburg-Prussia, 339; Byzantine, 175–76; Carthaginian, 97; as characteristic of civilization, 5; in Early Middle Ages, 172; in France, 337; Germanic in Rome, 141; Greek, 49–50, 51; in Hundred Years' War, 236; Macedonian, 70; Mycenaean, 48; Persian, 42, *42*; Roman, 96, 98, *99*, 106–7, 116, 129–30, 138; Russian, 341; in Spain, 272, 338; Spartan, 53
Miltiades (Greece), 56
Minerva (goddess), 99
Ming dynasty (China), 320
Minoan civilization (Crete), 46–47, 48 (map)
Missi dominici (messengers), 165
Mission, The (movie), 325, *325*
Missions/ missionaries: in Americas, 313, 323, 324; in Asia, 317, 323; Jesuit, 293–94; in Latin America, 324; monks and, 148–49
Mita (labor system), 313
Mithraism, 130, 134
Moabites, 29
Moctezuma (Aztecs), 311
Modern Devotion movement, 281
Mohenjo-Daro, 5, 6 (map)
Molière, Jean-Baptiste, 353
Moluccas (Spice Islands), 305, 316

Monarchs and monarchies, 306; ancient, 8, 27, 15–16, 19–22, 29–30, 40–41, 76; in 14th century, 239–41; absolutism and, 332; Aristotle on, 62; Austrian, 340; Dutch, 344; in eastern Europe, 273; in England, 206–7, 242, 271; in France, 207–11, 238, 242, 271; Germanic, 137–38, 141–46; Hellenistic, 76–81, 77 (map); in Italy, 260; medieval, 206–15, 216–27; "new monarchies," 271; papal, 217; in Rome, 91–92; in Spain, 271–73. *See also* specific kingdoms
Monasticism. *See* Monks and monasticism
Mongols, 238, 319; Black Death and, 231; empire of, 214 (map), 230; invasions by, 214–15, 305
Monks and monasticism, 147–51; Benedictine, 148; Cluniac, 216; in Ireland, 148–49; Luther on, 283; in Middle Ages, 147–51, 188, 196, 216; social services of, 219–20; women and, 148, 150. *See also* Religious orders
Monogamy: in Carolingian Empire, 167
Monotheism: of Judaism, 30–32
Montefeltro, Federigo da, 259–60
Moors: Spanish Muslims as, 212
Moravia, 178–79, 288
Mortality rates: from Black Death, 231, 233–34; childbearing and, 258; in slave trade, 314
Mosaics: in Ravenna, *154*
Moses (Bible), 28, 31–32, 156
Mother, The (de Hooch), 345, *345*
Muawiya, 158
Mughal Empire (India), 319, 319 (map)
Muhammad, 156–57, 159 (map)
Mühlberg, Battle of, *287*
Mulattoes, 323
Mumbai (Bombay), *308*
Mummification: in Egypt, 17, 18
Murad I (Ottoman Turks), 274
Murals: Etruscan, *92*
Muscovites, 340. *See also* Russia
Museum: of Alexandria, 81
Muslims, 221, 305; Byzantines and, 175; Classical culture and, 198–99; Crusades and, 221, 227; in India, 319; invasions by, 169; monasteries and, 216; on Rus people, 178; in Spain, 143, 158, 211, 211 (map), 212, 223, 271, 273. *See also* Islam
Myanmar. *See* Burma (Myanmar)
Mycenaean Greece, 47–48, 48 (map)
Mystery religions, 85, 130; Christianity and, 85, 130, 134

Nagasaki: Portuguese in, 321, *321*
Nantes, Edict of, 297
Naples, 194; French occupation of, 260; kingdom of, 242, 259, 285
Narva, Battle of, 342
Naseby, Battle of, 347
Native Americans. *See* American Indians
Natural philosophy, 358
Navarre, 211, 271, 297
Neanderthals, 3
Near East, 1–24, 7 (map), 26–43
Nebamun (Egypt), *20*
Nebuchadnezzar II (Chaldeans), 38
Neo-Babylonian Empire, 35 (map), 38
Neolithic Revolution, 3–5; in Europe, 27
Neoplatonism, 264
Nepotism: in Catholic Church, 276
Nero (Rome), 117, 132
Nerva (Rome), 117
Netherlands, 298 (map); Anabaptists in, 288, 290; England and, *298*; Habsburg-Valois Wars and, 286; revolt against Spain, 297–98; Scientific Revolution and, 361; United Provinces of, 344. *See also* Dutch
Neustria, 144
Nevsky, Alexander, 15
New Basilica (Rome), *140*
New Cicero (Bruni), 263
New Comedy (Hellenistic), 81
Newfoundland: Vikings in, 171
New Kingdom (Egypt), 15, 18, 19–22
New Model Army (England), 346, *346*
New monarchies, 271
New Netherland, 322
New Rome: Constantinople as, 140
New Spain, 313
New Stone Age. *See* Neolithic Revolution
New Testament: in Greek language, 151; translations of, 132, 152, 284
Newton, Isaac, 359, 361–64, *364*
New World. *See* America(s)
Nicholas (Saint), 220, 293
Nicholas of Cologne, 227
Nile River, 6, 13–14. *See also* Egypt
Nimrud, Assyria, 37
Nineteenth dynasty (Egypt), 22
Ninety-Five Theses: of Luther, 282–83
Nineveh, Assyria, *29,* 34, 37, *37,* 38
Ninhursaga (god), 12
Nippur, Sumer, 11
Noah: *Epic of Gilgamesh* and, 14
Nobiles (Rome), 105
Nobility: in 14th century, 239; in Carolingian Empire, 165; in Code of Hammurabi, 9; in Crusades, 224; in England, 206, 207; in France, 297, 337; in Germany, 213 (map); in High Middle Ages, 206; in Renaissance, 256–57; in Rome, 138; in Russia, 215; as Second Estate, 211, 256. *See also* Aristocracy; Second Estate (nobility)
Nogarola, Isotta, 264
Nomarch (Egyptian governor), 16
Nomes (Egyptian provinces), 16
Norman Conquest: of England, 206, *207*
Normandy, 171, 190, 210; English loss of, 207; in Hundred Years' War, 238
Normans: Comneni defeat of, 223
North Africa: Belisarius in, 152; Carthage in, 96; Greek settlements in, 51; Islam in, 180; Phoenicians in, 34; Rome and, 107
North America: British colonies in, 322; Europeans and, 308; French colonies in, 322; Vikings in, 171
Northern Europe, 214 (map); artistic Renaissance in, 269–71; Jews in, 221; kingdoms in, 213–14; Scientific Revolution in, 361–64
Northern Renaissance humanism, 280
Northmen (Norsemen). *See* Vikings
Northumbria, 150, 167
Norway, 213; Vikings and, 169, 170 (map)
Notre-Dame Cathedral (Paris), *202,* 220; school of, 197
Novgorod, 171, 179, 215
Nubia: Egypt and, 16, 19, 22
Number system: Indian and Muslim, 181; Mesopotamian, 13
Nuns, 148, 150, 219, *219*, 323. *See also* Monks and monasticism
Nystadt, Peace of, 342

Observations upon Experimental Philosophy and Grounds of Natural Philosophy (Cavendish), 366
Obsidian, 5
Octavian (Rome). *See* Augustus
Odoacer, 141
Odyssey (Homer), 49, 50
Oeconomicus (Xenophon), 65
Oedipus the King (Sophocles), 59
Old Babylonians. *See* Amorites
Old Kingdom (Egypt), 15–16
Old Testament. *See* Hebrew Bible
Oleg (Kiev), 179
Oligarchies: in Florence, 243; in Greece, 52, 58
Olivares (count), 339
Olympia, 46, 63
Olympic Games, 46, 63
Olympus, Mount, 63
"On Chastity" (Phintys), 79
Onesti, Nastagio degli, *259*
On the Fabric of the Human Body (Vesalius), 365
On the Family (Alberti), 258–59
On the Freedom of a Christian Man (Luther), 283–84
On the Laws (Cicero), 103
On the Motion of the Heart and Blood (Harvey), 365
On the Republic (Cicero), 103
On the Revolutions of the Heavenly Spheres (Copernicus), 359, *360,* 362
Optimates (Rome), 105–6
Oracles: in Greece, 63
Orange: house of, 344
Oration on the Dignity of Man (Pico), 264
Ordeal, 145, 146, 200
"Ordeal of Hot Water, An" (Gregory of Tours), 146
Orders (classes) in Rome, 93, 105–6, 116. *See also* Estates (social orders)
Oresteia (Aeschylus), 59
Origen of Alexandria, 133–34
Orléans: dukes of, 238, 242
Orthodox Christianity. *See* Eastern Orthodox Christianity
Osiris (god), 17, *17*
Ostia (port city), 121, *122*
Ostracism: in Athens, 56
Ostrogoths, 141, 143, 152
Otto I (Germany), 212
Ottoman Empire, 343; Austrian Empire and, 340; conquests by, 305; Holy Roman Empire and, 286 (map). *See also* Ottoman Turks; Turkey
Ottoman Turks: Byzantine Empire conquered by, 227, 273–74; Constantinople conquered by, 309; in Holy Roman Empire, 286. *See also* Ottoman Empire; Turkey
Otto of Friesing (historian), 219
Ovid (poet), 124; *Art of Love, The,* 124, 125
Oxford University, 197, 199

Pachakuti (Inca), 311
Padua, 248
Painting. *See* Art(s)
Pakistan, 72
Paleolithic Age, 3
Palestine: Alexander the Great and, 72; Arabs in, 154; Crusades and, *225*; Egypt and, 19
Pantheon (Rome), 117
Papacy, 207, 243, 244; in Avignon, 243, 245; Charlemagne and, 165–66; Crusades and, 223; in Italy, 242; reforms of, 216–17, 294–96; in Renaissance, 275. *See also* Popes; specific popes
Papal curia, 217
Papal monarchy, 275
Papal States, 212, 216, 245, 259
Papal supremacy, 243, 244

Paper, 181
Papyrus, 33
"Paradise" (*Divine Comedy,* Dante), 246
Paraguay: Guaraní Indians in, 324
Paris, University of, 197
Parlement (France), 211
Parliament (England), 235; address of Elizabeth I to, 299; authority of, 350; Charles I and, 344–46; English civil war and, 346; Henry VII and, 271; James I and, 344; taxation and, 207, 241
Parliament and parliamentary system: in France, 211; in Spain, 272; taxes and, 241. *See also* Parliament (England); Reichstag
Parnassus, Mount, 63
Parthenon (Athens), *60,* 61
Pascal, Blaise, 371–73
Paterfamilias (Rome), 100, 101, 125
Patriarch: in Byzantine Empire, 175, 223
Patricians: in medieval cities, 194; in Renaissance, 257; in Rome, 93, 105
Paul III (Pope), 294
Paul IV (Pope), 294, 295–96
Paul of Tarsus (Saint), 132, 134, 167
Peace of Augsburg, 286 (map), 287
Peace of Nystadt, 342
Peace of the Pyrenees, 339
Peace of Westphalia, 334, 339, 344
Peasants: after Black Death, 235; diet of, 188; free vs. serfs, 187; *235;* lifestyle of, *187,* 187–88; in Middle Ages, *175,* 185; in Renaissance, 257; revolts of, *235,* 235–36, 336; as Third Estate, 256, 257; in western Europe, 328. *See also* Serfs and serfdom
Peasants' Crusade, 224
Peasants' Revolt (England, 1381), 235
Peasants' War (Germany), 285, 288
Pechenegs, 223
Peloponnesian War, 58
Peloponnesus, 46, 48, 58
Penitential of Cummean, 149
Pensées (Thoughts) (Pascal), 372
Pepin (Franks), 163, 166
Pergamum, 76, *78,* 98
Pericles (Athens), 56–57, 58, 64; Funeral Oration of, 45–46
Perioikoi (Sparta), 53
Perpetua (Christian woman), 134
Persepolis, 72
Persia, 179; Mongols and, 215; Sassanid, 129. *See also* Persian Empire
Persian Empire, 22, 30, 38–42; Alexander the Great and, 69, 72; Arabs and, 158; Assyrian Empire and, 36; under Darius, 39 (map); expansion of, 39; government of, 40; Greece and, 39, 55–56; kings in, 41; military in, 42, *42;* religion in, 42; Seleucids and, 76; Sparta and, 58
Persian language, 28
Persian Wars, The (Herodotus), 58–59
Persis, Iran, 38
Peru, 6, 6 (map), 311, 313, 326
Peter (Saint), 132, 147
Peter the Great (Russia), 341–42
Peter the Hermit, 224
Petition of Right (England), 344
Petrarch, 263
Petrograd. *See* Saint Petersburg, Russia
Phalanx, 51, 70
Pharaohs (Egypt), 15, 16, 22, 76
Pharisees, 131
Philip II (Macedonia), 46, 55, 58, 69, 70; Demosthenes and Isocrates on, 71
Philip II (Spain), 290, 297–98, 299–301, 338
Philip II Augustus (France), 207, 210 (map), 217, 224–25
Philip III (Spain), 338
Philip IV ("the Fair," France), 211, 243, 244, *244*
Philip IV (Spain), 338–39
Philip VI (France), 236
Philippines: Magellan in, 305, 308
Philistines, 28–29, 33
Philosophy: Greek, 61–63; Hellenistic, 83–85; humanism and, 263–64; in Rome, 103. *See also* Intellectual thought
Philoxenos of Eretria, *73*
Phintys: "On Chastity," 79
Phoenicians, 33–34, 33 (map); alphabet of, 34, *34,* 48; in Carthage, 96
Phonetic writing, *12,* 48
Photian schism, 175
Photius (Patriarch), 175
Physiology, 365
Pi (mathematics), 83
Pico della Mirandola, Giovanni, 264
Pictographs, *12,* 34
Pietas (Rome), 105
Pilate, Pontius, 131
Piraeus, 64
Pisa: Council of, 246; in Crusades, 224, 227; trade and, *122*
Pisistratus (Athens), 55
Pius V (Pope), 255
Pizarro, Francisco, 312–13
Plague, 231; in Athens, 58; reactions to, 234. *See also* Black Death
Planets, 359, 362–64
Plantagenets (England), 206, 210, 210 (map)
Plantations: in Americas, 314, 321, 323
Plassey, Battle of, 319–20
Plataea, Battle of, 56
Plato, 62; in Arabic, 181; mathematics and, 359; Renaissance study of, 263–64, 358
Plautus (playwright), 103
Plebeians (Rome), 93, 105
Plebiscita (Rome), 93
Pliny the Younger, 123, 133
Plotina (Rome), 126
Plows, 186
Plutarch: *Lycurgus,* 54, 65–66
Pogroms, 234
Poland/Poles, 178; Anabaptists in, 288; Jews in, 221; kingdom in, 214; monarchy in, 273; Mongols in, 214, 215; Ottomans and, 274; Slavs in, 178
Polis (Greek city-state), 50–51, 53, 63, 70. *See also* Athens; Sparta
Politics: as characteristic of civilization, 5; Machiavelli on, 261
Politics (Aristotle), 62, 65
Politiques (France), 297
Poll tax: in England, 235
Polo family (Marco, Niccolò, Maffeo), 305
Poltava, Battle of, 342
Polybius, 81–82, 98
Polyclitus (sculptor), 61
Polytheism, 12
Pompey (Rome), 100, 107
Pondicherry, India, 319
Popes, 175; in 15th century, 259; Charlemagne and, 166; Holy Roman Empire and, 212; Luther and, *284;* in Middle Ages, 147, *147;* Renaissance, 281. *See also* Papacy; specific popes
Popular culture: elite culture and, 371; Protestantism and, 293; religion and, 293. *See also* Culture
Populares (Rome), 105–6, 107
Popular religion: in High Middle Ages, 220
Population: in 17th century, 332; of Americas, 313; Black Death and, 234; of British North America, 322; of China, 231; of French North America, 322; in High Middle Ages, 185, *185;* of Inca Empire, 311; of medieval cities, 194; of Roman slaves, 101; of Rome, 130
Portugal: Asia and, 317; Brazil and, 321; exploration by, 305, 306–7; Japan and, 321, *321;* revolts in, 336; slave trade and, 313; Southeast Asia and, 315–16; spheres of influence of, 310
Portunus, temple of, *100*
Porus (India), 74
Poseidon (god), 63
Postumus (Rome), 139
Potatoes, 326
Potosí mines, 326
Pottery, 5, 121, *122*
Praetorian guard, 116
Praetors (Rome), 92
Praise of Folly, The (Erasmus), 281
Predestination, 291
Prehistory, 2
Presbyterians: in England, 344
Prester John (legendary king), 305
Price revolution, 327; in Spain, 326
Prince, The (Machiavelli), 261, *261,* 262
Princeps (Rome), 114–15, 116
Principate (Rome), 114
Principes (Rome), 98
Principia (Newton), 361–62
Printing: in Renaissance, 264–66; Scientific Revolution and, 358, 365
Priscus: *Account of the Court of Attila the Hun, The,* 142–43
Proconsul (Rome), 92
Procurator (Russia), 341
Prolegomena (Ibn Khaldun), 193–94
Prophets: Hebrew, 32–33; Muhammad as, 156
Propraetor (Rome), 92
Protestant Reformation: Anabaptists and, 288–90; Calvin and, 291; in England, 290–91; events leading to, 280–82; in Germany, 285–87; Luther and, 282–85; social impact of, 292–93; spread of, 287–91
Protestants and Protestantism: in Europe by 1560, 294 (map); in France, 297, 337; popular culture and, 293; in Switzerland, 287–88; witchcraft trials and, 334
Protestant Union, 335 (map)
Provence: French rule of, 271
Prussia, 339; East Prussia, 214. *See also* Brandenburg-Prussia
Psalm 104 (Hebrew Bible), 21
Ptah-hotep (Egyptian vizier), 22
Ptolemaic kingdom (Egypt),76, 81, 85
Ptolemy (astronomer), 198, 358, 359; world map by, 306, *306*
Punic Wars, 96 (map), 97, 106
"Purgatory" (*Divine Comedy,* Dante), 246
Puritans (England), 293, 344, 346, 348
Puteoli (port city), 121
Pyramids: Egyptian, 15, 18, *19*
Pyrenees, Peace of the, 339

Qianlong (China), 320
Qing Empire (China). *See* Manchu Empire
Quadrivium, 152
Quaestors (Rome), 92
Quakers: abolition of slave trade and, 315

Quetzalcoatl (god), 311
Qur'an, 156, 157

Ramadan, *158*
Ramesses II (Egypt), 22
Raphael, *26,* 268, *269*
Rationalism: Descartes and, 369
Ravenna: Church of San Vitale in, *164,* 167
Razzia (raid), 157
Re (god), 17
Realism: in art, 248, 351–52
Reason: vs. faith, 200, 363–64; Pascal on, 371–73
Reconquista (Spain), 211, 211 (map), 224, 273
Reformation: Catholic, 293–96; printing and, 266; Protestant, 279–93; Radical, 288–90. *See also* Religion
Reform Commission (Catholic Church), 294
Reformed church: Lutheran, 285
"Regulations of Avignon, The," 222
Reichstag, 273
Relics: of saints, 220, 281
Relief sculpture: Assyrian, 37, *37*
Religion: in Americas, 313; in Assyria, 37; printing and, 266; as characteristic of civilization, 5; of Charles I (England), 346; Crusade against Albigensians and, 220; in eastern Europe, 273; in Egypt, 17–18, 19; in England, 344–48; in France, 297, 336, 337; in Greece, 60, 63; of Hebrews, 29; in Hellenistic world, 85–86; in High Middle Ages, 220; in Holy Roman Empire, 334; in Mesopotamia, 11–13; Pascal on, 371–73; Persian, 38, 42; popular culture and, 293; in Rome, 99–100, 130–34, 140; in Russia, 215; science and, 371–73; in Spain, 273; in Thirty Years' War, 334; witchcraft trials and, 334. *See also* Reformation; Religious wars; Secularism; Witchcraft; specific groups
Religious orders: Benedictine monasticism and, 148; in Middle Ages, 217–18; women in, 219
Religious wars, 296–301; Thirty Years' War as, 334–35, 335 (map)
Rembrandt van Rijn, 352, *353*
Rémy, Nicholas, 334
Renaissance, 253–54; ancient authors in, 358; arts in, 248, *248, 266,* 266–71, *267, 268, 269, 270, 271,* 358; banquets in, 255, *259;* Carolingian, 166–67; Catholic Church in, 274–76; education in, 264; families in, 257–59; hermeticism in, 264; intellectual thought in, 261–66; Italian, 254, 255–69, 260 (map); magic in, 359; nobility in, 256–57; in northern Europe, 269–71; papacy in, 275; printing in, 264–66; society in, 254, 255–59; trade in, 255–56
Republic(s): Dutch, 344; in England, 346; Roman, 92–107
Republic, The (Plato), 62
Res Gestae (Augustus), 115
Restoration: in England, 346–48
Revolts and rebellions: in 17th century, 335–36; against Assyrians, 34; in Athens, 58; in cities, 236; in France, 336; in Germany, 285; in Hungary, 336; by Jews against Rome, 131; in Netherlands, 297–98; peasant, *235,* 235–36; by Roman slaves, 101, 107; in Russia, 340. *See also* Peasant revolts
Rhetoric, 61
Rhine River region, 116, 118, *141,* 171, 286
Ribbed vault, 201–2
Richard I the Lionhearted (England), 224–26
Richard II (England), 236, 241
Richard II (Shakespeare), 354
Richard III (England), 271
Richelieu (Cardinal), 336
River valley civilizations, 5–6
Roads and highways: Persian, 40; Roman, 91, *95,* 105
Roman alphabet, 34, *34*
Roman Catholicism. *See* Catholic Church
Roman Confederation, 95, 96
Roman Empire, 110 (map), 113–35, 118 (map); agriculture in, 121–22; Augustus in, 105, 109, 113, *114,* 114–17; Christianity and, 130–34, 137, 140; cities in, 119, 126–27, 126 (map); crises in 3rd century, 129–30; culture in, 123–25; daily life in, 123; economy in, 120–22, 130, 138–39; Egypt in, 22; families in, 125–26; frontiers and provinces of, 116, 117–18, *119;* Greek influence on, 138; Julio-Claudians in, 117; Justinian and, 152; in late period, 139 (map), 141; law in, 119–20; military in, 138; religion in, 130–34; society in, 116, 125–27, 130, 138–39; trade in, 120–22, 120 (map), 121, *122;* Visigoths and, 141; women in, 125–26. *See also* Byzantine Empire; Eastern Roman Empire; Roman Republic; Rome (ancient); Western Roman Empire
Romanesque architecture, 201, *201*
Romania, 117
Roman Inquisition, 221, 361, 371
Romanization: of Germanic peoples, 141; of Roman provinces, 119–20
Roman law, 145
Romanov dynasty: Michael, 340
Roman peace, 114
Roman Republic, 92–96, 110 (map); conquest of Italy by, 93–96; fall of, 105–9; government of, 92–93; military in, 98; Punic Wars and, 96 (map). *See also* Roman Empire; Rome (ancient)
Rome (ancient), 89–90; art and architecture in, 105; Attalid kingdom to, 76; Carthage and, 96–97; citizenship in, 90, 93, 95–96; colonies of, 107; culture of, 103–5; Egypt and, 76; engineering in, 105; entertainment in, 100, 126–27; Etruscans and, 90, 91; expansion by, 92, 95–98, 96 (map); family in, 100, 101–2; geography of, 90; Greece and, 90, 91, 95; Hellenistic world and, 97–98; Jews and, 130–31; law of, 93, 103, 119–20, 199–200; legendary founding of, 91; literature in, 103; military in, 96, 98, *99,* 103, 106–7, 116; religion in, 99–100; roads in, 91, *95,* 105; slavery in, 100–101; society in, 93, 99–102, 105–6; values and attitudes in, 105; women in, *101,* 101–2. *See also* Roman Empire; Roman Republic
Rome (city): ancient, 91 (map), 126–27, 126 (map), *127;* destruction of, 143; Holy Roman Empire and, 212; papacy in, 245; sacks of, 141, 260
Romulus and Remus, 91
Romulus Augustulus (Rome), 141
Rossi, Luigi de', 275
Royal Academy of Sciences (France), 367, 370, *370,* 371
Royal Road (Persian Empire), 40
Royal Society (England), 366, 370–71
"Royal Standard": of Ur, *8*
Rubens, Peter Paul, 351, *351*
Rubicon River, Caesar at, 107
Rudel, Jaufré, 200
Rudolf of Habsburg, 213
Rules of Saint Benedict, 220
Runnymede, 207
Rurik (Vikings), 179
Russia, 214, 342 (map); absolutism in, 340–42; China and, 320; Christianity in, 215; eastern Slavs from, 179; military in, 341; Mongols in, 215; Peter the Great in, 341–42; plague in, 233; princes of Moscow and, 273; reforms in, 341–42; revolts in, 336; as state, 273; Vikings in, 171; women in, 342
Russian Orthodox Church, 340, 341

Sabines, 93
Sacred Way (Roman road), 91
Sadducees, 131
Saint(s), 220; Protestantism and, 293; relics of, 220, 281. *See also* specific saints
Saint-Denis, abbey of, 186, 202
Saint-Domingue. *See* Haiti
Saint Petersburg, Russia, 342
Saint-Simon (duc de), 332
Saladin, 226, 227
Salamis, Battle of, 56
Sallust (historian), 107
Samaria, *29,* 29–30
Samarkand, 231
Samnites: Roman wars with, 95
Samson (abbot of Bury Saint Edmonds), 206
San Lorenzo, Church of (Florence), 267, *267*
Sanskrit language, 28
San Vitale, Church of (Ravenna), *154,* 167
Sardinia, 27, 34, 96
Sardis, 39
Sargon (Akkad), 9
Sassanid Persians, 129
Satrap/satrapy (Persian Empire), 38, 39, 40
Saul (Israel), 29
Saxons, 145, 163
Saxony, elector of, 284, 285
Scandinavia, 27; kingdoms in, 213–14; Lutheranism in, 285; plague in, 233; trade and, 191; Vikings from, 169, 170 (map)
Schliemann, Heinrich, 4, 47
Scholasticism, 200
School of Athens (Raphael), 268, *269*
Schools. *See* Education; Universities and colleges
Science: Arabic works in, 198; Hellenistic, 82–83; Islamic, 181; medieval, 198; Mesopotamian, 13; religion and, 371–73; Renaissance arts and, 358; society and, 371. *See also* Scientific Revolution
Scientific method, 369–70
Scientific Revolution, 357–58; astronomy in, 359–64; chemistry in, 365–66; medicine in, 365; scientific method and, 369–70; women in, 366–67
Scientific societies, 370–71
Scipio Africanus, Publius Cornelius, 97
Scotland, 149, 291
Scriptoria (writing rooms), 166–67
Scriptures: Christian, 152
Sculpture: ancient, 4, *4;* Assyrian, 37, *37;* Greek, 61; Hellenistic, 82, *82, 83;* Roman, 105
Scutage, 239
Sea Peoples, 28, 33
Second Crusade, 224
Second Estate (nobility), 211, 256
Second Punic War, 97, 106
Secularism, 261–62, 331
Secularization, 331

Seeman, Enoch: on Newton, *364*
Sejm (Polish parliament), 273
Seleucus/Seleucids, 76, 85, 97–98
Seljuk Turks, 223, 274
Semitic languages and people; 9, 19, 28, 34, 37, 38, 155–56
Senate (Rome), 93, 106, 107, 114–15, 116
Seneca, 124
Sennacherib (Nineveh), *29*, 36
Septimius Severus (Rome), 129, *130*
Serbia/Serbs, 176, 274
Serfs and serfdom, 174–75; in Egypt, 16; free peasants and, 187. *See also* Peasants
Sermon on the Mount, 131
Servian Wall (Rome), 92
Seth (god), 17
Seven Years' War, 320
Sex and sexuality: in Babylon, 11; Christianity and, 167–68; in Islam, 156; Luther on, 283; marriage and, 292; women's status and, 367. *See also* Homosexuality
Seymour, Jane, 290
Sforza, Francesco, 259
Shakespeare, William, 352, 354
Shang dynasty (China), 6
Shari'a (Islamic law), 156–57
Sheriff: office of, 206
Shi'ite Muslims, 158, 223
Shikoku, 325
Siam (Thailand), 317
Sicily, 34, 90, 101, 169, 227, 233, 242, 259; Carthage and, 96, 97
Sidon, 33
Silesia, 215
Silk/Silk Road, 121 (map), 152, 231
Silver: in Americas, 121, 313, 316, 321, 326; mercantilists and, 328
Silver Age: of Latin literature, 124–25
Simeon the Stylite (Saint), 148
Simons, Menno, 290
Sistine Chapel: Michelangelo and, *253*, 254, 268
Sixtus IV (Pope), 276
Slavery/slave trade, 316; African, 313–15, 323; in Athens, 64; in Haiti, 322; in Latin America, 314; Middle Passage and, 314; Quakers and, 315; in Rome, 100–101, 107; in Sumer, 9
Slavic peoples, 163, 175, 214; migrations of, 177–79, 177 (map)
Slavonic language, 179
Slovenia, 340
Smallpox, 311, 312
Society: Arab, 156; Assyrian, 37; Black Death and, 234–35; in Egypt, 16; in France, 337; in Germanic kingdoms, 145–46; in Greece, 63–64; in Later Middle Ages, 248–50; in Latin America, 323; Mycenaean, 48; Protestant Reformation and, 292–93; in Renaissance, 254, 255–59; Roman, 93, 99–102, 105–6, 116, 117, 125–27, 130, 138; Russian, 340–42; science and, 371; in 17th century, 332–36; in Spain, 338–39; in Sumer, 8–9; Thirty Years' War and, 334–35; Viking, 170. *See also* Law codes
Society of Friends. *See* Quakers
Society of Jesus. *See* Jesuits
Socrates, 62
Socratic method, 62
Solomon (Israel), 26, *26*, 29, 29 (map)
Solon (Athens), 54–55
Song of Roland, The, 200–201
Sophists, 61
Sophocles, 59, 263
Sousse, Tunisia: Roman trade and, *122*
South Africa: humans in, 2
South America. *See* America(s)
South Asia, 5–6
Southeast Asia, 315–21, 315 (map)
Southern Slavs, 178–79
Southwest Asia, 1; civilizations in, 5–6. *See also* Near East
Spain, 34, 51, 233, 305; in 17th century, 332; Americas and, 306, 307, 310, 311–13, 338; Bourbon ruler in, 338; Carthage and, 96, 97; Catholic Church in, 272, 339; Christianity in, 211–12; Crusades and, 227; decline in 17th century, 338–39; England and, 290–91, 299–301; France and, 339; golden century of theater in, 352–53; Habsburg-Valois Wars and, 286; Holy Roman Empire and, 285; Italy and, 260; monarchy in, 271–73; Muslims in, 143, 158, 169, 180; Netherlands revolt against, 297–98; Ottomans and, 343; Philip II in, 297–98; price revolution in, 326; *Reconquista* in, 211, 211 (map), 224; Rome and, 107, 119; in Thirty Years' War, 334, 339; unification of, 271–72; Visigoths in, 143
Spanish Inquisition. *See* Inquisition
Sparta, 46, 53, 56, 58; Peloponnesian War and, 45– 46, 58; women in, 53, 65–66, 79
Spartacus, revolt by, 101, 107
Speyer, Germany: Jews in, 221
Spice Islands. *See* Moluccas
Spices and spice trade, 305, 308, 309, *309*, 316, 328
Spinoza, Benedict de, 368
Spiritual Exercises, The (Loyola), 295
Sri Lanka. *See* Ceylon (Sri Lanka)
Stadholders, 344
Stained-glass windows, 202
Starry Messenger, The (Galileo), 361
States General (United Provinces), 344
Statute of Laborers (England, 1351), 235
Stephen (Saint), 178
Stoicism, 84–85, 103
Stonehenge, 27, *27*
Strategoi (generals), 56
Strozzi family, 258; Alessandra, 257
Struggle of the orders: in Rome, 93
Stuart dynasty (England), 344, 346
Styria, 340
Subinfeudation, 172
Suetonius: on Caesar, 107, 164
Sugar industry, 314, 321
Suger (abbot of Saint-Denis), 186, 202
Suleiman I (Ottoman), 286, 343
Sulla, Lucius Cornelius, 106–7
Sultan, 223
Sumatra, 317
Sumer and Sumerians, 7–9, *12*, 13
Summa Theologica (Thomas Aquinas), 200
Sun-centered view. *See* Heliocentric conception
Sunni Muslims, 158
Supe River region (Peru), 6
Suppiluliumas I (Hittite), 28
Surat, India, 319
Susa, 41, 72
Sweden, 213, 334, 336; Russia and, 342; Vikings and, 169, 170 (map), 179
Swiss Brethren, 288
Switzerland: Calvin in, 291; Zwinglianism in, 287–88
Syncretism, 85
Syracuse: Archimedes and, 83
Syria, 16, 27, 34, 72; Arabs in, 154, 157; Byzantine Empire and, 177; Hittites in, 28; Seleucids in, 76; Zenobia and, 130
Tacitus (historian), 115, 117, 124, 127
Taille (French tax), 271
Tale of the Heike, 173
Tamerlane, 319
Tariffs, 328
Tarquinia: Etruscan tomb at, *92*
Tartuffe (Molière), 353
Taxation: in Egypt, 16; in England, 207, 241, 344–46; in France, 243, 271, 337; in Rome, 139
Technology, 3, 5; agricultural, 185–86; printing and, 264–65; Scientific Revolution and, 358–59. *See also* Science; Scientific Revolution; Weapons
Telescope, 358, *360*
Tell el-Amarna, 19
Temples: in Egypt, 23; Greek, 60–61, 63; in Jerusalem, 29, 86, 131; Mesopotamian, 11; Roman, *100*; in Sumer, 8
"Ten lost tribes," 29 (map), 30
Tenochtitlán, 311, 312
Tertullian, 151
Test Act (England, 1673), 346–48
Testelin, Henri, *370*
Tetzel, Johann, 282
Teutoburg Forest, Battle of, 116
Teutonic Knights, 214, 215
Texcoco, Lake, 310
Thailand. *See* Siam
Thebes, Boeotia (Greece), 46, 58
Thebes, Egypt, 19, 23
Theocracy, 8
Theocritus, 81
Theodoric (Ostrogoths), 141, 143, 152
Theodosius "the Great" (Rome), 140
Theology, 140, 200. *See also* Religion
Thera (island), 47
Thermopylae, Battle of, 56
Thessaly, 46
Third Crusade, 224–26
Third Estate (peasants, city dwellers, workers), 211, 256, 257
Third Philippic, The (Demosthenes), 71
Thirty Years' War, 334–35, 335 (map)
Thomas à Kempis, 281
Thomas Aquinas. *See* Aquinas, Thomas
Thrace, 39, 51, 70
Three-field system, 187
Throne of Saint Peter (Bernini), 351
Thucydides (historian), 58, 59, 81, 263
Thutmosis III (Egypt), 23
Tiberius (Rome), 117, 121
Tiberius Gracchus (Rome), 106
Tiber River, 90
Tigris River, 6, 34, 179
Time of Troubles (Russia), 340
Tin, 5
Titian: Charles V by, *287*
Titus (Rome), 127, *127*
Tlaxcala, 311
Tokugawa Ieyasu (Japan), 320, 321
Tokugawa shogunate (Japan), 320
Toleration Act (England, 1689), 348
Tonkin: Louis XIV (France) and, 318–19
Topa Inca, 311
Tordesillas, Treaty of, 307 (map), 310
Touraine: English loss of, 207
Tournaments, 189, *189*
Tours (Poitier), Battle of (732), 158
Trade: Arab, 156, 180; Assyrian, 37; in Athens, 55, 64; Byzantine, 176; in Carthage, 96–97; with China, 320; commercial capitalism and, 327–28; in Constantinople, 153;

Crusades and, 224, 227; in Early Middle Ages, 175; of eastern Slavs, 179; in Egypt, 14, 16; fairs for, 191; in Flanders, 191, 191 (map); globalization in, 328; Greek, 51–52; Hellenistic, 79; in High Middle Ages, 190–91, 192 (map); in Mauryan Empire, 76; Phoenician, 33 (map); protectionist, 328; in Renaissance, 255, 256; in Roman Empire, 120 (map), 121, *122*; Russian, 215; on Silk Road, 121, 231; spice, 305, 309, *309*; Sumerian, 8–9; triangular, 314; views of, 193–94. *See also* Commerce; Slavery/slave trade
Tragedy (drama): Greek, 59
Trajan (Rome), *99*, 117, 118 (map), 119; Pliny the Younger and, 133
Transubstantiation, 285, 296
Transylvania: Austrian Empire and, 340
Travels (Polo), 305
Travels of John Mandeville, The, 305
Traversaro, Paulo, *259*
Treaties. *See* specific treaties
Trent, Council of, 294, 296
Triangular trade, 314, 315 (map)
Triarii (Rome), 98
Tribunes of the plebs (Rome), 93
Tribute Money (Masaccio), *266*
Trier: Roman Empire and, *119*
Trinh family, 318–19
Trip-hammers, 186
Tripoli: as Crusader State, 224
Triumvirate (Rome): Caesar and, 107, *107*
Trivium, 152
Trojan War: *Iliad* (Homer) and, 48–49, *49*
Troubadours, 200
Troy, 48, 49, 59, 123
Tsar (Russia), 340, 342
Tudor dynasty (England), 271, 344
Tullia (Rome), 102
Turkey, 4, 28; holy league against, 297. *See also* Ottoman Empire; Ottoman Turks
Turkmenistan, 6
Turks: Ottoman, 273–74; Seljuk, 223, 274. *See also* Ottoman Empire; Ottoman Turks
Tuscany, 213, 243
Tutankhamun (Egypt), 19
Twelve Tables (Rome), 103, 104
Twentieth dynasty (Egypt), 22
Two Treatises of Government (Locke), 350
Two Women Teach a Child to Walk, 345
Tyler, Wat, 236
Tyrants: in Greece, 52–53, 55; in Italy, 243
Tyre, 33, 96
Tyrol, 340
Tyrrhenian Sea, 90

Ukrainians, 179
Ulpian (Roman jurist), 120
Ultra-Catholics: in France, 297
Umayyad caliphate, 158, 179, 180, 181
Umma, Mesopotamia, 7
Unam Sanctam (Boniface VIII), 243, 244
United Kingdom of Great Britain. *See* England (Britain)
United Provinces of the Netherlands, 298, 336, 344. *See also* Dutch
Universe: geocentric conception of, 82, 358, 359; heliocentric view of, 82, 359; medieval conception of, *360*; Scientific Revolution and, 357–64
Universities and colleges: in High Middle Ages, 196–98, *198*
University of Oxford, 197
University of Paris, 197
Upper Austria, 340
Upper Egypt, 14, 15
Ur, Mesopotamia, 7, 9; "Royal Standard" of, *8*
Urban II (Pope), 224
Urban areas: after Black Death, 248–50; as characteristic of civilization, 5; Hellenistic, 76, 78; in Italian Renaissance, 254. *See also* Cities and towns
Urbino, 259–60
Ur-Nammu (Ur), 9
Uruk, Mesopotamia, 1, 7
Utnapishtim (flood hero), 14
Uzbekistan, 6

Valencia, 211, 212
Valerian (Rome), 129
Valley of Mexico, 310
Valois monarchy (France), 236, 285–86
Vandals, 141
Van Eyck, Jan, 269, *270*
Varangians, 179
Varus (Rome), 116
Vasari, Giorgio: on Michelangelo, 254
Vassals/vassalage, 171–72, 207
Vault (architecture), *201*, 201–2, *202*
Venice, 194, 213, 243; in Crusades, 224, 227; population of, 194; trade of, 191, 255
Veracruz, 311
Verdun: Treaty of, 169 (map)
Vernacular languages, 200, 246–47
Versailles, 337; Hall of Mirrors in, *338*
Vesalius, Andreas, 365, 367
Vespasian (Rome), 117, *127*
Vespucci, Amerigo, 308
Via Appia (Appian Way), *95*
Viceroys: in Latin America, 313
Vienna: Ottomans and, 286, 340, 343
Vietnam: Europeans in, 317
Vikings, 169–70, 170 (map), 179; Christianity and, 216; in England, *171*; exploration by, 171; in Russia, 171; Slavs and, 179
Villages. *See* Cities and towns
Virgil (poet), 123–24, 246, 263
Virginity: cult of, 151
Virgin Mary, 220
Visconti family (Italy), 213, 243, 259
Visigoths, 141, 143
Vladimir (Kiev), 179
Volga region, 179
Volscian people, 93
Vulgate Bible, 152

Wales, 145
Wallachia, 274
Warka, mound of, 1
War of the Roses (England), 241, 271
Wars and warfare: Assyrian, 35; in Early Middle Ages, 172, *172*; in France, 337–38; Greek, 46; Hussite, 275; Spartan, 53. *See also* Military; Weapons; specific battles and wars
Wars of Religion: in 16th century, 296–301
Wartburg Castle: Luther at, 284
War with Cataline, The (Sallust), 108
Watermill, 187
Weapons, 3, 5; Archimedean, 83; in Early Middle Ages, 172; in Egypt, 19; gunpowder and, 238, 250, 274; in Hundred Years' War, 236; Macedonian, 70; Portuguese, 308
Wergeld (fine), 145
West Africa: slave trade and, 314
Western Europe: absolutism in, 336–39; in Later Middle Ages, 241–43; Renaissance state in, 271–74 *See also* Europe
Western Hemisphere. *See* America(s)
Western Roman Empire, 140–41, 144 (map). *See also* Eastern Roman Empire; Roman Empire
Western Slavs, 178
West Indies, 321–22 (map)
Westphalia: Peace of, 334, 339
Wet nurses, 257
Wheel: in Sumer, 9
White Russians, 179
William III (Netherlands), 344
William and Mary (England), 348, 349
William of Aquitaine, 216
William of Nassau (prince of Orange), 298
William of Normandy (England), 206
William of Orange (Netherlands), 344, 348
Wimborne: abbess of, 150
Windmills, 186–87
Winkelmann, Maria, 367
Witchcraft/witch trials, 332–34
Wittenberg: Luther in, 282, 284, *284*
Women: aristocratic, 189–90; Aristotle on, 62–63; in arts, 351; in Athens, 64–66; after Black Death, 248–50; in Carolingian Empire, 167; Cato the Elder on, 102; Christianity and, 134, 148, 150–51; debates on nature of, 367; education for, 80, 102; in Egypt, 22–23, 81, *81*; in Frankish society, 145–46; Gratian on, 190; in Hellenistic world, 79–81; humanist education for, 264; in Italian city-states, 260; literature by, 246–47; in Mesopotamia, 10–11; in Middle Ages, 248–50; Neolithic, 5; Paleolithic, 3; peasant, 188; Protestantism and, 292–93; in religious orders, 219; in Rome, *101*, 101–2, 125–26; in Russia, 342; in Scientific Revolution, 366–67; in Spanish America, 326; in Sparta, 53, 65–66, 79; Spinoza on, 368; witchcraft trials and, 332–34
Woolen industry: *ciompi* revolt in, 236
World economy, 327–28
World-machine (Newton), 364
Worms: Concordat of, 216–17; Diet of, 284; Edict of, 284; Jews in, 221
Writing, 5; in Central Asia, 6; as characteristic of civilization, 5; cuneiform, *12*, 13; Egyptian, 19; in Mesopotamia, *12*, 13; Phoenician, 34, *34*, 48. *See also* Alphabet
Wyclif, John, 274

Xenophon: *Constitution of the Spartans,* 65; *Oeconomicus,* 65
Xerxes (Persia), 56

Yahweh, 30, 31–32
Yarmuk, Battle of, 157
Yellow River region (China), 6, 6 (map)
York, house of (England), 271
Yucatán peninsula, 310. *See also* Maya civilization

Zama, Battle of, 97
Zarathustra (Zoroaster), 42
Zealots, 131
Zemsky Sobor (Russian assembly), 340
Zeno, 84
Zenobia (Syria), 130
Zeus (god), 63
Ziggurats, 8
Zoroaster (Zarathustra), 42
Zoroastrianism, 42, 130
Zürich, Swiss Brethren in, 288; Zwingli in, 287, 288 (map)
Zwingli, Ulrich/Zwinglianism, 287–88, 288 (map)